S0-BBX-003

ORGANIZATION

Text, Cases, and Readings
on the Management of
Organizational Design and Change

The Irwin Series in Management and The Behavioral Sciences
L. L. Cummings and E. Kirby Warren *Consulting Editors*
John F. Mee *Advisory Editor*

ORGANIZATION

Text, Cases, and Readings on the Management of Organizational Design and Change

John P. Kotter
Professor of Organizational Behavior
Graduate School of Business Administration
Harvard University

Leonard A. Schlesinger
Executive Vice President and Managing Officer
Au Bon Pain

Vijay Sathe
Professor of Organizational Behavior
Graduate Management Center
The Claremont Graduate School

1986 Second Edition

Homewood, Illinois 60430

ISBN 0-256-03228-9

Library of Congress Catalog Card No. 85–81340

Printed in the United States of America

4 5 6 7 8 9 0 K 3 2 1 0 9

Preface

We have prepared this new edition to make available several new cases and readings that have appeared since the book was first published. The text material remains unchanged; the basic concepts and analytical techniques presented in the first edition continue to be both valid and useful for the study and practice of organization design and change. Special topics, such as the design of innovative organizations and the influence of corporate culture, are covered in carefully selected readings which supplement the text material.

We would like to thank the many users who have provided us with feedback on the first edition. As before, our appreciation of the work of those who have contributed the readings and cases used in this edition is acknowledged by name where their work appears.

John P. Kotter
Leonard A. Schlesinger
Vijay Sathe

Preface to the First Edition

The existing literature on organizational design and organizational change falls into two major categories. On the one hand, most of the research and theorizing is being done by social scientists (psychologists, sociologists, anthropologists, social psychologists, and, most recently, organizational behaviorists) who write primarily for others in their profession. Few managers read this literature. On the other hand, what the practitioners do read is frequently based only on personal experience and observation or "armchair theorizing."

This book represents an attempt to bridge the widening gap between these two bodies of literature. We have written it for both students of management and practicing managers. It is based on the best social science research available, with the emphasis being on practical application. We hope this effort will stimulate and help those who are engaged in designing and managing today's organizations as well as those who will bear this responsibility in the future.

As the citations in the text, cases, and readings of the book will indicate, we have drawn on the research and systematic thinking of many people. What is less obvious is the substantial contribution made on a more informal basis by numerous individuals who were involved in developing and teaching the first-year Harvard MBA course titled Organizational Problems, on which this book is based. Without the benefit of this groundwork, which was laid over the past ten years, this book could not have been written.

We also owe special thanks to our students in that course, who provided us with useful feedback, to Connie Bourke, who helped us manage the development of the first and second drafts of this manuscript, and to Irwin consulting editors Larry Cummings and Kirby Warren, who provided useful suggestions regarding the shaping of those drafts.

But most of all, we owe thanks to two of our colleagues, Paul Lawrence and Jay Lorsch, on whose work we have attempted to build. It is to them that we dedicate this book.

December 1978

John P. Kotter
Leonard A. Schlesinger
Vijay Sathe

Contents

Part Five 459

Chapter 1

Introduction

The real secret of the greatness of the Romans was their genius for organization.

James Mooney, *Vice President*
General Motors, 1931

It was on the strength of their extensive organization that the peasants went into action and within four months (in 1926) brought about a great revolution in the countryside, a revolution without parallel in history.

Mao Tse-tung, 1927

Organizing Human Resources

An important aspect of managerial work in any setting involves organizing human resources—that is, ensuring that the right people are focusing on the right tasks; that they have the proper information, tools, incentives, and controls to perform these tasks effectively and efficiently;[1] and that their efforts are coordinated such that the organization's overall objectives are accomplished. Generally, the higher one goes in an organization, the more responsibility managers have for large numbers of human resources and the more time and effort they spend on this aspect of managerial work.

In a very small group of people, a manager can create and maintain an appropriate organization through face-to-face interaction with his or her employees. The manager can verbally assign tasks, watch that they are carried out, coordinate activities personally, compensate people fairly, and so on. If the organization begins to break down, the manager can spot this immediately and deal with it. The only real "tool" such a manager needs is interpersonal skills.

[1] Effectiveness is measured by the degree to which an organization meets its goals. Efficiency is measured by the amount of resources expended in achieving results.

Figure 1–1
The Human Organization

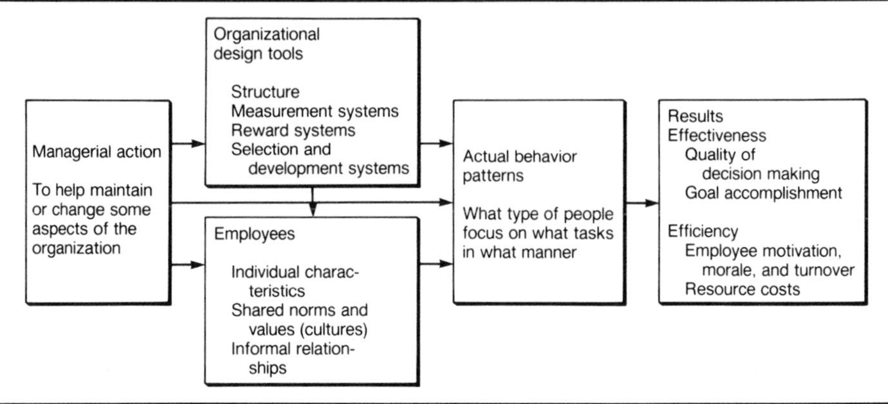

As the number of people a manager is responsible for grows, interpersonal skills soon prove to be insufficient to maintain an appropriate organization. A single manager can no longer deal with everyone face to face, coordinate everything personally, and always be around to deal with breakdowns. Many entrepreneurs have learned this lesson the hard way.

To organize large numbers of people, or people who are often spatially separated from one another, managers use a number of different organization design tools. These tools include, for example, job design, compensation systems, performance appraisal systems, and training programs. Considerable evidence today suggests that the design and implementation of these tools can have a major impact on an organization's financial performance as well as on the quality of work life of its employees (see Figure 1–1). Furthermore, research indicates that improper design can undermine an organization's performance and generate a variety of disruptive problems.

Organizational Problems

Inappropriate organizational designs often lead to the following types of recurring problems:

— Ineffective decision making. (Production personnel in one company continuously made poor decisions about inventory levels, which created a variety of problems.)
— High employee turnover. (One firm's management turnover was 30 percent per year, compared with less than 5 percent for other companies in its industry.)
— Low morale. (Nearly 50 percent of the employees in one company

complained that they didn't like their jobs and felt the company was a poor place to work.)

— Expensive conflict among individuals and groups. (The production and sales personnel within one company literally plotted against one another.)
— A lack of employee motivation. (The sales employees in one firm worked, on average, a five-hour day.)
— Wasted employee energy. (Using the same equipment and working just as hard, the production employees in one firm produced only 60 percent of the daily output of a similar firm.)
— A general lack of goal accomplishment. (The sales department in one company missed its sales objectives for 10 consecutive quarters.)

An important characteristic of these organizational problems and one that differentiates them from other types of problems is that they *recur*. They do so because they are not caused by an idiosyncratic individual, group, or environmental event but by the organizational design itself.

In addition, inappropriate attempts to introduce changes in organizational design can also be very costly. They can disrupt a company's operations, generate resistance and hostility among employees, and lead to any of the organizational problems previously listed. Such improper strategies can simply fail to produce a needed change, or they can generate a change at an unnecessarily burdensome cost to an organization.

The Purpose and Organization of This Book

The basic purpose of this book is to increase the reader's understanding of how to avoid potential organizational problems through organizational planning and how to solve existing organizational problems through organizational analysis and action planning. Specifically, our objectives are:

1. To provide the reader with examples that illustrate a wide variety of real situations in which managers are trying to deal with organizational issues.
2. To provide the reader with the best available research-based conceptual maps that can help in the analysis of organizational design and change issues.
3. To provide the reader with a sequence of material that will allow for the efficient development of new awarenesses, ideas, and skills related to organizational design and change.

To achieve these objectives, the book contains text, cases, and readings. The text provides an integrated analytical framework based on recent organizational research. The readings explore questions and issues identified in the text, but in greater detail and from more diverse viewpoints. The cases, most of which have been written in the past five years, focus on the most common organizational problems and questions that managers face today.

The book is organized into six parts, each of which builds on the previous one. It begins by looking at organizational design questions within the basic building block of modern organizations—the specialized department. Primary issues in Part One relate to turnover and morale, personnel selection and development, performance appraisal, employee motivation, job design, career paths, compensation, equity, and management by objectives. In the second part, the focus moves up one level in complexity, and the material deals with multiple, interdependent departments within single-business companies. Major issues relate to coordination, interdepartmental conflict, management control systems, and organizational structure. In Part Three, the focus once again moves up one level to large multidivisional and multinational organizations, each of which is made up of numerous single-business units. Primary issues at this point relate to coordination and control, the management of extreme diversity, cross-cultural conflict, group structures, and the misuse of power. Part Four focuses on organizational change processes that are initiated to correct the types of organizational design problems dealt with in the first three parts. Important issues here relate to resistance to change, planning change processes, questions of timing and speed, and power and influence. In Part Five, the focus shifts to a longer time horizon and to questions relating to developing an organization for long-run survival and effectiveness. The key issue here concerns the systematic development of adaptability while coping with short-run realities. The book concludes with a brief summary of the analytical and action-planning frameworks developed and presented in previous parts.

ORGANIZATION DESIGN

Chapter 2

Organization Design Tools

There are many ways one can conceptualize the formal elements of organizational design. In this book, we will do so in terms of structure, measurement systems, reward systems, and selection and development systems.

Structure

The elements of formal structure include individual jobs, subunits (departments/divisions), a management hierarchy, rules and plans, and committees and task forces. These design tools are generally used to influence behavior by clearly specifying what individuals are responsible for, where in the organization they should work and with whom, what authority they have and to whom they are responsible, and how they should go about performing their tasks.

A job is simply a set of tasks assigned to an individual. These tasks can be very clearly defined, perhaps in a detailed job description, or left very vague. Most organizations, except for those which are very small, are made up of many different kinds of jobs. Some of these jobs contain very similar tasks which can either be relatively difficult (staff specialists) or simple (many clerical and assembly-line jobs), while others require a more varied set of tasks (many managerial jobs).

Organizational structure generally groups jobs into subunits such as departments, and subunits into large subunits such as divisions. This grouping is usually based on functional similarity (all marketing jobs or subunits are grouped into a marketing department); product or service similarity (all jobs or subunits dealing with consulting are grouped into the consulting service department); or geographical area (all jobs or

Figure 2–1
Examples of Some Basic Types of Structural Groupings

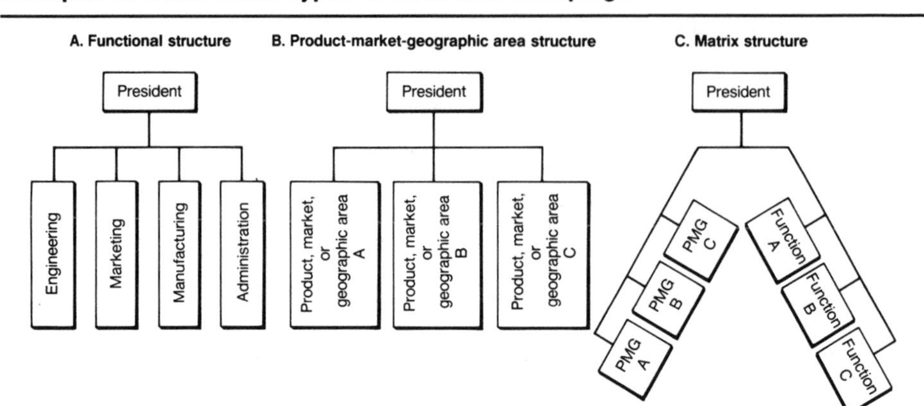

subunits dealing with Europe are grouped into the European division). While most organizations place a single job into just one subunit, so-called matrix organizations group individual jobs into two or even more subunits (e.g., a job may be in both the marketing department and the consulting services department). See Figure 2–1.

Closely related to such groupings is a management hierarchy which specifies reporting relationships and distributes formal authority for people and decisions to managers throughout the organization. Typically, the head of an organization is given the most formal authority. The people who report to him or her, some or all of whom are in charge of the organization's largest subunits, are given somewhat less formal authority. And so on down into the organization. Organizations are commonly called centralized if the formal authority is heavily concentrated in the hands of a few top people. If authority is widely distributed throughout the organization, the organization is often called decentralized. Hierarchies are sometimes described as "tall" and "flat," depending on the number of people reporting to each manager. A small span of control (few people reporting to each manager) creates relatively tall structures, and vice versa.

A fourth part of the structure of organizations includes rules, procedures, goals, and plans. Rules and procedures simply inform employees of how to perform their jobs. An organization with many rules and procedures is often called very bureaucratic. Plans and goals may be thought of as temporary rules and procedures; they also more clearly define what people are to do, although for a limited period of time.

A final part of structure consists of committees and task forces. These devices formalize team (as opposed to individual) efforts to work on some task. The only significant difference between the two devices is that task forces tend to be more temporary in nature. Both sometimes contain as few as 3 or as many as 20 members, who often come from different subunits within the organization.

Measurement Systems

Measurement systems attempt to influence human behavior by gathering, aggregating, disseminating, and evaluating information on the activities of individuals and groups within the organization. Measurement helps managers ask and answer such questions as: Are our managers achieving the organization's objectives? Do our employees perform according to the organization's expectations?

Measurement systems are either focused on the monitoring of ongoing activities or are designed primarily to appraise past performance. Either type can be based on financial, quantitative (other than financial), and/or qualitative data. The two most common types of measurement systems are management control systems and performance appraisal systems.

Management control systems are generally aimed at ensuring that the organization's (or its subunits') resources are being used in ways that are consistent with its goals and objectives. These systems focus on financial data and are usually referred to by the way in which information is collected and assessed: standard cost centers, revenue centers, discretionary expense centers, profit centers, or investment centers.

Performance appraisal systems attempt to measure factors associated with individual employees. These systems commonly ask a supervisor or a group of managers to rate individuals periodically on some scale regarding general characteristics of their work or personal traits. Other types of performance appraisal systems include those in which managers must rank all their employees from best to worst performers, those which are closely tied to Management by Objectives systems (MBO) or Assessment Centers, and those in which managers periodically write essays about their employees' performance.

Reward Systems

Reward systems are generally designed to induce people to join the organization, to work as its structure directs, and to work toward certain measured objectives. The two main characteristics of a reward system are the criteria used to allocate rewards and the nature of the rewards themselves.

Reward systems are sometimes closely tied to measurement systems, so that rewards are allocated primarily on the basis of measured results. Other common criteria for the allocation of rewards include past (as opposed to current) achievements, seniority, loyalty, and other factors such as the cost of living in the local area, family size, and education.

The most common rewards used by organizations include money, fringe benefits (both monetary and nonmonetary), promotions, job assignments which are intrinsically satisfying, and job security.

Organizations typically offer money either as a base salary or as a base plus incentives. Incentive plans can be based on individual performance, group performance, or organizationwide performance. Fringe benefits typically include an allowance for overtime work; holidays, vacations, and sick days off with pay; various types of insurance; and special employee services (e.g., inexpensive lunches at the cafeteria). Additional fringes for managers include bigger and better offices, a company-owned or -leased car, first-class travel on business trips, stock options, and so forth. Promotions reward an individual with more status, more power, and more responsibility. A job assignment that the individual likes can give him or her any number of different kinds of rewards—challenge, agreeable social relations, a comfortable work pace, excitement, and so on. Job security provides a stable flow of income as well as other types of rewards over time.

Selection and Development Systems

Selection and development are separate but interrelated formal organizational systems. They have an indirect effect on behavior patterns by influencing the knowledge, skills, values, and personalities of those people who work on the organization's tasks.

Selection systems range from very simple to very elaborate, and the selection process can even vary within an organization, depending on the job requirements and experience of the candidates. At one extreme, new employees may be selected on the basis of a relatively simple form that they are asked to fill out. At the other extreme, an applicant's past work experience may be carefully examined, and he or she may be asked to take a series of tests and undergo a large number of interviews with various managers. In either case, data on the person, once compiled, are sometimes compared to clear selection criteria, but more often are given to one or more individuals who then make a judgment.

Development systems also range from the simple to the elaborate. Some organizations provide only informal on-the-job training and development, which is based entirely on the skills and interests of individual managers. At the other extreme, some organizations offer formal internal training courses or send their employees to university programs. Some also systematically keep track of skill levels and work experience of certain employees with manpower planning systems and periodically make development decisions (transfer, rotation, promotion, training) based on that data. These organizations, through their measurement and reward systems, might also systematically encourage managers to develop their subordinates' skills.

Choices

In designing the overall structure as well as the measurement, reward, and selection and development systems of an organization, managers face many choices. Should they use a functional structure, for example, or a product structure? How many people should report to each manager? What type of people should be hired for each subunit? What is the best way to measure the performance of individuals? Should people be paid for performance, or for their seniority, or for their potential for the future?

In some cases, making these choices is relatively easy. For example, a small company that produces only one product for a limited geographical area will probably not have to think very long before adopting a functional structure. But in many cases, the best choice is not so obvious. For example, how much of a salesperson's income should depend on current sales performance—0 percent (a flat salary), 25 percent, 50 percent, 75 percent, or 100 percent (all commission)? Or how much money should an organization spend on management training programs—none, 1 percent of net income, or 10 percent of net? Or how many people should be assigned to a multibusiness company's corporate staff?

The basic purpose of the first three parts of this book is to help you develop the ability to analyze the available design alternatives and make these difficult choices.

Part One

The first part of this book focuses on the most basic of organizational building blocks: the specialized subunit that performs a limited functional task. Examples of such subunits which are included as cases in Part One are a corporate finance department (Megalith/Hay Associates) and a sales organization (Alcon Laboratories).

Managers of specialized subunits, as the cases illustrate, often face a variety of human resource problems associated with high turnover, inadequate individual performance, and low morale. The text provides a research-based framework for analyzing these problems and for deciding how to address them successfully through the use of organization design tools. The readings focus in greater detail on those four tools which tend to be particularly important at the subunit level—job design, reward systems, performance appraisal systems, and management by objectives (MBO).

Chapter 3

Organizing Human Resources within Specialized Subunits

In the late 18th century, Adam Smith convincingly demonstrated the significant economic advantages of applying the concept of specialization in organizations. Through specialization, he argued, people develop expertise in performing a limited set of activities and thus become highly effective at accomplishing those activities. In addition, Smith noted, specialization often produces significant economies of scale, thus helping an organization to be more efficient in its use of resources.

Virtually all of today's organizations consist of parts based on the Smithian notion of specialization. If we are to understand the organizational issues that confront modern corporations, we must begin by focusing on the most basic organizational building block: the subunit which performs a limited, specialized function.

Conceptualizing Organization Design within Specialized Subunits

The logical objective of the organizational design of a specialized subunit is to select, develop, direct, motivate, and control a group of human resources in order to accomplish a limited set of assigned tasks efficiently and effectively and in the short and long run. Recent research suggests that a useful way of conceptualizing how the organization design of a subunit achieves this objective is in terms of the three-way "fit" shown in Figure 3–1.[1] It indicates that an organization design that fits both

[1] Jay Lorsch and John Morse, *Organizations and Their Members* (New York: Harper & Row, 1974).

Figure 3–1
Conceptualization of the Function of Organization Design within a Specialized Subunit

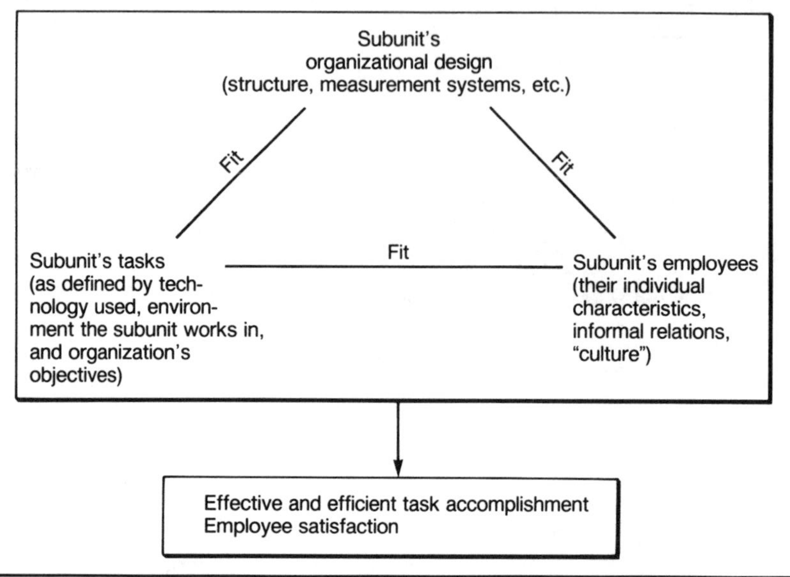

the subunit's tasks and its employees will lead toward efficient and effective task accomplishment as well as satisfied employees.

Organizational designs that do not exhibit the type of three-way fit presented in Figure 3–1 typically generate a number of problems. If either the design or the employees do not fit the tasks, the subunit tasks will usually not be accomplished effectively. If either the design or the tasks do not fit the employees, the subunit's employees will become dissatisfied and may exhibit the corresponding negative organizational outcomes—turnover, absenteeism, lateness, and so on.

When conceptualized as in Figure 3–1, the task of organizing a specialized subunit may appear to be quite simple. In reality it seldom is. Achieving an appropriate three-way fit in a specific situation is generally difficult because of the large number of relevant task, human, and organizational design variables. (Figure 3–2 presents a list of such variables.) It is possible to have a situation where task, human, and organizational design variables all *fit* on dozens of dimensions, and yet organizational problems will result because of a misfit on one or two additional dimensions. And since the people as well as the tasks in a subunit can change, even in the short run, misfits on a dimension or two and the resultant organizational problems can easily develop.

Because there are so many potentially relevant variables and rela-

Figure 3–2
Some Examples of Relevant Task, People, and Design Variables

Task	Organizational Design
Amount of diversity within the task	Number of rules and procedures
Task complexity	Diversity of the activities in each job
Routineness of task	Span of control of first-line supervision
Time span of task completion	Amount of detail on job descriptions
Amount of personal contact involved	Dimensions measured in performance evaluation system
Magnitude of task	Frequency of appraisal reviews
Relevant dimensions on which task accomplishment can be measured	Criteria under which people receive rewards
People	Percent of compensation that is fixed or variable (due to incentive, bonus, etc.)
Age	Selection criteria
Education	Amount of money allocated to formal training programs
Expectations (re work)	
Native ability	
Nature of special skills	
Needs/drives/motives	
Values	
Adaptability	

tionships implied in Figure 3–1, it is impossible to provide an exhaustive listing. It is possible, however, to examine some of the more important relationships and the more common mismatches that cause organizational problems.

The Organization Design–People Relationship

A fit between a specialized subunit's organizational design and its employees implies that the subunit's structure measurement, reward, and selection and development systems are congruent with its employees' needs, abilities, personalities, and expectations.

Structure

Perhaps the most obvious and important aspect of this relationship is the link between job design and employee skills and abilities. All jobs require some type of cognitive and interpersonal skills on the part of their incumbents. A mismatch between job requirements and employee abilities obviously creates problems.

A variety of techniques has been developed in the past 30–40 years to assist in matching job requirements with employee skills and abilities, such as systems for job content measurements, psychological tests, and assessment centers.[2] While these techniques can help eliminate job de-

[2] Edgar Schein, *Organizational Psychology* (Englewood Cliffs, N.J.: Prentice-Hall, 1965), pp. 19–26.

sign–people mismatches and are widely used today, they have their drawbacks. The more complex techniques, such as assessment centers, can be very expensive to develop and use. The simpler methods, such as tests, can be relatively ineffective in dealing with complex jobs or with jobs where requirements tend to change over time. As a result, managers still tend to rely heavily on their own judgments in trying to match job design and employees. Successful managers seem to be generally effective in making these kinds of judgments.

Job-people mismatches are typically the result of insufficient analysis of a job's requirements or of inappropriate measurement of people's abilities and skills. The underlying problem in both cases is usually that managers make assumptions (which are usually a function of *past* events) about what a job demands or what certain people can provide without testing those assumptions in a serious analysis of the current situation.

Many factory jobs, for example, have been designed in extremely narrow, routine, and predictable ways. Such jobs may well have fit the needs and abilities of a poor, uneducated, largely immigrant work force, but they are becoming increasingly inconsistent with the characteristics of today's worker who is better educated, more affluent, and holds considerably higher expectations for job variety and challenge. The most widely used solutions to this type of organizational problem are called "job enlargement" and "job enrichment," both of which involve changing job designs to correct the misfit. With job enlargement, elements of several routine jobs are combined to increase the variety of the work. With job enrichment, job designs are altered to allow for more challenge, responsibility, and autonomy.[3] Though both of these techniques have been used successfully in a large number of situations, both have also failed in numerous situations.[4]

The common theme in these failures is that job designs were altered without a clear objective of matching the current tasks involved or the current employee groups. In some cases, the "enlarged" or "enriched" jobs simply did not fit the existing set of technologically determined tasks, and costs went up considerably. In other situations, they provided employees with more variety, ambiguity, and challenge than they wanted or could handle and so led to poor performance and angry employees.[5]

Job design–people mismatches are also often created by changes in the subunit's task environment. These changes lead management to redesign jobs, which then do not fit the skills of current employees. Manage-

---

[3] John J. Morse, "A Contingency Look at Job Design," *California Management Review*, Fall 1973, p. 68.

[4] Ibid., p. 69.

[5] For a good discussion of the problems job enrichment programs have encountered, see J. Richard Hackman, "Is Job Enrichment Just a Fad?" *Harvard Business Review*, September–October 1975.

ment subsequently is faced with the choice of either training its employees to fit the new job demands or replacing them.

In growing organizations, for example, the nature of managerial jobs at the subunit level tends to change continuously. The job of an advertising manager in a company with sales of $5 million a year and an advertising department with only 2 people, for instance, is very different from the job of advertising manager in a $100 million company that has an advertising department with 20 people in it. Constantly replacing managers because their jobs outgrow them can be a very expensive and demoralizing solution to this problem. But getting managers to grow or change with their jobs can also be difficult, especially if the changes occur regularly.[6]

Changes in an organization's size, usually due to growth, can produce a variety of other structure-people mismatches. For example, research shows that as organizations add more and more people, subunit structure usually changes by adding more levels in the hierarchy, increasing the amount of specialization in jobs, increasing the number of formal rules and procedures, and decentralizing decision-making authority.[7]

Many other aspects of subunit structure can also, upon occasion, be found to be mismatched with the current employees. The structure, for example, might include many committees and meetings, while the employees are highly independent and not group oriented. The management hierarchy might have a very wide span of control (many people reporting to one supervisor), while many of the employees are new and unskilled and need fairly close supervision. A large and old corporation might have many rules and procedures, while its newer college-educated managers and professionals might be used to a more informal and permissive environment. In all of these cases, the subunits involved will experience a continuing series of problems unless the mismatch is identified and corrected.

Measurement Systems

Another significant aspect of the organization design–people relationship that often creates problems is related to the type and frequency of feedback that performance appraisal and other measurement systems provide. It is possible for measurement systems to provide too little, too much, or the wrong kind of information to fit the needs and expectations of employees.

---

[6] See, for example, Peter Drucker, *The Practice of Management* (New York: Harper & Row, 1975), pp. 246–62.

[7] See Chapters 2 and 3 in John Child, *Organization* (New York: Harper & Row, 1977). For a good discussion of the decentralization question, see Howard Carlisle, "A Contingency Approach to Decentralization," *Advanced Management Journal,* July 1974.

It is not uncommon, for example, to find a mismatch between relatively new, college educated employees and the almost nonexistent performance appraisal systems in some organizations. A person with a bachelor's degree has typically received concrete, often quantitative performance feedback within short and predictable intervals for most of his or her life. When such a person begins to work in an organization that provides nothing equivalent to what he or she has come to expect, one predictably finds problems.

In contrast, where elaborate appraisal systems do exist, they sometimes ignore the social psychological research that identifies types of feedback which cause people to become defensive and angry, thus creating a different kind of mismatch. Ideal feedback, this research suggests, should be descriptive rather than evaluative, directed at something the person can control, timely, specific rather than general (with clear and preferably recent examples), and not given in overly large amounts at any one particular time.[8] Some performance appraisal systems, on the other hand, are designed to provide a large amount of evaluative feedback about a person's traits (e.g., one's aggressiveness, good humor, leadership potential, etc.) in very general terms on an annual basis.

Performance appraisal systems often are inconsistent with the objectives or skills of the people who must implement them—the subunit's managers. For example, the systems sometimes require providing feedback at appraisal interviews—a skill that many managers do not possess. They sometimes generate strains in a manager's relationships with either subordinates (if the ratings seem low) or with peers (if the ratings seem high).[9] They also sometimes put supervisors in the uncomfortable and conflicting roles of both evaluators and coaches/helpers.[10] As a result of one or more of these mismatches, many managers resist using performance appraisal systems altogether.[11]

Virtually any aspect of a measurement system can in certain situations be out of phase with the employees involved. An information/control system, for example, might provide data on a subunit's results only once every three months, completely frustrating a group of employees whose high achievement motivation leads them to seek more frequent

---

[8] See John Anderson, "Giving and Receiving Feedback," in *Organizational Change and Development,* ed. Gene Dalton, Paul Lawrence, and Larry Greiner (Homewood, Ill.: Richard D. Irwin, 1970).

[9] Alan Patz, "Performance Appraisal: Useful but Still Resisted," *Harvard Business Review,* May–June 1975.

[10] See Herbert Meyer, Emanuel Kay, and John French, Jr., "Split Roles in Performance Appraisal," *Harvard Business Review,* January–February 1965, pp. 123–29.

[11] For a good discussion of the underlying problem and some ideas for solutions, see L. L. Cummings and Donald P. Schwab, "Designing Appraisal Systems for Different Purposes and Performance Histories," *California Management Review,* in press.

feedback.[12] Or a performance appraisal system could force supervisors and employees to interact in appraisal interviews in ways that are completely inconsistent with their normal interaction preferences, such as scientists in a research laboratory who work as colleagues and view one another accordingly.

Reward Systems

Possibly the most important aspect of the organization design–people relationship deals with the fit between reward systems and people's needs and perceptions of what they deserve from the organization. Reward systems can create severe problems for a company if they do not provide both the type and the amount of rewards that employees perceive as appropriate and fair.

The *types* of rewards that an individual or group of people will find attractive are affected by many factors, including their cultural backgrounds, education, age, career aspirations, off-the-job lifestyles, and work experiences to date.[13] Effective reward systems take these factors into account and attempt to offer different types of individuals and groups different reward possibilities. Pay may be stressed in some cases, while in others promotion opportunities, job security, challenging assignments, or fringe benefits may be emphasized.[14]

A second related group of factors affects the *amount* of rewards that an employee group will perceive as fair. These include general economic conditions, the nature of the jobs people have, people's perception of their performance on those jobs, seniority, and the rewards employees in other companies receive.[15] To help match pay levels and employees' feelings of equity, many large organizations have developed elaborate personnel systems that:

1. Periodically measure the skills required for all jobs, often assigning each a specific numerical score to represent its "content."
2. Assign a pay range to all jobs. The higher the content score, the higher the pay range.
3. Periodically compare the company's compensation with other companies—those in the same locale and/or in the same industry.

---

[12] See David McClelland, "That Urge to Achieve," *Think Magazine,* 1966.

[13] See Robert Suttermeister, ed., *People and Productivity* (New York: McGraw-Hill, 1976), chap. 5.

[14] Edward E. Lawler III, "Reward Systems," in *Improving Life at Work,* ed. J. Richard Hackman and J. Lloyd Suttle (Santa Monica, Calif.: Goodyear Publishing, 1977), p. 167.

[15] Ibid.

4. Devise detailed formulas to determine a person's compensation within his or her job's pay range (usually a function of performance and/or seniority).[16]

Selection and Development Systems

The selection and development systems in a company's subunits can be inappropriate for its employees if they do not provide the training people expect or need for their jobs or if they bring in people who are unable to get along with fellow employees.

In one study, for example, recently graduated M.B.A.s reported that the largest discrepancy between their expectations of what they would receive in their first jobs and what their companies expected to offer them related to personal and professional development opportunities. The M.B.A.s expected more than they received.[17] Where this was an important expectation from the M.B.A.'s standpoint, the person quit and moved on to another employer.

Another problem many organizations face is related to environmental change and its impact on the nature of the subunit tasks. For example, one company's customers began to change, subsequently causing the selling task to also change in important ways. The sales management responded by beginning to hire a different type of salesperson. When the older employees realized what was happening, many began to actively oppose the new selection criteria. Because these criteria represented a clear signal that their skills and abilities were no longer valued as much, some fought long and hard against the new standards. The disruptive fighting continued for nearly two years.

The Organization Design–Task Relationship

A fit between a specialized subunit's organization design and its tasks implies a fit between the various organization design tools and the attributes of the subunit's activities.

Structure

A subunit structure that fits its assigned tasks is one that directs employees to work on those tasks in effective and efficient ways. One of the more important aspects of the fit between a subunit's structure and its tasks is the relationship between task certainty/uncertainty and struc-

---

[16] For a further discussion of these types of systems, see Milton Rock, ed., *Handbook of Wage and Salary Administration* (New York: McGraw-Hill, 1972).

[17] John P. Kotter, "The Psychological Contract: Managing the Joining-Up Process," *California Management Review*, Spring 1973, p. 91.

tural formality/informality. Extensive research suggests that subunits that deal with very certain, predictable tasks are most effective when they are structured very formally, with clear job descriptions, rules, and procedures, while subunits that deal with very uncertain, unpredictable tasks are best structured informally.[18] The logic behind this relationship is simple. If a subunit's tasks are routine and predictable, careful study can determine the most efficient ways to perform them. These conclusions can then be programmed into job descriptions and rules. If, on the other hand, a subunit's tasks are highly uncertain, nonroutine, and unpredictable, such an analysis would be extremely difficult and would not identify a single best way to perform the tasks. In this kind of situation, detailed job descriptions and rules would generally be impossible and inappropriate. More informality and flexibility are required.

The relationship between the degree of predictability of tasks and formality of structure can be seen by comparing a factory with a research laboratory. Most manufacturing plants are technologically designed to contain fairly routine and predictable tasks; such plants typically are structured very formally. Research laboratories, on the other hand, engage in highly uncertain and nonroutine tasks and are usually structured very loosely and informally. These differences in structure are not random or accidental; rather, they are created by managers who explicitly or intuitively recognize this structure-task relationship.

A second important aspect of the subunit structure–task relationship concerns job design. In general, job designs that fit task requirements tend to be those that facilitate the completion of tasks effectively at a minimum cost.

For example, the vice president of sales in a clothing manufacturing firm was presented with two primary options for the design of his sales force. In Option 1, each salesperson would carry one of the firm's three lines of clothing (men's, women's, and juniors') and sell to about 60 customers in a geographical area. In Option 2, each salesperson would carry all three lines and sell to about 20 customers in a smaller area. In making his choice, the manager focused on three critical questions: (1) Is product knowledge or customer relations the more important factor in successful selling in our business? (2) How difficult and costly is it for a salesperson to learn a product line versus building a relationship with a customer? (3) How much more will the product-line specialization option cost in travel expenses and in the costs of coordinating the three salespeople that work together in a sales area? Based on an analysis of the situation, the vice president of sales decided that the customer relationship was more important than product knowledge. While training a salesperson in all three lines was expensive, it was not as expensive as the travel

---

[18] Paul Lawrence and Jay Lorsch, *Organization and Environment* (Boston: Harvard Business School, 1967).

and coordination costs associated with Option 1. Therefore, he chose the second option and designed sales jobs to carry all three lines for about 20 customers.

Still another aspect of the structure-task relationship that can cause problems for managers relates to span of control. Research shows that the number of people who can effectively report to a single manager can vary a great deal—literally from only one or two employees to two or three dozen—depending on a number of different task characteristics. For example, the more complex the tasks, the more time it will take a manager to hire, train, and evaluate a single subordinate and thus the smaller the span of control needed. Likewise, the more interdependent the tasks performed by different employees, the more time it will take the manager to manage that interdependence and thus the smaller the span of control required.[19]

Measurement Systems

To fit a set of subunit tasks, measurement systems need to focus on the more important task-related variables and provide feedback on these variables to people who can control them. When measurement systems focus on the wrong variables, feed information to the wrong people, or provide untimely information, they can cause serious problems.[20]

A rather extreme example of a measurement system that did not fit task requirements was once created by the new director of a corporation's research laboratory. Under this system, all professional personnel received a monthly report that indicated the total number of patents the laboratory had filed that month and that year to date, as well as the number of patents attributable to the individuals receiving the report. This system, intended to help motivate the scientists to work on the laboratory's tasks, created some serious problems for a number of reasons. First, the research projects the division worked on that led to profitable ventures for the corporation tended, in many cases to take 5 to 10 years to complete, while the measurement system focused on monthly accomplishments. Second, the successful research projects were accomplished by teams, not individuals, yet the measurement system focused on individual accomplishment. Finally, while successful research projects did usually lead to patents, the patent itself was only a by-product. The result of the company's focus on patents as an end product was an increase in the number of patents filed and a decrease in the number of successful research projects.

---

[19] For a further discussion of this issue, see H. Stieglitz, "Optimizing Span of Control," *Management Record* 24 (1962).

[20] Edward E. Lawler III and John Grant Rhode, *Information and Control in Organizations* (Santa Monica, Calif.: Goodyear Publishing, 1976), chap. 8.

Probably the most common problem that organizational subunits encounter in the measurement system–task linkage is a result of utilizing "off the shelf" performance appraisal systems. These systems (designed to be used by anybody, anywhere) sometimes measure people's personal characteristics, sometimes their behavior, and sometimes the results of their efforts. But they provide these measurements without consideration of the subunit's specific tasks. These systems are designed without serious attention to questions such as:

- What type of behavior and results are needed to effectively and efficiently achieve the subunit's tasks?
- How can these be measured?
- In light of an analysis of the tasks, how often should they be measured?

The fact that performance appraisal systems so often ignore these questions is a major contributor to their ineffectiveness.[21]

Reward Systems

For a reward system to fit a set of subunit tasks, it must motivate the type of behavior that is necessary, and it must do so at a cost that is reasonable in light of the importance of those tasks.[22] The most common reward system–task misfits occur when relatively unimportant behavior is rewarded while more important task-related behavior is not rewarded or when uncontrolled task outcomes are rewarded while outcomes under a person's control are not rewarded.

For example, the president of one organization decided to change the compensation system for marketing managers to one in which *(a)* the variable component in the average salary was higher and the fixed component was lower than before and *(b)* the variable was calculated in a way that was based 25 percent on individual performance and 75 percent on corporate earnings. Three years later, he abandoned this scheme after his managers bitterly protested its unfairness. They argued that they had very little control over corporate profits and that it just did not make sense to reward (or punish) them so heavily based on corporate profits.

In another situation, the compensation plan for the managers of a manufacturing plant was revised to provide up to a 50 percent bonus if they kept their costs within a fixed annual budget. This change was

---

[21] A 1974 Bureau of National Affairs survey revealed that while 93 percent of the firms polled had performance appraisal programs, only 10 percent of these firms' personnel executives felt that their appraisal programs were effective.

[22] Lyman W. Porter and Edward E. Lawler III, "What Job Attitudes Tell about Motivation," *Harvard Business Review,* January–February 1968, pp. 118–26.

made when the company's sales were flat but its costs were rising. The plan worked well until the company's business changed three years later. As a result of introducing new products, its sales started to increase dramatically beyond forecasts. But the sales increase soon died out because the company could not make timely delivery on its orders. Regardless of how much the sales department pleaded with the plant to quickly increase its output, the plant managers refused to budge until the company's president granted them a change in their expense budget.

Reward system–task mismatches sometimes occur, as in the previous example, because the subunit's tasks change. They occur even more often because some managers have a pet compensation, bonus, or commission system that they think fits all situations. Sometimes, a manager has learned about such a system from friends, books, or a consultant, but most often it is one that the manager has observed working very effectively somewhere else and simply does not recognize that the tasks in that environment are different from those in his or her own subunit.

Selection and Development Systems

Selection and development systems that fit task demands are those that help staff a subunit with the quantity and quality of people needed to perform the tasks effectively. The creation of good selection and development systems is central to facilitating a dynamic fit between a subunit's tasks and its employees.

As is the case with many of the organizational problems one finds in specialized subunits, mismatches between selection and development systems and subunit tasks are often caused by changes in the subunit's tasks. Alterations in an organizations's technologies, external environment, or mission are inevitable over long periods of time, and these changes will often cause the subunit's tasks to change. A selection and development system that is consistent with a given set of tasks can become completely inappropriate if there is a significant change in those tasks.[23]

For example, over a period of 15 years, one small company manufacturing predominantly industrial products developed a large number of consumer products. As a part of a general audit of the company's human resources, a consulting firm found that its sales force had an abnormally high turnover and a low morale. Further investigation found that the selection process for a salesperson had changed very little over the preceding 15 years, despite the shift in the company's business and despite other organizational changes such as the addition of product managers. The company was still hiring salespeople whose skills and expectations

[23] Leonard Schlesinger and Richard Walton, "Supervisory Roles in Participative Work Systems," *Academy of Management Proceedings,* August 1978.

were better suited to the old industrial products, which accounted for only about 25 percent of their total sales.

In another case, a technological change in a plant modified the nature of a number of tasks, including routine supervisory ones. Job descriptions were changed, and employees were given special training to help them adjust to the new jobs. But no one changed the routine training and development activities that the plant had used for years. Three years later, plant management determined that many new employees and newly promoted employees were not performing well. An investigation finally identified the mismatch between the old training activities and the new tasks.

Managing the Relationships among Organization Design, People, and Tasks

One of the major responsibilities of any subunit manager is to manage the relationships among organization design, employee, and task variables. While in some situations this responsibility is relatively simple, often it is not. A subunit's tasks can sometimes be so complex that they are difficult to comprehend completely. But without a clear understanding, it is extremely difficult for a manager to keep task variables aligned with the subunit's organizational design and employees. When a subunit has a large number of employees with diverse backgrounds, it can be equally difficult to comprehend the people accurately. And if either the tasks or the employees change very frequently, the potential problems are even greater.

Over the last few decades, a variety of techniques has been developed to help managers better manage the relationships among organization design, people, and task variables. One of the most widely used is called management by objectives, or simply MBO.

MBO

Championed by Peter Drucker,[24] Douglas McGregor,[25] and George Odiorne,[26] MBO has taken many specific forms in actual practice, but usually involves five basic steps:

1. A job description is developed for every job.
2. A list of objectives is developed for each employee in light of the job description. The objectives typically focus on both task accom-

---

[24] Peter Drucker, *Management* (New York: Harper & Row, 1974), chap. 34.

[25] Douglas McGregor, *The Human Side of Enterprise* (New York: McGraw-Hill, 1960), chap. 5.

[26] George Odiorne, *Management by Objectives* (Marshfield, Mass.: Pitman, 1965).

plishment and employee development. These objectives cover some specific period of time, typically one year.

3. The employee and supervisor determine how and when they will be able to tell how well the objectives have been achieved. This step involves deciding how to measure the achievement of objectives and when to review the results.
4. In accordance with the plan determined in Step 3, employee and supervisor review the employee's results against the plan.
5. At the end of the period for which objectives have been established, the employee and supervisor repeat the cycle, starting at either Step 1 or 2.

Within this basic framework, MBO is practiced in many different ways.[27] For example, sometimes the employee is responsible for writing the first draft of the job description, the objectives, and the appraisals; sometimes the supervisor is. Regardless of these details, however, the underlying logic for the approach remains the same. That is, by emphasizing the five steps, one can systematically get people throughout the organization to:

— Design jobs, plans, goals, and measurement systems to fit task requirements.

— Create employee expectations and develop employee abilities that are consistent with job designs, plans, goals, and potential rewards.

Under the right circumstances, MBO can be extremely helpful in managing the fit among organization design, task, and people variables. Nevertheless, despite MBO's popularity, it often ironically creates more organizational problems than it solves.[28]

Many managers have adopted specific MBO systems from consultants or books and have tried to implement them in all of their subunits without carefully considering how appropriate they are, given the subunit's tasks, employee groups, and organizational designs. Predictably, misfits have caused problems, leading a significant number of organizations to abandon their MBO systems.[29]

The most common problems companies have encountered with MBO systems are:

1. MBO-employee misfit: MBO systems are sometimes implemented without adequately training employees to use them. Setting appropriate, measurable objectives, for example, does not come naturally or easily

---

[27] Stephen Singular, "Has MBO Failed?" *MBA,* October 1975, pp. 47–50.

[28] Dallas T. DeFee, "Management by Objectives: When and How Does It Work?" *Personnel Journal,* January 1977, pp. 37–42.

[29] Singular, "Has MBO Failed?"

for most people. In fact, some people, even if taught, cannot use such a system effectively, because it is so much at odds with their natural styles.

2. MBO-task misfits: MBO systems must be used in an environment where task results are at least somewhat measurable, and where goal setting is a meaningful activity. If, for example, tasks are so predictable that goal setting is unnecessary or if tasks are so unpredictable that goal setting is impossible, MBO will not work.

3. MBO–organization design misfits: MBO systems are sometimes simply added onto an organization, not integrated into its existing design. Inconsistencies between an MBO system and the prevailing measurement systems, job designs, and so on, can create serious problems.

No panaceas exist for managing the relationships among a subunit's organization design, tasks, and people. Ultimately, only careful attention and monitoring by managers equipped with skills in organizational analysis will do the job.

Organizational Analysis

Within the context of the specialized subunit (see Figure 3–3), an organizational analysis consists of the following steps:

1. Clearly identify and understand the subunit's tasks. To do this, one needs to consider:
   - The organization's and subunit's environment in terms of general characteristics and key success factors.
   - The organization's overall strategy and its relationship to the subunit.
   - The subunit's technology (especially if it is a manufacturing subunit).
2. Clearly identify and understand the most relevant characteristics of a subunit's current employees, such as their:
   - Number.
   - Background.
   - Skills and abilities.
   - Values and norms.
   - Expectations, especially regarding their work and the organization.
3. Clearly identify the elements of the current organizational design:
   - Structure.
   - Measurement systems.
   - Reward systems.
   - Selection and development systems.

Figure 3–3
Organizational Analysis at the Subunit Level

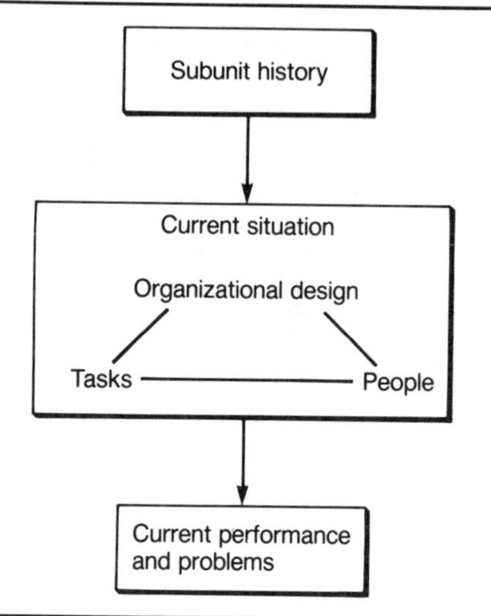

4. Identify the current performance of the subunit as well as any problems or symptoms of problems.
5. Trace the history of the subunit, with special attention to important changes that have occurred in its tasks, people, or organization design. Has the subunit grown in the recent past? Have its tasks changed as the result of a change in technology, business strategy, size, or the organization's environment? How has the organization design changed during this period?
6. Identify the relationships between the subunit's history, its current tasks/people/organization design, and its current performance. A good analysis is characterized by intelligent inferences about these relationships.

Competent organizational analysis not only provides one with a basis for designing viable action alternatives to correct organization design/people/task misfits but it also helps one decide if there really is a problem and, if so, how important it is. Unlike some types of managerial problems, significant organizational problems may sometimes be invisible to most people, while conspicuous problems may be unimportant. Under such circumstances, doing what seems obvious is not a very effective way to manage, and skillful organizational analysis becomes particularly important.

Case 3–1

Megalith, Inc.—Hay Associates (A)

John A. Seeger, John P. Kotter, Anne Harlan, George W. Baird, Jr.

Frank, there's no question about it. We're out of line. Way out of line. The situation is real. It's hurting us, and I have two resignations here to prove it.

John C. Boyd, senior vice president of Finance for Megalith, Inc., paced across his office in agitation. Near the door stood Frank C. Nicodemus, Megalith's vice president for Human Resources. The two men, long-time colleagues in the successful multinational firm, were continuing a debate begun much earlier, when Boyd had attempted to raise the salaries of his key managers by 25 percent.

You'd told me last June that these people were too young and inexperienced to be worth the money, Boyd continued. *And I told you we'd have to pay based on their competence, not their seniority. Now it's October, and two of them have given notice in the past month. You know both of them—Lonny Jackson and George Arnold are two of the best managers in the company. They're half of the team I brought in here to bring the Finance Group out of the stone age, and they've been absolutely vital to the development of the group. And now they're both leaving—to get salaries I wanted to pay them months ago.*

Boyd turned and shook his head. *Frank, I know that what's done is done, and we're not going to get Lonny and George back. But what if my other key people take off, too? Where would that leave us? I've got to have more room in*

Harvard Business School case 476–107.

the salary schedule to take care of the exceptional people who've made this group click!

Boyd paused, and Frank Nicodemus responded. *John, you'll remember I showed you that all four of your key people were right at the top of our scale. Megalith's compensation system isn't something we've arbitrarily picked out of the air; every year we check the schedule against trade associations' published data, and we adjust it to make sure we're above average—that we're competitive with the best in the labor market. To make exceptions to a well-grounded scale would be both hasty and rash. It would raise hell around here, throwing everything out of balance.*

So I held the line. But since then I've been checking to see just how sound our schedules are. We found a consulting firm that has a very good reputation in comparative compensation, and for the past month I've been working with one of their partners. His name is Ed Rogers, and the firm is Hay Associates. You know them: they're the people conducting the climate study right now, and reviewing all our corporate-level job descriptions. Would you like to talk to Rogers?

Frank, I've got the comparisons I need, right here, John Boyd waved a file folder at his friend. *Lonny Jackson will start with an extra $12,000 a year in direct salary and will make a bonanza if he does well as executive vice president of R. G. Miller, and I'm sure he'll succeed. Megalith will have to pay at least $12,000 to find and break in a replacement vice president for Information Systems. What are we saving by putting our budget into search instead of salary?*

And the same thing goes for George Arnold, my treasurer. He's going to take over a new leasing division for Rockwell, and his chance for profit incentive payments there puts anything we can offer to shame.

I just can't compete, Frank. You've got us locked in with a pay schedule that looks competitive on the surface, but when the chips are down, it's a loser." John Boyd hesitated, then continued slowly, *We've never before failed to reach agreement, Frank, but I'm afraid I'll have to fight you on this one. If we haven't solved the problem by the time Allen Whitfield (Megalith's president) gets back from Europe, I intend to ask him to call the board's Compensation Committee in, to review the whole damn system.*

A silence of several seconds was finally broken by the Human Resources vice president. *John, what could the Com-Com really do? They'd* have *to call in professional help, and they'd probably rely on our CPAs or a firm of specialists, like the ones I've already brought in. Wouldn't it make sense to hear what Rogers has to say, before we admit defeat? Won't you talk to him?*

Megalith, Inc.

In its 50 years of operations, Megalith, Inc. had grown to international prominence as a manufacturer of printing equipment, as a publisher, as a supplier of office equipment and supplies, and more recently as a builder of computer-related printers, plotters, and data recorders. From its beginnings, the firm had led the field in development of lithography and photo-offset printing techniques; basic patents in both printing and

Exhibit 1
Corporate Organization Chart, 1982

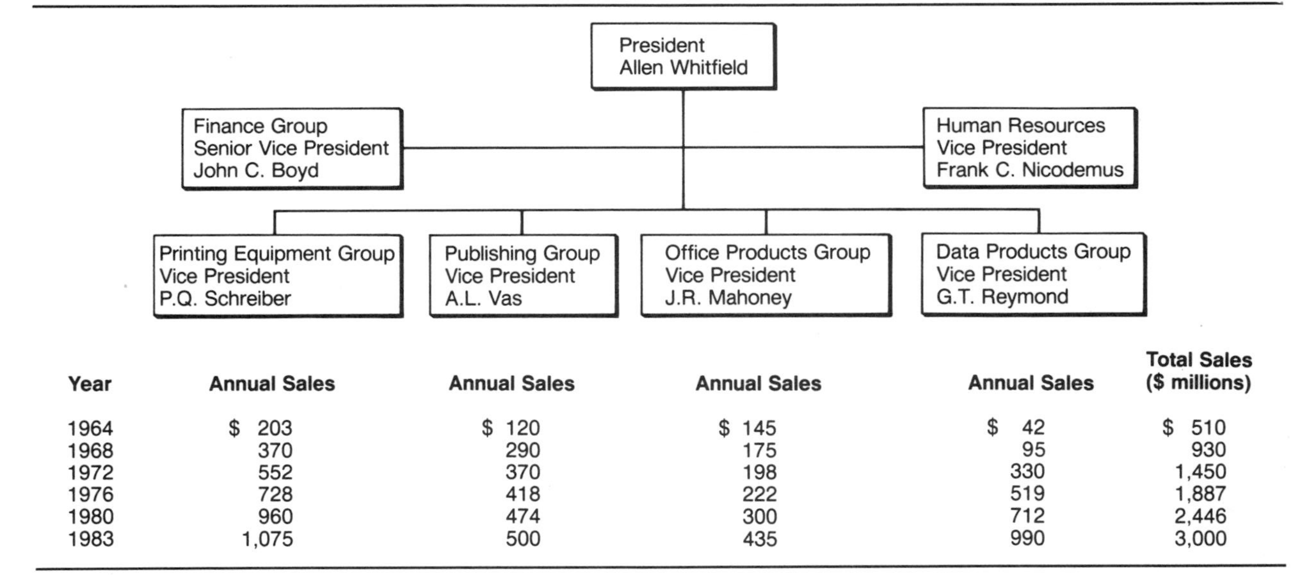

Year	Annual Sales	Annual Sales	Annual Sales	Annual Sales	Total Sales ($ millions)
1964	$ 203	$ 120	$ 145	$ 42	$ 510
1968	370	290	175	95	930
1972	552	370	198	330	1,450
1976	728	418	222	519	1,887
1980	960	474	300	712	2,446
1983	1,075	500	435	990	3,000

plate-making equipment had allowed Megalith to penetrate international markets early in its history. Megalith trademarks were found in virtually every job-shop printing house in the world.

Shortly after World War II the company diversified into publishing; by 1975 it operated large-scale printing plants in seven countries. In the late 1950s Megalith attacked the office equipment industry; primarily through acquisitions it had achieved significant shares of markets in copying equipment, dictating systems, and typewriters—although it had failed to threaten the dominance of Xerox or IBM in these fields. Megalith's newest diversification strategy recognized that computers had come of age as sources of the written word; the firm began acquiring technology-based companies making high-speed line printers, plotters, microfilm output printers, and data recorders. By 1978, Megalith was a leading producer of computer peripheral equipment under its own name, as well as a leading supplier to the computer industry itself. Worldwide sales volume reached $3.0 billion in 1982, and profitability remained at traditionally high levels, in spite of generally poor economic conditions. (Exhibit 1 shows Megalith's corporate-level organization chart, with annual sales by product group since 1964.)

Megalith executives credited the company's success to well-chosen strategy (dominance in printed communication), to technological leadership, and to strength in financial control. They were quick to admit that the company's only failure to reach market dominance—in the office equipment field—was due to the relative unimportance there of financial controls and engineering leadership; marketing genius was required to displace the leaders there. Still, the Megalith Office Products Group contributed significantly to profits and was considered a good investment.

Behind the desk of Megalith President Allen G. Whitfield hung a large, ornately framed poster, loudly proclaiming, "WE PRINT MONEY." The poster had been commissioned when the company had closed the order to equip the United States Mint; it had become an informal slogan of the firm, and smaller reproductions of the poster were common in executive offices and factory washrooms. Megalith people were proud of their "blue chip" reputation.

Hay Associates

In its own, much different market, Hay Associates was also proud of its leadership position. Founded in Philadelphia in 1943, with a psychological assessment and job content measurement focus, the firm now provided the process, skills, and data to help management link business needs with effective human resources management. Hay's integrated business included recognized competence in all aspects of strategic compensation, corporate culture, performance planning and measurement, search, and outplacement. As a multinational, approximately half of

Hay's 1982 revenues of over $100 million came from its 40 offices outside of the United States. Its 10-year growth from 1970 to 1980 averaged 30 percent per year.

Hay Associates brought an approach to compensation problems which began with an understanding of business issues and the corporate culture and developed a design which supported needed objectives. Typically they audited the firm's base salary, short-term and long-term incentives, and benefits to determine the effectiveness of the present system.

Interviews with jobholders were used to develop descriptions acceptable to both the organization and the incumbent. These descriptions were used by a top managment team led by a Hay consultant as a basis of measuring relative job content.

A comprehensive data base, collected annually from hundreds of client firms, permitted the client to compare its base salary practice and total remuneration including benefits with those of a broad industrial or financial base. Since many companies had many businesses, and varied competitive needs, compensation comparisons could be made by appropriate market, geographic, and specific job segments. All contributors to the data base used the same measurement process; therefore, comparisons were always made on the basis of uniform content values for any position.

* * * * *

John Boyd sat comfortably in a leather-upholstered chair beside the window of his Manhattan office. Across a low coffee table, Edmund Law Rogers, partner in the firm of Hay Associates, leaned forward intently, listening.

So there's my situation, Ed. With this team of four really outstanding managers, we've built the Finance Group from a skeleton crew of budget assemblers into one of the finest, most professional teams in industry. Now I'm losing the people responsible for breathing life into this outfit, because our bureaucratic salary system doesn't recognize the difference between talent and mediocrity. Can your system tell the difference?

John, that's a judgment no formal system can make. Only the responsible executive—the man in your own shoes—can tell how well his people are performing, or how high they can go. But a formal system can say something about the jobs themselves. We can compare the jobs in the Finance Group to each other, based on their contents, to give you a measure of internal equity—of how fairly you're paying your people relative to each other. Then we can compare your salaries to those paid for similar-content jobs by a broad spectrum of industry. We can help define what end results each position is accountable for, and those definitions can sharpen your measurements of performance. That can help you decide what "outstanding" means, and how much you're willing to pay for it.

I'd like to know more about these key positions. Do you have a group organization chart handy?

The Megalith Finance Group

In early 1976, Allen Whitfield had asked John Boyd to move from the group vice presidency for Office Products to the new position as senior vice president for Finance. The corporation, with advice from a major American consulting firm, had decided to increase the size of its central financial staff, to bring together in the New York headquarters the analytic and control talents which were then scattered rather unevenly between the operating companies. Whitfield wanted a proven leader to build a coherent finance group, and Boyd was his first choice.

The Finance Group, Whitfield and Boyd decided, should be responsible for end results in the areas of strategy, planning, policy, and control. Exhibit 2 details the specifics of the Finance Group mandate.

Under Boyd's direction, the Finance Group had grown from 350 to 630 employees. (The 1982 organization chart for the department is included in Exhibit 3.) The expansion had required new personnel, and Boyd had consciously decided to seek out energetic, competent, young people who could respond to the challenge, and to bring his new recruits up through the ranks of the group as fast as possible. This "fast track" policy had helped attract the four key people who, Boyd said, had made the concept work. All four of the "young stars" had performed beyond all expectations, impressing the entire senior management group with their imagination, forcefulness, and effectiveness. All four had received every possible commendation, promotion, salary increase, and incentive bonus. (Exhibit 4 shows annual salaries and brief personal data on the key group personnel.)

Exhibit 2
Expected Outcomes for the Finance Group's Activities

1. Financial strategy which significantly contributes to corporate profit and growth objectives.
2. Financial policies, processes, and controls to provide timely and accurate information, comply with accepted practices and regulatory authorities, and protect assets.
3. Corporate planning and measurement process which provides an effective means to integrate group operations, evaluate achievement, and assure top management awareness of problems and opportunities.
4. Continuity of a corporate financial management team organized and competent to achieve functional objectives and a significant contribution to group financial management continuity and competence.
5. Effective asset and liability management which contribute to corporate short-term profit objective and long-term growth and stability.
6. Significant contribution to acquisition strategy and effective implementation through development of objectives, evaluations, and analysis.
7. Systems and control capability to provide effective management information services.
8. An informed top management and board of directors aware of financial results and projections.

Exhibit 3
Organization Chart, Finance Group: July 1, 1982

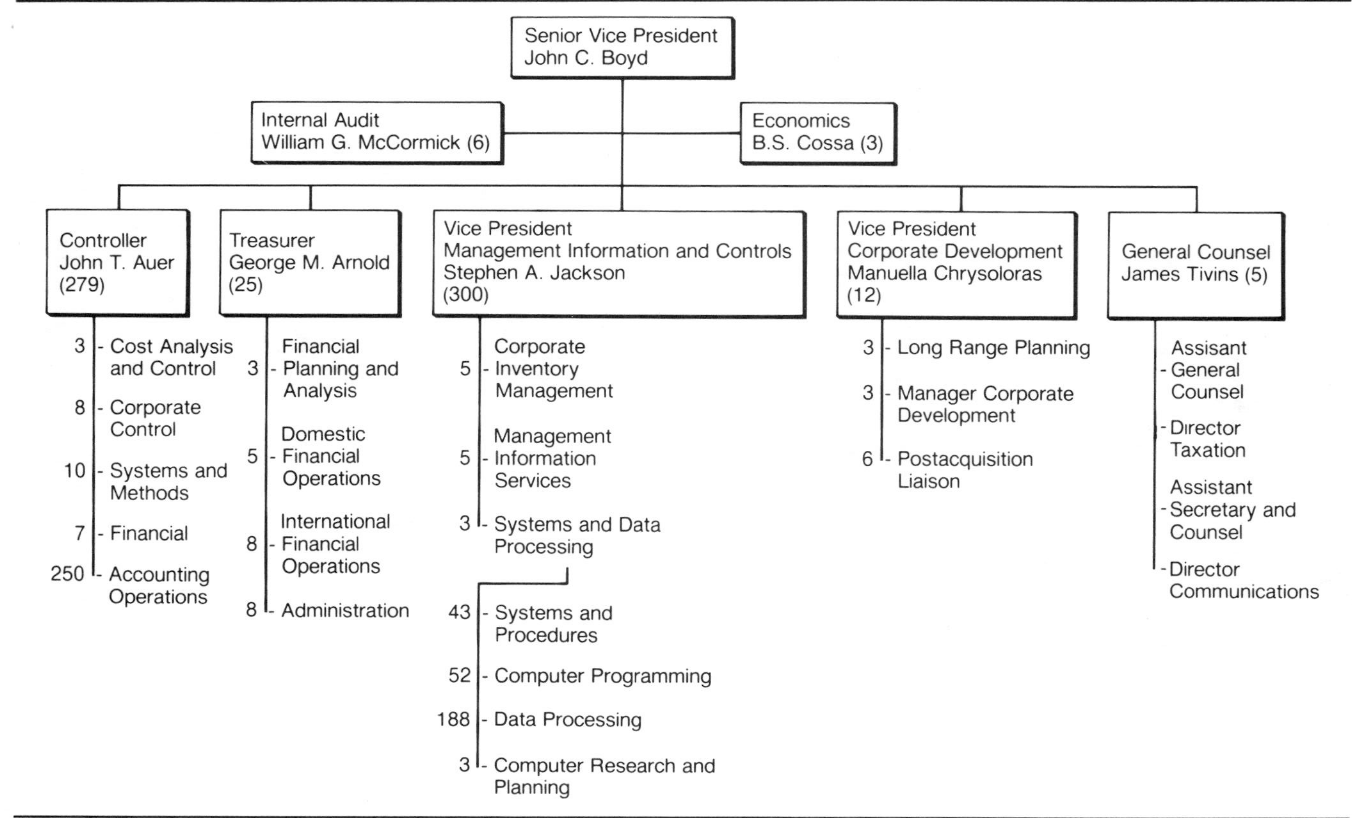

Exhibit 4
Excerpts from Personnel Resources Reference, July 1, 1983

Senior Vice President, Finance: John Covert Boyd, age 54, M.B.A., Harvard, 1955. Founded Duplicopy, Inc. and served as its president until its acquisition by Megalith in 1963. Became group vice president, Office Products, in 1967, and SVP in 1976.
1983 salary: $230,000 plus $35,500 incentive.*

Controller: John T. Auer, age 39. M.B.A., Wharton, 1971. Financial analyst, then assistant controller of Itek International until 1974, when he joined a small consulting firm as an associate. Recruited by Boyd in 1976 to head the controller's Systems and Methods Group. Promoted to director of Accounting Operations in 1980, and to controller in 1982.
1983 salary: $125,000 plus $25,000 incentive.

Treasurer: George Miles Arnold, age 43. M.S., London School of Economics, 1969. Lecturer in finance, University of Bologna, then joined a major international oil company as coordinator of financial planning for Europe and the Middle East. Joined Barclay International in 1974 to form a new consulting services group in international money management. Recruited in 1977 by Boyd to head Megalith International Financial Operations Department; set up the Domestic Financial Operations office in 1979, and reorganized the Accounting Operations department in 1980. Promoted to treasurer in 1982.
1983 salary: $135,000 plus $33,750 incentive (plus car).

Vice President, Management Information Systems: Stephen Alonzo Jackson, age 35. B.S., MIT, 1970. Partner in a small, Boston-based software consulting firm for three years, then head of systems analysis for McGraw-Hill West Coast operations. M.B.A., Stanford, 1977. Joined Megalith as director of Systems and Procedures; became director of Management Information Services in early 1979; director of Systems and Data Processing in 1980; and VP for MIS in 1983.
1983 salary; $110,000 plus $22,000 (plus car).

Vice President, Corporate Development: Manuella Chrysoloras, age 41. M.B.A., Darden, 1969. Joined an investment banking firm, and three years later set up her own brokerage in mergers and acquisitions. Retained by Megalith to assist in acquisition of four small computer peripheral manufacturers, and became executive vice president of the largest one. Drafted into Finance Group by Allen Whitfield in early 1978.
1983 salary: $130,000 plus $25,000 incentive.

General Counsel: James Tivins, age 61. L.L.B., University of Virginia, 1956. Joined legal staff of one of Megalith's printing equipment companies in 1963. Extensive work in antitrust, finance, and tax law. Appointed corporate secretary in 1966, and general counsel in 1975.
1983 salary: $165,000 plus $25,000 incentive.

* Incentive plan payments are based on results for fiscal year ended June 30, 1983; they were approved by the Compensation Committee of the board of directors on September 1, and were paid the following week.

John Boyd stated to Ed Rogers, *It was in June's performance planning meetings with people, I began to feel uneasy. There had been more and more complaints coming from people, about money. Most of them could be handled all right, but with my key people, we were up against the ceilings in both direct salaries and management incentive opportunity. I couldn't offer them enough, and I couldn't get Frank Nicodemus to relax the constraints. You know those personnel people, they always seem to stand in your way.* (See Exhibit 5 for a summary of the Megalith compensation system.) *It's clear now: I should have fought harder. Lonny and George both gave notice in September. Now I'm waiting for the other shoe to drop; if John Auer and Manuella should also leave, it would be like starting over from scratch, to build a new team.*

Was there any connection between the two resignations?

No, Ed. Neither man knew the other was going to quit, and they both feel badly that the group here will suffer. But the money was too much for them to resist.

Are you sure it's money that made them go?

That's what they both said, and I'm sure they're leveling with me. If we'd been competitive, neither of them would have given the time of day to the recruiters who contacted them. Besides, it all fits in with other comments I've heard—that the pay is inadequate.

I've got two issues. First I know that all your comparisons are based on how the job gets measured, and I'm not sure I fully understand how that is done. Second, I believe we should be more imaginative. For example, I've been reading about junior stock plans and believe these would be the type of reward we need around here for my top risk takers.

But let me get back to the question: would your compensation system allow for the exceptional managers? Can we get Frank to give in on those damn ceilings? I need a fast answer, because I'm starting to recruit replacements, and I have to tell them what they can look forward to.

John, I can appreciate your concern. We don't like to lose good people either. You asked several questions, and I'll try to respond to both. First, as you know, a compensation system is made up of many integrated pieces. The measurement of internal relationship of jobs is a basic fundamental, but only one piece. It is not a system. The system includes determination of market posture base, short- and long-term incentives, benefits and perquisites, administration, performance measurements, and so forth. Second, junior stock, as anything else, has to be considered in light of the total reward system.

Boyd and Rogers spend the next half hour discussing the Hay evaluation system, which provides a systematic approach to relative job content measurement. Rogers briefly described the evaluation process. Responding to Boyd's questions, he detailed how a specific job might be evaluated.

Know-how, in the Hay system, is scored according to three different aspects of the job's requirements—technical or practical knowledge, how-

Exhibit 5
Summary: Compensation Policy, Revised July 1, 1977

Compensation objective: To attract and motivate professional management people, enhancing their positive identification with corporate strategy and goals. Total compensation practice shall be competitive with an appropriate market mix of similar high-growth companies.

Compensation components: Cash compensation shall consist of a base salary (determined by comparison with appropriate markets), and management incentive opportunity (determined by formula and approved in each case by the Compensation Committee of the board).

Noncash compensation includes pension plan; deferred savings plan; group life insurance; medical plan; short-term disability and long-term disability plans. These combined benefits approximate 35 percent of base salary expenditures for the company; details of all plans are available from the vice president, Human Resources.

Compensation procedures: All positions shall be described in writing whenever changed or filled following a vacancy; all descriptions shall be audited annually by the Human Resources staff. Changed or added descriptions shall be evaluated by the appropriate HR Review Committee to maintain internal consistency and equity.

Management incentive opportunity plan: MIO payments apply to all positions specifically determined by the Compensation Committee of the board to have both a direct impact on corporate earnings and a distinct requirement for individual discretion in their performance.

Corporate threshold: Before any MIO awards are paid, Megalith must earn a targeted earnings per share as set by the Executive Committee. The EPS goal must equal or exceed the average EPS of the latest three years' operations. The Executive Committee may make an exception to the threshold for a division or group which achieves exceptional results.

Performance planning: Each MIO participant shall agree with his supervisor, before the beginning of each year, on his own performance goals and implementation plans. Group and functional heads are responsible for coordination of these goals within the framework of corporate strategy, and shall inform each participant of his own potential MIO earnings for the forthcoming year, at different levels of performance.

Performance growth plan: Participants will be eligible for annual awards, determined by the Compensation Committee and calculated as a percentage of the MIO payments received during the immediately preceding four years.

Participants may accept awards wholly in Megalith stock (with a 20 percent inducement premium for doing so), or half in stock and half in cash. PGP awards may be deferred until after retirement, and taken over a period not to exceed 10 years, at the participant's option. Cash-deferred awards will accrue interest at the prime rate; stock-deferred options shall reinvest dividends in additional stock.

Exhibit 6

Sample Evaluation

KNOW-HOW

Technical/practical know-how required: SCIENTIFIC DISCIPLINES / SPECIALIZED TECHNIQUES / PRACTICAL PROCEDURES

	● ● MANAGERIAL KNOW-HOW												
●	I. LIMITED Performance or supervision within a single function with operational regard for relevant activities.			II. RELATED Primarily within a single function with some internal or external integration with related fields.			III. DIVERSE Integration and coordination of diversified activities in an operating unit, or in a corporate-wide function.			IV. COMPREHENSIVE Comprehensive integration and coordination in a major management complex, or of a corporate-wide activity.			
	1.	2.	3.	1.	2.	3.	1.	2.	3.	1.	2.	3.	
A. PRIMARY: Elementary plus some secondary (or equivalent) education, plus work indoctrination.	50	57	66	66	76	87						152	A
	57	66	76	76	87	100						175	
	66	76	87	87	100	115						200	
B. ELEMENTARY VOCATIONAL: Uninvolved, standardized work routines and/or use of simple equipment and machines.	66	76	87	87	100	115						200	B
	76	87	100	100	115	132						230	
	87	100	115	115	132	152						264	
C. VOCATIONAL: Procedural or systematic proficiency, which may involve the use of specialized equipment.	87	100	115	115	132	152						264	C
	100	115	132	132	152	175						304	
	115	132	152	152	175	200	200	230	264	264	304	350	
D. ADVANCED VOCATIONAL: Some specialized (generally nontechnical) skills, however acquired, giving additional depth to a generally single function.	115	132	152	152	175	200	200	230	264	264	304	350	D
	132	152	175	175	200	230	230	264	304	304	350	400	
	152	175	200	200	230	264	264	304	350	350	400	460	
E. BASIC TECHNICAL-SPECIALIZED: Sufficiency in a technique requiring a grasp either of involved practices and precedents; or of scientific theory and principles; or both.	152	175	200	200	230	264	264	304	350	350	400	460	E
	175	200	230	230	264	304	304	350	400	400	460	528	
	200	230	264	264	304	350	350	400	460	460	528	608	
F. SEASONED TECHNICAL-SPECIALIZED: Proficiency, gained through wide experiences in a specialized or technical field.	200	230	264	264	304	350	350	400	460	460	528	608	F
	230	264	304	304	350	400	400	460	528	528	608	700	
	264	304	350	350	400	460	460	528	608	608	700	800	
G. TECHNICAL-SPECIALIZED MASTERY: Determinative mastery of techniques, practices and theories gained through wide seasoning and/or special development.	264	304	350	350	400	460	460	528	608	608	700	800	G
	304	350	400	400	460	528	528	608	700	700	800	920	
	350	400	460	460	528	608	608	700	800	800	920	1056	
H. PROFESSIONAL MASTERY: Exceptional competence and unique mastery in scientific or other learned discipline.	350	400	460	460	528	608	608	700	800	800	920	1056	H
	400	460	528	528	608	700	700	800	920	920	1056	1216	
	460	528	608	608	700	800	800	920	1056	1056	1216	1400	

Human Relations Skills required by the position:
1 = basic (courtesy)
2 = intermediate (get along well)
3 = critical (motivate people)

KH	PS	AC	TOTAL
152			

SUPERVISOR KEY PUNCH

KH	PS	AC	TOTAL
304			

ACTUARIAL SPECIALIST
RESEARCH ASSOCIATE

KH	PS	AC	TOTAL
700			

AREA MANAGER

ever acquired; managerial knowledge, in terms of degree of integration and coordination with other functions or activities required by the position; and human relations skills needed to perform the job, classified as basic, important, or critical. (A sample section of the guide chart, used by Rogers to demonstrate the rating of three typical jobs, is included in Exhibit 6.)

A similar, but more comprehensive guide chart has been developed for Megalith's own job evaluations, Rogers said.

Problem-solving requirements of a job are rated according to two dimensions—the thinking environment, ranging from strictly routine to abstractly defined; and the thinking challenge of the job, ranging from repetitive choice making to creative concept formation.

Accountability, the last major area for rating, is measured on three dimensions—the position's freedom to act, ranging from totally prescribed to unconstrained except for broad policy; its impact on end results, ranging from indirect-remote to direct-primary; and the dollar magnitude of the area most clearly affected by the job.

Given a large number of jobs, consistently described and rated, we can compare the salaries, and incentives paid for job contents, rather than job titles, Rogers summed up. *You can't compare on the basis of title, because incumbents, organizations' needs, and/or organizations' styles make the jobs different.*

Here in Megalith, we've finished with the updating of job descriptions (see Exhibit 7 for a sample description), *and I expect to submit our final report to Frank Nicodemus in two weeks. He's said you'll be the first one he sends a copy to.*

John Boyd thought for a moment as he lit a cigarette. *OK,* he said. *You'll tell us how our pay scale stacks up in terms of the jobs we pay for. But you're not going to evaluate the individuals involved, or the problem of identifying exceptional talent and holding it. Is that right?*

John, that's got to be your job. We can help, by giving you information, and an analysis of your own system's strengths and weaknesses, and our suggestions for changing the system.

Our numbers data will *show Megalith's current salary practice, compared with the practice of a broad industrial spectrum. We* will *include an analysis showing what your current salaries would be, if they were fully consistent with the measured content of the jobs. But Frank Nicodemus hasn't asked us to go beyond that in this report.*

In addition to the numbers, you'll see the results of the climate study we've just finished here. About 50 of your finance people have filled out our survey forms, and we'll digest that information for you, relating it to the answers given by several thousand other respondents.

Boyd stubbed out his cigarette and stood. *I'll look forward to seeing that report. And I assume we'll meet again to talk about what it means—probably with Frank.* Boyd smiled. *I've tried a couple of times to pin you down on an answer to this, but you've dodged me. Before you go, I'd like to ask you directly. Do you have any opinion yet on raising these ceilings of ours?*

No way, John, Rogers smiled in return. *But I'll look forward to seeing you again after the report is finished.*

Exhibit 7
Position Description, November 1, 1982

POSITION:	Treasurer	ORGANIZATION UNIT:	Financial
INCUMBENT:	George M. Arnold	LOCATION:	New York

Accountability Objective:

This position is accountable for planning of debt-equity financing and the direction and coordination of cash mobilization, short-term investment, insurance, and benefit plan services.

Dimensions:

Department operating expenses:	$1.0 million
Short-term investment earnings:	$2–5 million
Department employees:	24

Nature and Scope:

Megalith, Inc. is a major, multinational corporation with financing requirements and cash management operations throughout the world. Major outlays of cash are anticipated to continue an upward trend during the next 8–10 years. Possible changes in accounting for and reporting of off-book financing, the need to generate increased amounts of capital overseas for use in overseas operations, and the uncertainties created by new international monetary arrangements pose formidable challenges to the corporation's financial capability and plans for growth. The treasurer's function has been recently reorganized to concentrate on these problems.

Reporting to the treasurer are four directors. Their areas of concentration are:

1. *Financial Planning and Analysis* (3 employees)—This unit conducts overall analysis of debt-equity financing and performs similar analyses in developed plans for financing foreign operations from foreign financing sources; develops plans for the management of foreign exchange; makes buy/lease analyses of property from the financial point of view; and generates regularly total forecasts of cash requirements worldwide for short- and mid-term periods of time, and updates forecasts periodically during the year.

2. *Domestic Financial Operations* (5 employees)—This unit makes short-term investments in the money market including treasury notes, CDs and banker's acceptances; gathers and deposits cash through the operation and collection of 500 bank accounts throughout the United States, and monitors compensating balances in relation to lines of credit.

Exhibit 7 *(concluded)*

3. *International Financial Operations* (8 employees)—This unit coordinates overseas project financing; manages more than 40 bank accounts in approximately 12 different foreign countries, including the transfer of funds between accounts; deals with a variety of currencies; borrows money from other than offshore finance companies; and provides advice and counsel to management on the implications of the cash management and financing support for their operations.

4. *Administration* (8 employees)—This unit develops working company policies, including those having to do with credit and collection, for the guidance of all operating groups; buys insurance (premiums amounting to $2–3 million per year) for the corporation in the form of blanket policies covering worldwide risks (a $3 million deductible provision is a feature of all covered risks). In addition, this unit performs cost-benefit analyses of group benefit plans and participates in negotiating and placing benefits with carriers.

Principal End Results:

1. Financial plans, and forecasts which reliably project the financing needs of the company.
2. Optimum cash availability for current needs through effective use of cash mobilization systems and policies, and efficient financial operations.
3. Maximum return on short-term investments consistent with the company needs for liquidity.
4. A worldwide system of banking relationships that facilitates the management of funds, the availability of cash, short-term investments, and assures required borrowings.
5. Risk and benefits plan placement which effectively meets company objectives.
6. Knowledgeable advice and counsel to management concerning proposed capital expenditures and investments for domestic expansions, acquisitions, mergers and other business ventures.
7. Continuity and development of a professionally competent staff of financial managers and specialists.

Case 3–2

Alcon Laboratories, Inc. (Condensed)

Paul H. Thompson, Joseph Seher, John P. Kotter

In the summer of 1966, George Leone, national sales manager of Alcon Laboratories, initiated an appraisal of the organization and morale of his 70-member sales force. Leone expressed particular concern over the high turnover in the sales force (28 percent in the fiscal year 1965–1966). He had considered a number of changes that might reduce the turnover but was unsure as to just what action he should take. While he was willing to make any changes that might improve the situation, he felt it would be better to do nothing than to attempt changes that were inappropriate to the needs of his organization.

Company History

In Fort Worth, Texas, two pharmacists founded Alcon Laboratories in 1947 on the principle that more accurate, sterile, and stable pharmaceutical compounds could be manufactured by Alcon on a large-scale basis than was possible in retail drugstores, where most prescribed drugs were being compounded at that time.

In early years Alcon management decided to achieve growth by concentrating its marketing efforts in specialty fields. The field in which Alcon first specialized was ophthalmological drugs (drugs used in the

Harvard Business School case 472–115.

Table 1
Highlights of Operating and Financial Data

	1966	1965	1964	1963	1962	1961	1960	1959	1958
Earnings per share	$1.30	$1.05	$1.20	$0.86	$0.66	$0.50	$0.40	$0.30	$0.13
Current ratio	3.24	3.06	2.39	1.96	1.87	1.31	2.25	2.03	2.02
					($000)				
Net sales	$9,114	$8,749	$8,697	$7,718	$6,392	$3,057	$3,094	$2,035	$1,347
Net income	821	663	750	534	404	268	215	163	69
Working capital	3,262	2,448	1,846	1,065	734	186	532	381	169
Total assets	7,016	6,007	5,426	4,413	3,648	2,606	1,810	1,478	545

Table 2
Income Statement*

	Year Ended April 30, 1966
Net sales	$9,114
Costs and expenses	
Costs of goods sold	3,129
Selling, general and administrative expenses†	4,411
Total cost and expenses	7,540
Income before provision for federal taxes	1,574
Provision for federal income taxes	753
Net income	$ 821

* Dollars in thousands.

† R&D represented a significant portion of general and administrative expenses.

treatment of defects and diseases of the eye). In 1947, 85 percent of all eye-care drugs were being compounded in drug stores.

As doctors became familiar with the company's products and their quality, they prescribed them more and more, and Alcon prospered. By 1957 a sales force of 30 people was promoting the company's eye-care products nationally, and sales had grown to nearly $1 million.

Alcon Laboratories continued to grow both domestically and internationally. In fiscal 1966 total sales were $9.1 million. Domestic sales of 33 products were about $6 million and were promoted by a 70-member sales force. In addition, by purchasing another small, specialized pharmaceutical firm, Alcon entered a second specialty field. Furthermore, the company had achieved some backward integration by purchasing a manufacturer of plastic containers for pharmaceutical products. Alcon manufactured and sold its product line internationally through foreign subsidiaries and joint agreements. Table 1 shows selected historical operating and financial information for the period 1958 to 1966. Table 2 gives the consolidated income statement for 1966.

Alcon's Eye-Care Products: Use and Distribution

Alcon manufactured products for a wide array of eye problems, ranging from treatments for serious eye diseases to less serious infections and cleansing agents. Similarly, Alcon sold products used in diagnostics and for surgical assists. These products were available either directly or through wholesalers, both to hospitals and to retail drugstores. Ninety percent of total sales were prescribed by one of the 6,000 ophthalmologists (medical doctors specializing in the treatment of eye diseases and defects) or by one of 2,000 eye-ear-nose-throat doctors who practiced in the United States. Alcon salespeople regularly visited these doctors.

The Market and Competition

In 1965, total retail sales of ophthalmological drugs in the United States were $30 million. Alcon Laboratories' share of the total domestic ophthalmological drug market was nearly 20 percent. Small, specialized manufacturers like Alcon, which attempted to find a niche in the total market by catering specifically to the ophthalmic market, competed directly with Alcon. The company also competed with large, diversified drug manufacturers for whom certain segments of the ophthalmic market were large and lucrative enough to warrant attention. Alcon management stated that in 1966 two large drug manufacturing firms controlled about 30 percent of the domestic ophthalmic market.

The active chemical compounds used in various ophthalmological preparations were essentially the same, regardless of manufacturer. Competing products were differentiated primarily on the basis of their form[1] and vehicle.[2] Competing manufacturers were constantly looking for new preparations that would have performance superior to existing ones. While Alcon was interested in developing compounds of active ingredients, the major thrust of its research was to improve the performance of existing compounds by developing better or new forms and vehicles.

Marketing Department

Organization. The Marketing Department of Alcon Laboratories was under the direction of the marketing director, who was also a vice president of Alcon and a member of the company's executive management group. Ed Schollmaier, who currently held this position, was 32 years old and had risen rapidly at Alcon. After receiving his M.B.A. at the Harvard Business School in 1958, he had started as a salesman with Alcon, and in a short time he had been promoted to district sales manager. After less than two years with Alcon, he had been called into the home office to assist in directing the sales effort. In 1963 he was appointed director of marketing. Reporting to Schollmaier were the national sales manager, product managers (marketing responsibility other than direct sales), and the director of market research.

The primary responsibility of the Marketing Department was to assure the success of the sales effort. The home office was responsible for the design of the sales program, while the field sales organization was responsible for the program's execution. A great deal of time and effort

---

[1] *Form* referred to whether the compounds came in solution, ointment, cream, pill, and so forth.

[2] The *vehicle* comprised the inactive ingredients that were important in determining such product qualities as the stability of the product, how well the product stayed in the eyes (instead of "sweating out"), the irritation and/or side effects of the product, and so forth.

were typically spent on both areas. According to a 1965 study, drug and pharmaceutical firms' selling costs were twice those of U.S. industry as a whole. The survey showed that in 1964 the cost of selling pharmaceuticals amounted to 30.5 percent of gross sales revenue. This study included as selling costs such items as seminars held for doctors to acquaint them with new drugs, and samples sent out as part of a product's introductory stage. Other industries did not have such expenses to the degree that the drug industry had, and some companies included similar costs in R&D for accounting purposes. Another factor to consider in comparing drug industry costs with those of other industries was that most consumer goods manufacturers shared costs of advertising with retailers; drug companies, on the other hand, bore most of these costs alone. In addition, allowances for returned merchandise were higher in the drug industry, since companies regularly took back unopened stock that was out of date. The study presented the following breakdown of total selling costs (see Table 3). Between 1961 and 1966, Alcon's total annual expenses for advertising, merchandising, and promotion increased from $90,000 to $750,000.

The central activity of the Marketing Department was the planning of promotion programs, a joint responsibility of the product managers and the national sales manager. Prior to the beginning of each fiscal year, the product managers would meet with George Leone, the national sales manager. This group would draw up a list of the particular products to be promoted in the coming year, on the basis of the size of the total promotion budget, the length of time since a product had been actively promoted. Leone's estimate of market potential, the current share of market held by the products involved, and competitive activity. Products on the list were then assigned specific dates for promotion. This promotion schedule was then approved by the marketing director.

The promotional campaign was developed by the product managers, who first consulted with the national sales manager for his ideas on market positioning. After the campaign had been designed, the national sales manager and his subordinates taught the sales force how to carry

Table 3
Total Selling Costs

	Drug Industry	Average, All Industries
Sales force		
Compensation	37.3%	45.2%
Travel and other expenses	13.6	12.8
Sales management costs	14.0	16.2
Advertising, merchandising, and promotion	29.9	14.2
Servicing	3.0	7.4
All other costs	2.2	4.2
Total	100.0%	100.0%

it out. To provide the sales force with the information that was desired by doctors, the Marketing department needed the aid of the Medical Department and the Research Department.

The Medical Department was responsible for professional contact with members of the medical profession. Through a clinical liaison group, the medical department engaged physicians doing clinical research to conduct studies to test the uses or find new uses for Alcon's products. These findings were frequently used in the form of professional articles, technical bulletins, or promotional campaigns. It was not uncommon for a member of the Marketing Department to ask the Medical Department to help in developing some technical data to support particular claims for a product.

Alcon's R&D Department was also important to the marketing effort. The development of new chemical compounds, new uses of existing compounds, and improvements in existing compounds, were all considered to be of prime importance. Introducing new and improved drug preparations was considered to be one of the most effective ways to increase sales and enhance the company's reputation in the medical community. Sales of various ophthalmological preparations tended to be more stable than the sales of the pharmaceutical preparations in general, which were characterized by extreme volatility due to the frequent introduction of new chemical compounds that made existing compounds, in all types of forms and vehicles, obsolete. Alcon management stated, however, that "the impact of new products (i.e., new formulations of existing ophthalmological compounds) since 1960 accounted for more than half of Alcon's growth, and half of that growth was attributable to innovations in the steroid product category in particular."

The mutual interests of the Marketing, Medical, and R&D Departments were coordinated through meetings of the Product Committee whose members included Ed Schollmaier, marketing vice president; Dr. Earl Maxwell, medical director and director of R&D; Frank Buhler, director of International Operations; and William Conner, chairman of the board and president. For example, through the Product Committee the time and resources of the R&D Department might be allocated to fill gaps in the product line, as determined by sales management and product managers. The need for providing technical data from the medical department was also coordinated through the Product Committee.

The National Sales Manager. George Leone headed the 70-member sales force in 1966. He had been with Alcon since 1950, when there were only six salespeople in the company. After doing an outstanding job as a salesman, he was made a district sales manager in 1955, a regional sales manager in 1961, and national sales manager in 1963.

As national sales manager, Leone was responsible for the overall administration and performance of the sales force and for coordinating the activities of the sales force with other groups in the Marketing Department. In his administrative capacity, Leone was primarily concerned with the establishment of company programs in the areas of recruitment and selection, training and development, supervision, standards of performance appraisal, and compensation and benefits. He was also responsible for identifying and developing field sales managers.

Leone directed three groups of personnel: regional managers, district sales managers, and medical sales representatives. The latter were more commonly known within the industry as salespeople, and were frequently identified by physicians as "detail men." Exhibit 1 shows a chart of the sales organization.

Regional Sales Managers. Alcon divided the United States into four large sales regions, each supervised by a regional sales manager. The job description in the company's supervisory manual listed five major functions for the regional sales manager (RSM):

1. Recruitment and selection of candidates for field sales work (medical service representatives) with special emphasis on applicants with management potential.
2. Training and developing the district managers.

Exhibit 1
Sales Group: Organization Chart

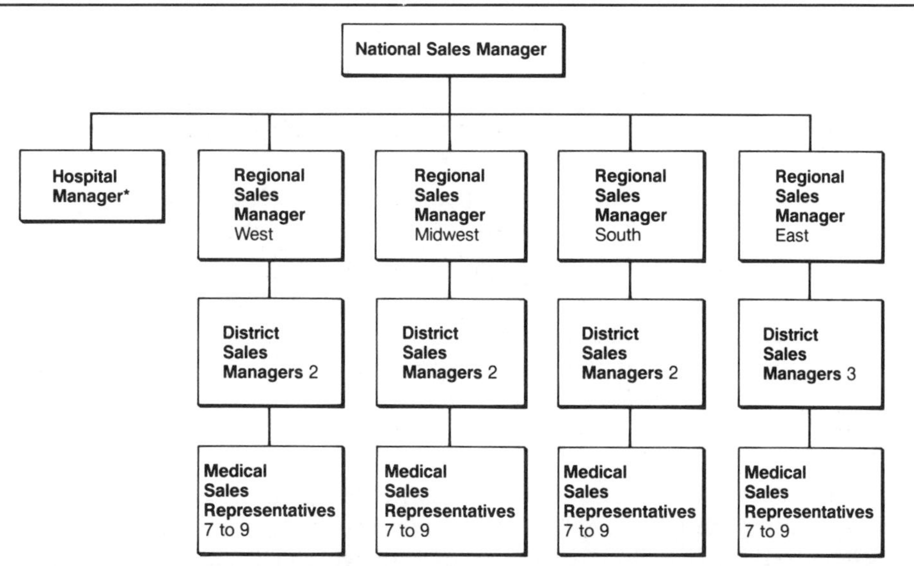

* From 1963 to mid-1965 only; dropped in 1965 because of the overlap between calls on doctors when they were at the hospital and when they were at their private office.

3. Supervising, directing, and controlling the activities of the district sales managers.
4. Maintaining communications with the home office through weekly reports and with the sales force through quarterly regional sales meetings.
5. Planning and organizing to help set the objectives for the region and to help the district sales managers set their goals.

The job description stated that RSMs should spend a minimum of 35 percent of their time in personal field visits with their district sales managers. They had no direct customer responsibilities.

Three of the four regional sales managers worked in the home office and spent a good deal of their time working with Leone in planning the national sales effort. They were involved in sales promotion, planning, meetings, and developing company policies and procedures for recruiting, selection, training, and supervision of the sales force. The fourth RSM was in the process of moving from Chicago to the home office.

District Sales Managers. Reporting to each of the four regional sales managers were two to three district sales managers (DSMs). An Alcon district was a subdivision of a region (for example, the New England states constituted one district of Alcon's eastern region). The district sales manager's job description listed five major duties:

1. Recruiting, selecting, and with approval from RSM, hiring salespeople to become medical sales representatives.
2. Training and developing the field sales force.
3. Supervising, directing, and controlling the activities of the field sales force.
4. Maintaining communications with home office and with RSM, and conducting quarterly district sales meetings.
5. Planning and organizing operation of districts through setting objectives for field salespeople.

The job description further stated that the DSM should allocate his or her time as follows: "a minimum of 75 percent of his time in personal field visits with the medical sales representatives, and the remainder (25 percent) at medical meetings, sales meetings, and visits with regional sales manager." The DSMs, like the RSMs, had no direct customer responsibilities.

Sales Force. Reporting to each of the nine district sales managers were seven to nine medical sales representatives (MSRs). These 70 salespeople were responsible for Alcon's direct customer contacts. Each MSR covered one Alcon territory. The medical sales representative's job description listed six major duties:

1. Call on each of the following:
   a. All eye physicians within territory.
   b. All pharmacies on call list.
   c. All hospitals on call list.
   d. All wholesalers on call list.
2. Follow the sales program, including using all sales tools outlined by the program.
3. All MSRs must fulfill their performance standards and objectives each month in the following areas:
   a. Doctor call standards (*a* above).
   b. Retail call standards (*b* above).
   c. Wholesale call standards (*d* above).
   d. Increase sales objective (the DSM and MSR together set a specific objective as to how much sales will increase in the current year over the previous year).
   e. Ratio of increased sales to sales cost; for example:

$$\begin{array}{lcc} & \textbf{1966} & \textbf{1965} \\ \dfrac{\text{Total territory sales}}{\text{Total territory costs}} & \dfrac{\$100{,}000}{12{,}000} = \dfrac{8}{1} & \dfrac{\$120{,}000}{20{,}000} = \dfrac{6}{1} \end{array}$$

   f. Featured product (the one being promoted or detailed) objective.
   g. Turnover order objective.[3]
4. Planning and organizing territory coverage by maintaining territory coverage plan and territory records.
5. Maintaining communications with supervisor and the home office by submitting the required daily, weekly, and monthly reports.
6. Meeting standards of self-development by attaining an adequate product knowledge, and knowing and complying with company policies on appearance, conduct, and maintaining company property.

Top management described the sales force's activities as falling into two distinct categories: *creating demand* (when the MSR is in the doctor's office, trying to get the doctor to prescribe Alcon's products), and *distribution* (supporting demand by getting the product to the wholesaler and retailer).

Selling in the Drug Industry

Salespeople in the drug industry as a whole made an average of 48 calls per week. A typical day for a member of Alcon's sales force started by

[3] Turnover orders were those that the drug salespeople wrote for the drug retailer and hand carried or mailed to the drug wholesaler to be filled.

driving 50 miles to a city to make calls, waiting up to 30 minutes to see a doctor, actually seeing only five of the nine doctors called on, and spending only about 5 minutes with each doctor because of busy schedules. In a normal day, the sales representative also called on one drug wholesaler and three drug retailers, spending only about 15 minutes with each.

Alcon salespeople typically saw their DSM only once a month, but maintained weekly contact by telephone. Alcon salespeople generally saw each other only at their bimonthly sales meetings. Although they had infrequent contact with other Alcon salespeople, the typical MSR had the opportunity for more frequent contact with other companies' salespeople detailing the same area.

The Doctor Call. Alcon, as well as other drug companies, considered "detailing" the doctor as one of the best ways to create demand for both new and existing products; thus salespeople called on eye doctors once a month. On a typical visit to an eye specialist, the Alcon MSR was ecpected to detail one primary product, one secondary product, and one "door handle" product (one that was just mentioned on the way out). Any one product was usually detailed for three consecutive months, though some were detailed for only one month, while others were detailed for as long as seven consecutive months.

The MSR was supposed to discuss with the doctor whether he now used the product being detailed, or would use it in the near future. Because doctors were so busy, the salespeople had only a brief period to make their presentations. One doctor commented: "The detail men have to see you at your office. I'm very busy there, so it is hard to find time to see them. I can only give them 5 to 10 minutes and that is time away from seeing my patients." Alcon's management hoped that the MSR's brief presentation would make a lasting impression on the doctor. Journal advertising and direct-mail promotions from Alcon were timed to support the salespeople's message to the doctor.

The Retailer Call. The Alcon sales force also called on retail druggists. There were 55,000 drugstores in the United States, but according to Alcon management the Alcon sales force called only on the 10 percent that did the most business in ophthalmological drugs. In the course of calls on retail druggists, salespeople would make it known which product(s) were being detailed in the area and thus which drug(s) doctors would probably be prescribing. If Alcon had any promotional deals on over-the-counter items (usually an offer of free goods with each purchase, e.g., 1 free item with each 12 purchased), the MSR would bring these to the druggist's attention. During the call, the MSR checked the druggist's stock of Alcon products and indicated which areas the druggist should replenish. The MSR attempted to persuade the druggist to stock at least one bottle of all Alcon products and several bottles of the fast-moving items. The MSR would write up the order and mail it or take it to the druggist's wholesaler.

The Wholesaler Call. To obtain adequate distribution of a product, it was also important to call on drug wholesalers. The average Alcon territory contained six drug wholesalers who served as intermediaries between drug manufacturers and drug retailers. Wholesalers maintained sales staffs on their own by which they contacted many more retail druggists than Alcon's MSRs were able to see. A wholesaler's sales force would make calls on each retail druggist once a week and would have daily contact with each druggist by telephone. Thus wholesalers, once sold on Alcon products, could shoulder a considerable part of the sales effort.

When a new product was being introduced, or when an existing product was being promoted, the Alcon MSR was expected to call on each wholesaler to gain support for the product(s) in question. The purpose of this effort was to persuade the wholesaler's sales manager to use his or her sales force to give special attention to Alcon's product. The Alcon MSR was supposed to show the sales manager the detail piece on the product, along with any available literature. While at the wholesaler's, the MSR also attempted to see the buyer or purchasing agent to ensure that a six- to eight-week supply of Alcon's products was maintained.

The casewriter observed that few Alcon salespeople were able to execute promotion of new products. The buyer and sales manager of the wholesaler saw about 100 drug salespeople per week and were pressed for time.

The Call Mix. Alcon's management explained that the same MSR called on the doctor, the retailer, and the wholesaler because the calls were highly related and needed careful coordination. For instance, since no order was written in the doctor's office, the MSR would not know if the doctor would actually prescribe the detailed product or not. One of the best ways to find out was to call on the pharmacist a few days after detailing the doctor and inquire whether Dr. X was prescribing the product in question. If the MSR had established a good relationship with the pharmacist, the pharmacist would, in all likelihood, tell the MSR. In fact, the pharmacist often went so far as to let the salesperson check through the pharmacy's prescription file to see what all of the doctors were prescribing. With this type of information, the MSR knew which products were selling well and which products should be discussed with a doctor on the next visit.

In addition, Alcon managers emphasized that distribution and demand creation had to be closely coordinated. By handling all three types of calls, the sales force could assure the doctors that the pharmacists had the drug they prescribed in stock, and they could assure pharmacists that doctors would prescribe the drugs they stocked.

Alcon managers observed that the retailer calls and the wholesaler calls were directly related. First, they were both distribution calls. Secondly, the turnover order took the MSR back to the wholesaler with a definite order from a retailer, thus giving the MSR an opportunity to urge further purchases of Alcon's products.

While Alcon's management had agreed that one MSR should handle both demand creation (doctor calls) and distribution (wholesaler and retailer calls), in the past there had been a difference of opinion in the Marketing Department as to which of the two areas should receive the greatest emphasis. As a result, emphasis had shifted from time to time.

In the past, when a new product was introduced, Alcon management had emphasized demand creation. Historically, this had resulted in a sales increase that was consistent with top management's commitment to rapid growth. As sales began to level off, however, an easy way to boost sales was to emphasize distribution by loading up the wholesaler and retailer with inventory. The distribution campaigns had included deals, the use of promotion money to the wholesaler's sales force, and sales contests for Alcon's salespeople. In addition, automatic shipments (i.e., shipments of goods which Alcon estimated could be sold, but which had not been ordered by the wholesaler) would often be made to wholesalers during these periods.

There had been a number of distribution campaigns during periods of slow sales growth. One had been held in May 1964, when a six-month distribution campaign was launched and a sales contest was initiated, in which the winner from each of the four regions won a trip to Mexico. When the contest was over, however, some wholesalers shipped goods back to Alcon (all of Alcon's sales were guaranteed; i.e., Alcon agreed to take back products that were unsold after a specific time). In one winner's territory, returns exceeded sales for a month or two. During the nine months following the contest, three of the four winners left Alcon.

Such distribution campaigns caused wide fluctuations in sales, and strained relations with wholesalers and retailers. Management recognized the undesirable consequences of such actions and concluded that enduring sales growth came only from demand creation. With this in mind, in October 1964 George Leone shifted the emphasis of the sales effort to demand creation. He instructed salespeople to spend 75 percent of their time calling on doctors (compared with 40 percent during the distribution campaign). The salespeople told the casewriter they welcomed this shift in their call mix because they preferred doctors calls to distribution calls. Management believed that MSRs who preferred distribution calls, such as the four contest winners, left the company when the shift in emphasis took place.

Alcon maintained this emphasis on demand creation, and managers stated that they did not intend to return to the practice of using distribution campaigns to boost sales in periods of slow growth.

Administration of Sales Force

Alcon, like the rest of the industry, had found that it was difficult to find and keep a person who could perform all of the required functions of the medical sales representative. In the past six years the annual turnover of Alcon's sales force had averaged approximately 33 percent.

Recruiting and Selection. District sales managers were responsible for recruiting and selecting salespeople for each of their territories—they had an instruction manual to help them. One page was entitled "The Man You Want"[4] and listed the following characteristics:

> 25 to 35 years of age; preferably married—stable domestic life; college degree; scientific and business courses; above-average grades in school; good work history, preferably in sales/marketing; good grooming and physical appearance; good health, past and present; sound financial position; good diction and use of grammar—articulate, able to understand and project emotions and ideas; has self-confidence and poise; self-starter; doesn't object to travel; enjoys working with people; ambitious with maturity, honesty, and integrity; and enthusiasm and capacity for work.

The district managers used several techniques to find people with these qualifications. When a vacancy occurred in an area, the district manager typically first contacted schools if the opening occurred around commencement time.

George Leone said that Alcon recruited at business schools in particular because Alcon liked to hire M.B.A.s. He felt that the training and ambition of M.B.A.s made them compatible with Alcon's objectives and organization. Leone believed that Alcon had hired approximately 20 M.B.A.s within the last 10 years; 4 to 8 had left the company. Leone identified those still with Alcon; he believed that there were two others whom he had not included on the list (see Table 4).

A brochure in the Harvard Business School Placement Office contained the following statement: "The company is small by usual standards, but it offers the opportunity for easy recognition of contribution and rapid promotion to greater management responsibilities. Initial as-

---

[4] At that time, Alcon's sales force consisted entirely of men.

Table 4
Alcon's Sales Force

Employee	M.B.A. Received	Present Position
A	HBS '57	Financial vice president
B*	HBS '58	Marketing vice president
C	HBS '60	Comptroller's Department
D	HBS '59	Product manager
E*	HBS '62	Product manager
F*	HBS '64	Assistant product manager
G	Chicago	International comptroller
H*	N. Texas	Salesperson
I*	Northwestern	District manager
J	Wharton '65	n.a.

* Began by working as an MSR.

signments are in field sales. M.B.A.s are expected to reach district manager level within 18–24 months."

If qualified applicants were unavailable at business schools, the district sales manager next contacted an employment agency, where typically about 40 people were interviewed. After the first round of interviews, the sales manager would narrow the field to 10–12 applicants for second interviews. If the sales manager was unable to fill the vacant positions on the sales force, using these sources, a district sales manager would then use a classified advertisement to recruit applicants. One district sales manager had used the following ad several times under such circumstances:

Careers in Sales

Leading to sales management for qualified men based on performance. Young dynamic pharmaceutical company, growth rate of 47 percent per year. Leader in its field has openings local and away. Creative ambitious men with drive and determination, college degree. Science background helpful. Unusual remuneration and incentive plan tops in the industry. Excellent training program, liberal benefits, insurance, pension, stock options, profit sharing. Rare opportunity for growth for self-motivators. Men with an outstanding record of success in selling considered. Call OL 3–4818, Sunday, 1 to 5 P.M.

Resumes to
Box X
[City, State]

This district sales manager reported that the ad brought an average of 75 resumes each time it was used in a large East Coast city; 40 to 45 of these resumes could be discarded immediately on the basis of age or educational background. After telephone interviews with the remaining 30 to 35 applicants, the sales manager would discard 10 to 15 more. Personal interviews would be held with the remaining 10 to 15 applicants.

One district manager explained his selection process:

My selection is generally made during the second interview as to my first, second, and third choices for a man to fill a vacancy. Then I have two or three more interviews with these men and their wives. The average interview time for a man who is hired is a total of approximately 10 hours. By the time he is hired we really know one another and what we expect from one another. In rare instances, where there is competition for manpower from other industries in a given area, I may make a tentative offer on the spot during the first interview. In a case like this, the first interview would run one and a half to two hours.

Selection was based primarily on the characteristics listed previously under "The Man You Want." The extent to which applicants fulfilled these characteristics was determined on the basis of information gathered through interviews, on application forms, and testing.

The district sales manager was required to spend a good deal of time recruiting because of the high turnover rate in the sales force. In 1965–66 the region with the highest turnover had 6 people out of 19 leave. This region had the equivalent of four sales territories vacant for the year.

Training. Each new MSR entered a four-week training program, which was under the direction of the DSM and took place in the field. In the first week, the DSM worked with the new MSR, demonstrating calls on the doctor, the wholesaler, and the retailer. In the evening the new MSR was expected to learn company policies and procedures and to gain an adequate product knowledge, including the following: *(a)* basic anatomy, physiology, and pathology of the eye; *(b)* basic ocular therapy and medical concepts; *(c)* basic pharmacology; *(d)* Alcon product advantages; and *(e)* competitive products.

During the second and third weeks, the new MSR went into the territory of a senior salesperson in the district and made as many field calls with the senior salesperson as possible to perfect the first week's training. In addition, the MSR was expected to continue spending evenings on gaining product knowledge.

In the fourth week, new MSRs worked in their own areas under the supervision of the DSM. At this point the MSR was supposed to make most of the calls while the DSM observed. The DSM made sure that the new MSR was prepared to handle the territory.

This concluded the formal training of the new MSR. After this initial training, the DSM worked with the MSR only periodically, giving additional training as necessary. The new salespeople reported to the casewriter that while an effort was made to do this, the DSM was often too busy to carry out the training as planned.

To develop field sales managers, at the end of 1964, Alcon introduced a program for training managers called the advanced development program (ADP). Outstanding salespeople who were interested in advancement were included in this program (there were nine ADPs in the summer of 1966). The program consisted of each ADP doing a number of individual projects that were usually performed by field managers; for example, the ADP would recruit and train new salespeople. George Leone said, "Four of our best field managers today came from this program."

Control and Evaluation. To keep track of what each MSR was doing, Alcon required that two reports be submitted by each salesperson to the DSM and the home office, including the following:

1. A daily report of all calls made, by type of call, and the number and amount of turnover orders. This report was cumulative on a monthly basis.
2. An expense voucher to be filled in daily and mailed to Fort Worth on Saturday morning.

In addition, the MSR was required to keep territory records, including a doctor call book with information such as the doctor's day off, the best time to call, the doctor's specialty, and so forth.

Once a year the district sales manager conducted a performance appraisal of the MSR. The DSM then made a recommendation for a salary increase based on this performance appraisal and the MSR's commission for the past year. Management maintained that the introduction of regular performance appraisals greatly improved the compensation of the sales force at Alcon, making it more equitable by relating salary increases more closely to performance. In addition, the company made it a practice to terminate salespeople who did not meet the high standards set by the company.

Compensation. Compensation for salespeople was in the form of salary plus commission. Alcon's starting salaries ranged from $400 to $700 per month, depending on the training and experience of the new person.

Table 5
Salespeople's Salaries at Alcon

Year Ending April 30	Average Annual Salary of All Salespeople*
1962	$5,760
1963	6,168
1964	6,744
1965	6,900
1966	6,960

* Excludes commissions.

Table 6
Drug Industry's Total Compensation for Salespeople, Salary and Commission: 1964

100th percentile	$25,000
75th percentile	9,000
50th percentile	8,000
25th percentile	7,000
1st percentile	5,000

A group of 28 companies manufacturing drugs, chemicals, and cosmetics reported the following data concerning the compensation (salary and commission) of their salespeople:

Compensation for:	Midpoint	Range
Highest person	$12,000	$8,000–25,000
Top half of sales force	9,000	8,000–10,000
Lowest person	6,000	5,000– 7,000
Lowest half of sales force	7,000	6,000– 8,000

Source: *Sales Management,* January 21, 1966.

In 1966, Alcon's salespeople's salaries ranged from $500 to $916 per month, and averaged $580 per month. Each MSR was eligible for a yearly salary increase, and the annual increase could be up to one half of the commission received the preceding year. Table 5 presents MSRs' salaries from 1962 to 1966.

Management expressed the opinion that although Alcon had been behind the industry in compensation before, significant salary increases had made Alcon quite competitive with the drug industry. Table 6 presents data on the drug industry's compensation of salespeople in 1964.

Commissions were handled in the following manner: A new MSR was placed on commission after three months of employment with Alcon, following a performance review and approval by all levels of field supervision. Commissions were paid twice each fiscal year and were based on 10 percent of increased sales after total MSR expenses (including car expenses, motel, telephone, meals) had been deducted. The following is an illustration of the commission plan:

MSR's sales:	1965	$75,000
	1964	50,000
Sales increase		25,000
Salesperson's expenses		−12,000
		13,000
		×.10
Commission		$ 1,300

The commission plan had been introduced in 1960 when the company was having trouble controlling salespeople's expenses. Some Alcon managers had expressed the feeling that this plan was not equitable because it penalized those with large territories requiring overnight travel. Total commissions paid to the 70 salespeople in 1965–66 were $26,000, ranging from $0 to $1,500 individually, but Leone observed that 80 percent of the commission payments went to 20 percent of the sales force.

Thirty-eight salespeople had been hired and retained since 1964. Of these, more than two thirds were between the ages of 25 and 30 and more than three fourths were married. Virtually all of them had earned a bachelor's degree, in a wide range of fields. Prior to joining Alcon, they had 31 collective years of sales experience and 52 years' experience in a variety of occupations.

Attitudes of Managers, Salespeople, and Customers

In the course of gathering material for the case, the casewriter interviewed individuals at different organizational levels within Alcon. In addition, he interviewed a number of eye doctors, drug retailers, and drug wholesalers concerning their attitudes toward drug salespeople.

The two DSMs interviewed by the casewriter reported that other activities prevented them from spending 75 percent of their time with the MSR as their job description required. With a high turnover in the sales force, it was necessary for them to spend a great deal of time on recruiting and selecting new salespeople. One DSM had three vacancies to fill in a four-month period, and it was necessary for him to spend nearly all his time trying to fill those vacancies during that period. The DSM also reported that "the job has changed a lot in the past two to three years. Before, I just worked with the men, but now I am running an organization. I hire, fire, train, and evaluate men. I also run a good bit of the sales meetings. We have one about every two months."

Views of Selected MSRs. Don Wade, an Alcon salesman for eight years, expressed the following comments, which seemed typical of Alcon's older salespeople:

> *The most important thing is to sell the doctor and create demand for your product. If you just get it into the retailer and then the doctor doesn't write it, you have problems because the retailer will send it back. I provide information to the doctor. The doctors ask me about drugs, ours and our competition's; they ask me what they are and what they do, etc. If I don't know about a product, I don't try to bluff it, so they trust me. If a competitor's product is good, I tell the doctor it is. I've been with Alcon a long time, so I know the doctors and they write my products. When I come around with a new drug, the doctors trust me, so they'll start right in and use it.*
>
> *The doctor call is indirect selling; you don't write up an order, and you don't know if you have sold him. That's what makes it such a challenge. I enjoy trying to match wits with the doctor, and I can tell 80 percent of the time whether*

I have sold him or not. But you have to know what he is saying. A doctor will promise you anything. They want to be nice to you like they are to their patients, so they will say they will use your drug and then they won't follow up and do it.

You have to use finesse with the doctor—it's a soft sell. You have to know where he went to school, his likes and dislikes. The more you can get him to talk, the better you can sell him. The doctor is more professional and more ethical.

A distribution call, on the other hand, is direct selling. The pharmacist is more interested in money, so you have to show how your product will make him a profit. The pharmacist trusts me, so I just check his inventory, decide what he needs, and write up the turnover order. Usually he doesn't even see it. I just send it to the wholesaler. It's the same way with the wholesalers. I have a good relationship with them, and they just let me write up the orders.

An interview with John Cook revealed the attitude of the younger, more ambitious salespeople. Cook had been with Alcon just one year and was described by the DSM as a good management prospect. He said:

It's a hard sell with the doctor. You're in there as a salesman to sell your product. You really have to know your doctors because you can really pin some of them down and get a commitment to write your product, but with others you can't do much. So you have to know which ones to push. You have to get to know the receptionist too, because she guards the doctor and can prevent you from seeing him.

I would rather call on the doctor because he treats me like a professional man. It's just a chore to make retail calls. I spend 85 percent of my time calling on doctors because I'd rather call on them. Some of our wholesalers are upset because they say Alcon is high pressure as a result of the distribution campaign two years ago.

Bob Jensen, a salesman with three years' experience at Alcon, commented:

I studied premed in college, but I didn't have good enough grades to get into medical school. However, I still wanted some dealings with the medical profession, so after I got some sales experience I came with Alcon. Because the eye doctors know that Alcon only calls on eye doctors, they like to see the Alcon man. So I am accepted more by doctors than the detail men from other companies are.

I enjoy calling on the doctor because he is more professional—ethical. The only problem is that you don't know when you've sold the doctor. You get better feedback from the pharmacist because you write up an order there.

Ninety-nine percent of the doctors accept me very well; about 50 percent of them call me by my first name, but it's taken two years to get on a first-name basis. The doctor would rather discuss products with a friend, so if you have been calling on him a while and he knows you, he'll listen.

Comments from Doctors. Doctor Jones was about 45, had a large practice, and also did some work with a well-respected eye clinic in the large eastern city where he practiced. His views were typical of the busy, successful ophthalmologist.

The detail man keeps the doctor informed. He makes the information available before it comes out in the journals (the journals are always months behind), and you can ask questions of him directly.

I like a detail man who is pleasant and sincere, and one who has a knowledge of his product or at least is honest enough to let you know when he doesn't. I also prefer one that makes no demands. Some of them will say, "I'll be back in 10 days to see how you've gotten along with my product," and it puts you on the spot.

When asked which companies were doing the best job of promoting their products, Dr. Jones replied:

The question really should be which ones see you most frequently? The answer is Alcon; Smith, Miller & Patch; and Upjohn, I guess. I tend to write more of their products when they call frequently and I have more knowledge of their products. I depend on the detail man to get information on things like products, sizes, availability, etc. They keep me up-to-date on new developments.

Dr. Barron was about 50 years old. Barron, less busy than some other eye doctors, commented that detail men could be quite helpful:

I am influenced by the detail man. I have an emotional affinity for him, and he leaves a lot of samples. I feel an obligation to him, and I'll write his drugs. But I don't like the overpowering salesman. I like a neat, well-dressed, polite man who just gives me information. I think all detail men are frustrated doctors—you wouldn't really want to be a detail man. Generally, the salesmen are very nice people and very cooperative.

Pharmacist's View of the Sales Force. A pharmacist was asked about his feelings toward the sales force and the companies they represented. He expressed his views as follows:

The ethical drug salesman tells us about new products, price changes, and what's being detailed, because that's what sells. He comes in and writes up the order. Then we check it over and cut back if he's put in too much of any product.

All the major companies do a good job. Upjohn, Merck, etc. But the small companies have high turnover. They'll have a new man in here about every month. We sometimes have a problem with them.

The salesman expects us to keep his products in stock; he sells the products to the doctor. He also asks for information on what the doctors are writing. We have a prescription file, and he's welcome to look through it.

Wholesaler's View of the Sales Force. The following interview with a buyer at a busy wholesaler gives an indication of his attitude toward the sales force:

I like salesmen who take care of the details on their products, such as price changes, returns, checking inventory, and giving us information on new items.

Also, I don't like pressure. We are trying to sell merchandise and in order to sell we have to buy. We don't need anyone to pressure us. It's just the new man or the fly-by-night guy who gets this pitch from the home office and tries to shove it down our throat. But by and large they tend to be quite professional in their approach.

When asked specifically about Alcon, the buyer said: "They're a little pushy, a little bang-bang. But they are less so now than in the past. They tended to put up these deals at the home office and then put them off on us."

Sales Force's View of the Marketing Effort. A number of managers and salespeople pointed out that the quality of the promotion developed by the product managers could greatly influence an MSR's success. With a high-quality program and the support of direct-mail and journal advertising, the MSR could significantly increase sales of featured products. The salespeople appeared to agree that the work of the product managers had improved a great deal in the past two to three years, and that they were doing an excellent job. Many of the sales force expressed concern, however, about the infrequency with which Alcon had introduced new products. One MSR said that in the past six years Alcon had introduced only "two big new products," and that it was only in those periods that the company had experienced rapid sales growth. One manager pointed out that Alcon had significantly expanded its R&D effort in the past two years and that "we now have in R&D more Ph.D.s per sales dollar than anyone else in the industry, and we are currently spending 10 percent of sales for that purpose."

Sales Force's Views of the Company, Compensation, and Opportunity for Advancement. The following is another part of the interview with Don Wade, who had been with Alcon over eight years:

You can't make big money in the drug business, and if you compare Alcon with the others in the industry, their salary is not the best, but they hit a happy medium. I've been offered more money by other drug companies, but Alcon has a great future and they have a good relationship with the doctors.

Alcon has the best opportunity for advancement in the industry, if you're looking for that. I'm not. I just want to be a salesman. The DSM has to travel too much and I don't want to be away from my family any more than I am now.

Our company has been weak in supervision compared with other drug companies. At least we've been weak in the past. But now they're doing a better job of training a man before they make him a DSM. Nobody can learn the drug business in two years, so our managers just haven't had enough field experience.

When asked why so many salespeople had left Alcon, Wade replied: "Alcon promises you the sky in terms of advancement and then they just don't come through. So, when the boys have been here awhile and they don't get a promotion as soon as they were told they would, they leave."

Nearly all of the Alcon employees interviewed said they believed that there were excellent opportunities for advancement with Alcon. Management indicated, however, that there were no plans to expand the sales force or the number of field managers in the immediate future. When the casewriter presented this apparent contradiction to Dave Colton, a salesman who had been with Alcon for five months, Colton replied that he expected to advance with Alcon. He believed that there would be an opportunity for him to be promoted into a management position in one of the companies that had been acquired or would be acquired by Alcon.

Management Concern

Management was aware that turnover was high among sales personnel throughout the drug industry (12.1 percent in 1964), but Alcon turnover was a great deal higher than at other drug companies. In fact, it had been as high as 42 percent in 1964. (Table 7 shows the turnover in Alcon's sales force from 1961 to 1966, and the length of service of those leaving.)

Management was concerned about the high turnover for several rea-

Table 7
Alcon's Sales Force Turnover Data

A. Turnover of Alcon's Sales Force

Year Ending April 30	Percent Turnover
1961	35
1962	27
1963	35
1964	42
1965	34
1966	28

B. Length of Service of Salespeople Terminating

Number of Months Employed	Personnel		Cumulative Personnel	
	Number	Percent*	Number	Percent*
6 or less	4	14%	4	14%
12 or less	8	28	12	41
18	4	14	16	55
24	2	7	18	62
30	5	17	23	80
36	1	4	24	83
42	1	4	25	87
48	1	4	26	90
60	3	10	29	100

* Figures do not add to 100 due to rounding.

sons. First of all, it was costly. Although Alcon's figures were not available, one survey reported, "The cost of selecting, training, and supervising a new drug salesman averages $7,612 excluding salary." Just as important as cost was the fact that it took one to two years for an MSR to establish a relationship with the doctor, the wholesaler, and the retailer. Most of the men who left had been with Alcon less than two and one half years; they just barely got to know the customers before leaving.

George Leone was uncertain about why so many people had left Alcon. He indicated that almost all of them said they were leaving because they were not earning enough money, but he was not sure that was the whole reason. Alcon had raised salaries considerably in the past three years, but people were still leaving. Leone felt that part of the problem may have been the shift in emphasis from demand to distribution and then back to demand. Leone noted that Alcon's higher turnover had occurred in the years when they had distribution campaigns.

Reading 3–1

Reward Systems*

Edward E. Lawler III

Organizations distribute a large number of rewards to their members every day. Pay, promotions, fringe benefits, and status symbols are perhaps the most apparent but certainly not all of the important rewards. Because these rewards are important, the ways they are distributed have profound effects on the quality of work life that employees experience as well as on the effectiveness of organizations.

Despite the importance of rewards in organizations, most of the writings concerned with quality of work life have tended to ignore or play down their impact. This is a serious oversight and one that needs to be corrected if organizations are to be designed in ways that provide a high quality of work life. One reason for this oversight may be the often made assumption that there is a very simple and direct relationship between the amount of reward received and the quality of work life. If this view is accepted, then improving the quality of work life is simply a matter of giving everyone more rewards. The research that has been done, however, shows that this is too simple a view. Some rewards have been found to contribute more to a high quality of work life than others, and problems of equity cannot be solved simply by giving more rewards. These findings will be reviewed later in this chapter when we focus on the characteristics of different rewards and on some of the approaches to reward system design that promise to increase both the quality of work life and organizational effectiveness. But before specific rewards and reward practices are considered, it is necessary to review briefly

---

* Reprinted by permission from chap. 3, "Reward Systems," in *Improving Life at Work: Behavioral Science Approaches to Organizational Change,* ed. J. R. Hackman and J. L. Suttle (Santa Monica, Calif.: Goodyear Publishing, 1977).

what is known about the determinants of people's affective reactions to rewards, and about the impact of reward systems on organizational effectiveness.

Reward Systems and Individual Satisfaction

A great deal of research has been done on what determines whether individuals will be satisfied with the rewards they receive from a situation. This research has shown that satisfaction is a complex reaction to a situation and is influenced by a number of factors. The research can be summarized in five conclusions:

1. *Satisfaction with a reward is a function of both how much is received and how much the individual feels should be received.* Most theories of satisfaction stress that people's feelings of satisfaction are determined by a comparison between what they receive and what they feel they should receive or would like to receive (Locke, 1969). When individuals receive less than they believe they should, they are dissatisfied; when they receive more than they believe they should, they tend to feel guilty and uncomfortable (Adams, 1965). Feelings of overreward seem to be easily reduced by individuals and therefore are very infrequent (surveys often show about 5 percent of an employee group feel overpaid). Feeling of overreward are usually reduced by individuals changing their perceptions of the situation. For example, they increase their perceptions of their worth, or their perceptions of the amount of pay deserved. Feelings of underreward are less easily reduced and often can be reduced only by an actual change in the objective situation—by higher pay or a new job.

2. *People's feelings of satisfaction are influenced by comparisons with what happens to others.* A great deal of research has shown that people's feelings are very much influenced by what happens to others like themselves (Patchen, 1961). People seem to compare what others do and what others receive with their own situations. These comparisons are made both inside and outside the organizations they work in, but are usually made with similar people. As a result of these comparisons, people reach conclusions about what rewards they should receive. When the overall comparison between their situations and those of others is favorable, people are satisfied. When the comparison is unfavorable, they are dissatisfied.

People consider such inputs as their education, training, seniority, job performance, and the nature of their jobs when they think about what their rewards should be. There are often substantial differences among people in which inputs they think should be most important in determining their rewards. Typically, people believe that the inputs that they excel in should be weighed most heavily (Lawler, 1966). This, of course, means that it is very difficult to have everyone satisfied with their rewards, because people tend to make their comparisons based on what is most favorable to them. Individuals also tend to rate their inputs higher than do others. It has often been noted, for example, that average employees rate their job performances at the 80th percentile (Meyer, 1975). Given this and the fact that the average person cannot be rewarded at the 80th percentile, it is not surprising that many individuals often are dissatisfied with their rewards. Still, it is possible to influence how satisfied employees are by altering the total amount of rewards that are given and by altering how those rewards are distributed. Some distribution patterns clearly are seen as more equitable and satisfying, because they are more closely related to the inputs of individuals and therefore to what people feel they should receive.

It is because individuals make comparisons that people who receive less of a given reward often are more satisfied with the amount of the reward they receive than are those who receive more (Lawler, 1971). For example, people who are highly paid in comparison to others doing the same job often are more satisfied than are individuals who receive more (for a different job) but are poorly paid in comparison to others doing the same kind of job.

3. *Overall job satisfaction is influenced by how satisfied employees are with both the intrinsic and extrinsic rewards they receive from their jobs.* A number of writers have debated the issue of whether extrinsic rewards are more important than intrinsic rewards in determining job satisfaction. No study has yet been done that definitely establishes one as more important than the other. Most studies show that both are very important and have a substantial impact on overall satisfaction (Vroom, 1964). It seems quite clear, also, that extrinsic and intrinsic rewards are not directly substitutable for each other, because they satisfy different needs. To have all their needs satisfied, most individuals must receive both the intrinsic and the extrinsic rewards they desire and feel they deserve. This means, for example, that money will not make up for a boring, repetitive job, just as an interesting job will not make up for low pay.

4. *People differ widely in the rewards they desire and in how important the different rewards are to them.* Probably the most frequently and hotly debated topic related to the quality of work life concerns how important different rewards are to employees. One group of writers says money is the most important, while another group says interesting work is *(Work in America, 1971).* Both groups, of course, are able to find examples to support their points of view, because for some people money is most important and for others job content is most important. People differ substantially and in meaningful ways in what is important to them. Some groups, because of their backgrounds and present situations, value extrinsic rewards more than do others. For example, one review gave the following description of a person who is likely to value pay highly: "The employee is a male, young (probably in his 20s); he has low self-assurance and high neuroticism; he comes from a small town or farm background; he belongs to few clubs and social groups, he owns his own home or aspires to own it and probably is a Republican and a Protestant" (Lawler, 1971). People with different personal and background characteristics, on the other hand, value an interesting job more highly.

The research on the importance of different rewards also quite clearly shows that the amount of reward a person has strongly influences the importance attached to it (Alderfer, 1969). In the case of extrinsic rewards, for example, those individuals who have a small amount of a reward typically value it the most. It also appears that the importance individuals attach to rewards shifts as they acquire and lose quantities of different rewards. Some evidence suggests that minimal amounts of the rewards that are required to maintain a person's physical well-being and security are needed before other rewards become very important (cf. Cofer and Appley, 1964).

Overall, reward systems seem to have a greater influence on individuals' satisfaction with rewards than on the importance attached to those rewards (Lawler, 1971). Both satisfaction and importance can be influenced by the amount of rewards that organizations provide. But satisfaction seems to be much more susceptible to influence, because it is directly affected by reward levels. The importance of rewards, on the other hand, is influenced by things that are beyond the control of organizations (such as family background and the economic climate), as well as by satisfaction.

5. *Many extrinsic rewards are important and satisfying only because they lead to other rewards.* There is nothing inherently valuable about many of the things that people seek in organizations. They are important only because they lead to other things or because of their symbolic value. A particular kind of desk or office, for example, often is seen as a reward because it is indicative of power and status. Money is important only because it leads to other things that are attractive, such as food, job security, and status. If money were to stop leading to some or all of these things, it would decrease in importance (Vroom, 1964). Because extrinsic rewards typically lead to other rewards, they can satisfy many needs and thus remain important even when conditions change.

Necessary Reward System Properties

On the basis of what has been said so far about rewards and satisfaction, we can identify four important properties that any organizational reward system must have if it is to produce a high quality of work life. First, the system must make enough rewards available so that individuals' basic needs are satisfied. If these needs are not met, employees will not be satisfied even if external comparisons are favorable. Fortunately in most work situations the employees' basic needs are satisfied, often because of the requirements of federal legislation and union contracts. It is often pointed out, however, that sometimes these needs are not met, particularly the need for security. When the need is not met, action to increase job security must be taken before a high quality of work life will be present. Just meeting basic needs is not enough.

Second, the reward levels in the organization must compare favorably with those in other organizations. Unless the reward levels compare favorably with what other organizations provide, individuals will not be satisfied with their rewards because they will inevitably note that they are not as well off as others.

Third, the rewards that are available must be distributed in a way that is seen as equitable by the people in the organization. People compare their own situations with those of others inside the organization. And they are likely to be dissatisfied if, in their organization, people they perceive as less deserving receive more rewards, even though they themselves are in a favorable position with respect to the outside market. People have a sense of equity, which involves considerations of how much they receive in comparison to what others around them receive, regardless of the absolute amount they receive or their position in the outside market. To construct a reward system that is high on internal (within-organization) equity, it is necessary to base that system on the perceptions of the people in the organization. As will be emphasized later, the most direct way to take these perceptions into account is to have people in the organization make the decisions about how much different individuals will be rewarded.

Finally, the reward system must deal with organization members as individuals. This means recognizing their individuality by giving them the kinds of rewards they desire. This point is crucial because of the large differences among people in what rewards they want. Unless these differences are explicitly recognized, it is unlikely that a reward system will be broad enough and flexible enough to encompass the full range of individual differences.

In summary, because of the nature of people's reactions to reward systems, a reward system must be built in a way that allows it to provide four things: (1) enough rewards to fulfill basic needs, (2) equity with the external market, (3) equity within the organization, and (4) treatment of each member of the organization in terms of his or her individual needs.

Reward Systems and Organizational Effectiveness

In looking at the role of rewards in organizations it is not enough to look only at their impact on the quality of work life. Consideration must also be given to the impact of rewards on organizational effectiveness. Indeed, the adoption of any reward system hinges partially on the impact it is expected to have on organizational effectiveness. A reward system that substantially reduces organizational effectiveness is not likely to be voluntarily adopted, no matter how much it contributes to a high quality of work life. Further, quality of work life and organizational effectiveness are closely tied together, because without some level of organizational effectiveness, there is no organization and no work life at all. Thus, the challenge is to find reward systems that contribute to both organizational effectiveness and a high quality of work life.

Organizations typically rely on reward systems to do four things that contribute to organizational effectiveness: (1) motivate employees to join the organization, (2) motivate employees to come to work, (3) motivate employees to perform effectively, and (4) reinforce the organizational structure by indicating the position of different individuals in the organization. The considerable amount of research that has been concerned with each of these functions of reward systems is summarized in the following four sections.

Reward Systems and Organizational Membership

There is a great deal of evidence which shows that the rewards an organization offers directly influence the decisions people make about whether to join an organization, as well as their decisions about when and if to quit (see Lawler, 1971, and Yoder, 1956, for reviews). All other things being equal, individuals tend to gravitate toward and remain in those organizations that give the most desirable rewards. This behavior seems to be explainable because high reward levels lead to high satisfaction. Many studies have found that turnover is strongly related to job satisfaction and somewhat less strongly related to satisfaction with the extrinsic rewards a person receives (Porter and Steers, 1973). Apparently this is true because individuals who are presently satisfied with their jobs expect to continue to be satisfied and as a result want to stay with the same organization.

The relationship between turnover and organizational effectiveness is not so simple. It is often assumed that the lower the turnover rate, the more effective the organization is likely to be. This probably is a valid generalization, because turnover is expensive. Studies that have actually costed it out have found that it often costs an organization five or more times an employee's monthly salary to replace him (Macy and Mirvis, 1974). However, not all turnover is harmful to organizational effectiveness. Clearly, organizations can afford to lose some individuals, and indeed may profit from losing them. Thus, turnover is a matter of both rate *and* who turns over.

The objective should be to design a reward system that is very effective at retaining the most valuable employees. To do this a reward system must distribute rewards in a way that will lead the better performers to feel satisfied when they compare their rewards with those received by individuals performing similar jobs in other organizations. The emphasis here is on *external* comparisons, because turnover means leaving an organization for a better situation elsewhere. One way to accomplish this, of course, is to reward everyone at a level that is above the reward levels in other organizations. However, this strategy has two drawbacks. In the case of some rewards (for example, money), it is very costly. And it can cause feelings of intraorganizational inequity, because the better performers are likely to feel inequitably treated when they are rewarded at the same level as poor performers in the same organization, even though they are fairly treated in terms of external comparisons. Faced with this situation the better performers may not quit, but they are likely to be dissatisfied, complain, look for internal transfers, and mistrust the organization.

What, then, is the best solution? It would seem to be to have competitive reward levels and to base rewards on performance. This should encourage the better performers to be satisfied and to stay with the organization. It is important to note, however, that not only must the better performers receive more rewards than the poor performers, but they also must receive *significantly* more rewards because they feel they deserve more (Porter and Lawler, 1968). Just rewarding them slightly more may do no more than make the better and poorer performers *equally* satisfied.

In summary, managing turnover means managing satisfaction. This depends on effectively relating rewards to performances, a task that is often difficult. When it cannot be done, about all an organization can do is to try to reward individuals at an above-average level. In situations where turnover is costly, this should be a cost-effective strategy even if it involves giving out expensive rewards.

Organizational Effectiveness and Absenteeism

Absenteeism, like turnover, is expensive. Like its twin, tardiness, it leads to overstaffing. Another result is that untrained and inexperienced individuals do the jobs of those who are absent. Thus, it makes sense for organizations to adopt reward policies that minimize absenteeism. What kind of reward policies will do this? A great deal of research has shown that absenteeism and satisfaction are related. When the workplace is pleasant and satisfying, individuals come regularly; when it isn't, they don't. Basically, therefore, reward policies that make work a satisfying place to be and that tie rewards to attendance will reduce absenteeism.

Several studies have shown that absenteeism can be reduced by tying pay bonuses and other rewards to attendance. This approach is costly, but sometimes it is less costly than absenteeism. It seems to be a particularly useful strategy in situations where both the work content and the working conditions are poor and do not lend themselves to meaningful improvements (see, for example, Hackman, 1977). In situations where work content or conditions can be improved, such improvements are often the most effective and cost-efficient way to deal with absenteeism. Thus, reward system policies are only one of several ways to influence absenteeism, but they are potentially effective if an organization is willing to tie important rewards to coming to work. In many ways this is easier to do than tying rewards to performance, because attendance is more measurable and visible.

Reward Systems and Motivation

When certain specifiable conditions exist, reward systems have been demonstrated to motivate performance (Lawler, 1971; Vroom, 1964; Whyte, 1955). What are those conditions? Important rewards must be perceived to be tied in a timely fashion to effective performance. Stated another way, research shows that organizations get the kind of behavior that is seen to lead to rewards employees value. In many ways this is a deceptively simple statement of the conditions that must exist if rewards are to motivate performance. It is deceptive in the sense that it suggests all an organization has to do is to actually relate pay and other frequently valued rewards to performance. Not only is this not the only thing an organization has to do, but it is very difficult to accomplish (Tosi, House, and Dunnette, 1972; Whyte, 1955). Tying rewards to performance requires a good measure of performance, the ability to identify which rewards are important to particular individuals, and the ability to control the amount of these rewards that an individual receives. None of these things are easy to accomplish in most organizational settings, a fact that has led some to conclude that it is not worth trying to relate rewards to performance (Meyer, 1975).

Organizations must not only tie important rewards to performance, but they must do so in a manner that will lead to employees' perceiving the relationship. This means that the connection between performance and rewards must be visible, and that a climate of trust and credibility must exist in the organization. The reason why visibility is necessary should be obvious; the importance of trust may be less so. The belief that performance will lead to rewards is essentially a prediction about the future. For individuals to make this kind of prediction they have to trust the system that is promising them the rewards. Unfortunately, it is not entirely clear how a climate of trust can be established. However, some research suggests that a high level of openness and the use of participation can contribute to trust.

Reward Systems and Organizational Structure

In all complex organizations there is division of labor. Organizations differ, however, in the degree to which members have unique, highly specialized jobs, and in the degree of hierarchical differentiation that exists (Galbraith, 1973; Lawrence and Lorsch, 1967; Lorsch and Morse, 1974; Perrow, 1967). Some organizations, for example, are characterized by relatively flat structures and only a few levels of management; others have many levels—often as many as 20 in very large organizations. Some organizations are broken up into many departments, each of which has a function; others as a matter of policy try to discourage a high level of functional specialization.

In any organization, reward systems can be used to reinforce the existing or desired structure, and to help it operate effectively. The military is perhaps the clearest example of an organization that uses the reward system very effectively to differentiate between people in different positions. Each rank in the military has different privileges; there are even separate officer clubs and housing areas on bases. The argument in favor of such differentiation is that is helps make the organization more effective, because it clearly establishes who has authority and makes it easier for subordinates to take orders because they come from the position rather than from the person. Thus, the whole use of rewards in military organizations is designed to be congruent with the reliance on steep, strict hierarchies with decision making centered at the top.

At the other extreme are organizations that consciously try to give everyone the same fringe benefits, parking spaces, and offices, to diminish the distance between different organizational levels. The argument here is that the lack of differentiation among people in terms of rewards and symbols of office, when combined with a relatively flat organization structure, produces an organization that is highly participative, equalitarian, and flexible. The further argument is that large differences among people in a more participative organization are incongruent with this style of management and organization structure and would be counterproductive. This is an interesting argument but one lacking substantial research support. Nevertheless, as various reward system practices are considered, it is important to think about whether they lead to differential or similar treatment of organization members who are at different management levels.

Reward System Requirements

Table 1 summarizes what has been said so far about what a reward system must do if it is to contribute to organizational effectiveness and the quality of work life. Although there is not perfect agreement between the reward system characteristics that lead to a high quality of work

Table 1
Overview of Reward System Requirements

Quality of work life	
a. Reward level	A reward level high enough to satisfy the basic needs of individuals.
b. External equity	Rewards equal to or greater than those in other organizations.
c. Internal equity	A distribution of rewards that is seen as fair by members.
d. Individuality	Provision of rewards that fit the needs of individuals.
Organizational effectiveness	
a. Membership	High overall satisfaction, external equity, and higher reward level for better performers.
b. Absenteeism	Important rewards related to actually coming to work (high job satisfaction).
c. Performance motivation	Important rewards perceived to be related to performance.
d. Organization structure	Reward distribution pattern that fits the management style and organization structure.

life and those that lead to organizational effectiveness, there is a high degree of overlap. Rewards that are seen to be fair in terms of both internal and external comparisons are functional for both, because they lead to high satisfaction, low absenteeism, and low turnover. Tailoring the rewards to the needs of the individual can also contribute to both a high quality of work life and organizational effectiveness. This approach leads to high satisfaction and can help make a performance motivation system more effective by assuring that valued or important rewards are tied to effective job performance.

Tying rewards to performance contributes to motivation. It can also contribute to satisfaction because people only feel equitably treated when rewards are based on their contributions, one of the most important of which is job performance. Satisfaction of basic needs and provision of high overall reward levels contribute primarily to a high quality of work life; congruence with organization structure seems to contribute primarily to organizational effectiveness. In order for reward systems to operate in the manner that we have identified as optimally effective, there are five identifiable characteristics that the rewards themselves should have. These include (1) importance, (2) flexibility, (3) frequency with respect to administration, (4) visibility, and (5) low cost.

A reward must be *important* to some individual or group of individuals if it is to influence organizational effectiveness and employee satisfaction. Thus, the first question that needs to be asked about any reward is whether it is valued by the particular individuals involved. Although it is possible to identify some rewards as more important than others *on the average,* there are large individual differences in how important rewards are.

A reward system that relies solely on generally important rewards inevitably is going to miss some employees, because even rewards that are important to most employees are not important to everyone. This creates the need for individualizing rewards (Lawler, 1971) so that employees will receive the rewards each specifically desires. In some situations, individualization can be accomplished—and the quality of work life improved—by giving people the choice of which extrinsic rewards they will receive. For example, one company allows workers who have finished their daily production quota the choice of going home or receiving extra pay. If rewards are to be tailored to individuals, those rewards must be flexible with respect to both the amount given and whether it is given to everyone in the organization. It is impossible to create individualized reward packages without flexibility. Further, unless there is flexibility in who receives rewards, it is impossible to vary rewards according to the performance of individuals; thus, equity is difficult to achieve. Overall then, *flexibility* is a desirable characteristic for a reward to have.

Related to the issue of flexibility is the issue of *frequency.* Giving rewards frequently is often helpful for sustaining extrinsic motivation and satisfaction. Thus, the best rewards are those that can be given frequently without losing their importance.

The *visibility* of rewards is important because it influences the ability of the reward to satisfy esteem and recognition needs. Low-visibility rewards cannot satisfy these needs and therefore often are less valued by employees. Visibility is also important in clarifying the relationship between rewards and performance.

Finally, the *cost* of the reward is relevant because it is a constraint that the organization must consider. A high-cost reward simply cannot be given as often, and when used reduces organizational effectiveness as a result of its cost.

Table 2 presents an evaluation of the common rewards that are used by organizations in terms of their average importance, flexibility, visibility, frequency, and cost. As can be seen from the table, none of the rewards rate high on all of the criteria. Interestingly, pay seems to possess all the characteristics that are necessary to make it the perfect extrinsic reward except one—low cost. It is particularly expensive to use as an extrinsic reward, because individuals need to receive frequent pay increases or bonuses in order for sustained extrinsic motivation and satisfaction to be present.

Promotion, dismissal, and tenure are all low in flexibility. They cannot be easily varied in amount according to the situation. They also cannot be given very regularly. This makes it difficult to tie them closely to performance over a long period of time. Job tenure or a guarantee

Table 2
Evaluation of Extrinsic Rewards

	Average Importance	Flexibility in Amount	Visibility	Frequency	Dollar Cost
Pay	High	High	Potentially high	High	High
Promotion	High	Low	High	Low	High
Dismissal	High	Low	High	Low	High
Job tenure	Moderate	Low	High	Low	High
Status symbols	Moderate	High	High	Low	Moderate
Special awards, certificates, and medals	Low	High	High	Low	Low
Fringe benefits	High	Moderate	Moderate	Low	High

of permanent employment, for example, is a one-shot reward, and once it is given it loses all ability to motivate. These rewards also tend to be expensive. Their high cost is not as visible and obvious as is the cost of pay, but it is real. Special awards, certificates, and medals are examples of rewards with quite a different set of characteristics. They are high in flexibility and visibility. However, they can only be given a few times before they lose their value. And because many people do not value them at all, their average importance is relatively low.

In summary, there is no one reward or class of rewards that meets all the criteria for being a good extrinsic reward. Furthermore, organizations have little control over how important different outcomes are to individuals. However, organizations do control which outcomes they use. It is important that each organization carefully diagnose its situation and use the one or ones that are right for its particular situation. Failure to do this assures that the reward system will fail to contribute to a high quality of work life and organizational effectiveness.

Table 2 points out that promotion, fringe benefits, and pay are the extrinsic rewards that can have the greatest impact on the quality of work life as well as on organizational effectiveness, because they are important to most individuals. Each of these rewards also has other characteristics that make it potentially effective.

References

Adams, J. S. "Injustice in Social Exchange." In *Advances in Experimental Social Psychology,* vol. 2, ed. L. Berkowitz. New York: Academic Press, 1965, pp. 267–99.

Alderfer, C. P. "An Empirical Test of a New Theory of Human Needs." *Organizational Behavior and Human Performance* 4 (1969), pp. 142–75.

Cofer, C., and Appley, M. *Motivation: Theory and Research.* New York: John Wiley & Sons, 1964.

Galbraith, Jay. *Designing Complex Organizations.* Reading, Mass.: Addison-Wesley Publishing, 1973.

Hackman, J. Richard. "Work Design." In *Improving Life at Work,* ed. J. Richard Hackman and J. Lloyd Suttle. Santa Monica, Calif.: Goodyear Publishing, 1977.

Lawler, E. E. III. "Managers' Attitudes toward How Their Pay Is and Should Be Determined." *Journal of Applied Psychology* 50 (1966), pp. 273–79.

Lawler, E. E. III. *Pay and Organizational Effectiveness: A Psychological View.* New York: McGraw-Hill, 1971.

Lawrence, Paul R., and Lorsch, Jay W. *Organization and Environment.* Boston: Division of Research, Graduate School of Business Administration, Harvard University, 1967.

Locke, E. "What Is Job Satisfaction?" *Organizational Behavior and Human Performance* 4 (1969), pp. 309–36.

Lorsch, Jay W., and Morse, John. *Organizations and Their Members: A Contingency Approach.* New York: Harper & Row, 1974.

Macy, B., and Mirvis, P. "Measuring Quality of Work and Organizational Effectiveness in Behavioral Economic Terms." Paper presented at American Psychological Association Convention, New Orleans, La., September 1974.

Meyer, H. "The Pay-for-Performance Dilemma." *Organizational Dynamics,* Winter 1975, pp. 39–50.

Patchen, M. *The Choice of Wage Comparisons.* Englewood Cliffs, N. J.: Prentice-Hall, 1961.

Perrow, C. "A Framework for the Comparative Analysis of Organizations." *American Sociological Review* 32 (1967), pp. 194–208.

Porter, L. W., and Lawler, E. E. *Managerial Attitudes and Performance.* Homewood, Ill.: Dorsey Press, 1968.

Porter, L., and Steers, R. "Organizational, Work and Personal Factors in Employee Turnover and Absenteeism." *Psychological Bulletin* 80 (1973), pp. 151–76.

Tosi, H., House, R., and Dunnette, M., eds. *Managerial Motivation and Compensation.* East Lansing: Michigan State University Business Studies, 1972.

Vroom, V. *Work and Motivation.* New York: John Wiley & Sons, 1964.

Whyte, W. F., ed. *Money and Motivation: An Analysis of Incentives for Industry.* New York: Harper & Row, 1955.

Work in America. Cambridge, Mass.: MIT Press, 1973.

Yoder, D. *Personnel Management and Industrial Relations.* Englewood Cliffs, N. J.: Prentice-Hall, 1956.

Reading 3–2

*Performance Appraisal: Dilemmas and Possibilities**

Michael Beer

> *It completely refused to run* (a) *when the waves were high,* (b) *when the wind blew,* (c) *at night, early in the morning, and evening,* (d) *in rain, dew, or fog,* (e) *when the distance to be covered was more than 200 yards. But on warm, sunny days when the weather was calm and the white beach close by—in a word, on days when it would have been a pleasure to row, it [the outboard motor] started at a touch and would not stop.*
>
> John Steinbeck

Steinbeck's description of an outboard motor is a very apt introduction to an article on performance appraisal. When performance and potential are good, when superior and subordinates have an open relationship, when promotions or salary increases are abundant, when there is plenty of time for preparation and discussion—in short, whenever it's a pleasure—performance appraisal is easy to do. Most of the time, however, and particularly at the times when it is most needed and most difficult to do, performance appraisal refuses to run properly.

The difficulties managers and subordinates experience in the appraisal interview may be traced to the quality of their relationship, to the manner and skill with which the interview is conducted, and to the appraisal system itself—that is, the objectives the organization has for it, the administrative system in which it is embedded, and the forms and procedures that make up the system. This article will explore the

---

* Reprinted, by permission of the publisher, from *Organizational Dynamics,* Winter 1981

difficulties, the many causes of these difficulties, and what might be done about them.

Goals of Performance Appraisal

Both the organization and the individual employee want the performance appraisal to meet particular objectives. In some cases these objectives or goals are compatible, but in many cases they are not. The potential for conflict between the employee's goals and the organization's objectives for performance appraisal has been discussed by Lyman W. Porter, Edward E. Lawler III, and Richard J. Hackman, and the subject will be reviewed and expanded in this article.

The Organization's Goals

Performance evaluation is an important element in the information and control system of most complex organizations. It can be used to obtain information about the performance of employees—so that decisions about placement, promotions, terminations, and pay can be made.

Performance appraisal systems and, more important, discussions between supervisor and subordinate about performance, can also influence the employee's behavior and performance. This is true of management by objectives (MBO) systems, as well as various performance rating systems. The process of influencing behavior is an important part of the organization's efforts to develop future human resources, and it is of utmost importance to managers in their attempts to obtain the results for which they are accountable. From the manager's and the organization's points of view, the performance appraisal process is a major tool for changing individual behavior.

The following lists summarize the organization's objectives for performance appraisal. First, the *evaluation goals:*

1. To provide feedback for subordinates so that they will know where they stand.
2. To develop valid data for pay (salary and bonus) and promotion decisions and to provide a means for communicating these decisions.
3. To help the manager in making discharge and retention decisions and to provide a means for warning subordinates about unsatisfactory performance.

Next, the *coaching and development goals:*

1. To counsel and coach subordinates so they will improve their performance and develop future potential.
2. To develop commitment to the larger organization through discus-

sion with subordinates of career opportunities and career planning.

3. To motivate subordinates through recognition and support.
4. To strengthen supervisor-subordinate relations.
5. To diagnose individual and organizational problems.

Note that this list includes many goals and, as the vertical arrow on the left of Exhibit 1 shows, they are in conflict. When the performance appraisal is being conducted to meet evaluation goals, the system is a tool by which managers make difficult judgments that affect their subordinates' futures. When they communicate these judgments, they may well have to justify their appraisal in response to, or in anticipation of, subordinates' disagreement. The result can be an adversary relationship, faulty listening, and low trust. None of these are conducive to the coaching and development objectives of performance appraisal. When coaching and development are the goals, managers must play the role of helper. If they are to help, they must draw out subordinates, listen to their problems, and get them to understand their own weaknesses. The different communication processes required to achieve the conflicting goals of performance appraisal create difficult problems for the manager involved.

The Individual's Goals

As the vertical arrow on the right of Exhibit 1 shows, the employee also has conflicting goals for the performance appraisal. Employees want and desire feedback about their performance because it helps them learn about themselves, how they are doing, and what management values. If this information is favorable, it helps satisfy their psychological needs for competence and success; if it is not, they tend to experience failure, and the feedback may be difficult to accept. Thus, even when people in organizations ask for or demand feedback, they are really looking for favorable feedback that will affirm their concept of themselves. When rewards, such as pay and promotion, are tied to the evaluation, employees have even more reason for wanting to avoid unfavorable evaluations.

An employee's self-development goals require him or her to be willing to accept feedback and ideas for alternative approaches to the job. Subordinates must be willing to drop their defenses and consider accepting the manager's view of their performance. They need an inquisitive attitude about their performance and what might be done to improve it. However, to protect their self-image or to obtain valued rewards, subordinates may gloss over, if not deny, problems. Often without realizing it, individuals may present themselves in a more favorable light than warranted by the facts. The simultaneous needs to be open and to be protective create difficult problems for the individual.

Exhibit 1
Conflicts in Performance Appraisal

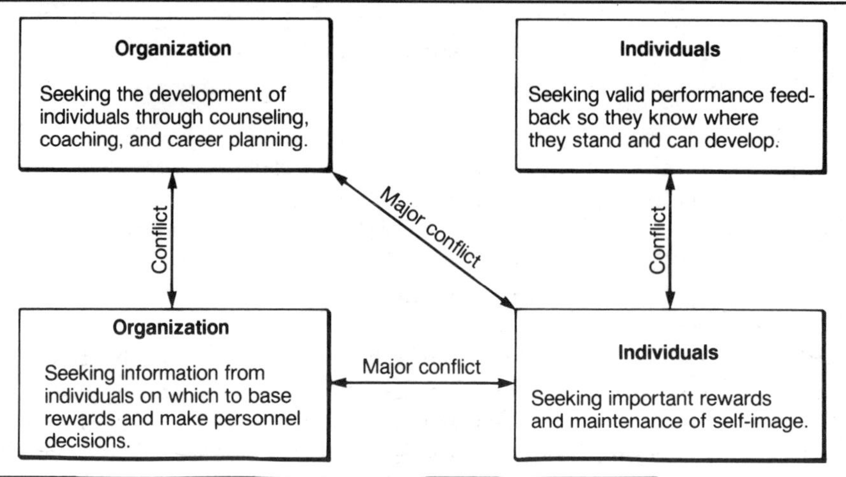

Adapted from Porter, Lawler, and Hackman, 1975.

Conflicting Individual and Organizational Goals

The biggest conflict, however, is between individual and organizational goals or objectives. The individual desires to confirm a positive self-image and to obtain organizational rewards, such as promotion or pay. The organization wants individuals to be receptive to negative information about themselves in order to improve their performance and promotability. It also wants individuals to be helpful in supplying necessary information. The conflict is over the exchange of valid information. As long as individual employees see the appraisal process as having an important influence on their reward (pay, recognition), on their career (promotions and reputation), and on their self-image, there will be a reluctance to engage in the kind of open dialogue required for valid evaluation and personal development. The poorer the employee's performance, the worse the potential conflict, and the less likely that there'll be an exchange of valid information. Major conflicts between the individual and the organization are shown by the diagonal and horizontal arrows in Exhibit 1 and are the reasons why performance appraisals run like Steinbeck's outboard motor.

Problems with Performance Appraisal

Several identifiable problems develop around the performance appraisal process. Some of the most troublesome follow.

Ambivalence and Avoidance

Given the conflicts that are present in the performance appraisal process, it is not surprising that supervisors and subordinates are often ambivalent about participating in it.

Supervisors are uncomfortable because their organizational role places them in the position of being both judge and jury. They must make decisions that affect people's careers and lives in significant ways. Furthermore, most managers are not trained to handle the difficult interpersonal situations that are likely to arise when feedback is negative. This is a problem particularly because managers must maintain good relations with their subordinates to perform their own jobs effectively. All this leads to uncertainty about their subjective judgments and anxiety about meeting with subordinates to discuss performance. Yet supervisors also know they must have performance discussions because the organization expects it and subordinates want it. Finally, supervisors often feel personally and legally bound to let people know where they stand. If they are not open with their subordinates, mutual trust suffers because subordinates usually sense when supervisors have been less than truthful. Then, too, there's the growing threat that supervisor's actions can lead to legal action against the organization if an individual feels he or she has been treated unfairly. Furthermore, as I have already pointed out, subordinates usually want constructive feedback, but they're very ambivalent about receiving negative feedback.

The ambivalence of both superiors and subordinates has led to what some behavioral scientists have called the "vanishing performance appraisal." In many organizations, supervisors report that they hold periodic appraisal interviews and give honest feedback, while their subordinates report they have not had a performance appraisal for many years or that they heard nothing negative. The appraisals conducted by the supervisors seem to "vanish." What probably happens is that supervisors, fearful of the appraisal process, have talked in very general terms to the subordinates, alluding only vaguely to problems. There are many ways this can occur. One of the most common is the "sandwich approach"—that is, the supervisor provides negative feedback between heavy doses of positive feedback. He or she may choose to conduct an appraisal on an airplane or during a car ride where the setting blurs its serious purpose. There are other ways, too, to obscure the process—for example, the supervisor makes very general statements and doesn't refer to specific problems. Or when the supervisor's own anxiety or the subordinate's defensiveness signals potential problems, the supervisor does provide negative feedback, but immediately counterbalances it with positive statements.

The subordinate's fear of learning things that will diminish his or her self-image often leads to the lack of initiative in seeking negative feedback and an unconscious collusion with the supervisor that results in avoidance. Thus the supervisor and subordinate engage in long conversations that are only marginally related to the purpose of the appraisal interview. Or they may engage in small talk or humor that conveys an oblique message, or they may develop a pattern of communication in which phrases do not convey a clear meaning to either of them. Thus there is no in-depth exploration of negative feedback, and it is not fully understood and internalized by the subordinate.

Defensiveness and Resistance

The conflict between the organization's evaluation objectives and its coaching and development objectives tends to place the manager in the incompatible roles of judge and helper during the appraisal interview. Some managers feel obligated to fulfill their organizational role as judge by explaining to the employee all facets of his or her evaluation. They want to be sure they fulfill their obligation to let the subordinate know where he or she stands by going down a rating form or discussing all "shortfalls" in performance. This tactic can naturally elicit appraisees' resistance as they defend against threats to their self-esteem.

Defensiveness may come in a variety of forms. Subordinates may try to explain away their "shortfalls" by blaming others or uncontrollable events; they may question the appraisal system itself; they may minimize the importance of the appraisal process; they may demean the source of the data; they may insincerely apologize and say they will not do it again, just to cut short their exposure to negative feedback; or they may seem to agree readily to the information while inwardly denying its validity or accuracy.

The core of the problem is that the supervisors' organizational role as judge can lead them into communicating and defending their evaluation to subordinates at the very time they are trying to develop an open two-way dialogue for a valid information exchange and development. The defensiveness that results may take the form of open hostility and denials, but it may also take the form of passivity and "surface" compliance. In either case, the subordinate doesn't really accept or understand the feedback. Thus, those subordinates who may need development the most may learn the least.

The Worst of All Interviews: Avoidance and Defensiveness Combined

The problems created by ambivalence and avoidance can combine with the problems of defensiveness and resistance in the same appraisal interview. For example, when managers go through a perfunctory performance appraisal to fulfill their supervisory duty, ambivalence leads them to avoid direct and meaningful talk about performance, while the need to fulfill the judge's role leads them to a complete but mechanical review of the evaluation form. Thus even though they avoid delving into subordinates' performance problems, they elicit defensive behavior from subordinates by going through the evaluation form in detail. Thus neither the benefits of avoidance (that is, maintenance of good relations and personal comfort) nor the benefits of accurate feedback (that is, clear understanding and development) are reaped, and none of the problems of avoidance and resistance are resolved.

Nonevaluative Evaluation

The basic dilemma of the appraisal process is how to have an open discussion of performance that meets the employee's need for feedback and the organization's need to develop employees, yet prevents damage to the employee's self-esteem and to his or her security about organizational rewards. This is, of course, a paradox, and thus both goals are not fully achievable. In the rest of this article, I will offer some ideas and suggestions on dealing with this paradox.

Potential Solutions to Appraisal Problems

There are three major ways in which the problems I have outlined can be dealt with. First, the appraisal system can be designed to minimize the negative dynamics outlined above. (The manager often has only marginal control over these matters.) Second, more attention can be paid to the ongoing relationship between supervisors and subordinates. Third, the interview process itself—that is, the quality of communication between supervisor and subordinate—can be improved. Let's look at how these approaches can be directed toward solving appraisal problems.

Designing the Appraisal System

The following corrective steps can improve performance appraisal systems.

Uncoupling Evaluation and Development. Herbert Meyer and his associates have suggested that less defensiveness and an open dialogue result when the manager splits her or his role as helper from that as judge. This can be done by having two separate performance appraisal interviews: one that focuses on evaluation and the other that focuses on coaching and development. The open problem-solving dialogue required for building a relationship and developing subordinates should be scheduled at a different time of the year than the meeting in which the supervisor informs the subordinate about her or his overall evaluation and its implications for retention, pay, and promotion. Such a split recognizes that managers cannot help and judge at the same time without the behavior required by one role interfering with the behavior required by the other.

Many performance appraisal systems inadvertently encourage managers to mix the role of judge and helper by providing only one evaluation form that ends up in the subordinate's personnel record. What is needed are two distinct forms and procedures. The evaluation form becomes part of the personnel record while the form that guides the development discussion does not.

Choosing Appropriate Performance Data. A manager can minimize defensiveness and avoidance by narrowly focusing feedback on specific behaviors or specific performance goals. For example, rating a person as unsatisfactory on a characteristic as broad as motivation is likely to be perceived as a broadside attack and as a threat to self-esteem. Feedback about specific incidents or aspects of "how" a person is performing the job is more likely to be heard than broad generalizations, and it will be more helpful to the individual who wants to improve performance. Thus an appraisal discussion that relies on a report card rating of traits or performance is doomed to failure because it leads the supervisor into general evaluative statements that threaten the subordinate.

Fortunately, some appraisal techniques are available to guide the supervisor toward more specific behavioral observations. One example is the behavioral rating scale that asks supervisors to indicate the degree to which subordinates fulfill certain behavioral requirements of their job (for example, participating actively in meetings or communicating sufficiently with other departments). Another technique is the critical-incident method in which the supervisor records important examples of effective or ineffective performance.

Similarly, there are various management by objectives (MBO) techniques that can be used to guide the appraisal discussion toward reviewing specific accomplishments.

Robert Ruh and I have suggested elsewhere that a comprehensive performance management system include both MBO and behavioral ratings. MBO is a means of managing *what* the individual should do, while behavioral ratings are a means for helping employees examine *how* they should do it. They are different but complementary tools in managing and appraising performance. A behavioral rating form might very well be the tool an organization can provide to managers as a guide for the developmental interview.

Separating Evaluations of Performance and Potential. Current performance, as measured by the attainment of results, is not necessarily correlated with potential for promotion. Yet many appraisal systems do not adequately provide for separate evaluations of these dimensions. In the case of a subordinate who rates high in current performance and low in potential for advancement (or vice versa), a manager is placed in the situation of averaging his or her unconscious assessment of these qualities and then defending an evaluation that may be inconsistent with his or her perception and the subordinate's self-perception of either performance of potential alone. Even if separate evaluations of these dimensions do not reduce subordinate defensiveness, they can reduce the manager's need to defend a composite rating that he or she cannot justify. Systems that separate assessments of performance and potential increase the likelihood of a constructive dialogue and therefore reduce the likelihood of avoidance.

Recognizing Individual Differences in System Design. Individuals differ in their needs for performance evaluation and development. Upwardly mobile employees may desire and need more feedback about performance and promotability than less upwardly mobile employees. They will also need longer and more frequent developmental discussions. Similarly, more confident and open employees will be able to handle these discussions better than will employees who lack self-esteem and are defensive. Performance appraisal policies should permit managers to use different methods depending on the particular employee being appraised. An appraisal every two or three years may be enough for an employee who has reached the peak of his or her capabilities. Such an appraisal could be limited to a rating and discussion of current performance, but omit any discussion of promotion potential. Uniform systems and procedures stand in the way of such differential treatment.

Upward Appraisal. The appraisal dynamic that contributes most to defensiveness and/or avoidance is the authoritarian character of the supervisor-subordinate relationship. The simple fact that one person is the boss and responsible for evaluation places him or her in a dominant role and induces submissive behavior on the part of the subordinate. Furthermore, the boss holds and controls rewards. In order to develop the open, two-way dialogue required in the coaching and developmental interview, power must be equalized or at least brought into better balance during the interview. One way to achieve this is to ask subordinates to appraise their supervisor.

An upward appraisal can help a supervisor create the conditions needed for an effective performance appraisal interview for several reasons. It gives subordinates a real stake in the appraisal interview and an opportunity to influence a part of their environment that ultimately influences their performance. Thus it makes them more equal and less dependent, increasing their motivation to enter the appraisal process with an open frame of mind. It also offers the supervisor an opportunity to demonstrate nondefensive behavior and a willingness to engage in a real two-way dialogue (assuming the supervisor is capable of behaving nondefensively).

Organizations can encourage the use of upward appraisals by providing forms and developing policies that support this approach. If the organization doesn't do so, the supervisor can develop his or her own form or seek informal feedback sometime during the appraisal interviews.

Self-Appraisal. Experience with self-appraisal suggests that it often results in lower ratings than the supervisor would have given. Subordinates appraising themselves before an interview do so with the knowledge that an unrealistic or obviously self-serving rating will affect their manager's perception of them. Thus performance appraisal systems that include self-appraisal before either the coaching or evaluation interview are likely to result in a more realistic rating and a greater acceptance of the final rating by subordinates and supervisors.

Some or all of the system design elements described in this section can be used to minimize manager avoidance and subordinate resistance. But by themselves they are not sufficient. Good relationships and interpersonal competence are also required.

Improving Supervisor-Subordinate Relationship

Not surprisingly, the quality of the appraisal process depends on the nature of the day-to-day supervisor-subordinate relationship. First, an effective relationship means that the supervisor is providing feedback and coaching on an ongoing basis. Thus the appraisal interview is merely a review of issues that have already been discussed. Second, the appraisal interview is only a small segment of the broader supervisor-subordinate relationship, and expectations for it are likely to be shaped by the broader relationship. If a relationship of mutual trust and supportiveness exists, subordinates are more apt to be open in discussing performance problems and less defensive in response to negative feedback.

There is no substitute for a good supervisor-subordinate relationship. Without such a relationship, no performance appraisal system can be effective. Although the development of such a relationship is not the subject of this article, it is important to understand that the appraisal interview itself can be used to build a relationship of mutual trust, provided the interview is modeled after some of the ideas discussed in the next section.

Improving the Appraisal Interview

The appraisal interview has multiple objectives. Therefore, it isn't surprising that different objectives are best met by somewhat different interview methods.

Directive Interviews. If the interview's objective is to communicate a performance evaluation or pay decision that has already been made, the interview should take a more directive form. The manager tells the subordinate what the evaluation is and, to assure the subordinate about its fairness, the process by which it was determined. The manager then listens actively, accepting and trying to understand the employee's reactions and feelings without signaling that the performance evaluation is open to change.

If the manager has already evaluated the subordinate, any attempt to conduct an open and participative dialogue to motivate the subordinate will fail. Such an approach encourages the subordinate to try to influence the manager's rating—a move that puts the manger in the position of defending a final decision. In this situation, the subordinate not only has to accept an evaluation that may be inconsistent with his or her self-perception, but may also have to leave the interview frustrated by unsuccessful attempts to influence the manager.

As stated earlier, managers may be drawn into this situation by systems that provide only one form for evaluation. An open dialogue cannot occur, because the manager follows the form mechanically in an effort to communicate accurately judgments that he or she has already committed to paper. Corporate procedures that require the manager's boss to review the evaluation before the appraisal interview only increase the manager's need to defend the rating and reduce even further the likelihood of an open dialogue.

Participative Problem-Solving Interview. If the interview's objective is to motivate subordinates to change their behavior or improve their performance, an open process that includes mutual participation is required. This approach takes the manager out of the role of judge and puts him or her into the role of helper. The objective is to help subordinates discover their own performance deficiencies and help them take the initiative to develop a joint plan for improvement. The problem-solving interview makes no provision for communicating the supervisor's unilateral evaluation. The assumption underlying this type of interview is that self-understanding by subordinates and motivation to improve performance cannot occur in a setting where the manager has already made judgments and psychologically separates her- or himself from the subordinate to avoid being swayed. The problem-solving interview is therefore less structured, relies on the subordinate to lead the discussion into problem areas, and relies on the manager to listen, reflect, care, guide, and coach.

Individual Differences and the Interview. The subordinate's characteristics should also determine the interview method. Subordinates differ in their age, experience, sensitivity about negative feedback, attitude

Exhibit 2
Mixed-Model Interview

Interview Begins

1. Open-ended discussion and exploration of problems, in which the subordinate leads and the supervisor listens.
2. Problem-solving discussion, in which the subordinate leads, but supervisor takes somewhat stronger role.
3. Agreement between supervisor and subordinate on performance problems and a plan for improvements.
4. Closing evaluation, in which the supervisor gives his or her views and final evaluation if the subordinate has not dealt with important issues.

Interview Ends

toward the supervisor, and desire for influence and control over their destiny. For example, if the subordinate is young, inexperienced, and dependent and looks up to the supervisor, a more directive interview in which the supervisor does most of the talking may be appropriate—unless, of course, it is the supervisor's objective to help the subordinate become more independent. On the other hand, if the subordinate is older, more experienced, and sensitive about negative feedback, and has a high need for controlling his or her destiny, the same objective is best met by a less directive approach.

Mixed-Model Interviews. When situational factors such as corporate policies, practices and forms, available time, and subordinate expectations prevent separate evaluation and developmental interviews, it is possible to design one interview to achieve both purposes. The most effective way of implementing a mixed-model appraisal interview is to start the appraisal process with the open-ended problem-solving approach and end with the more directive approach. If the supervisor starts off with one-way communication, real two-way communication and in-depth exploration of personal and job performance issues are unlikely to occur. Thus, as Exhibit 2 shows, the interview should start with an open-ended exploration of perceptions and concerns, with the subordinate taking the lead, and it should finish with a more closed-ended agreement on what performance improvements are expected. Performance problems and improvements are agreed to jointly, but if such agreement is not possible, ultimate responsibility rests with the supervisor. The supervisor may choose to tell the subordinate what is expected if crucial problems have not been discussed or solutions agreed on.

There are many ways in which a mixed-model interview can be implemented. I have outlined one possible pattern for an effective appraisal interview with multiple purposes below. The following assumptions underlie the recommended interview process:

1. It is possible to defuse the potential negative effects of corporate systems and traditional expectations through joint supervisor-subordinate agreement on interview content and process before the interview.
2. Joint planning of the interview enhances the probability that the interview goals and process will be compatible.
3. Joint supervisor-subordinate agreement on ground rules for effective communication before the interview increases control over the process.
4. It is necessary to equalize the power of the appraiser and appraisee to achieve developmental objectives and maintain good relations. However, this should not prevent the supervisor from taking a more directive role later in the interview if it is necessary.
5. A good appraisal interview can occur only in a context of good supervisor-subordinate relations or when both parties are motivated to use the interview as a means of improving relations.
6. Managers can mix the inherently incompatible judging and helping roles only if the latter is the primary role and goal.
7. A mixed interview requires the manager to assume a substantial range of styles and to have the ability to shift between them quickly and appropriately.

The following proposed interview sequence is only illustrative:

1. *Scheduling.* Notify the subordinate well in advance when the appraisal discussion is scheduled. The interview should be set at a time when both parties are alert and undisturbed by external organizational or personal matters. The discussion should be scheduled as long after the salary review as possible.

2. *Agreeing on content.* Before the interview, discuss the nature of the interview with the subordinate and work toward agreement on the goals of the interview and what will be discussed (for example, rating forms to be used or performance issues to be discussed). This gives the subordinate a chance to prepare for the interview (including self-rating or rating the supervisor if this is to be part of the session), and to come to the interview on a more equal footing with the supervisor. If necessary, it also permits supervisor and subordinate to devise a form and procedure compatible with their goals for the interview.

3. *Agreeing on process.* Agree on the process for the appraisal discussion with the subordinate before the interview. For example, agreement should be reached on the sequencing of interview phases. If an open, exploratory discussion is to come first, followed by problem solving, action planning, and upward appraisal, this is the time to tell the subordinate about these phases. Similarly, ground rules for communications can be established that will ensure constructive feedback and good listening. (See Step 7.)

4. *Setting location and space.* If possible, meet on neutral territory or in the subordinate's office. In this way, a relationship of more equal power that's so crucial to open communication can be established.

5. *Opening the interview.* Review the objectives of the appraisal interview that were previously agreed to. This review sets the stage and allows supervisor and subordinate to prepare themselves psychologically.

6. *Starting the discussion.* Give the initiative to the subordinate in the discussion that follows the opening statement. Specifically start the discussion by asking, "How do you feel things are going on the job? What's going well and what problems are you experiencing? How do you see your performance?" Such general questions will stimulate the subordinate to take the initiative in the problem identification and solving discussion. To facilitate this, a subordinate may be asked to appraise his or her own performance. If the manager starts by expressing views about the employee's performance, the interview inevitably becomes directive.

7. *Exchanging feedback.* Follow well-accepted ground rules for giving and receiving feedback. A supervisor who sets up these methods for effective communication encourages the exchange of valid information.

In giving feedback, a supervisor can reduce employee's defensiveness by being specific about the performance and behavior-causing problems (that is, what was said and done?). Citing specific examples of observed behavior and describing the consequences of that behavior in terms of effects on others, on the supervisor's feelings, and on the department's performance can help an employee identify what needs to be changed. To prevent defensive reactions, the supervisor should avoid making general statements, imputing motives to behavior (that is, you are lazy or you aren't committed), blaming, or accusing.

The supervisor should set up ground rules for receiving feedback and encourage the subordinate to follow them. Defensiveness should be avoided at all costs; negative feedback is usually cut off by the giver when signs of defensiveness appear in the receiver, and this reduces the amount of information transmitted. Active listening can encourage receptiveness to and understanding of negative feedback. The receiver should paraphase what is being said, request clarification, and summarize the discussion periodically. The receiver can maintain openness and keep information coming by exploring the negative feedback and showing a willingness to examine him- or herself critically. On the other hand, feedback is usually cut off and understanding reduced by justifying actions, apologizing, blaming others, explaining, and "building a case."

The ground rules for receiving feedback are not meant to imply that supervisors and subordinates should not help each other understand why they are doing what they are doing. However, the timing of explanations is critical in stimulating openness instead of defensiveness. Active listening first, followed by explanations later, is a better sequence than the reverse.

8. *Presenting the supervisor's views.* The supervisor should provide a summary of the subordinate's major improvement needs based on the previous discussion. This summary sets the agenda for the next phase of the discussion in which plans for improvement are developed jointly. However, the summary should also include the subordinate's strengths—those things that should be continued.

9. *Developing a plan for improvement.* Let subordinates lead with what they think is an adequate plan for improvement on the basis of the previous discussion and summary. It is much easier to prevent defensiveness if the supervisor reacts to and perhaps expands on the subordinate's plans for changing instead of making such suggestions directly. A problem-solving rather than blame-placing approach should be maintained. However, if subordinates cannot formulate good action plans, or seem to be unmotivated to do so, the supervisor can take a more directive approach at this point. It is critical that the interview end in a concrete plan for performance improvement or else no change is likely to occur.

10. *Closing the discussion.* Close the discussion with a view of the individual's future. However, this is relevant only in organizations where opportunities for promotion exist and for individuals who clearly have potential—unless, of course, the individual brings it up and wants to know. If the individual needs to be told what his or her evaluation is, this should be done at the very end of the interview if it cannot take place in a separate interview.

Summary

This article attempts to summarize what is known about the underlying causes of problems experienced with performance appraisal and to suggest some means for overcoming these. The central thrust has been to find means for dealing with the main barrier to effective appraisals—that is, avoidance by the supervisor and defensiveness from the subordinate. We have suggested a number of ways in which supervisors and subordinates might negotiate the difficult dilemma of discussing an evaluation of performance in a nonevaluative manner.

Selected Bibliography

A discussion of the many organizational and contextual factors affecting performance appraisal can be found in Morgan W. McCall and David L. DeVries's "Appraisal in Context: Clashing with Organizational Realities," presented in symposium "Performance Appraisal and Feedback: Fleas in the Ointment," David DeVries, Chair, *84th Annual Convention of the American Psychological Association,* Washington, D.C., September 5, 1976.

The section on performance appraisal goals draws extensively on discussions of this subject in Lyman W. Porter, Edward E. Lawler III, and Richard J. Hackman's *Behavior in Organizations* (McGraw-Hill, 1975).

An example of a performance appraisal system designed to deal with some of the dilemmas discussed in this article can be found in Michael Beer and Robert A. Ruh's "Employee Growth through Performance Management," *Harvard Business Review,* July–August 1976.

The phenomenon of the "vanishing performance appraisal" was first discussed by Douglas T. Hall and Edward E. Lawler III in "Job Characteristics and Pressures and Organizational Integration of Professionals," *Administrative Science Quarterly,* Third Quarter 1970.

The effects of performance feedback on a person's self-esteem were discussed by Alvin Zander in "Research on Self-Esteem, Feedback and Threats to Self-Esteem," in A. Zander (Ed.), *Performance Appraisals: Effects on Employees and Their Performance* (Foundation for Research in Human Behavior, 1963).

The classic study of performance appraisal that first posited the importance of splitting evaluation from developmental interviews is Herbert H. Meyer, Emanuel Kay, and John R. P. French, Jr.'s "Split Roles in Performance Appraisal," *Harvard Business Review,* January–February 1965.

The critical-incident technique in which managers record incidents of effective or ineffective performance by subordinates as data for appraisals was first discussed by John C. Flanagan and Robert K. Burns in "The Employee Performance Record," *Harvard Business Review,* September–October 1955.

The idea that different types of individuals have different performance appraisal purposes was articulated by Norman R. F. Maier in "Three Types of Appraisal Interviews," *Personnel,* March–April 1958.

Problem-solving performance appraisal interviews that rely heavily on nondirective counseling were first discussed by Carl R. Rogers in "Releasing Expression," *Counseling and Psychotherapy* (Houghton Mifflin, 1942).

A number of ideas in this article about methods for improving the performance appraisal interviews were discussed by Herbert H. Meyer in "The Annual Performance Review Discussion—Making It Constructive" (University of South Florida, unpublished and undated paper.)

Guidelines for giving and receiving feedback are cited in this article as important in guiding a constructive dialogue between boss and subordinate. This was discussed in more detail in John Anderson's "Giving and Receiving Feedback" in G. W. Dalton, P. R. Lawrence, and L. E. Greiner (Eds.), *Organizational Change and Development* (Richard D. Irwin and Dorsey Press, 1970).

Reading 3–3

*Designing the Innovating Organization**

Jay R. Galbraith

Innovation is in. New workable, marketable ideas are being sought and promoted these days as never before in the effort to restore U.S. leadership in technology, in productivity growth, and in the ability to compete in the world marketplace. Innovative methods for conserving energy and adapting to new energy sources are also in demand.

The popular press uses words like *revitalization* to capture the essence of the issue. The primary culprit of our undoing, up until now, has been management's short-run earnings focus. However, even some patient managers with long-term views are finding that they cannot buy innovation. They cannot exhort their operating organizations to be more innovative and creative. Patience, money, and a supportive leadership are not enough. It takes more than these things to achieve innovation.

It is my contention that innovation requires an organization specifically designed for that purpose—that is, such an organization's structure, processes, rewards, and people must be combined in a special way to create an innovating organization, one that is designed to do something for the first time. The point to be emphasized here is that the innovating organization's components are completely different from and often contrary to those of existing organizations, which are generally operating organizations. The latter are designed to efficiently process the millionth loan, produce the millionth automobile, or serve the millionth client.

---

* Reprinted by permission of the author.

An organization that is designed to do something well for the millionth time is not good at doing something for the first time. Therefore, organizations that want to innovate or revitalize themselves need two organizations, an operating organization and an innovating organization. In addition, if the ideas produced by the innovating organization are to be implemented by the operating organization, they need a transition process to transfer ideas from the innovating organization to the operating organization.

This article will describe the components of an organization geared to producing innovative ideas. Specifically, in the next section of this article, I describe a case history that illustrates the components required for successful innovation. Then I will explore the lessons to be learned from this case history by describing the role structure, the key processes, the reward systems, and the people practices that characterize an innovating organization.

The Innovating Process

Before I describe the typical process by which innovations occur in organizations, we must understand what we are discussing. What is innovation? How do we distinguish between invention and innovation? Invention is the creation of a new idea. Innovation is the process of applying a new idea to create a new process or product. Invention occurs more frequently than innovation. In addition, the kind of innovation in which we are interested here is the kind that becomes necessary to implement a new idea that is not consistent with the current concept of the organization's business. Many new ideas that are consistent with an organization's current business concept are routinely generated in some companies. Those are not our current concern; here we are concerned with implementing inventions that are good ideas but do not quite fit into the organization's current mold. Industry has a poor track record with this type of innovation. Most major technological changes come from outside an industry. The mechanical typewriter manufacturers did not introduce the electric typewriter; the electric typewriter people did not invent the electronic typewriter; vacuum tube companies did not introduce the transistor, and so on. Our objective is to describe an organization that will increase the odds that such nonroutine innovations can be made. The following case history of a nonroutine innovation presents a number of lessons that illustrate how we can design an innovating organization.

The Case History

The organization in question is a venture that was started in the early 70s. While working for one of our fairly innovative electronics firms, a group of engineers developed a new electronics product. However, they were in a division that did not have the charter for their product. The ensuing political battle caused the engineers to leave and form their own company. They successfully found venture capital and introduced their new product. Initial acceptance was good, and within several years their company was growing rapidly and had become the industry leader.

However, in the early 1970s Intel invented the microprocessor, and by the mid- to late 70s, this innovation had spread through the electronics industries. Manufacturers of previously "dumb" products now had the capability of incorporating intelligence into their product lines. A competitor who understood computers and software introduced just such a product into our new venture firm's market, and it met with high acceptance. The firm's president responded by hiring someone who knew something about microcomputers and some software people and instructing the engineering department to respond to the need for a competing product.

The president spent most of his time raising capital to finance the venture's growth. But when he suddenly realized that the engineers had not made much progress, he instructed them to get a product out quickly. They did, but it was a half-hearted effort. The new product incorporated a microprocessor but was less than the second-generation product that was called for.

Even though the president developed markets in Europe and Singapore, he noticed that the competitor continued to grow faster than his company and had started to steal a share of his company's market. When the competitor became the industry leader, the president decided to take charge of the product development effort. However, he found that the hardware proponents and software proponents in the engineering department were locked in a political battle. Each group felt that its "magic" was the more powerful. Unfortunately, the lead engineer (who was a cofounder of the firm) was a hardware proponent, and the hardware establishment prevailed. However, they then clashed head-on with the marketing department, which agreed with the software proponents. The conflict resulted in studies and presentations, but no new product. So here was a young, small (1,200 people) entrepreneurial firm that could not innovate even though the president wanted innovation and provided resources to produce it. The lesson is that more was needed.

As the president became more deeply involved in the problem, he received a call from his New England sales manager, who wanted him to meet a field engineer who had modified the company's product and programmed it in a way that met customer demands. The sales manager suggested, "We may have something here."

Indeed, the president was impressed with what he saw. When the engineer had wanted to use the company's product to track his own inventory, he wrote to company headquarters for programming instructions. The response had been: It's against company policy to send instructional materials to field engineers. Undaunted, the engineer bought a home computer and taught himself to program. He then modified the product in the field and programmed it to solve his problem. When the sales manager happened to see what was done, he recognized its significance and immediately called the president.

The field engineer accompanied the president back to headquarters and presented his work to the engineers who had been working on the second-generation product for so long. They brushed off his efforts as idiosyncratic, and the field engineer was thanked and returned to the field.

A couple of weeks later the sales manager called the president again. He said that the company would lose this talented guy if something wasn't done. Besides, he thought that the field engineer, not engineering, was right. While he was considering what to do with this ingenious engineer, who on his own had produced more than the entire engineering department, the president received a request from the European sales manager to have the engineer assigned to him.

The European sales manager had heard about the field engineer when he visited headquarters, and had sought him out and listened to his story. The sales manager knew that a French bank wanted the type of application that the field engineer had created for himself; a successful application would be worth an order for several hundred machines. The president gave the go-ahead and sent the field engineer to Europe. The engineering department persisted in their view that the program wouldn't work. Three months later, the field engineer successfully developed the application, and the bank signed the order.

When the field engineer returned, the president assigned him to a trusted marketing manager who was told to protect him and get a product out. The engineers were told to support the manager and reluctantly did so. Soon they created some applications software and a printed circuit board that could easily be installed in all existing machines in the field. The addition of this board and the software temporarily saved the company and made its current product slightly superior to that of the competitor.

Elated, the president congratulated the young field engineer and gave him a good staff position working on special assignments to develop software. Then problems arose. When the president tried to get the personnel department to give the engineer a special cash award, they were reluctant. "After all," they said, "other people worked on the effort, too. It will set a precedent." And so it went. The finance department wanted to withhold $500 from the engineer's pay because he had received a $1,000 advance for his European trip, but had turned in vouchers for only $500.

The engineer didn't help himself very much either; he was hard to get along with and refused to accept supervision from anyone except the European sales manager. When the president arranged to have him permanently transferred to Europe on three occasions, the engineer changed his mind about going at the last minute. The president is still wondering what to do with him.

There are a number of lessons about the needs of an innovative organization in this not uncommon story. The next section elaborates on these lessons.

The Innovating Organization

Before we can draw upon the case history's lessons, it is important to note that the basic components of the innovating organization are no different from those of an operating organization. That is, both include a task, a structure, processes, reward systems, and people, as shown in Exhibit 1. Exhibit 2 compares the design parameters of the operating organization's components with those of the innovating organization's components.

This figure shows that each component must fit with each of the other components and with the task. A basic premise of this article is that the task of the innovating organization is fundamentally different from that of the operating organization. The innovating task is more uncertain and risky, takes place over longer time periods, assumes that failure in the early stages may be desirable, and so on. Therefore, the organization that performs the innovative task should also be different.

Exhibit 1
Organization Design Components

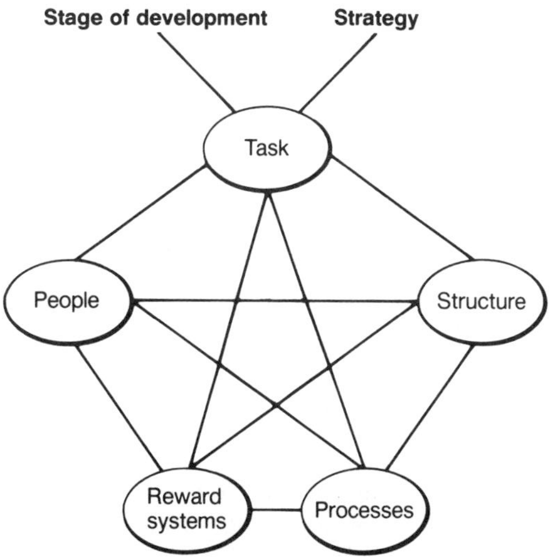

Exhibit 2
Comparison of Components of Operating and Innovating Organizations

	Operating Organization	Innovating Organization
Structure	Division of labor Departmentalization Span of control Distribution of power	Roles: Orchestrator Sponsor Idea generator (champion) Differentiation Reservations
Processes	Providing information and communication Planning and budgeting Measuring performance Linking departments	Planning/funding Getting ideas Blending ideas Transitioning Managing programs
Reward systems	Compensation Promotion Leader style Job design	Opportunity/autonomy Promotion/recognition Special compensation
People	Selection/recruitment Promotion/transfer Training/development	Selection/self-selection Training/development

Obviously, a firm that wishes to innovate needs both an operating organization and an innovating organization. Let's look at the latter.

Structure of the Innovating Organization

The structure of the innovating organization encompasses these elements: (1) people to fill three vital roles—idea generators, sponsors, and orchestrators; (2) differentiation, a process that differentiates or separates the innovating organization's activities from those of the operating organization; and (3) "reservations," the means by which the separation occurs—and this may be accomplished physically, financially, or organizationally.

The part that each of these elements plays in the commercialization of a new idea can be illustrated by referring to the case history.

Roles

Like any organized phenomenon, innovation is brought about through the efforts of people who interact in a combination of roles. Innovation is not an individual phenomenon. People who must interact to produce a commercial product—that is, to innovate in the sense we are discussing—play their roles as follows:

• Every innovation starts with an *idea generator* or idea champion. In the above example, the field engineer was the person who generated the new idea—that is, the inventor, the entrepreneur, or risk taker on whom much of our attention has been focused. The case history showed that an idea champion is needed at each stage of an idea's or an invention's development into an innovation. That is, at each stage there must be a dedicated, full-time individual whose success or failure depends on developing the idea. The idea generator is usually a low-level person who experiences a problem and develops a new response to it. The lesson here is that many ideas originate down where "the rubber meets the road." The low status and authority level of the idea generator creates a need for someone to play the next role.

• Every idea needs at least one *sponsor* to promote it. To carry an idea through to implementation, someone has to discover it and fund the increasingly disruptive and expensive development and testing efforts that shape it. Thus idea generators need to find sponsors for their ideas so they can perfect them. In our example, the New England sales manager, the European sales manager, and finally the marketing manager all sponsored the field engineer's idea. Thus one of the sponsor's functions is to lend his or her authority and resources to an idea to carry the idea closer to commercialization.

The sponsor must also recognize the business significance of an idea. In any organization, there are hundreds of ideas being promoted at any one time. The sponsor must select from among these ideas those that might become marketable. Thus it is best that sponsors be generalists. (However, that is not always the case, as our case history illustrates.)

Sponsors are usually middle managers who may be anywhere in the organization and who usually work for both the operating and the innovating organization. Some sponsors run divisions or departments. They must be able to balance the operating and innovating needs of their business or function. On the other hand, when the firm can afford the creation of venture groups, new-product development departments, and the like, sponsors may work full time for the innovating organization. In the case history, the two sales managers spontaneously became sponsors, and the marketing manager was formally designated as a sponsor by the president. The point here is that by formally designating the role or recognizing it, funding it with monies earmarked for innovation, creating innovating incentives, and developing and selecting sponsorship skills, the organization can improve its odds of coming up with successful innovations. Not much attention has been given to sponsors, but they need equal attention because innovation will not occur unless there are people in the company who will fill all three roles.

• The third role illustrated in the case history is that of the *orchestrator*. The president played this role. An orchestrator is necessary because new ideas are never neutral. Innovative ideas are destructive; they destroy investments in capital equipment and people's careers. The management of ideas is a political process. The problem is that the political struggle is biased toward those in the establishment who have authority and control of resources. The orchestrator must balance the power to give the new idea a chance to be tested in the face of a negative establishment. The orchestrator must protect idea people, promote the opportunity to try out new ideas, and back those whose ideas prove effective. This person must legitimize the whole process. That is what the president did with the field engineer; before he became involved, the hardware establishment had prevailed. Without an orchestrator, there can be no innovation.

To play their roles successfully, orchestrators use the processes and rewards to be described in the following sections. That is, a person orchestrates by funding innovating activities and creating incentives for middle managers to sponsor innovating ideas. Orchestrators are the organization's top managers, and they must design the innovating organization.

The typical operating role structure of a divisionalized firm is shown in Exhibit 3. The hierarchy is one of the operating functions reporting to division general managers who are, in turn, grouped under group executives. The group executives report to the chief executive officer (CEO). Some of these people play roles in both the operating and the innovating organization.

The innovating organization's role structure is shown in Exhibit 4. The chief executive and a group executive function as orchestrators.

Exhibit 3
Typical Operating Structure of Divisionalized Firm

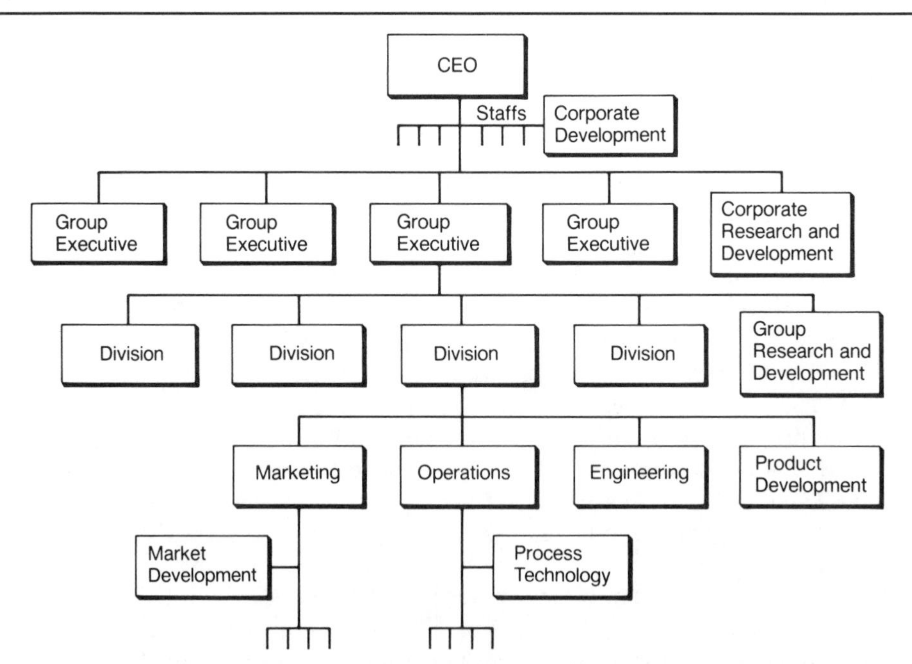

Exhibit 4
An Innovating Role Structure (Differentiation)

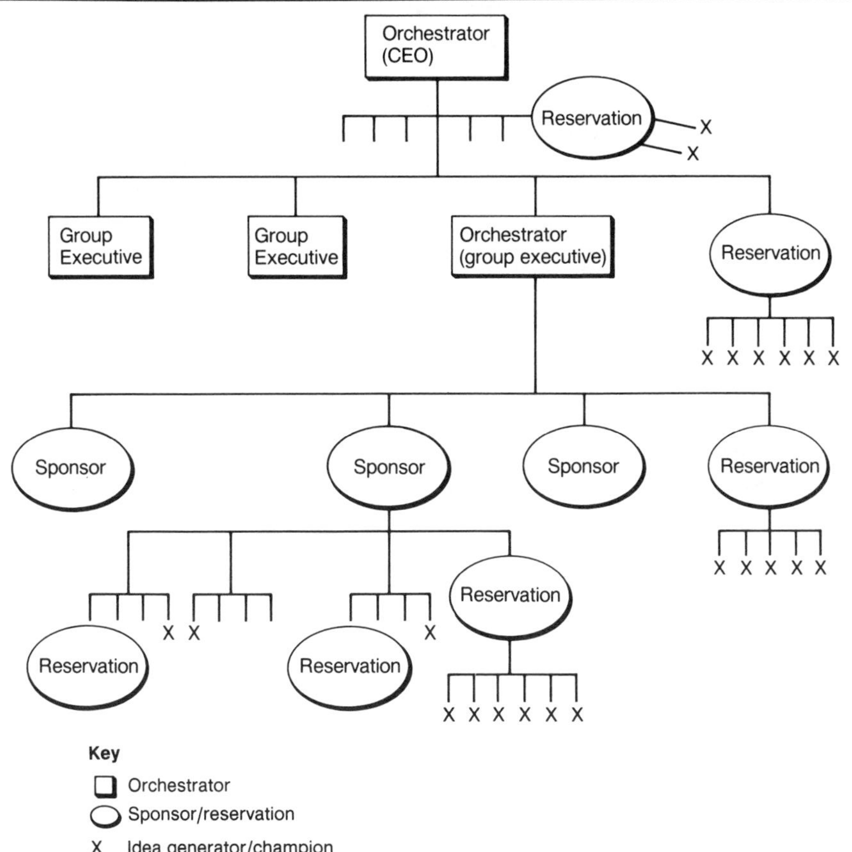

Division managers are the sponsors who work in both the operating and the innovating organizations. In addition, several reservations are created in which managers of research and development (R&D), corporate development, product development, market development, and new-process technology function as full-time sponsors. These reservations allow the separation of innovating activity from the operating activity. This separation is an organizing choice called differentiation. It is described next.

Differentiation

In the case history, we saw that the innovative idea perfected at a remote site was relatively advanced before it was discovered by management.

The lesson to be learned from this is that if one wants to stimulate new ideas, the odds are better if early efforts to perfect and test new "crazy" ideas are differentiated—that is, separated—from the functions of the operating organization. Such differentiation occurs when an effort is separated physically, financially, and/or organizationally from the day-to-day activities that are likely to disrupt it. If the field engineer had worked within the engineering department or at company headquarters, his idea probably would have been snuffed out prematurely.

Another kind of differentiation can be accomplished by freeing initial idea tests from staff controls designed for the operating organization. The effect of too much control is illustrated by one company in which a decision on whether to buy an oscilloscope took about 15 to 30 minutes (with a shout across the room) before the company was acquired by a larger organization. After the acquisition, that same type of decision took 12 to 18 months because the purchase required a capital appropriation request. Controls based on operating logic reduce the innovating organization's ability to rapidly, cheaply, and frequently test and modify new ideas. Thus, the more differentiated an initial effort is, the greater the likelihood of innovation.

The problem with differentiation, however, is that it decreases the likelihood that a new proven idea will be transferred back to the operating organization. Herein lies the differentiation/transfer dilemma: The more differentiated the effort, the greater the likelihood of producing a new business idea, but the less likelihood of transferring the new idea into the operating organization for implementation. The dilemma occurs only when the organization needs both invention and transfer. That is, some organizations may not need to transfer new ideas to the operating organization. For example, when Exxon started its information systems business, there was no intention to have the petroleum company run this area of business. Exxon innovators had to grow their own operating organizations; therefore, they could maximize differentiation in the early phases. Alternatively, when Intel started work on the 64K RAM (the next generation of semiconductor memories, this random-access memory holds roughly 64,000 bits of information), the effort was consistent with their current business and the transfer into fabrication and sales was critical. Therefore, the development effort was only minimally separated from the operating division that was producing the 16K RAM. The problem becomes particularly difficult when a new product or process differs from current ones, but must be implemented through the current manufacturing and sales organizations. The greater the need for invention and the greater the difference between the new idea and the existing business concept, the greater the degree of differentiation required to perfect the idea. The only way to accomplish both invention and transfer is to proceed stagewise. That is, differentiate in the early phases and then start the transition process before development is completed so that only a little differentiation is left when the product is ready for implementation. The transition process is described below in the section on key processes.

In summary, invention occurs best when initial efforts are separated from the operating organization and its controls—because innovating and operating are fundamentally opposing logics. This kind of separation allows both to be performed simultaneously and prevents the establishment from prematurely snuffing out a new idea. The less the dominant culture of the organization supports innovation, the greater is the need for separation. Often this separation occurs naturally as in the case history, or clandestinely as in "bootlegging." If a firm wants to foster innovation, it can create reservations where innovating activity can occur as a matter of course. Let us now turn to this last structural parameter.

Reservations

Reservations are organizational units, such as R&D groups, that are totally devoted to creating new ideas for future business. The intention is to reproduce a garagelike atmosphere where people can rapidly and frequently test their ideas. Reservations are havens for "safe learning." When innovating, one wants to maximize early failure to promote learning. On reservations that are separated from operations, this cheap, rapid screening can take place.

Reservations permit differentiation to occur by housing people who work solely for the innovating organization and by having a reservation manager who works full time as a sponsor. They may be located within divisions and/or at corporate headquarters to permit various degrees of differentiation.

Reservations can be internal or external. Internal reservations may include some staff and research groups, product and process development labs, and groups that are devoted to market development, new ventures, and/or corporate development. They are organizational homes where idea generators can contribute without becoming managers. Originally, this was the purpose of staff groups, but staff groups now frequently assume control responsibilities or are narrow specialists who contribute to the current business idea. Because such internal groups can be expensive, outside reservations like universities, consulting firms, and advertising agencies are often used to tap nonmanagerial idea generators.

Reservations can be permanent or temporary. The internal reservations described above, such as R&D units, are reasonably permanent entities. Others can be temporary. Members of the operating organization may be relieved of operating duties to develop a new program, a new process, or a new product. When developed, they take the idea into the operating organization and resume their operating responsibilities. But for a period of time they are differentiated from operating functions to varying degrees in order to innovate, fail, learn, and ultimately perfect a new idea.

Collectively the roles of orchestrators, sponsors, and idea generators working with and on reservations constitute the structure of the innovating organization. Some of the people, such as sponsors and orchestrators, play roles in both organizations; reservation managers and idea generators work only for the innovating organization. Virtually everyone in the organization can be an idea generator, and all middle managers are potential sponsors. However not all choose to play these roles. People vary considerably in their innovating skills. By recognizing the need for these roles, developing people to fill them, giving them opportunity to use their skills in key processes, and rewarding innovating accomplishments, the organization can do considerably better than just allowing a spontaneous process to work. Several key processes are part and parcel of this innovating organizational structure. These are described in the next section.

Key Processes

In our case history, the idea generator and the first two sponsors found each other through happenstance. The odds of such propitious matchups can be significantly improved through the explicit design of processes that help sponsors and idea generators find each other. The chances of successful matchups can be improved by such funding, getting ideas, and blending ideas. In addition, the processes of transitioning and program management move ideas from reservations into operations. Each of these is described below.

Funding

A key process that increases our ability to innovate is a funding process that is explicitly earmarked for the innovating organization. A leader in this field is Texas Instruments (TI), a company that budgets and allocates funds for both operating and innovating. In essence the orchestrators make the short-run/long-run trade-off at this point. They then orchestrate by choosing where to place the innovating funds—with division sponsors or corporate reservations. The funding process is a key tool for orchestration.

Another lesson to be learned from the case history is that it frequently takes more than one sponsor to launch a new idea. The field engineer's idea would never have been brought to management's attention without the New England sales manager. It would never have been tested in the market without the European sales manager. Multiple sponsors keep fragile ideas alive. If engineering had been the only available sponsor for technical ideas, there would have been no innovation.

Some organizations purposely create a multiple sponsoring system and make it legitimate for an idea generator to go to any sponsor who has funding for new ideas. Multiple sponsors duplicate the market system of multiple bankers for entrepreneurs. At Minnesota Mining & Manufacturing (3M), for example, an idea generator can go to his or her division sponsor for funding. If refused, the idea generator can then go to any other division sponsor or even to corporate R&D. If the idea is outside current business lines, the idea generator can go to the new-ventures group for support. If the idea is rejected by all possible sponsors, it probably isn't a very good idea. However, the idea is kept alive and given several opportunities to be tested. Multiple sponsors keep fragile young ideas alive.

Getting Ideas

The process of getting ideas occurs by happenstance as it did in the case history. The premise of this section is that the odds of matchups between idea generators and sponsors can be improved by organization design. First, the natural process can be improved by network-building actions such as multidivision or multireservation careers or companywide seminars and conferences. All of these practices plus a common physical location facilitate matching at 3M.

The matching process is formalized at TI, where there is an elaborate planning process called the objectives, strategies, and tactics (or OST) system, which is an annual harvest of new ideas. Innovating funds are distributed to managers of objectives (sponsors) who fund projects based on ideas formulated by idea generators, and these then become tactical action programs. Ideas that are not funded go into a creative backlog to be tapped throughout the year. Whether formal, as at TI, or informal, as at 3M, it is noteworthy that these are known systems for matching ideas with sponsors.

Ideas can also be acquired by aggressive sponsors. Sponsors sit at the crossroads of many ideas and often arrive at a better idea by putting two or more together. They can then pursue an idea generator to champion it. Good sponsors know where the proven idea people are located and how to attract such people to come to perfect an idea on their reservation. Sponsors can go inside or outside the organization to pursue these idea people.

And finally, formal events for matching purposes can be scheduled. At 3M, for example, there's an annual fair at which idea generators can set up booths to be viewed by shopping sponsors. Exxon Enterprises held a "shake the tree" event at which idea people could throw out ideas to be pursued by attending sponsors. The variations of such events are endless. The point is that by devoting time to ideas and making innovation legitimate, the odds that sponsors will find new ideas are increased.

Blending Ideas

An important lesson to be derived from our scenario is that it is no accident that a field engineer produced the new product idea. Why? Because the field engineer spent all day working on customer problems and also knew the technology. Therefore, one person knew the need and the means by which to satisfy that need. (An added plus: The field engineer had a personal need to design the appropriate technology.) The premise here is that innovation is more likely to occur when knowledge of technologies and user requirements are combined in the minds of as few people as possible—preferably in that of one person.

The question of whether innovations are need stimulated or means stimulated is debatable. Do you start with the disease and look for a cure, or start with a cure and find a disease for it? Research indicates that two thirds of innovations are need stimulated. But this argument misses the point. As shown in Exhibit 5A the debate is over whether use or means drives the downstream efforts. This thinking is linear and sequential. Instead, the model suggested here is shown in Exhibit 5B. That is, for innovation to occur, knowledge of all key components is simultaneously coupled. And the best way to maximize communication among the components is to have the communication occur intrapersonally—that is, within one person's mind. If this is impossible, then as

Exhibit 5
Linear Sequential Coupling Compared with Simultaneous Coupling of Knowledge

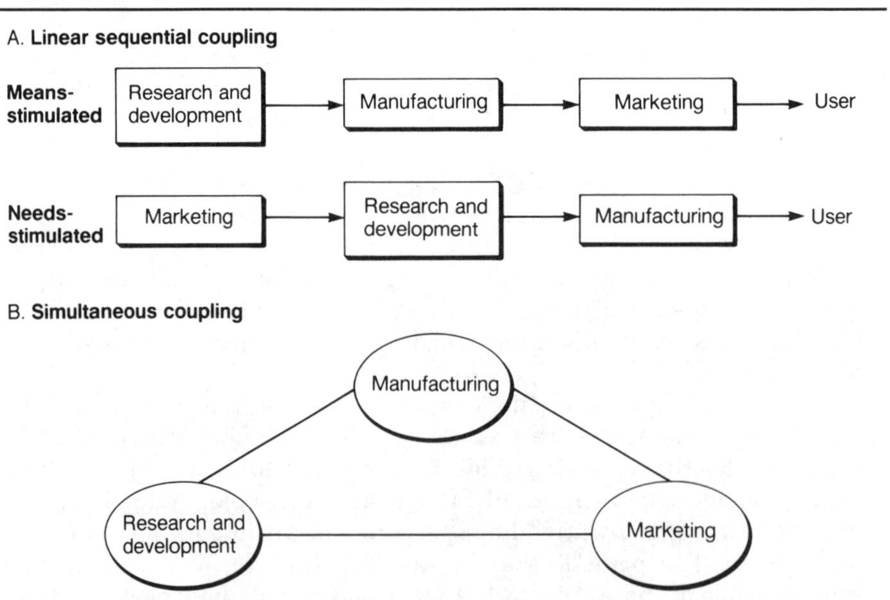

few people as possible should have to communicate or interact. The point is that innovative ideas occur when knowledge of the essential specialties is coupled in as few heads as possible. To encourage such coupling, the organization can grow or select individuals with the essential skills, or it can encourage interaction between those with meshing skills. These practices will be discussed in a "People" section.

A variety of processes are employed by organizations to match knowledge of need and of means. At IBM they place marketing people directly in the R&D labs where they can readily interpret the market requirement documents for researchers. People are rotated through this unit, and a network is created. Wang holds an annual users' conference at which customers and product designers interact and discuss the use of Wang products. Lanier insists that all top managers, including R&D management, spend one day a month selling in the field. It is reported that British scientists made remarkable progress on developing radar after actually flying missions with the Royal Air Force. In all these cases there is an explicit matching of the use and the user with knowledge of a technology to meet the use. Again these processes are explicitly designed to get a user orientation among the idea generators and sponsors. They increase the likelihood that inventions will be innovations. The more complete a new idea or invention is at its inception, the greater the likelihood of its being transferred into the operating organization.

Transitioning

Perhaps the most crucial process in getting an innovation product to market is the transitioning of an idea from a reservation to an operating organization for implementation. This process occurs in stages, as illustrated in the case history. First, the idea was formulated in the field before management knew about it. Then it was tested with a customer, the French bank. And finally, at the third stage, development and full-scale implementation took place. In other cases, several additional stages of testing and scale-up may be necessary. In any case, transitioning should be planned in such stages. At each stage the orchestrator has several choices that balance the need for further invention with the need for transfer. The choices and typical stages of idea development are shown in Exhibit 6.

At each stage these choices face the orchestrator: Who will be the sponsor? Who will be the champion? Where can staff be secured for the effort? At what physical location will work be performed? Who will fund the effort? How much autonomy should the effort have, or how differentiated should it be? For example, at the initial new-idea formulation stage the sponsor could be the corporate ventures group with the champion working on the corporate reservation. The effort could be staffed with other corporate reservation types and funded at the corporate

Exhibit 6
Transitioning Ideas by Stages

	Stages			
Choices	**I**	**II**	**Nth**	**Implementation**
Sponsor	Corporate	Corporate	. . .	Division
Champion	Corporate	Corporate	. . .	Division
Staffing	Corporate	Corporate-division	. . .	Division
Location	Corporate	Corporate	. . .	Division
Funding	Corporate	Corporate	. . .	Division
Autonomy	Complete	Complete	. . .	Minimal

level. The activity would be fully separate and autonomous. If the results were positive, the process could proceed to the next stage. If the idea needed further development, some division people could be brought in to round out the needed specialties. If the data were still positive after the second stage, then the effort could be transferred physically to the division, but the champion, sponsor, and funding might remain at the corporate level. In this manner, by orchestrating through choices of sponsor, champion, staff, location, funding, and autonomy, the orchestrator balances the need for innovation and protection with the need for testing against reality and transfer.

The above is an all too brief outline of the transition process; entire books have been written on the subject of technology transfer. The goal here is to highlight the stagewise nature of the process and the decisions to be made by the orchestrator at each stage. The process is crucial because it is the link between the two organizations. Thus to consistently innovate, the firm needs an innovating organization, an operating organization, and a process for transitioning ideas from the former to the latter.

Managing Programs

Program management is necessary to implement new products and processes within divisions. At this stage of the process, the idea generator usually hands the idea off to a product/project/program manager. The product or process is then implemented across the functional organization within the division. The systems and organizational processes for managing projects have been discussed elsewhere and will not be discussed here. The point is that a program management process and skill is needed.

In summary, several key processes—that is, funding, getting ideas, blending ideas, transitioning, and managing programs—are basic components of the innovating structure. Even though many of these occur naturally in all organizations, our implicit hypothesis is that the odds for successful innovation can be increased by explicitly designing these processes and by earmarking corporate resources for them. Hundreds of people in organizations choose to innovate voluntarily, as did the field engineer in the case history. However, if there were a reward system for people like these, more would choose to innovate, and more would choose to stay in the organization to do their innovating. The reward system is the next component to be described.

Reward System

The innovating organization, like the operating organization, needs an incentive system to motivate innovating behavior. Because the task of innovating is different from that of operating, the innovating organization needs a different reward system. The innovating task is riskier, more difficult, and takes place over longer time frames. These factors call for some adjustment of the operating organization's reward system, the amount of adjustment depending on how innovative the operating organization is and how attractive outside alternatives are.

The functions of the reward system are threefold: First, the rewards must attract idea people to the company and the reservations and retain them. Because various firms have different attraction and retention problems, their reward systems must vary. Second, the rewards provide motivation for the extra effort needed to innovate. After 19 failures, for example, something has to motivate the idea generator to make the 20th attempt. And, finally, successful performance deserves a reward. These rewards are primarily for idea generators. However, a reward measurement system for sponsors is equally important. Various reward systems will be discussed in the next sections.

Rewards for Idea Generators

Reward systems mix several types of internal motivators, such as the opportunity to pursue one's ideas, promotions, recognition, systems, and special compensation. First, people can be attracted and motivated intrinsically by simply giving them the opportunity and autonomy to pursue their own ideas. A reservation can provide such opportunity and autonomy. Idea people—who are internally driven—such as the field engineer in our story can come to a reservation, pursue their own ideas, and be guided and evaluated by a reservation manager. This is a reward in itself, albeit a minimal reward. If that minimal level attracts and motivates idea people, the innovating organization need go no further in creating a separate reward system.

However, if necessary, motivational leverage can be obtained by promotion and recognition for innovating performance. The dual ladder—that is, a system whereby an individual contributor can be promoted and given increased salary without taking on managerial responsibilities—is the best example of such a system. At 3M a contributor can rise in both status and salary to the equivalent of a group executive without becoming a manager. The dual ladder has always existed in R&D, but it is now being extended to some other functions as well.

Some firms grant special recognition for high career performance. IBM has its IBM fellows program in which the person selected as a fellow can work on projects of his or her own choosing for five years. At 3M, there is the Carlton Award, which is described as an internal Nobel Prize. Such promotion and recognition systems reward innovation and help create an innovating culture.

When greater motivation is needed, and/or the organization wants to signal the importance of innovation, special compensation is added to the aforementioned systems. Different special compensation systems will be discussed in the order of increasing motivational impact and of increasing dysfunctional ripple effects. The implication is that the firm should use special compensation only to the degree that the need for attraction and for motivation dictates.

Some companies reward successful idea generators with one-time cash awards. For example, International Harvester's share of the combine market jumped from 12 percent to 17 percent because of the introduction of the axial flow combine. The scientist whose six patents contributed to the product development was given $10,000. If the product continues to succeed, he may be given another award. IBM uses the "Chairman's Outstanding Contribution Award." The current program manager on the 4300 series was given a $5,000 award for her breakthrough in coding. These awards are made after the idea is successful and primarily serve to reward achievement rather than to attract innovators and provide incentive for future efforts.

Programs that give a "percentage of the take" to the idea generator and early team members provide even stronger motivation. Toy and game companies give a royalty to inventors—both internal and external—of toys and games they produce. Apple Computer claims to give royalties to employees who write software programs that will run on Apple equipment. A chemical company created a pool by putting aside 4 percent of the first five years' earnings from a new business venture, which was to be distributed to the initial venture team. Other companies create pools from percentages that range from 2 to 20 percent of cost savings created by process innovations. In any case, a predetermined contract is created to motivate the idea generator and those who join a risky effort at an early stage.

The most controversial efforts to date are attempts to duplicate free-market rewards within the firm. For example, a couple of years ago, ITT bought a small company named Qume that made high-speed printers. The founder became a millionaire from the sale; he had to quit his previous employer to found the venture capital effort to start Qume. If ITT can make an outsider a millionaire, why not give the same chance to entrepreneurial insiders? Many people advocate such a system but have not found an appropriate formula to implement the idea. For example, one firm created five-year milestones for a venture, the accomplishment of which would result in a cash award of $6 million to the idea generator. However, the business climate changed after two years, and the idea generator, not surprisingly, tried to make the plan work rather than adapt to the new, unforeseen reality.

Another scheme is to give the idea generator and the initial team some phantom stock, which gets evaluated at sale time in the same way that any acquisition would be evaluated. This process duplicates the free-market process and gives internal people the same venture capital opportunities and risks as they would have on the outside.

The special compensation programs produce motivation and dysfunctions. People who contribute at later stages frequently feel like second-class citizens. Also, any program that discriminates will create perceptions of unfair treatment and possible fallout in the operating organization. If the benefits are judged to be worth the effort, however, care should be taken to manage the fallout.

Rewards for Sponsors

The case history also demonstrates that sponsors need incentives, too. In the example, because they were being beaten in the market, the salespeople had an incentive to adopt a new product. The point is that sponsors will sponsor ideas, but these may not be innovating ideas unless there's something in it for them. The orchestrator's task is to create and communicate those incentives.

Sponsor incentives take many forms. At 3M, division managers have a bonus goal that is reached if 25 percent of their revenue comes from products introduced within the previous five years. When the percentage falls below the goal, and the bonus is threatened, these sponsors become amazingly receptive to new product ideas. The transfer process becomes much easier as a result. Sales growth, revenue increase, numbers of new products, and so on, may be the bases for incentives that motivate sponsors.

Another controversy can arise if the idea generators receive phantom stock. Should the sponsors who supervise these idea people receive phantom stock, too? Some banks have created separate subsidiaries so that sponsors can receive stock in the new venture. To the degree that sponsors contribute to idea development, they will need to be given such stock options, too.

Thus, the innovating organization needs reward systems for both idea generators and sponsors. It should start with a simple reward system and move to more motivating, more complex, and possibly more upsetting types of rewards only if and when attraction and motivation problems call for them.

People

The final policy area to be considered involves people practices. The assumption is that some people who are better at innovating are not necessarily good at operating. Therefore, the ability of the innovating organization to generate new business ideas can be increased by systematically developing and selecting those people who are better at innovating than others. But first the desirable attributes must be identified. These characteristics that identify likely idea generators and sponsors are spelled out in the following sections.

Attributes of Idea Generators

The field engineer in our case history is the stereotype of the inventor. He is not mainstream. He's hard to get along with, and he wasn't afraid to break company policy to perfect his idea. Such people have strong egos that allow them to persist and swim upstream. They generally are not the type of people who get along well in an organization. However, if an organization has reservations, innovating funds, and dual ladders, these people can be attracted and retained.

The psychological attributes of successful entrepreneurs include great need to achieve and to take risks. But, to translate that need into innovation, several other attributes are needed. First, prospective innovators have an irreverence for the status quo. They often come from outcast groups or are newcomers to the company; they are less satisfied with the way things are and have less to lose if there's a change. Successful innovators also need "previous programming in the industry"—that is, an in-depth knowledge of the industry gained through either experience or formal education. Hence, the innovator needs industry knowledge, but not the religion.

Previous start-up experience is also associated with successful business ventures, as are people who come from incubator firms (for example high-technology companies) and areas (such as Boston and the Silicon Valley) that are noted for creativity.

The amount of organizational effort needed to select these people varies with the ability to attract them to the organization in the first place. If idea people are attracted through reputation, then by funding reservations and employing idea-getting processes, idea people will, in effect, select themselves—they will want to work with the organization—and over time their presence will reinforce the organization's reputation for idea generation. If the firm has no reputation for innovation, then idea people must be sought out or external reservations established to encourage initial idea generation. One firm made extensive use of outside recruiting to accomplish such a goal. A sponsor would develop an idea and then attend annual conferences of key specialists to determine who was most skilled in the area of interest; he or she would then interview appropriate candidates and offer the opportunity to develop the venture to those with entrepreneurial interests.

Another key attribute of successful business innovators is varied experience, which creates the coupling of a knowledge of means and of use in a single individual's mind. It is the generalist, not the specialist, who creates an idea that differs from the firm's current business line. Specialists are inventors; generalists are innovators. These people can be selected or developed. One ceramics engineering firm selects the best and the brightest graduates from the ceramics engineering schools and places them in central engineering to learn the firm's overall system. They are then assigned to field engineering where they spend three to five years with customers and their problems and then they return to central engineering product design. Only then do they design products for those customers. This type of internal coupling can be created by role rotation. Some aerospace firms rotate engineers through manufacturing liaison.

People who have the characteristics that make them successful innovators can be retained, however, only if there are reservations for them and sponsors to guide them.

Atttributes of Sponsors and Reservation Managers

The innovating organization must also attract, develop, train, and retain people to manage the idea development process. Because certain types of people and management skills are better suited to managing ideas than others, likely prospects for such positions should have a management style that enables them to handle idea people, as well as early experience in innovating, the capability to generate ideas of their own, the skills to put deals together, and generalist business skills.

One of the key skills necessary for operating an innovating organization is the skill to manage and supervise the kind of person who is likely to be an idea generator and champion—that is, people who, among other characteristics, do not take very well to being supervised. Idea generators and champions have a great deal of ownership in their ideas. They gain their satisfaction by having "done it their way." The intrinsic satisfaction comes from the ownership and autonomy. However, idea people also need help, advice, and sounding boards. The successful sponsor learns how to manage these people in the same way that a producer or publisher learns to handle the egos of their stars and writers. This style was best described by a successful sponsor.

It's a lot like teaching your kids to ride a bike. You're there. You walk along behind. If the kid takes off, he or she never knows that they could have been helped. If they stagger a little, you lend a helping hand, undetected preferably. If they fall, you catch them. If they do something stupid, you take the bike away until they're ready.

This style is quite different from the hands-on, directive style of managers in an operating organization. Of course, the best way to learn this style is to have been managed by it and seen it practiced in an innovating organization. Therefore, experience in an innovating organization is essential.

More than the idea generators, the sponsors need to understand the logic of innovation and to have experienced the management of innovation. Its managers need to have an intuitive feel for the task and its nuances. Managers whose only experience is in operations will not have developed the managerial style, understanding, and intuitive feel that is necessary to manage innovations because the logic of operations is counterintuitive in comparison with the logic of innovations. This means that some idea generators and champions who have experienced innovation should become managers as well as individual contributors. For example, the president in our case history was the inventor of the first-generation product and therefore understood the long, agonizing process of developing a business idea. It is also rare to find an R&D manager who hasn't come through the R&D ranks.

The best idea sponsors and idea reservation managers, therefore, are people who have experienced innovation early in their careers and are comfortable with it. They will have been exposed to risk, uncertainty, parallel experiments, repeated failures that led to learning, coupling rather than assembly-line thinking, long time frames, and personal control systems based on people and ideas, not numbers and budget variances. Sponsors and reservation managers can be developed or recruited from the outside.

Sponsors and reservation managers need to be idea generators themselves. Ideas tend to come from two sources. The first is at low levels of the organization where the problem gap is experienced. The idea generator who offers a solution is the one who experienced the problem and goes to a sponsor for testing and development. One problem with these ideas is that they may offer only partial solutions because they come from specialists whose views can be parochial and local. But sponsors are at the crossroads of many ideas. They may get a broader vision of the emerging situation as a result. These idea sponsors can themselves generate an idea that is suitable for the organization's business, or they can blend several partial ideas into a business-adaptable idea. Sponsors and reservation managers who are at the crossroads of idea flow are an important secondary source of new ideas. Therefore, they should be selected and trained for their ability to generate new ideas.

Another skill that sponsors and especially reservation managers need is the ability to make deals and broker ideas. Once an idea has emerged, a reservation manager may have to argue for the release of key people, space, resources, charters, for production time, or a customer contact. These deals all require someone who is adept at persuasion. In that sense, handling them is no different than project or product management roles. People do vary in their ability to make deals and to bargain, and those who are particularly adept should be selected for these roles. However, those who have other idea management skills may well be able to be trained in negotiating and bargaining.

And, finally, sponsors and reservation managers should be generalists with general business skills. Again, the ability to recognize a business idea and to shape partial ideas into business ideas is needed. Sponsors and reservation managers must coach idea generators in specialties in which the idea generator is not schooled. Most successful research managers are those with business skills who can see the business significance in the good ideas that come from scientists.

In summary, the sponsors and reservation managers who manage the idea development process must be recruited, selected, and developed. The skills that these people need relate to their style, experience, idea-generating ability, deal-making ability, and generalist business acumen. People with these skills can either be selected or developed.

Thus some of the attributes of successful idea generators and idea sponsors can be identifed. In creating the innovating organization, people with these attributes can be recruited, selected, and/or developed. In so doing, the organization improves its odds at generating and developing new business ideas.

Summary

The innovating organization described is one that recognizes and formalizes the roles, processes, rewards, and people practices that naturally lead to innovations. The point we have emphasized throughout this article is that the organization that purposely designs these roles and processes is more likely to generate innovations than is an organization that doesn't plan for this function. Such a purposely designed organization is needed to overcome the obstacles to innovation. Because innovation is destructive to many established groups, it will be resisted. Innovation is contrary to operations and will be ignored. These and other obstacles are more likely to be overcome if the organization is designed specifically to innovate.

Managers have tried to overcome these obstacles by creating venture groups, by hiring some entrepreneurs, by creating "breakthrough funds," or by offering special incentives. These are good policies but by themselves will not accomplish the goal. Exhibit 1 conveyed the message that a consistent set of policies concerning structure, process, rewards, and people are needed. The innovating organization is illustrated in Exhibit 7. It is the combination of idea people, reservations in which they can operate, sponsors to supervise them, funding for their ideas, and rewards for their success that increase the odds in favor of innovation. Simply

Exhibit 7
An Innovating Organization's Design Components

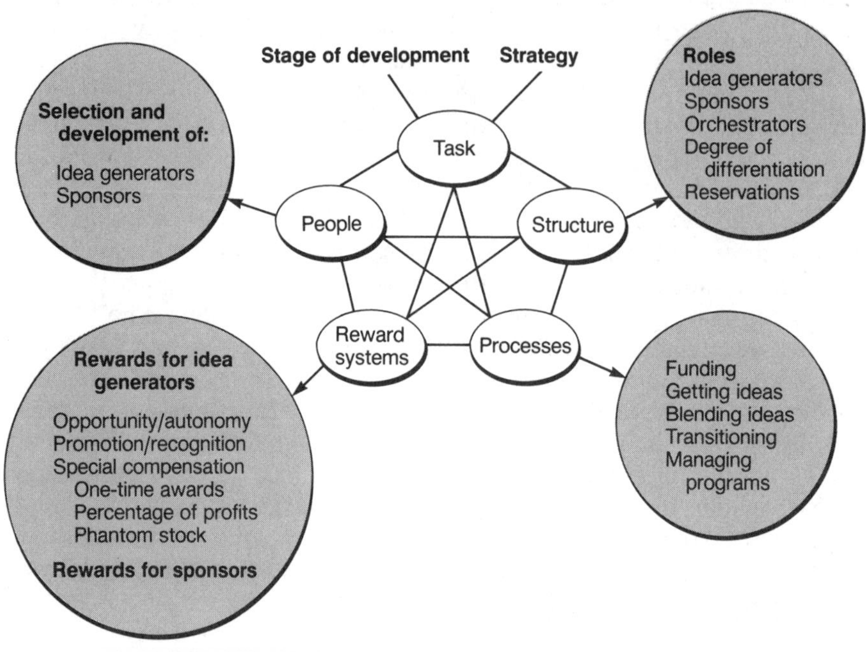

implementing one or two of these practices will result in failure and will only give people the impression that such practices do not work. A consistent combination of such practices will create an innovating organization that will work.

Selected Bibliography

The basic ideas of organization design and of blending structure, processes, rewards, and people practices are described in my earlier book. *Organization Design* (Addison-Wesley Publishing, 1978). The idea of differentiation comes from Paul Lawrence and Jay Lorsch's *Organization and Environment* (Harvard Business School, 1967). One can also find there the basic ideas of contingency theory.

The structure of the innovative organization and the three roles involved are similar to those identified in the investment idea and capital-budgeting process. These have been identified by Joseph Bower in *The Resource Allocation Process* (Division of Research at Harvard University, 1968).

Innovation itself has been treated in various ways by many people. Some good ideas about technological innovation can be found in Lowell Steele's *Innovation in Big Business* (Elsevier, 1975).

Part Two

This part of the book expands our domain of analysis from the specialized subunit to the single-business company, which consists of two or more specialized subunits. These organizations may be independent corporations or divisions of still larger organizations.

Managers of single-business companies, as the cases illustrate, face a number of organizational issues that are most often associated with coordinating and controlling their interdependent subunits. The text suggests an analytical framework for thinking about those and other single-business unit issues. The cases provide a range of situations, from relatively simple subunit interdependence (Continental Can of Canada) to relatively complex interdependence (TRW Systems), in which one can practice using that framework. Finally, the readings provide a more in-depth description of a number of the design tools used by single-business unit managers to deal effectively with subunit interdependence.

Chapter 4

Organizing Human Resources in a Single-Business Company

Designing the organization of human resources for a company operating in a single business area requires answers to three basic questions:

1. *Where do we draw the boundaries that define the company's major and minor specialized subunits? Exactly what tasks should we assign to each of these subunits?* For example, should the company be divided into three major parts, one of which focuses on marketing activities, another on manufacturing, and another on administration? Or should it be divided into two major parts, one of which focuses on all activities associated with Product X, and a second of which focuses on all activities associated with Product Y? Or would still another alternative be better? How should each major part be subdivided, if at all? If there is a manufacturing department, for example, should it be subdivided into two plants—one that produces Product X and one that produces Product Y? Or should it be subdivided into an East Coast plant and a West Coast plant, each manufacturing both X and Y? Or is there a still better alternative?

2. *How do we organize each of the major and minor specialized subunits we have created? That is, how do we structure each of these units, and what types of measurement, reward, selection, and development systems are appropriate?* For example, suppose that a company is divided into three major parts—the Product X group, the Product Y group, and administration. Further, suppose that the two product groups are each made up of a manufacturing department and a marketing department and that the administrative unit is made up of a finance group, an EDP group, and personnel. This second design question then addresses the internal organization of each of these groups. That is, should the two

engineering departments be organized in the same way? If not, how should they be different? Should a single performance appraisal system be used companywide, or should different systems be used by each of the three major subunits? How should jobs be designed in the finance group? In the personnel group? What type of training is needed in the two marketing departments? And so on.

3. *How do we integrate these specialized subunits so that their individual contributions add up to achieve the company's overall objectives? How do we avoid a situation in which each part performs its role adequately and yet the whole doesn't accomplish its goals?* For example, how should a company organize itself to ensure that its manufacturing and sales departments collaborate in the manner needed to achieve adequate levels of sales and profits? Would some type of companywide incentive bonus system based on profits encourage the managers in manufacturing and sales to collaborate? Or should the company just work out a set of clearly understood ground rules concerning what each department is expected to do under different circumstances so that their contributions integrate into a whole? Or is still some other method needed?

We have discussed the second of these three questions in Chapter 3. In this chapter, we will deal with the other two questions, starting with the third. After gaining a basic understanding of the factors involved in the second and third questions, it will be much easier to discuss the fundamental choices in the first question.

Interdependence: The Factor Creating a Need for Integration

All organizations are composed of specialized parts that are to some degree interdependent. It is because of this interdependence that organizations must design ways to integrate their parts. If their parts were totally independent, this would not be necessary. Furthermore, if the nature of the interdependence among parts or organizations was always the same or almost the same, then achieving integration would be relatively simple from a design point of view; there would exist some standard solution that could always be used. In reality, however, the nature of subunit interdependence varies significantly within and among organizations because of three important factors: (1) a company's external environment, (2) a company's technologies, and (3) a company's strategies and objectives. (See Figure 4–1).

Consider, for example, Company A—a small company that makes and sells a standard product in a limited geographical area. The company's external environment is characterized by a stable and loyal customer base and little direct competition. The company develops no new products and relies on a relatively simple manufacturing technology. It is a family-

Figure 4–1
Factors Affecting the Nature of the Interdependence among a Company's Parts

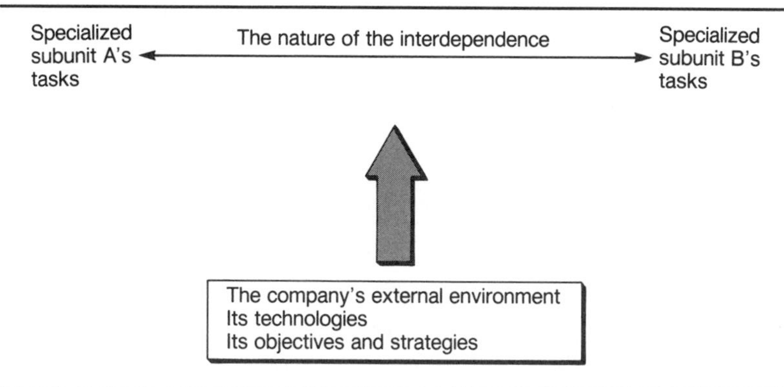

owned business whose primary objective is to generate a stable income.

This company's sales and manufacturing activities are interdependent in a relatively simple way. The manufacturing people depend on the salespeople to give them orders in an accurate and timely manner. Without those orders the manufacturing people cannot accomplish their tasks effectively and efficiently. The salespeople, however, have no similar dependence on manufacturing. They can do their job for weeks at a time without ever even thinking about the plant. Only if something catastrophic happens at the plant, for example, something that stops shipments to customers, would the salespeople be affected.

Company B, which operates in the same geographic area as Company A, is in quite a different situation. Company B operates in a much more competitive environment and sells a nonstandard set of products that are almost always custom made. Although also a family business, the family's business objectives are focused on profitable growth.

Sales and manufacturing in Company B are interdependent in very different ways than in A, due to differences in their environments, technologies, and business objectives. Sales at B depend on manufacturing for timely and accurate cost and delivery estimates, because B's products do not have standard cost and delivery times like A's. If the plant doesn't respond quickly or if it responds with cost and delivery times that are high, the salespeople will have great difficulty accomplishing their sales objectives. The salespeople (who deliver and install) also depend on the plant for supplying them with completed orders that are on time and of the quality promised. Again, if the plant does not cooperate, sales will have difficulty doing its job. At the same time, manufacturing depends on sales for orders, as was the case in Company A, as well as for other types of customer data. Because the plant does not make stan-

Figure 4–2
Sales/Manufacturing Interdependence in Two Different Companies

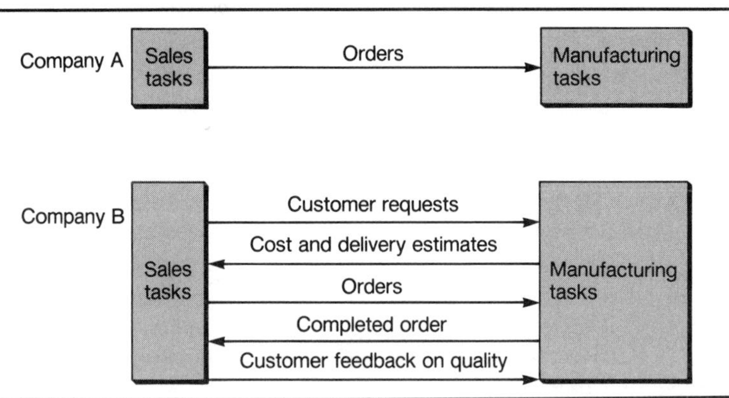

dard products, it needs to know both what types of products customers want and what customers think about the products it makes. Without this information from sales, manufacturing cannot effectively accomplish its task.

The differences between the sales/manufacturing interdependence at Company A and Company B are summarized in Figure 4–2. These differences place dissimilar demands on the mechanisms that are needed to integrate sales and manufacturing. The key implication for organizational design is obvious: one would not use the same mechanisms in these two companies to integrate manufacturing and sales. One would use a different set of tools in each case—tools that are designed to fit the particular nature of the interdependence involved.[1]

To design mechanisms that can most appropriately integrate the parts of an organization requires that one understand how those parts are interdependent. But that alone, or even in conjunction with an understanding of the organization design tools that can be used to create integration, is not enough. One also needs an appreciation of those factors that make achieving integration economically difficult.

Factors that Make It Difficult to Cope with Interdependence

In organizing an entire corporation, quite possibly the largest problem is related to the successful integration of its subunits. In talking to com-

[1] For a further discussion of interdependence see James Thompson, *Organizations in Action* (New York: McGraw-Hill, 1967), chap. 5; and Pradip Khandwalla, *The Design of Organizations* (New York: Harcourt Brace Jovanovich, 1977), chap. 13.

pany presidents, it is not at all uncommon to have them report problems such as these:

Our line and staff departments just won't cooperate with each other, and it's costing us a lot of money.

The manufacturing-sales interface is a constant source of problems, and this is giving us a bad reputation among our customers.

We just can't seem to get the interdepartmental coordination we need to bring out new products quickly.

Complexity

A number of factors typically contribute to these kinds of integration problems, one of which has to do with the complexity and intensity of the interdependence itself.

Sometimes, because of the nature of a business's environment, technology, or strategy, its subunits will be interdependent in relatively simple ways. Such was the case of Company A in Figure 4–2. Other times, subunit interdependence can be moderate to very complex because of:

1. The volume of information (per unit of time) that must go from one unit to another.
2. The multidirectionality of that information (e.g., it is not just A → B, but A ⇄ B).
3. The nonstandard nature of the information.

Consider, for example, a large, technologically complex manufacturer whose strategy is to achieve high profit margins by developing new products before any of its competitors. It has four major functional units: engineering, manufacturing, marketing, and administration (accounting, personnel, etc.). Bringing out complex new products that are successful in the marketplace requires hundreds of daily decisions, and often these decisions require expertise from many people in more than one functional unit. Consequently, a great deal of information needs to be transmitted among the functional units each day, and it would be difficult to predict, even a few days in advance, exactly what that information would be in any specific case. In situations like this, where the interdependence is intense and complex, achieving successful integration economically is obviously much more difficult than in situations where the interdependence is less complex.[2]

---

[2] For further discussion of how organizations cope with varying amounts and types of information processing among functional units, see Jay Galbraith, *Designing Complex Organizations* (Reading, Mass.: Addison-Wesley Publishing, 1973), chap. 2.

Differentiation

A second factor that contributes to integration problems is differentiation, that is, systematic differences in the values, attitudes, and behaviors of employees in different subunits. Social scientists have long established that communication and understanding usually are easiest to achieve among people who are very similar.[3] With similar goals, values, expectations, and world views, the potential for conflict or for simple misunderstandings is minimized. Through specialization, organizations purposely create differences among their subunits so that they can most effectively accomplish different kinds of tasks. But once created, these differences in objectives, personalities, education, time frames, and so on, can make the coordination of the subunits even more difficult.[4]

The following scene, for example, has probably been repeated, with slight variations, thousands of times.[5]

Factory supervisor: I'd like to get this work done as quickly as possible.

Laboratory group leader: Well, it will take us some time to understand the factors involved, and I also have to free up a person to work on it.

Factory supervisor: I understand that, but this work is critical to my operation. We've got a high spoilage rate now.

Laboratory group leader: [*To himself*—Hell, this isn't a challenging problem, none of my people will want to work on it.] I suspect we might make some progress in a month's time.

Factory supervisor: A month? You've got to be kidding! That's a month of bad products and reduced output. [*To himself*—My boss will eat me alive if we don't get this solved before then.] I was hoping you could do it this week.

Laboratory group leader: No way.

In analyzing this type of situation, people often assume the problem is a function of the specific individuals involved, without realizing that the organization itself has systematically created the basis of their conflict. To do a good job at the research task, the company in the example staffed the laboratory with managers who enjoyed working on unstructured tasks and gave them a great deal of autonomy. They measured and rewarded these managers on their long-term effect on innovation and knowledge building. At the same time, however, to achieve its produc-

---

[3] See Carl R. Rogers and F. J. Roethlisberger, "Barriers and Gateways to Communication," *Harvard Business Review*, July–August 1952, pp. 46–52.

[4] See Paul Lawrence and Jay Lorsch, *Organization and Environment* (Boston: Harvard Business School, 1967).

[5] From Jay Lorsch, "Organization Design" (Boston: Intercollegiate Case Clearing House) 9–476–094, pp. 10–11.

tion goals the company organized the factory so that its managers thought in terms of costs, quality, and productivity in the short run, and liked a "no surprises," orderly operation. Under these circumstances, it is hardly surprising that a factory manager and a lab manager might find themselves arguing with one another.

Poor Informal Relationships

A third factor that leads to integration problems is poor informal relationships among subunits. For example, if an organization's history has created informal norms that encourage subunit independence and if informal relationships among people in subunits have been characterized by suspicion and distrust, then the potential for conflict and problems will certainly exist if the subunits become interdependent.

When the type of conflict characterized by the factory manager and the laboratory manager continues over a period of time, it is relatively easy for the subunits involved to grow resentful of each other. Once distrust has developed, it can perpetuate itself even without much direct group-to-group contact. For example, a new factory manager may seldom, if ever, interact with anyone from the lab but may nevertheless be very distrustful of those "long-haired crazies" simply because that attitude is pervasive in the factory.[6]

One of the most common types of integration problems found in organizations, line-staff conflict is created by a combination of all three of the factors discussed so far. Line and staff organizations are usually designed so that they are highly interdependent. Specifically, the staff often depends on the line managers to take their advice, act on it, and give them proper recognition for their achievements. The line depends on the staff to give them helpful advice that does not interfere with their efforts either to achieve their job objectives or to relate to their superiors. In addition, staff and line units tend to be made up of different types of people, who are measured and rewarded differently. The staff are generally more specialized and are not measured on bottom-line results as are line executives. These built-in differences produce conflict which, over time, may lead to a deterioration in the relations between line and staff people. The complex interdependence, the different orientations, and the bad relationships then produce even more conflict. Under these circumstances it is hardly surprising that line managers often accuse the staff of being too specialized, of making unrealistic recommendations, of taking credit when things go well and hiding when they don't, and of acting as a spy for top management. Nor is it unusual that staff managers often complain that line people are resistant to change and

---

[6] Edgar Schein, *Organizational Psychology* (Englewood Cliffs, N.J.: Prentice-Hall, 1965), chap. 5.

are unwilling to provide the staff with proper recognition or adequate authority.[7]

Poor informal relationships among subunits can sometimes be traced to personality incompatibility. Although this factor is much less important than historical circumstances, occasionally one finds integration problems that are created by two subunit heads or two key people in different subunits who would have difficulty relating to each other under any circumstance.

Size and Physical Distance

A fourth factor that can make integration difficult is size. As the number of employees in a firm increases, the number of potentially interdependent relationships among individuals in different subunits also increases. To take a simple example, in a firm with just one sales and one production employee, there is obviously just one interdependent human relationship between the sales unit and the production unit. In a firm with 100 sales and 100 production employees, each salesperson or sales manager easily might have an interdependent relationship with half a dozen production people—that is, people that he or she needs to communicate with regularly. Overall then, there could be hundreds of relevant interdependent relationships between the sales and production units. And as the number of relationships grows, the potential for creating integration problems also grows.[8]

A final factor that can contribute to integration problems is physical distance. It is much easier for people to manage their interdependence when they work in close proximity to one another. In large corporations, offices may be separated by as much as 10,000 miles. Although technological advances in communications and transportation make it much easier to integrate distant operations, physical separation can still create problems.[9]

A sensitivity to all of the factors that can contribute to integration problems is important. If several are involved in a specific situation, then achieving effective integration will probably require considerable effort. (Figure 4–3). Moreover, in designing solutions it is important to know exactly which factors are involved; just as was the case with differ-

---

[7] For an interesting description of line-staff conflict, see Melville Dalton, *Men Who Manage* (New York: John Wiley & Sons, 1969), chap. 4.

[8] William G. Ouchi and Reuben T. Harris, "The Dynamic Organization: Structure, Technology, and Environment," in *Organizational Behavior—Issues and Research,* ed. George Strauss et al. (Madison, Wis.: Industrial Relations Research Association, 1974).

[9] Harold J. Leavitt, *Managerial Psychology* (Chicago: University of Chicago Press, 1964), p. 236.

Figure 4–3
Factors that Make Achieving Effective Integration Difficult

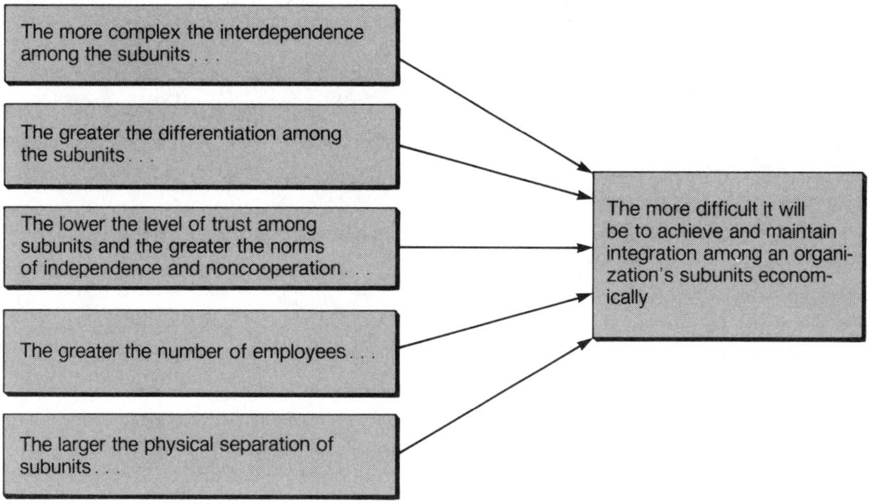

ent types of interdependence, different complicating factors tend to require different types of organizational design solutions.

Commonly Used Integrating Devices

Virtually all organizational design tools can be used to solve certain types of integration problems. The key to using them efficiently and effectively is knowing exactly what each can accomplish and at what cost.

Management Hierarchy

Perhaps the most common solution to solving an integration problem among two or more subunits has been to have them report to the same supervisor, who would then see to it that their activities were properly integrated by facilitating communications, resolving conflicts, and the like.[10] Furthermore, by having a continuous chain of command or set of management positions that link all the organization's major and minor subunits, one has a built-in mechanism for resolving conflict and coordinating activities throughout the organization. For example, if the head of the eastern sales office and the supervisor for an assembly line cannot

[10] For example, "the most ancient, as well as the most important, device for achieving coordination is the supervisor." Harold Koontz and Cyril O'Donnell, *Principles of Management* (New York: McGraw-Hill, 1955), p. 38.

settle a conflict regarding delivery delays, the problem would be communicated up the chain from both departments until both messages came to the same person (perhaps the division manager), who would then resolve the problem.

If staffed with appropriate individuals, a management hierarchy can be very effective in fostering subunit integration. By itself, however, the hierarchy can easily become overloaded with conflicts to resolve, information to pass on, etc. In such cases, executives find themselves working long hours trying to coordinate activities personally while the backlog grows of conflicts and decisions to be made. Of course, one could reduce the overload by adding more positions in the hierarchy, thus reducing the span of control. Up to a point, this solution can help; but it can also become expensive and create a large number of levels in the hierarchy that can ultimately distort communication.[11]

Staff

The problem of hierarchy overload can also be alleviated to some degree through the use of staff. By giving a line manager assistants or functional specialists, one can increase the amount of information that position in the hierarchy can process, the number of decisions it can make, and the amount of conflict it can resolve. However, there are two drawbacks to using staff as an integrating device. The first is cost. It is not surprising that the smaller the company, the less staff its managers usually have. The second drawback, as already mentioned, is that a staff group can create integration problems as well as solve them—especially between themselves and line managers in the subunits.

Rules and Procedures

Rules and procedures are another mechanism that can be used to keep the management hierarchy from becoming overloaded. When decision situations routinely arise that affect two or more parts of an organization, it is sometimes possible to establish rules or procedures regarding how they should be handled. For example: "Whenever a salesman receives an order over $5,000, he or she should inform the plant's production scheduler, by phone or in person, within four hours."

The biggest advantage of this mechanism is that it is a very economical way to achieve integration. Compare, for example, the one-time cost of developing and implementing a set of procedures with the ongoing cost of using an entire management hierarchy or a large staff. The problem with these integration devices, however, is that they only work when

---

[11] Jay Galbraith, *Organization Design* (Reading, Mass.: Addison-Wesley Publishing, 1977), pp. 48–49; and Richard H. Hall, *Organizations: Structure & Process* (Englewood Cliffs, N.J.: Prentice-Hall, 1972), chap. 9.

intelligent rules can be established and when the situation is stable enough that the company does not have to be constantly changing the rules. Furthermore, when organizations rely heavily on rules for integration or other purposes, there are a variety of dysfunctional consequences. For example, since rules have to be policed, they create stress between managers (policers) and workers. And since rules and procedures inevitably specify minimum acceptable behavior, they often cause behavior to settle at that minimum level.[12] Moreover, excessive reliance on rules and procedures can lead to "goal displacement," where the pursuance of those rules and procedures becomes an end in itself rather than a means toward the end of achieving the goals of the organization. That, in turn, can produce rigidity of behavior and an inability to respond to changing circumstances.[13]

Goals and Plans

Goals and plans can serve a function similar to that of rules and procedures, but for a limited time. That is, once established, they allow two or more parts of an organization to operate relatively independently and yet have their outputs integrated. For example, by setting exact specifications for modifying a product and by determining timetables for its production and introduction dates, the engineering, marketing, and manufacturing departments of a company can work independently on their part of the new-product development task and at the same time be assured that it will still fit with the other parts. Coordination is thus achieved.

Except in circumstances where planning and goal setting are infeasible, perhaps because events are too unpredictable, these devices can be very useful in facilitating integration. The major drawback to using goals and plans is their cost. It takes time and energy to create realistic and intelligent goals and plans. In some circumstances, this cost simply precludes the use of these devices, particularly when compared with other devices (such as rules and procedures).[14]

Committees and Task Forces

Still another set of structural devices that can be used to facilitate integration consists of meetings, committees, task forces, and the like. To help coordinate sales and production, for example, the heads of the two

---

[12] A. W. Gouldner, *Patterns of Industrial Bureaucracy* (New York: Free Press, 1954).

[13] R. K. Merton, "Bureaucratic Structure and Personality," *Social Forces* 18 (1970), pp. 560–68.

[14] Jay Galbraith, *Designing Complex Organizations* (Reading, Mass.: Addison-Wesley Publishing, 1973), pp. 12–14.

units along with some of their staff might meet for a few hours each week.

Committees, task forces, and meetings are attractive in that they can solve integration problems that some other devices cannot. Unlike rules or plans, they can deal with nonroutine, spur-of-the-moment issues. Unlike a management hierarchy, they can process a lot of information and make many decisions in a relatively short period of time. The primary drawback of this device is cost. One committee of eight middle-level managers that meets once a week for two hours can easily cost an organization (in salary, benefits, and support services) over $15,000 a year. A second drawback is related to the need for small-group decision-making skills on the part of those participating in committees or task forces. Without these skills, the groups can become inefficient and ineffective, and employees can become frustrated and angry.[15]

Integrating Roles

Under certain circumstances where coordination is particularly difficult to achieve and yet is particularly important, organizations can create special integrating roles or departments. A product manager position, for example, might be created to integrate the marketing and production subunits for a specific product or product line. Or a project manager position might be created to help integrate personnel from different subunits working on a project.

Typically, the integrator does not have direct authority over the personnel he or she coordinates. This prevents the integrator from "railroading" decisions against the better judgment of the specialists being coordinated. This lack of authority can be frustrating, because the coordinator is forced to rely on considerable initiative and personal skills (enthusiasm, energy, tact, judgment) to bring about the necessary integration. Accordingly, the selection of people with the appropriate background and skills for the integration roles becomes crucial. To be effective, an integrator must be a good leader and have a somewhat "generalist" orientation—one that is different from that of the specialized subunits, yet allows understanding of each of them. Similarly, integrating departments seem to work best when they are structured in a way that is not identical to any of the subunits they must integrate but rather is in between them on important dimensions.[16]

---

[15] For a good description of the types of skills that are needed and why, see Edgar Schein, *Process Consultation* (Reading, Mass.: Addison-Wesley Publishing, 1969), chaps. 3–7.

[16] For a further discussion of integrating roles, see Paul R. Lawrence and Jay W. Lorsch, "New Management Job: The Integrator," *Harvard Business Review*, November–December 1967.

Full-time integrators can be an expensive addition to an organization. The cost of just eight product managers can easily approach half a million dollars a year for salary and fringe benefits alone. A small company would have great difficulty justifying or affording such an expense.

Formal Authority

Still another element of structure that can help or hinder effective integration is the distribution of formal authority in the organization, i.e., whether it is relatively centralized or decentralized and whether subunits such as manufacturing and sales have equal power. To facilitate integration, authority should be distributed so that people or groups who have information relevant to making integrating decisions also have the power to make the decisions. For example, if a company depends on teams, meetings, and task forces to achieve integration, then power should be relatively decentralized. If a company relies almost exclusively on rules and a management hierarchy, then power should be relatively centralized.

The major problem with relying on formal authority to help achieve subunit integration is that once in place, it can be difficult to change when necessary. People seldom give up formal power without a fight.[17]

Measurement and Reward Systems

Measurement and reward systems are often used as integrating devices. In such cases, systems are set up to measure the variables related to the successful integration of certain subunits. This information is then sent to those decision makers who have the most control over the successful integration of these subunits, and their rewards are made partially contingent on their success at achieving it.[18]

For example, it is not uncommon for companies that utilize product managers to establish accounting systems which measure profitability, sales, and costs by individual product line. This information can be used by the product manager and is often tied in to his or her compensation.

While well-designed measurement and reward systems can motivate behavior that focuses on effective integration, they also have drawbacks. The first, again, is the direct cost of establishing and maintaining these systems. Other drawbacks relate to the indirect costs associated with the dysfunctional behavior these systems sometimes produce. To obtain the desired rewards these systems promise, people sometimes ignore im-

---

[17] Gene Dalton, Louis Barnes, and Abraham Zaleznik, *The Distribution of Authority in Formal Organizations* (Boston: Harvard Business School, 1968), chap. 3.

[18] J. Leslie Livingstone, "Managerial Accounting and Organizational Coordination," in *The Accountant in a Changing Business Environment*, ed. Willard E. Stone (University of Florida Press, 1973), pp. 42–45.

portant but unrewarded behaviors. Supervisors will, for example, stop helping others or investing time in their development unless their actions produce measured results. They will sometimes even focus on finding ways to fool the system into reporting invalid data that are favorable to them. In still other cases, they will simply stop working as hard or cooperating as much because of their resentment toward the "carrot and stick" system.[19]

Selection and Development Systems

Selection and development systems can serve as integration devices in two different ways. First, they can provide an organization with individuals who are capable of effectively playing key integrating roles. Second, by providing formal training programs, they can help build better relationships between individuals or groups whose subunits require integration.

By seeking and hiring people who have the characteristics of good integrators, selection systems provide organizations with people who can serve integrating roles. Development systems can achieve similar results by taking existing personnel and, either with formal training programs or job rotation through specialist departments, developing them into effective integrators.

Selection systems can help improve relations between individuals or groups through occasional hiring and promotion decisions. For example, to help maintain good relations between sales and manufacturing personnel, some organizations periodically promote a few people across departmental lines.

Development systems also help provide integration among representatives of an organization's subparts through team development and intergroup development activities. Team development activities are usually focused on task forces, committees, or other groups that perform an integrating function. The objective of team development is to help these groups perform better. The method usually involves meeting in a nonwork setting for one to four days, with an agenda that focuses on group process and group problems. An expert in small-group process usually meets with the team to help the members identify and solve any communication, interpersonal, or leadership problems that impede their effectiveness.[20] Intergroup development activities focus on improving the relationships among the people in two or more subunits. They also usually involve an offsite meeting for one or two days with an expert facilitator.

---

[19] E. E. Lawler and J. G. Rhode, *Information and Control in Organizations* (Santa Monica, Calif.: Goodyear Publishing, 1976), chap. 6.

[20] For more information on team development, see Shel Davis, "Building More Effective Teams," *Innovation* 15 (1970), pp. 32–41.

The activities typically focus on breaking down distorted beliefs on both sides, on helping each side understand the other better, and on building relationships and communication channels across the groups.[21] Both team and intergroup development activities are also used to encourage members to share norms in a company's culture that will facilitate effective integration. For example, there is considerable evidence that successful companies have norms that favor confronting conflicts and dealing with them through problem solving, rather than smoothing over or avoiding conflict, or solving it by forcing one person's solution on another.[22] Team and intergroup development activities usually try to foster the development and maintenance of confronting and problem-solving norms.

Physical Setting

Another element of organizational design that is sometimes used to facilitate integration is architecture. Because physical proximity makes communication easier, some organizations design their offices, conference areas, and open space with an eye toward meeting critical integration needs. For example, one money management firm felt that its 45-minute daily morning meeting was such an important device for facilitating coordination between the research and portfolio management departments that it spent over $100,000 to build a room that was specially designed for that meeting.[23]

Architecture has the same drawbacks as some of the other integrating devices. It can be expensive, and it can inadvertently reduce a company's needed specialization. For example, putting all the specialists that are associated with Product X in the same office area and providing them with team-building activities will clearly help integration efforts concerning Product X, but it might also lead to an erosion of the specialists' particular expertise. This can be threatening to specialists who view their career development as contingent on continued specialization.

Departmentalization

A final way that managers can solve integration problems is to redesign subunit boundaries so as to include the required interdependence *within* the new subunit boundaries, where it can be more easily managed.

---

[21] For more information on intergroup development, see Robert Blake and Jane Mouton, *Managing Intergroup Conflict for Industry* (Houston: Gulf Publishing, 1964).

[22] See, for example, Lawrence and Lorsch, *Organization and Environment.*

[23] For an in-depth look at physical settings as an integrating device, see Fritz Steele, *Physical Settings and Organizational Development* (Reading, Mass.: Addison-Wesley Publishing, 1973).

One of the most common examples of the use of departmentalization as an integrating device is an organization that switches from a functional to a product, market, or geographical structure. Small manufacturing firms typically use a functional structure; however, many switch to a product division structure after achieving a certain size. One of the key reasons they make this change is that integration across functions becomes increasingly difficult and expensive as they grow larger and larger. Increased size usually means a greater volume of information must flow between functions, thus increasing the complexity of the interdependence. With larger size come additional people and thus more interdependent relationships to be managed across functions. Specialization also tends to increase with size, and with it the differences among specialists in different functions are multiplied. The physical proximity of people in different functions tends to decrease with increases in size, and with it the possibility for easy face-to-face interaction. By shifting to product divisions, a company reduces the size of the functional units being integrated around each product, the amount of information flowing between the small functional units, and sometimes the physical distance between people in various functional units. These changes make functional integration around the designated products or product line easier.

Nevertheless, the switch from a functional to a product (or market or geographic) structure has some drawbacks. Achieving integration across the products can be more difficult. And often some functional specialization and/or economics of scale are sacrificed.[24]

Organizations that need both strong functional specialization and a high degree of integration across functions sometimes use a matrix structure. In bipolar matrix structures (the most common),[25] all jobs and minor departments are grouped into two major departments: usually one is associated with some function and the other is associated with some product or market. Everyone thus has two bosses.

In a sense, a matrix is an attempt to gain the benefits of *both* functional and product/market structures. It can do so, but not without its own costs. Because a matrix calls for two hierarchies and because it requires time and effort to manage the ambiguity and tension which result from having multiple bosses for each person and subunit, a matrix can be expensive and difficult to maintain. In a matrix organization it is easy for unresolved conflicts between the two dimensions to slow down information flow and decisions. It is also possible for one side of the

---

[24] For a further discussion of the trade-off between product and functional structures, see Jay Lorsch and Art Walker, "Organizational Choice: Product versus Function," *Harvard Business Review,* November–December, 1968.

[25] Matrix structures can contain more than two dimensions. For an example of how a three-dimensional matrix is designed, see William C. Goggin, "How the Multidimensional Structure Works at Dow Corning," *Harvard Business Review,* January–February 1974.

matrix to overpower the other, thus turning it back into a functional or a product/market organization for all practical purposes.[26]

Most organizations use some combination of functional, product, market, geographical, and matrix structures. For example, a manufacturing company might have five major subunits, four of which are functional departments (manufacturing, marketing, engineering, and administration) and one of which is a geographical department (international—all non-U.S. sales, manufacturing, etc.). The marketing department might be further divided into a number of market-oriented subunits. Manufacturing might be divided geographically, with plants in different regions of the country. Engineering might be structured as a matrix, where one side represents engineering functions (electrical, mechanical, etc.) while the other side represents new-product development projects.

Selecting a Set of Integrating Mechanisms

In selecting a set of integrating mechanisms, an awareness of their individual strengths and weaknesses (Figure 4–4) is required. In addition, two generalizations may be made:

1. *The larger the number of factors that make achievement of integration difficult, the more costly the needed integration devices will be.* In an organization where there is little interdependence among the parts, where the parts are not highly specialized, and where informal relations among the parts are good, effective integration might well be achieved through a management hierarchy along with some rules and procedures. In a large and geographically dispersed organization where there is intense interdependence among the parts, where the parts are highly specialized, and where informal relations among the parts are poor, effective integration might require a hierarchy, rules, plans and goals, teams or task forces, integrating personnel, special measurement and reward systems, team building, and maybe more.

Lawrence and Lorsch, for example, in a study of companies in three different industries, found just this type of correlation between integration needs and integrating devices used[27] (see Figure 4–5).

2. *The effective solution to any integration problem is the one that costs the least and that does not seriously undermine the effectiveness of the specialized subunits.* One of the most common problems managers encounter when trying to solve integration problems is related to cost.

---

[26] For more on matrix organizations, see Leonard Sayles, "Matrix Management," *Organizational Dynamics,* Autumn 1976, pp. 2–17; and Paul Lawrence, Harvey Kolodny, and Stanley Davis, "The Human Side of the Matrix," *Organizational Dynamics,* Summer 1977, pp. 43–61.

[27] Lawrence and Lorsch, *Organization and Environment.*

Figure 4–4
Costs and Benefits of Alternative Integration Methods

Integrating Methods	Advantages	Drawbacks
The management hierarchy/ span of control	Provides a network that links together all of an organization's major and minor functional units.	Can become overloaded and break down. A very narrow span can be expensive and cumbersome.
Staff	Can supplement the management hierarchy and help it perform a larger integration function.	Cost. Also can create its own integration problems (between staff and line).
Rules and procedures	Economical way to achieve integration around routine issues.	Limited to routine issues. Heavy use can create dysfunctional consequences.
Plans and goals	Can handle many nonroutine issues that rules and procedures cannot.	Cost, in time and effort.
Meetings, committees, task forces, etc.	Can deal with a large number of unpredictable problems and decisions.	Cost. People involved need skills at group decision making.
Integrating roles	Can deal with a large number of unpredictable problems and decisions.	Cost. Can be difficult to find people with the right characteristics to fill the role.
Formal authority	No direct cost.	Can be abused; difficult to shift when shifts are needed.
Measurement and reward systems	Can motivate behavior directed at integration.	Cost. Activities or outcomes not measured and rewarded can be ignored or undermined. Can produce dysfunctional behavior.
Selection and development systems	Can solve certain types of problems more efficiently than other devices.	Can be expensive. Can erode specialized expertise.
Architecture	Under some circumstances, can be very inexpensive solution.	Can be expensive. Can erode specialized expertise.
Departmentalization:		
Functional structure	Facilitates integration within functions.	Does not facilitate integration across functions.
Product/market/ geographic structure	Promotes integration within and among functions associated with each product/market/ geographical area.	Does not promote integration between product/market/ geographic area.
Matrix structure	Promotes integration between each side.	Expensive. Generates conflict and tension.

Figure 4–5
The Relationship of Integrating Needs to Integrating Devices Used*

	Industry		
	Container	**Foods**	**Plastics**
Integration needs	Low	Moderate	High
Structural integration devices used	Hierarchy Procedures Some plans	Integrators Plans Hierarchy Procedures	Cross-functional teams Integrators Departments of integrators Hierarchy, plans, and procedures

* Adapted from Paul R. Lawrence and Jay W. Lorsch, *Organization and Environment* (Boston: Harvard Business School, 1967).

A second common problem is related to side effects. A good solution to any problem is one that does not create even more serious problems of a different kind. In solving integration problems, managers sometimes seriously undermine the types of organization needed at the subunit level. More than one well-intentioned company president has managed to "get his people to start pulling together," but in the process, made them each less effective at their respective specialized tasks.

Drawing Subunit Boundaries

In designing organizations, managers must make fundamental choices regarding not only how to organize subunits and how to integrate them but also where to draw subunit boundaries in the first place. We have saved this issue until this point, because addressing it involves making trade-off judgments between:

1. The benefits to be gained from the development of specialized expertise and/or the economies of scale that are possible within subunit boundaries.
2. The cost of establishing, maintaining, and achieving effective integration across subunit boundaries.

An example will help clarify this issue. A manufacturing company with 400 employees sold one product line to customers in three different industries. The firm was organized functionally, with marketing, engineering, manufacturing, and administrative departments reporting to the president (Figure 4–6A). In 1973, in response to an increasing number of recurring problems, the president decided to analyze the company's organization. A summary of his analysis follows:

a. While we are currently serving customers in three industries, only eight years ago we were much smaller and were selling to customers in one industry

Figure 4–6

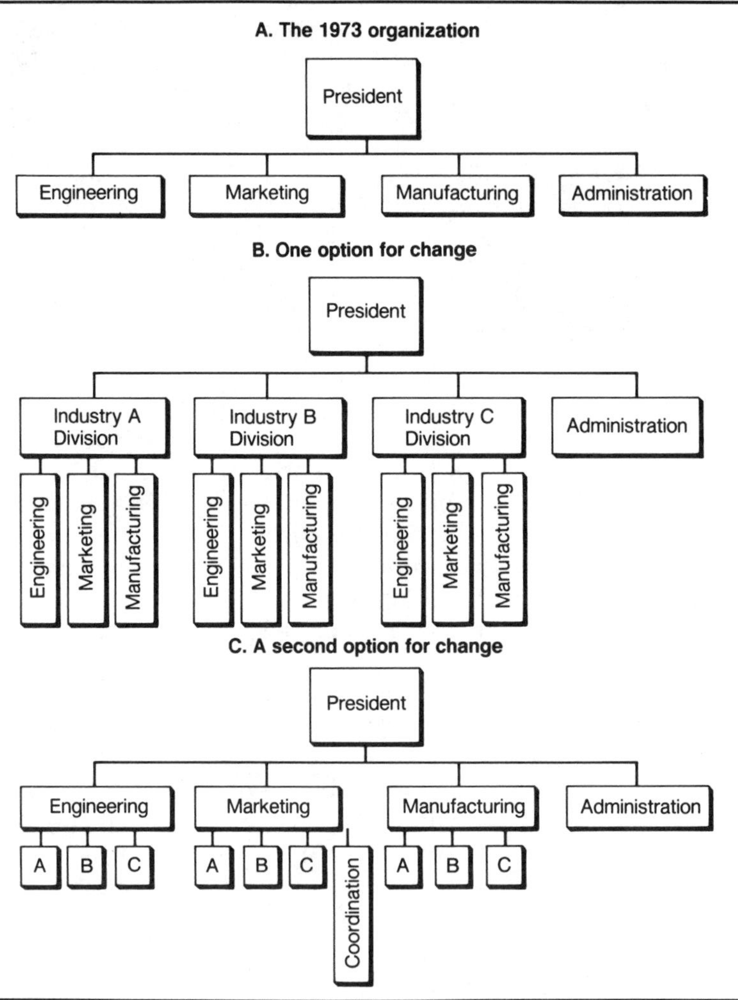

only. This change is important because the demands that the customers in the three industries place on us are very different. The amount and type of special engineering that has to be done, the nature of selling and customer relations, and the way we can manufacture our products vary considerably between customers in different industries, but are very similar between customers in the same industry.

b. Our organization, which has grown in size but has not changed its structure in the past eight years, is just not able to effectively handle all three industries. We still do the best job and are most profitable in our original industry. That, I believe, is due to the fact that our engineering, sales, and manufacturing are still basically geared to that industry. I'm convinced that the key to increased sales and profitability is to better serve the different needs of customers in our two newer industries while retaining our ability to serve our older customers.

c. A number of people have suggested to me that we should reorganize into three industry-oriented groups (Figure 4–6B). *I think that such a redefinition of our departmental boundaries would solve some problems but would create others. The industry-oriented structure would clearly allow us to develop expertise in serving customers in each of the three industries. But I think it is an impractical solution for a company of our size. It would require a number of additional managers. It would sacrifice a number of economies of scale we now have. It would be difficult to switch some slack engineering availability from one division to another, for example, which we can easily do with our current structure. And I'm not sure how we could keep from reinventing wheels within the three sales groups, the three engineering groups, etc., unless we had a lot of time-consuming meetings.*

d. So I have tentatively decided on a modification of our current structure (Figure 4–6C), *which essentially leaves the main department boundaries as they are, but creates a new set of groups within each department and adds three "industry coordinators" within marketing. This solution is economically feasible, and it will allow us to gain the expertise we need to serve all three industries.*

This solution was implemented during 1973, and after a period of adjustment, the company experienced large increases in sales and profits in 1975 and 1976.

Deciding where to draw major and minor subunit boundaries always involves an analytical and judgmental process similar to the one just described. The decision cannot be made according to any formula, and it must be made while considering the implications for organizing as well as integrating the subunits thus defined. The key to making this judgment, as well as to answering the other two major organizational questions raised at the beginning of this chapter, is a thorough analysis of the specific situation.

Summary

Designing an organization or trying to solve an organizational problem from the point of view of an entire company requires a form of analysis that can be summarized in the following steps:

1. First one needs to identify the company's key activities, their diversity, and their interdependence. This business analysis can be accomplished only by thoroughly examining the company's external environment, its technology, and its strategy or goals. It is important here to be specific regarding exactly what the important characteristics of the activities are, how they are different, what the nature of the interdependence among them is, and what is really critical for success. If any of these factors have changed in the past five years or so, it is important to identify that as well as the reasons for the changes.

Figure 4–7

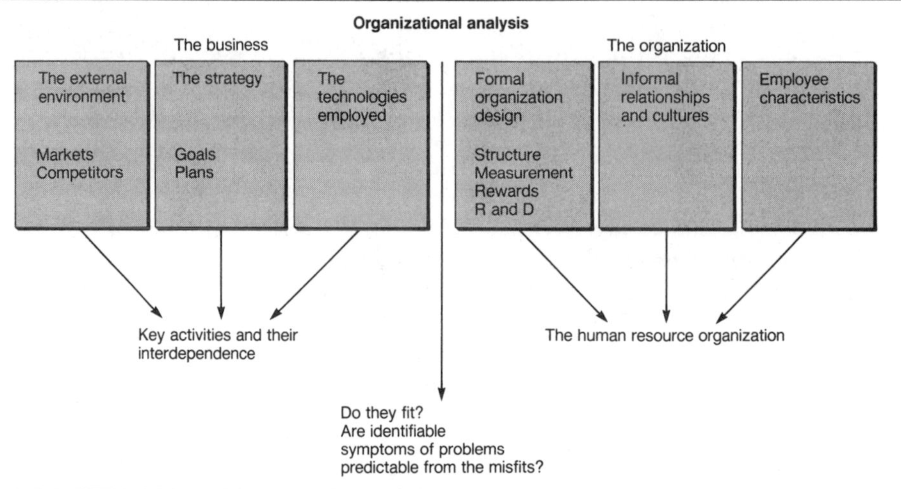

Probably the biggest mistake that managers and consultants make in dealing with organizational issues is to begin defining problems and considering solutions without having completed a thorough examination of the business involved. Subunit boundary structure, integrating devices, and subunit organizational designs cannot be evaluated in the abstract. Rules, matrixes, and profit centers are not "good" or "bad" by themselves. They are only appropriate or inappropriate in light of how well they fit a specific situation.

2. One must identify the company's current human resource organization in terms of staff characteristics, formal arrangements, and informal relationships. It is essential that one go beyond an analysis of the formal design. What is important is the actual human resource organization that has emerged in the situation. And that organization is very much a function of not only the formal design but also of informal relations and employee characteristics. Again, if any of these factors have changed recently, it is important to recognize that and the forces creating the change.

3. One should next make a judgment regarding how well the organization fits the company's business (see Figure 4–7).[28] This judgment can be compared with one's knowledge of the existence or absence of any recurring problems. If the analysis is sound, the logical consequences of the misfits should actually exist as problems in the organization.

---

[28] For an example of this type of analysis as it pertains specifically to selecting management control systems, see Richard F. Vancil, "What Kind of Management Control Do You Need?" *Harvard Business Review,* March–April 1973.

4. Finally, one needs to identify alternative organizational designs that might solve the problems. That is, develop different solutions to the three basic questions raised at the beginning of this chapter. The answers can then be tested against the analysis, and a choice can be made.

There is no question that this mode of analysis involves making difficult judgments. No simple rule will dictate how a company should be organized. Nevertheless, the concepts and techniques outlined in this chapter provide analytical tools that can aid a manager in arriving at a decision that best fits the situation.

Case 4–1

Continental Can Company of Canada, Ltd. (B)*

Paul R. Lawrence, John P. Kotter

By the fall of 1963, Continental Can Company of Canada had developed a sophisticated control system for use in its plants. This control system, begun in the years following World War II, stressed competition within the company as well as against other companies in the industry. Within its division at Continental, the can manufacturing plant at St. Laurent, Quebec, had become a preferred site for production management trainees as a result of its successful use of control systems. According to a division training executive:

> *The St. Laurent people look at the controls as tools. They show trainees that they really work. The French-Canadian atmosphere is good too. In a French-Canadian family everything is open and aboveboard. There are no secrets. Trainees can ask anyone anything, and the friendliness and company parties give them a feel for good employee relations.*

Products, Technology, and Markets

Continental Can Company of Canada in 1963 operated a number of plants in Canada. The principal products of the St. Laurent plant were Open Top food cans, bottle caps and crowns, steel pails, and general-line containers. Of these, Open Top cans constituted the largest group. These were manufactured for the major packers of vegetable products—peas,

---

* This case is a revision of Empire Glass (B), from which the disguise has been removed.

Harvard Business School case 478–017.

beans, corn, and tomatoes—and for the soup manufacturers. Beer and soft-drink cans were a growing commodity, and large quantities of general-line containers of many different configurations were produced to hold solvents, paints, lighter fluids, waxes, antifreeze, and so on. Several styles of steel pails of up to 5-gallon capacity were also produced to hold many specialized products.

Most of the thousands of different products varying in size, shape, color, and decoration were produced to order. Typical lead times between the customer's order and shipment from the plant were two to three weeks in 1963, having been reduced from five and one-half to six weeks in the early 1950s, according to St. Laurent plant executives.

Quality inspection in the can manufacturing operation was critical, as the can maker usually supplied the closing equipment and assisted in or recommended the process to be used in the final packing procedure. In producing Open Top food cans, for example, the can body was formed, soldered, and flanged at speeds exceeding 400 cans per minute. After the bottom or end unit was assembled to the body, each can was air tested to reject poor double seams or poor soldering or plate inclusions that could cause pin holes. Both side seams and double seams underwent periodic destruction testing to ensure that assembly specifications were met. Although a number of measuring devices were used in the process, much of the inspection was still visual, involving human inspection and monitoring. The quality of the can also affected the filling and processing procedure: it had to withstand internal pressures from expansion of the product as it was heated, and then it had to sustain a vacuum without collapsing when it was cooled. Costly claims could result if the container failed in the field and the product had to be withdrawn from store shelves.

Almost all of the containers required protective coatings inside and out, and the majority were decorated. The coating and decorating equipment was sophisticated and required sizable investment. This part of the operation was unionized, and the lithographers or press men were among the highest paid of the various craftsmen in the plant.

Most of the key equipment was designed and developed by the parent organization over many years. The St. Laurent plant spent substantial sums each year to modernize and renovate its equipment. Modernization and the implementation of new techniques to increase speed, reduce material costs, and improve quality were a necessity as volume increased. Over the years, many of the small-run, handmade boxes and pails were discontinued and the equipment scrapped. Other lines were automated and personnel retrained to handle the higher mechanical skills and changeovers required. In spite of these changes, however, according to a general foreman, a production worker of the 1940s could return in 1963 and not feel entirely out of place. Many of the less skilled machine operators were required to handle several tasks on the higher-speed equipment. In general, most of the jobs in the plant were relatively unskilled, highly repetitive, and gave the worker little control over method or pace. The die makers, who made and repaired the dies, and machine repairmen and those who made equipment setup changes between different products were considered to possess the highest level of skill.

All production workers below the rank of assistant foreman were unionized; however, there had never been a strike at the plant. Wages were high compared to other similar industries in the Montreal area. The union was not part of the master agreement that governed all other plants in Canada and most of the plants in the U.S., but management made every effort to apply equality to this plant. Output standards were established for all jobs, but no bonus was paid for exceeding standards.

The metal can industry was relatively stable with little product differentiation. The St. Laurent plant to some extent shipped its products throughout Canada, although transportation costs limited its market primarily to eastern Canada. While some of the customers were large and bought in huge quantities (between 300 and 500 million cans), many were relatively small and purchased a more specialized product.

The Plant Organization

Plant Management

Andrew Fox, the plant manager at St. Laurent since 1961, had risen from an hourly worker through foreman up to plant manufacturing engineer in the maintenance of the business. He had developed an intimate, first-hand knowledge of operations and was frequently seen around the plant, a cigar clenched between his teeth.

As plant manager, Fox had no responsibility for sales or research and development activities. In fact, both Fox and the district sales manager in his area had separate executives to whom they reported in the division headquarters, and it was in the superior of these executives that responsibility for both sales and production first came together.

Fox commented about the working relationships at the St. Laurent plant:

> *You will see that frequently two managers with different job titles are assigned responsibility for the same task.* (He implied that it was up to them to work out their own pattern of mutual support and cooperation.) *However, I don't have to adhere strictly to the description. I may end up asking a lot more of the man at certain times and under certain conditions than is ever put down on paper.*
>
> *In effect, the staff*[1] *runs the plant. We delegate to the various staff department*

[1] The personnel reporting directly to Fox. The organization chart (see Exhibit 1) was prominently displayed on the wall of the lobby. See Exhibit 2 for other information on personnel.

Exhibit 1
St. Laurent Plant: Organization Chart March 1, 1963

- Plant Manager
  Andrew Fox
  - Plant
    Engineer
    B. McDonald
    - Machine Shop
      Foreman
      - Assistant
        Foreman
    - Engineer
  - Production
    Control Manager
    A. Whitelaw
  - Plant
    Controller
    A. Hunter
  - Industrial
    Relations Manager
    H. Stone
  - Assistant Plant
    Manager
    R. Andrews
    - Batch
      Department
    - Tank
      Department
      - Assistant
        Foreman
    - General
      Foreman
      G. Jacques
      - Forming
        Department
        - Assistant
          Foreman
      - Packing
        Department
        - Assistant
          Foreman
    - Night
      Foreman
      H. F. Ford
    - General
      Foreman
      H. LaSalle
      - Forming
        Department
        - Assistant
          Foreman
      - Packing
        Department
        - Assistant
          Foreman
        - Assistant
          Foreman
    - Warehouse
      and Shipping
  - Plant
    Industrial Engineer
    J. Herman
  - Purchasing
    Agent
    A. Jordan
  - Quality
    Control Manager
    T. Voorhees

Exhibit 2
Information about Certain Personnel

Name	Position	Approximate Age	Approximate Length of Service: St. Laurent	Approximate Length of Service: CCC	College Education
Andrew Fox	Plant manager	40–45	8	18	None
Robert Andrews	Assistant plant manager	35	3	8	Agricultural engineering
A. Hunter	Plant controller	50	15	23	None
A. Whitelaw	Production control supervisor	45	18	18	None
Harold Stone	Personnel supervisor	45–50	5	29	None
Joe Herman	Plant industrial engineer	30–35	1	10	Engineering
Tom Voorhees	Quality control supervisor	30	5	5	Engineering in Netherlands
G. E. Jacques	General foreman	45–50	25	25	None
Henri LaSalle	General foreman	50	18	18	None
L. G. Adams	District sales manager	45–50	18	18	None

heads the authority to implement decisions within the framework of our budget planning. This method of handling responsibility means that staff members have to be prepared to substantiate their decisions. At the same time, it gives them a greater sense of participation in and responsibility for plant income. We endeavor to carry this principle into the operating and service departments. The foreman is given responsibility and encouraged to act as though he were operating a business of his own. He is held responsible for all results generated in his department and is fully aware of how many decisions of his affect plant income.

Our division personnel counsel and assist the plant staff and the plant staff counsel and assist the department foremen. Regular visits are made to the plant by our division manager and members of his staff. The principal contact is through the division manager of manufacturing and his staff, the manager of industrial engineering, the manager of production engineering and the manager of quality control. [There was no division staff officer in production control.]

However, the onus is on the plant to request help or assistance of any kind. We can contact the many resources of Continental Can Company, usually on an informal basis. That is, we deal with other plant managers directly for information when manufacturing problems exist without going through the division office.

Each member of the staff understands that we, as a plant, have committed ourselves through the budget to provide a stated amount of income, and regardless of conditions which develop, this income figure must be maintained. If sales are off and a continuing trend is anticipated, we will reduce expenses wherever possible to retain income. Conversely, if we have a gain in sales volume, we look for the complete conversion of the extra sales at the profit margin rate. However, this is not always possible, especially if the increase in sales comes at a peak time when facilities are already strained.

Fox was assisted by Robert Andrews, the assistant plant manager. Andrews, promoted from quality control manager in 1961, was responsible for all manufacturing operations within the plant. Andrews appeared more reserved than Fox, talked intently, and smiled easily while working with the persons that reported to him. Fifteen salaried supervisors reported to Andrews and helped him control the three-shift operation of the plant and its 500 hourly workers. (During peak periods during the summer, the plant employed as many as 800 people; most of the additional workers were the sons and daughters of plant employees.) Andrews noted:

Our foremen have full responsibility for running their departments; quality, conditions of equipment, employee relations, production according to schedule, control of inventory through accurate reporting of spoilage and production, and cost control. He is just as accountable for those in his department as the plant manager is for the entire plant.

Andrews added that supervisory positions carried a good deal of status. Each supervisor had a personal parking spot and office and was expected to wear white shirts.[2] Andrews spoke of these symbols as an important aspect of the supervisor's position of authority. "He is no longer the best man with the wrench—he is the man with the best overall supervisory qualification."

Production Control

Al Whitelaw, the production control manager, had worked all of his 18 years with Continental Can at the St. Laurent plant. He was responsible for planning and controlling plant inventories and production schedules to meet sales requirements consistent with efficient utilization of facilities, materials, and manpower. Whitelaw spoke quickly and chain-smoked cigarettes. According to him the main task of his job was "to try to achieve the maximum length of run without affecting service or exceeding inventory budgets."

Whitelaw was assisted by a scheduler for each major operating department and clerks to service the schedulers. The schedulers worked closely with the department foreman in the plant and were in frequent telephone contact with the sales offices. Whitelaw commented: "We in production control are the buffer between sales and operating people."

To facilitate their work, Whitelaw and Andrews headed biweekly production control meetings, each lasting about one hour. Fox, the plant manager, was a frequent observer. These meetings were attended by the two general foremen. Each production foreman and the production control scheduler working for his department came into the meeting

---

[2] The plant manager, management staff, foremen, and clerks in the office all wore white shirts and ties but no coat. The union president (a production worker) wore a white shirt but no tie. All other personnel wore colored sports shirts.

at a prearranged time, and when their turn came they reported on operations in their department and on problems they were encountering. Most of the questions as well as instructions given in the meeting came from Andrews. It was also he who usually dismissed one foreman/scheduler pair and called on the next. Questions from Andrews or Whitelaw were seldom clearly addressed to either the foreman or scheduler. They were answered more frequently by the scheduler than the foreman, and often a scheduler would supplement comments made by the foreman. Generally the schedulers were younger but spoke with more self-assurance than the foremen.

In these meetings, there were frequent references to specific customers, their needs, complaints, and present attitudes toward Continental Can. Both Whitelaw and Andrews tended to put instructions and decisions in terms of what was required to satisfy some particular customer or group of customers.

A recent meeting involving a foreman, Maurice Pelletier, and the scheduler for his department, Dan Brown, is illustrative of the process. It was observed that while Dan presented the status report, Maurice shook his head in disagreement without saying anything. Dan was discussing his plan to discontinue an order being processed on a certain line on Friday to shift to another order and then to return to the original order on Tuesday.

Andrews: I don't think your plan makes much sense. You go off on Friday and then on again Tuesday.

Maurice (to Dan): Is this all required before the end of the year? (This was asked with obvious negative emotional feeling and then followed by comments by both Andrews and Whitelaw.)

Dan: Mind you—I could call sales again.

Whitelaw: I can see the point, Dan. It is sort of nonsensical to change back after so short a run.

Maurice: This would mean our production would be reduced all week to around 300 instead of 350. You know it takes four hours to make the changeover.

Dan: But the order has been backed up.

Andrews: It is backed up only because their [sales] demands are unreasonable.

Dan: They only asked us to do the best we can.

Andrews: They always do this. We should never have put this order on in the first place.

Maurice: If you want to, we could . . . (Makes a suggestion about how to handle the problem.)

Andrews: Productionwise, this is the best deal. (Agreeing with Maurice's plan.)

Dan: Let me look at it again.

Andrews: Productionwise, this is best; make the changeover on the weekend.

Whitelaw (Summarizes; then to Dan): The whole argument is the lost production you would have.

Maurice: It'll mean backing up the order only one day.

Andrews: (After another matter in Maurice's department has been discussed and there is apparently nothing further, Andrews turns to Dan and smiles.) It's been a pleasure, Dan. (Dan then returned the smile weakly and got up to leave, somewhat nervously.)

As Whitelaw left the conference room after the meeting he was heard to comment: "Danny got clobbered as you could see. I used to stand up for him, but he just doesn't come up here prepared. He should have the plans worked out with his foreman before they come up."

When discussing his job, Whitelaw frequently commented on how he thought a decision or problem would affect someone else in the plant:

If all you had to do was manage the nuts and bolts of production scheduling and not worry about the customer or how people were going to react, this would be the easiest job in the whole plant. You could just sit down with a paper and pencil and lay it out the best way. But because the customer is so important and because you've got to look ahead to how people are going to react to a given kind of schedule, it makes the whole job tremendously complicated. It isn't easy!

Other Personnel and Functions

Hunter, the plant accountant, reported directly to the plant manager, although he was functionally responsible to the division controller. The major tasks for Hunter's department were the development and application of many thousands of individual product costs and the coordination of the annual sales and income budget, developed by the responsible operating and staff groups. Explaining another of his duties, Hunter noted:

We are the auditors who see that every other department is obeying rules and procedures. It is our responsibility to know all that is in the instruction manuals. There are 12 volumes of general instructions and lots of special manuals.

Joe Herman, the plant industrial engineer, explained the responsibilities of his department:

We're active in the fields of time study, budgetary control, job evaluation, and methods improvement. Our company is on a standard cost system—that is, all our product costs are based on engineered standards, accurately measuring all labor, direct and indirect, and material that is expended in the manufacture of each and every item we make in our plants. All the jobs in the St. Laurent plant, up to and including the foreman, have been measured and standards set. However, all our standards are forwarded to division which checks them against standards in use at other plants. There are companywide benchmarks for most standards, since most of the machinery is the same in other Continental Can plants.

Herman noted that the budgeted savings from methods improvement was approximately $600,000 for the year, and he expected to exceed that by a substantial amount.

Harold Stone, the industrial relations manager, was proud that the St. Laurent plant had never experienced a strike and that formal written grievances were almost unheard of. Stone ran training programs and monitored safety, absenteeism, and turnover data. The St. Laurent plant had an outstanding record in these areas. Stone attributed this to the high wages and fringe benefits of the plant. He also maintained campaigns on housekeeping and posted slogans and comments, in both French and English, on job security and industrial competition. Also he was responsible for the display of a five-foot chart on an easel near the main entrance which showed the manufacturing efficiency rating (actual production cost versus standard cost) of the previous month for each of the Continental Can Company plants and their standing within the division. On Continental Can's personnel policy, Stone stated:

We believe that it is important that the supervisor and the employee understand each other, that they know what the other person thinks about business, profit, importance of satisfying the customer, and any other aspect of business. We also believe that rapport between the supervisor and the employee can be improved in the social contacts which exist or can be organized. For this reason we sponsor dances, bowling leagues, golf days, fishing derbies, picnics, baseball leagues, supervision parties, management weekends, and many unofficial get-togethers. Over many years we have been convinced that these activities really improve management-labor relations. They also provide a means for union and management to work closely together in organizing and planning these events. These opportunities help provide a mutual respect for the other fellow's point of view.

It was Stone's responsibility to maintain the confidential file in connection with Continental's performance appraisal program for salaried employees. Procedures for handling the program were spelled out in one of the corporate manuals. Two forms were completed annually. One called for a rating of the employee by his supervisor, first on his performance of each of his responsibilities outlined in the Position Analysis Manual and then on each of 12 general characteristics such as cooperation, initiative, job knowledge, and delegation. In another section the supervisor and the appraised employee were jointly required to indicate what experience, training, or self-development would improve performance or prepare for advancement by the employee prior to the next appraisal. The appraisal was to be discussed between the supervisor and the employee; the latter was required to sign the form, and space was given for any comments he might want to make. The second form was not shown to the employee. It called for a rating on overall performance, an indication of promotability, and a listing of potential replacements. It was used for manpower planning, and after comments by the supervisor of the appraiser, it was forwarded to the division office.

Managerial Practices

Managing with Budgets

Management at the St. Laurent plant coordinated their activities through a number of informal, as well as scheduled, meetings. Impromptu meetings of two or more members of management were frequent, facilitated by the close proximity of their offices. Among the formal meetings, the most important was the monthly discussion of performance against the budget. This meeting was attended by all of the management staff as well as production supervisors. Other regularly scheduled meetings included the production control meeting (twice weekly) and the plant cost reduction committee meetings.

In discussing the budget, Fox explained that the manufacturing plant was organized as a profit center. Plant income was determined by actual sales, not a transfer price. Therefore income was adversely affected when either sales failed to come up to the forecast on which the budget was based or sales prices were reduced to meet competition. Fox also explained that sales managers also have their incentives based on making or exceeding the budget and that their forecasts had tended to be quite accurate. Overoptimism of one group of products had usually been offset by underestimation of sales on other products. However, because no adjustment was permitted in budgeted profit when sales income was below forecast, the fact that sales were running 3 percent below the level budgeted for 1963 was forcing the plant to reduce expenses substantially in order to equal or exceed the profit budgeted for the year.

When asked whether the budget was a straight jacket or if there were some accounts which left slack for reducing expenses if sales fell below forecast, Fox replied:

> *We never put anything in the budget that is unknown or guessed at. We have to be able to back up every single figure in the budget. We have to budget our costs at standard assuming that we can operate at standard. We know we won't all the time. There will be errors and failures, but we are never allowed to budget for them.*

Hunter agreed with Fox, stating that "in this company there is very little opportunity to play footsy with the figures."

Fox conceded that there were some discretionary accounts like overtime and outside storage which involved arguments with the division. For example, "I might ask for $140,000 for overtime. The division manager will say $130,000, so we compromise at $130,000." As far as cost reduction projects are concerned, Fox added that "we budget for more than the expected savings. We might have $100,000 in specific projects and budget for $150,000."

Fox went on to note that equipment repairs and overhauls could be delayed to reduce expenses. But even the overhaul schedule was included as part of the budget, and any changes had to be approved at the division level.

Robert Andrews complained that the budget system didn't leave much room for imagination. He felt that overly optimistic sales estimates were caused by the salespeople being fearful of sending a pessimistic estimate up to the division. These estimates, according to Andrews, were a major source of manufacturing inefficiency.

Andrews was asked whether he was concerned about increasing production volume, and he replied:

We have standards. So long as we are meeting the standards, we are meeting our costs and we do not worry about increasing production. We don't tell the foreman that he needs to get more goods out the door. We tell him to get rid of the red in his budget. I'm content with a 100 percent performance. I'd like 105 percent, but if we want more production it is up to industrial engineering to develop methods change.

Andrews talked about the necessary skills for a foreman:

The foreman should be good at communications and the use of available control procedures. The foreman is expected to communicate effectively with all plant personnel, including staff heads. Our control procedures are easy to apply. In each department there is an engineered standard for each operation covering labor, materials, and spoilage. Without waiting for a formal statement from accounting, a foreman can analyze his performance in any area and take corrective action if necessary. Then he receives reports from accounting to assist him in maintaining tight cost control. One is a daily report which records labor and spoilage performance against standard. The monthly report provides a more detailed breakdown of labor costs, materials and supplies use, and spoilage. It also establishes the efficiency figure for the month. This report is discussed at a monthly meeting of all my supervisors. Generally the plant industrial engineer and a member of the accounting staff are present. Each foreman explains his variances from standard and submits a forecast for his next month's performance.

The Bonus Plan

Andrew Fox indicated that the budget was also used in rewarding employees of Continental Can. The incentive for managers was based on performance of the plant compared to budget. According to Fox:

The bonus is paid on the year's results. It is paid as a percentage of salary to all who are eligible—they are the ones on the organization chart [see Exhibit 1]. *There are three parts to it—one part is based on plant income, one on standards improvement or cost cutting, and the third on operating performance. We can make up to 20 percent by beating our plant income target and 25 percent on cost reduction and operating efficiency together. But we have to make 90 percent of our budgeted income figure to participate in any bonus at all.*

I think we have the 25 percent on efficiency and cost reduction pretty well sewn up this year. If we go over our budgeted income, we can get almost 35 percent bonus.

In years past, St. Laurent managers had made about 10 percent of their salaries from the bonus. The improved performance was the result of a change in the design of the bonus plan. Hunter explained the effect of the change:

At one time the bonus plan was based on departmental results and efficiency. Under this there was a tendency for the departments to work at cross-purposes, to compete rather than cooperate with each other. For the last seven or eight years, the emphasis has been on the plant, not the department. The latest plan is geared not only to the attainment of budgeted cost goals, but also the attainment of budgeted income. This is consistent with the attention we are placing on sales. I think the company was disturbed by what they sensed was a belief that those at the plant level can't do much about sales. Now we are trying to get the idea across that if we make better cans and give better service, we will sell more.

Foremen and Production Workers

General Foremen

Guillaume Jacques and Henri LaSalle were the general foremen on two of the three shifts. They described their jobs as working closely with both the assistant plant manager and the production control manager, but more with the latter. Jacques and LaSalle were asked how they balanced employee satisfaction with the requirements of the budget. Jacques commented:

Management not only asks me to meet the budget but do better. So, you've got to make the worker understand the importance of keeping the budget. I get them in the office and explain that if we don't meet the budget we'll have to cut down somewhere else. It is mathematical. I explain all this to them; management has given me a budget to meet, I need them for this, they need me to give them work. We work like a team. I try to understand them. All supervisors work under tension. Myself, I ask the men to go out to have a beer with me, to go to a party. It relaxes them from our preoccupations. Right now, for example, there is this party with the foremen coming up. At these gatherings it is strictly against the rules to talk about work. These things are necessary.

LaSalle explained that while foremen have a copy of the budget for their department, the workers see only a machine operating standard. The standard was set so that if he works the machine at full capacity he achieves 110 percent of standard. LaSalle told of his way of handling workers:

Well, there is usually some needling when a man is down below standard. He's told, "Why don't you get to be part of the crew?" It doesn't hurt anything . . . you only get a good day's work out of people if they are happy. We strive to keep our people happy so they'll produce the standard and make the budget. We try to familiarize them with what is expected of them. We have targets set for us. The budget is reasonable, but it is not simple to attain. By explaining our problems to the workers, we find it easier to reach the budget.

Foremen

Most of the foremen were aware of, and accepted, the necessity of keying their activities to the work standards and budgets. One young, and purportedly ambitious, foreman commented about his job:

What I like about this department is that I am in charge. I can do anything I like as long as I meet up with the budget. I can have that machine moved—send it over there—as long as I have good reasons to justify it. The department, that's me. I do all the planning, and I'm responsible for the results. I'm perfectly free in the use of my time (gives examples of his different arrival times during the past week and the fact that he came in twice on Saturday and once on Sunday for short periods).

While other foremen expressed dislike for some of the pressures inherent in their jobs, there was general satisfaction. One notable exception was a foreman with many years' service, who said:

We have a meeting once a month upstairs. They talk to us about budgets, quality, etc. That's all on the surface; that's b---s---. It looks good. It has to look good but it is all bull. For example, the other day a foreman had a meeting with the workers to talk about quality. After that an employee brought to his attention a defect in some products. He answered, "Send it out anyway." And they had just finished talking to us about quality.

Foremen tended to view the production worker as irresponsible and interested, insofar as his job is concerned, only in his paycheck and quitting time. One foreman said, "We do all the work; they do nothing." Even an officer of the union, speaking about the workers, commented:

They don't give a damn about the standards. They work nonchalantly, and they are very happy when their work slows up. If the foreman is obliged to stop the line for two minutes, everyone goes to the toilet. There are some workers who do their work conscientiously, but this is not the case with the majority.

Comments from Workers

Several of the production workers expressed feelings of pressure although others declared they were accustomed to their work and it did not bother them. One said: "Everyone is obsessed with meeting the standards—the machine adjuster, the foreman, the assistant foreman. They all get on my nerves."

One old-timer clearly differentiated the company, which he considered benevolent, from his foreman:

> *I can understand that these men are under tension as well as we are. They have meetings every week. I don't know what they talk about up there. The foremen have their standards to live up to. They're nervous. They don't even have a union like us. So if things go bad, well, that's all. They make us nervous with all this. But there's a way with people. We don't say to a man, "Do this, do that." If we said, "Would you do this?" it is not the same thing. You know a guy like myself who has been here for 35 years knows a few tricks. If I am mad at the foreman I could do a few little things to the machine to prevent it from keeping up with the standards and no one would know.*

While some workers stated they would work for less money if some of the tension were relieved, the majority were quite content with their jobs.[3]

Enforcing the Budget

By November 1963, sales for the year had fallen below expectations, and the management bonus was in jeopardy as a result.

One day in early November there was an unusual amount of activity in the accounting section. Fox came into the area frequently, and he and Hunter from time to time would huddle with one of the accountants over some figures. Hunter explained that the extra activity was in response to a report on the October results that had been issued about a week before.

Fox decided to schedule a joint meeting of the management staff and the line organization to go over the October results. This was a departure from the usual practice of having the groups in separate meetings. Prior to the meeting, Fox outlined what he hoped to accomplish in the meeting:

> *Those figures we got last week showed that some of the accounts did what they were expected to do, some did more, and some did a good deal less. The thing we have to do now is to kick those accounts in the pants that are not*

---

[3] In a Harvard research study of 12 plants in the United States and Canada, the St. Laurent plant workers ranked highest of the 12 plants in job satisfaction.

making the savings they planned to make. What we've been doing is raising the expected savings as the time gets shorter. It may be easy to save 10 percent on your budget when you've got six months; but with only six weeks, it is an entirely different matter. The thing to do now is to get everybody together and excited about the possibility of doing it. We know how it can be done. Those decisions have already been made. It's not unattainable even though I realize we are asking an awful lot from these men. You see we are in a position now where just a few thousand dollars one way or the other can make as much as 10 percent difference in the amount of bonus the men get. There is some real money on the line. It can come either from a sales increase or an expense decrease, but the big chunk has to come out of an expense decrease.

Fox did not feel there would be a conflict in the meeting about who is right and who is wrong:

We never fight about the budget. It is simply a tool. All we want to know is what is going on. There are never any disagreements about the budget itself. Our purpose this afternoon is to pinpoint those areas where savings can be made, where there is a little bit of slack, and then get to work and pick up the slack.

Fox talked about his style in handling cost and people problems:

When budgeted sales expenses get out of line, management automatically takes in other accounts to make up the losses. We'll give the department that has been losing money a certain period of time to make it up. Also, anytime anybody has a gain, I tell them I expect them to maintain that gain.

The manager must make the final decisions and has to consider the overall relationships. But there are some things I can't delegate—relations with sales for example. The manager, and not production control, must make the final decisions.

Larry Adams, the sales manager in our district, feels that the budget gets in the way of the customer's needs. He thinks the budget dominates the thinking and actions around here. Maybe he's right. But I have to deal with the people and problems here.

The manager must be close to his people. I take a daily tour of the plant and talk to the people by name. My practice as a manager is to follow a head-on approach. I don't write many memos. When I have something to say I go tell the person or persons right away. That's why I'm holding a meeting this afternoon.

Bob Andrews commented on the methods used to pick up the projected savings:

When you have lost money in one sector, you have to look around for something else that you can "milk" to make up the difference. But we don't ask for volunteers, we do the "milking." Those guys just have to do what we say. How much we can save pretty much depends on how hard the man in the corner office wants to push on the thing. I mean if we really wanted to save money we probably could do it, but it would take a tremendous effort on everybody's part and Fox would really have to crack the whip.

Because of Fox's comments on relationships with sales, Larry Adams, the district sales manager, was asked about his feelings on working with the production people at the St. Laurent plant:

> *The budget comes to dominate people's thinking and influence all their actions. I'm afraid even my salesmen have swallowed the production line whole. They can understand the budget so well they can't understand their customers. And the St. Laurent plant boys are getting more and more local in their thinking with this budget. They're not thinking about what the customer needs today or may need tomorrow, they just think about their goddamned budget.*
>
> *If the customer will not take account of your shortcomings, and if you can't take account of the customer's shortcomings, the two of you will eventually end up at each other's throats. That's what this budget system has built into it. Suppose, for example, you want to give a customer a break. Say he has originally planned for a two-week delivery date, but he phones you and says he really has problems and if you possibly could he would like about four days knocked off that delivery date. So I go trotting over to the plant, and I say, "Can we get it four days sooner?" Those guys go out of their minds, and they start hollering about the budget and how everything is planned just right and how I'm stirring them up. They get so steamed up I can't go running to them all the time but only when I really need something in the worst way. You can't let those plant guys see your strategy, you know. It is taking an awful lot out of a guy's life around here when he has to do everything by the numbers.*

Special Budget Meeting

The meeting was held in the conference room at 4 P.M. Fox and Hunter sat at the far end of the table, facing the door, with an easel bearing a flip chart near them. The chart listed the projected savings in budgeted expenses for November and December, account by account. The group of about 30 arranged themselves at the table so that, with only a couple of exceptions, the management staff personnel and general foremen sat closest to Fox and Hunter and the foremen and assistant foremen sat toward the foot of the table.

Fox opened the meeting and declared that performance against the budget for October would first be reviewed, followed by discussion of the November and December projections. He stated rather emphatically that he was "disappointed" in the October performance. Although money had been saved, it represented good performance in some areas but rather poor performance in others. The gains made in the areas where performance had been good must be maintained and the weak areas brought up, Fox declared.

He then turned the meeting over to Hunter who reviewed the October results, reading from the report which everyone had in front of him. Where performance was not good, he called on the individual responsible for that area to explain. The typical explanation was that the original budgeted figure was unrealistic and that the actual amount expended was as low as it could possibly be under the circumstances. Fox frequently broke into the explanation with a comment like, "Well, that is not good enough" or "Can you possibly do better for the rest of the year?" or "I hope we have that straightened out now." When he sat down, the person giving the explanation was invariably thanked by Hunter.

Next, Hunter, followed by Whitelaw, commented on the sales outlook for the remainder of the year. They indicated that for two months as a whole sales were expected to be about on budget. After asking for questions and getting one from a foreman, Fox said:

Well now, are there any more questions? Ask them now if you have them. Everybody sees where we stand on the bonus, I assume. Right?

Fox then referred to the chart on plant expense savings and began to discuss it, saying:

The problem now is time. We keep compressing the time and raising the gain [the projected savings for the year had been raised $32,000 above what had been projected in October]. *You can only do that so long. Time is running out, fellows. We've got to get on the stick.*

Several times Fox demanded better upward communication on problems as they came up. Referring to a specific example, he said:

This sort of thing is absolutely inexcusable. We've got to know ahead of time when these mix-ups are going to occur, so that we can allow for and correct them.

As Hunter was covering manufacturing efficiency projections for November, he addressed Andrews. "Now we have come to you, Bob. I see you're getting a little bit more optimistic on what you think you can do."

Andrews replied:

Yes, the boss keeps telling me I'm just an old pessimist and I don't have any faith in my people. I'm still a pessimist, but we are doing tremendously. I think it's terrific, fellows (pointing to a line graph). *I don't know whether we can get off the top of this chart or not, but at the rate this actual performance line is climbing, we might make it. All I can say is, keep up the good work.*

I guess I'm an optimistic pessimist.

During the discussion of projected savings for December in the equipment maintenance account, Hunter commented, "Where in the world are you fellows going to save $8,000 more than you originally said you would save?"

Jones responded:

I'd just like to say at this point to the group that it would be a big help if you guys would take it easy on your machines. That's where we are going to save an extra $8,000—simply by only coming down to fix the stuff that won't *run. You're really going to have to make it go as best you can. That's the only way we can possibly save the kind of money we have to save. You have been going along pretty well, but all I've got to say is I hope you can keep it up and not push those machines too hard.*

Although Jones spoke with sincerity, a number of foremen sitting near the door exchanged sly smiles and pokes in the ribs.

Fox concluded the meeting at about 5:30, still chewing on his cigar:

There are just a couple of things I want to say before we break up. First, we've got to stop making stupid errors in shipping. Joe [foreman of shipping], *you've absolutely* got *to get after those people to straighten them out. Second, I think it should be clear, fellows, that we can't break any more promises. Sales is our bread and butter. If we don't get those orders out in time we'll have no one but ourselves to blame for missing our budget. So I just hope it is clear that production control is running the show for the rest of the year. Third, the big push is on* now! *We sit around here expecting these problems to solve themselves, but they don't! It ought to be clear to all of you that no problem gets solved until it's spotted. Damn it, I just don't want any more dewy-eyed estimates about performance for the rest of the year. If something is going sour we want to hear about it. And there's no reason for not hearing about it!* (Pounds the table, then voice falls and a smile begins to form.) *It can mean a nice penny in your pocket if you can keep up the good work.*

That's all I've got to say. Thank you very much.

The room cleared immediately, but Whitelaw lingered on. He reflected aloud on the just-ended meeting.

I'm afraid that little bit of advice there at the end won't make a great deal of difference in the way things work out. You have to play off sales against production. It's built into the job. When I attend a meeting like that one and I see all those production people with their assistants and see the other staff managers with their assistants, and I hear fellows refer to corporate policy that dictates and supports their action at the plant level, I suddenly realize that I'm all alone up there. I can't sit down and fire off a letter to my boss at the division level like the rest of those guys can do. I haven't got any authority at all. It is all based strictly on my own guts and strength. Now Bob is a wonderful guy, I like him and I have a lot of respect for him, but it just so happens that 80 percent of the time he and I disagree. He knows it and I know it; I mean it's nothing we run away from, we just find ourselves on opposite sides of the question, and I'm dependent upon his tact and good judgment to keep from starting a war.

Boy, it can get you down—it really can after a while, and I've been at it for—God—20 years. But in production control you've just got to accept it—you're an outcast. They tell you you're cold, that you're inhuman, that you're a bastard, that you don't care about anything except your schedule. And what are you going to say? You're just going to have to swallow it because basically you haven't got the authority to back up the things you know need to be done. Four nights out of five I am like this at the end of the day—just completely drained out—and it comes from having to fight my way through to try to get the plant running as smoothly as I can.

And Andrews up there in that meeting. He stands up with his chart, and he compliments everybody about how well they are doing on efficiency. You know, he says, "Keep up the good work," and all that sort of stuff. I just sat there—shaking my head. I was so dazed you know, I mean I just keep saying to myself, "What's he doing? What's he saying? What's so great about this?" You know if I could have, I'd have stood up and I'd have said, "Somebody go down to my files in production control and pick out any five customer orders at random—and letters—and bring them back up here and read them—at random, pick any five." You know what they would show? Broken promises and missed delivery dates and slightly off-standard items we've been pushing out the door here. I mean, what is an efficient operation? Why the stress on operating efficiency? That's why I just couldn't figure out why in the world Andrews was getting as much mileage out of his efficiency performance as he was. Look at all the things we sacrifice to get that efficiency. But what could I do?

In early 1964 the report being sent by Fox to division would show, despite the fact that sales had fallen about 3 percent below budget, that profits for 1963 had exceeded the amount budgeted and that operating efficiency and cost reduction had both exceeded the budget by a comfortable margin. This enabled the managers and supervisors at the St. Laurent plant to attain the salary bonuses for which they had been striving.

Case 4–2

People Express

Debra Whitestone, Leonard A. Schlesinger

We're now the biggest air carrier in terms of departures at any New York airport. We've flown almost 3 million passengers and saved the flying public over one quarter of a billion dollars (not including the savings from fares reduced by other airlines trying to compete with us). We expect to see a $3 million profit this year. . . . We have a concept that works and is unique.

But with no growth horizon, people have been disempowered. We've started slowing down, getting sleepy. So, we've decided to set a new growth objective. Instead of adding 4 to 6 aircraft as we planned for this year, we are now thinking in terms of 12 or more new aircraft a year for the next few years.

With this announcement, Don Burr, founder, president, and CEO of People Express airline, concluded the business portion of the company's third quarterly financial meeting of 1982, graciously received rousing applause from several hundred of his stockholder-managers there to hear about and celebrate the success of their young company, and signaled for the music to begin.

Origins and Brief History

People Express had been incorporated on April 7, 1980. In July of that year it had applied to the Civil Aeronautics Board (CAB) for permission to form a new airline to be based in the New York–Newark metropolitan area and dedicated to providing low-cost service in the eastern United

States. Organized specifically to take advantage of provisions of the 1978 Airline Deregulation Act, People Express was the first airline to apply for certification since its passage. (The act, which was designed to stimulate competition, allowed greater flexibility in scheduling and pricing and lowered the barriers to new entrants.)

In applying to the CAB for a "determination of fitness and certification of public convenience and necessity," People Express committed itself to:

1. Provide "a broad new choice of flights" with high-frequency service.
2. Keep costs low by "extremely productive use of assets."
3. Offer "unrestricted deep discount price savings" through productivity gains.
4. Focus on several high-density eastern U.S. markets which had yet to reap the pricing benefits of deregulation.
5. Center operations in the densely populated New York–Newark metropolitan area with service at the underutilized, uncongested, highly accessible Newark International Airport.

The Civil Aeronautics Board was sufficiently impressed with this stated intent that it approved the application in three months (compared to the usual year or more). On October 24, 1980, People Express had its certificate to offer air passenger service between the New York–New Jersey area and 27 major cities in the eastern United States.

Start-Up

People Express's managing officers proceeded to work round the clock for the next six months to turn their plans and ideas into a certificated operating airline. They raised money, leased a terminal, bought planes, recruited, trained, established routes and schedules, and prepared manuals to meet the FAA's fitness and safety standards. "We were here every night . . . from November until April when they (the Federal Aviation Administration) gave us our certificate. . . . It was hell" (Burr). People's operating certificate was granted April 24, 1981.

Operations Begin

Flight service began on April 30, with three planes flying between Newark and Buffalo, New York; Columbus, Ohio; and Norfolk, Virginia. By the following year, the company employed a work force of over 1,200, owned 17 airplanes, and had flown nearly 2 million passengers between the 13 cities it was servicing. People Express had grown faster than any other airline and most businesses. It had managed to survive a start-up year filled with environmental obstacles, a severe national economic recession, a strike of air traffic controllers, and bad winter weather—all of which had serious negative effects on air travel. By June 1982, though the airline industry in general was losing money, and though competition resulting from deregulation was intense, People had begun showing a profit. Exhibit 1 lists milestones in the growth of People Express.

In the spring and summer of 1982, People underwent an extensive review of its infrastructure, added resources to the recruitment function so as to fill a 200-person staffing shortfall, and modified and attempted to implement more systematically a governance and communication system for which there had been little time during start-up. By the fall of 1982 three more planes were about to arrive, and three more cities were scheduled to be opened for service.

Background and Precursors

Donald Burr had been president of Texas International Airlines (TI) before he left it to found People Express with a group of his colleagues. The airline business was a "hobby business" for Burr; his love of airplanes went back to his childhood, and he began flying in college, where as president of the Stanford Flying Club he could get his flight instruction paid for. After receiving an M.B.A. from Harvard Business School in 1965 he went to work for National Aviation, a company specializing in airline investments, thus combining his affinity for aviation with his interest in finance. In 1971 he was elected president of National Aviation. While at National Aviation, Burr began a venture capital operation which involved him in the start-up of several companies, including one which aimed at taking advantage of the recently deregulated telecommunications industry.

Exhibit 1
Major Events

April 1980	Date of incorporation.
May 1980	First external financing—Citicorp venture.
October 1980	CAB certificate awarded.
November 1980	Initial public offering—$25.5 million common.
March 1981	First aricraft delivered.
April 1981	First scheduled flight.
August 1981	PATCO strike.
October 1981	Florida service emphasized.
January 1982	1 millionth passenger carried.
March 1982	17th aircraft delivered.
April 1982	Reported first quarterly operating profit.
July 1982	Filed 1.5 million shares of common stock.

Eighteen months later he decided he wanted to get into the "dirty fingernails" side of the airline business. He left Wall Street and joined Texas International Airlines as a director and chairman of the Executive Committee. In June 1973 he became executive vice president and in 1976 assumed the responsibilities of chief operations officer. Between 1973 and 1977, Texas International moved from a position close to bankruptcy to become a profitable business. In June 1979 he was made president of Texas International. Six months later, he resigned.

Looking for a new challenge, one option he considered at that time was starting a new airline. The day after Burr left TI, Gerald Gitner, his VP of planning and marketing, and Melrose Dawsey, his own and the CEO's executive secretary at TI, both submitted their resignations and joined Burr to incorporate People Express.

By the fall of 1980, 15 of Texas International's top managers and several more experienced staff from the ranks followed Burr to become part of the People Express management team and start-up crew. Some gave up their positions even before they knew where the new company would be based, how it would be financed, whether they would be able to acquire planes, or what their exact jobs would be. In spite of the personal and financial risks, the opportunity to start an airline from scratch, with people they liked and respected, was too good to pass up. It was an adventure, a chance to test themselves. Burr at 39 was the oldest of the officers. Even if People Express failed, they assumed that they could pick themselves up and start again.

According to Hap Paretti, former legal counsel and head of government relations at Texas International, who became the fifth managing officer at People Express:

> *We weren't talking about my job description or what kind of a budget I would have. It was more, we're friends, we're starting a new airline, you're one of the people we'd like to have join us in starting the company. . . . What you do will be determined by what your interests are. The idea of getting involved and letting my personality and talents come through to determine my job appealed to me. I'm not happy doing just one thing.*

Bob McAdoo, People's managing officer in charge of finance, had been corporate comptroller at Texas International. For MacAdoo, joining People Express "was an easy decision, though I was having a good time at Texas International. . . . I happen to be a guy driven by things related to efficiency. This was a chance to build an airline that was the most efficient in the business."

Lori Dubose had become director of human resources at TI—the first female director there—within a year after being hired.

> *When Burr called to offer me the "People" job he explained that we would all be working in different capacities. I'd get to learn operations, get stock—I*

didn't know anything about stock, never owned any. At 28 how could I pass it up?

She came even though she was married and her husband decided not to move with her to Newark.

Financing and Airplane Acquisition

To finance this adventure, Burr put up $355,000, Gitner put in $175,000, and the other managing officers came up with from $20,000 to $50,000 each. Burr secured an additional $200,000 from FNCB Capital Corp., a subsidiary of CitiCorp. The papers for the CitiCorp money, People Express's first outside funds, were signed on May 8, 1980, Burr's 40th birthday. Subsequently, the investment firm of Hambrecht & Quist agreed to help raise additional start-up funds. Impressed with Burr's record and the quality of his management team, and aware of the opportunities created by airline deregulation, William Hambrecht agreed to Burr's suggestion of taking People Express public. (No other airline had ever gone public to raise start-up money.)

As soon as the CAB application was approved in October 1980 all eight managing officers went on the road explaining their business plan and concepts to potential investors throughout the country. They were able to sell over $24 million worth of stock—3 million shares at $8.50 per share.

The official plan stated in the CAB application had called for raising $4–5 million, buying or leasing one to three planes, and hiring 200 or so people the first year. According to Hap Paretti, "We thought we'd start by leasing three little DC–9s, and flying them for a few years until we made enough money to buy a plane of our own." According to Burr, however, that plan reflected Gitner's more cautious approach and what most investors would tolerate at the beginning. Even with the additional money raised, Gitner thought they should buy at most 11 planes, but Burr's ideas were more expansive. From the beginning he wanted to start with a large number of planes so as to establish a presence in the industry quickly and support the company's overhead.

With cash in hand they were able to make a very attractive purchase from Lufthansa of an entire fleet of 17 Boeing 737s, all of which would be delivered totally remodeled and redecorated to People's specifications. While other managing officers recalled being a bit stunned, Burr viewed the transaction as being "right on plan."

Burr's Personal Motivation and People's Philosophy

Government deregulation appeared to provide a "unique moment in history," and was one of several factors which motivated Burr to risk his personal earnings on starting a new airline. At least as important was his strong conviction that people were basically good and trustworthy, that they could be more effectively organized, and if properly trained, were likely to be creative and productive.

I guess the single predominant reason that I cared about starting a new company was to try and develop a better way for people to work together. . . . That's where the name People Express came from [as well as] *the whole people focus and thrust. . . . It drives everything else that we do.*

Most organizations believe that humans are generally bad and you have to control them and watch them and make sure they work. At People Express, people are trusted to do a good job until they prove they definitely won't.

From its inception, therefore, People Express was seen as a chance for Burr and his management team to experiment with and demonstrate a "better" way of managing not just an airline but any business.

While Burr recognized that his stance was contrary to the majority of organized structures in the United States, he rejected any insinuation that he was optimistic or soft.

I'm not a "goody two-shoes" person, I don't view myself as a social scientist, as a minister, as a do-gooder. I perceive myself as a hard-nosed businessman, whose ambitions and aspirations have to do with providing goods and services to other people for a return.

In addition, however, he wanted PE to serve as a role model for other organizations, a concept which carried with it the desire to have an external impact and to contribute to the world's debate about "how the hell to do things well, with good purpose, good intent, and good results for everybody. To me, that's good business, a good way to live. It makes sense, it's logical, it's hopeful, so why not do (it)?"

Prior to starting service, Burr and the other managing officers spent a lot of time discussing their ideas about the "right" way to run an airline. Early on, they retained an outside management consultant to help them work together effectively as a management team and begin to articulate the principles to which they could commit themselves and their company. Over time, the principles evolved into a list of six "precepts," which were written down in December of 1981 and referred to continually from then on in devising and explaining company policies, hiring and training new recruits, structuring and assigning tasks. These precepts were: (1) service, commitment to growth of people; (2) best provider of air transportation; (3) highest quality of management; (4) role model for other airlines and other businesses; (5) simplicity; (6) maximization of profits.

From Burr's philosophy as well as these precepts and a myriad of how-to-do-it-right ideas, a set of strategies began to evolve. According to People's management consultant, the "path" theory was the modus operandi—management would see what route people took to get somewhere, then pave the paths that had been worn naturally to make them more visible.

Thus, by 1982, one could articulate fairly clearly a set of strategies that had become "the concept," the way things were done at People Express.

The People Express Concept: The Philosophy Operationalized

The People Express business concept was broken down and operationalized into three sets of strategies: marketing, cost, and people. (Over Burr's objections, the presentation prepared by investment company Morgan Stanley for PE investors began with the marketing and cost strategies rather than the people strategies.)

Marketing Strategy

Fundamental to People's initial marketing strategy was its view of air travel as a commodity product for which consumers had little or no brand loyalty. (See Exhibit 2 for a representative advertisement.) People Express defined its own version of that product as a basic, cut-rate, no-nonsense, air trip. A People Express ticket entitled a passenger to an airplane seat on a safe trip between two airports, period. The marketing strategy was to build and maintain passenger volume by offering extremely low fares and frequent, dependable service on previously overpriced, underserviced routes. In keeping with this strategy, the following tactics were adopted:

1. Very Low Fares. On any given route, People's fares were substantially below the standard fares prevailing prior to PE's announcement of service on that route. For instance, People entered the Newark-to-Pittsburgh market with a $19 fare in April 1982, when U.S. Air was charging $123 on that route. Typically, peak fares ran from 40 percent to 55 percent below the competition's standard fares and 65 percent to 75 percent below during off-peak hours (after 6 P.M. and weekends).

2. Convenient Flight Schedules. For any route that its planes flew, People tried to offer the most frequent flight schedule. With low fares and frequent flights, People could broaden its market segment beyond those of established airlines to include passengers who would ordinarily have used other forms of transportation. In an effort to expand the size of the air travel market, People's ads announcing service in new cities were pitched to automobile drivers, bus riders, and even those who tended not to travel at all. People hoped to capture most of the increase as well as some share of the preexisting market for each route.

Exhibit 2

Particularly a new airline, with the audacity to consistently charge two-thirds less than you're accustomed to paying.

For example, before we flew to Columbus, the standard air fare was $146. People Express charges $40 off peak and $65 peak. What's more, our price to Florida is just $75 off peak and $89 peak.

In short, People Express offers low prices every seat. Every flight. Every day.

And we always will.

But even if paying much less takes a little getting used to, you'll appreciate our other attributes. In no time flat.

OUR SCHEDULES ARE GEARED TO YOUR SCHEDULE.

Because we know how hectic your life can be, instead of the usual frequent excuses, we give you frequent flights — 98 non-stops each business day.

And, unlike any other major airline, People Express doesn't accept freight or mail. So you don't sit on a plane cooling your heels while mail bags and freight cartons are loaded and unloaded.

ALL OUR PEOPLE TREAT YOU AS ATTENTIVELY AS IF THEY OWNED THE AIRLINE. BECAUSE THEY DO.

At People Express, we don't offer jobs. We offer careers. From the person who welcomes you on the plane to the person who pilots the plane, each and every full time member of our staff owns an average of — amazing as it sounds — $13,000 of our stock. (And the stock of the company founders was not averaged in.)

The result quite simply, is the first airline where attitude is as important as altitude.

NON-STOP CHECK IN.

And to save a little more time and hassle, we've done away with another nemesis: the ticket counter. Purchase your ticket through your travel agent. Or phone in your reservation in advance with us and purchase your ticket right on the plane.

YOU AND YOUR LUGGAGE NEED NEVER BE SEPARATED.

Someone whose time is as valuable as yours has no intention of wasting it waiting for luggage. So instead of hassling you about carry-on luggage, we actually encourage you — by providing unusually spacious overhead and underseat areas. But if you have luggage you want us to handle, we're happy to do it for $3 a bag.

TASTEFUL BOEING 737's. WITHOUT THE INDIGESTION OF AIRLINE FOOD.

People Express flies the finest equipment in the air: Boeing 737's. Easy on your eyes . . . thanks to our clean, tasteful appointments. Easy on your weary bones . . . thanks to our comfortable seats. And easy on your stomach . . . because we don't serve airline food. Of course, if you're willing to spend a little of all that money you're saving, you can get a first rate beverage or snack on board.

THE FASTEST MOVING AIRLINE IN THE WORLD.

People Express offers more flights out of convenient Newark Airport than any other airline.

And we've already flown over a million passengers.

After only ten months of operation.

Perhaps it was our attitude. Or our prices. Or our frequency to all ten cities.

But no other airline has come this far this fast. Which proves we've offered the public something it's been waiting for a long time . . . a better way to fly.

And nobody will appreciate us more than someone who has been around as much as you.

PEOPLExpress

FLY SMART

NEW YORK/NEWARK, BOSTON, WASHINGTON/BALTIMORE, SYRACUSE, BUFFALO, NORFOLK, COLUMBUS, JACKSONVILLE, SARASOTA, WEST PALM BEACH

Exhibit 2 *(concluded)*

WHEN YOU FLY PEOPLE EXPRESS, AN OWNER IS NEVER MORE THAN A FEW STEPS AWAY.

Our planes are staffed by the most attentive people in the world: stockholders.

Each and every full time member of our staff owns an average of $38,000 of our stock. (That's not including the stock of the company founders.)

Which helps us attract talented people.

Which makes for a more efficiently run airline.

Which enables us to charge less.

Which is how you get both low prices and great service on People Express.

PEOPLExpress
FLY SMART

3. Regionwide Identity. People set out to establish a formidable image in its first year as a major airline servicing the entire eastern United States. Large, established airlines could easily wage price wars and successfully compete with a new airline in any one city, but they would probably have to absorb some losses and would be hard pressed to mount such a campaign on several fronts at once.

4. Pitch to "Smart" Air Travelers. In keeping with its product definition, People's ads sought to identify People Express not as exotic or delicious or entertaining, but as the smart travel choice for smart, thrifty, busy travelers. The ads were filled with consumer information, as well as information about PE's smart people and policies. Unlike most airlines, for instance, every People Express plane had roomy overhead compartments for passengers' baggage, thereby saving them money, time, and the potential inconvenience of loss.

5. Memorable Positive Atmosphere. Burr's long-term marketing strategy, once the airline was off the ground financially, was to make flying with People Express the most pleasant and memorable travel experience possible. The goal was for passengers to arrive at their destination feeling very well served. Thus, People Express's ultimate marketing strategy was to staff every position with competent, sensitive, respectful, upbeat, high-energy people who would create a contagious positive atmosphere. The message to staff and customers alike was: "At People Express, attitude is as important as altitude."

Cost Structure

People's cost structure was not based on a clear-cut formula so much as on an attitude that encouraged the constant, critical examination of every aspect of the business. According to Bob McAdoo, the management team "literally looked for every possible way to do things more simply and efficiently." McAdoo could point to at least 15 or 20 factors he felt were important in keeping costs down while preserving safety and quality. "If you look for one or two key factors, you miss the point." Cost savings measures affecting every aspect of the business included the following:

1. Aircraft. Since fuel was the biggest single cost for an airline, People chose, redesigned, and deployed its aircraft with fuel efficiency in mind. Its twin engine Boeing 737–100 planes were thought to be the most fuel-efficient planes for their mission in the industry. By eliminating first-class and gallery sections, interior redesign increased the number of all coach-class seats from 90 to 118 per plane. Overhead racks were expanded to accommodate more carry-on baggage. The planes were redecorated to convey a modern image and reassure potential passengers that low fares did not mean sacrificing quality or safety.

PE scheduled these planes to squeeze the most possible flying time out of them: 10.36 hours per plane per day, compared with the industry average of 7.08 hours. Finally, plane maintenance work was done by other airlines on a contract basis, a practice seen as less expensive than hiring a maintenance staff.

2. Low Labor Costs. Labor is an airline's second biggest expense. Though salaries were generally competitive, and in some cases above industry norms, People's labor costs were relatively small. The belief was that if every employee was intelligent, well trained, flexible, and motivated to work hard, fewer people (as much as one-third fewer) would be needed than most airlines employed.

People kept its work force deliberately lean, and expected it to work hard. Each employee, carefully selected after an extensive screening process, received training in multiple functions (ticketing, reservations, ground operations, and so on) and was extensively cross-utilized, depending on where the company's needs were at any given time. If a bag needed to be carried to a plane, whoever was heading towards the plane would carry the bag. Thus, peaks and valleys could be handled efficiently. This was in sharp contrast with other airlines which hired people into one of a variety of distinct "classes in craft," (such as flight attendants, reservations, baggage), each of which had a fairly rigid job description, was represented by a different union, and therefore was precluded from being cross-utilized.

3. In-House Expertise and Problem Solving. In addition to keeping the work force small and challenged, cross-utilization and rotation were expected to add the benefits of a de facto ongoing quality and efficiency review. Problems could be identified and solutions and new efficiency measures could be continually invented if people were familiar with all aspects of the business and motivated to take managementlike responsibility for improving their company.

The Paxtrac ticketing computer was commonly cited as a successful example of how PE tapped its reservoir of internal brain power rather than calling in outside consultants to solve a company problem. Many of PE's longer routes were combinations of short-haul flights into and out of Newark. The existing ticketing system required a separate ticket for each leg of the trip, resulting in higher fares than PE wanted. Burr spotted the problem when he was flying one day (he tried to spend some time each month on board the planes or in the ground operations area). An ad hoc team of managers was sent off to a hotel in Florida for a week to solve the problem. They came up with a specially designed microprocessor ticketing machine with the flexibility to accommodate the company's marketing plans and fast enough (7 seconds per ticket versus 20 seconds) to enable on-board ticketing of large passenger loads.

4. Facilities. Like its aircraft, People Express's work space was low cost and strictly functional. The main Newark terminal was located in the old North Terminal building, significantly cheaper to rent than space at the West and South terminals a mile away. People had no ticket counters. All ticketing was done either by travel agents in advance or by customer service managers on board the planes once they were airbound. Corporate headquarters, located upstairs over the main terminal, had none of the luxurious trappings associated with a major airline. Offices were shared, few had carpeting, and decoration consisted primarily of People Express ads, sometimes blown up poster size, and an occasional framed print of an airplane.

5. Reservations. The reservations system was kept extremely simple, fast, and therefore inexpensive. There were no interline arrangements with other airlines for ticketing or baggage transfer; no assistance was offered with hotel or auto reservations in spite of the potential revenue leverage to be derived from such customer service. Thus, calls could be handled quickly by hundreds of easily trained temporary workers in several of the cities People served, using local lines (a WATS line would cost $8,000 per month) and simple equipment ($900 versus the standard $3,000 computer terminals).

6. No "Freebies." Costs of convenience services were unbundled from basic transportation costs. People Express offered none of the usual airline "freebies." Neither snacks nor baggage handling, for example, were included in the price of a ticket, though such extras were available and could be purchased for an additional fee.

People

Burr told his managers repeatedly that it was People's people and its people policies that made the company unique and successful. "The people dimension is the value added to the commodity. Many investors still don't fully appreciate this point, but high commitment and participation, and maximum flexibility and massive creative productivity are the most important strategies in People Express."

Structure and Policies

As People moved from a set of ideas to an operating business, People's managers took pains to design structures and develop policies consistent with the company's stated precepts and strategies. This resulted in an organization characterized by minimal hierarchy, rotation and cross-utilization, work teams, ownership, self-management, participation, compensation, selective hiring and recruitment, multipurpose training, and team building.

1. Minimal Hierarchy. People's initial organizational structure consisted of only three formal levels of authority. At the top of the organization was the president/CEO and six managing officers, each of whom provided line as well as staff leadership for more than 1 of the 13 functional areas (see Exhibit 3 for a listing of functions).

Reporting to and working closely with the managing officers were eight general managers, each of whom provided day-to-day implementation and leadership in at least one functional area, as well as planning for and coordinating with other areas. People's managing officers and general managers worked hard at exemplifying the company's philosophy. They worked in teams, rotated out of their specialties as much as possible to take on line work, filling in at a gate or on a flight. Several had gone through the full "in-flight" training required of customer service

Exhibit 3
Organizational Structure: November 1982—Author's Rendition (CEO, president*—chairman of the board, Don Burr)

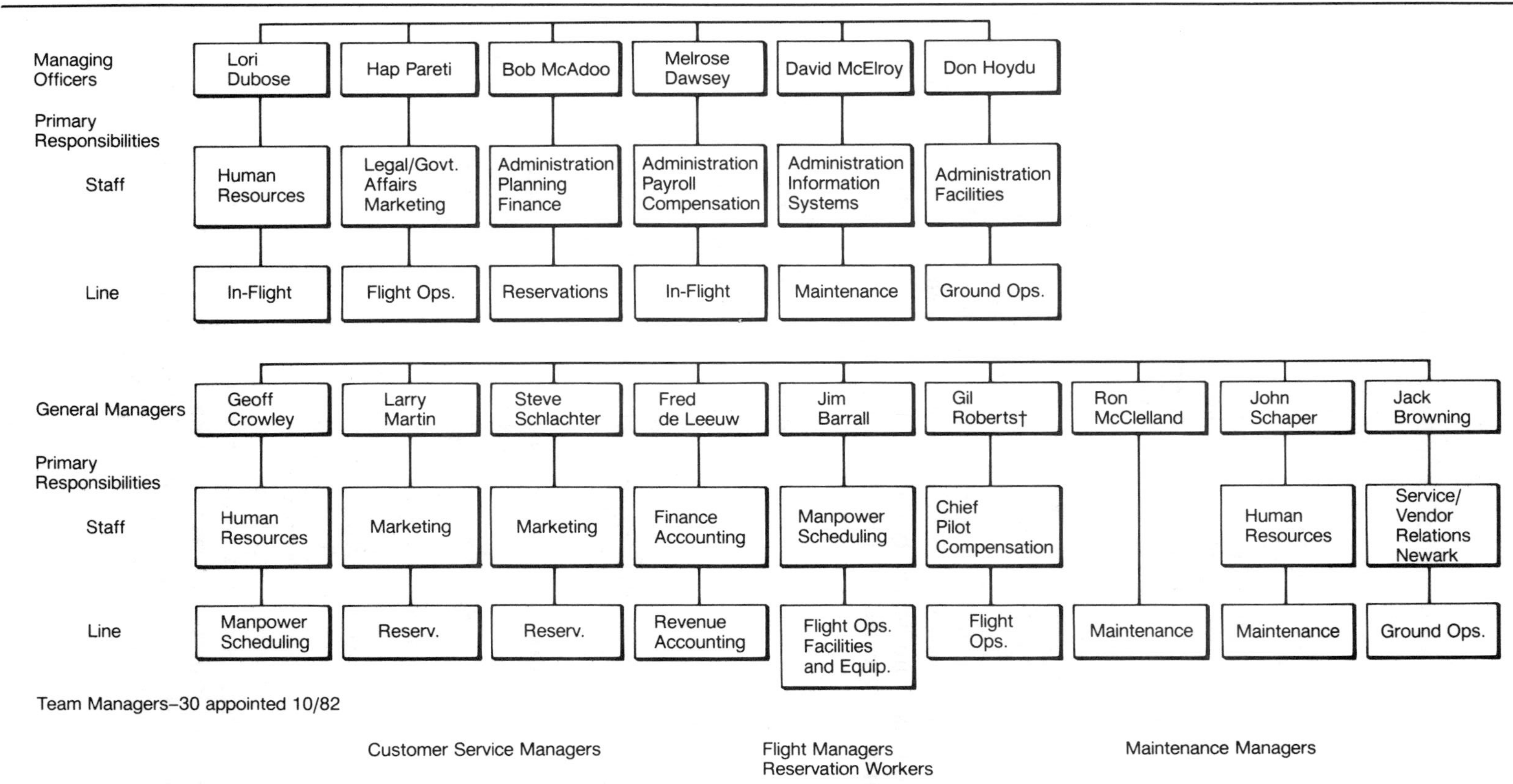

* Original president, Gerald Gitner, resigned in March 1982, and Burr assumed the presidency.
† Gil Roberts appointed chief pilot in November 1982.

managers. They shared office furniture and phones. Burr's office doubled as the all-purpose executive meeting room; if others were using it when he had an appointment, he would move down the hall and borrow someone else's empty space.

There were no executive assistants, secretaries, or support staff of any kind. The managers themselves assumed the activities that such staff would ordinarily perform. Individuals, teams, and committees did their own typing, which kept written communications to a minimum. Everyone answered his or her own phone. (Both practices were seen as promoting direct communication as well as saving money.)

Beyond the top 15 officers, all remaining full-time employees were either flight managers, maintenance managers, or customer service managers. The titles indicated distinctions in qualifications and functional emphasis rather than organizational authority. *Flight managers* were pilots. Their primary responsibility was flying, but they also performed various other tasks, such as dispatching, scheduling, and safety checks, on a rotating basis, or as needed. *Maintenance managers* were technicians who oversaw and facilitated maintenance of PE's airplanes, equipment, and facilities by contract with other airlines' maintenance crews. In addition to monitoring and assuring the quality of the contracted work, maintenance managers were utilized to perform various staff jobs.

The vast majority of People's managers were *customer service managers*, generalists trained to perform all passenger-related tasks, such as security clearance, boarding, flight attending, ticketing, and food service, as well as some staff function activities (see Exhibit 3).

By and large, what few authority distinctions did exist were obscure and informal. Managing officers, general managers, and others with seniority (over one year) had more responsibility for giving direction, motivating, teaching, and perhaps coordinating, but *not* for supervising or managing in the traditional sense.

2. Ownership, Lifelong Job Security. Everyone in a permanent position at PE was a shareholder, required as a condition of employment to buy, at a greatly discounted price, a number of shares of common stock, determined on the basis of his or her salary level. It was expected that each employee, in keeping with being a manager-owner, would demonstrate a positive attitude towards work, and participate in the governance of the company. As Managing Officer Lori Dubose pointed out, "We'll fire someone only if it is (absolutely) necessary. . . . For instance, we won't tolerate dishonesty or willful disregard for the company's policies, but we don't punish people for making mistakes." In exchange, People Express promised the security of lifetime employment and opportunities for personal and professional growth through continuing education, cross-utilization, promotion from within the company, and compensation higher than other companies paid for similar skills and experience.

3. Cross-Utilization and Rotation. No one, regardless of work history, qualifications, or responsibility, was assigned to do the same job all the time. Everyone, including managing officers, was expected to be "cross-utilized" as needed and to rotate monthly between in-flight and ground operations and/or between line and staff functions. (The terms *line* and *staff* in PE differentiated tasks which were directly flight related from those related to the business of operating the company.)

Seen by some as unnecessarily complicated and troublesome, cross-utilization and rotation was justified by PE in several ways. According to Burr, they were conceived primarily as methods of continuing education, aimed at keeping everyone interested, challenged, and growing. Bob McAdoo appreciated the flexible staff utilization capability which eventually would result from everyone having broad exposure to the company's functions. Rotation did create some difficulties:

> *It takes people a while to master each job. It might seem better to have an expert doing a given job. Cross-utilization also means you need high-quality people who are capable of doing several jobs. This in turn limits how fast you can recruit and how fast you can grow.*

These were seen, even by McAdoo, the efficiency expert, as short-term inconveniences well worth the long-term payoff.

> *When you rotate people often, they don't develop procedures that are too complicated for newcomers to learn and master fast. This forces the work to be broken down into short, simple packets, easily taught and easily learned.*

4. Self-Management. People were expected to manage themselves and their own work in collaboration with their teams and co-workers. According to Jim Miller, coordinator of training:

> *We don't want to teach behaviors—we want to teach what the end result should look like and allow each individual to arrive at those results his or her own way. . . . When desired results aren't achieved, we try to guide people and assist them in improving the outcome of their efforts.*

The written, though never formalized, guidelines regarding "self-management" read as follows:

> Within the context of our precepts and corporate objectives, and with leadership direction but no supervision, individuals and/or teams have the opportunity (and the obligation) to self-manage, which encompasses the following:
>
> — Setting specific, challenging, but realistic objectives within the organizational context.
> — Monitoring and assessing the quantity/quality/timeliness of one's own performance ("How am I doing?") by gathering data and seeking input from other people.
> — Inventing and executing activities to remedy performance problems that appear and exploiting opportunities for improved performance.

— Actively seeking the information, resources, and/or assistance needed to achieve the performance objectives.

When it came time for performance reviews, each individual distributed forms to those six co-workers from whom feedback would be useful. Again, growth rather than policing was the objective.

5. Work Teams. Dubose observed that "even with smart, self-managed people, one person can't have all the components to be the answer to every situation." People Express therefore had decided to organize its work force into small (3–4 person) work groups as an alternative to larger groups with supervisors. "If you don't want a hierarchical structure with 40 levels, you have to have some way to manage the numbers of people we were anticipating." Teams were seen as promoting better problem solving and decision making as well as personal growth and learning.

Every customer service manager belonged to a self-chosen, ongoing team with which he or she was assigned work by a lottery system on a monthly basis. Though monthly staff assignments were made individually according to interests, skills, and needs, staff work was expected to be performed in teams. This applied to flight managers and maintenance managers as well as customer service managers. Each team was to elect a liaison to communicate with other teams. Each staff function was managed by a team of coordinators, most of whom were members of the start-up team recruited from Texas International. Managing officers also worked in teams and rotated certain responsibilities to share the burden and the growth benefits of primary leadership.

6. Governance, Broad-Based Participation. People's governance structure was designed with several objectives: policy development, problem solving, participation, and communication.

While Burr was the ultimate decision maker, top management decisions, including plans and policies, were to be made by management teams with the assistance of advisory councils. Each of the eight managing officers and eight general managers was responsible for at least 1 of the 13 functional areas (see Exhibit 3) and served on a management team for at least 1 other function. The 13 function-specific management teams were grouped into 4 umbrella staff committees: operations, people, marketing, and finance and administration. For each staff committee, composed of managing officers and general managers from the relevant functional areas, there was an advisory council made up of selected customer service managers, flight managers, and maintenance managers serving on relevant line and staff teams. The councils were intended to generate and review policy recommendations, but until August 1982 they followed no written guidelines. A study done by Yale University students under the direction of Professor Richard Hackman, showed considerable confusion as to their purposes (influencing, learning, solving, communicating issues) and role (advising versus making decisions).

To minimize duplication and maximize communication, each advisory council elected a member to sit on an overarching "coordinating council" which was to meet regularly with Don Burr (to transmit information to and from him and among the councils). These ongoing teams and councils were supplemented periodically by ad hoc committees and task forces which could be created at anyone's suggestion to solve a particular problem, conduct a study, and/or delevop proposals.

In addition to maximizing productivity, all of the above practices, teams, and committees were seen essentially to promote personal growth and keep people interested in and challenged by their work.

7. Compensation—High Reward for Expected High Performance. People's four-part compensation package was aimed at reinforcing its human resource strategy. Base salaries were determined strictly by job category on a relatively flat scale, ranging in 1981 from $17,000 for customer service managers to $48,000 for the managing officers and CEO. (Competitor airlines averaged only $17,600 for flight attendants after several years of service, but paid nearly double for managing officers and more than four times as much for their chief executives.)

Whereas most companies shared medical expenses with employees, People paid 100 percent of all medical and dental expenses. Life insurance, rather than being pegged to salary level, was $50,000 for everyone.

After one year with PE all managers' base salary and benefits were augmented by three forms of potential earnings tied to the company's fortunes. There were two profit-sharing plans: (1) a dollar-for-dollar plan, based on quarterly profits and paid quarterly to full-time employees who had been with PE over one year; and (2) a plan based on annual profitability. The former was allocated proportionally according to salary level and distributed incrementally. If profits were large, those at higher salary levels stood to receive larger bonuses, but only after all eligible managers had received some reward. The sustained profits were distributed annually and in equal amounts to people in all categories. Together, earnings from these plans could total up to 50 percent or more of base salary. The aggregate amount of PE's profit-sharing contributions after the second quarter of 1982 was $311,000.

Finally, PE awarded several stock option bonuses, one nearly every quarter, making it possible for managers who had worked at least half a year to purchase limited quantities of common stock at discounts ranging from 25 percent to 40 percent of market value. The company offered five-year, interest-free promissory notes for the full amount of the stock purchase required of new employees, and for two thirds the amount of any optional purchase. As of July 1982, 651 employees, including the managing officers, held an aggregate 513,000 shares of common stock under a restricted stock purchase plan. Approximately 85 percent were held by employees other than managing officers and general managers. The total number of shares reserved under this plan was, at that time, 900,000.

8. Selective Hiring of the People Express "Type." Given the extent and diversity of responsibilities People required of its people, Lori Dubose, managing officer in charge of the company's "people" as well as in-flight functions, believed firmly that it took a certain type of person to do well at People Express. Her recruiters, experienced CSMs themselves, looked for people who were bright, educated, well groomed, mature, articulate, assertive, creative, energetic, conscientious, and hard working. While they had to be capable of functioning independently and taking initiative, and it was desirable for them to be ambitious in terms of personal development, achievements, and wealth, it was also essential that they be flexible, collaborative rather than competitive with co-workers, excellent team players, and comfortable with PE's horizontal structure. "If someone needed to be a vice president in order to be happy, we'd be concerned and might not hire them" (Miller).

Recruiting efforts for customer service managers were pitched deliberately to service professionals—nurses, social workers, teachers—with an interest in innovative management. No attempt was made to attract those with airline experience or interest per se (see Exhibit 4). Applicants who came from traditional airlines where "everyone memorized the union contract and knew you were only supposed to work x number of minutes and hours," were often ill-suited to People's style. They were not comfortable with its loose structure and broadly defined, constantly changing job assignments. They were not as flexible as People Express types.

The flight manager positions were somewhat easier to fill. Many pilots had been laid off by other airlines due to economic problems, and People Express had an abundant pool of applicants. All licensed pilots had already met certain intelligence and technical skill criteria, but not every qualified pilot was suited or even willing to be a People Express flight manager. Though flying time was strictly limited to the FAA's standard 30 hours per week (100/month, 1,000/year), and rules regarding pilot rest before flying were carefully followed, additional staff and management responsibilities could bring a flight manager's work week to anywhere from 50 to 70 hours.

Furthermore, FMs were expected to collaborate and share status with others, even nonpilots. In return for being flexible and egalitarian—traits which were typically somewhat in conflict with their previous training, and job demands—pilots at PE were offered the opportunity to learn the business, diversify their skills and interests, and benefit from profit sharing and stock ownership, if and when the company succeeded.

Exhibit 4

TEAMWORK TAKES ON A WHOLE NEW MEANING AT PEOPLExpress!

TOTAL PROFESSIONALISM

Customer Service Managers

PEOPLExpress has a whole new approach to running an airline! As a Customer Service Manager, you'll be a vital part of our management team, working in all areas from In-Flight Service, Ground Operations, and Reservations to staff support functions such as Marketing, Scheduling, Training, Recruiting, Accounting, and more.

This cross-utilization takes a lot of hard creative work—but it's the best way we know to achieve greater professionalism and productivity! Instead of doing just one limited job, you'll be involved in both line and staff activities—so you can learn the airline business fully. Faced with our variety of challenge, you'll develop and *use* all your decision-making skills. That's how bright people grow at PEOPLExpress . . . by finding simple creative solutions to complex problems . . . solutions that contribute to our productivity and growth . . . and *yours*.

Even better, your productivity can show a direct return. As a Customer Service Manager, you'll have the opportunity to participate in our unique STOCK PURCHASE PROGRAM (subject to legal requirements) and our profit-sharing plan.

If challenge stimulates you, if you really want to pursue management and growth, . . . and are willing to invest the time it takes to achieve TOTAL PROFESSIONALISM, joining PEOPLExpress could be the turning-point in your career (we're already one of the phenomenal success stories in the history of American business).

Our basic requirements are that, preferably, you've had previous business management experience—and that you be poised, personable, have some college education—and be between 5′2″ and 6′4″ with weight proportional.

If you would like to learn more about the opportunities available to you . . .

THE GRAND HYATT NEW YORK
Park Ave. at Grand Central Station, NYC

NO PHONE CALLS ACCEPTED
SATURDAY, APRIL 23, 1983
11 A.M. to 4 P.M.

PEOPLExpress

We are an Equal Opportunity Employer M/F

9. Recruitment Process. As many as 1,600 would-be CSMs has shown up in response to a recruitment ad. To cull out "good PE types" from such masses, Dubose and her start-up team, eight CSMs whom she recruited directly from TI, designed a multistep screening process.

Applicants who qualified after two levels of tests and interviews with recruiters were granted a "broad interview" with at least one general manager and two other senior people who reviewed psychological profiles and character data. In a final review after a day-long orientation, selected candidates were invited to become trainees. One out of 100 CSM applicants was hired (see Exhibit 5 for a CSM profile).

In screening pilots, "the interview process was very stringent. Many people who were highly qualified were eliminated." Only one out of three flight manager applicants was hired.

10. Training and Team Building. The training program for CSMs lasted for five weeks, six days a week, without pay. At the end, candidates went through an in-flight emergency evacuation role-play and took exams for oral competency as well as written procedures. Those who tested at 90 or above were offered a position.

The training was designed to enable CSMs, many without airline experience, to perform multiple tasks and be knowledgeable about all

Exhibit 5
Profile of a Customer Service Manager

Look for candidates who:

1. Appear to pay special attention to personal grooming.
2. Are composed and free of tension.
3. Show self-confidence and self-assurance.
4. Express logically developed thoughts.
5. Ask intelligent questions; show good judgment.
6. Have goals; want to succeed and grow.
7. Have strong educational backgrounds; have substantial work experience, preferably in public contact.
8. Are very mature, self-starters with outgoing personality.
9. Appear to have self-discipline, good planners.
10. Are warm but assertive personalities, enthusiastic, good listeners.

*Appearance guidelines:**

Well-groomed, attractive appearance.
Clean, tastefully worn, appropriate clothing.
Manicured, clean nails.
Reasonably clear complexion.
Hair neatly styled and clean.
Weight strictly in proportion to height.
No offensive body odor.
Good posture.
For women, make up should be applied attractively and neatly.
Good teeth.

* Above listed guidelines apply to everyone regardless of ethnic background, race, religion, sex, or age.

aspects of an airline. Three full days were devoted to team building, aimed at developing trainees' self-awareness, communication skills, and sense of community. "We try to teach people to respect differences, to work effectively with others, to build synergy" (Miller).

On the last team-building day, everybody chose two or three others to start work with. These groups became work teams, People's basic organizational unit. Initially, according to Miller, these decisions tended to be based on personalities, and many trainees were reluctant to choose their own work teams. They were afraid of hurting people's feelings or being hurt. Trainers would remind them that People Express gave them more freedom than they would get in most companies, more than they were used to, and that "freedom has its price. . . . It means you've got to be direct and you've got to take responsibility" (Kramer).

Over time, trainers learned to emphasize skills over personalities as the basis of team composition and to distinguish work teams from friendship groups. Choosing a work team was a business decision.

Bottom Lines: Business Indicators

As of the second quarter of 1982, People was showing a $3 million net profit, one of only five airlines in the industry to show any profit at that time. In addition to short-term profitability, Burr and his people enjoyed pointing out that by several other concrete indicators typically used to judge the health and competitive strength of an airline, their strategies were paying off and their innovative company was succeeding.

Marketing Payoff. Over 3 million passengers had chosen to fly with People Express. The size of air passenger markets in cities serviced by People had increased since People's entrance. In some instances the increase had been immediate and dramatic, over 100 percent. Annual revenue rates were approaching $200 million.

Cost Containment. Total costs per available seat-mile were the lowest of any major airline (5.2 cents compared to a 9.4 cents industry average). Fuel costs were .5–.75 cents per seat-mile lower than other airlines.

Productivity. Aircraft productivity surpassed the industry average by 50 percent (10.36 hours/day/plane compared to 7.06). Employee productivity was 145 percent above the 1981 industry average (1.52 compared to .62 revenue passenger miles per employee) for a 600-mile average trip. Return on revenue was 15.3 percent, second only to, and a mere .9 percent below, Southwest—the country's most successful airline. (Exhibit 6 shows operating statements through June 1982, and Exhibit 7 presents industry comparative data on costs and productivity.)

Exhibit 6
People Express

Statement of Operations
(in thousands, except per share data)

	April 7, 1980, to March 31, 1981	Nine Months Ended December 31, 1981	Six Months Ended June 30, 1982 (unaudited)
Operating revenues:			
Passenger	—	$37,046	$59,998
Baggage and other revenue, net	—	1,337	2,302
Total operating revenues	—	38,383	62,300
Operating expenses:			
Flying operations	—	3,464	4,240
Fuel and oil	—	16,410	22,238
Maintenance	21	2,131	3,693
Passenger service	—	1,785	2,676
Aircraft and traffic servicing	—	7,833	10,097
Promotion and sales	146	8,076	7,569
General and administrative	1,685	3,508	2,498
Depreciation and amortization of property and equipment	6	1,898	3,087
Amortization—restricted stock purchase plan	—	479	434
Total operating expenses	1,858	45,584	56,532
Income (loss) from operations	(1,858)	(7,201)	5,768
Interest:			
Interest income	1,420	1,909	763
Interest expense	14	3,913	5,510
Interest expense (income), net	(1,406)	2,004	4,747
Income (loss) before income taxes and extraordinary item	(452)	(9,205)	1,021
Less: Provision for income taxes	—	—	(470)
Income (loss) before extraordinary item	(452)	(9,205)	551
Extraordinary item—utilization of net operating loss carryforward	—	—	470
Net income (loss)	$ (452)	$ (9,205)	$ 1,021
Net income (loss) per common share:			
Income (loss) before extraordinary item	$ (.20)	$ (1.92)	$ .11
Extraordinary item	—	—	.09
Net income (loss) per common share	$ (.20)	$ (1.92)	$ .20
Weighted average number of common shares outstanding	$ 2,299	$ 4,805	$ 5,046

Explanations of Success

How could a new little airline with a funny name like People Express become such a formidable force so fast in such difficult times? Burr was fond of posing this question with a semipuzzled expression on his face and answering with a twinkle in his eye! The precepts and policies repre-

Exhibit 7

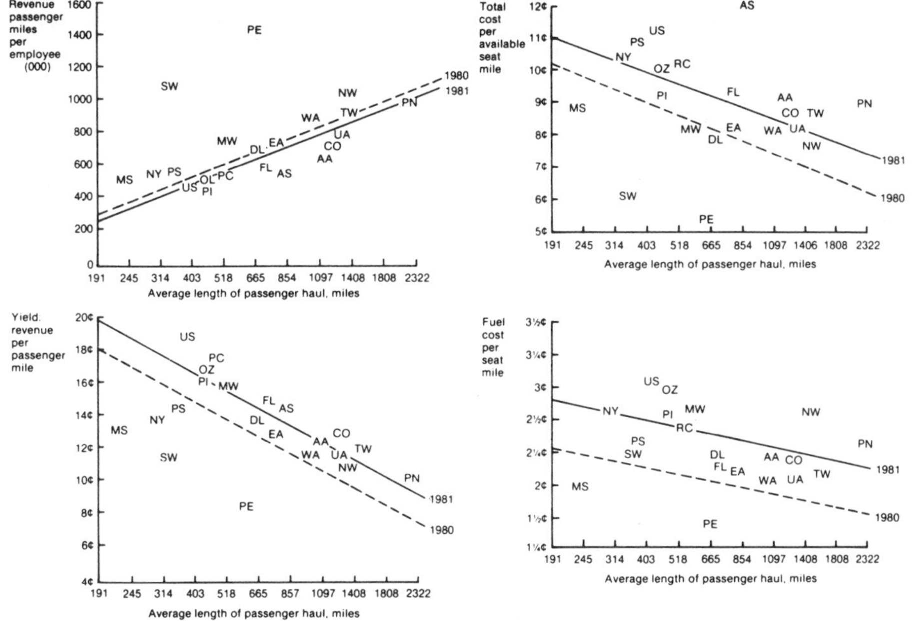

Key to Charts

Symbol	*Airline*	*Symbol*	*Airline*
AA	American	PN	Pan American
AS	Alaska	PS	Pacific Southwest
CO	Continental	PE	People Express
DL	Delta	PI	Piedmont
EA	Eastern	RC	Republic
FL	Frontier	SW	Southwest
MW	Midway	TW	Trans World
MS	Muse	WA	Western
NY	New York Air	UA	United
NW	Northwest Orient	US	USAir
OZ	Ozark		

Notes:

— All data has been drawn from calendar 1981 results, except People Express and Muse, for which the first quarter of 1982 is used in order to offer comparisons not influenced by the start-up of operations.

— Total cost is operating cost plus interest expense net of capitalized interest and interest income.

— Yield represents passenger revenues divided by revenue passenger miles (RPM).

— Average length of passenger haul is plotted on a logarithmic scale.

— The average line in each graph is a least-squared linear regression curve, based on 16 carriers which evolved in the regulated environment. Southwest, People Express, New York Air, Muse, and Alaska were not used in the calculations to determine the average. The 16 carriers were assigned equal weightings in the average.

Source: Hambrecht and Quist, June 1982.

sented by that "funny" name—People—had made the difference. To back up this assertion, Burr and the other managing officers gave examples of how the people factor was impacting directly on the company's bottom line.

Consumer research showed that, notwithstanding heavy investments in award-winning advertisements, the biggest source of People's success was word of mouth; average customer ratings of passenger courtesy and personal treatment on ground and on board were 4.7 out of 5.

Several journalists had passed on to readers their favorable impressions of People's service: "I have never flown on an airline whose help is so cheerful and interested in their work. This is an airline with verve and an upbeat spirit which rubs off on passengers." Others credited the commitment, creativity, and flexibility of People's people with the company's very survival through its several start-up hurdles and first-year crises.

Perhaps the biggest crisis was the PATCO strike which occurred just months after PE began flying. While the air traffic controllers were on strike, the number of landing slots at major airports, including Newark, were drastically reduced. This made People's original hub-and-spoke, short-haul route design unworkable. To overfly Newark and have planes land less frequently without reducing aircraft utilization, People Express took a chance on establishing some new, previously unserviced, longer routes between smaller, uncontrolled airports—such as Buffalo, New York, to Jacksonville, Florida. This solution was tantamount to starting a new airline, with several new Florida stations, new advertising, and new route scheduling arrangements. The costs were enormous. According to Hap Paretti:

> *We could have run out of $25 million very quickly, and there wouldn't be any People Express. The effort people made was astronomical, and it was certainly in their best interest to make that effort. Everybody recognized truly and sincerely that the air traffic controllers strike was a threat to their very existence. They rearranged their own schedules, worked extra days, really put the extra flying hours in, came in on their off days to do the staff functions, all things of that nature; people just really chipped in and did it and did a damned good job. So when we went into these markets from Buffalo to Florida, we could go in at $69. If we went in at $199 like everybody else, we wouldn't have attracted one person. We could go in very low like that because we had a cost structure that allowed us to do that. That's where the people strategy, from a cost standpoint, resulted in our survival. If it wasn't there, we'd be in the same situation many other carriers are today, hanging on by a toenail.*

By way of comparison, New York Air, a nonunion airline started by others from Texas International around the same time as People Express with plenty of financial backing, economical planes, and a similar concept of low-cost, high-frequency service, but different people policies, was losing money.

The Human Dimensions: Positive Climate and Personal Growth

In addition to becoming a financially viable business, People Express had shown positive results in the sphere of personal growth, the number one objective of its "people strategy." High levels of employee satisfaction showed up in the first-year surveys done by the University of Michigan. Less tangible but nevertheless striking were the nonverbal and anecdotal data. A cheerful, friendly, energetic atmosphere permeated the planes and passenger terminals as well as the private crew lounge and hallways of corporate headquarters. Questions about the company were almost invariably answered articulately, confidently, and enthusiastically. Stories of personal change, profit, and learning were common:

Ted E., customer service manager:

I was a special education teacher making $12,000 a year, receiving little recognition, getting tired, looking for something else. I started here at $17,000, already have received $600 in profit sharing, and will soon own about 800 shares of stock worth $12 on the open market, all bought at very reduced rates. [Two months after this statement the stock was worth $26 a share.]

Glenn G., customer service manager:

I was running a hot line and crisis program, then was assistant manager of a health food store before seeing the People Express recruitment ad in the newspaper and coming to check it out. I'm about to sell my car in order to take advantage of the current stock offer to employees.

Both Glenn and Ted had worked primarily in training but had also done "in-flight" and "ground operations" jobs. They wanted more responsibilities, hoped to get them, but even if they didn't get promoted soon they expected to continue learning from and enjoying their work.

Michael F., a flight captain:

I'm making $36,000. With my profit-sharing checks so far I've got $43,000 and on top of that I'll get sustained profit-sharing deals. . . . I'm doing OK. . . . Granted, at [another company] *a captain might be making $110,000 working 10 days a month* [but] *they're not really worth it.* [In other companies] *the top people might make over $100,000, but they throw on 200 guys at the bottom so they can continue to make their salary. Is that fair?* [Also, the seniority system would have kept Michael from being a captain at most other airlines.] *We're radically different and I believe radically better.*

Most pilots know very little about what's going on in their company. In a People flight manager position, the knowledge people gain in this ratty old building is incredible. It's a phenomenal opportunity. It's very stimulating and exciting. I never thought I would have this much fun.

The stories of People's start-up team members and officers were even more dramatic. Each had profited and diversified substantially in their two years with People.

Melrose Dawsey, Burr's secretary at Texas International, was a managing officer at People with primary responsibility for administration. She owned 40,000 shares of stock, purchased at $.50 a share and worth, as of November 1982, over $20 per share. For her own career development, she had also begun to assume some line management responsibilities in the in-flight area. In her spare time, she had earned her in-flight certification and run the New York marathon (as had Burr).

Lori Dubose, the youngest officer, had come to People to head the personnel function. In addition, she had taken on primary responsibility for the "in-flight" function as well as assuming the de facto role of key translator and guide vis-à-vis the company's precepts. As others came to see the value and purpose of People's precepts and human resource policies, Dubose's status among the officers had also risen.

Jim Miller had been a flight attendant for a year and base manager of in-flight services for four years at Texas International. As part of Dubose's start-up team, he had been coordinator of training, played a key role in recruitment, and then took on added responsibility for management and organizational development as well.

Hap Paretti, who began as legal counsel and head of government relations, quickly became involved in all aspects of the marketing function, and then went on to head flight operations, a move he acknowledged was "a little out of the ordinary" since he didn't have a technical background as a pilot. He spoke for all of the officers in saying, "As a managing officer you're expected to think about virtually every major decision that comes up for review."

Many spoke of the more subtle aspects of their personal development. Hap Paretti enjoyed the challenge of motivating other people and "managing by example" so as to enhance the growth of others.

Geoff Crowley, general manager in charge of ground operations and manpower scheduling, talked of becoming "less competitive" and "less uptight about winning alone" and more interested in working together with others to accomplish group and company goals.

The Downside of People's Growth and Strategies

People Express's growth rate and strategies were not without significant organizational, financial, and human costs. By Burr's own observation,

> *I would say at best, we're operating at 50 percent of what we'd like to be operating at in terms of the environment for people to do the best in. So we're nowhere near accomplishing what we would really like to accomplish in that regard.* [But] *I think we're better off today than we ever have been. And I think we're gaining on the problem.*

Chronic Understaffing

Lori Dubose saw the hiring rate as the most difficult aspect of the company's growth process, causing many other problems:

> *If we could get enough people to staff adequately in all three areas of the company so that people got some staff and some line responsibility and would*

have some time for management development. . . . I think things would be a lot different. [There's been] *constant pressure to hire, hire, hire, and we just haven't gotten enough.*

She was adamant, however, about not relaxing People's requirements.

When Dubose came to PE she expected to have to staff a company flying three planes, which would have required rapid hiring of perhaps 200–300 people. The purchase of the Lufthansa fleet meant five or six times as many staff were needed. Given the time consumed by the selective recruiting process, and the low percentage of hires, the staffing demands for supporting and launching 17 planes stretched People's people to the limit. The result was chronic understaffing even by People's own lean staffing standards.

As of November 1982 the 800 permanent "managers" were supplemented with over 400 temporaries, hired to handle telephone reservations, a function trained CSMs were originally expected to cover. Some of these "res" workers had been there a year or more, but still were not considered full-fledged People people, though many would have liked to be. They received little training, did not work in teams, own stock, receive profitsharing bonuses, or participate in advisory councils. They were just starting to be invited to social activities. For a while those wishing to be considered for permanent CSM positions were required to leave their temporary jobs first on the theory that any bad feelings from being rejected could be contagious and have a bad effect on morale. That policy was eventually seen as unfair, and dropped. Indeed, some managers saw the res area as a training ground for CSM applicants.

In August 1982 several MOs estimated that aside from reservation workers, they were short by about 200 people, though the recruiting staff was working 10 to 12 hours daily, often six days a week, as they had since January 1981. This understaffing in turn created other difficulties, limiting profits, policy implementation, and development of the organization's infrastructure.

If we had another 100 to 150 CSMs without adding an additional airplane we could just go out and add probably another half a million to a million dollars a month to the bottom line of the company. . . . There is additional flying out there that we could do with these airplanes. . . . We could generate a lot more money . . . almost double the profits of the company. [MacAdoo]

The policy of job rotation, critical to keeping everyone challenged and motivated, had been only partially implemented. Initial plans called for universal monthly rotations, with 50 percent of almost everyone's time spent flying, 25 percent on ground line work and another 25 percent in "staff functions." Due to staffing shortages, however, many people had been frozen in either line jobs without staff functions or vice versa. Some had become almost full-time coordinators or staff to a given function like recruiting and training, while others had done mostly line work and had little or no opportunity to do what they expected when they were hired as "managers." Since neither performance appraisal nor governance plans had been fully carried out, many felt inadequately recognized, guided, or involved.

There were also certain inherent human costs of People's people strategies. Rotating generalists were less knowledgeable and sometimes performed less efficiently than specialists on specific tasks. High commitment to the company plus expectations of flexibility in work hours could be costly in terms of individual's personal and family lives. For many who were single and had moved to Newark to join People Express, there "was no outside life." As one customer service manager described it, "People Express is it. . . . You kind of become socially retarded . . . and when you do find yourself in another social atmosphere it's kind of awkard."

For those who were married, the intense involvement and closeness with co-workers and with the company was sometimes threatening to family members who felt left out. Of the initial 15 officers, three had been divorced within a year and a half. The very fact of People's difference, in spite of the benefits, was seen by some as a source of stress; keeping the hierarchy to a minimum meant few titles and few promotions in the conventional sense.

> *You might know personally that you're growing more than you would ever have an opportunity to grow anywhere else, but your title doesn't change,* [which] *doesn't mean that much to you but how does your family react?* [Magel]

Even People's biggest strengths, the upbeat culture, the high-caliber performance, and positive attitude of the work force could be stressful. "It's not a competitive environment, it's highly challenging. Everybody's a star. . . . But, you know," said one customer service manager, "maintaining high positive attitude is enough to give you a heart attack."

High commitment and high ambition, together with rapid growth and understaffing, meant that most of People's managers were working long, hard hours and were under considerable stress. Said one CSM, "Nobody is ever scheduled for over 40 hours (a week), but I don't know anybody who works just 40 hours."

Dubose recognized that the situation had taken a toll on everybody's health:

> *I was never sick a day in my life until I worked for People Express and in the last two years I've been sick constantly.* [Other managing officers, including Burr, had also been sick a lot, as had general managers.] *And start-up team members—oh my God, they've got ulcers, high blood pressure, allergies, a divorce. . . . It's one thing after another. . . . We've all been physically run down.*

She adds, however, "It's not required that we kill ourselves," asserting that personality traits and an emotionally rewarding workplace accounted for the long hours many worked.

Burr's stance on this issue was that there were no emotional or human costs of hard work. "Work is a very misunderstood, underrated idea. In fact human beings are prepared and can operate at levels far in excess of what they think they can do. If you let them think they're tired and ought to go on vacation for two years or so, they will."

By the fall of 1982, though people were still generally satisfied with their jobs and motivated by their stock ownership to make the company work, many of People's managers below the top level were not as satisfied or optimistic as they once were. A University of Michigan 18-month climate survey taken in September 1982 showed signs of declining morale since December 1981.

> *People are feeling frustrated in their work (and feel they can't raise questions), cross-utilization is not being well received, management is viewed as less supportive and consultative, the total compensation package (including pay) is viewed less favorably. Clearly there is work to be done in several areas.* [Exhibit 8 contains excerpts from the 1982 survey.]

Exhibit 8
Excerpts from the 1982 Survey

Changes since the December 1981 Climate Survey

In comparing the responses from the December 1981 and September 1982 surveys, the following significant changes have apparently taken place:*

- Getting help or advice about a work-related problem is not as easy.
- What is expected of people is not as clear.
- People are not being kept as well informed about the performance and plans of the airline.
- Satisfaction with work schedules has decreased.
- The number of perceived opportunities to exercise self-management is lower.
- The process used to create initial work teams is viewed less favorably.
- The work is generally perceived to be less challenging and involving.
- The overall quality of upper management is being questioned more.
- Fewer opportunities for personal growth and career development are apparent.
- People are not very comfortable about using the "open door" policy at People Express.
- People feel that their efforts have less of an influence on the price of People Express stock.
- The buying of discounted company stock is being perceived as less of a part of the pay program.
- The compensation package is thought to be less equitable considering the work people do.
- People feel they have to work too hard to accomplish what is expected of them.
- The team concept at People Express is being questioned more.
- Officers and general managers are thought to be nonconsultative on important decisions.
- People Express is thought to be growing and expanding too fast.
- There is a stronger perception that asking questions about how the airline is managed may lead to trouble.

All of these changes are in a negative direction. Clearly, people are frustrated with the "climate" at People Express: morale and satisfaction are on the decline.

On the positive side, people's expectations of profiting financially were somewhat greater.

* Responses on many of these items were still quite positive in an absolute sense, though showing statistically significant decline from earlier studies.

The report found significant differences in the perceptions of FMs and CSMs: flight managers were more skeptical of cross-utilization and more uncertain of what self-management meant; they felt most strongly that management was nonconsultative.

When questioned about such problems, those in leadership positions were adamant that both business and personal difficulties were short term, and the costs were well worth the long-term benefits. They felt that virtually every problem was soluble over time with better self-management skills—including time management and stress management, which everyone was being helped to develop—and with evolving improvements in organizational structure. Even those responsible for recruitment insisted, "The challenge is that it seems impossible and there's a way to do it" [Robinson].

> *I don't think the long-term effects on the individual are going to be disastrous because we are learning how to cope with it. And I think the short-term effects on the organization will not be real bad because I think we're trying to put in place all the structure modifications at the same time that we're continuing the growth. That makes it take longer to get the structure modifications on the road. Which isn't real good. But they'll get there. Long term I think they will have a positive effect. I think. I wish I knew for sure.* [Dubose]

Within two months of the climate survey report, Dubose and others from the People advisory council made a video presentation to address many of the items raised in the report. For almost every major item a solution had been formulated.

In spite of all the new initiatives, each of which would entail considerable time and energy to implement, People's officers did not believe they should slow down the company's rate of growth while attending to internal problems. Their standard explanations were as follows:

> *If you don't keep growing then the individual growth won't happen. People here have a very high level of expectation anyway, I mean unrealistic, I mean there's no way it's going to happen. They're not going to be general managers tomorrow, they're not going to learn each area of the airline by next month. But they all want to. And even a reasonable rate of growth isn't going to be attainable for the individual if we don't continue to grow as a company. And the momentum is with us now we're on a roll. If we lose the momentum now we might never be able to pick it up again.* [Dubose]

Burr put it even more strongly:

> *Now there are a lot of people who argue that you ought to slow down and take stock and that everything would be a whole lot nicer and easier and all that; I don't believe that. People get more fatigued and stressed when they don't have a lot to do. I really believe that, and I think I have tested it. I think it's obvious as hell, and I feel pretty strongly about it.*

He was convinced that the decrease in energy and decline in morale evident even among the officers were not reason to slow down but to speed up. For himself, he had taken a lot of time to think about things in his early years and had only really begun to know what was important to him between his 35th and 40th years. Then he had entered what he hoped would be an enormous growth period, accelerating "between now and when I get senile. It's sensational what direction does. The beauty of the human condition is the magic people are capable of when there's direction. When there's no direction, you're not capable of much."

Approaching 1983, the big issue ahead for People Express, as Burr saw it, was not the speed or costs of growth. Rather, it was how he and People's other leaders would "keep in touch with what's important" and "not lose sight of their humanity."

Case 4-3

TRW Systems Group (A and B Condensed)*

Joseph Seher, John P. Kotter, Paul H. Thompson

History of TRW Inc. and TRW Systems Group[1]

TRW Inc. was formed in 1957 by the merger of Thompson Products, Inc. and the Ramo-Wooldridge Corporation. Thompson Products, a Cleveland-based manufacturer of auto and aircraft parts, had provided $500,000 to help Simon Ramo and Dean Wooldridge get started in 1953.

Ramo-Wooldridge Corporation (R–W) grew quickly by linking itself with the accelerating ICBM program sponsored by the Air Force. After winning the contract for technical supervision of the ICBM program, R–W gradually expanded its capabilities to include advance planning for future ballistic weapons systems and space technology, and technical advice to the Air Force.

R–W was considered by some industry specialists to be a quasi-government agency. In fact, some of their competitors in the aerospace industry resented R–W's opportunities for auditing and examining their operations. Because of this close relationship with the Air Force, R–W was

* It is a condensation and merger of the TRW Systems Group (A) and (B) cases.

[1] In its brief history, this part of TRW Inc. had several names: the Guided Missiles Division of Ramo-Wooldridge, Ramo-Wooldridge Corporation, Space Technology Laboratories (S.T.L.), and most recently, TRW Systems Group. Frequently used abbreviations of TRW Systems Group are TRW Systems and Systems Group.

prohibited from bidding on hardware contracts. This prevented them from competing for work on mainframes or on assemblies. In 1959, after the merger with Thompson, TRW decided that the hardware ban was too great a liability and moved to free the Systems Group from its limited relationship with the Air Force.

The Air Force was reluctant to lose the valued services of the Systems Group. But they agreed to a solution that called for the creation by the Air Force of a nonprofit organization, the Aerospace Corporation, to take over the advance planning and broad technical assistance formerly given by the Systems Group. TRW agreed to recruit, from its own personnel, a staff of top technicians to man Aerospace, and in 1960, about 20 percent of Systems' professionals went over to Aerospace.

The Systems Group underwent a difficult transition from serving a single customer to becoming a competitive organization. The change involved worrying about marketing, manufacturing, and dealing with different types of contracts. Previously, Systems had worked on a cost-plus-fixed-fee basis but now worked on incentive contracts, rewarding performance and specified delivery dates while penalizing failures.

Systems thrived in the new competitive arena (see Table 1), winning a number of important contracts. Nestled in the sunny Southern California region at Redondo Beach, the Systems Group worked in a free and open atmosphere. According to an article in *Fortune,* Systems' competitive advantage was its professional personnel:

> S.T.L. is headed by 38-year-old Rube Mettler, who holds the title of president of the subsidiary. A Ph.D. from Caltech, he served with Hughes Aircraft, and was a consultant at the Pentagon before coming to Ramo-Wooldridge in 1955, where he made his mark directing the Thor program to completion in record time. Of his technical staff of 2,100, more than 35 percent hold advanced degrees, and despite their youth they average 11 years of experience per man: in other words, most of them have been in the space industry virtually since the space industry began. They are housed mostly in a group of four long, low buildings for research, engineering, and development in the campuslike Space Center at Redondo Beach. Some of them are occupied in the various labs for research in quantum physics, programming, and applied mathematics, inertial guidance and control, etc.; others simply sit in solitude in their offices and think, or mess around with formulas on the

Table 1
Comparative Profile of TRW Systems Group

	June 1960	February 1963
Customers	8	42
Contracts	16	108
Total personnel	3,860	6,000
Technical staff	1,400	2,100
Annual sales rate	$63 million	$108 million

> inevitable blackboard. But typically, the materialization of all this brainpower is accomplished in one medium-sized manufacturing building called FIT (fabrication, integration, and testing), which has but 800 employees all told. FIT has a high bay area to accommodate its huge chamber for simulating space environment and other exotic testing equipment.[2]

The Aerospace Industry

Observers have described the industry in which Systems competed as a large job shop subject to frequent changes. An article entitled "Strategies for Survival in the Aerospace Industry" described it as follows.

> Because of rapid changes in technology, in customer requirements, and in competitive practices, product lines in the aerospace industry tend to be transitory. The customers' needs are finite and discrete. . . . Although the aerospace industry as a whole has grown steadily during the last decade, the fluctuations of individual companies underscore the job-shop nature of defense work. Aerospace industry planners must be constantly aware of the possibility of cancellation or prolongation of large programs.[3]

The rapid changes and temporary nature of the programs had several effects on companies within the industry. Sales and profits fluctuated with the number and size of contracts the company had; the level of activity in the company fluctuated, which meant hiring and later laying off large numbers of employees; and each plant went from full utilization of physical facilities to idle capacity.

The fluctuations resulted in a highly mobile work force that tended to follow the contracts, moving from a company that had finished a contract to one that was beginning a new contract. But the employees were highly trained and could find other jobs without difficulty. Miller and Kane pointed out that "the industry's ratios of technical employment to total employment and of technical employment to dollar volume of sales are higher than those in any other industry. Moreover, 30 percent of all persons privately employed in research and development are in the aerospace industry.[4]

TRW Systems tried to minimize these fluctuations and their effects by limiting the size of a contract for which they might compete. They would rather have had 10 $10 million contracts than 1 $100 million contract. They also had a policy of leasing a portion of their facilities to maintain flexibility in their physical plant.

---

[2] *Fortune,* February 1963, p. 95.

[3] T. C. Miller, Jr., and L. P. Kane, "Strategies for Survival in the Aerospace Industry," *Industrial Management Review,* Fall 1965, pp. 22–23.

[4] Ibid., p. 20.

In pursuing a conscious policy of growth, they competed for many contracts. By winning a reasonable number of these contracts, the company grew; when one contract ran out, there were always others starting up. As a result, between 1953 and 1963, Systems did not have a single major layoff.

Another characteristic of the industry was the complexity of the products being produced. There were thousands of parts in a space rocket, and they had to interrelate in numerous subtle ways. If one part didn't come up to specifications, it might harm hundreds of others. Since the parts and systems were so interdependent, the people in the various groups, divisions, and companies who made and assembled the parts were also highly interdependent. These interdependencies created some organizational problems for the companies in the industry, which forced them to develop a new type of organization called the matrix organization.

TRW Systems' Organization

Exhibit 1 shows an organization chart for TRW in 1963 with the various functional divisions and the offices for program management (the word *project* is often used interchangeably for *program*). These different systems interrelated in a matrix organization. The relationship between program offices and the functional divisions was complex but can best be explained by noting that instead of setting up, for example, a systems engineering group for the Atlas missile program and another separate systems group for the Titan missile program, all systems engineers were assigned organizationally to the Systems Division. This division was one of five technical divisions, each staffed with MTS (members technical staff) working in a particular functional area. The various program offices coordinated the work of all the functional groups working on their particular programs and, in addition, handled all relationships with the contracting customer. The program offices were formally on the same organizational level as the functional divisions.

The engineers in these functional divisions were formally responsible to the director of their division, but they might also have a dotted-line responsibility to a program office. For example, an electrical engineer would be responsible to his manager in the Electronics Division even though he might spend all of his time working for the Atlas program office. While working on the program he would report to the Atlas program director through one of his assistants.

Functional Organization

Each functional division served as a technology center and focused on the disciplines and skills appropriate to its technology. Generally, a num-

Exhibit 1
TRW Systems Group: Organization Chart, 1963

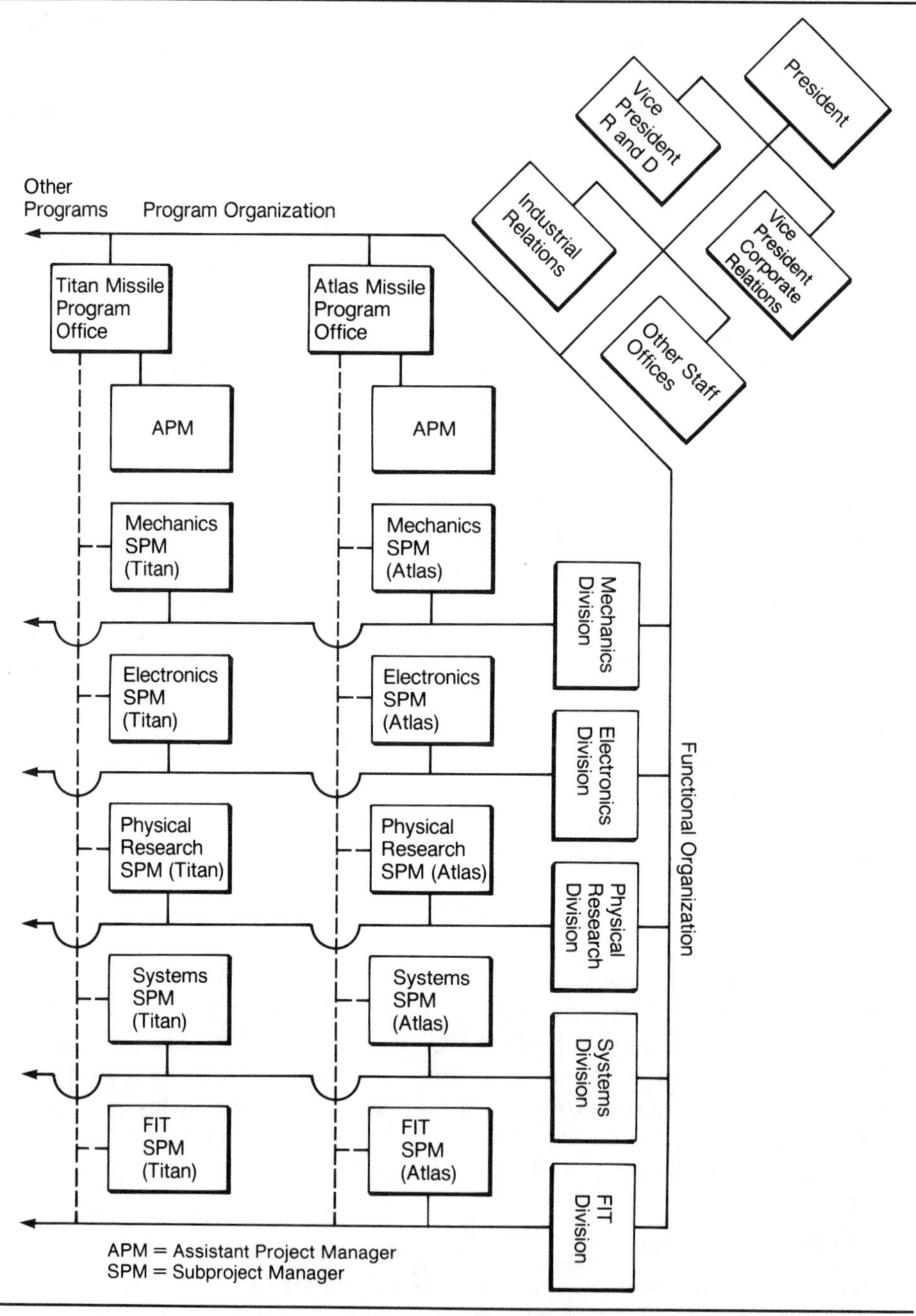

ber of operations managers reported to the division manager, each of whom was in charge of a group of laboratories dealing with similar technologies. The laboratory directors who reported to the operations managers were each responsible for a number of functional departments organized around technical specialties. The engineers in these laboratory departments were the people who performed the actual work on program office projects.

Program Office Organization

A program manager maintained overall management responsibility for pulling together the various phases of a particular customer project. His office was the central location for all projectwide activities such as the project schedule, cost and performance control, system planning, system engineering, system integration, and contract and major subcontract management. Assistant project managers were appointed for these activities as warranted by the size of the project.

The total project effort was divided into subprojects, each project being assigned to a specific functional organization according to the technical specialty involved. The manager of the functional organization appointed a subproject manager with the concurrence of the project manager. The subproject manager was assigned responsibility for the total subproject activity and was delegated management authority by the functional division management and by the assistant project manager to whom he reported operationally for the project. The subproject manager was a full-time member of the project organization, but he was not considered a member of the project office; he remained a member of his functional organization. He was accountable for performance in his functional specialty to the manager of his functional area, usually a laboratory manager. The functional manager was responsible for the performance evaluation of the subproject manager. The subproject manager thus represented both the program office and his functional area and was responsible for coordinating the work of his subproject with the engineers within the functional area. Normally each functional area was involved in work on several projects simultaneously. One manager defined the subproject manager's responsibility this way:

The subproject manager is a prime mover in this organization, and his job is a tough one. He is the person who brings the program office's requirements and the lab's resources together to produce a subsystem. He has to deal with the pressures and needs of both sides of the matrix and is responsible for bringing a subsystem together. He has to go to the functional department managers to get engineers to work on his project, but about all he can say is, "Thanks for the work you've done on my subproject." But he does have program office money as a source of power, which the functional managers need to fund their operations. The technical managers are strong people. They are not yes-men; they have their own ideas about how things ought to be done. You do not want them to be yes-men either. Otherwise you've lost the balance you need to make sure that technical performance is not sacrificed for cost and schedule expediencies which are of great importance to the program office. The functional managers also are interested in long-range applications of the work they are doing on a particular project.

This often puts the subproject manager in a real bind; he gets caught between conflicting desires. It is especially difficult because it is hard for him not to identify with the program office because that's the focus of his interest. But he is paid by the lab and that is also where he must go to get his work done. If he is smart he will identify with his subsystem and not with either the program office or the lab. He must represent the best course for his subproject, which sometimes means fighting with the program office and the departments at different times during the life of the subproject. If he reacts too much to pressures from either side, it hurts his ability to be objective about his subproject, and people will immediately sense this.

The casewriter asked Jim Dunlap, director of the Industrial Relations Department, what happened when an engineer's two bosses disagreed on how he should spend his time. He replied:

The decisions of priority on where a person should spend his time are made by Rube Mettler because he is the only common boss. But, of course, you try to get them to resolve it at a lower level. You just have to learn to live with ambiguity. It's not a structural situation. It just can't be.

You have to understand the needs of Systems Group to understand why we need the matrix organization. There are some good reasons why we use a matrix. Because R&D-type programs are finite programs—you create them, they live, and then they die—they have to die or overhead is out of line. Also, there are several stages in any project. You don't necessarily need the same people on the project all the time. In fact, you waste the creative people if they work until the end finishing it up. The matrix is flexible. We can shift creative people around and bring in the people who are needed at various stages in the project. The creative people in the functions are professionals and are leaders in their technical disciplines. So the functional relationship helps them to continue to improve their professional expertise. Also, there is a responsiveness to all kinds of crises that come up. You sometimes have 30 days to answer a proposal—so you can put together a team with guys from everywhere. We're used to temporary systems; that's the way we live.

Often an engineer will work on two or three projects at a time, and he just emphasizes one more than others. He's part of two systems at the same time.

The key word in the matrix organization is interdependency. Matrix means multiple interdependencies. We're continually setting up temporary systems. For example, we set up a project manager for the Saturn project with 20 people under him. Then he would call on people in systems engineering to get things started on the project. Next he might call in people from the Electronics Division, and after they finish their work the project would go to FIT where it would be manufactured. So what's involved is a lot of people coming in and then leaving the project.

There is a large gap between authority and responsibility, and we plan it that way. We give a person more responsibility than he has authority, and the only way he can do his job is to collaborate with other people. The effect is that the system is flexible and adaptive, but it's hard to live with. An example of this is that the project manager has no authority over people working on the project from the functional areas. He can't decide on their pay, promotion, or even how much time they'll spend on his project as opposed to some other project. He has to work with the functional heads on these problems. We purposely set up this imbalance between authority and responsibility. We design a situation so that it's ambiguous. That way, people have to collaborate and be flexible. You just can't rely on bureaucracy or power to solve your problems.

The casewriter talked to a number of people in various positions at TRW Systems Group, and their comments about the matrix could be summarized as follows: "It is difficult to work with because it's flexible and always changing, but it does work; and it's probably the only organization that could work here."

Nearly everyone the casewriter talked with indicated that Systems Group was a "good place to work" and that they enjoyed the freedom they had. However, one critic of the system, a member of the administrative staff, presented his complaints about the system as follows:

People think this is a country club. It's a college campus atmosphere. Top management thinks everyone is mature, and so they let them work as if they were on a college campus. They don't have rules to make people come to work on time or things like that. Sixty to 70 percent of the assigned parking spaces are empty at 8:30 A.M. Davis's group did a study of that—people are late. It's a good place to work for people who want complete freedom. But people abuse it. They don't come to work on time; they just do what they want around here. It's very democratic here. Nobody is telling you what to do and making all the decisions, but it can border on anarchy.

The management philosophy is that everybody will work harmoniously and you don't need a leader. But I think there has to be leadership—some one person who's responsible.

The casewriter then asked the question: "Isn't the project engineer responsible?" The response was:

The project engineer is a figurehead—in many cases he doesn't lead. I know one project engineer who provides no leadership at all. Besides, the matrix is constantly agitating. It's changing all the time, so it's just a bucket of worms. You never know where you stand. It's like ants on a log in a river and each one thinks he's steering—when none of them are. It's true that the top-level managers can make this philosophy work on their level. But we can't on our level. Let me give you an example. Mettler says he wants everything microfilmed, but he doesn't tell others to let me do it. I have responsibility but no authority in the form of a piece of paper or statement that I can do it. I just can't walk into some guy's empire and say I'm here to microfilm all of your papers. It's like an amoeba, always changing so you never know where your limits are or what you can or can't do.

As a contrasting view, one of the laboratory heads felt that the lack of formal rules and procedures was one of the strengths of the organization. He commented as follows:

This is not a company which is characterized by a lot of crisp orders and formal procedures. Quite honestly, we operate pretty loosely as far as procedures are concerned. In fact, I came from a university environment, but I believe there's more freedom and looseness of atmosphere around here than there was as a faculty member.

I think if you have pretty average people, you can have a very strict line type of organization and make it work, and maybe that's why we insist on being different. You see, I think you can also have a working organization with no strict lines of authority if you have broader-gauged people in it. I like to think that the individuals in the company are extremely high caliber, and I think there is some evidence to support that.

Another manager supported the matrix organization with the following comments:

The people around here are really committed to the job. They'll work 24 hours a day when it is necessary, and sometimes it's necessary. I was on a team working on a project proposal a few months ago, and during the last week of the proposal there were people working here around the clock. We had the secretaries come in on different shifts, and we just stayed here and worked. I think that Mettler makes this matrix organization work. It's a difficult job, but people have faith that Mettler knows what he's doing so they work hard and it comes out all right.

Evolution of Career Development

In 1962, TRW Systems Group began a management development program called career development. Jim Dunlap, the director of Industrial Relations, had responsibility for this program along with his other duties in Industrial Relations (see Exhibit 2).

Early History of Career Development (1957–1965)

"What are we doing about management development?" Simon Ramo was asked in 1957. Ramo replied: "We don't believe in management development. We hire bright, intelligent people, and we don't plan to insult their intelligence by giving them courses in courage."

In 1961, as Systems was trying to expand its customer base and cope with its new competitive environment, Rube Mettler became president. Mettler asked a consulting firm for advice on how best to make the transition to a competitive firm. "Systems needs people with experience in business management," the consultants said. "You will have to hire experienced top-level administrators from outside the firm. There aren't any here." Mettler agreed with them about needing top-level ad-

Exhibit 2
Industrial Relations: Organization Chart, 1962

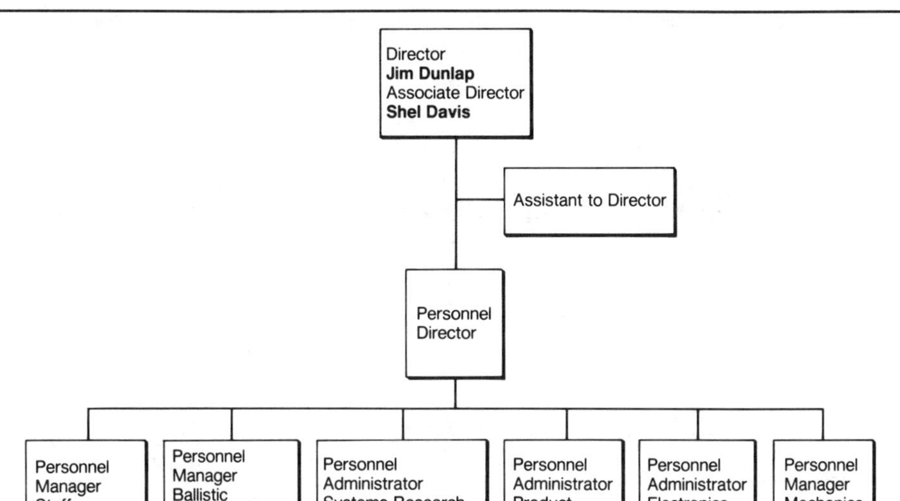

ministrators. "But we'll develop our own people," Mettler added. He confided in others that he feared a manager with experience in another organization would have to unlearn a lot of bad habits before he could be successful at TRW.

Mettler put Dunlap in charge of the development program at TRW. Mettler made it clear to Dunlap that he wanted a task-oriented, dynamic development program to fit the special needs of the Systems Group.

Dunlap felt he needed assistance to implement the kind of program Mettler wanted. "The one thing I did was to entice Shel Davis to come into Industrial Relations," commented Dunlap. "He impressed me as a restless, dynamic, creative sort of guy." Davis had worked in a line position in one of TRW's other divisions.

With the help of an outside consultant, Dunlap and Davis began to design a development program. Early in 1962, 40 top managers were interviewed about what they felt was needed. One manager characterized the feelings of the entire group: "We need skills in management. Every time a new project starts around here, it takes half of the project schedule just bringing people on board. If we could have a quicker start-up, we'd finish these projects on time."

Dunlap, Davis, and the consultant went to work on a plan to fit these needs. Dunlap set up a two-day offsite meeting to discuss their plans and recommendations with some of the top managers. At the meeting, Dunlap and Davis talked about two relatively new applied behavioral science techniques called team development and T-groups[5] as ways of meeting the needs of managers. Dave Patterson was there and was impressed by this approach. Patterson had recently been appointed head of a new project and had asked for their assistance: "I have a new team, and I'm ready to hold a team-building meeting next week. Can you arrange it?"

Shel Davis, along with a consultant, held an offsite team development session for Patterson. After the meeting, Patterson's project group improved its working relationships with manufacturing. The success of this experiment became well known throughout the company. Mettler asked Patterson what effect the meeting had had. "It saved us six weeks on the program. About a million bucks," Patterson replied. This impressed people.

Late in 1962, Davis and Dunlap prepared a "white paper" on possible approaches in career development and sent it to the top 70 people. Most of the managers responded that TRW should improve its skills in three areas: communications and interpersonal skills, business management skills, and technical skills. Davis described the conversation he and Dunlap had with Mettler:

Jim and I talked with Mettler about the kind of program we wanted in the company and what we did and didn't want to do. As it turned out, we were in agreement with Mettler on almost every issue. For example, we decided not to make it a crash effort but to work at it and to take a lot of time making sure people understood what we wanted to do and that they supported it. We also decided to start at the top of the organization rather than at the bottom. During these discussions, they decided to call the training effort career development rather than organizational development or management development because Mettler didn't want to give the impression that they were going to concentrate on administrative training and neglect technical training.

Shortly after the white paper came out, Shel Davis and Jim Dunlap began to invite people to T-groups run by professionals outside of TRW. About 12 people took advantage of this opportunity between January and May of 1963. Ten of the 12 later reported that it was a "great experience." As a result, Mettler continued to support Dunlap and Davis, telling them–"Try things—if they work, continue them; if they don't, modify them, improve them, or drop them."

In April 1963, Davis and Dunlap decided to hold a team development meeting for the key people in Industrial Relations. The two men felt that once employees at the Systems Group started going to T-groups

---

[5] *Team development* (or team building) refers to a development process designed to improve the performance and effectiveness of people who work together. *Laboratory T-groups* (training groups) are a form of experiential learning away from the normal environment. Using unstructured groups, participants attempt to increase their sensitivity to their own and others' behavior as well as to factors that hinder group interaction and effectiveness.

there would be a growing demand for career development activities that the IR group would be asked to meet. The team development session, they felt, would help train the IR staff to meet this demand.

Dunlap and Davis next decided to run some T-groups themselves, within TRW. Dunlap argued for limiting this effort to 20 people. Davis wanted 40, saying, "Hell, let's go with it. Let's do too much too fast and then it will really have an effect on the organization. Otherwise it might not be noticed." Dunlap and Davis eventually decided to run four T-groups of 10 people each.

The chain of events following that activity was described by Frank Jasinski, who become director of career development in 1964:

> *After that, things really started to move. There was a strong demand for T-group experience. But we didn't just want to send people through labs like we were turning out so many sausages. We wanted to free up the organization, to seed it with people who had been to T-groups. The T-groups were to be just the beginning of a continuing process.*
>
> *This continuing process was in several stages and developed over the three-year period. Maybe I can describe it in terms of one manager and his work group. First, the manager volunteered to go to a T-group (we have kept the program on a voluntary basis). Before he went to the T-group, there was a pre-T-group session where the participants asked questions and got prepared for the T-group experience. Then they went through the T-group.*
>
> *After the T-group, there were three or four sessions where the group participants got together to discuss the problems of applying the T-group values back home. After the manager had been through the T-group, some of the members of his work group could decide to go to a T-group. The next stage was when the manager and his group decided they wanted to undertake a team development process where they could work on improving intragroup relations.*
>
> *Following a team development effort could be an interface meeting. This is the kind Alan East had. It seems Alan's department, Product Assurance, was having trouble getting along with a number of different departments in the organization. Alan felt if they were going to do their job well they had to be able to work effectively with these other groups. So he got three or four of his people together with the key people from five or six other departments and they worked on the interdepartmental relationship. Still another type of meeting that is similar is the intergroup meeting. If two groups just can't get along and are having difficulties, they may decide to hold an offsite meeting and try to work on the problems between them.*
>
> *We also started doing some technical training and business management training. As with all of our training we try to make it organic: to meet the needs of the people and the organization. We tend to ask, What is the problem? Specific skill training may not be the answer.*

Such a large increase in career development activities required a rapid buildup of uniquely trained personnel. This problem was met in part by the use of outside consultants. Systems Group was able to interest a number of the national leaders in T-group-type activities to act as consultants, to serve as T-group trainers, and to work with the divisions on team-building activities. By December 1964, they had built up a staff of nine outside consultants.[6]

In order for the program to work on a day-to-day basis, they felt a need to build a comparable internal staff. It was decided that the personnel manager in each division would not only be responsible for traditional personnel activities but would also be an internal consultant on career development activities. Lynn Stewart, one of the outside consultants working with the Systems Group, described how TRW obtained a group of trained personnel managers.

Systems Group needed to build some internal agents, which meant expanding the industrial relations effort. It required the development of the skills of people in Industrial Relations, especially the personnel managers. They were able to retool some of the people in Industrial Relations by sending them to T-groups. Some were not able to make the transition. They were transferred or fired. All of this was done to provide a staff that could service the needs created when people returned from T-groups.

In December 1964, Jim Dunlap announced that he had been promoted to vice president of human relations for TRW Inc. and would be moving to Cleveland. He also announced that Shel Davis would succeed him as director of industrial relations. Exhibit 3 presents an organization chart of Industrial Relations as of January 1965.

A number of the personnel managers became concerned about the future of Industrial Relations. They knew Shel Davis had openly referred to the day-to-day personnel activities as "personnel crap," and they wondered what changes he would make. One personnel manager expressed this feeling when he said of the December 28 meeting: "There were some undertones of a threat in Jim's leaving which might break the balance of prudence and loose Shel upon the group, forcing us to work exclusively on career development and then neglect our day-to-day personnel responsibilities."

By summer 1966, however, most of the people in Industrial Relations felt that Shel Davis had adjusted to his role as director and was doing a good job balancing the demands of career development and day-to-day personnel activities.

Career Development in 1966

By 1966, career development activities had greatly increased since their initiation in 1963 (see Exhibit 4). While T-groups continued to be used, the major effort of the department was in facilitating team building and intergroup labs.

---

[6] This group consisted of senior professors at some of the largest business schools in the country and nationally recognized private consultants.

Exhibit 3

A. Industrial Relations: Organization Charts, January 1965

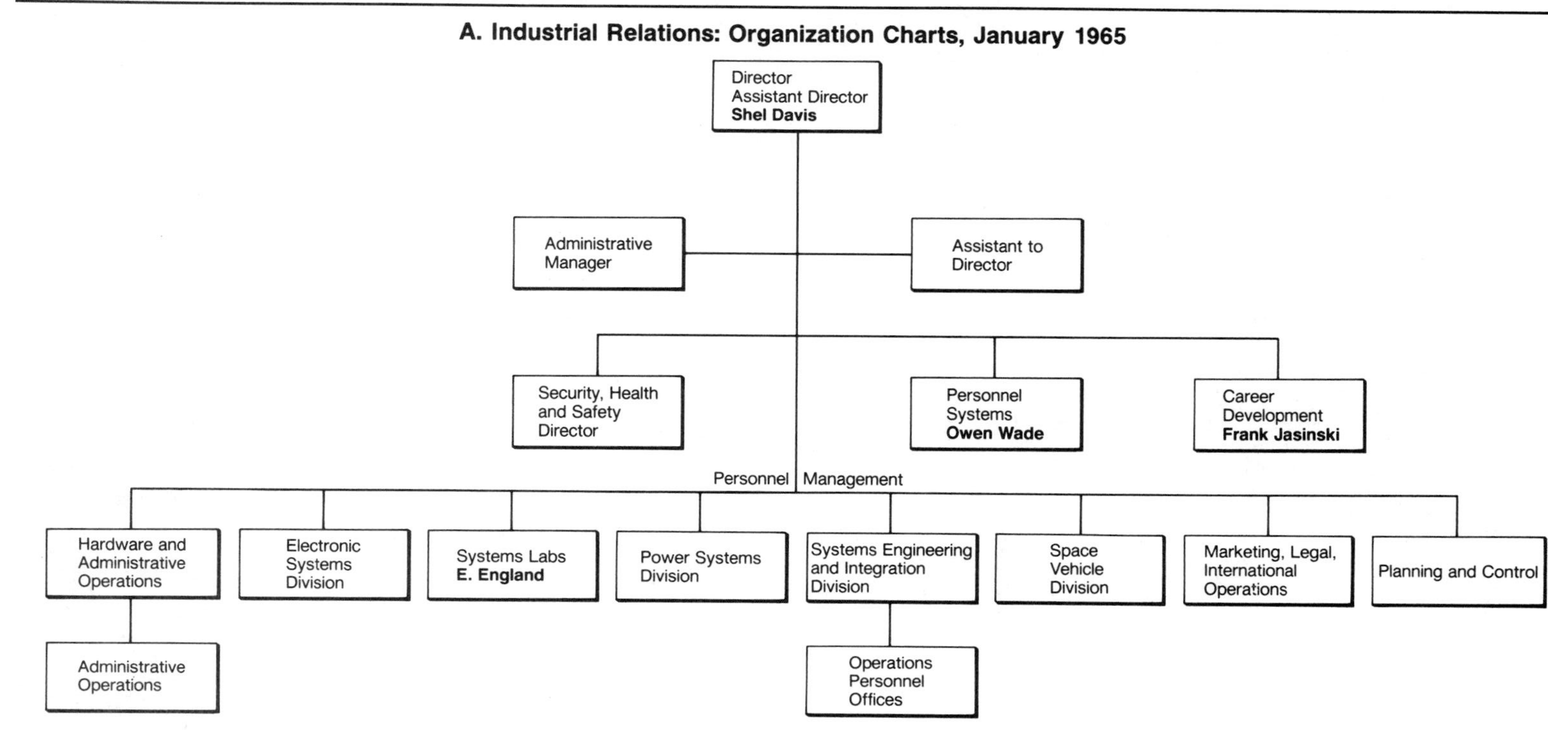

Exhibit 3 *(continued)*

B. Industrial Relations—Career Development

Exhibit 3 ***(concluded)***

C. Industrial Relations—Personnel Systems

Director
Owen Wade

Systems and Policies

Wage and Salary Administration
Owen Wade

Executive Compensation

Employee Benefits

Functional Reporting

Wage and Salary Analysis

D. Industrial Relations—Security, Health, and Safety

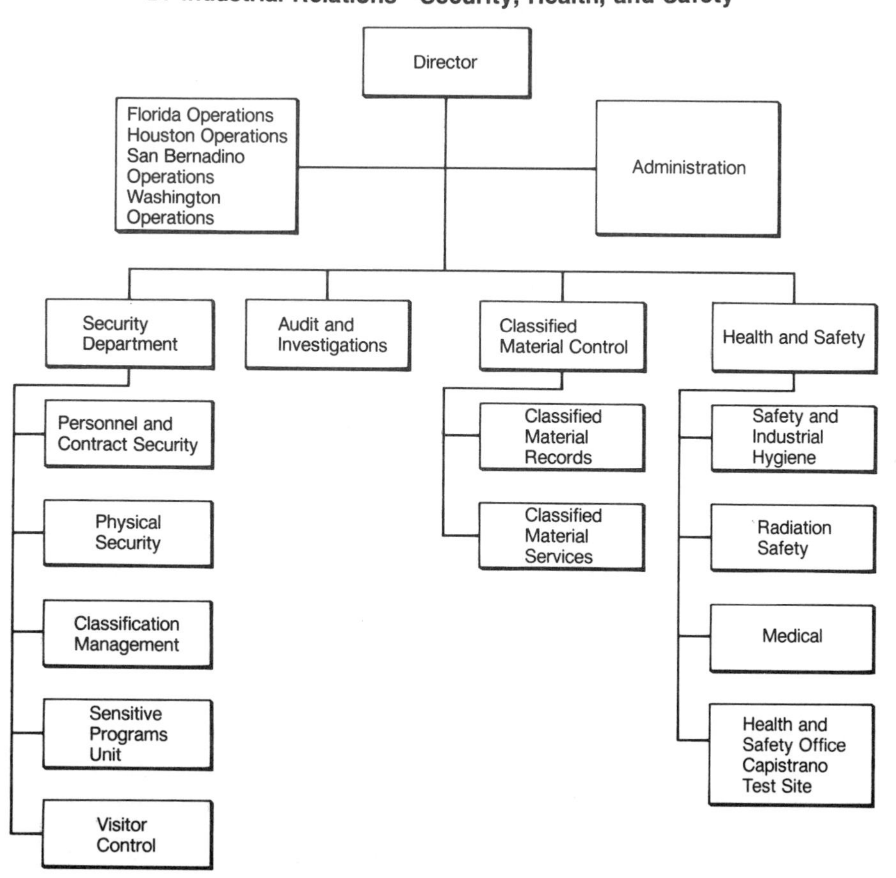

Exhibit 4
Career Development Activities, 1963–1965

	1963		1964		1965	
Activities	**Courses**	**Attendees**	**Courses**	**Attendees**	**Courses**	**Attendees**
Orientation	49	627	32	369	32	1,146
Colloquia	51	3,060	31	5,580	7	1,525
Invited lectures	2	800	4	1,600	—	—
Evening courses	12	261	17	438	16	651
Staff education	—	767	—	1,066	—	1,166
Technical courses	—	—	3	97	6	377
Internal leadership laboratories (T-groups)	1	45	4	104	4	151
External leadership laboratories (T-groups)	—	20	—	17	—	27
Team development meetings	—	—	4	76	44	671

Team Development

There were a number of different types of team development activities. One was an effort to get a new team started faster. TRW repeatedly created temporary teams to accomplish recurring tasks. The tasks were quite similar, but the team membership changed considerably. One example was a team established to prepare a proposal to bid on a particular contract. More than a dozen organizations would contribute to the final product: the written proposal. On major proposals, the representative from the administrative and nontechnical areas remained fairly constant. The technical staff, however, varied with the task and usually was entirely new from proposal to proposal. This changing team membership required constant "bringing up to speed" of new members and repeated creation of a smoothly working unit. As the new team came together, a team development session, usually offsite, helped to get the team working together sooner and saved time in the long run. A session would last one or two days, and the participants would try to identify potential problems and begin to develop solutions for such problems. Lynn Stewart, an outside consultant, described a team development session for a launch team:

> *TRW has a matrix organization so that any one person is a member of many systems simultaneously. He has interfaces with many different groups. In addition, he is continually moving from one team to another, so they need team development to get the teams off to a fast start. On a launch team, for example, you have all kinds of people that come together for a short time. There are project directors, manufacturing people, the scientists who designed the experiments, and those who launch the bird. You have to put all of those people together into a cohesive group in a short time. At launch time they can't be worrying about an organizational chart and how their respective roles change as preparation for the launch progresses. Their relationships do change over time, but they should work that through and discuss it beforehand, not when the bird is on the pad. The concept of the organization is that you have a lot of resources and you need to regroup them in different ways as customers and contracts change. You can speed up the regrouping process by holding team development sessions.*

Another type of team development activity was one with an ongoing group. Typically the manager would come to the personnel manager in his division and express an interest in team development for his group. If both agreed it would be beneficial, they would begin to plan such a session. First, an effort would be made to identify an agenda for the one- or two-day offsite meetings. This would be developed in one of two ways. The personnel manager or the consultant could interview, on an individual basis, all the people who would be attending the session to identify problem areas they needed to work on. He would then summarize the problems identified in his interviews and distribute this summary to the participants a day or two before the session was held. Another method sometimes used to develop an agenda was to get all of the participants together onsite for two or three hours several days before the offsite staff meeting. The participants would then be divided into subgroups and would identify problem areas. At the extended offsite staff meeting, the group would be task oriented, addressing itself to the question, How can we improve the way our group works together? They would look at how the group's process got in the way of the group's performance. The manager of the group would conduct the meeting, but the personnel manager and an outside consultant would be there to observe and raise issues for the group. There had been a number of similar team development sessions at TRW. The people involved felt that they had been worthwhile and had improved the group's effectiveness.

Another type of team development activity that was carried out on a continuous basis was the critiquing of the organization's many meetings. The casewriter sat in on a staff meeting of the Industrial Relations Department which was attended by the personnel managers—Ed, Don, and Bob—and key people in the staff groups of Personnel Systems and Career Development. The purpose of the meeting was to plan the projects to be undertaken by Personnel Systems and Career Development throughout the remainder of the year. This included a discussion of what projects the personnel managers wanted undertaken and a priority listing of which were most important. Owen Wade, director of personnel systems, led the discussion during the first hour and a half of the meeting, while the group discussed projects for Personnel Systems. Frank Jasinski, director of career development, led the discussion in the last hour when projects for his department were discussed. Near the end of the meeting the following discussion took place:

Shel Davis: We only have 10 minutes left so we had better spend some time on a critique of the meeting. Does anyone have any comments?

Ed: We bit off more than we could chew here. We shouldn't have planned to do so much.

Don: I felt we just floated from 10:30 to 10:45. We got through with Frank and his subject, and then nothing was done until the break.

Bob: Why didn't you make the observation at 10:30, Don, so we could do something about it? Do you feel intimidated about making a process observation?

Don: No. I felt like I was in the corner earlier. But not after making this observation. Besides, I did say earlier that we weren't doing anything and should move on, but I guess I didn't say it loud enough for people to hear me.

Ed: Don, that is the first time you've made a process observation in six months. I wish you'd make more of them.

Shel Davis: I think Owen's presentation was very good because he had estimated the number of man-weeks of work required for each of the projects. Frank's presentation was less effective because his didn't have that.

Frank Jasinski: I have a question on the manpower requirements. I spent seven or eight hours preparing for this meeting in setting priorities on all the projects we had listed and then it wasn't followed up in this meeting. [Two or three people echoed support for this statement.]

Bob: I thought we were asked to do too much in preparing for this meeting. It was just too detailed and too much work, so I rebelled and refused to do it.

Owen Wade: Well, from my point of view on the staff side of the fence, I feel pressured and as if I'm asked to do too much. The personnel managers have a very different set of rules. You don't plan as much as we have to, and I think you should plan more.

One of the participants commented that a large number of the meetings at TRW were critiqued in a similar manner.

Intergroup and Interface Labs

As a result of the nature of TRW's work and of the matrix organization, there was a great deal of interaction between the various groups in the organization. Sometimes this interaction was characterized by conflict; the Career Development staff began to work on ways to help groups deal with this conflict. One such effort, the first interface lab, was developed by Alan East, director of product assurance. East commented.

I came to Product Assurance from a technical organization so I knew very little of what Product Assurance was about. First, I tried to find out what our objectives were. I talked to our supervisors, and I found there was a lack of morale. They thought they were second-class citizens. They were cowed by the domineering engineers, and they felt inferior. I decided one of the problems was that people outside Product Assurance didn't understand us and the importance of our job. I concluded that that was easy to solve: We'd educate them. So we set out to educate the company. We decided to call a meeting, and we drew up an agenda. Then, as an afterthought, I went to see Shel Davis to see if he had some ideas on how to train people. But he just turned it around. He got me to see that rather than educating them, maybe we could find out how they really saw us and why. Well, we had an offsite meeting, and we identified a lot of problems between Product Assurance and the other departments. After the meeting, we came back and started to work to correct those problems.

After East's successful interface meeting, the idea caught hold, and similar meetings were held by other groups. Harold Nelson, the director of finance, held an interface meeting between four members of his department and a number of departments that had frequent contact with Finance. The purpose of the meeting was to get feedback on how Finance was seen by others in the organization. Commenting on the effectiveness of the meeting, Nelson added, "They were impressed that we were able to have a meeting, listen to their gripes about us, and not be defensive. The impact of such meetings on individuals is tremendous. It causes people to change, so these meetings are very productive."

Del Thomas, a participant in the interface meeting with Finance, represented another department. Thomas observed that, prior to the meeting, his group felt Finance was too slow in evaluating requests and that Nelson and his subordinates "were too meticulous, too much like accountants." Thomas felt the meeting improved the performance of Finance:

> *I think Harold [Nelson] got what he was looking for, but he may have been surprised there were so many negative comments. I think there are indications that the meeting has improved things. First, Harold is easier to get hold of now. Second, since the meeting, Harold brought in a new person to evaluate capital expenditures, and he's doing a top job. He's helpful and he has speeded up the process. I think the atmosphere of the whole Finance group is changing. They are starting to think more of "we the company" and less of "us and them."*

Evaluation of the Career Development Effort

Jim Dunlap, the vice president for human relations, was asked to evaluate the effect of career development on TRW Systems. Dunlap pulled two studies from his desk drawer. The first, a report by a government official, titled "Impulse for Openness," noted in its summary:

> It is not our intention, nor certainly that of TRW Systems, to imply that either the company reorganization or the physical progress are results solely of the career development program, but it does appear that the program had a substantial impact on the success of the company. The data shown complete the picture of changes in the company during the period under discussion. Employment at 6,000 in 1962 and over 11,000 in March 1966 will most likely double by the end of this year. Sales more than tripled between 1962 and 1965. Professional turnover decreased from 17.1 percent in 1962 to 6.9 percent in March 1966. The average for the aerospace industry in this area of California is approximately 20 percent.

Dunlap also revealed the results of a study by a professional organization to which many of Systems Group employees belonged. It had taken a survey of its members, asking them to rank 54 firms in the aerospace industry on six different factors. The respondents ranked TRW Systems first in "desirability as an employer," seventh for "contribution to aerospace," and second in "salary."

Dunlap also added his personal comments on the efforts of the career development program:

It's very hard to make an evaluation of the program and say it has saved us X million dollars. But there are several indications that it has been effective. Turnover is down significantly, and I've heard a lot of people say, "I stayed at TRW because of the career development activities." Some people make more definite claims for the program. Dave Patterson says our team development process saved us $500,000. Rube Mettler is convinced the program has improved our skills so that we've won some contracts we wouldn't have gotten otherwise. I believe it has improved our team performance. All of our proposal teams spend two days on team building before they start on the proposal. Every program starts with an offsite team development lab. They help build a team esprit de corps, and it creates an openness, so they are better able to solve problems.

A number of employees were willing to discuss their attitudes toward the career development program. Denis Brown, a member of the administrative staff and a participant in the activities of career development, felt the program was valuable. Denis noted:

They took the OGO launch crew offsite and improved their effectiveness. Well, a launch is very tense, and if one person is hostile toward another it may mean failure which costs $20 million. I don't know how much they spent on career development, but say it's a quarter of a million dollars. If one person improves his relationship with another and it saves a launch and $20 million, you've made it back many times over. The company feels it is a good thing, and it has worked well, so they'll continue it.

Jim Whitman, a subproject manager, had high praise for career development. Whitman credited the program for making groups more effective in communicating and working with one another. Recounting his own experiences, Whitman added that the program led to better collaboration and working conditions between the design engineer and the fabrication engineer.

But other employees were less enthusiastic. John Ward, a member of a program office, discussed his participation in career development activities. Ward felt that some of the offsite sessions were "rather grueling affairs, particularly when you are the center of attention." But Ward added that the session he attended was valuable.

In my opinion, the reason it was worthwhile is that under the pressure of work, people cannot—I use the word cannot *when I should say* will not*—take the time to sit down and discuss some very basic issues to get the air cleared. Even in a small group, people tend to wear blinders. You think about your own problems because you have so many of them, so you tend to build up a fence to keep some of the other person's problems from getting through. He talks about them but you don't hear them; you don't get the significance of what he's trying to tell you. But if you go away with instructions that people are not to bother you unless it is really important, you create an environment where there is time to work out some of these things.*

One member of the administrative staff, Dan Jackson, had very different views on career development. Jackson noted:

Idealistically, it's a good thing. If in the real world people lived that way, were open and sincere and could tell each other their feelings without getting hurt, it would be excellent. But people just aren't that way in the real world. The people who are enthusiastic about this, Mettler, Hesse, Davis, and so forth, are at a level in the company where they can practice this. They're just dealing with other vice presidents and top-level people. But down on my level it won't work. We've got to produce things down here, and people just aren't responsible and we can't just be nice to people all the time. We have to get some work done.

I think that the trainers at the lab live that way, and that's all right, but they tend to be frustrated headshrinkers. They want to be psychiatrists, but they don't have the training—so they do sensitivity training. It's kind of like running a therapy group. I think the techniques they use are pretty good, like having one group inside talking and one group on the outside observing, but the people running it aren't well enough trained. They may be the best that are available, but they are not good enough. Frankly, I think these trainers are really just trying to find out their own problems, but they do it by getting mixed up in other people's problems.

Jackson continued, observing that participation in these activities was not completely voluntary:

Oh, it's voluntary, but you are kind of told you had better go. You aren't fired if you don't, but there's pressure put on you to go. One of our Ph.Ds walked out after two days at a T-group. I don't think it has hurt his career, but people know he took a walk. He just felt it was a sin, morally wrong, what was going on up there.

While Jackson seemed to express the most negative attitudes toward career development, there was a widely circulated story about an employee who had suffered a nervous breakdown after attending a T-group. Jim Dunlap was asked to comment on the incident:

Yes, one person had a traumatic experience, or as they say, "cracked up." Very early in the program we decided that the people in personnel should go to a T-group so they'd understand what we were going to do. I asked this fellow if he'd like to go. He took it as an order and he went. But I was only asking him to go. If I'd known more about him, I wouldn't have asked him if he wanted to go. But I just saw him at work, and he seemed to be getting along all right, although I knew that he didn't enjoy his job. He wanted to get into education. But I didn't know he was having troubles at home and that things weren't going very well for him in general. He was just kind of holding himself together as best he could. He went to the T-group, and it caused him to start thinking about his situation and he fell apart; he had a nervous breakdown. After the T-group was over he went home, but he didn't come to work. He stayed home for a week or two. Finally, he decided he needed help and began to see a psychiatrist. Apparently that was just what he needed because he then decided to get that job in education which he liked very much. He seems to have solved his problems, so everything has turned out for the best. But it scared the hell out of us at the time.

Reading 4–1

Fit, Failure and the Hall of Fame*

Raymond E. Miles, Charles C. Snow

There is currently a convergence of attention and concern among managers and management scholars across basic issues of organizational success and failure. Whether attention is focused on the very survival of organizations in aging industries, the pursuit of excellence in mature industries, or the preparation of organizations for the rapidly approaching challenges of the 21st century, the concern is real and highly motivated. U.S. managers and organizations have been indicted for low productivity, and management scholars have recognized the fragmentation of their literature and called for a new synthesis.

Clearly, neither organizational success nor failure has an easy explanation. Nevertheless, it is becoming increasingly evident that a simple though profound core concept is at the heart of many organization and management research findings as well as many of the proposed remedies for industrial and organizational renewal. The concept is that of *fit* among an organization's strategy, structure, and management processes.

Successful organizations achieve strategic fit with their market environment and support their strategies with appropriately designed structures and management processes. Less successful organizations typically exhibit poor fit externally and/or internally. A conceptual framework can be built upon the process of fit that will prove valuable to both managers and management scholars as they sift through current theories, perspectives, and prescriptions in search of an operational consensus. The main features of such a framework are structured around four main points:

- *Minimal* fit among strategy, structure, and process is essential to all organizations operating in competitive environments. If a misfit occurs for a prolonged period, the result usually is failure.
- *Tight fit,* both internally and externally, is associated with excellence. Tight fit is the underlying causal dynamic producing sustained, excellent performance and a strong corporate culture.
- *Early fit*—the discovery and articulation of a new pattern of strategy, structure, and process—frequently results in performance records which in sporting circles would merit Hall of Fame status. The invention or early application of a new organization form may provide a more powerful competitive advantage than a market or technological breakthrough.
- *Fragile* fit involves vulnerability to both shifting external conditions and to inadvertent internal unraveling. Even Hall of Fame organizations may become victims of deteriorating fit.

Minimal Fit, Misfit, and Failure

The concept of fit plays an undeniably important role in managerial behavior and organizational analysis. Fit is a process as well as a state—a dynamic search that seeks to *align* the organization with its environment and to *arrange* resources internally in support of that alignment. In practical terms, the basic alignment mechanism is *strategy,* and the internal arrangements are *organization structure* and *management processes.* Because in a changing environment it is very difficult to keep these major organizational components tightly integrated, perfect fit is most often a condition to be strived for rather than accomplished.

Although fit is seldom referred to explicitly, it has appeared as the hallmark of successful organizations in a variety of settings and circumstances. For example, in our own studies or organizational behavior in many widely different industries, we have regularly found that organizations of different types can be successful provided that their particular configuration of strategy, structure, and process is internally and externally consistent.[1] In his landmark historical analysis, Alfred Chandler found that the companies now recognized as the pioneers of the divisional organization structure were among the first to identify emerging markets, to develop diversification strategies to meet these market needs, and to revamp their organization structures to fit the new strategies.[2] In their study of the management of innovation in electronics firms, Tom Burns and G. M. Stalker found that organizations pursuing innovation strategies had to use flexible, organic structures and management processes; rigid, mechanistic approaches did not fit with such strategies.[3] Finally, in another highly acclaimed study, Paul Lawrence and Jay Lorsch found that successful organizations in three quite different industries were those that were sufficiently differentiated to deal with the complexities of their industrial environments while simultaneously being tightly integrated internally.[4]

These and other studies conducted by organization theorists have essentially if not directly reaffirmed the importance of fit. In addition, recent research in sociology and economics has supported the idea that achieving at least minimal fit is closely associated with organizational success. Industrial economists have identified a set of generic strategies that generally fit most industries, as well as some of the organizational and managerial characteristics associated with these strategies.[5] Sociologists, borrowing concepts and theories from biology, have examined, within different populations of organizations, certain features that fit (or do not fit) particular environments.[6] In sum, the concept of fit may at first glance appear to be obvious, but many studies from several disciplines indicate that while fit is fundamental to organizational success, it is enormously difficult to achieve and/or maintain.

Fit and Survival

It is appropriate to distinguish between degree of fit as well as the nature of fit, specifically that *minimal fit is required for organizational survival.* Under some circumstances, organizations that are "misfits" in their industries may survive, but sooner or later they must adjust their behavior or fail. For example, in one of our studies, the objective was to determine if certain strategies were both feasible and effective in different industries.[7] The industries selected for study were air transportation, autos, plastics, and semiconductors. We found that in general some strategies were effective and others were not. Organizations that we called "defenders," "prospectors," and "analyzers" were all effective; i.e., they met the test of minimal fit in each industry. On the other hand, organizations identified as "reactors" were generally ineffective, except in the air transportation industry, which was highly regulated at the time (1975). Reactors are organizations that have either a poorly articulated strategy, a strategy inappropriate for the industrial environment, or an organization structure and management system that does not fit the strategy. The findings from this study suggest that in competitive industries, there is a set of feasible strategies (e.g., defender, prospector, analyzer) each of which can be effective. Moreover, misfits—organizations whose behavior lies outside of the feasible set—tend to perform poorly unless they are in a "protected" environment such as that provided by government regulation.

Fit and Misfit

The line of demarcation between minimal fit and misfit, however, is not obvious. No whistles blow warning an organization that its internal or external fit is coming undone. The process is more likely to be marked by a general deterioration whose speed is affected by competitive circumstances. For example, an in-depth study of the major firms in the tobacco industry during the years 1950–1975 illustrates the point.[8] Few American industries have experienced the degree of negative pressure that was exerted on the tobacco industry during these years, and the experiences of four companies (Philip Morris, R. J. Reynolds, American Brands, Liggett & Myers) pointedly show how organizations struggle to maintain an alignment with their shifting environments over time.

Each of the companies responded differently to severe, uncontrollable jolts such as the Sloan-Kettering report linking smoking to cancer (1953), the Surgeon General's report reaffirming this conclusion (1964), and events leading to and concluding with a ban on broadcast advertising of cigarettes (1970). Philip Morris, relying on a prospector strategy, engaged in a series of product and market innovations that propelled the company from last among the major firms in 1950 market share to first today. R. J. Reynolds largely pursued an analyzer strategy—rarely the first-mover in product market innovations but always an early adopter of the successful innovations of its competitors—and today it ranks a close second to Philip Morris. Both of these companies currently exhibit a minimal if not strong fit with environmental conditions in the tobacco industry.

American Brands followed a defender strategy in which it tried to maintain its traditional approach in the face of these environmental changes. This strategy essentially amounted to continued reliance on nonfiltered cigarettes even though the filtered cigarette market segment was growing steadily. American Brands, probably not wanting to cannibalize its sales of nonfiltered cigarettes, was at least 10 years behind Philip Morris and R. J. Reynolds in entering the filtered cigarette market, and during this period, the company fell from first to fourth place in overall market share. The company's internal fit among strategy, structure, and process was a good one throughout the mid-1950s to mid-1960s, but its strategic fit with the market underwent a gradual decline. Certainly, in retrospect, one could argue that American Brands was a misfit during this time, and the firm paid for it in declining performance.

Lastly, Liggett & Myers behaved almost as a classic reactor throughout this quarter-century period. It demonstrated substantially less internal consistency than its competitors, fared poorly in its product/market strategy, and doggedly hung on to its approach despite unfavorable performance. Described by one source as "always too late with too little," Liggett & Myers in the late 1970s was searching for someone to purchase its tobacco business. Here was a misfit bordering on failure.

In the case of the tobacco industry, major environmental changes resulted in declining fit and performance for one company and near-failure for another. Organizational misfit does not, however, have to come from external changes; it can result from internal shifts generated by the organization itself. To illustrate internally generated misfit, consider the well-known case of organizational disintegration and resurrection, the Chrysler Corp.[9]

From a strong position as the country's second largest automobile manufacturer in the 1930s, Chrysler arguably began to decline in the post-World War II period when it changed its strategy without significantly altering its organization structure or management processes. Prior to the 1950s, Chrysler kept its capital base as small as possible, subcontracted out a substantial part of its production, and rode its suppliers hard to keep costs down. But then Chrysler decided to emulate both General Motors and Ford, even to the point of matching their product lines model for model. From the early 1960s until its federal bailout in the 1970s, Chrysler seemed determined to be a full-line, worldwide, direct competitor of Ford and GM.

To support this product/market strategy, however, Chrysler was late in forming a subsidiary to monitor its distributors, late in making the necessary foreign acquisitions, and often late in designing its greatly broadened product line which was done mostly by a single, centralized engineering group. In fact, Chrysler largely remained a functionally departmentalized and centralized organization long after it adopted a strategy of diversification. Managerial problems in the areas of cost control, inventory, and production merely added to the misfit between Chrysler's strategy and its structure and management system. Despite its recent public attention and economic rebound, the company has not yet achieved stable performance.

In sum, the consequence of misfit is declining performance if not complete failure. Organizational misfits can be protected by a benign environment, sometimes for lengthy periods of time, but minimal fit is required for survival in competitive environments. However, minimal fit, as the term implies, does not guarantee excellent performance.

Tight Fit: The Foundation for Excellence

Corporate excellence requires more than minimal fit. Truly outstanding performance, achieved by many companies, is associated with tight fit—both externally with the environment and internally among strategy, structure, and management process. In fact, *tight fit is the causal force* at work when organizational excellence is said to be caused by various managerial and organizational characteristics.

In the late 1940s and early 1950s, Peter Drucker studied a number of top U.S. corporations, including General Motors, General Electric, IBM, and Sears, Roebuck.[10] Based on his observations, Drucker associated the widely acclaimed achievements of these organizations with such managerial characteristics as delegation and joint goal setting (MBO) and with organizational characteristics emphasizing the decentralization of operating decisions. He saw overstaffing as a threat to corporate responsiveness and argued that the best performance comes when jobs are enriched rather than narrowed. Finally, he felt that the overall key to the success of these companies was that they knew what business they were in, what their competencies were, and how to keep their efforts focused on their goals.

Some 30 years later, Thomas Peters and Robert Waterman studied 62 U.S. companies and produced their own checklist of characteristics associated with corporate excellence.[11] As had Drucker before them, they noted that organizations with records of sustained high performance tended to have a clear business focus, a bias for action, and lean structures and staffs that facilitated the pursuit of strategy.

Drucker clearly acknowledged the importance of organization structure and was convinced at the time that the federally decentralized (i.e., multidivisional) organization structure was the design of the future. He did not, however, probe the relationship between alternative strategies and their appropriate structures and management processes. Similarly, while Peters and Waterman stressed structural leanness and responsiveness as universally valuable characteristics, they also noted the requirement of achieving a close fit among the seven "S's" of strategy, structure, skills, systems, style, shared values, and staff (people). Again, however, Peters and Waterman did not discuss the possible alternative organization forms appropriate for different strategies. In our view, the observations of Drucker, Peters, and Waterman are accurate and extremely valuable. The discovery 30 years apart of the association of similar characteristics with organizational excellence is a powerful argument for the validity of that association—but it is not an explanation of why that association exists nor of the causal force that may be involved.

Both the managerial and organizational characteristics described by these observers, and the outstanding performance achieved by the organizations that they have examined, are the result of the achievement—by discovery or by design—of tight fit. That is, such characteristics as convergence on a set of core business values—doing what one does best, a lean, action-oriented structure that provides opportunities for the full use of people's capabilities at all levels, etc.—essentially flow from the achievement of tight fit with the environment and among strategy, structure, and process. In short, the causal dynamic of tight fit tends to operate in four stages:

- First, the discovery of the basic structure and management processes necessary to support a chosen strategy create a *gestalt* that becomes so obvious and compelling that complex organizational and managerial demands appear to be simple.

- Second, *simplicity* leads to widespread understanding which reinforces and sustains fit. Organization structure and key management processes such as reward and control systems "teach" managers and employees the appropriate attitudes and behaviors for maintaining focus on strategic requirements.
- Third, simplicity *reduces the need for elaborate coordinating mechanisms,* thereby creating slack resources that can be reallocated elsewhere in the system.
- Fourth, as outstanding performance is achieved and sustained, its *association* with the process by which it is attained is reinforced, and this serves to further simplify the basic fit among strategy, structure, and process.

It should be emphasized that we do not specify "finding the right strategy" as an important element of this causal linkage. In fact, finding strategy-structure-process fit is usually far more important and problematic. It may be that there is less to strategy than meets the eye. At any moment, in any given industry, it is likely that several organizations are considering the same strategic moves: to diversify, retrench, acquire other firms, etc. For example, in the 1920s, the top executives of Sears, Roebuck did not have a secret crystal ball that forecast the effects of the automobile on retail trade. Indeed most organizations—including Sears' major competitor, Montgomery Ward—saw similar trends. It was the case, however, that well ahead of competitors Sears developed a structure that would allow it to operate as a high-quality, low-cost nationwide retailing organization.

It is valuable, of course, that the chosen strategy be articulated—for example, Sears pursued the image of "a hometown store with nationwide purchasing power." Nevertheless, it is when the blueprint of how to achieve such strategic goals is drawn that real understanding begins to emerge throughout the system. As clarity involving means emerges, that which was enormously complex and apparently beyond accomplishment now seems straightforward and easy to achieve.

The process of searching for, discovering, and achieving tight fit is pervasive. At the individual level, for instance, learning to drive a car, fly an airplane, or serve a tennis ball are all activities that at first appear complex and difficult to learn but once mastered seem to be relatively simple. Mastery occurs, however, only when the gestalt is apprehended, felt, and understood. The same learning process occurs within organizations. The Baltimore Orioles, for example, believe they know how and why they won the recent World Series and have enjoyed success over the years. Strategy, structure, and process fit and are well understood by members at all levels of the organization. From the front office to the manager, coaches, and players (including those in the farm system), it seems clear how one goes about building a world-champion team. Much of the same could be said for Procter & Gamble, Johnson & Johnson, Minnesota Mining & Manufacturing, McDonald's, Schlumberger, and other excellent companies.

In sum, what we are suggesting is that focus, leanness, action, involvement, identification, etc., are likely *products* of tight fit. Fit simplifies complex organizational and managerial arrangements, and simple systems facilitate leanness, action, and many other observed manifestations of excellence. As one understands the system, one feels more a part of it, and as one's role becomes clear to self and others, participation is facilitated, almost demanded. Closeness and understanding provide a common culture, and stories and myths emerge that perpetuate key aspects of culture.

Early Fit: A Key to the Hall of Fame?

To this point we have argued that minimal fit is necessary for an organization's survival and that tight fit is associated with excellent performance. We now suggest that *early fit—the discovery and articulation of a new organization form—can lead to sustained excellence* over considerable periods of time and thus a place in some mythical Hall of Fame.

Picking a Hall of Fame company is difficult. In sports, Hall of Fame performers are individuals who have been selected only after their careers are over, and sometimes selection is preceded by an interval of several years so that the decision is relatively objective, based on complete information, and final. Organizations, in the other hand, are ongoing systems; therefore, any given Hall of Fame nominee might immediately have one or more "off" years. Nevertheless, some organizations would be likely to appear on every pundit's Hall of Fame list, and we believe that most of these organizations would share the characteristic of an early organizational breakthrough that was not quickly or easily matched by their competitors at the time.

There are, of course, many ways that companies can achieve a competitive advantage. For example, obtaining a patent on a particular product or technology gives a firm an edge on its competitors. Cornering the supply of a key raw material through location or judicious buying may permit a company to dominate a particular business. An innovative product design or the development of a new distribution channel can provide an organization with a competitive lead that is difficult to overcome. Yet all of these competitive advantages are more or less temporary—sooner or later, competitors will imitate and improve upon the innovation, and the advantage will disappear. Such abilities, therefore, do not guarantee induction into the Hall of Fame.

Sustained corporate excellence seems to have at least one necessary condition: the invention or early application of—and rapid tight fit around—a new organization form. Achieving early fit succeeds over the proprietary advantages mentioned above, because a new organization form cannot be completely copied in the short or even intermediate run. In this century, certain firms would appear to merit Hall of Fame nomination based on broad criteria such as product excellence, management performance, market share and responsiveness, and the like. We will discuss five of our own nominees, all of which meet these criteria but also share the characteristic of early fit through invention or application of a new organization form: Carnegie Steel, General Motors, Sears, Roebuck, Hewlett-Packard, and IBM.

Carnegie Steel

Carnegie Steel was one of the first companies to employ the fully integrated functional organization form complete with centralized management and technical specialization.[12] In his early 30s, Andrew Carnegie left a position with the railroad to concentrate on manufacturing steel rails. Convinced that the management methods he and others had pioneered on the railroad could also be applied to the manufacturing sector, Carnegie essentially started the modern steel business in the United States, and he played a major role in forging the world's first billion-dollar corporation, U.S. Steel.

At the heart of Carnegie Steel's success was its reliance on centralized management (particularly cost accounting and control) and full vertical integration. Carnegie recognized early the benefits of vertical integration in the fragmented, geographically dispersed steel industry in the latter half of the 19th century, and his company integrated backward into the purchase of ore deposits and the production of coke as well as forward into manufacture of finished steel products. Vertical integration permitted a new external alignment in the steel industry: substantially larger market areas could now be served much more quickly, efficiently, and profitably. Carnegie Steel supplemented its functional organization structure with careful plant design and transportation logistics, continuous technological improvements, successful (though limited) product diversification, and innovative human resources management practices and labor relations. Thus, internally, there was rapid development of a tight fit between management processes and the company's pioneering strategy and structure.

Carnegie Steel, of course, did not invent the vertically integrated, functional organization form; elements of this model were already available. However, the company's early and complete use of this form dramatically altered the steel business in a way that was not matched by competitors for decades. (See Table 1 for the evolution of major organization forms and our prediction of the next new form.)

Table 1
Evolution of Organization Forms

	Product/Market Strategy	Organization Structure	Inventory or Early User	Core Activating and Control Mechanisms
1800	Single product or service. Local/regional markets.	Agency.	Numerous small, owner-managed firms.	Personal direction and control.
1850	Limited, standardized product or service line. Regional/national markets.	Functional.	Carnegie Steel.	Central plan and budgets.
1900	Diversified, changing product or service line. National/international markets.	Divisional.	General Motors, Sears, Roebuck, Hewlett-Packard.	Corporate policies and division profit centers.
1950	Standard and innovative products or services. Stable and changing markets.	Matrix.	Several aerospace and electronics firms (e.g., NASA, TRW, IBM, Texas Instruments).	Temporary teams and lateral resource allocation devices such as internal markets, joint planning systems, etc.
2000	Product or service design. Global, changing markets.	Dynamic network.	International/construction firms; global consumer goods companies; selected electronics and computer firms (e.g., IBM).	Broker-assembled temporary structures with shared information systems as basis for trust and coordination.

General Motors

General Motors has the strongest claim as the inventor of the "federally decentralized" or divisional organization structure. Among the early automobile makers, William C. Durant was one of the strongest believers in the enormous potential market for the moderate-priced car.[13] Acting on his beliefs, Durant put together a group of companies engaged in the making and selling of automobiles, parts, and accessories. In 1919, the total combined assets of Durant's General Motors made it the fifth largest company in the United States. But although Durant had spotted a potentially large opportunity, and had moved rapidly to create an industrial empire to take advantage of it, he had little interest in developing an organization structure and management system for the enterprise he had created.

Indeed, in combining individual firms into General Motors Durant relied on the same organizational approach of volume production and vertical integration that he had used in his previous managerial positions and that was popular at the time. However, this approach led to little more than an expanding agglomeration of different companies making automobiles, parts, accessories, trucks, tractors, and even refrigerators. An unforeseen collapse in the demand for automobiles in 1920 precipitated a financial crisis at General Motors, which was quickly followed by Durant's retirement as president. Pierre du Pont, who had been in semiretirement from the chemical company, agreed to take the presidency of GM. One of du Pont's first actions was to approve a plan devised by Alfred P. Sloan, a high-level GM executive whose family firm had been purchased by Durant, that defined an organization structure for General Motors.

Sloan's plan, which went into effect in early 1921, called for a general office to coordinate, appraise, and set broad goals and policies for the numerous, loosely controlled operating divisions of GM. The general officers individually were to supervise and coordinate different groups of divisions and collectively were to help make policy for the corporation as a whole. Staff specialists were to advise and serve both the division managers and the general officers and to provide business and financial information necessary for appraising the performance of the individual units and for formulating overall policy. Although most of Sloan's proposals had been carried out by the end of 1921, it was not until 1925 that the original plan resulted in a smooth-running organization. The multidivisional decentralized structure allowed GM to diversify a standard product, the automobile, to meet a variety of consumer needs and tastes while maintaining overall corporate financial synergy.

From 1924–1927, General Motors' market share rose from 19 to 43 percent. Unlike its major competitor, Ford, which was devastated by the Depression, GM's profits grew steadily throughout the Depression and World War II. It has been the leading automobile manufacturer in the world since its implementation of the divisional structure and for years was the corporate model for similar structural changes in other large American industrial enterprises.

Sears, Roebuck

Just as General Motors can make a strong claim to the invention of the divisional structure for product diversification, Sears, Roebuck can claim to have been one of the earliest users of this structure outside of manufacturing. Sears has long enjoyed its reputation as the world's most successful retailer.[14] Since its inception in 1895, Sears has undergone two periods where it achieved an "early fit" among its competitors. The first phase of the Sears story began in 1895 when Julius Rosenwald, a consummate administrator, joined Richard Sears, a brilliant merchandiser, and together they built a company catering to the American farmer. Sears, Roebuck's Chicago mail-order plant was a major innovation in the retailing business. Designed by Otto Doering in 1903, this modern mass-production plant preceded by five years Henry Ford's acclaimed automobile assembly line, and it ushered in the "distribution revolution" that was so vital a factor in early 20th century America's economic growth.

The second phase of the Sears story began in 1924 when Robert E. Wood left Montgomery Ward to join the company. Since farmers could now travel to cities in their automobiles and the urban population was more affluent, retail selling through local stores appeared to be more promising than mail-order sales. Promoted to president in 1928, Wood, with his new handpicked management team, moved ahead rapidly to create a nationwide retail organization. Montgomery Ward and other retail chains of the period (e.g., J. C. Penney, Eaton's, Woolworth's, Grant's, Kresge's) have not been able to this day to match Sears' performance.

The organization form developed at Sears bore many similarities to GM's multidivisional structure, but it was geared toward retailing rather than manufacturing. Whereas GM diversified by product, Sears diversified by geographic territory. Each of the territorial units became full-fledged autonomous divisions with their managers responsible for overall operating results, and the Chicago headquarters remained a central office with staff specialists and general executives. Sears' ultimate tight internal and external fit was not accomplished nearly as rapidly as those of Carnegie Steel or General Motors, but it was achieved first among Sears' competitors and gave the company a competitive advantage that has not, until recently, been seriously threatened.

Hewlett-Packard

The decentralized, divisional structure developed by General Motors and Sears (along with a few other outstanding companies such as Du Pont and Standard Oil of New Jersey) flourished in the 1950s under the spotlight of publicity from management consulting firms and from academics like Peter Drucker. For most companies, however, the divisional structure did not serve as a proprietary advantage but merely as a necessary means of maintaining alignment with a market demanding diversity. Nevertheless, one outstanding company, a Hall of Fame nominee on many early ballots, has taken this organization structure to new heights in its pursuit of leading-edge technological developments in an emerging industry. The company is Hewlett-Packard, and the industry, of course, is electronics. Founded in 1939 by William Hewlett and David Packard, this company is the world's largest manufacturer of test and measurement instruments as well as a major producer of small computers. The company is noted for its strong corporate culture and nearly continuous high performance in a very demanding industrial environment.

From the beginning, Hewlett-Packard has pursued a strategy that brings the products of scientific research into industrial application while maintaining the collegial atmosphere of a university laboratory. This means that the firm concentrates on advanced technology and offers mostly state-of-the-art products to a variety of industrial and consumer markets. A given product line and market are actively pursued as long as the company has a distinctive technological or design advantage. When products reach the stage where successful competition depends primarily on low costs and prices, Hewlett-Packard often moves out of the arena and turns its attention to a new design or an entirely new product. As a company that achieved early fit, its technological diversification rivals General Motors' product diversification and Sears' territorial diversification.

Hewlett-Packard's strategy of technological innovation is supported by an organization structure and management system that may be unparalleled in flexibility. The fundamental business unit is the product division, an integrated, self-sustaining organization with a great deal of independence. New divisions arise when a particular product line becomes large enough to support its continued growth out of the profit it generates. Also, new divisions tend to emerge when a single division gets so large that the people involved start to lose their identification with the product line. Most human resources management practices—especially those concerning hiring, placement, and rewards—are appropriately matched with the company's structural and strategic decentralization.

International Business Machines

Any Hall of Fame list must include IBM.[15] One of the largest producers of calculating, computing, and office machinery, IBM is arguably the best-managed company in the United States, perhaps the world. Paradoxically, IBM's nomination to the Hall of Fame cannot be based on the invention of a particular organization form—nor, for that matter, a management innovation or technological breakthrough. The company is simply good at everything it does; it is a polydextrous organization that is consistently quick to adopt and refine any approach that it can use to its advantage.

The company was born when Thomas Watson, Sr. joined the Computing-Recording Corporation in 1914 and renamed it International Business Machines in 1924. However, the modern IBM dates to the stewardship of Thomas Watson, Jr., who was chief executive officer from 1956 to 1971. Today IBM is the most profitable U.S. industrial company, and its form of organization is a combination of time-honored and advanced approaches.

IBM takes advantage of two key characteristics of the functional organization, vertical integration and production efficiency. For example, IBM is the world's largest manufacturer of memory chips and installs its entire output in its own machines. And beginning in the late 1970s, a series of huge capital improvements has made IBM one of the most automated and lowest-cost producers in the industry.

IBM has also relied to a limited extent on acquisitions, a characteristic most often associated with the divisional organization. Unlike many large conglomerates, the company is very selective about its acquisitions, the most recent of which is intended to help IBM create the futuristic electronic office.

Finally, IBM uses a variety of the most advanced approaches to organization and management. First, the company has created at least 15 internal new ventures groups in the last few years to explore new business opportunities. The new units are independently run, but they can draw on IBM resources. Second, the company has increased its use of subcontracting. In its most recent product venture, the personal computer, IBM relied largely on parts obtained from outside suppliers and is selling the machine through retail outlets like Sears and ComputerLand as well as its own sales network. Software for the machine was developed by inviting numerous software firms to supply ideas and materials. Third, besides being a vigorous competitor, IBM has formed many successful cooperative agreements with other companies, especially in Japan and Europe. It is generally acknowledged that substantially more cooperative arrangements involving business firms, as well as governments and universities, will be needed in coming years to supplement traditional competitive practices. And, lastly, IBM is international in scope. It is the leading computer firm in virtually every one of the approximately 130 countries where it does business.

In sum, a close, current look at the Hall of Fame companies just described would probably not uncover the maintenance of perfect fit. As suggested earlier, even these organizations are vulnerable to external and internal slippage, perhaps even distortion. Therefore, it is important to explore the processes by which tight fit may be eroded.

The Fragility of Fit

As noted earlier, fit is a process as well as a state. Environmental factors outside an organization's control are constantly changing and may require incremental or major strategic adjustment. Strategic change, in turn, is likely to require changes in organization structure and/or management processes. When environmental jolts are extreme, some organizations may be unwilling or unable to adjust—recall the earlier examples from the tobacco industry and witness the recent plight of several airline companies under deregulation.

However, environmental change is not the only cause of alignment deterioration. For example, misfit may occur when organizations voluntarily change their strategies but fail to follow through with appropriate structural and managerial adjustments, as illustrated by the case of Chrysler. An even more intriguing alignment-threatening process is also demonstrable, one which may well account for more deterioration of fit than either environmental jolts or unsupported strategic changes.

This process involves voluntary internal structure and process changes that are made without concern for their longer-run consequences for strategy and market responsiveness. Although usually subtle and long term in its development, this process of internal unraveling underscores the point that an organization's fit at any given time may be quite fragile.

Recall the earlier description of how the discovery of tight fit results in system simplicity: When strategy, structure, and process are completely aligned, both goals and means are visible, and task requirements are obvious and compelling. Resources previously required for coordination or troubleshooting can be redeployed in the primary system, and even tighter fit may result. However, as the spotlight of tight fit illuminates the overall system for everyone to see and understand, its bright glare may also begin to highlight the organization's inherent deficiencies. That is, each pattern of fit has its own distinct contribution to make. For example, the functional organization form is ideal for efficient production of standard goods or services, and the divisional form is most appropriate for diversification. Each form not only has its own strengths but also its own builit-in limitations. The form best suited for efficiency is vulnerable to market change, and the form suited to diversification is sometimes clearly redundant.

As the pattern of fit becomes increasingly clear to managers and employees of excellent (tight fit) companies, they can easily describe why the organization prospers. But at least some members of these same companies can also point to the system's shortcomings. For example, in a vertically integrated, centralized, functional organization, perceptive managers will advocate the creation of task forces, project groups, or even separate divisions to facilitate quick development of new products or services. Conversely, one can anticipate in a decentralized, divisional structure that cost-conscious managers will suggest standardizing certain components or services across divisions in order to reduce redundancy and achieve scale economies. Most organizations regularly make minor adjustments in their structures and processes to accommodate demands for which their systems were not designed. In some organizations, however, what begins as a limited adjustment may over time grow into a crippling, step-by-step unraveling of the entire system. Moreover, this may occur without conscious long-term planning or even awareness. Two brief examples, both associated with companies on our Hall of Fame list, serve as illustrations.

At General Motors, once Sloan's federally decentralized structure was fully in place, managers began to recommend standardization of various product components and production processes. Some aspects of engineering and production had been coordinated across divisions from the beginning, but the advocates of full-scale standardization finally began to override the divisional structure in the 1950s. Many readers may recall the "scandal" that occurred when buyers discovered that the General Motors' engine in their cars had not been made by that division and, in some cases, even by a division of lower status. In fact, those engines had been manufactured according to policies that reflected increasing interdivisional coordination and centralization of decision making. During the 1950s and 1960s when General Motors appeared invulnerable to competition—foreign or domestic—the cost of increased centralization and coordination was probably not visible. It almost appeared that the company could have its diversity and its cost savings, too. One wonders how much more rapidly General Motors might have responded to the challenge of foreign competition if it had been able to do so by simply aiming the operations of one autonomous division toward Japan and another toward Europe. In general, the more attention that is devoted to the known shortcomings of a particular organization form, the more likely is the possibility of unraveling a successful fit.

Could a similar process occur at Hewlett-Packard in the 1980s? In recent months, the company has been beset with problems caused by its decentralized management system and entrepreneurial culture, including overlapping products, lagging development of new technology, and a piecemeal approach to key markets.[16] The response to these problems was the launching of several programs to improve planning, coordinate marketing, and strengthen the firm's computer-related research and development efforts.

Hewlett-Packard's current CEO, John Young, recognizes that these organizational changes involve trade-offs; the benefits obtained from cross-divisional coordination have to be weighed against the threats to the entrepreneurial spirit of the various divisions. That is, the use of program managers and strategic coordinators to align product designs, to force the divisions to share components, and to coordinate pricing and marketing strategies has generated a number of successful cross-divisional development projects. However, these successes have been offset by a wave of manager and engineer defections to other companies. Thus, only time will tell if this reorganization improves the company's internal fit or begins to unravel the core threads among strategy, structure, and process that have produced Hewlett-Packard's success.

The moral of these examples is not that managers of excellent companies should not try to improve performance. Rather, it is that rearranging organization structure and management systems may in some cases preclude an organization from pursuing its desired strategy. Managers of truly outstanding companies recognize the strengths and limitations of alternate organization forms, and they will not undo a crucial link among strategy, structure, or process in order to "solve" predictable problems.

Future Fit: A New Organization Form

Our argument concerning the effects of minimal, tight, and early fit on organizational performance is based on the belief that the search for fit has been visible in organizations for at least the past 100 years. But will this search continue in the future? We believe it will. In fact, many managers are now considering a new organization form and are experimenting with its major components and processes in their organizations. The reality of this new form, therefore, simply awaits articulation and understanding.

In this century, there have been three major breakthroughs in the way organizations have been designed and managed (see again Table 1). The first breakthrough occurred at the turn of the century in the form of the functional organization. Prior to that time, small firms had relied on an informal structure in which the owner-manager's immediate subordinates acted as all-purpose "agents" of the chief executive, solving whatever problems arose. There was very little of the technical specialization found in today's organizations. The functional form allowed those companies that adopted it to become very large and to specialize in a limited set of products and markets. Next came the divisional form, which facilitated even more organizational growth, but, more importantly, it facilitated diversification in both products and markets. The third breakthrough was the matrix structure in which elements of the functional and divisional forms were combined into a single system able to accommodate both standard and innovative products or projects.

Now a promising new organization form is emerging, one that appears to fit the fast-approaching conditions of the 21st century. As was true of previous forms, elements of this new form are sprouting in several companies and industries simultaneously.

Large Construction Firms. The construction industry has long been known for its use of subcontracting to accomplish large, complex tasks. Today, the size and complexity of a construction project can be immense, as evidenced by the multinational consortium of companies now building an entire city in Saudi Arabia. Under such circumstances, companies must be able to form a network of reliable subcontractors, many of them large firms which have not worked together before. Some companies, therefore, have found it advantageous to focus only on the overall design and management of a project, leaving the actual construction to their affiliates.

Global Consumer Goods Companies. Standardized products such as clothes, cameras, and watches can be designed, manufactured, and marketed throughout the world. Companies engaged in this type of business are prime examples of the "world enterprise": buying raw materials wherever they are cheapest, manufacturing wherever costs are lowest, and selling wherever the products will bring the highest price. To do so, however, requires many different brokers—individuals and groups who bring together complementary resources. All of the participants in the process—designers, suppliers, manufacturers, distributors, etc.—must be coupled into a smooth-running operation even though they are continents apart.

Electronics and Computer Firms. Certain firms in these industries already are dealing with conditions that in the future will be widespread: rapid change, demassification, high technology, information abundance, and so on.[17] In these companies, product life cycles are often short, and all firms live under the constant threat of technological innovations that can change the structure of the industry. Individual firms must constantly redesign their processes around new products. Across the industry, spin-off firms are continually emerging. Thus, a common development model includes venture capitalists working with high-technology entrepreneurs in the development, manufacture, and distribution of innovative products or services.

Across these three examples, some key characteristics of the new organization form are clearly visible. Organizations of the future are likely to be *vertically disaggregated:* functions typically encompassed within a single organization will instead be performed in independent organizations. That is, the functions of product design and development, manufacturing, and distribution, ordinarily integrated by a plan and controlled directly by managers, will instead be brought together by *brokers* and held in temporary alignment by a variety of *market mechanisms.*

For example, one form of a vertically disaggregated organization held together by a market mechanism is the franchise system, symbolized by McDonald's or H & R Block. In a franchise system, both the product or service and its basic recipe are provided by the parent corporation to a local management group. Such a model, however, seems appropriate only for a limited set of standard goods or services. In our view, a more flexible and comprehensive approach—and hence a better analogue of the organization of the future–is the "designer" system associated with companies such as Yves St. Laurent or Gucci. In these companies, design skills can be applied in a variety of arenas, from electronics to household goods to personal products or services. Similarly, production expertise can be contracted for and applied to a wide array of products or services, as can skills in marketing and distribution. Thus, we expect the 21st century firm to be a temporary organization, brought together by an entrepreneur with the aid of brokers and maintained by a network of contractual ties. In some instances, a single entrepreneur will play a lead role and subcontract for various services. This same individual may also serve as a consultant to others attempting to form their own organizational networks. In other cases, linkages among equals may be created by request through various brokers specializing in a particular service.

Given these characteristics, we have found it useful to refer to this emerging form as the *dynamic network* organization. However, the full realization of this new type of organization awaits the development of a core activating and control mechanism comparable to those that energized the previous organization forms (e.g., the profit center in the divisional form). Our prediction is that this mechanism essentially will be a broad-access computerized information system. Note that most of today's temporary organizations (e.g., a general contractor) have been put together on the basis of lengthy experience among the key participants. Under future conditions of high complexity and rapid change, however, participants in the network organization will first have to be identified, trust between the parties will be a major issue, and fixed-fee contracts specified in advance will usually not be feasible. Therefore, as a substitute for lengthy trust-building processes, participants will have to agree on a general structure of payment for value added and then hook themselves together in a full-disclosure information system so that contributions can be mutually and instantaneously verified. Properly constructed, the dynamic network organization will display the technical expertise of the functional form, the market focus of the divisional form, and the efficient use of resources characteristic of the matrix. And, especially important, it will be able to quickly reshape itself whenever necessary.

Conclusion

The United States is in a period of economic challenge and organizational upheaval. There are myriad prescriptions for industrial and organizational renewal, and many of the factors linked to organizational success are being rediscovered today after a 30-year hiatus. Our own analysis, however, indicates that these characteristics, while important, are merely manifestations of a more fundamental, dynamic process called fit—the search for an organization form that is both internally and externally consistent. We have argued that minimal fit is necessary for survival, tight fit is associated with corporate excellence, and early fit provides a competitive advantage that can lead to the organization Hall of Fame. Tomorrow's Hall of Fame companies are working on new organization forms today.

References

1. Raymond E. Miles and Charles C. Snow, *Organizational Strategy, Structure, and Process* (New York: McGraw-Hill, 1978).
2. Alfred D. Chandler, Jr., *Strategy and Structure* (Garden City, N.Y.: Doubleday Publishing, 1962).
3. Tom Burns and G. M. Stalker, *The Management of Innovation* (London: Tavistock, 1961).

4. Paul R. Lawrence and Jay W. Lorsch, *Organization and Environment* (Boston: Harvard Graduate School of Business Administration, 1967).
5. Michael E. Porter, *Competitive Strategy* (New York: Free Press, 1980).
6. Michael T. Hannan and John H. Freeman, "The Population Ecology of Organizations," *American Journal of Sociology* 82 (March 1977), pp. 929–64; and Howard E. Aldrich, *Organizations and Environments* (Englewood Cliffs, N.J.: Prentice-Hall, 1979).
7. Charles C. Snow and Lawrence G. Hrebiniak, "Strategy, Distinctive Competence, and Organizational Performance," *Administrative Science Quarterly* 25 (June 1980), pp. 317–36.
8. Robert H. Miles, *Coffin Nails and Corporate Strategies* (Englewood Cliffs, N.J.: Prentice-Hall, 1980).
9. The description of Chrysler Corp. was adapted from James Brian Quinn, *Chrysler Corporation,* copyrighted case, the Amos Tuck School of Business Administration, Dartmouth College, 1977.
10. Peter F. Drucker, *The Practice of Management* (New York: Harper & Row, 1954).
11. Thomas J. Peters and Robert H. Waterman, *In Search of Excellence: Lessons from America's Best Run Companies* (New York: Free Press, 1983), chap. 3.
12. The description of Carnegie Steel was adapted from Paul R. Lawrence and Davis Dyer, *Renewing American Industry* (New York: Free Press, 1983). chap. 3.
13. The description of General Motors was adapted from Chandler, *Strategy,* chap. 3.
14. The description of Sears, Roebuck was adapted from Chandler, *Strategy,* chap. 5; and from Drucker, *Practice,* chap. 4.
15. The description of IBM was adapted from "The Colossus that Works," *Time,* July 11, 1983, pp. 44–54.
16. "Can John Young Redesign Hewlett-Packard?" *Business Week,* December 6, 1982, pp. 72–78.
17. For a complete discussion of these conditions, see Alvin Toffler, *The Third Wave* (New York: Bantam Books, 1981); and John Naisbitt, *Megatrends* (New York: Warner Books, 1982).

Reading 4–2

The Human Side of the Matrix*

Paul R. Lawrence, Harvey F. Kolodny, Stanley M. Davis

Matrix management and organization have become increasingly common in recent years. If we were pressed to pick one word that characterizes the potential of the matrix organization, it would have to be *flexibility*. The matrix structure offers the potential of achieving the flexibility that is so often missing in conventional, single-line-of-command organizations and of reconciling this flexibility with the coordination and economies of scale that are the historic strengths of large organizations. (See the box on pages 244–45 for the basic elements of matrix design.)

Now that the use of the matrix structure is so widespread, it has become apparent that it calls for different kinds of managerial behavior than are typical in conventional line organizations. This article will identify the key management roles in a matrix organization and describe the essential aspects called for in each of them.

Envision the matrix structure as a diamond [Exhibit 1]. The general executive, who heads up the matrix, is at the top of the diamond. The matrix bosses, or matrix managers, who share common subordinate(s), are on the sides of the diamond. The person at the bottom is the 2-boss manager.

---

* Reprinted, by permission of the publisher, from *Organizational Dynamics*, Summer 1977 © 1977 AMACOM, a division of American Management Associations, New York.

Top Leadership

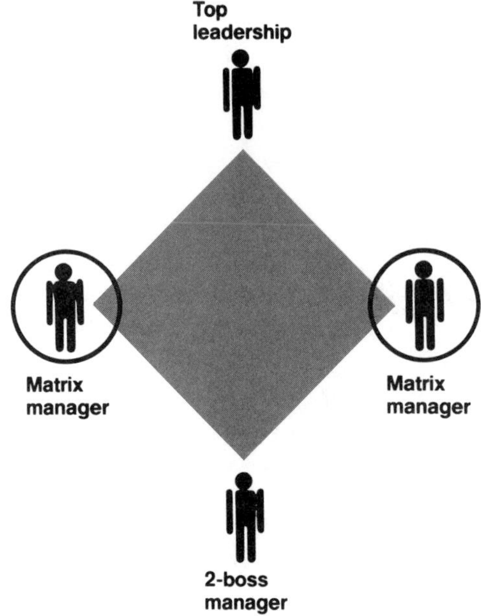

The top leadership is literally atop, or outside of, the matrix organization. This is not generally appreciated. Even in totally matrix organizations, the top executives are not *in* the matrix. Despite this, however, they are *of* it: It is the top leaders who oversee and sustain the balance of power.

In a corporationwide matrix, the top leaders are the chief executive and a few other key individuals; in a product group or a division matrix, the top leader is the senior manager. This individual does not share power with others, and there is no unequal separation of authority and responsibility. Formally, the role itself is the same as in any traditional organization. What distinguishes it from the traditional top slot is the leadership process as it is applied to the people in the next levels down.

The top leader is the one who must "buy" the matrix approach. He must be convinced of its merits to the point that he believes it is the best (although not necessarily the ideal) of all alternative designs. He must also "sell" it; he must be very vocal and articulate in developing the concept and arousing enthusiasm for it among the ranks.

One of the several paradoxes of the matrix approach, then, is that it requires a strong, unified command at the top, to ensure a balance of power at the next level down. In some senses, this is the benevolent dictator: "You will enjoy democracy (shared power), and I will enjoy

Exhibit 1

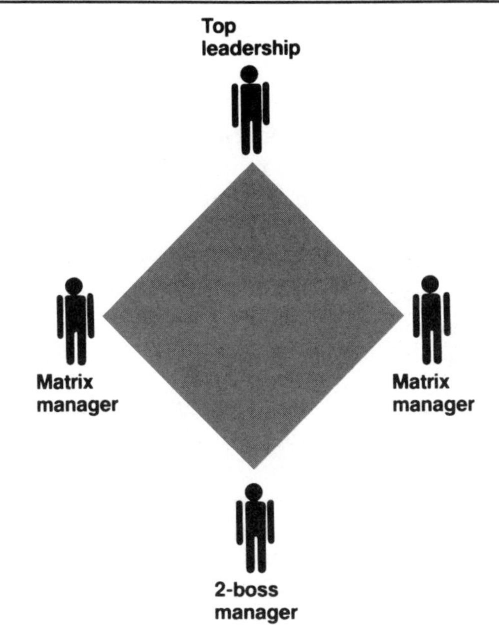

autocracy (ultimate power)"; or "I'm OK, you're OK; but I'm still the boss."

Balancing power as a top leader therefore calls for a blend of autocratic and participative leadership styles. A clear example of this comes from Bastien Hello, head of the B–1 bomber division at Rockwell International. The *New York Times* called his project the most costly and complex plane project in history. In an interview he said:

Today I have some formidable people working for me. When you have a group like that, you have two choices, running a Captain Bligh operation, or a Mr. Roberts operation. I would call one autocratic, the other group therapy.

If I have to lean in one direction, I would shave a little closer to group therapy. It's not because I, and the fellows who work for me, don't have autocratic tendencies: We do. But if you're going to keep everybody working in the same direction, you've got to have group participation in the decisions.

So I like to get my team of managers together and thrash out problems with them, and I like to hear all sides. It's not that I'm a goody-goody about it; there is malice aforethought to it.

Once they have participated in and agreed to the decision, you can hold their noses right to it. It's not that I like group sessions—I don't, they're painful—but they do bring the team along. And once you get them signed up, then *you become autocratic about it.*

The general executive of a matrix organization has the unique role of heading up both of its dual command structures, administrative and technical. As we understand this role, it involves three unique aspects: *power balancing, managing the decision context,* and *standard setting.* These three processes, while of concern to any top executive, take on a very special importance in a mature matrix organization. The reason for this importance is not hard to find. It stems directly from three basic reasons as to why a matrix can be a desirable organizational form.

1. The existence of dual pressures calls for balanced decision making that considers both aspects simultaneously. The general executive's critical role in achieving such decision making is to establish and sustain a reasonable balance of power between the two arms of the matrix.

2. The second necessary condition for a matrix organization to be effective is that a very high volume of information be processed and focused for use in making key decisions. If the organization is to cope with such an information-processing load, the top leader must be only one among several key decision makers—he must delegate. However, he cannot delegate to other decision makers the job of setting the stage; he must himself manage the decision context.

3. Last, the top executive must set the standards of expected performance. Others contribute to this process, but unless the top individual has high expectations for the organization, it is unlikely that the matrix organization will respond adequately to the environmental pressure for resource redeployment, which we have identified as a third necessary condition for a matrix organization. Let us look at each of these three special aspects of the top leader's role in the matrix organization in more detail.

Power Balancing

The power-balancing element of the general executive's role is, in our experience, vital to mature matrix organization performance. Any general manager must of course pay attention to this process, but it is uniquely critical in matrix organizations. If we contrast the pyramid diagram of a conventional hierarchy and the matrix diamond diagram, we have a clue as to why this is true. The diamond diagram, unlike the pyramid, is inherently unstable. For the structure to remain in place despite environmental pushing and pulling that lead to changed administrative and technical requirements, its emphasis and activities must be constantly rebalanced by hands-on top leadership. The analogy is crude but relevant. Managers in a leadership role are usually quite explicit about this requirement of their job. The "tuning" of a matrix organization needs continuing attention.

The basic methods that general executives use to establish a power balance are both obvious and important. The two arms of a matrix organization are, first of all, usually described in the formal documents that establish the structure as being of equal power and importance. The top executive uses every possible occasion to reinforce this message, and one way that is often used is by establishing dual budgeting systems and dual evaluation systems.

Most mature matrix organizations adopt dual budgeting systems, in which a complete budget is generated within each arm of the matrix. As with a double-entry accounting system, the dual budgets count everything twice—each time in a different way and for a different purpose. Functional budgets are primarily cost budgets—unless the functions sell their services outside. The budgets begin with product- and business-area estimates of work required from each functional area, usually expressed in man-hours and materials requirements. Functional groups then add indirect and overhead costs to these direct hours and come up with an hourly rate for services to the product or business managers.

Product or business units accept these rates or challenge them, sometimes by threatening to buy from the outside. This is the time when the difference in outlook is most striking. Business units, for example, have little sympathy for functional desires to hold people in an overhead category for contingencies or for the development of long-term competence. A business unit is hard pressed to see the need to develop competence that may be required three years hence, or for another business, when its own central concern is with short-term profit and loss. When the rates are approved for all the different functions, the product or business units develop their own profit and loss budgets for each of their product lines.

The parallel accounting systems provide independent controls that are consistent with the characteristic of the work in each type of unit and that recognize the partial autonomy of each organizational subunit. Each unit has the means to evaluate its own performance and to be evaluated independent of others. The CEO of one organization described the dual control systems in his organization as follows:

> *The accounting system matches the organization precisely; so that's an aspect the product manager and I don't have to talk about. He can see how he's doing himself. When resources seem to be a problem, then I must get involved.*
>
> *Both product managers and functional managers get accounting evaluations. The functional shops have budgets but little spending money. They have a cost budget, but in theory it's all released into the projects. From the functional side, the accounting system locates and isolates unused capacity. As soon as the task requirement disappears the excess capacity turns up. The functional shop then has a "social" problem. The key thing is that the excess turns up immediately. There is no place to hide. Matrix is a free organization, but it's a tough organization.*

With dual budgets, some interesting possibilities arise in achieving flexibility of organizational response. In the aforementioned organization, the CEO resolved an internal dispute: A product group was lobbying for control of repair and overhaul contracts on products in the field that it had developed and sold, over the protests of a functional group that had always managed the organization's field repair and overhaul activity. In the resolution of the dispute, the function remained in charge of the activity, but the product group was credited with the profits from all repair and overhaul contracts on its products. Both sides were satisfied.

Dual personnel evaluation systems go hand in hand with dual budgeting to help sustain a power balance. If a person's work is to be directed by two superiors, in all logic both should take part in that person's evaluation. Occasionally, the duality is nothing more than a product or business group sign-off of an evaluation form prepared by the functional boss. At other times, the initiative comes from the other side, primarily because the individual involved may have been physically situated within the product or business unit and had limited contact with the functional unit during the period covered by the evaluation.

Essential Characteristics of Matrix Organizations

- The identifying feature of a matrix organization is that some managers report to two bosses rather than to the traditional single boss—there is a dual rather than a single chain of command.
- Firms tend to adopt matrix forms when it is absolutely essential that they be highly responsive to two sectors, such as markets and technology; when they face uncertainties that generate very high information-processing requirements; and when they must deal with strong constraints on financial and/or human resources. The matrix form can help provide flexibility and balanced decision making, but at the price of complexity.
- Matrix organization is more than matrix structure. It must also be reinforced by matrix systems such as dual control and evaluation systems, by matrix leadership behavior that operates comfortably with lateral decision making, and by a matrix culture that fosters open conflict management and a balance of power.
- Most matrix organizations assign dual command responsibilities to functional departments (marketing, production, engineering, and so on) and to product/market departments. The former are oriented to specialized resources while the latter focus on outputs. Other matrix organizations are area-based departments for either products or functions.
- Every matrix organization contains three unique and critical roles: the top manager who heads up and balances the dual chains of command; the matrix bosses (functional, product, or area) who share subordinates; and the 2-boss managers who report to two different matrix bosses. Each of these roles has its own unique requirements.

- The matrix organization started in aerospace companies, but now firms in many industries (chemical, banking, insurance, package goods, electronics, computer, and so on) and in different fields (hospitals, government agencies, professional organizations) are turning to different forms of the matrix structure.

Regardless of the particular system design, the person with 2-bosses must know that both have been a part of the evaluation if that person is to feel committed to consider both orientations in his activities. For this reason many matrix organizations insist that both superiors sit in on the evaluation feedback with the employee and that both advise the employee of salary changes so that rewards will not be construed as having been secured from only one side of the matrix.

These basic formal arrangements for setting up a reasonable balance of power are essential in a mature matrix, but they are seldom sufficient. Too many events can upset the balance, and a loss of balance needs to be caught by the general manager or it can degenerate into a major power struggle and even an ill-advised move away from the matrix organization. The matrix can be thrown off balance in many ways, but a common cause of a loss of balance is a temporary crisis on one side of the matrix structure that is used as an excuse for mobilizing resources in that direction. Up to a point such a reaction to a true crisis is certainly appropriate, but it can be the start of a lasting imbalance unless it is corrected by the general manager.

A more lasting source of instability arises from the fact that product- and business-area managers manage a whole business and thereby have that special mystique associated with bottom-line responsibility. This is a source of power. They are seen as the sources of revenue—the people who make the cash register ring. The general manager needs to be alert to this one-sided source of power to avoid its unbalancing potential. The profit center manager is often tempted to argue that he must have complete control over all needed resources, but this argument has no place in a matrix organization.

Given the inherent power instability of the matrix, the general managers of mature matrix organizations use a wide variety of supplemental ways to maintain the balance of the matrix. These methods are not new, but they are worth remembering as especially relevant for use in a matrix. Here are five such means:

1. Pay levels, as an important symbol of power, can be marginally higher on one side of the matrix, thus acting as a countervailing force.
2. Job titles can be adjusted between the two sides as a balancing item.
3. Access to the general manager at meetings and informal occasions is a source of power that can be controlled as a balancing factor.

4. Situation of offices is a related factor that carries a status or power message.
5. Reporting level is a frequently used power-balancing method. For instance, product managers can report up through a second in command while functional managers report directly to the general manager.

We have talked about the unbalancing potential possessed by profit center managers. But this imbalance of potential fluctuates from situation to situation. In many cases, the organization traditionally gave top priority to the functional side. Here the general manager employs his stratagems to shore up the prestige and position of the business-area or product managers and to make them, in fact as well as in name, the equals of the functional managers.

Managing the Decision Context

There is no substitute in a matrix organization for the sensitive management of the decision context by the top leadership. The existence of a matrix structure is an acknowledgment that the executive leaders cannot make all the key decisions in a timely way. There is too much relevant information to be digested, and too many points of view must be taken into account. But the general manager must set the stage for this decision making by others. He must see that it happens.

We have already seen that dual environmental pressures and complexity make conflict inevitable. To cope with this situation, the top manager must sponsor and act as a model of a three-stage decision process:

1. The conflicts must be brought into the open. This is fostered in the matrix structure, with its dual arms; but beyond this, the given manager must reward those who bring the tough topics to the surface for open discussion.

2. The conflicting positions must be debated in a spirited and reasoned manner. Relevant lines of argument and appropriate evidence must be presented. The executive manager's personal behavior has to encourage this in others.

3. The issue must be resolved and a commitment made in a timely fashion. The leader cannot tolerate stalling by others or passing the buck up the line.

All these decision processes call for a high order of interpersonal skills and a willingness to take risks. They also call for a minimum of status differentials from the top to the bottom ranks. Top leaders can favorably influence these factors by their own openness to dissent and willingness to listen and debate. One of the noticeable features of most leaders of matrix organizations is the simplicity of their offices and the relative informality of their manner and dress. The key point here is that this behavior must start at the top as part of setting the decision context.

Standard Setting

The leadership of matrix organizations is where high performance standards start. We earlier identified environmental pressures for high performance as a necessary condition for matrix organizations. But it is all too easy for organizational members to insulate themselves from these outside pressures. The general executive in a mature matrix organization internalizes the outside pressures and articulates them in the form of performance standards. Each subsystem on both sides of the matrix structure will of course be making its own projections and setting specific targets for higher review. But the overall level of aspiration in the organization begins with the general executive. This is a duty, as we said before, that he cannot afford to delegate.

The Matrix Boss

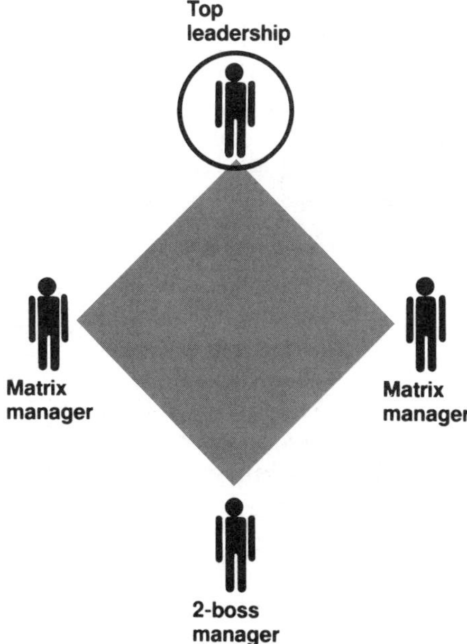

The matrix organization boss shares subordinates in common with another boss. As matrixes evolve, this means that the matrix structure boss will find himself positioned on one of the dimensions in the power balance. Whether the dimension is the one that is given or the one that is grown can make a significant difference for the perspective that evolves. Since one of the most typical evolutions is from a functional structure through a project overlay to a business function balance, let us examine the matrix boss role for each of these two dimensions in detail. The same lessons, however, apply to matrix structure bosses who are in charge of areas, markets, services, or clients.

The Functional Manager

One of the greatest surprises of the matrix organization form comes in the changing role of functional managers. In a functional organization, managers have authority over the objectives of their function, the selection of individuals, the priorities assigned to different tasks, the assignment of subordinates to different tasks and projects, the evaluation of progress on projects, the evaluation of subordinates' performance, and decisions on subordinate pay and promotions. They consult or take direction only from their boss in these matters, but much of the function is self-contained.

In a matrix organization, by contrast, none of these responsibilities is the sole responsibility of the functional manager. He must share many of the decisions with program or business managers or other functional managers at his level. Many matrix structures require dual sign-offs on performance evaluations and on pay and promotion decisions. Even when this is not so, consultation on these matters with others is essential for the effective functioning of the matrix and the power balance discussed previously. Tasks, assignments, and priority decisions have to be shared with business managers and indeed often come about as the result of decisions made by project or business teams. Even a function's objectives are partially determined by the resource demands of projects and businesses. The functional manager in his matrix role is responding in areas in which he has traditionally been the initiator. A manufacturing manager, for example, struggled against and for several years resisted the notion that many of the plant managers who reported to him had to set their goals in response to a business team's needs and that review of goal accomplishment, from a time point of view, was the business manager's and team's responsibility. He had difficulty in understanding that his responsibility was to review goal accomplishment from the point of view of a functional specialty.

Thus, for the functional manager, a matrix organization is often experienced as involving a loss of status, authority, and control. He becomes less central and less powerful as parts of his previous role as initiator move from the function to the business manager. The ultimate example of this is the increased confrontation of functional managers by their functional subordinates, who are now also members of a business team that provides the legitimate need and social support for such upward initiation and confrontation. For managers who have been in relative control of their domain, this is a rude awakening that can create initial hostility and a quite predictable resistance to a matrix form of management.

As a matrix organization matures, however, functional managers adapt to these changes, and they find the role not only tolerable but highly challenging. Even though in matrix organizations it is the business managers who tend to control the money that buys human resources, functional managers must engage in very complex people planning.

They must balance the needs of the different product lines and/or businesses in the organization, they must anticipate training needs, and they must handle union negotiations if layoffs or promotions are involved. They must also administer support staff (supervisors, managers, secretaries, clerks) and accompanying resources (equipment, facilities, space, maintenance), many of which must be shared with the business units.

To accomplish this with any degree of efficiency, functional managers must balance workloads to avoid excessive peaks and valleys in resources. They must do this in any organization, but in a matrix, business managers act with relative autonomy, and functional managers cannot be effective by holding to some central plan prepared primarily for budget purposes. It is imperative that they know the product- and business-workload projections and changes well in advance; that they negotiate constantly with these managers to speed up, slow down, schedule, plan, and replan the pace and amount of their activities. In other words, they must go to the business unit managers and be *proactive* if they are to manage their functions effectively.

Some comments from managers in 2 matrix organizations serve to underscore this need for proactive behavior:

> *Functional managers have to learn that they're losing some of their authority to product units, and they will have to take direction from the product bosses. They have to segment their work along product lines, not functional lines, and they must be willing to establish communication channels with product lines.*
>
> *Functional managers have to learn to become more aware of the impact of their decisions on our productmarket success and become more responsive to the product organization needs that reflect the market. They have to remove their blinders and look around them while they turn the crank.*

One functional manager concurred heartily:

> *We have to learn to serve as well as dictate; become more customer oriented—where the customer is the product line. We must realize that the function's mission is to perform the function and prove that the function is the best available. There is a burden of proof in matrix that did not exist in functional organization.*

The Business Manager

As we have pointed out, in a matrix organization various functional specialists are brought together in temporary (project) or permanent (business or product) groupings. These groups are led by product or business managers who have the responsibility for ensuring that the efforts of functional members of the team are integrated in the interest of the project or business. In this regard they have the same responsibilities as a general executive; their objective is project accomplishment or the long-term profitability of a business.

However, in a matrix organization these business managers do not have the same undivided authority as does the general executive. People on the team do not report to them exclusively since many also report to a functional manager. Thus, as many such managers have complained, "We have all the responsibility and little of the required authority."

Top leaders in traditional organizations have the benefit of instant legitimacy because people understand that reporting to them means being responsive to their needs. This is because their boss not only has formal title and status, but influences their performances evaluation, their pay, their advancement, and, in the long run, their careers. In a matrix organization these sources of authority are shared with functional managers, thus lessening, in the eyes of team members, the power of the project or business manager. He does not unilaterally decide. He manages the decision process so that differences are aired and trade-offs made in the interest of the whole. Thus he is left with the arduous task of influencing with limited formal authority. He must use his knowledge, competence, relationships, force of personality, and skills in group management to get people to do what is necessary to the success of the project or business.

This role of the matrix organization (business) boss creates both real and imagined demands for new behaviors that can be particularly anxiety producing for individuals who face the job for the first time. The matrix (business) manager must rely more heavily on his personal qualities, on his ability to persuade through knowledge about a program, business, or function. He must use communication and relationships to influence and move things along. His skills in managing meetings, in bringing out divergent points of view and, it is to be hoped, working through to a consensus are taxed more than the skills of general managers in conventional organizations.

Thus, for individuals who face these demands for the first time, the world is quite different. They can easily experience frustration, doubt, and loss of confidence as they begin to rely on new behaviors to get their job done. They begin to question their competence as they experience what in their eyes is a discrepancy between final and complete responsibility for a program and less certain means of gaining compliance from others. Some individuals learn the required new behaviors; others never do.

Not only does the actual and required change in behavior create a problem for new matrix organization business managers, but so does their own attitude toward the change. In our experience, individuals assigned to this role must first break through their perception of the job as impossible. Individuals who have spent all their time in traditional organizations have firmly implanted in their minds the notion of hierarchy and formal authority as the source of influence and power. They are convinced that the job cannot be done because they have never had to think through how power and influence, in reality, are wielded in the traditional organization. They cling to the myth that the formal power a boss has is what gives him influence.

This myth remains even after they themselves have developed and used other means of gaining influence. The myth about power and influence is often the first barrier that must be broken before the individual can be motivated to address the real demands for new behavior.

In his relations with his peers in both arms of the matrix organization, a business manager needs to assume a posture that blends reason and advocacy; bluster and threats are out. It is through these relations that he obtains the human resources needed to accomplish his goals. He has to expect that a number of these resources will be in short supply and that competing claims will have to be resolved.

In these dialogues the business manager must stand up for his requirements without developing a fatal reputation for overstating them. He must search with his peers for imaginative ways to share scarce resources. He must reveal any developing problems quickly while there is still time for remedial action. These actions do not come easily to managers conditioned in more traditional structures.

Last, in his relations with the various functional specialists represented on his team, the matrix organization business manager must establish a balanced or intermediate orientation. He cannot be seen as biased toward one function. He cannot have an overly long or short time horizon. His capacity to obtain a high-quality decision is dependent on an approach that seeks to integrate the views and orientations of all the various functions. If he shows a bias, team members will begin to distrust his objectivity and his capacity to be a fair arbiter of differences. This distrust can be the seed of a team's destruction.

For many individuals, this is a difficult task. A career spent in one side of the matrix structure creates a bias imperceptible to the individual but quite obvious to others. The need to wear multiple hats believably and equally well creates heavy attitudinal and behavioral demands.

It requires of an individual the capacity to have empathy with people in a number of functional areas and to identify with them while at the same time maintaining a strong personal concept and orientation that guides his own behavior and role performance.

Since the heir to the chief executive office is likely to come from this rank, there is generally a great, though diplomatic, battle going on for supremacy among the shared-subordinate bosses. The statesman's posture is an ingredient essential to success. The appearance of being threatened by sharing subordinates is fatal: This brands the individual as not being top management material.

Top leadership often uses the matrix structure to let the candidates for the top spar with each other in a constructive arena. The matrix structure is a better form than the pyramid for testing managers' ability to make things happen because of the strength of their personalities, their ability to lead, and the validity of their perceptions rather than because of their superior position in the hierarchy.

The perceptive matrix organization manager is aware that subordinates have other voices to attend to, other masters to please. Orders that seem irrational or unfair can more easily be circumvented under the protection of the other boss, than they can in a single chain of command. More care is therefore given to making clear the logic and importance of a directive.

For senior managers who must share their people with other senior managers, the matrix organization is both a training ground for how to assume the institutional reins and an incentive to go beyond having to share those reins equally with anyone else.

The rule for success in this role is to accept that while it can place contradictory demands on people, it is the best solution to accommodate simultaneous competing demands. Assume that there is no one best way to organize; each alternative has equally important claims, and the correct choice is both—in varying proportions.

2-Boss Managers

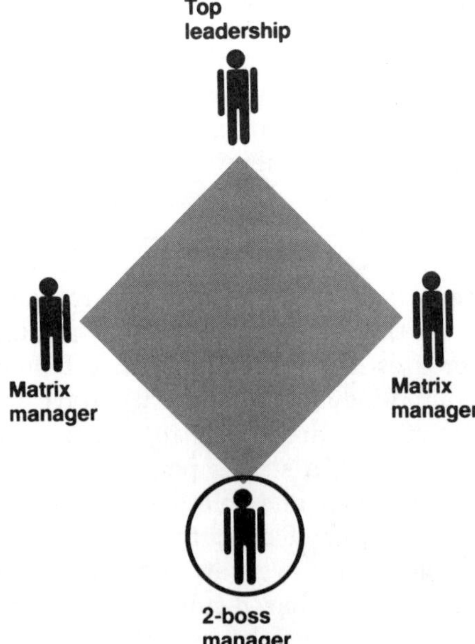

The most obvious challenge built into this matrix organization role is the sometimes conflicting demands of two bosses. For example, a representative from a manufacturing plant on a business team may know that his plant is having profitability problems and that the last thing the plant manager wants is to disrupt ongoing production activities with developmental work such as making samples or experimenting with a new process. Yet, as a business team member, the plant's representative may see the importance of doing these things immediately to achieve project success.

In this situation the individual in a 2-boss position experiences a great deal of anxiety and stress. These come from the difficulties of weighing the conflicting interests of his function and his project team. Both have legitimate viewpoints. But which is the more important viewpoint from the perspective of the whole organization? This is not an easy question to answer or an easy conflict to resolve. But added to this are the questions of identification and loyalty to the individual's function or business team and the consequences of rejection or even punishment from the side of the matrix organization that perceives it has lost in a given conflict. To compound the problem, even if the plant representative on a project team decides that he needs to go against what he knows is in the interest of his plant, how does he communicate this back to his organization members and convince them of the merits of his views? The same problem would exist if he were to favor his functional orientation and have to persuade the team that sample runs will have to be delayed.

We can see from this description and the earlier discussion that there are problems of dual group membership—new demands for communication, uncertainty about the kinds of commitment that can be made, uncertainties about how to influence other people in the function or team, and uncertainties created by a more generalist orientation not demanded in a conventional functional organization. There are of course differences in the capacity of individuals to deal with ambiguity, but all individuals new to matrix management lack some of the knowledge and the skills needed to navigate through the ambiguities and conflicts generated by a matrix organization.

Remember that this manager is also at the apex of his or her own pyramid—subordinates to this role need not be shared. It is the multiple demands from above and beyond the immediate command that must be managed. But his approach, to be successful, must be no different from that of the top role: Both must pay heed to competing demands, make trade-offs, and manage the conflicts that cannot be resolved. Any skillful politician knows that alternative sources of power increase one's flexibility. It is the unimaginative 2-boss manager who would trade extra degrees of freedom for finite and singular sources of action.

One operating manual for this role, developed after about a year's experience in a matrix organization, included the following points in a section titled "Practices for Managing Matrix Relationships":

- Lobby actively with relevant 2-boss counterparts and with your matrix bosses to win support before the event.
- Understand the other side's position in order to determine where trade-offs can be negotiated; understand where your objectives overlap.
- Avoid absolutes.
- Negotiate to win support on key issues that are critical to accomplishing your goals; try to yield only to the less critical points.
- Maintain frequent contact with top leadership to avoid surprises.
- Assume an active leadership role in all committees and use this to educate other matrix players; share information/help interpret.
- Prepare more thoroughly before entering any key negotiation than you would in nonmatrix situations; and use third-party experts more than normally.
- Strike bilateral agreements prior to meetings to disarm potential opponents.
- Emphasize and play on the supportive role that each of your matrix bosses can provide for the other.
- If all else fails:
    a. You can consider escalation (going up another level to the boss-in-common).
    b. You can threaten escalation.
    c. You can escalate.
- Before traveling this road, however, consider your timing. How much testing and negotiating should be done before calling for senior support? Does the top leadership want to be involved? When will they support and encourage your approach? Does escalation represent failure?

This kind of advice relies on managerial behavior, not on organization structure, for success. It sees personal style and influence as more important than power derived from either position or specialized knowledge. Success flows from facilitating decisions more than it does from making them. To remain flexible in this managerial role, it suggests, the manager must minimize the formal elements, move from fixture to actor, from bureaucracy to process.

The role problems of the 2-boss manager can of course become manageable in a mature matrix organization. This happens primarily because for the most part the functional and business managers learn to avoid making irreconcilable demands of their shared subordinates. This will still happen on occasion, however, even in a smoothly functioning matrix organization. In a familiar instance, the 2-boss manager may be directed to be in two places at the same time.

In addition to a balanced structure and shared roles, a matrix organization should have mechanisms for processing information along overlapping dimensions simultaneously. In a product-area matrix organization, a way of dealing with such situations is to establish the norm that the 2-boss individual is expected, and even directed, to convene a meeting between his two bosses to resolve any such conflict. The 2-boss manager is reprimanded only if he suffers such a conflict in silence.

Beyond handling such occasional problems, the 2-boss manager learns in a mature matrix organization that his role gives him a degree of influence not usually experienced at his level in a conventional organization. He not infrequently finds himself striking a balance in a discussion with his two bosses over some point of conflict. If he knows his facts and expresses his judgment on the merits of the particular issue, he often finds it is taken very seriously. This is the heart of training for general management.

This is exactly how the matrix organization is intended to work—with decisions being made at a level where the relevant information is concentrated and where time is available for a thorough airing of the options. In such a framework a higher percentage of decisions will, in fact, be given careful attention and decided on for their unique merits rather than in terms of a single orientation.

In reviewing the general characteristics of the mature matrix organization, we have emphasized the quality of flexibility. By looking in some detail at the four roles unique to the matrix, we have discovered where that flexibility comes from—from the individuals in key roles who have been challenged by the matrix structure to respond to each new situation in a fresh and flexible fashion. This constant pressure for fresh thinking and for learning in the mature matrix organization has, in fact, seemed to greatly increase the organization's productivity, especially at middle management levels. This may be fine for the organization, but how about the individuals as they initially face new and demanding role expectations? Is this a problem or an opportunity? In most cases it is probably both.

The Future of the Mature Matrix

A matrix organization includes matrix behavior, matrix systems, and a matrix culture, as well as a matrix structure. After years of working with a matrix, some organizations find that they no longer need the contradictory architecture of the matrix structure to accomplish their goals. Instead, they revert to the simpler pyramid for their structural form, while at the same time retaining the dual or multiple perspective in their managerial behavior, in their information processing, and in the culture of their firms.

This interpretation suggests that the matrix organization is not likely to become the dominant feature in the *structure* of American organizations. Its utility is more likely to be in helping organizations become more flexible in their responses to environmental pressures. Structures are intended to channel people's behavior in desired ways. Like laws, they are strongest when they are not invoked or tested. To the extent that managers behave effectively, they have little need to bump up against formal structures and reporting walls. In traditional pyramids, managers were always bumping against something—either the structure was centralized, and there wasn't enough freedom, or it was decentralized, and there wasn't enough control.

Organizations with mature matrix structures therefore appear to follow one of two paths, and the extent to which the structural framework survives depends on the path an organization takes. One is to maintain dual command, shared use of human resources, and an enriched information-processing capacity. The other is to maintain matrix behavior, matrix systems, and a matrix style or culture, but without using the matrix's structural form. Some organizations tear down the matrix entirely and revert to the traditional forms, practices, and managerial behavior of the pyramid.

The distinction between a pathological breakdown and an evolutionary rotation, where the matrix is a transitional form, is a matter of interpretation. As we observe the change in these organizations we may ask, was the matrix thrown out or did the firm grow beyond it? The distinction is more than academic. As long as the environmental pressures that initially propelled an organization into a matrix structure remain, the original inadequacies of the pyramid form will reappear if the matrix structure is actually abandoned. Our observations suggest that this would be fairly evident in three to six months and painfully obvious within one to one and a half years.

Because the structural element of the matrix is fo fiendishly difficult to many, we observe organizations trying to shed the form while maintaining the substance. Our diagnosis is that it can be done successfully only where appropriate matrix behavior is so internalized by all significant members that no one notices the structural shift. Even then, however, we anticipate that through the years the structural imbalances will increase.

Where We Stand on the Learning Curve

Not too many years ago few managers in our classrooms had heard of matrix organization, and today nearly half of them raise their hands when asked whether they work in a matrix organization. Objectively, this self-reporting is inaccurate. What is relevant, however, is the perception itself. Like Molière's gentleman who was surprised to learn that he had been speaking prose all his life, many managers find that they have been "matrixing" all along. The word is jargon, but the grammar connotes people's behavior more than the form of their organization. The unrealistically high self-reporting also demonstrates an increasing comfort and familiarity with the idea among a very large body of executives.

Our major purposes have been to broaden traditional treatments of the matrix structure by demonstrating its applicability in diverse settings and by suggesting ways to change a seemingly radical conception into a familiar and legitimate design. The matrix structure seems to have spread despite itself. It is complex and difficult; it requires human flexibility in order to provide organizational flexibility. But the reverse is also true. For these reasons, we believe, many managers shied away. The academic literature, until now, has limited the utility of the matrix structure to high-technology project organizations. We have shown how both in organization theory and in application, the matrix structure has a much broader applicability. Behavioral descriptions were replete with words like "tension," "conflict," and "confusion." For many it was not pleasant, but it seemed to improve performance. Success gave it legitimacy, and as the concept spread, familiarity seemed to reduce the resistance.

Matrix structure gained acceptance in the space age of the late 1960s. In fact, for a while in the early 1970s it almost seemed to be a fad. Organizations that should never have used it experimented with the form. It was in danger of becoming another hot item from the behavioral science grab bag for business. When this occurred, the results were usually disastrous, thus fueling the sense that if an organization played with the matrix structure it might easily get burned. Despite many misadventures, however, the matrix structure gained respectability. What was necessary was made desirable.

More organizations are feeling the pressure to respond to two or more critical aspects of their businesses simultaneously—that is, to consider and organize by function *and* by product, by service *and* by market area at the same time. There is also increasing pressure to improve information-processing capacity, and recent technological advances make multiple matrix systems feasible. Last, it is clear that there is an increased sense of the scarcity of all resources and hence pressures for achieving economies of scale. As we described, these were the necessary and sufficient conditions for the emergence of matrix organizations in the first place. Because these conditions are increasingly prevalent, we feel that more organizations will be forced to consider the matrix organizational form.

Each organization that turns to the matrix structure has a larger and more varied number of predecessors that have charted the way. Despite our belief that matrix structures must be grown from within, the examples of wider applicability must nevertheless suggest that we are dealing less and less with an experiment and more and more with a mature formulation in organization design. Familiarity, here, reduces fear. As more organizations travel up the matrix structure learning curve, the curve itself becomes an easier one to climb. Similarly, as more managers gain experience operating in matrix organizations they are bound to spread this experience as some of them move into other organizations on their career journeys.

When pioneers experiment with new forms of organization, the costs are high and there are usually many casualties. In the case of the matrix structure, this has been true for both organizations and individuals. As the matrix has become a more familiar alternative, however, the costs and pressures have been reduced. Today, we believe that the concept is no longer a radical one; the understanding of the design is widespread, and the economic and social benefits have increased.

People in the Middle Ages had a very clear view of the world order. Galileo changed that. Newton changed the view of universal order once more, and Einstein did too in a later age. In each period there was certainty of the logic and correctness of the structure of the universe. And each period lasted until a new formulation posed a previously unthinkable question. After varying periods of resistance or adjustment, people become comfortable with the new formulation and in each instance assume it to be the final word.

The organization of large numbers of people to accomplish uncertain, complex, and interdependent tasks is currently nowhere as susceptible to the same exactness in calculation as the physical world. And there are those who would say that to compare the world of physics and the world of organizations is to compare the sacred with the profane. But the process of acceptability and then increased applicability of new formulations is similar, even if rather more humble. We believe, therefore, that in the future, matrix organizations will become almost commonplace and that managers will speak less of the difficulties of the matrix structure and will take more of its advantages almost for granted.

Selected Bibliography

Chris Argyris's "Today's Problems with Tomorrow's Organizations" (*Journal of Management Studies,* February 1967, pp. 31–55) is an empirical study of nine British matrix organizations. The study is positive about the structure, but demonstrates how implementation has been unsuccessful because of traditional management behavioral styles. Arthur G. Butler's "Project Management: A Study in Organizational Conflict" (*Academy of Management Journal,* March 1973, pp. 8–101) contains an excellent review of the project management literature and deals extensively with the conflict faced by professionals involved in project work. David I. Cleland and William R. King's *Systems Analysis and Project Management* (McGraw-Hill, 1968) is one of the best and most thorough books available that explains project management and locates it in the larger setting of systems and organization theory. And Stanley M. Davis's "Two Models of Organization: Unity of Command versus Balance of Power" (*Sloan Management Review,* Fall 1974, pp. 29–40) spells out the basic theories and how they evolved in both domestic and international organizations.

Jay R. Galbraith's "Matrix Organization Design" (*Business Horizons,* February 1971, pp. 29–40) contains a fictitious case through which the author describes the decisions involved in adding a product orientation to a functional organization until an appropriate balance is reached. The article delimits the boundaries of matrix organization. William C. Goggin's "How the Multidimensional Structure Works at Dow-Corning" (*Harvard Business Review,* January–February 1974, pp. 54–65) is a case description of how Dow-Corning expanded a matrix form of organization into one that added an area dimension to the product and function areas plus a fourth dimension to consider organizational evolution. And Sherman K. Grinnell and Howard P. Apple's "When Two Bosses Are Better than One" (*Machine Design,* January 9, 1975, pp. 84–87) includes brief but practical guidelines on when to use a matrix organization and how to make it work.

Leonard R. Sayles's recent article in *Organizational Dynamics,* "Matrix Management: The Structure with a Future" (Autumn 1976, pp. 2–18), expresses a viewpoint similar to our own and has developed a suggestive typology that encompasses five different types of matrix structures.

Reading 4–3

From Control to Commitment in the Workplace*

Richard E. Walton

The larger shape of institutional change is always difficult to recognize when one stands right in the middle of it. Today, throughout American industry, a significant change is under way in long-established approaches to the organization and management of work. Although this shift in attitude and practice takes a wide variety of company-specific forms, its larger shape—its overall pattern—is already visible if one knows where and how to look.

Consider, for example, the marked differences between two plants in the chemical products division of a major U.S. corporation. Both make similar products and employ similar technologies, but that is virtually all they have in common.

The first, organized by businesses with an identifiable product or product line, divides its employees into self-supervising 10- to 15-person work teams that are collectively responsible for a set of related tasks. Each team member has the training to perform many or all of the tasks for which the team is accountable, and pay reflects the level of mastery of required skills. These teams have received assurances that management will go to extra lengths to provide continued employment in any economic downturn. The teams have also been thoroughly briefed on such issues as market share, product costs, and their implications for the business.

Not surprisingly, this plant is a top performer economically and rates well on all measures of employee satisfaction, absenteeism, turnover,

* Reprinted by permission of the *Harvard Business Review.* "From Control to Commitment in the Workplace" by Richard E. Walton (March/April 1985).

and safety. With its employees actively engaged in identifying and solving problems, it operates with fewer levels of management and fewer specialized departments than do its sister plants. It is also one of the principal suppliers of management talent for these other plants and for the division manufacturing staff.

In the second plant, each employee is responsible for a fixed job and is required to perform up to the minimum standard defined for that job. Peer pressure keeps new employees from exceeding the minimum standards and from taking other initiatives that go beyond basic job requirements. Supervisors, who manage daily assignments and monitor performance, have long since given up hope for anything more than compliance with standards, finding sufficient difficulty in getting their people to perform adequately most of the time. In fact, they and their workers try to prevent the industrial engineering department, which is under pressure from top plant management to improve operations, from using changes in methods to "jack up" standards.

A recent management campaign to document an "airtight case" against employees who have excessive absenteeism or subpar performance mirrors employees' low morale and high distrust of management. A constant stream of formal grievances, violations of plant rules, harassment of supervisors, wildcat walkouts, and even sabotage has prevented the plant from reaching its productivity and quality goals and has absorbed a disproportionate amount of division staff time. Dealings with the union are characterized by contract negotiations on economic matters and skirmishes over issues of management control.

No responsible manager, of course, would ever wish to encourage the kind of situation at this second plant, yet the determination to understand its deeper causes and to attack them at their root does not come easily. Established modes of doing things have an inertia all their own. Such an effort is, however, in process all across the industrial landscape. And with that effort comes the possibility of a revolution in industrial relations every bit as great as that occasioned by the rise of mass production the better part of a century ago. The challenge is clear to those managers willing to see it—and the potential benefits, enormous.

Approaches to Work Force Management

What explains the extraordinary differences between the plants just described? Is it that the first is new (built in 1976) and the other old? Yes and no. Not all new plants enjoy so fruitful an approach to work organization; not all older plants have such intractable problems. Is it that one plant is unionized and the other not? Again, yes and no. The presence of a union may institutionalize conflict and lackluster performance, but it seldom causes them.

At issue here is not so much age or unionization but two radically different strategies for managing a company's or a factory's work force, two incompatible views of what managers can reasonably expect of workers and of the kind of partnership they can share with them. For simplicity, I will speak of these profound differences as reflecting the choice between a strategy based on imposing *control* and a strategy based on eliciting *commitment*.

The "Control" Strategy

The traditional—or control-oriented—approach to work force management took shape during the early part of this century in response to the division of work into small, fixed jobs for which individuals could be held accountable. The actual definition of jobs, as of acceptable standards of performance, rested on "lowest common denominator" assumptions about workers' skill and motivation. To monitor and control effort of this assumed caliber, management organized its own responsibilities into a hierarchy of specialized roles buttressed by a top-down allocation of authority and by status symbols attached to positions in the hierarchy.

For workers, compensation followed the rubric of "a fair day's pay for a fair day's work" because precise evaluations were possible when individual job requirements were so carefully prescribed. Most managers had little doubt that labor was best thought of as a variable cost, although some exceptional companies guaranteed job security to head off unionization attempts.

In the traditional approach, there was generally little policy definition with regard to employee voice unless the work force was unionized, in which case damage control strategies predominated. With no union, management relied on an open-door policy, attitude surveys, and similar devices to learn about employees' concerns. If the work force was unionized, then management bargained terms of employment and established an appeal mechanism. These activities fell to labor relations specialists, who operated independently from line management and whose very existence assumed the inevitability and even the appropriateness of an adversarial relationship between workers and managers. Indeed, to those who saw management's exclusive obligation to be to a company's shareowners and the ownership of property to be the ultimate source of both obligation and prerogative, the claims of employees were constraints, nothing more.

At the heart of this traditional model is the wish to establish order, exercise control, and achieve efficiency in the application of the work force. Although it has distant antecedents in the bureaucracies of both church and military, the model's real father is Frederick W. Taylor, the turn-of-the-century "father of scientific management," whose views about the proper organization of work have long influenced management practice as well as the reactive policies of the U.S. labor movement.

Recently, however, changing expectations among workers have prompted a growing disillusionment with the apparatus of control. At the same time, of course, an intensified challenge from abroad has made the competitive obsolescence of this strategy clear. A model that assumes low employee commitment and that is designed to produce reliable if not outstanding performance simply cannot match the standards of excellence set by world-class competitors. Especially in a high-wage country like the United States, market success depends on a superior level of performance, a level that, in turn, requires the deep commitment, not merely the obedience—if you could obtain it—of workers. And as painful experience shows, this commitment cannot flourish in a workplace dominated by the familiar model of control.

The "Commitment" Strategy

Since the early 1970s, companies have experimented at the plant level with a radically different work force strategy. The more visible pioneers—among them, General Foods at Topeka, Kansas; General Motors at Brookhaven, Mississippi; Cummins Engine at Jamestown, New York; and Procter & Gamble at Lima, Ohio—have begun to show how great and productive the contribution of a truly committed work force can be. For a time, all new plants of this sort were nonunion, but by 1980 the success of efforts undertaken jointly with unions—GM's cooperation with the UAW at the Cadillac plant in Livonia, Michigan, for example—was impressive enough to encourage managers of both new and existing facilities to rethink their approach to the work force.

Stimulated in part by the dramatic turnaround at GM's Tarrytown assembly plant in the mid-1970s, local managers and union officials are increasingly talking about common interests, working to develop mutual trust, and agreeing to sponsor quality-of-work-life (QWL) or employee involvement (EI) activities. Although most of these ventures have been initiated at the local level, major exceptions include the joint effort between the Communication Workers of America and AT&T to promote QWL throughout the Bell System and the UAW–Ford EI program centrally directed by Donald Ephlin of the UAW and Peter Pestillo of Ford. In the nonunion sphere, the spirit of these new initiatives is evident in the decision by workers of Delta Airlines to show their commitment to the company by collecting money to buy a new plane.

More recently, a growing number of manufacturing companies have begun to remove levels of plant hierarchy, increase managers' spans of control, integrate quality and production activities at lower organizational levels, combine production and maintenance operations, and open up new career possibilities for workers. Some corporations have even begun to chart organizational renewal for the entire company. Cummins

Engine, for example, has ambitiously committed itself to inform employees about the business, to encourage participation by everyone, and to create jobs that involve greater responsibility and more flexibility.

In this new commitment-based approach to the work force, jobs are designed to be broader than before, to combine planning and implementation, and to include efforts to upgrade operations, not just maintain them. Individual responsibilities are expected to change as conditions change, and teams, not individuals, often are the organizational units accountable for performance. With management hierarchies relatively flat and differences in status minimized, control and lateral coordination depend on shared goals, and expertise rather than formal position determines influence.

People Express, to cite one example, started up with its management hierarchy limited to three levels, organized its work force into three- or four-person groups, and created positions with exceptionally broad scope. Every full-time employee is a "manager": Flight managers are pilots who also perform dispatching and safety checks; maintenance managers are technicians with other staff responsibilities; customer service managers take care of ticketing, security clearance, passenger boarding, and in-flight service. Everyone, including the officers, is expected to rotate among functions to boost all workers' understanding of the business and to promote personal development.

Under the commitment strategy, performance expectations are high and serve not to define minimum standards but to provide "stretch objectives," emphasize continuous improvement, and reflect the requirements of the marketplace. Accordingly, compensation policies reflect less the old formulas of job evaluation than the heightened importance of group achievement, the expanded scope of individual contribution, and the growing concern for such questions of "equity" as gain sharing, stock ownership, and profit sharing. This principle of economic sharing is not new. It has long played a role in Dana Corporation, which has many unionized plants, and is a fundamental part of the strategy of People Express, which has no union. Today, Ford sees it as an important part of the company's transition to a commitment strategy.

Equally important to the commitment strategy is the challenge of giving employees some assurance of security, perhaps by offering them priority in training and retraining as old jobs are eliminated and new ones created. Guaranteeing employees access to due process and providing them the means to be heard on such issues as production methods, problem solving, and human resource policies and practices is also a challenge. In unionized settings, the additional tasks include making relations less adversarial, broadening the agenda for joint problem solving and planning, and facilitating employee consultation.

Underlying all these policies is a management philosophy, often embodied in a published statement, that acknowledges the legitimate claims of a company's multiple stakeholders—owners, employees, customers, and the public. At the center of this philosophy is a belief that eliciting employee commitment will lead to enhanced performance. The evidence shows this belief to be well grounded. In the absence of genuine commitment, however, new management policies designed for a committed work force may well leave a company distinctly more vulnerable than would older policies based on the control approach. The advantages—and risks—are considerable.

The Costs of Commitment

Because the potential leverage of a commitment-oriented strategy on performance is so great, the natural temptation is to assume the universal applicability of that strategy. Some environments, however, especially those requiring intricate teamwork, problem solving, organizational learning, and self-monitoring, are better suited than others to the commitment model. Indeed, the pioneers of the deep-commitment strategy—a fertilizer plant in Norway, a refinery in the United Kingdom, a paper mill in Pennsylvania, a pet-food processing plant in Kansas—were all based on continuous-process technologies and were all capital and raw material intensive. All provided high economic leverage to improvements in workers' skills and attitudes, and all could offer considerable job challenge.

Is the converse true? Is the control strategy appropriate whenever—as with convicts breaking rocks with sledgehammers in a prison yard—work can be completely prescribed, remains static, and calls for individual, not group, effort? In practice, managers have long answered yes. Mass production, epitomized by the assembly line, has for years been thought suitable for old-fashioned control.

But not any longer. Many mass producers, not least the automakers, have recently been trying to reconceive the structure of work and to give employees a significant role in solving problems and improving methods. Why? For many reasons, including to boost in-plant quality, lower warranty costs, cut waste, raise machine utilization and total capacity with the same plant and equipment, reduce operating and support personnel, reduce turnover and absenteeism, and speed up implementation of change. In addition, some managers place direct value on the fact that the commitment policies promote the development of human skills and individual self-esteem.

The benefits, economic and human, of worker commitment extend not only to continuous-process industries but to traditional manufacturing industries as well. What, though, are the costs? To achieve these gains, managers have had to invest extra effort, develop new skills and relationships, cope with higher levels of ambiguity and uncertainty, and experience the pain and discomfort associated with changing habits and attitudes. Some of their skills have become obsolete, and some of their careers have been casualties of change. Union officials, too, have had to face the dislocation and discomfort that inevitably follow any upheaval in attitudes and skills. For their part, workers have inherited more responsibility and, along with it, greater uncertainty and a more open-ended possibility of failure.

Part of the difficulty in assessing these costs is the fact that so many of the following problems inherent to the commitment strategy remain to be solved.

Employment Assurances

As managers in heavy industry confront economic realities that make such assurances less feasible and as their counterparts in fiercely competitive high-technology areas are forced to rethink early guarantees of employment security, pointed questions await.

Will managers give lifetime assurances to the few—those who reach, say, 15 years' seniority—or will they adopt a general no-layoff policy? Will they demonstrate by policies and practices that employment security, though by no means absolute, is a higher priority item than it was under the control approach? Will they accept greater responsibility for outplacement?

Compensation

In one sense, the more productive employees under the commitment approach deserve to receive better pay for their better efforts, but how can managers balance this claim on resources with the harsh reality that domestic pay rates have risen to levels that render many of our industries uncompetitive internationally? Already, in such industries as trucking and airlines, new domestic competitors have placed companies that maintain prevailing wage rates at a significant disadvantage. Experience shows, however, that wage freezes and concession bargaining create obstacles to commitment, and new approaches to compensation are difficult to develop at a time when management cannot raise the overall level of pay.

Which approach is really suitable to the commitment model is unclear. Traditional job classifications place limits on the discretion of supervisors and encourage workers' sense of job ownership. Can pay systems based on employees' skill levels, which have long been used in engineering and skilled crafts, prove widely effective? Can these systems make up in greater mastery, positive motivation, and work force flexibility what they give away in higher average wages?

In capital-intensive businesses, where total payroll accounts for a small percentage of costs, economics favor the move toward pay progression based on deeper and broader mastery. Still, conceptual problems remain with measuring skills, achieving consistency in pay decisions, allocating opportunities for learning new skills, trading off breadth and flexibility against depth, and handling the effects of "topping out" in a system that rewards and encourages personal growth.

There are also practical difficulties. Existing plants cannot, for example, convert to a skill-based structure overnight because of the vested interests of employees in the higher classifications. Similarly, formal profit- or gain-sharing plans like the Scanlon Plan (which shares gains in productivity as measured by improvements in the ratio of payroll to the sales value of production) cannot always operate. At the plant level, formulas that are responsive to what employees can influence, that are not unduly influenced by factors beyond their control, and that are readily understood, are not easy to devise. Small stand-alone businesses with a mature technology and stable markets tend to find the task least troublesome, but they are not the only ones trying to implement the commitment approach.

Yet another problem, very much at issue in the Hyatt-Clark bearing plant, which employees purchased from General Motors in 1981, is the relationship between compensation decisions affecting salaried managers and professionals, on the one hand, and hourly workers, on the other. When they formed the company, workers took a 25 percent pay cut to make their bearings competitive but the managers maintained and, in certain instances increased, their own salaries in order to help the company attract and retain critical talent. A manager's ability to elicit and preserve commitment, however, is sensitive to issues of equity, as became evident once again when GM and Ford announced huge executive bonuses in the spring of 1984 while keeping hourly wages capped.

Technology

Computer-based technology can reinforce the control model or facilitate movement to the commitment model. Applications can narrow the scope of jobs or broaden them, emphasize the individual nature of tasks or promote the work of groups, centralize or decentralize the making of decisions, and create performance measures that emphasize learning or hierarchical control.

To date, the effects of this technology on control and commitment have been largely unintentional and unexpected. Even in organizations otherwise pursuing a commitment strategy, managers have rarely appreciated that the side effects of technology are not somehow "given" in the nature of things or that they can be actively managed. In fact, computer-based technology may be the least deterministic, most flexible technology to enter the workplace since the industrial revolution. As it becomes less hardware dependent and more software intensive and as the cost of computer power declines, the variety of ways to meet business requirements expands, each with a different set of human implications. Management has yet to identify the potential role of technology policy in the commitment strategy, and it has yet to invent concepts and methods to realize that potential.

Supervisors

The commitment model requires first-line supervisors to facilitate rather than direct the work force, to impart rather than merely practice their technical and administrative expertise, and to help workers develop the ability to manage themselves. In practice, supervisors are to delegate away most of their traditional functions—often without having received adequate training and support for their new team-building tasks or having their own needs for voice, dignity, and fulfillment recognized.

These dilemmas are even visible in the new titles many supervisors carry—"team advisers" or "team consultants," for example—most of which imply that supervisors are not in the chain of command, although they are expected to be directive if necessary and assume functions delegated to the work force if they are not being performed. Part of the confusion here is the failure to distinguish the behavioral style required of supervisors from the basic responsibilities assigned them. Their ideal style may be advisory, but their responsibilities are to achieve certain human and economic outcomes. With experience, however, as first-line managers become more comfortable with the notion of delegating what subordinates are ready and able to perform, the problem will diminish.

Other difficulties are less tractable. The new breed of supervisors must have a level of interpersonal skill and conceptual ability often lacking in the present supervisory work force. Some companies have tried to address this lack by using the position as an entry point to management for college graduates. This approach may succeed where the work force has already acquired the necessary technical expertise, but it blocks a route of advancement for workers and sharpens the dividing line between management and other employees. Moreover, unless the company intends to open up higher-level positions for these college-educated supervisors, they may well grow impatient with the shift work of first-line supervision.

Even when new supervisory roles are filled—and filled successfully—from the ranks, dilemmas remain. With teams developed and functions delegated, to what new challenges do they turn to utilize fully their own capabilities? Do those capabilities match the demands of the other managerial work they might take on? If fewer and fewer supervisors are required as their individual span of control extends to a second and a third work team, what promotional opportunities exist for the rest? Where do they go?

Union-Management Relations

Some companies, as they move from control to commitment, seek to decertify their unions and, at the same time, strengthen their employees' bond to the company. Others—like GM, Ford, Jones & Laughlin, and AT&T—pursue cooperation with their unions, believing that they need their active support. Management's interest in cooperation intensified in the late 1970s, as improved work force effectiveness could not by itself close the competitive gap in many industries and wage concessions became necessary. Based on their own analysis of competitive conditions, unions sometimes agreed to these concessions but expanded their influence over matters previously subject to management control.

These developments open up new questions. Where companies are trying to preserve the nonunion status of some plants and yet promote collaborative union relations in others, will unions increasingly force the company to choose? After General Motors saw the potential of its joint QWL program with the UAW, it signed a neutrality clause (in 1976) and then an understanding about automatic recognition in new plants (in 1979). If forced to choose, what will other managements do? Further, where union and management have collaborated in promoting QWL, how can the union prevent management from using the program to appeal directly to the workers about issues, such as wage concessions, that are subject to collective bargaining?

And if, in the spirit of mutuality, both sides agree to expand their joint agenda, what new risks will they face? Do union officials have the expertise to deal effectively with new agenda items like investment, pricing, and technology? To support QWL activities, they already have had to expand their skills and commit substantial resources at a time when shrinking employment has reduced their membership and thus their finances.

The Transitional Stage

Although some organizations have adopted a comprehensive version of the commitment approach, most initially take on a more limited set of changes, which I refer to as a "transitional" stage or approach. The challenge here is to modify expectations, to make credible the leaders' stated intentions for further movement, and to support the initial changes in behavior. These transitional efforts can achieve a temporary equilibrium, provided they are viewed as part of a movement toward a comprehensive commitment strategy.

The cornerstone of the transitional stage is the voluntary participation of employees in problem-solving groups like quality circles. In unionized organizations, union-management dialogue leading to a jointly sponsored program is a condition for this type of employee involvement, which must then be supported by additional training and communication and

Exhibit 1
Work Force Strategies

	Control	Transitional	Commitment
Job design principles	Individual attention limited to performing individual job.	Scope of individual responsibility extended to upgrading system performance, via participative problem-solving groups in QWL, EI, and quality-circle programs.	Individual responsibility extended to upgrading system performance.
	Job design deskills and fragments work and separates doing and thinking.	No change in traditional job design or accountability.	Job design enhances content of work, emphasizes whole task, and combines doing and thinking.
	Accountability focused on individual.		Frequent use of teams as basic accountable unit.
	Fixed job definition.		Flexible definition of duties, contingent on changing conditions.
Performance expectations	Measured standards define minimum performance. Stability seen as desirable.		Emphasis placed on higher, "stretch objectives," which tend to be dynamic and oriented to the marketplace.
Management organization: structure, systems, and style	Structure tends to be layered, with top-down controls.	No basic changes in approaches to structure, control, or authority.	Flat organization structure with mutual influence systems.
	Coordination and control rely on rules and procedures.		Coordination and control based more on shared goals, values, and traditions.
	More emphasis on prerogatives and positional authority.		Management emphasis on problem solving and relevant information and expertise.
	Status symbols distributed to reinforce hierarchy.	A few visible symbols change.	Minimum status differentials to deemphasize inherent hierarchy.

Compensation policies	Variable pay where feasible to provide individual incentive.	Typically no basic changes in compensation concepts.	Variable rewards to create equity and to reinforce group achievements: gain sharing, profit sharing.
	Individual pay geared to job evaluation.		Individual pay linked to skills and mastery.
	In downturn, cuts concentrated on hourly payroll.	Equality of sacrifice among employee groups.	Equality of sacrifice.
Employment assurances	Employees regarded as variable costs.	Assurances that participation will not result in loss of job.	Assurances that participation will not result in loss of job.
		Extra effort to avoid layoffs.	High commitment to avoid or assist in reemployment.
			Priority for training and retaining existing work force.
Employee-voice policies	Employee input allowed on relatively narrow agenda. Attendant risks emphasized. Methods include open-door policy, attitude surveys, grievance procedures, and collective bargaining in some organizations.	Addition of limited, ad hoc consultation mechanisms. No change in corporate governance.	Employee participation encouraged on wide range of issues. Attendant benefits emphasized. New concepts of corporate governance.
	Business information distributed on strictly defined, "need to know" basis.	Additional sharing of information.	Business data shared widely.
Labor-management relations	Adversarial labor relations; emphasis on interest conflict.	Thawing of adversarial attitudes; joint sponsorship of QWL or EI; emphasis on common fate.	Mutuality in labor relations; joint planning and problem solving on expanded agenda.
			Unions, management, and workers redefine their respective roles.

by a shift in management style. Managers must also seek ways to consult employees about changes that affect them and to assure them that management will make every effort to avoid, defer, or minimize layoffs from higher productivity. When volume-related layoffs or concessions on pay are unavoidable, the principle of "equality of sacrifice" must apply to all employee groups, not just the hourly work force.

As a rule, during the early stages of transformation, few immediate changes can occur in the basic design of jobs, the compensation system, or the management system itself. It is easy, of course, to attempt to change too much too soon. A more common error, especially in established organizations, is to make only "token" changes that never reach a critical mass. All too often managers try a succession of technique-oriented changes one by one: job enrichment, sensitivity training, management by objectives, group brainstorming, quality circles, and so on. Whatever the benefits of these techniques, their value to the organization will rapidly decay if the management philosophy—and practice—does not shift accordingly.

A different type of error—"overreaching"—may occur in newly established organizations based on commitment principles. In one new plant, managers allowed too much peer influence in pay decisions; in another, they underplayed the role of first-line supervisors as a link in the chain of command; in a third, they overemphasized learning of new skills and flexibility at the expense of mastery in critical operations. These design errors by themselves are not fatal, but the organization must be able to make midcourse corrections.

Rate of Transformation

How rapidly is the transformation in work force strategy, summarized in Exhibit 1 occurring? Hard data are difficult to come by, but certain trends are clear. In 1970, only a few plants in the United States were systematically revising their approach to the work force. By 1975, hundreds of plants were involved. Today, I estimate that at least a thousand plants are in the process of making a comprehensive change and that many times that number are somewhere in the transitional stage.

In the early 1970s, plant managers tended to sponsor what efforts there were. Today, company presidents are formulating the plans. Not long ago, the initiatives were experimental; now they are policy. Early change focused on the blue-collar work force and on those clerical operations that most closely resemble the factory. Although clerical change has lagged somewhat—because the control model has not produced such overt employee disaffection, and because management has been slow to recognize the importance of quality and productivity improvement—there are signs of a quickened pace of change in clerical operations.

Only a small fraction of U.S. workplaces today can boast of a comprehensive commitment strategy, but the rate of transformation continues to accelerate, and the move toward commitment via some explicit transitional stage extends to a still larger number of plants and offices. This transformation may be fueled by economic necessity, but other factors are shaping and pacing it—individual leadership in management and labor, philosophical choices, organizational competence in managing change, and cumulative learning from change itself.

Suggested Readings

Irving Bluestone, "Labor's Stake in Improving the Quality of Working Life," *The Quality of Working Life and the 1980s,* ed. Harvey Kolodny and Hans van Beinum (New York: Praeger Publishers, 1983).

Robert H. Guest, "Quality of Work Life—Learning from Tarrytown," *Harvard Business Review,* July–August 1979, p. 76.

Janice A. Klein, "Why Supervisors Resist Employee Involvement," *Harvard Business Review,* September–October 1984, p. 87.

John F. Runcie, " 'By Days I Make the Cars'," *Harvard Business Review,* May–June 1980, p. 106.

W. Earl Sasser and Frank S. Leonard, "Let First-Level Supervisors Do Their Job," *Harvard Business Review,* March–April 1980, p. 113.

Leonard A. Schlesinger and Janice A. Klein, "The First-Line Supervisor: Past, Present and Future," *Handbook of Organizational Behavior,* ed. Jay W. Lorsch (Englewood Cliffs, N.J.: Prentice-Hall, 1983).

Richard E. Walton, "Work Innovations in the United States," *Harvard Business Review,* July–August 1979, p. 88; "Improving the Quality of Work Life," *Harvard Business Review,* May–June 1974, p. 12; "How to Counter Alienation in the Plant," *Harvard Business Review,* November–December 1972, p. 70.

Richard E. Walton and Wendy Vittori, "New Information Technology: Organizational Problem or Opportunity?" *Office: Technology and People,* No. 1, 1983, p. 249.

Richard E. Walton and Leonard A. Schlesinger, "Do Supervisors Thrive in Participative Work Systems?" *Organizational Dynamics,* Winter 1979, p. 25.

Part Three

In this part, our scope of attention once again expands, this time to multibusiness and multinational corporations.

As the cases illustrate, the size, product/market diversity, and geographical dispersion of multibusiness and multinational companies all contribute to presenting managers with organizational issues which can be different from, and often more complex than, those addressed in earlier parts. However, as the text demonstrates, the basic conceptual framework introduced in Parts One and Two can be applied to multibusiness and multinational companies as well.

Chapter 5

Organizing Human Resources for Multibusiness and Multinational Companies

Because of their greater size, the greater diversity of their products and markets, and their greater geographical dispersion, multibusiness and multinational companies face organizational problems that are somewhat different from, and often more complex than, those faced by single businesses. For example, many companies included in the *Fortune* 500 list of largest industrial corporations operate in dozens of different countries, making and selling hundreds of different products through an organization staffed by thousands of people. In doing so, these companies must deal with questions such as:

- How can we coordinate and control our divisions and subsidiaries when no one has the necessary breadth of experience and knowledge to fully understand our diverse businesses?
- How can we simultaneously cope with the need to adapt our major product lines to the unique cultural and marketing characteristics of each country we operate in, as well as the need to achieve economies of scale worldwide and to coordinate all of our new-product development efforts?
- How can we make sure that our many dispersed employees do not misuse our significant economic power?

Throughout this chapter we will discuss these and other questions related to organizational issues in multibusiness and multinational companies. Initially, however, we will attempt to show that despite differences in size, product/market diversity, and geographical spread, the basic approach of organization design in single businesses can be applied to multibusiness and multinational companies as well.[1]

The Three Design Questions

Question 1: Drawing Subunit Boundaries

Just as in single businesses, in drawing subunit boundaries for multibusiness and multinational firms, one needs to consider the diversity and interdependence of the activities the coporation is engaged in; the tradeoff between the gains of specialization and economies of scale that can occur within subunit boundaries; and the costs of establishing these subunits and integrating across their boundaries.

For example, in one large multinational company, the president's staff reviewed its organization in 1970 in response to numerous complaints and problems within its European operations. Specifically, after an initial period of success in Europe, the company was having great difficulty penetrating new and larger markets. The staff report concluded that its functional organization in Europe should be changed to a national organization—that is, its major subunit boundaries should include all activities within a country and not all European activities associated with particular functions, such as manufacturing and marketing. Their rationale, in summary, was the following:

> *When we originally established the European organization, our sales were $10 million. Today they are $300 million. Back then we had to organize Europe by functions because we couldn't afford any other option—our sales just would not support separate manufacturing facilities and sales forces in each country. But today we can afford a country-by-country organization, and we desperately need one. The cultural, economic, and legal conditions in each European country are different. Our current organization serves none of these differences very well. We need an organization that can sell a French variation of our product with a French sales force, for example. If we organize our European operation by countries, we can achieve this.*

In another moderate-sized ($700 million in sales) American multibusiness company, a second type of boundary choice problem arose in 1975 regarding long-range planning activities. The chairman of the board believed that the company had grown to the point where it managed a very large amount of assets for its stockholders and that it had a duty to do some long-range thinking (10–20 years) to protect those assets. This raised the question of where the long-range planning activity should

[1] We are really talking about three different types of companies in this chapter: domestic multibusiness, single-product multinational, and multiproduct multinational. Although one could devote a chapter to each, as we have done with domestic single-product companies, that is beyond the scope of this book.

be carried out. While one executive suggested that long-range planning should be included in all management jobs—that is, that a special function or set of functions should not be created—the suggestion was quickly disregarded. Almost everyone agreed that the long-range planning task was sufficiently different from most of the tasks managers did that it would not be carried out very well, if at all, by line managers. Two options then emerged. In the first, a special long-range planning function would reside at the divisional level. Operationally, that meant a staff person would report to each of the company's six division managers. Their efforts would be coordinated by a planner who reported to the president. In the second option, a corporate long-range planning subunit would be created and staffed with seven planners reporting to the president. This latter arrangement was eventually chosen because "the advantages to be gained by having long-range planning better integrated into operating divisions were more than offset, we felt, by the need for a group of a certain minimum size—that is, a group that could include a Ph.D. economist, a political scientist, a professional planner, and so on."

Because the situations are sometimes more complex than in single-business contexts, judgments about where to draw subunit boundaries can be more difficult in multibusiness and multinational firms. Nevertheless, the process is the same in both cases.

Question 2: Organizing within Subunits

The major subunits of multibusiness organizations are usually single-product companies themselves or groups of such companies. (You will recall that a number of the cases in Part Two concerned divisions of multibusiness companies.) The major subunits of multinational companies are sometimes single-business companies and sometimes functional units or geographical organizations. We have already dealt with the question of internally organizing these units in Part One (subunits specialized by function, area, or product) and Part Two (single-business companies).

An example will help demonstrate the applicability of these approaches to an international setting. Consider a company that makes and sells about $20 million a year in specialized electrical equipment. In 1969 it was organized functionally (see Figure 5–1).

When establishing a fourth geographical subunit in the international department, the sales manager had to deal with the following types of decisions:

Should I hire local nationals as salespeople, and train them as best I can? Or should I bring in some of our experienced salespeople from other countries? (He decided the sales task required salespeople to be from the same culture as the buyer, so he hired local nationals and trained them.)

Should I compensate the sales force at the local wage rate and risk upsetting them when they learn how much more their colleagues in the other areas get?

Figure 5–1

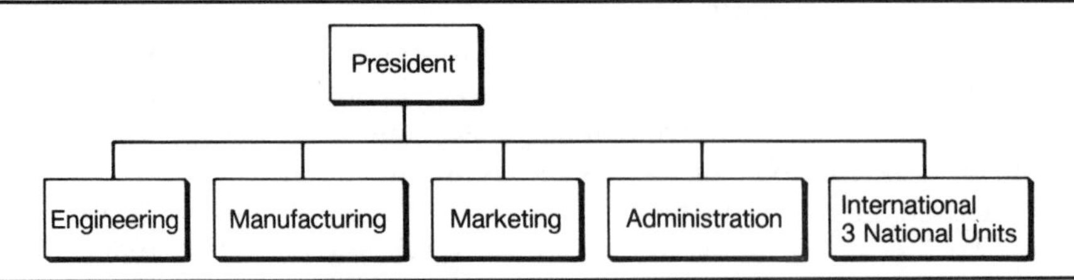

Or should I hire them at a higher rate and accept the direct economic consequences? (He decided to set the base salaries above local wages but below salaries for his salespeople in other areas.)

How can I best deal with the culturally based reluctance of most of the nationals to be away from their homes on sales trips? (He eventually decided to draw small sales territories for six salespersons in the six most densely populated areas, which contained about 85 percent of all potential buyers. He then hired six people, each of whom lived within one of the six territories. Thus overnight travel was not necessary.)

Regardless of the setting, the key to organizing effectively within subunits is a thorough knowledge of the tasks (or the business) and the employees (or the organization) involved, as well as the organizational design tools that can be used. In multibusiness settings, this means understanding a diverse set of businesses. And in multinational settings, this usually means understanding a diverse group of people and cultures.[2]

Question 3: Integrating the Subunits

Essentially the same integrating devices that are used by single-business companies are also used by multibusiness and multinational companies. For example, to integrate its 12 product/market divisions, one multibusiness company relies on:

1. Three key positions in the management hierarchy, called group vice presidents. These managers, who are stationed at corporate headquarters, each have four divisions reporting to them.
2. Goals and plans jointly agreed on each year by corporate headquarters and each of the divisions.
3. A corporate staff that helps the company's president and group vice presidents examine divisions' plans and establish reasonable goals.

---

[2] For a discussion of the importance of understanding foreign work forces and some of the common problems managers face in doing so, see David Sirota and J. Michael Greenwood, "Understanding Your Overseas Work Force," *Harvard Business Review*, January–February 1971, pp. 53–60.

4. A monthly meeting of division managers, group vice presidents, the president, and some of the corporate staff to review results to date.
5. A financial measurement system that focuses on each division separately and the company as a whole.
6. A compensation system that rewards division managers for both corporate and divisional results.

Just as in the case of a single-business company, the problem of integration is probably the one organizational issue that most plagues multibusiness and multinational managers, despite the fact that subunits in multiproduct and multinational firms are often much less interdependent than the subunits in a typical domestic single-product company. The large volumes of complex information that must move among subunits can sometimes make the nature of the interdependencies very complex. But more important, the high degree of subunit differentiation caused by the diverse products, markets, and cultures these organizations deal with, in addition to the large number of employees involved and their geographical dispersion, all make achieving effective integration very difficult.

Organizational Problems Caused by High Diversity, Large Size, and Geographical Dispersion

In a typical multibusiness organization the problem of achieving effective integration among the subparts operationally means getting thousands of people—most of whom are thousands of miles apart and have never met each other, and none of whom really understand all of the businesses the others are involved in—to behave in ways that facilitate the achievement of corporate goals.[3]

Consider, for example, the case of a diversified American corporation that acquired its first consumer goods manufacturing business. The acquisition came into the company as a division reporting to a group vice president, but since no one at corporate headquarters knew much about this new business, it operated with a fairly high degree of autonomy (a fact which some other division managers quickly spotted and resented). The new division was required to report financial results monthly and for the first 12 months met its sales and profit objectives each month. In the 13th month, however, sales were off 20 percent, and profits were down 35 percent.

The group vice president in charge of the new division requested an immediate report from the division manager outlining the reasons

[3] See R. N. Anthony and J. Dearden, *Management Control Systems,* 3d ed. (Homewood, Ill.: Richard D. Irwin, 1976), chap. 8.

for the declining sales and profits as well as corrective actions being taken. The report arrived three weeks later and satisfied neither the group vice president nor those on the corporate staff who read it. The group vice president asked for a more detailed report. Before this report arrived, the next month's financial figures reported that sales were off 25 percent and profits were wiped out completely. The corporation's president became very concerned at this point because he felt the division's performance could cause the company to miss its overall profit goals for the year. He urged the group vice president to take more aggressive action, so the group vice president and five other corporate staff people immediately went to visit the division. The division manager and his staff resented the "interference" and indicated that they were doing the best they could to deal with an unusual situation; and they were reluctant to talk with the corporate staff. Division and corporate staff did negotiate a new budget as well as a set of specific actions the division manager was to take. The next financial report showed that the division almost broke even; yet the following month it again lost a large amount of money. The corporate president thereupon fired the division manager and replaced him.

The new division manager encountered a variety of unexpected problems. He quickly discovered that his background with the company's other manufacturing divisions had not adequately prepared him to understand this division's business; he found he would have to go through a learning period. He also found a company culture that was very different from those in his past experiences. Meanwhile, the division continued to lose money. The losses increased when another of the company's divisions pulled out of a joint venture, leaving the troubled division with excess capacity in a partially built facility. Despite pressure from the corporation's president, the other division refused to have anything to do with what they referred to as a "snake pit."

After 16 months the corporation did get this situation under control. But the cost was high, even in corporate terms. Although this example illustrates problems resulting from an acquisition, they typify the type of control and collaboration issues that business diversity can cause in multibusiness organizations.

Multinational organizations can sometimes operate in even more diverse environments than the one just illustrated. Not only do they often have considerable product diversity, they also must cope with cultural and legal diversity.[4] Successful integration within and among prod-

---

[4] For example, many European countries have laws regarding worker participation on management boards (so-called codetermination), while most of the rest of the world does not. But even within Europe, each country has slightly different laws regarding worker participation. See, for example, Robert Kuhne, "Co-Determination: A Strategy Restructuring of the Organization," *Columbia Journal of World Business,* Summer 1976, pp. 17–25.

ucts and cultures can, as the following example illustrates, be very difficult.[5]

> To hear officials of some multinational companies talk, there is a surefire success formula for any large corporation with global facilities. First of all, they say the multinational should unify its product lines around the world to obtain mass-production efficiency. Second, it should make its parts wherever such manufacturing is most economical. Third, it should focus its sales efforts on countries where markets are growing fastest. The result, say the formula's proponents, is a maximization of profits.
>
> If all this sounds reasonable, not to say obvious, one might consider the fact that Ford Motor Co. has been following just that formula in recent years and is finding that the scheme isn't as surefire as it seems. This by no means implies that the giant automaker is thinking of abandoning its integrated approach; however, it does mean that Ford is finding some major flaws in the approach—a finding that is emphasized by talking to Gerd Maletz, an owner of one of the biggest Ford dealerships in Germany.
>
> "Take spare parts," Mr. Maletz says. "An engine for one Ford model now must come from Britain, and we may wait months for it. And if the British workers are on strike—and they're always on strike—we wait and wait and wait. We could get a German engine in a couple of days."
>
> Ford decided on integration in 1967. At the time the company's rationale for so doing seemed sound indeed: integration would avoid unnecessarily duplicating the amount—some $100 million—that it costs to engineer and produce a new auto model.
>
> So Ford decided to produce just one European line in place of the completely different cars that used to be turned out by its British and German plants. And the single line began to reduce costs in another way, since the company began to buy parts in bigger volumes—meaning lower prices—from its outside suppliers.
>
> To achieve integration, Ford began to weave a complex manufacturing web that stretched from its big plants in Britain and Germany to its smaller units in Belgium, France, Ireland, the Netherlands, and Portugal. It was planned that some units would make parts, some would assemble finished autos, and some would do both, with the entire operation being directed from Ford of Europe's headquarters in Warley, outside of London.
>
> But even in the very early stages, there were problems. One Ford executive, an American who moved from Detroit to Britain to help set up Ford of Europe, says he quickly ran into nationality differences. "It was easy to get our British people to agree (to a plan), but five minutes later they were always back questioning it," the American recalls. "It seemed almost impossible to get the German Ford people to agree to anything; but once they did, they just kept marching even if they were marching right off the end of the earth."
>
> The first all-new auto launched by Ford of Europe was a medium-sized

[5] From William Carley, "A Giant Multinational Finds Unified Activities Aren't Easy to Set Up." Reprinted with permission of *The Wall Stree Journal,* © Dow Jones & Company, Inc. 1974. All rights reserved.

> car that was called the Cortina Mark III in Britain and the Taunus in Germany. The launch, which began in 1970, was a disaster, and the aftereffects are still plaguing Ford. "There's no question we screwed that one up," one official concedes.
>
> The fiasco stemmed partly from British inexperience with the metric system. Ford's British workers had just converted to that system, long used by Germany and other Continental countries; but, says one of the British workers, "we were still thinking in inches." As a result, the British and German parts often didn't mesh. "The doors didn't fit, the bonnet (hood) didn't fit, nothing fit," says Arthur Naylor, a metal finisher in Ford's Dagenham, England, body plant.
>
> It has also been argued by British workers that some of the German-designed parts were too precise. "Our men often work with a one-16th inch tolerance, but on the German engine suspension system, we had to work down to two or three 1000ths of a bloody inch," contends Jock Macraw, a union shop steward at Dagenham. "The Germans wanted an engineering job done on the production line, and that's impossible."
>
> Because of all the snafus, the Cortina-Taunus assembly line in Dagenham barely moved along. By January 1971, when some kinks had been ironed out, the line was speeded up—much to the displeasure of some workers, Mr. Macraw says. Coincidentally, Ford's wage contract was expiring at the time; and on January 20, 1971, unions struck Ford in Britain, halting production for nine weeks. It wasn't until September, nearly a year after initial production of the new car had begun, that Dagenham hit peak production. Ford says the peak should have been reached in two months.

Significant geographical dispersion, beyond that found in this example of Ford in Europe, can significantly intensify the organizational problems faced by multinational and multibusiness companies. It is possible for an important message in such companies to pass through dozens of people before it reaches its appropriate destination. Because the potential for distortion and miscommunication increases with each additional person involved, it is relatively easy for information to be lost or distorted.

Perhaps an even more troubling consequence of large size and geographical dispersion relates to the potential for power misuse. The substantial resources of large companies can lead to an inherently dangerous situation. Because a great deal is at stake, because managers have considerable power available to them to protect those stakes, and because there are many geographically separated managers who can be difficult to control, some managers have involved corporations in unethical and illegal activities.[6] The result for large corporations in general, and large multinational enterprises in particular, has been the development of a cadre of vocal critics.[7]

---

[6] "The Pressures to Compromise Personal Ethics," *Business Week,* January 31, 1977, p. 107. See also Steven N. Bresner and Earl A. Molander, "Is the Ethics of Business Changing?" *Harvard Business Review,* January–February 1977, pp. 57–71.

[7] See Richard Barnet and Ronald E. Muller, *Global Reach: The Power of the Multinational Corporation* (New York: Simon & Schuster, 1974).

Finally, a problem common to all organizations is that what is best for the whole is not necessarily best for each of its parts. The inevitable conflict, and the problems it can cause, is exacerbated in multibusiness and multinational organizations for two reasons. First, the conflict is often more visible because the performance measures for the whole and the parts are clearer. For example, one parts plant, instead of separate ones in each European country, might increase a corporation's net income through economies of scale, but it might also reduce the net income of a subsidiary that lost sales while waiting for spare parts. Second, getting the subparts to do what is in the best interest of the corporation is often more difficult, for all of the reasons previously mentioned (e.g., a corporate president might desperately want to enforce a rule that no bribes be paid by his company's employees but not be able to do it).

Coping with Extreme Diversity, Size, and Geographical Dispersion

Multibusiness and multinational organizations rely on a variety of mechanisms to help them cope with difficult integration problems, the most common of which is modern communication and transportation facilities. The airplane and the telephone/telex, which we tend to take for granted today, play an enormously important role in tying together the distant parts of large enterprises. Likewise, future technological advances in transportation and communication could significantly help multinational enterprises in particular.

Other integrating mechanisms which are used more selectively include group structures, corporate staffs, elaborate measurement and reward systems, selective transfers, area structures, and presidential "offices."

Group Structures with Corporate Staff

Multibusiness firms often rely heavily on group structures as integrating devices. In a typical case, product divisions that are related because of technology or markets are grouped together under a group vice president. The group vice president then becomes a specialist in that product/market group and attempts to identify and manage any interdependence among the divisions in the group. He also helps the president, with the aid of corporate staff, to make decisions regarding funding requests, financial objectives, and business plans from his divisions. And he works with the president and the staff to monitor division performance on the measurement systems they have developed (which often involve a monthly or quarterly reporting requirement). When designed properly to fit the business situation, these arrangements can significantly increase a corporation's ability to process relevant information and make effective integrating decisions, as well as to take speedy action when problems develop.

The size of a corporate staff group, the complexity of the reporting systems, and the number of decisions made or reviewed at corporate headquarters can vary significantly among companies that use this set of integrating devices. Companies that have relatively little diversity among their businesses and relatively high interdependence among them tend to rely on a large corporate staff and a relatively centralized decision-making system; with more business diversity and less interdependence, corporations often use a smaller corporate staff and more decentralized management. At the extreme, some multibusiness companies with very diverse and independent businesses do not use this device at all, but instead rely on other mechanisms, such as the careful selection and transfer of division managers.[8] In such cases the diversity among the businesses makes it impractical to try to actively manage them from corporate headquarters.

Companies that have varying degrees of diversity and interdependence among their divisions will often treat different divisions in different ways. As a rule, the lower a division's interdependence with other parts of the company, the higher the chances are that it will be allowed to operate autonomously, that it will be treated as a profit center, and that the division manager will be offered the opportunity for significant bonuses based on divisional profits.[9]

Selection and Transfer of Managers

Careful selection and transfer of people into subunit manager slots can be a key integrating device. To facilitate the integration of a subunit into the corporation, for example, the president might select someone with whom he or she has a good relationship, who can be trusted to pass on accurate and timely information, and who also has a background in the area of business that is the focus of the subunit's activities. Similarly, to facilitate the integration of two divisions that are highly interdependent, a company might rotate its division managers.[10] Probably the major reason this solution is not used more frequently is that companies often do not have the type of people needed to make it work. They do not always have someone the president knows and trusts, who has a

---

[8] Harold Stieglitz, "On Concepts of Corporate Structure," *The Conference Board Record,* February 1974, pp. 7–13; see also Jay Lorsch and Stephen Allen, *Managing Diversity and Interdependence* (Boston: Harvard Business School, 1973).

[9] Richard F. Vancil, *Decentralization* (New York: Financial Executive Research Foundation, 1978).

[10] For an interesting discussion of how corporations use management transfer to aid coordination and control, see Jay Galbraith and Anders Edstrom, "International Transfer of Managers: Some Important Policy Considerations," *Columbia Journal of World Business,* Summer 1976, pp. 100–112.

background in a certain product or area, and who is available to be moved. Some companies systematically try to develop a pool of people who might be used to support such a selection, promotion, and transfer policy.[11] They might, for example, hire some Europeans graduating from a U.S. business school, initially give them assignments at corporate headquarters and then give them a series of assignments in different European subsidiaries, all in order to prepare them for positions as European division managers. This approach can be quite expensive, however.

Product/Area Structure

Multinational organizations also rely heavily on a variety of product/area structures to help with their integration problems. In cases where they feel an area focus is more important than a product focus, companies depend on a geographic structure combined with some type of product management; those that emphasize a product focus rely on a product division structure aided by some type of area coordination.[12] Companies that feel they need to focus equally on products and markets (and sometimes on functions, too) may rely on a product/area matrix. All except the smallest multinational organizations are using one of these three structures or moving toward using one of them.[13]

The trend toward global product/area structures is relatively new; yet because of its advantages, that structure will undoubtedly become more important in the future.[14] The slowness with which companies have adopted this structure is very much a function of the problems it can cause, which are similar to those of matrix structures in single businesses. As a result, one writer has warned that multinational/multibusiness companies not implement a matrix unless:

1. There is diversification of both products and markets requiring balanced and simultaneous attention.
2. The opportunities lost and difficulties experienced by favoring either a product or geographic unity of command cannot be ignored.

---

[11] Robert A. Pitts, "Unshackle Your 'Comers'," *Harvard Business Review,* May–June 1977, pp. 127–36.

[12] Stanley Davis, "Trends in the Organization of Multinational Corporations," *Columbia Journal of World Business,* Summer 1976, p. 70.

[13] A typical multinational company evolves in the following way. When it first starts selling internationally, it sets up foreign subsidiaries. When the sales from these subsidiaries become significant or after its investment abroad becomes significant, the company establishes an "international division." Later it shifts to either a global product division or global area division. Finally, it reorganizes, using some form of product/area matrix.

[14] For a good discussion of the advantages of a complex matrix for a multibusiness and multinational company, see William Goggin, "How the Multidimensional Structure Works at Dow Corning," *Harvard Business Review,* January–February 1974, pp. 54–65.

3. Environmental pressure to secure international economies of scale require the shared use of scarce human resources.
4. There is a need for enriched information-processing capacity because of uncertain, complex, and interdependent tasks.
5. Information, planning, and control systems operate along the different dimensions of the structure simultaneously.
6. As much attention is paid to managerial behavior as to the structure. The corporate culture and ethos must actively support and believe in negotiated management.[15]

Office of the President

Some multibusiness and multinational organizations have recently developed still another mechanism to promote integration. Usually called "the office," this device is most commonly used at the presidental level. Instead of having one person act as president, under an "office" arrangement three or four people work together in that role. When it is successful, this device fosters faster and more competent information processing.[16] One significant requirement for this arrangement to be successful is that excellent relationships exist among the people in the office.

Corporate Culture

Another integrative device that is used by multibusiness and multinational organizations is a corporate "culture" which is developed and maintained by top management. Through their words and deeds, top managers attempt to clearly set norms and values.[17] For example, if a corporate president can establish the norm that "we do not engage in illegal activities even if the countries we operate in expect it," that norm can have an effect more powerful than the most expensive control systems or the most elaborate hierarchies.

That more companies do not actively try to create and maintain an integrating culture attests to its difficulty. Establishing certain norms and values in a global organization is a slow and time-consuming process, and one that may not be practical under many circumstances.

---

[15] Stanley Davis, "Trends in the Organization of Multinational Corporations," *Columbia Journal of World Business,* Summer 1976, p. 70.

[16] For an example of an "office," how it was developed, and how it works, see Gilbert Burck, "Union Carbide's Patient Schemers," *Fortune,* December 1965.

[17] Roger Harrison, "Understanding Your Organization's Character," *Harvard Business Review,* May–June 1972.

Summary

The approach we outlined for dealing with organizational questions in single-business companies is equally applicable to multibusiness and multinational companies. Nevertheless, because of their greater product/market diversity, their greater size, and their geographical dispersion, the latter type of company often faces even more difficult integration problems. To cope with these problems, they tend to use all of the integration devices used by single-business companies plus additional ones that are appropriate for their specific problems (see Figure 5–2).

In designing a solution to an organizational problem in a multibusi-

Figure 5–2
Multinational Business Integrating Devices: Pros and Cons

Integrating Device	Advantages	Drawbacks
Modern communications and transportation facilities	To some degree, available to everyone.	Cost, especially in time and energy for traveling managers.
Group structures, with corporate staff and elaborate measurement/reward systems	Can significantly increase a corporation's ability to make optimizing decisions and spot problems quickly.	Absorbs subunit manager's time. If businesses are extremely diverse, this option just may not work.
Selection and transfer of subunit managers	Can be less expensive and cumbersome than structural solutions.	It is sometimes not possible to find the types of individuals needed. Extensive transfers can be expensive.
Product/area structure:		
Area subunits with product managers	Best when area focus is most important.	Does not provide best product focus.
Product subunits with area coordination	Best when product focus is most important.	Does not provide best area focus.
Matrix	Can achieve integration within and across products, areas, and other dimensions (e.g., functions).	Can be very difficult to maintain the balance in the system and to manage the tensions and conflicts.
Office of the president	Allows a key "office" to process information faster and more competently than if it were staffed with a single individual.	Requires the development and maintenance of excellent working relationships among the people involved.
Corporate culture	Once established, can be much more powerful and less expensive than other solutions.	Difficult and slow to develop.

ness or multinational corporation, one needs to consider, just as in single-business contexts, the diversity and interdependence of the activities the corporation engages in and the current organization (formal, informal, people). One needs to make judgments about what fits and what does not. And one needs to avoid the temptation to solve troublesome integration problems by ignoring important aspects of the corporation's product/market diversity and reducing needed differentiation in the organization.

One of the most common mistakes that managers in multinational and multibusiness organizations make is to ignore important aspects of their product/market diversity—often because they are not happy with the implications of organizationally taking that diversity into account. Corporate staff managers, for example, often try to implement uniform compensation and performance appraisal systems throughout a worldwide corporation, regardless of important differences among divisions and countries.[18] After acquiring a new division in a different business or in a different country, corporate managers often try to treat it like the rest of the corporation, regardless of important differences. This type of behavior leads eventually to organizational problems—sometimes very serious ones.

---

[18] See, for example, Howard Perlmutter and David Heenan, "How Multinational Should Your Managers Be?" *Harvard Business Review,* November–December 1974, p. 129.

Case 5–1

*Texana Petroleum Corporation**

Jay W. Lorsch, Paul R. Lawrence, James A. Garrison

During the summer of 1966, George Prentice, the newly designated executive vice president for domestic operations of the Texana Petroleum Corporation, was devoting much of his time to thinking about improving the combined performance of the five product divisions reporting to him (see Exhibit 1). His main concern was that corporate profits were not reflecting the full, potential contribution that could result from the close technological interdependence of the raw materials utilized and produced by these divisions. As Prentice saw it, the principal difficulty was that the division general managers reporting to him were not working well together:

> *As far as I see it, the issue is where do we make the money for the corporation? Not how do we beat the other person. Nobody is communicating with anybody else at the general-manager level. In fact they are telling a bunch of secrets around here.*

Recent Corporate History

The Texana Petroleum Corporation was one of the early major producers and marketers of petroleum products in the southwest United States. Up until the early 1950s, Texana had been almost exclusively in the

* This case was made possible by the cooperation of a firm which remains anonymous.

Harvard Business School case 413–056.

Exhibit 1
Texana Petroleum: Partial Organization Chart, 1966

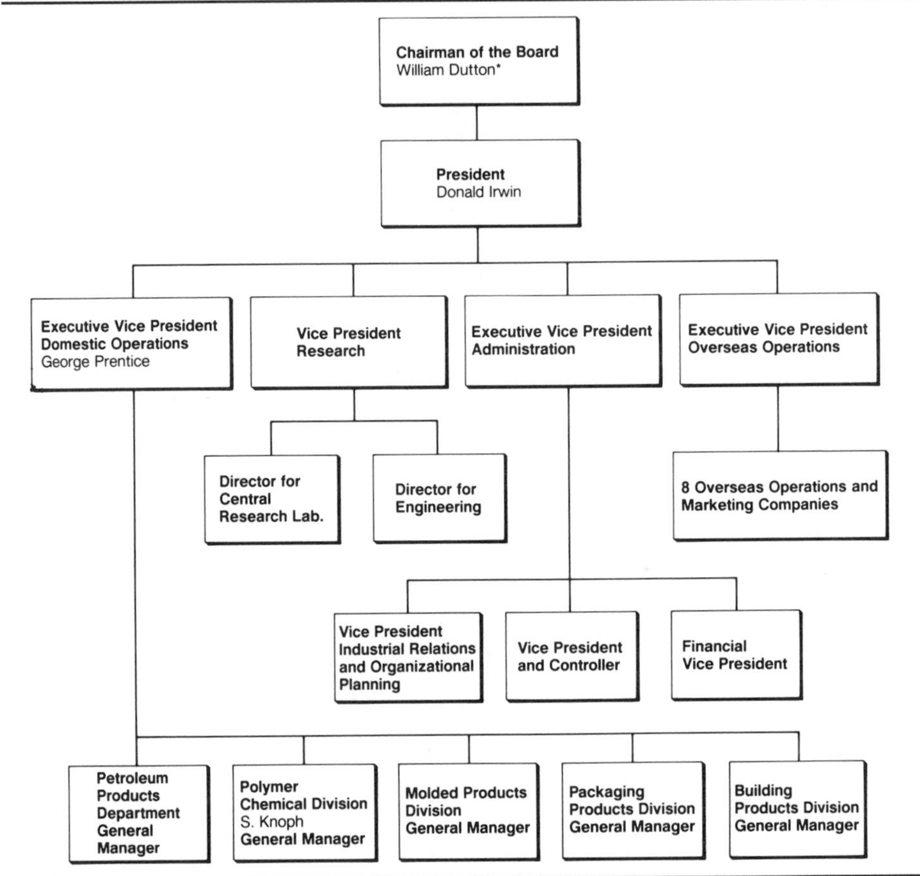

* Names are included for those mentioned in the case.

business of processing and refining crude oil; it was also involved in selling petroleum products through a chain of company-operated service stations in the southwestern states and in Central and South America. By 1950, company sales had risen to approximately $500 million, with accompanying growth in profits. About 1950, however, Texana faced increasingly stiff competition at the retail service station level from several larger, national petroleum companies. As a result sales volume declined sharply during the early 1950s. By 1955 sales had fallen to only $300 million, and the company was operating at just above the break-even point.

At that time, Roger Holmes, who had been a dominant force in the company since its founding, retired as president and chief executive officer because of his age. He was replaced by Donald Irwin, 49, who had been a senior executive with a major chemical company. William Dutton, 55, who had spent his entire career with Texana, was appointed chairman of the board to replace the retiring board chairman. Prior to his appointment as chairman, he had been senior vice president for petroleum products, reporting to Holmes.

Irwin and Dutton, along with other senior executives, moved quickly to solve the problems facing Texana. They gradually divested the company of its retail outlets and abandoned the domestic consumer petroleum markets. Through both internal development and acquisition they expanded rapidly, increasing the company's involvement in the business of processing petroleum for chemical and plastics products. By moving in this direction, they were further expanding on initial moves made by Texana in 1949, when the company built its first chemical processing plant and began marketing these products. To speed the company's growth in these areas, Irwin and Dutton selected aggressive general managers for each division and gave them a wide degree of freedom in decision making. Top management's major requirement was that each division general manager create a growing division with a satisfactory return on investment capital. By 1966 top management had reshaped the company so that it was an integrated producer of chemicals and plastic materials in both domestic and foreign markets. In foreign operations, the company continued to operate service stations in Latin America and in Europe. This change in direction was successful; by 1966 company sales had risen to $750 million, along with a healthy rise in profits.

In spite of this success, management believed that there was a need for an increase in return on invested capital. The financial and trade press, which had been generous in its praise of the company's recovery, was still critical of the present return on investment, and top management shared this concern. Dutton, Irwin, and Prentice were in agreement that one important method of increasing profits was to take further advantage of the potential cost savings that could come from increased coordination among the domestic operating divisions as they developed new products, processes, and markets.

Domestic Organization 1966

The product divisions reporting to Prentice represented a continuum of producing and marketing activities, from the production and refining of crude oil to the marketing of several types of plastics products to industrial consumers. Each division was headed by a general manager. While there was some variation in the internal organizational structure of the several divisions, they were generally set up along functional lines (manufacturing, sales, research and development). Each division also had its own controller and engineering activities, although these were supported and augmented by the corporate staff. While divisions had their own research efforts, there was also a central research laboratory at the corporate level that carried out longer-range research of a more fundamental nature, thus outside the scope of any of the product division's activities.

The Petroleum Products Division was the remaining nucleus of the company's original producing and refining activities. It supplied raw materials to the Polymer and Chemicals Division and also sold refining products under long-term contracts to other petroleum companies. In the early and mid-1950s this division's management had generated much of the company's revenue and profits through its skill in negotiating these agreements. In 1966 top corporate management felt that this division's management had accepted its role as a supplier to the rest of the corporation, and they also felt that there were harmonious relations between it and its sister divisions.

The Polymer and Chemicals Division was developed internally during the late 1940s and early 1950s as management saw its share of the consumer petroleum market declining. Under the leadership of Seymour Knoph (who had been general manager for several years) and his predecessor (who was executive vice president, administration in 1966), the division had rapidly developed a line of chemical and polymer compounds derived from petroleum raw materials. Most of the products of this division were manufactured under licensing agreements, or they were materials with well-understood formulations. Nevertheless, technical personnel in the division had developed an industrywide reputation for their ability to develop new and improved processes. Top management of the division took particular pride in this ability. From the beginning the decisions of what products to manufacture were based, to a large extent, upon the requirements of the Molded and Packaging Products Divisions. Moreover, Polymer and Chemicals Division executives had always attempted to market these same products to external customers, and at this they had been highly successful. These external sales were extremely important to Texana, for they assured the company a large enough volume of operation to process a broad product line of polymer chemicals profitably. As the other divisions had grown, however, they required a larger proportion of the division's capacity, which meant that Polymer and Chemicals Division managers had to reduce their commitment to external customers.

The Molded Products Division was also an internally developed division, which had been formed in 1951. It produced a variety of molded plastic products, ranging from toys and household items to automotive and electronic parts. This division's major strengths were its knowledge of molding technology and in particular, its marketing ability. While it depended on the Polymer and Chemicals Division for its raw materials, its operations were largely independent of those of the Packaging Products and Building Products Divisions.

The Packaging Products Division was acquired in 1952. Its products were plastic packaging materials, including films, cartons, bottles, and so forth. All of these products were marketed to industrial customers. Like the products division, the packaging division depended on the Polymer and Chemicals Division as a source of raw materials, but it was largely independent of other end-product divisions.

The Building Products Division was acquired in 1963 to give Texana a position in the construction materials market. The division produced and marketed a variety of insulation roofing materials and similar products to the building trade. It was a particularly attractive acquisition for Texana, since it had achieved some success with plastic products for insulation and roofing materials prior to the acquisition. Although the plastic products accounted for less than 20 percent of total division sales in 1965, plans called for these products to account for over 50 percent of division sales in the next five years. Its affiliation with Texana gave this division a stronger position in plastic raw materials through the Polymer and Chemicals Division.

Selection and Recruitment of Management Personnel

The rapid expansion of the corporation into these new areas had created the need for much additional management talent, and top management had not hesitated in bringing new people in from outside the corporation, as well as advancing promising younger people inside Texana. In both the internally developed and acquired divisions, most managers had spent their careers inside the division, although some top division managers were moved between divisions or into corporate positions.

In speaking about the type of people he had sought for management positions, Donald Irwin described his criterion in a financial publication: "We don't want people around who are afraid to move. The attraction of Texana is that it gives the individual responsibilities which aren't diluted. It attracts the person who wants a challenge."

Another corporate executive described Texana managers: "It's a group of very tough-minded, but considerate individuals with an enormous drive to get things done."

Another manager, who had been with Texana for his entire career and considered himself to be different from most Texana managers, described the typical Texana manager as follows:

> *Texana attracts a particular type of person. Most of these characteristics are personal characteristics rather than professional ones. I would use terms such as cold, unfeeling, aggressive, and extremely competitive, but not particularly loyal to the organization. He is loyal to dollars, his own personal dollars. I think this is part of the communication problem. I think this is done on purpose. The*

selection procedures lead in this direction. I think this is so because of contrast with the way the company operated 10 years ago. Of course I was at the plant level at that time. But today the attitude I have described is also in the plants. Ten years ago the organization was composed of people who worked together for the good of the organization, because they wanted to. I don't think this is so today.

Location of Division Facilities

The Petroleum Products, Polymer and Chemicals, and Packaging Products Divisions had their executive offices on separate floors of the Texana headquarters building in downtown Chicago. The plants and research and development facilities of these divisions were spread out across Oklahoma, Texas, and Louisiana. The Molded Products Division had its headquarters, R&D facilities, and a major plant in an industrial suburb of Chicago. This division's other plants were at several locations in the Middle West and East Coast. The Building Products Division's headquarters and major production and technical facilities were located in Fort Worth, Texas. All five divisions shared sales offices in major cities from coast to coast.

Evaluation and Control of Division Performance

The principal methods of controlling and evaluating the operations of these divisions were the semiannual review of division plans and the approval of major capital expenditures by the executive committee.[1] In reviewing performance against plans, members of the executive committee placed almost sole emphasis on the division's actual return on investment against budget. Corporate executives felt that this practice, together with the technological interdependence of the divisions, created many disputes about transfer pricing.

In addition to these regular reviews, corporate executives had frequent discussions with division executives about their strategies, plans, and operations. It had been difficult for corporate management to strike the proper balance in guiding the operations for the divisions. This problem was particularly acute with regard to the Polymer and Chemicals Division, because of its central place in the corporation's product line. One corporate staff member explained his view of the problem:

This whole matter of communications between the corporate staff and the Polymer and Chemicals Division has been a fairly difficult problem. Corporate management used to contribute immensely to this by trying to get into the nuts

---

[1] The executive committee consisted of Messrs. Dutton, Irwin, and Prentice, as well as the vice president of research, executive vice president–administration, and the executive vice president of foreign operations.

and bolts area within the Chemical and Polymer organization, and this created serious criticisms; however, I think they have backed off in this manner.

A second corporate executive in discussing the matter for a trade publication report put the problem this way: "We're trying to find the middle ground. We don't want to be a holding company, and with our diversity we can't be a highly centralized corporation."

Executive Vice President, Domestic Operations

In an effort to find this middle ground, the position of executive vice president, domestic operations, was created in early 1966, and George Prentice was its first occupant. Prior to this change, there had been two senior domestic vice presidents—one in charge of the Petroleum Products and Polymer and Chemicals Divisions and the other in charge of the end-use divisions. Prentice had been senior vice president in charge of the end-use divisions before the new position was created. He had held that position for only two years, having come to it from a highly successful marketing career with a competitor.

At the time of his appointment one press account described Prentice as "hard-driving, aggressive, and ambitious—an archetype of the self-actuated dynamo Irwin has sought out."

Shortly after taking his new position, Prentice described the task before him:

I think the corporation wants to integrate its parts better, and I am here because I reflect this feeling. We can't be a bunch of entrepreneurs around here. We have got to balance discipline with entrepreneurial motivation. This is what we were in the past, just a bunch of entrepreneurs, and if they came in with ideas we would get the money. But now our dollars are limited, and especially the Polymer and Chemicals people haven't been able to discipline themselves to select from within 10 good projects. They just don't seem to be able to do this, and so they come running in here with all 10 good projects which they say we have to buy, and they get upset when we can't buy them all.

This was the tone of my predecessors [*senior vice presidents*]. *All of them were very strong on being entrepreneurs. I am going to run it different. I am going to take a marketing and capital orientation. As far as I can see, there is a time to compete and a time to collaborate, and I think right now there has been a lack of recognition in the Polymer and Chemicals executive suite that this thing has changed.*

Other Views of Domestic Interdivisional Relations

Executives within the Polymer and Chemicals Division, the end-use divisions, and at the corporate level shared Prentice's view that the major breakdown in interdivisional relations was between the Polymer and Chemicals Division and the end-use divisions. Executives in the end-use divisions made these typical comments about the problem:

I think the thing we have got to realize is that we are wedded to the Polymer and Chemicals Division whether we like it or not. We are really tied up with them. And just as we would with any outside supplier or with any of our customers, we will do things to maintain their business. But because they feel they have our business wrapped up, they do not reciprocate in turn. Now let me emphasize that they have not arbitrarily refused to do the things that we are requiring, but there is a pressure on them for investment projects, and we are low man on the pole. And I think this could heavily jeopardize our chances for growth.

I would say our relationships are sticky, and I think this is primarily because we think our reason for being is to make money, so we try to keep Polymer and Chemicals as an arm's-length supplier. For example, I cannot see, just because it is a Polymer and Chemicals product, accepting millions of pounds of very questionable material. It takes dollars out of our pocket, and we are very profit centered.

The big frustration, I guess, and one of our major problems, is that you can't get help from them [Polymer and Chemicals]. You feel they are not interested in what you are doing, particularly if it doesn't have a large return for them. But as far as I am concerned this has to become a joint venture relationship, and this is getting to be real sweat with us. We are the guys down below yelling for help. And they have got to give us some relief.

My experience with the Polymer and Chemicals Division is that you cannot trust what they say at all, and even when they put it in writing you can't be absolutely sure that they are going to live up to it.

Managers within the Polymer and Chemicals Division expressed similar sentiments:

Personally, right now I have the feeling that the divisions' interests are growing further apart. It seems that the divisions are going their own way. For example, we are a polymer producer but the molding division wants to be in a special area, so that means they are going to be less of a customer to us, and there is a whole family of plastics being left out that nobody's touching, and this is bearing on our program. . . . We don't mess with the Building Products Division at all, either. They deal in small volumes. Those that we are already making we sell to them, those that we don't make we can't justify making because of the kinds of things we are working with. What I am saying is that I don't think the corporation is integrating, but I think we ought to be, and this is one of the problems of delegated divisions. What happens is that an executive heads this up and goes for the place that makes the most money for the division, but this is not necessarily the best place from a corporate standpoint.

We don't have as much contact with sister divisions as I think we should. I have been trying to get a liaison with people in my function but it has been a complete flop. One of the problems is that I don't know who to call on in these other divisions. There is no table of organization, nor is there any encouragement to try and get anything going. My experience has been that all of these operating divisions are very closed organizations. I know people up the line will say that I am nuts about this. They say to just call over and I will get an answer. But this always has to be a big deal, and it doesn't happen automatically, and it hurts us.

The comments of corporate staff members describe these relationships and the factors they saw as contributing to the problem:

Right now I would say there is an iron curtain between the Polymer and Chemicals Division and the rest of the corporation. You know, we tell our divisions they are responsible, autonomous groups, and the Polymer and Chemicals Division took it very seriously. However, when you are a three-quarter billion dollar company, you've got to be coordinated, or the whole thing is going to fall apart—it can be no other way. The domestic executive vice president thing has been a big step forward to improve this, but I would say it hasn't worked out yet.

The big thing that is really bothering [*the Polymer and Chemicals Division*] *is that they think they have to go develop all new markets on their own. They are going to do it alone independently, and this is the problem they are faced with. They have got this big thing, that they want to prove that they are a company all by themselves and not rely upon packaging or anybody else.*

Polymer and Chemicals Division executives talked about the effect of this drive for independence of the divisional operating heads on their own planning efforts:

The Polymer and Chemicals Division doesn't like to communicate with the corporate staff. This seems hard for us, and I think the [*a recent major proposal*] *was a classic example of this. That plan, as it was whipped up by the Polymer and Chemicals Division, had massive implications for the corporation both in expertise and in capital. In fact, I think we did this to be competitive and one up on the rest of our sister divisions. We wanted to be the best-looking division in the system, but we carried it to an extreme. In this effort, we wanted to show that we had developed this concept completely on our own. . . . Now I think a lot of our problems with it stemmed from this intense desire we have to be the best in this organization.*

Boy, a big doldrum around here was shortly after Christmas [*1965*] *when they dropped out a new plant, right out of our central plan, without any appreciation of the importance of this plant to the whole Polymer and Chemicals Division's growth. . . . Now we have a windfall, and we are back in business on this new plant. But for a while things were very black, and everything we had planned and everything we had built our patterns on were out. In fact, when we put this plan together, it never really occurred to us that we were going to get it turned down, and I'll bet we didn't even put the plans together in such a way as to really reflect the importance of this plant to the rest of the corporation.*

A number of executives in the end-use divisions attributed the interdivisional problems to different management practices and assumptions within the Polymer and Chemicals Division. An executive in the packaging division made this point:

We make decisions quickly and at the lowest possible level, and this is tremendously different from the rest of Texana. I don't know another division like this in the rest of the corporation.

Look at what Sy Knoph has superfluous to his operation compared to ours.

These are the reasons for our success. You've got to turn your people loose and not breathe down their necks all the time. We don't slow our people down with staff. Sure, you may work with a staff, the wheels may grind, but they sure grind slow.

Also, we don't work on detail like the other divisions do. Our management doesn't feel they need the detail stuff. Therefore, they're [Polymer and Chemicals] always asking us for detail which we can't supply; our process doesn't generate it and their process requires it, and this always creates problems with the Polymer and Chemicals Division. But I'll be damned if I am going to have a group of people running between me and the plant, and I'll be goddamned if I am going to clutter up my organization with all the people that Knoph has got working for him. I don't want this staff, but they are sure pushing it on me.

This comment from a molding division manager is typical of many made about the technical concerns of the Polymer and Chemicals Division management:

Historically, even up to the not too distant past, the Polymer and Chemicals Division was considered a snake pit as far as the corporate people were concerned. This was because the corporate people were market oriented and Polymer and Chemicals Division was technically run and very much a manufacturing effort. These two factors created a communication barrier, and to really understand the Polymer and Chemicals Division problems, they felt that you have to have a basic appreciation of the technology and all the interrelationships.

Building on this strong belief, the Polymer and Chemicals Division executives in the past have tried to communicate in technical terms, and this just further hurt the relationship, and it just did not work. Now they are coming up with a little bit more business or commercial orientation, and they are beginning to appreciate that they have got to justify the things they want to do in a business or commercial orientation rather than just a technical sense. This also helps the problem of maintaining their relationships with the corporation as most of the staff is nontechnical; however, this has changed a little bit in that more and more technical people have been coming on and this has helped from the other side.

They work on the assumption in the Polymer and Chemicals Division that you have to know the territory before you can be an effective manager. You have got to be an operating person to contribute meaningfully to their problems. However, their biggest problem is this concentration on technical solutions to their problems. This is a thing that has boxed them in the most trouble with corporate and the other sister divisions.

These and other executives also pointed to another source of conflict between the Polymer and Chemicals Division and other divisions. This was the question of whether the Polymer and Chemicals Division should develop into a more independent marketer, or whether it should rely more heavily on the end-use divisions to "push" its products to the market.

The following comments by end-use division executives are typical views of this conflict:

The big question I have about Polymer and Chemicals is what is their strategy going to be? I can understand them completely from a technical standpoint; this is no problem. I wonder what is the role of this company? How is it going to fit into what we and others are doing? Right now, judging from the behavior I've seen, Polymer and Chemicals could care less about what we are doing in terms of integration of our markets or a joint approach to them.

I think it is debatable whether the Polymer and Chemicals Division should be a new product company or not. Right now we have an almost inexhaustible appetite for what they do and do well. As I see it, the present charter is fine. However, that group is very impatient, aggressive, and they want to grow, but you have got to grow within guidelines. Possibly the Polymer and Chemicals Division is just going to have to learn to hang on the coattails of the other divisions, and do just what they are doing now, only better.

I think the future role of the Polymer and Chemicals Division is going to be, at any one point in time for the corporation, that if it looks like a product is needed, they will make it. . . . They are going to be suppliers because I will guarantee you that if the moment comes and we can't buy it elsewhere, for example, then I darn well know they are going to make it for us regardless of what their other commitments are. They are just going to have to supply us. If you were to put the Polymer and Chemicals Division off from the corporation, I don't think they would last a year. Without their huge captive requirements, they would not be able to compete economically in the commercial areas they are in.

A number of other executives indicated that the primary emphasis within the corporation on return on investment by divisions tended to induce, among other things, a narrow, competitive concern on the part of the various divisional managements. The comment of this division executive was typical:

As far as I can see it, we [his division and Polymer and Chemicals] are 180 degrees off on our respective charters. Therefore, when Sy Knoph talks about this big project we listen nicely and then we say, "God bless you, lots of luck," but I am sure we are not going to get involved in it. I don't see any money in it for us. It may be a gold mine for Sy, but it is not for our company; and as long as we are held to the high profit standards we are, we just cannot afford to get involved. I can certainly see it might make good corporate sense for us to get it, but it doesn't make any sense in terms of our particular company. We have got to be able to show the returns in order to get continuing capital, and I just can't on that kind of project. I guess what I am saying is that under the right conditions we could certainly go in but not under the present framework; we would just be dead in terms of dealing with the corporate financial structure. We just cannot get the kinds of returns on our capital that the corporation has set to get new capital. In terms of the long run, I'd like very much to see what the corporation has envisioned in terms of a hookup between us, but right now I don't see any sense in going on. You know my career is at stake here, too.

Another divisional executive made this point more succinctly:

Personally, I think that a lot more could be done from a corporate point of view, and this is frustrating. Right now all these various divisions seem to be viewed strictly as an investment by the corporate people. They only look at us as a banker might look at us. This hurts us in terms of evolving some of these programs because we have relationships which are beyond financial relationships.

The remarks of a corporate executive seemed to support this concern:

One of the things I worry about is where is the end of the rope on this interdivisional thing. I'm wondering if action really has to come from just the division. You know, in this organization when they decide to do something new it always has been a divisional proposal—they were coming to us for review and approval. The executive committee ends up a review board; not us, working downward. With this kind of pattern, the talent of the corporate people is pretty well seduced into asking questions and determining whether a thing needs guidelines. But I think we ought to be the idea people, as well, thinking about where we are going in the future, and if we think we ought to be getting into some new area, then we tell the divisions to do it. The stream has got to work both ways. Now it is not.

Case 5–2

*Bancil Corporation (A)**

Lawrence D. Chrzanowski and Ram Charan

Struggling to clear his mind, Remy Gentile, marketing manager in France for the Toiletry Division of Bancil, stumbled to answer the ringing telephone.

"Allo?"

"Remy, Tom Wilson here. Sorry to bother you at this hour. Can you hear me?"

"Sacre Bleu! Do you know what time it is?"

"About 5:20 in Sunnyvale. I've been looking over the past quarter's results for our Peau Doux . . ."

"Tom, it's after 2 A.M. in Paris; hold the phone for a moment."

Remy was vexed with Tom Wilson, marketing vice president for the Toiletry Division and acting division marketing director for Europe, since they had discussed the Peau Doux situation via telex no more than a month ago. When he returned to the phone, Remy spoke in a more controlled manner.

You mentioned the Peau Doux line, Tom.

Yes, Remy, the last quarter's results were very disappointing. Though we've increased advertising by 30 percent, sales were less than 1 percent higher. What is even more distressing, Remy, is that our competitors' sales have been growing

---

* This case was prepared by Lawrence D. Chrzanowski under the supervision of Ram Charan, associate professor of policy and environment, as a basis for class discussion rather than to illustrate either effective or ineffective handling of an administrative situation. The case was made possible by a corporation which prefers to remain anonymous. All names, figures, and locations have been disguised.

at nearly 20 percent per year. Furthermore, our percent cost of goods sold has not decreased. Has Pierre Chevalier bought the new equipment to streamline the factory's operation?

No, Pierre has not yet authorized the purchase of the machines, and there is little that can be done to rationalize operations in the antiquated Peau Doux plant. Also, we have not yet succeeded in securing another distributor for the line.

What! But that was part of the strategy with our increased advertising. I thought we agreed to . . .

Tom Wilson hesitated for a moment. His mind was racing as he attempted to recall the specifics of the proposed Toiletry Division strategy for France. That strategy had guided his earlier recommendation to Gentile and Pierre Chevalier, the Bancil general manager in France, to increase advertising and to obtain a new distributor. Tom wanted to be forceful but tactful to ensure Gentile's commitment to the strategy.

Remy, let's think about what we discussed on my last trip to Paris. Do you recall we agreed to propose to Chevalier a plan to revitalize Peau Doux's growth? If my memory serves me well, it was to increase advertising by 25 percent, groom a new national distributor, reduce manufacturing costs with new equipment, increase prices, and purchase the 'L'aube' product line to spread our marketing overhead.

Oui, oui. We explored some ideas, and I thought they needed more study.

Remy, as you recall, Peau Doux has a low margin. Cutting costs is imperative. We expected to decrease costs by 5 percent by investing $45,000 in new equipment. Our test for the new strategy next year was to increase advertising this quarter and next quarter while contracting for a new distributor. The advertising was for naught. What happened?

I really don't know. I guess Pierre has some second thoughts.

Tom spoke faster as he grew more impatient. Gentile's asking Tom to repeat what he had said made him angrier. Tom realized that he must visit Paris to salvage what he could from the current test program on Peau Doux. He knew that the recent results would not support the proposed Toiletry Division strategy.

Remy, I need to see what's going on and then decide how I can best assist you and Chevalier. I should visit Paris soon. How about early next week, say Monday and Tuesday?

Oui, that is fine.

I'll fly in on Sunday morning. Do you think you can join me for dinner that evening at the Vietnamese restaurant we dined at last time?

Oui.

Please make reservations only for two. I'm coming alone. Good night, Remy.

Oui. Bon soir.

Company Background

Bancil Corporation of Sunnyvale, California, was founded in 1908 by pharmacist Dominic Bancil. During its first half century, its products consisted primarily of analgesics (branded pain relievers like aspirin), an antiseptic mouthwash, and a first-aid cream. By 1974, some of the top management positions were still held by members of the Bancil family, who typically had backgrounds as pharmacists or physicians. This tradition notwithstanding, John Stoopes, the present chief executive officer, was committed to developing a broad-based professional management team.

Bancil sales, amounting to $61 million in 1955, had grown to $380 million in 1970 and to $600 million in 1974. This sales growth had been aided by diversification and acquisition of allied businesses as well as by international expansion. Bancil's product line by 1970 included four major groups:

	Sales ($ millions)	
	1970	**1974**
Agricultural and animal health products (weed killers, fertilizers, feed additives)	$ 52	$141
Consumer products (Bancil original line plus hand creams, shampoos, and baby accessories)	205	276
Pharmaceutical products (tranquilizers, oral contraceptives, hormonal drugs)	62	107
Professional products (diagnostic reagents, automated chemical analyzers, and surgical gloves and instruments)	60	76

In 1974, Bancil's corporate organization was structured around these four product groups which, in turn, were divided into two or three divisions. Thus, in 1973 the Consumer Products group had been divided into the Dominic Division, which handled Bancil's original product line, and the Toiletry Division, which was in charge of the newer product acquisitions. The objective of this separation was to direct greater attention to the toiletry products.

International Operations

International expansion had begun in the mid-1950s when Bancil exported through agents and distributors. Subsequently, marketing subsidiaries, called national units (NUs), were created in Europe, Africa, Latin America, and Japan. All manufacturing took place in the United States. Virtually the entire export activity consisted of Bancil's analgesic Domicil. An innovative packaging concept, large amounts of creative advertising, and considerable sales push made Domicil a common word in most of the free world, reaching even the most remote areas of Africa, Asia, and South America. A vice president of international operations exercised control at this time through letters and occasional overseas trips. By the mid-1960s, overseas marketing of pharmaceutical and professional products began, frequently through a joint venture with a local company. Increasing sales led to the construction of production facilities for many of Bancil's products in England, Kenya, Mexico, Brazil, and Japan.

Bancil's international expansion received a strong commitment from top management. John Stoopes was not only a successful business executive but also a widely read intellectual with an avid interest in South American and African cultures. This interest generated an extraordinary sense of responsibility to the developing nations and a conviction that the mature industrial societies had an obligation to help in their development. He did not want Bancil to be viewed as a firm that drained resources and money from the developing world; rather, he desired to apply Bancil's resources to worldwide health and malnutrition problems. His personal commitment as an ardent humanist was a guideline for Bancil's international operations.

While Bancil had been successful during the 1960s in terms of both domestic diversification and international expansion, its efforts to achieve worldwide diversification had given rise to frustration. Even though the International Division's specific purpose was to promote all Bancil products most advantageously throughout the world, the NUs had concentrated mainly on analgesics. As a result, the growth of the remaining products had been generally confined to the United States, and thus these products were not realizing their fullest worldwide potential.

According to Bancil executives, these problems had their roots in the fact that the various product lines, though generically related, required different management strategies. For consumer products, advertising consumed 28 percent to 35 percent of sales; since production facilities did not require a large capital investment, considerable spare capacity was available to absorb impulses in demand created by advertising campaigns. For agricultural and animal health products, promotion was less than 1 percent of sales, but the capital-intensive production (a facility of minimum economic scale cost $18 million) required a marketing effort to stimulate demand consistently near full production capacity. Furthermore, the nature of the marketing activity for the professional and pharmaceutical products placed the burden on personal selling rather than on a mass-promotion effort.

In response to this situation, a reorganization in 1969 gave each product division worldwide responsibility for marketing its products. Regional marketing managers, reporting to the division's vice president of marketing, were given authority for most marketing decisions (e.g., advertising, pricing, distribution channels) of their division's products in their area. The Manufacturing Division, with headquarters in Sunnyvale, had worldwide responsibility for production and quality control. (See Exhibit 1 for the 1969 organization chart.)

Exhibit 1
Bancil Corporation: 1969 Organization Chart

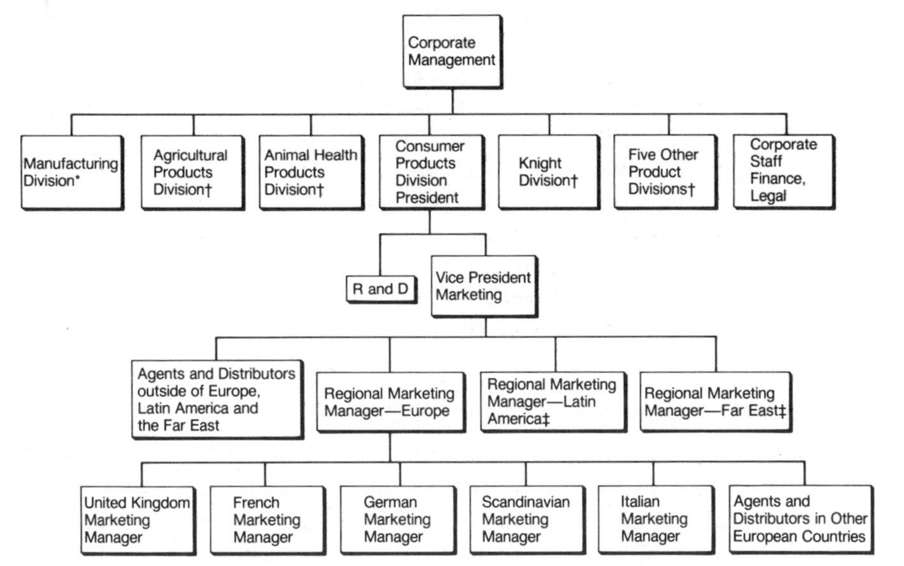

* The Manufacturing Division manufactured products for all the product divisions. Overseas manufacturing (not shown) reported to the Manufacturing Division in Sunnyvale.
† Organization similar to that of the Consumer Products Division.
‡ Organization similar to that for Europe.
Source: Company records.

Corporate management also identified a need in key countries for a single local executive to represent Bancil Corporation's interests in local banking and political circles. There was no single criterion for selecting, from the divisions' representatives in each country, the Bancil delegate, the title given to this position. A corporate officer remarked:

We chose whom we thought was the best business executive in each country. There was no emphasis on functional specialty or on selecting an individual from the division with the greatest volume. In one country, the major candidates were opinionated and strong willed, and we therefore chose the individual who was the least controversial. The Bancil delegate generally had a marketing background if marketing was the primary Bancil activity in the country or a production background if Bancil had several manufacturing facilities in the country.

While international sales had grown from $99 million in 1970 to $147 million in 1972, profit performance from 1971 to 1972 had been disappointing. A consultant's report stated:

There are excessive communications between the NUs and Sunnyvale. The marketing managers and all the agents are calling for product-line information from the divisional headquarters. Five individuals are calling three times per week on an average, and many more are calling only slightly less often.

It appeared that a great deal of management time was spent on telex, long-distance communications, and travel. In response to these concerns, the divisions' staffs increased in each country. Overhead nearly tripled, affecting the growth rate of profits from international operations.

With the exception of financial decisions which were dictated by corporate headquarters, most decisions on inventories, pricing, new-product offerings, and facility development were made by corporate headquarters in conjunction with the local people. Local people, however, felt that the key decisions were being postponed. Conflicting demands also were a problem as every division drew on the local resources for manpower, inventories, receivables, and capital investment. These demands had been manageable, however, because even though profits were below target no cash shortages had developed.

Current Organization of International Operations

To improve the performance of its international operations, Bancil instituted a reorganization in mid-1973. The new organization was a matrix of NU general managers and area vice presidents, who were responsible for total resource allocation in their geographic area, and division presidents, who were responsible for their product lines worldwide. (See Exhibit 2 for a description of the matrix in 1975.)

The general manager was the chief executive in his country in charge of all Bancil products. He also was Bancil's representative on the board and executive committee of local joint ventures. The Bancil delegate usually had been chosen as the general manager. He was responsible for making the best use of financial, material, and personnel resources; pursuing approved strategies; searching for and identifying new business opportunities for Bancil in his NU; and developing Bancil's reputation as a responsible corporate citizen. The general manager was assisted by a financial manager, one or more plant managers, product-line marketing managers, and other functional managers as required.

The divisions were responsible for operations in the United States and Canada and for worldwide expertise on their product lines. Divisions discharged the latter responsibility through local product-line marketing managers who reported on a line basis to the NU general manager and on a functional basis to a division area marketing director. The latter, in turn, reported to the divisional marketing vice president. Where divisions were involved in other functional activities, the organizational structure was similar to that for marketing. The flow of product-line expertise from the divisions to the NUs consisted of (1) operational inputs such as hiring/termination policies and the structure of merit programs and (2) technical/professional inputs to the NU marketing, production, and other staff functions on the conduct of the division's business within the NU.

Exhibit 2
Bancil's Shared-Responsibility Matrix

Vice President
International Operations
Clark B. Tucker

Product Group Vice Presidents	Division Presidents	Europe Andre Dufour			Latin America Juan Vilas			Far East	Area Vice Presidents
		France P. Chevalier	Germany D. Rogge	Four other national units	Argentina and Uruguay S. Portillo	Brazil E. Covelli	Two other national units	Four national units	General Managers
Agricultural and Animal Health (3 divisions)	Rodgers Division								
	Division B								
	Division C								
Consumer Products (2 divisions)	Dominic Division								
	Toiletry Division (Robert Vincent)								
Pharmaceuticals (2 divisions)	Division A								
	Division B								
Professional (3 divisions)	Knight Division								
	Division B								
	Division C								

Source: Company records.

Only the Dominic Division was represented in every NU. Some divisions lacked representation in several NUs, and in some cases a division did not have a marketing director in an area. For example, the Rodgers Division had area marketing directors in Europe, the Far East, and Latin America, all reporting to the divisional vice president of marketing to whom the division's U. S. marketing personnel also reported. However, the Knight Division, which had a structure similar to that of the Rodgers Division, could justify area marketing directors only in Europe and Latin America.

The new matrix organization established for each country a national unit review committee (NURC), with its membership consisting of the general manager (chairman), a financial manager, and a representative from each division with activities in the NU. Corporate executives viewed the NURC as the major mechanism for exercising shared profit responsibility. NURC met quarterly, or more frequently at the general manager's direction, to (1) review and approve divisional profit commitments generated by the general manager's staff; (2) ensure that these profit commitments, viewed as a whole, were compatible with and representative of the best use of the NU's resources; (3) monitor the NU's progress against the agreed plans; and (4) review and approve salary ranges for key NU personnel. When the division's representatives acted as members of the NURC, they were expected to view themselves as responsible executives of the NU.

Strategic Planning and Control

NURC was also the framework within which general managers and division representatives established the NU's annual strategic plan and profit commitment. Strategy meetings commenced in May, at which time the general manager presented a forecast of Bancil's business in his NU for the next five years and the strategies he would pursue to exploit environmental opportunities. The general manager and the divisional representatives worked together between May and September to develop a mutually acceptable strategy and profit commitment. If genuine disagreement on principle arose during these deliberations, the issue could be resolved at the next level of responsibility. The profit commitment was reviewed at higher levels both within the area and within the product divisions, with the final approval coming from the Corporate Executive Committee (CEC) which required compatible figures from the vice president of international operations and the product group executives. CEC, the major policymaking forum at Bancil, consisting of the chief executive officer, the group vice presidents, the vice president of international operations, and the corporate secretary, met monthly to resolve policy issues and to review operating performance.

For each country, results were reported separately for the various divisions represented, which, in turn, were consolidated into a combined NU statement. The NU as well as the divisions were held accountable, though at different levels, according to their responsibilities. The division profit flow (DPF) and NU net income are shown in the following example for the Argentine National Unit in 1974:

	Rodgers Division	Dominic Division	Toiletry Division	National Unit
Division sales	$250,000	$800,000	$1,250,000	$2,300,000
Division expenses	160,000	650,000	970,000	1,780,000
Division profit flow (DPF)	90,000	150,000	280,000	520,000
NU other expenses (general administrative, interest on loans, etc.)				350,000
NU income before taxes				$ 170,000
Less: Taxes				80,000
NU net income				$ 90,000
Working capital	$100,000	$300,000	$ 700,000	

The product divisions were responsible for worldwide division profit flow (DPF), defined as net sales less all direct expenses related to divisional activity, including marketing managers' salaries, sales force, and sales office expenses. The NU was responsible for net income after charging all local divisional expenses and all NU operating expenses such as general administration, taxes, and interest on borrowed funds. Because both the general managers and the divisions shared responsibility for profit in the international operations, the new structure was called a shared-responsibility matrix (SRM). The vice president of international operations and the division presidents continually monitored various performance ratios and figures (see Exhibit 3). In 1975, international operations emphasized return on resources, cash generation, and cash remittance, while the division presidents emphasized product-line return on resources, competitive market share, share of advertising, and dates of new-product introductions.

The impact of the 1973 organizational shift to the SRM had been greatest for the general managers. Previously, as Bancil delegates, they had not been measured on the basis of the NU's total performance for which they were now held responsible. Also, they now determined salary adjustments, hiring, dismissals, and appointments after consultations with the divisions. In addition, general managers continued to keep abreast of important political developments in their areas, such as the appointment of a new finance minister, a general work strike, imposition of punitive taxes, and the outbreak of political strife, a not infrequent occurrence in some countries.

Exhibit 3
Control Figures and Ratios

Vice President of International Operations for National Unit		Division President for Product Line
X*	Sales	X
X	Operating income: percent of sales	X
X	General manager expense: percent of sales	
X	Selling expense: percent of sales	X
X	Nonproduction expense: percent of operating income	
X	Operating income per staff employee	
X	Percent of staff turnover	
X	Accounts receivable (days)	X
X	Inventories (days)	X
X	Fixed assets	X
X	Resources employed	X
X	Return on resources	X
X	Cash generation	
X	Cash remittances	
X	Share of market and share of advertising	X
X	Rate of new-product introduction	X

* X indicates figure or ratio on organization's (national unit or division) performance of interest to the vice president of international operations and the division presidents.

Source: Company records.

Exhibit 4
Sales and Profits for Bancil Corporation, Domestic and International, ($ millions)

	Domestic		International		Total	
Year	**Sales**	**Profit**	**Sales**	**Profit**	**Sales**	**Profit**
1955	$ 61	$ 5.5	—	—	$ 61	$ 5.5
1960	83	8.3	$ 6	$ 0.2	89	8.5
1965	121	13.5	23	1.3	144	14.8
1969	269	26.7	76	9.2	345	35.9
1970	280	27.1	99	12.3	379	39.4
1971	288	28.7	110	14.2	398	42.9
1972	313	32.5	147	15.8	460	48.3
1973	333	35.3	188	21.4	521	56.7
1974	358	36.7	242	30.9	600	67.6

Source: Company records.

Under the new organizational structure, the area marketing directors felt that their influence was waning. While they were responsible for DPF, they were not sure that they had "enough muscle" to effect appropriate allocation of resources for their products in each of the countries they served. This view was shared by Nicholas Rosati, Knight Division marketing manager in Italy, who commented on his job:

The European marketing director for the Knight Division keeps telling me to make more calls on hospitals and laboratories. But it is useless to make calls to solicit more orders. The general manager for Italy came from the Consumer Products Division. He will neither allocate additional manpower to service new accounts for the Knight Division nor will he purchase sufficient inventory of our products so I can promise reasonable delivery times for new accounts.

Divisions, nevertheless, were anxious to increase their market penetration outside the United States and Canada, seeing such a strategy as their best avenue of growth. The recent increase in international sales and profits, which has by far exceeded that of domestic operations (see Exhibit 4), seemed to confirm the soundness of this view. Not all NU general managers shared this approach, as exemplified by a statement from Edmundo Covelli, the general manager of Brazil:

The divisions are continually seeking to boost their sales and increase their DPF. They are not concerned with the working-capital requirements to support the sales. With the inflation rate in Brazil, my interest rate of 40 percent on short-term loans has a significant effect on my profits.

The Peau Doux Issue

The telephone conversation described at the beginning of the case involved a disagreement between Tom Wilson, who was both marketing vice president for the Toiletry Division and acting division marketing director for Europe, and Pierre Chevalier, Bancil's general manager for France. It also involved Remy Gentile, who reported on a line basis to Chevalier and on a functional basis to Wilson.

Pierre Chevalier had been a general manager of France for 18 months after having been hired from a competitor in the consumer products business. Upon assuming the position, he identified several organizational and operational problems in France:

> *When I took this job, I had five marketing managers, a financial manager, a production manager, and a medical specialist reporting to me. After the Consumer products Division split, the new Toiletry Division wanted its own marketing manager. Nine people reporting to me was too many. I hired Remy for his administrative talents and had him assume responsibility for the Toiletry Division in addition to having the other marketing managers report to him. That gave me more time to work with our production people to get the cost of goods down.*

In less than two years as general manager, Chevalier had reduced the cost of goods sold by more than 3 percent by investing in new equipment and had improved the net income for the French NU by discontinuing products which had little profit potential.

Remy Gentile had been the marketing manager for the Toiletry Division in France for the past year. In addition, five other marketing managers (one for each Bancil Corporation division operating in France) reported to him. During the previous six years, Gentile had progressed from salesman to sales supervisor to marketing manager within the Knight Division in France. Although he had received mixed reviews from the Toiletry Division, particularly on his lack of mass-marketing experience, Chevalier had hired him because of his track record, his ability to learn fast, and his outstanding judgment.

The disagreement involved the Peau Doux line of hand creams which Bancil Corporation had purchased five years earlier to spread the general manager's overhead, especially in terms of marketing, over a broader product offering. Wilson's frustration resulted from Chevalier's ambivalence toward the division's strategy of increasing the marketing effort and cutting manufacturing costs on the Peau Doux line.

The total market in France for the Peau Doux product line was growing at an annual rate of 15–20 percent, according to both Wilson and Gentile. However, Peau Doux, an old, highly regarded hand cream, had been traditionally distributed through pharmacies, whereas recently introduced hand creams had been successfully sold through supermarkets. The original Peau Doux sales force was not equipped to distribute the product through other outlets. To support a second sales force for supermarket distribution, the Toiletry Division sought to acquire the L'aube shampoo and face cream line. When Gentile had informed Chevalier of this strategy, the latter had questioned the wisdom of the move. The current volume of the Peau Doux line was $800,000. Though less than 10 percent of Chevalier's total volume, it comprised the entire Toiletry Division volume in France.

Tom Wilson viewed the Peau Doux problems primarily in terms of an inadequate marketing effort. On three occasions within the past year, he or his media experts from Sunnyvale had gone to Paris to troubleshoot the Peau Doux problems. On the last trip, Robert Vincent, the Toiletry Division president, had joined them. On the return flight to Sunnyvale, Wilson remarked to Vincent:

> *I have the suspicion that Chevalier, in disregarding our expertise, is challenging our authority. It is apparent from his indifference to our concerns and his neglect in allocating capital for new machinery that he doesn't care about the Peau Doux line. Maybe he should be told what to do directly.*

Vincent responded:

> *Those are very strong words, Tom. I suggest we hold tight and do a very thorough job of preparing for the budget session on our strategy in France. If Chevalier does not accept or fundamentally revises our budget, we may take appropriate measures to make corporate management aware of the existing insensitivity to the Toiletry Division in France. This seems to be a critical issue. If we lose now, we may never get back in the French market in the future.*

After Wilson and Vincent had departed for Sunnyvale, Chevalier commented to Dufour, his area vice president:

> *I have the feeling that nothing we say will alter the thinking of Wilson and Vincent. They seem to be impervious to our arguments that mass advertising and merchandising in France do not fit the Peau Doux product concept.*

Andre Dufour had been a practicing pharmacist for six years prior to joining Bancil Corporation as a sales supervisor in Paris in 1962. He had progressed to sales manager and marketing manager of the Consumer Products Division in France. After the untimely death of the existing Bancil delegate for France in 1970, he had been selected to fill that position. With the advent of SRM he had become the general manager and had been promoted to vice president for Europe a year later. Dufour had a talent for identifying market needs and for thoroughly planning and deliberately executing strategies. He was also admired for his perseverance and dedication to established objectives. Clark B. Tucker, vice president of international operations and Dufour's immediate supervisor, commented:

> *When he was a pharmacist he developed an avocational interest in chess and desired to become proficient at the game. Within five years he successfully competed in several international tournaments and achieved the rank of international grand master.*

In the fall of 1974, Dufour had become the acting vice president of international operations while his superior, Clark Tucker, was attending the 13-week advanced management program at the Harvard Business School. Though Dufour had considerable difficulty with the English language, he favorably impressed the corporate management at Sunnyvale with his ability of getting to the heart of business problems.

The Toiletry Division had only limited international activities. In addition to the Peau Doux line in France, it marketed Cascada shampoos and Tempestad fragrances in Argentina. The Cascada and Tempestad lines had been acquired in 1971.

Tom Wilson and Manual Ramirez, Toiletry Division marketing director for Latin America, were ecstatic over the consumer acceptance and division performance of Cascada and Tempestad in Argentina. Revenue and DPF had quintupled since the acquisition. In his dealings with Gentile, Wilson frequently referred to the Toiletry Division's success in Argentina. Given this sales performance and the division's clearly stated responsibility for worldwide marketing of toiletry products, Wilson felt that his position in proposing the new strategy for France was strong.

On the other hand, Sergio Portillo, general manager of Argentina and Uruguay, and Juan Vilas, vice president for Latin American operations, had become alarmed by the cash drain from marketing the Toiletry Division products in Argentina. The high interest charges on funds for inventories and receivables seemed to negate the margins touted by the division executives. In describing the Cascada and Tempestad operation to Vilas, Portillo commented:

I have roughly calculated our inventory turnover for the Toiletry Division products marketed in Argentina. Though my calculations are crude, the ratio based on gross sales is about four, which is less than one half the inventory turnover of the remainder of our products.

Neither Portillo nor Vilas shared the Toiletry Division's enthusiasm, and they suspected that Cascada and Tempestad were only slightly above break-even profitability. Chevalier and Dufour were aware of this concern with the toiletry products in Argentina.

As Chevalier contemplated the Toiletry Division strategy, he became convinced that more substantive arguments rather than just economic ones would support his position. In discussing his concerns with Dufour, Chevalier asked:

Are the Toiletry Division product lines really part of what John Stoopes and we want to be Bancil's business? Hand creams, shampoos, and fragrances belong to firms like Colgate-Palmolive, Procter & Gamble, and Revlon. What is Bancil contributing to the local people's welfare by producing and marketing toiletries? We have several potentially lucrative alternatives for our resources. The Rodgers Division's revenues have been increasing at 18 percent. We recently completed construction of a processing plant for Rodgers, and we must get sales up to our new capacity. The Knight Division is introducing an electronic blood analyzer that represents a technological breakthrough. We must expand and educate our sales force to take advantage of this opportunity.

Chevalier senses that Gentile was becoming increasingly uneasy on this issue, and the feeling was contagious. They had never faced such a situation before. Under the previous organization, NUs had been required to comply, although sometimes reluctantly, with the decisions from Sunnyvale. However, SRM was not supposed to work this way. Chevalier and Gentile stood firmly behind their position, though they recognized the pressure on Tom Wilson and to a lesser degree on Vincent. They wondered what should be the next step and who should take it. Due to the strained relationship with Wilson, they did not rule out the possibility of Wilson and Vincent's taking the Peau Doux issue to the consumer products group vice president and having it resolved within the corporate executive committee.

Reading 5–1

On Concepts of Corporate Structure: Economic Determinants of Organization*

Harold Stieglitz

Just about 25 years ago, General Motors announced one of its most important products—the GM Formula. Its wage escalation clause negotiated then with the UAW provided for a 1 cent increase in hourly wages for each 1.14 point rise in the BLS index. Confronted with the inflationary period of Korea, many company negotiators copied GM and adopted the 1 for 1.14 formula for escalating wages. The fact that the formula had a specific relevance to GM's employees—that it reflected the ratio of average wages of the GM employees to the cost-of-living index at the time of adoption—seemed beside the point. The fact that a different formula might have more appropriately reflected the wage–cost-of-living relationship of their employees deterred few from just going ahead with 1 for 1.14. Evidently what was good enough for the sophisticates at GM was good enough for most of its emulators.

More than 50 years ago, however, GM had developed another product that proved to have an even larger impact. This was a management concept labeled "centralized coordination, decentralized administration"—or, "decentralization with coordination and control." While adoption of this concept came less rapidly, many companies turned to it—especially in the post–World War II growth period, when diversification and greater complexity characterized an increasing number.

In application, the concept meant reorganizing operations into divisionalized profit centers that operated with a high degree of decentralization; setting up corporate staffs to provide centralized coordination and control under corporatewide policies. Initially, the ambiguities and vaga-

* Reprinted by permission from *The Conference Board Record,* February 1974.

ries of the concept were not seen as deterrents to its adoption. GM's success in the marketplace showed it must be doing something right. If "decentralization with centralized control" was good enough for GM, it was good enough for others.

Since the early 1920s, however, the concept was subject to adaptation and development at GM itself. Even during Alfred P. Sloan's tenure, changes in technology and the marketplace brought an ebb and flow to the degree of decentralization versus centralized coordination—and, retrospectively, it's been more ebb than flow. But those who borrowed the concept sometimes missed the nuances of GM's later experience, so what seemed to work there didn't always work for them.

Emulation in structuring organization is not, of course, dead. Upon hearing of a major company that operates very effectively with a very small central staff, many a chief executive has envied the cost savings implicit in such a structure. Some have tried it. Similarly, the prospect of putting some young tigers at the head of their own decentralized profit centers had led others to reorganize. However, in more recent years, there is evidence that a more mature approach to organization planning has displaced such "me-too-ism."

The Reasons for Structuring Organization

Sloan, the prime mover in the development and adaptation of GM's concept of organization, at the close of his long career remarked, "An organization does not make decisions; its function is to provide a framework, based upon established criteria, within which decisions can be made."[1] The modifying phrase "based upon established criteria" is crucial, and maturity in corporate organization structuring has only developed as more top executives have been able to identify those criteria that condition the framework.

Admittedly, many a pragmatic top executive denies that there are any basic criteria that dictate key elements of the organization structure. The "situation," the "personalities," the "management style," and a host of other factors are presumably enough to make each organization and its structure unique.[2] Over the long run, however, one may observe that constant reorganizations and adaptation tend to move the structure in directions that seem almost independent of particular personalities or styles or whims.

Demonstrably, the spectrum of organizational structures throughout industry remains quite broad. It stretches from companies that are orga-

---

[1] Alfred P. Sloan, Jr., *My Years with General Motors* (Garden City, N. Y.: Doubleday Publishing, 1964).

[2] See *The Chief Executive and His Job,* Studies in Personnel Policy, No. 214 (National Industrial Conference Board, 1969).

nized virtually like holding companies to those that operate, basically, like one-man businesses. There are companies that operate in a highly centralized manner, others that are highly decentralized—and all shades in between. Similarly, some are functionally organized, some have certain elements set up as divisions, some are mixed. And staff within these companies come in all shapes and sizes.[3]

Still, the patterns of organization structure that have emerged indicate that there are company characteristics that are at the root of the developments, and they are primarily economic. Moreover, those that are evidently most influential in shaping organization structure can be specified:

1. *Degree of diversification* in terms of the variety of goods and services produced and/or markets served.
2. *Degree of interdependency,* integration, or overlap among the diversified operating components.

Such other factors as economies of scale, dispersion, or absolute size are significant, but largely to the extent that they affect diversification and overlap.[4]

The extent to which a company is diversified tends to determine whether its major operating activities will be structured by division or function and the nature of the groups that come into existence.

The extent to which the operations overlap—in terms of markets, technology, sources of supply, etc.—emerges as the key determinant of the degree of decentralization and the types and role of corporate staff.

In short, the emergence of the divisionalized decentralized form of organization is less a matter of managerial sophistication, more a matter of economic necessity. In an organizational sense, sophistication amounts to recognition of the inevitable.

A Continuum of Organizations

Relating structure to economic variables is more readily seen when the varieties of types of companies and apposite key structural elements are arrayed. Looking at diversity and overlap of operations, it's quite evident, for example, that companies range from those engaged in the

---

[3] For documentation of major organization trends, see *Corporate Organization Structures,* Studies in Personnel Policy, Nos. 183 and 210 (National Industrial Conference Board, 1961 and 1968), and *Corporate Organization Structures: Manufacturing* (1973). Also see *Organization Planning: Basic Concepts, Emerging Trends* (National Industrial Conference Board, 1969).

[4] See, for example, *Staff Services in Smaller Companies: The View from the Top,* Report No. 592 (The Conference Board, April 1973).

production and/sale of one good or service to those involved in a multiplicity of related and unrelated businesses. Indeed, when so arrayed, it is clear that the myriad variations form a continuum with no real discontinuities [see Exhibit 1].

A company at Point 1 of the continuum may be substantially different from one at Point 10, but to distinguish too sharply between companies at Points 4 and 5 would be fatuous. Even so, the continuum, as represented in the chart, can be divided for analytical purposes into four categories—each of which, in itself, covers a spectrum of companies:

I. ***Single businesses***—one company producing a single or homogeneous product for a single or homogeneous market.

II. ***Multiple businesses, related***—one company producing a variety of products for a variety of markets, but with a high degree of overlap in markets for the various products and/or a high degree of integration in materials or technology involved in manufacturing the products.

III. ***Multiple businesses, unrelated***—one company producing a variety of products for a variety of markets, but the overlap is absent. There are viturally no common denominators—no overlap—in the markets served or the resources or technology employed in producing the variety of goods or services.

IV. ***Multiple businesses, unrelated (no corporate identity)***—one company but little or no attempt to manage the unrelated businesses; little or no attempt to project a company identity. This, of course, is the holding company defined by Sloan as "a central office surrounded by autonomously operating satellites."

This continuum is not designed to suggest a strategy for growth. Nor does it imply that normal growth occurs through movement across the continuum. A company's growth pattern may keep it in Category I, move it from I to II, or from IV to III.

It bears repeating that the array is a continuum—there are no sharp discontinuities. For analytical purposes, a company can only be characterized as having "more or less" of the economic qualities of a particular category. Similarly, the key organizational elements that related to these categories can also only be referred to in terms of degree—more or less—i.e., more or less decentralized, more or less divisionalized. Overall, the tendency to divisionalize increases as one moves from Categories I to IV; more significantly, the degree of decentralization decreases as one moves from IV to I. The major related structural elements—makeup of the divisions, types and roles of staff, nature of the groups—also vary.

Exhibit 1
A Continuum of Corporations and Related Organization Structures

Elements of Organization	Single Businesses I (1 2 3 4)	Multiple Businesses, Related II (5 6 7 8)	Multiple Businesses, Unrelated III (9 10 11 12)	Multiple Businesses, Unrelated (no corporate identity) IV (13 14 15 16)
Structure of operations	Functional	Divisionalized	Divisionalized	Divisionalized (subsidiaries)
Functional elements within divisions	—	Production and sales (little staff)	Production and sales (more staff)	Production and sales (more complete staff)
Degree of decentralization	More centralized	Decentralized	Highly decentralized	Highly decentralized (virtual autonomy for divisions)
Corporate staff				
Type	Administrative and operational	Administrative and operational	Administrative	Administrative (if any)
Role	Services Advisory control	Advisory control	Advisory (consultant)	—
Groups	—	Superdivisions	Liaison	Unlikely

Functional versus Divisional Form of Organization

It is no accident that companies, regardless of size, that fall into Category I tend to be organized on a functional basis. At the extreme left of the spectrum there is usually little basis for coordinating specialized activities in any other way. Thus, inasmuch as all manufacturing and engineering activities serve a common product, they are organized under one head. Inasmuch as all marketing activities are designed to promote one product, they too are most effectively coordinated by one head.

As the company finds either its product or market spectrum broadening—as it diversifies—it often is able to segregate either its production activities or its marketing activities by product or market. But in terms of who is accountable for what, it's still functional—until such time as increased diversity allows both marketing and production of a given product for a specified market to be linked.

This move to link production and sales of a given product under one head—thus divisionalizing and forming a "profit center," as opposed to a "cost center"—characteristically occurs in companies whose diversification efforts result in *(a)* more discrete technologies for each product, *(b)* more discrete markets for each product. Under these circumstances, whether diversification has come from internal product development or external mergers or acquisition, product divisions emerge as the more effective operating components. Again, it is no accident that companies whose operational characteristics are those of Categories II, III, or IV tend to organize them into product or so-called market divisions. In short, they divisionalize.[5]

However, the divisions that are so characteristic of the more diversified companies vary in terms of the more specialized functional components that are assigned or report to the division head. In Category II, for example, the divisions undoubtedly have their own production and sales units; they may very well have their own accounting and engineering units. But it is most likely that corporate units in various areas—e.g., marketing, manufacturing, purchasing, or research and development—will exist, in part, to supply certain services that are common to several divisions. Thus the divisions of companies in Category II tend to truncate; they are not complete in terms of all the functions necessary to carry on their operations.

The divisions that make up companies in Categories III and IV, on the other hand, tend to be more self-sufficient, less reliant on common services. Indeed, in Category IV, many of the operating components exist as virtually self-sufficient subsidiaries. Obviously, the greater interdepen-

---

[5] For a more complete analysis of divisionalization, see *Top Management Organization in Divisionalized Companies*, Studies in Personnel Policy, No. 195 (National Industrial Conference Board, 1965).

dence and overlap of markets, technology, and resources in Category II accounts for the more truncated divisions in this class; the lack of commonality between the divisions or subdivisions of Categories III and IV makes for far greater self-sufficiency—at least in terms of functional components.

Centralization-Decentralization

Degree of overlap is even more closely related to the varying degrees of decentralization that are evident at various points in the continuum. Decentralization, in this context, has a specific meaning: the extent to which decision-making authority is delegated to lower levels of the organization and, by implication, the degree of constraint—of centralized control in the form, for example, of corporatewide policies—that curtails the area of discretion left to lower-level managers.

Generally, it can be observed that three factors have a major effect on the degree of delegated authority and/or decentralization:

1. *The confidence factor*—the confidence of superiors in the competence of subordinates.
2. *The information factor*—the extent to which the organization has developed mechanisms to feed information to the decision-making points, and the extent to which feedback systems have developed that allow accountable managers to evaluate results of their decisions.
3. *The scope-of-impact factor*—the extent to which a decision made by one unit head affects the operations of another unit.

It is this third factor—the scope of impact of decision—that, in the long run, becomes the key ingredient in determining the degree of decentralization. And, clearly, the scope of impact of decisions is directly related to the degree of integration, or overlap, or interdependence of the company's varied operations. With a greater degree of interaction, less decentralization is possible. As the operations become more highly varied and opportunities for operational synergy decrease, the greater the possible degree of decentralization, the greater the toleration of differences in approaches to personnel, customers, and the public.[6]

In terms of the continuum, it is evident that the operation of companies in Category I encourages a higher degree of centralized decision making than takes place in Category II. Similarly, companies in Category III can, and do, tolerate more decentralization than those in Category II. And while the operations, or the divisions of companies, in Categories III and IV might be very similar in terms of diversity and minimum

[6] Ibid.

overlap, the fact that companies in Category IV are not intent on projecting a corporate identity—and thus can eschew corporatewide policies—makes for a degree of decentralization that verges on virtual autonomy for the operating divisions or subsidiaries.

Corporate Staff: Functions and Roles

Size is undoubtedly a key factor that determines whether and when a particular staff unit will emerge within the corporation. Until there is a continuing need for a particular functional expertise, the company may well make use of outside or part-time consultants or services. But once the need is felt and a full-time staff unit is created, whether it be one person or a larger unit, the nature of the operations and the degree of decentralization tend to be strong determinants of the types of specialized staff that come into being and their role relative to the rest of the company.

For analytical purposes, it is useful to distinguish between: *(a)* administrative staff, the functional (staff) units that derive from the fact that a corporation exists as a legal and financial entity (the legal, financial, and public relations staff are typical), and *(b)* operational staff, the functional (staff) units that emerge because of the peculiar nature of the companies' operations (e.g., manufacturing, marketing, purchasing, and traffic).

An even more substantive distinction can be drawn between the various roles that characterize staff in its varied relationships. Again, for analytical purposes, whether it be administrative or operational staff, three roles can be distinguished.[7]

1. *Advisory or counseling role:* The staff unit brings its professional expertise to bear in analyzing and solving problems. In this role, staff acts as a consultant; its relationship is largely that of a professional to a client.

2. *Service role:* The staff unit provides services that can be more efficiently and economically provided by one unit with specialized expertise than by many units attempting to provide for themselves. Its relationship in this role is largely that of a supplier to a customer.

3. *Control role:* Because of its professional or specialized expertise in a given functional area, staff is called upon to assist in establishing the plans, budgets, policies, rules, standard operating procedures that act as major constraints on delegated authority; that set the parameters of decision making at lower levels. And it sets up mechanisms to audit

---

[7] For a more complete discussion, see also *Top Management Organization in Divisionalized Companies* [footnote 5], especially chap. 7, "Staff."

and evaluate performance vis-à-vis these controls. In exercising this role, its relationship to the rest of the organization is that of an agent for top management.

By combining the elements—type of staff and role—it is possible to draw a profile of corporate staff. And that profile tends to vary with companies in each of the four categories.

Thus the fact that Category I includes companies that are organized functionally, that are more centralized than decentralized, narrows the options for the character of staff units that come into being. Of necessity, staff units of both administrative and operational types become part of corporate structure—with the operational staff elements often reporting directly to the accountable operational head of manufacturing or sales. And while some staff units may be more service oriented than advisory, others more advisory than control, the fact that the functional organization is virtually one large profit center makes advice, service, and control a part of every staff unit's job.

Among Category II companies, whose diversification has fostered divisionalization and greater decentralization, the profile of corporate staff changes. The change is largely one of role rather than type.

Because the divisional operations are interdependent and overlap, there may well be need for operational staff as well as administrative units at the corporate level. But divisions may also have their own staff units to provide services that are unique to the division. Thus, in a divisionalized company there may be, for example, R&D at both corporate and division levels, with divisional staff emphasizing development, corporate staff emphasizing longer-range research. However, because more staff is created within the divisions of Category II companies to provide services locally, the service role of the corporate staff declines. As a result, the advisory and control roles of the corporate staff units assume primary emphasis.

However, this is not to suggest that the advisory and control roles become dominant merely as residual factors. To the contrary, they gain emphasis because: *(a)* In companies with the economic characteristics of Category II, corporate top management becomes relatively more future oriented; the divisions remain more oriented to the near term. The future emphasis underscores the corporate staff's advisory role in planning. *(b)* The decentralization occasioned by multiple profit centers heightens the need to discern areas of overlap as well as matters of overriding corporate concern that require consistency in decision making, i.e., the generation of corporate policies. And it puts greater emphasis on discerning and establishing more sophisticated control procedures. Thus the greater emphasis on staff as an agency of control.

Moving to companies whose economic characteristics are those of Category III, the profile of corporate staff again changes—this time in both type and role. Because the operating divisions have little in common, they share no markets; they don't overlap in technology and resources; there is little need for corporate staff in operational areas. Rather, operational staff units are more often housed within the divisions or at the group level. The corporate staff units more often are those in the general areas of administration—financial, legal—and often those that are closely tied to future development of the corporation.

More significantly, the corporate staff's role as a control agency, prominent in both Categories I and II, fades among Category III companies. The far greater degree of decentralization possible in any such company is synonymous with fewer overall constraints in the form of corporate policies and procedures. This fact accounts for the change in role. For the most part, staff units in Category III companies, with the possible exception of finance and planning, are primarily advisory in role—captive consultants.

The diminished need for operational staff and the shift to a primarily consulting relationship that characterizes corporate staff in Category III companies becomes even more pronounced in Category IV. Indeed, it becomes difficult even to see corporate staff—in the sense so far discussed—in the company that operates like a holding company. The parent corporation may have a strong financial unit and legal unit, but these exist primarily to serve the parent. Since the divisions or subsidiaries are encouraged to operate in a manner that verges on autonomy, they establish their own controls, have their own staffs whose profile undoubtedly varies with the economic characteristics of the particular division or subsidiary. If there is such a thing as "corporate staff" in companies at the extreme of Category IV, it may very well exist as a separate "management service" subsidiary from which the other divisions may purchase services as required.

Group Structures

The increased use of groups, headed by group executives, is relatively recent. The increase has resulted largely from the proliferation of operating divisions within corporations. It's another level of management introduced to secure better coordination of several presumably separate divisions.[8] Almost by definition, the group mechanism is confined to the divisionalized companies of Categories II and III. But not quite.

There are ambiguities in the group concept and variations in the structure of groups that can be linked to the same factors accounting for variations in the role of corporate staff.

Starting with Category IV, in this instance, there is little evidence of attempts to link operating units into groups headed by a group execu-

[8] Ibid., chap. 4, "Group Executives."

tive. This seems consistent with the parent corporation's hands-off approach to the highly independent divisions or subsidiaries.

In Category III companies, on the other hand, diverse though the divisions may be, there is an attempt to link the operations more closely with guidance from the corporation. There is an attempt to devise a corporate strategy and to project a corporate identity. Divisions very often are assembled into groups. But for the most part, the divisions within the groups have little in common—other than that they serve the "industrial market" or "consumer market" or operate under some such similarly broad umbrella. The group executive, in such instances, may serve as an advisor, a reviewer of plans, an appraiser of performance. But he is essentially a link pin between the division and their objectives and the corporation. His primary function may well be to plug the communication gap that emerges when the proliferation of divisions has caused too broad a span of control for the chief executive. Chances are that such a group will have no staff at the group level, or possibly just a controllership function that reports to the group executive.

Move to Category II companies, and the character of the group and the function of the group executive change. Here, the groups that emerge tend to be more closely knit, comprised of divisions that invite synergistic development. Indeed, in many such situations the group structure develops as a pragmatic mechanism for dealing with the fact that the "discrete and separate" divisions are not really all that discrete or separate. In many such companies, the divisions do share markets or do overlap in technology. The pulling together of these overlapping divisions makes it more possible to develop a business strategy for a total market, or to pool certain production facilities, or share common staff services.

The group, in such instances, actually becomes more of a superdivision composed of truncated or even functional divisions. And the group executive, rather than providing liaison between a series of unrelated divisions, becomes the head of a more encompassing profit center.

In Category I companies, the definition of group seems to preclude its existence—except possibly at Point 4 in the spectrum, where beginning attempts to diversify may lead to the creation of a group that pulls together newer businesses emerging as product divisions. The closest approximation of the group executive in the functionally organized company is the high-level executive who coordinates related staff and operating functions—e.g., an executive vice president whose domain covers manufacturing, engineering, R&D, and purchasing. However, he is still primarily a functional executive.

The Models in Perspective

These major elements of structure, when assembled by category, reveal organizational profiles that are significantly different. Each structural model is rooted in the dominant economic characteristics of the corporation as a total entity. It is worth underscoring the point that each category in itself covers a spectrum. The "more or less" caveat referred to earlier applies to each as well as the overall continuum. The profile of a company at Point 13 may be more like one at Point 12 than one at 16; or 5 and 4 may be more similar than 5 and 8.

Developments in organization structure make clear that companies, structurally, are trending toward more congruence with the economic realities of their businesses. But obviously there are many companies whose current structures seem to be at odds with their economic models. Indeed, complete congruence is more an ideal than a realizable goal.

In some companies, shorter-term pressures or more-immediate advantages take priority over what seems more logical in the longer term. Immediate pressure to penetrate special markets may induce a divisionalized structure even though there are longer-term advantages to greater integration on a functional basis. Or one phase of the company's operations, accounting for perhaps the larger part of the company's total sales and profits, may be so significant that the overall structure is organized functionally to accommodate it. Or the lack of management talent may require higher-level management to make more decisions and thus force a greater degree of centralization than seems warranted by the character of the operations. For these and many more highly practical reasons, the longer-term optimum organization structure is less than optimum to those whose performance is evaluated in the short term.

However, there is another set of factors, equally real, that impede achievement of the best fit. These lie in the psyche of the human organization. The incumbent staff may be so thoroughly familiar with the more specific organization problems of various elements of the organization that they have difficulty seeing the total corporation because of its divisions.

Even more inhibiting to achievement of the optimum structure are the inertial factors that restrict any major organization change—the comforts of sticking with past habits and traditions, of applying past practice to new situations.[9] A company's growth may be of a character that it moves from Category I to Category II. But the operating and staff personnel who move with it know how to operate in the environment of a functional organization with greater centralization and don't willingly assume new roles. As a result, some of the more poignant managerial tragedies, particularly those of chief executives, can be traced to their inability to mate individual "management styles" with the economic verities of the total company.

---

[9] For elaboration, see *Organization Change—Perceptions and Realities*, Report No. 561 (National Industrial Conference Board, July 1972).

Reading 5–2

*MNCs: Get Off the Reorganization Merry-Go-Round**

Christopher A. Bartlett

For many companies, international expansion has been the major strategic thrust of the postwar era. Yet even successful, well-established organizations face difficult problems in managing global operations. Heady years of overseas expansion have been followed by a persistent organizational hangover, unresponsive to traditional remedies.

In the 1960s, the answer to the international challenge seemed clear: managers simply needed to identify key strategic goals and restructure the corporation around them. But after two decades of experimentation, an "ideal international structure" remains elusive. Many companies still reorganize in the hope of finding it—but with only isolated cases of success.

With so many companies searching for this structural solution, why have results been so poor? Could it be that managers, obsessed with structure, were focusing on the wrong variable? A study I have made of 10 diverse and successful MNCs indicates that companies that persistently reorganize may be misdirecting their efforts. The companies I studied have *not* continually reorganized their operations. Each has retained for years a simple structure built around an international division—a form of organization that many management theorists regard as embryonic, appropriate only for companies in the earliest stages of worldwide growth.

These companies see the international challenge as one of building and maintaining a complex decision-making process rather than of find-

---

* Reprinted by permission of the *Harvard Business Review.* "MNCs: Get Off the Reorganization Merry-Go-Round" by Christopher A. Bartlett (March/April 1983).

ing the right formal structure. The critical task is to develop new management perspectives, attitudes, and processes that reflect and respond to the complex demands companies with international strategies face. Such a process might sound too time consuming, too subtle, or too difficult to imitate. But companies that want to better meet the challenge can use as a guide the patterns established by these successful companies.

Broken Promise

To understand why these companies have succeeded, we first should look at the reasons others have failed. As companies began to feel the strain of controlling fast-growing foreign operations, managements intuitively looked for structural solutions. This generation of top managers was on the front line when the wave of postwar product diversification led to the widespread shift from functional to multidivisional organization structures. They saw, firsthand, the powerful linkage between strategy and structure. The conventional wisdom was that if the divisional organization structure had helped managers implement the corporate strategy of diversification, surely an equivalent structure would facilitate their new international strategic thrust.

Managers had other reasons to reorganize. For one, changing the formal structure was recognized as a powerful tool through which management could redefine responsibilities and relationships. Top managers could make clear choices, have immediate impact, and send strong signals of change to all hierarchical levels. Furthermore, companies were encouraged to pursue such international reorganization because it seemed many others were doing likewise. In fact, the pattern of reorganization became so familiar that management theorists had documented and classified it.

Frustration came when managers discovered that no one structure provided a long-term solution. To many executives, it seemed they had no sooner developed a new set of systems, relationships, and decision-making processes than the international operations again needed to be reorganized. For example, Westinghouse disbanded its separate international division in 1971 when the 125 domestic-product division managers were given worldwide responsibilities. By early 1979, however, concern about the lack of coordination among divisions and the insensitivity to certain nations had mounted. A task force recommended a global matrix, and by midyear the new structure was in place. It was the third reorganization of international operations in one decade.

Like the executives at Westinghouse, many managers turned to a global matrix because they were frustrated by the one-dimensional biases built into a global-product or area-based structure. It was supposed to allow a company to respond to national and regional differences while simultaneously maintaining coordination and integration of worldwide business. But the record of companies that adopted this structure is disappointing. The promised land of the global matrix quickly turned into an organizational quagmire, forcing a large number of companies to retreat from it. Some of these cases were widely publicized, such as that of Dow Chemical.

Dow, which served as the textbook case study of the global matrix, eventually returned to a more conventional structure in which the emphasis is on geographically based managers. Citibank became the new case illustration in one important book on matrix organization.[1] Yet within a few years, Citibank was reportedly retreating from its global matrix structure.

The same problems with the global matrix kept coming up: tension and uncertainty built into dual reporting channels sometimes escalated to open conflict, complex issues were forced into a rigid two-dimensional decision framework, and minor issues became the subject of committee debates. More important, the design of matrix organization implied that managers with conflicting views or overlapping responsibilities communicate problems and confront and resolve differences. Yet barriers of distance, language, and culture impeded this vital process.

Managing the Process

The 10 companies that escaped the organizational merry-go-round had a number of things in common, but the most fundamental was their adaptability to complex demands without restructuring. Underlying the approach to global operations of managers of these companies was the way they thought about the strategic demands and the appropriate organizational response.

Two major forces exerted opposite pressures on international strategies during the 1970s. First, as global competitors emerged in many industries, skirmishes for single-country markets gave way to battles for worldwide market position and global-scale efficiencies. Second, host country governments raised their demands, and competition for market access tilted the bargaining power more in the governments' favor. MNCs had to increase local equity participation, transfer technology, build local manufacturing and research facilities, and meet export quotas.

With one set of pressures suggesting global integration and the other demanding local responsiveness, it is easy to see why executives of many companies thought in either-or terms and argued whether to centralize or decentralize control and whether to let the product or the geographic managers dominate corporate structure.

---

[1] See Stanley M. Davis and Paul R. Lawrence, *Matrix* (Reading, Mass.: Addison-Wesley Publishing, 1977). Citibank CEO Walter Wriston acknowledged in his foreword to this book the difficulty of managing in a global matrix.

While managers in the 10 companies remained sensitive to those conflicting demands, they resisted the temptation to view their tasks in such simple either-or terms. The managers understood that such clear-cut answers would not work since *both* forces are present to some degree in all businesses. Moreover, thinking of strategy in "global" or "local" terms ignored the complexity, diversity, and changeability of the demands facing them.

For example, a growing threat of Japanese competitors forced Timken, the leading bearings manufacturer, to become more globally competitive in the 1970s. Unlike the Japanese, Timken chose not to compete solely as the low-cost producer of standard bearings. Rather, the company opted to reinforce its position as the technological leader in the industry. While this strategy required the strengthening and integrating of a worldwide research function, Timken's management thought such global integration was unnecessary in manufacturing. It trimmed and standardized product lines to gain efficiencies, but plants still specialized on a regional—not a worldwide—basis. Moreover, because customer service and response time were at the core of Timken's strategy, sales forces and engineering services retained their strict local focus.

Savvy managers realize that it is often difficult to know how to focus responsibility even within a single function. For example, Corning Glass Works's TV tube marketing strategy required global decision making for pricing and local decision making for service and delivery.

The Challenge of Subtlety

It is not surprising that with this subtle perception of the nature of strategy, the managers in the 10 corporations set objectives, adopted a focus, and used tools that were different from those in most other MNCs. They realized that if the pressures in the international operating environment were intrinsically complex, diverse, and changeable, they had to create an internal management environment that could respond to these external demands and opportunities.

With this perception, managers viewed the organizational challenge not as one of finding and installing the right structure but as one of building an appropriate management process. As a result, they focused attention on the individual decision and the way it was reached rather than on the overall corporate structure. Questions changed from "Do we need worldwide product divisions or an area structure?" to "How can the company take the regional product group's perspective more into account in capacity expansion decisions?"

Finally, they looked for management tools with a finer edge than the blunt instrument of formal structural reorganization. Managers in other companies seemed so captivated by architectural problems that they forgot that the boxes they sketched on the back of an envelope represented not just positions but also people: the lines they casually erased and redrew stood not only for lines of authority but also for personal relationships. It was not unusual then to announce major reorganization very suddenly and install the structure in a few weeks or months. The result was often traumatic readjustment, followed by a long recovery. At Westinghouse, for example, the decision to reorganize into a global matrix structure was made by a senior management task force after a 90-day study of the problems and was put in place over the following 90 days.

Managers in the companies studied used tools that influenced individuals' behavior and attitudes or group norms and values in a more discrete and flexible manner.

A Multidimensional Decision Process

The experience of the companies studied suggests that development of the diverse and flexible organizational processes follows three closely related stages. First, because an organization must take into account the richness of the environment it faces rather than view the world through a single, dominant management perspective, the companies developed internal groups that allowed the organization to sense, analyze, and respond to a full range of strategic opportunities and demands.

In most companies, a necessarily formal organizational structure limits interaction between such diverse interests. Therefore, during the second stage, the company builds additional channels of communication and forums for decision making to allow greater flexibility.

Finally, in the third stage, the company develops norms and values within the organization to support shared decisions and corporate perspectives. Value is placed on corporate goals and collaborative effort rather than on parochial interests and adversary relationships.

Developing Multiple Management Perspectives

In this environment of changeable demands and pressures, managers must sense and analyze complex strategic issues from all perspectives. Top management's job is to eliminate the one-dimensional bias built into most organizations.

The traditional bias in companies with international divisions, for example, allowed country and regional managers to dominate decision making from their line positions, with product and functional staff groups relegated to support and advisory roles. As a result, the companies underestimated or even ignored strategic opportunities that might have been realized by global coordination and integration of operations.

Similarly, organization by product divisions fostered decisions favoring worldwide standardization and integration. The power of headquarters product managers over their geographic and functional counterparts was usually reinforced within the structure in formal as well as informal ways. For instance, the companies constructed information systems around products that allowed headquarters-based product management to collect and analyze data more easily than their functional or geographic counterparts. Furthermore, the strongest managers were appointed to product management positions, which reinforced their influence over the decision process.

Top management can begin to gradually eliminate these biases in the decision process by:

1. Upgrading Personnel. Assigning capable people to the right positions not only allows skills to be brought to bear in important areas but also sends strong signals that top management is serious about its objectives and priorities. For example, top managers of the hospital supply company Baxter Travenol decided to counterbalance the strength of country managers in the international division with a strong global business perspective. First, they replaced existing product managers with M.B.A.s who, while lacking the product expertise of their predecessors (ex-sales representatives), brought a more analytical and strategic perspective to the role. While this interim step upgraded the role, it was only with the appointment of more experienced managers from the domestic product divisions and foreign subsidiaries that the company achieved a strong global business perspective in its international strategy decisions.

2. Broadening Responsibilities. Aggressive, ambitious, and able managers will naturally resist transfer to positions viewed as less powerful and having fewer responsibilities and lower status. So companies must redefine the role of the positions at the same time they upgrade the personnel. In the example of Baxter Travenol, when top management appointed M.B.A.s to product manager positions, it enlarged the role from primarily a support responsibility to one that focused on monitoring and analyzing global product performance. When experienced product and country managers superseded the M.B.A.s, the company allowed them to get involved in the budgeting and strategic planning processes, making recommendations about the management of their lines of business worldwide.

Such progression of roles is fairly typical when a company is trying to develop groups previously underrepresented in the decision process. The company first broadens advisory and support roles to encompass responsibility for monitoring and control. Exposure to the information necessary to undertake these new tasks then helps develop the ability to make analyses and recommendations of key issues, and finally to implement strategy.

3. Changing Managerial Systems. The biggest impediment to these changes is often the existing line management group; as happened at Baxter Travenol, country subsidiary managers may greatly resent the increased "interference" of product and functional staff. So top management needs to back up the desired changes.

If the newly upgraded managers are to succeed, they need information tailored to their responsibilities. Management systems usually parallel the formal organization structure and give line managers a tremendous information advantage. Top executives must be sure managers representing other perspectives also have the information needed to support their proposals and arguments.

Originally, Corning consolidated data only by geographic entity. When the company decided to upgrade the role of product and functional managers, however, it found that consolidating data along these dimensions was both difficult and expensive. Inconsistent product-line definitions, different expense allocation practices, and numerous tangled cases of double counting were impediments to system restructuring. By the time management sorted out these problems (with the help of a consultant and a couple of high-powered software packages), the new systems had cost well over $1 million.

Through these three steps, the company elevates previously underrepresented management groups. The organization recognizes the need to monitor the environment from their perspective, acknowledges their competence to analyze the strategic implications of key issues, and accepts the legitimacy of representing such views in the decision process. Happily, many old distinctions between line and staff blur, and organization clichés about the locus of power become less relevant. As the president of Bristol-Myers' International Division told me: "The traditional distinctions between line and staff roles are increasingly unclear here. . . . But by motivating managers and giving them latitude rather than writing restrictive job descriptions, we believe we can achieve much more."

Creating Supplementary Information Channels

It is not enough for a company simply to develop an organization that can sense and analyze issues from various perspectives. Managers representing diverse points of view need access to the decision-making processes.

As I mentioned earlier, in most companies formal communication channels parallel formal organization structures. The focus is one-dimensional, and the decision-making process hierarchical and formal. The structure reinforces the power of dominant line managers while limiting the influence of managers representing other perspectives.

Top management must create forums for decision making that take many perspectives into account and are flexible. While the formal reporting lines and management systems provide one way to channel communications, management can use an equally strong set of informal channels.

Influencing Informality. Informal relationships among people, of course, naturally develop in any organization, and to date, many corporate executives have regarded them as an uncontrollable by-product of the formal organization. Increasingly, however, they recognize that they can, and indeed should, influence the organization's informal systems if the environment is to allow people representing diverse and frequently conflicting interests to influence decisions. In any MNC, managers are separated by barriers of distance, time, and culture; the extent to which top management works to overcome these barriers, the way in which it builds bridges, and the groups among which it develops contacts and relationships all have an important influence on the organization's informal network and processes.

A variety of tools is available. By bringing certain individuals together to work on common problems, for example, or by assigning a specific manager to a position that requires frequent contact with colleagues, management can influence the development of social relationships. Such personal bonds break down the defensiveness and misunderstanding that often build when line managers feel their power is threatened.

Senior management of Eli Lilly's International Division was conscious of this dynamic. As a normal part of career development, it transferred managers from line to staff positions, from one product line to another, and from headquarters to country subsidiaries. Although the original idea was to develop a broad perspective, an equally important benefit has been the development of an informal network of friends and contacts throughout the organization. In the words of one manager, "Those who moved about had far better information sources than computer reports, and more important, they developed the influence that comes with being known, understood, and respected."

Baxter Travenol's top management used frequent, well-planned meetings to help develop informal relationships. The company had long held annual general-manager's meetings in which country and regional line managers listened to formal presentations of the year's financial results, of the latest corporate plans, and of one or two new products. Recognizing that staff-line relationships were becoming very strained, the division president changed the traditional meeting into a senior management conference to which product managers and functional managers were also invited. He replaced most formal presentations with discussions, during which senior managers jointly identified and tried to resolve strategic and organizational issues.[2] The team formed bonds that endured far beyond the meetings.

Avoiding Strategic Anarchy. Of course a company cannot resolve complex issues by simply allowing different interests to clash in a trading-room-floor atmosphere. The formal hierarchy will still constrain and limit the influence of nonline managers as key issues are actually decided. There are, however, ways to ensure the representation of appropriate interests and at the same time allow headquarters to retain control.

Most managers are familiar with such things as task forces, interdepartmental teams, and special committees. These devices are often used ad hoc, after the formal decision process has failed, for example, or in response to a crisis. But managers can also use them in a more routine manner to pull certain issues out of the mainstream and to tailor the analysis and decision making.

Bristol-Myers' international organization, for instance, feared that the company was dissipating scarce research resources. Each project typically had the backing of a country subsidiary manager who claimed that the project was absolutely essential to his or her national strategy. By creating a "pharmaceutical council" comprised of senior geographic line managers and division-level business development staff managers, the division president forced these managers to make compromises and to combine these separate proposals into a single cohesive program. By appointing the business development director as the council's chairman, he increased this manager's influence and leverage and ensured that the deliberations would have a global perspective.

In Warner Lambert, country managers had for years influenced decisions on manufacturing capacity toward constructing local plants. Believing that such decisions compromised efficiency, the division president set up a task force of geographic and functional managers to conduct an 18-month review of global capacity needs. Recognizing the sensitivity of country managers to any loss of autonomy, he appointed regional managers to represent the line organization. The task force's manufacturing, finance, and marketing managers convinced regional managers of the need for greater coordination of manufacturing operations and rationalization of facilities to gain scale economies. With regional managers behind the idea, country managers were forced to recognize the program's considerable savings.

One note of caution: the purpose of such temporary task groups is to supplement rather than replace the mainstream decision process. The company must consider carefully which decisions cannot be resolved

[2] For a description of the process used, see my article, written with David W. De Long, "Operating Cases to Help Solve Corporate Problems," *Harvard Business Review*, March–April 1982, p. 68.

by the regular managerial process. It should clearly define and limit the number of issues taken "off-line" and keep them out of the mainstream only as long as necessary.

Building a Supportive Culture

There is no guarantee that decisions will reflect the mix of interests and views represented in the process. Simply putting people together does not mean they will interact positively and productively. It is necessary to build an organizational culture that supports multidimensional, flexible decision making.

In many companies, a culture that stresses internal competition has proven the major barrier to the development of a flexible decision process. In one of the companies studied, a well-known motto was that "only your final result counts." The company's formal structure and reward systems reinforced the value.

When internal competition is overemphasized, managers with different perspectives easily become entrenched adversaries and the decision-making process deteriorates, as protecting territory and even subversion become the norms. In fact, many companies discovered that upgrading nonline management groups and supplementing the hierarchical decision process triggered such adverse reactions.

To make the organization flexible, top management of the companies studied made certain that managers understood how their particular points of view fit with corporate strategies; it reinforced this understanding with a culture supportive of cooperation and compromise. The organizational norms and values creating such an environment obviously could not be established by management fiat. Rather, they were carefully developed through a variety of small actions and decisions.

Articulate Goals and Values. Elementary and simplistic as it may seem, one of the most powerful tools for top management is the precise formulation and communication of specific strategic objectives and behavioral norms. In a surprising number of companies, however, middle managers have only the vaguest notion of overall corporate objectives and of the boundaries of accceptable behavior.

Eli Lilly places great importance on mutual trust, openness, and honesty in all interpersonal dealings. In an orientation brochure for new employees, the late Eli Lilly, grandson of the founder, was quoted as saying: "Values are, quite simply, the core of both men and institutions. . . . By combining our thoughts and by helping one another, we are able to merge the parts [of this organization] into a rational, workable management system." It is clear that adversary relationships and parochial behavior do not fit in the culture he envisioned.

At Baxter Travenol, senior management conferences provided an ideal communication forum for the International Division president. In addition to articulating overall objectives and priorities, he acknowledged the conflicts implicit in particular important issues and encouraged managers to discuss how they might subjugate individual interests to the overall strategy. The participation of managers ensured not only their understanding of the issues but also their involvement in, and commitment to, corporate goals.

Modify Reward Systems. It is clear that a company cannot ask managers to compromise parochial interests for a broader good if it continues to evaluate and reward them on the basis of indicators tied tightly to a small area of responsibility. Successful international companies in the sample made sure managers understood they did not compromise career opportunities or expose themselves to other organizational risks by adopting a cooperative and flexible attitude. Many companies altered management evaluation criteria and modified formal reward systems.

As the decision-making processes became increasingly complex at Corning Glass Works, top managers changed the criteria for promotion. One top manager said to me:

> *In addition to the analytic and entrepreneurial capabilities we have always required, managers must now have strong interpersonal skills to succeed in key positions. To contribute to our decision-making process, they must be good communicators, negotiators, and team players. We had to move aside some individuals who simply could not work in the new environment.*

Eli Lilly's formal evaluation and reward systems are tied even more directly to the need for cooperation and flexibility. Rather than being evaluated only by a direct superior, each manager's performance is also appraised by others with whom he or she deals. This multiple review process not only encourages cooperative behavior but also serves as a control to identify those who are unwilling or unable to develop positive work relationships.

Provide Role Models. Top managers know that their words and actions are models that strongly influence values and behavioral norms in the organization. Yet few top managers routinely use these powerful tools. With a little thought and planning, they can send signals that encourage behavior conducive to achieving the organization's goals.

After one restructuring failed, Corning's president and vice chairman recognized that the role model they were providing as top management was one of the fundamental problems. They were simply not communicating and cooperating on efforts to integrate the international and domestic operations, and this lessened the willingness of domestic division managers to share information and cooperate with their overseas counterparts. Later, as these top managers made a strong effort to work closely on issues and to let the organization see their joint commitment to decisions, they saw their cooperative behavior reflected throughout the organization.

The Key Is Flexibility

Clearly, the approach outlined is vastly different from one in which a company installs a new structure to "force the product managers to interact with geographic specialists."[3] Building a multidimensional and flexible decision process means the company will sense and respond to the complex, diverse, and changeable demands most MNCs face.

Several benefits flow from this approach. First, matching decision processes with the task keeps managers' attention focused on the business issues. By contrast, in an organization going through a major restructuring, management's attention tends to be riveted on changes in formal roles and responsibilities, as people debate the implications of the new structure and jockey for position and turf.

Second, by working to achieve a gradual organizational evolution rather than a more rapid structural change, a company can avoid much of the trauma associated with reorganization. Changes in roles and relationships are best achieved incrementally.

Finally, by thinking in terms of changing behavior rather than changing structural design, managers free themselves from the limitations of representing organizations diagrammatically. They are not restricted by the number of dimensions that can be represented on a chart; they are not tempted to view the organization symmetrically; and they are not limited by the innately static nature of an organization diagram.

---

[3] This was the objective of the Westinghouse reorganization study, according to the report in "Westinghouse Takes Aim at the World," *Fortune,* January 14, 1980, p. 52.

ORGANIZATIONAL CHANGE

Chapter 6

Managing Organizational Change

Even an appropriate organizational design has a limited lifetime. Inevitable changes in a company's environment, whether cultural, economic, or technological, create misfits and their associated problems. Consequently, an important aspect of managerial work involves the *process* of managing changes in organizational design. The remainder of this book focuses on such processes.

Organizational Change Strategies and Tactics

Just as there are many different types of job designs, compensation systems, and training programs, there are also many different approaches to planning and implementing changes in those systems.

Strategically, managers sometimes try to introduce organizational change very quickly—in a matter of days or weeks, perhaps even before people realize what has happened. At other times they proceed much more slowly; change efforts have been known to take years before they are successfully completed. Managers sometimes involve virtually no one but themselves in the planning and execution of a change; at other times they involve many people—perhaps everyone who will be affected by the change.

In dealing with specific individuals or groups of individuals, managers can employ a large number of tactics to implement an organizational change. These tactics include:

- Persuading people of the merits of the change.
- Forcing or coercing people to accept the change without resistance.

- Offering people some form of compensation in lieu of what they will lose as a result of the change.
- Supporting people emotionally or with education to help them accept the change.
- Scaring people into accepting the change.
- Asking people to participate and help in the design or implementation of the change.
- Co-opting people—making them feel as if they are participating.

The appropriateness of any of these tactics varies significantly in different change efforts.

Problem-Solving Change versus Developmental Change

Organizational change efforts can be thought of as existing on a continuum where at one extreme a company attempts solely to solve some current organizational problem and at the other extreme attempts solely to prevent problems from emerging in the future. Most change efforts will, of course, be somewhere between the extremes, but will usually be aimed mainly at solving a current problem or developing the organization for the future.

Distinguishing between problem-solving and developmental change is also important because managers tend to approach these two different kinds of change efforts using different strategies and tactics.

Choices

In managing organizational change, managers are confronted with many choices. They must decide:

1. How much change to try to bring about.
2. How much effort will be directed at problem solving versus developmental change.
3. What specific strategy and tactics to use.

The difficulties inherent in making these choices are increased by the number of options that are possible in any instance.

The remainder of this book is designed to help you develop your decision-making abilities in these areas. Part Four focuses mostly on problem-solving change, while Part Five focuses on developmental change.

Part Four

Part Four shifts our attention from questions of organizational design to issues associated with implementing changes in design tools to solve organizational problems, regardless of the type of organization involved.

Managers who attempt to introduce major organizational changes often run into problems of human resistance. The text in this part provides a framework for analyzing such resistance and for selecting appropriate change strategies and tactics. The cases present examples of different change strategies and tactics. The readings provide specific discussions of two very different approaches to change: those aimed at minimizing any resistance and those aimed at overcoming resistance.

Chapter 7

Organizational Change Strategies and Tactics

Solving and avoiding organizational problems inevitably involve the introduction of organizational change. When the required changes are small and isolated, they can usually be accomplished without major problems. However, when they are large and involve many people and subunits, they can often bring about significant problems.

The following scenario illustrates a common pattern in the process of organizational change:

1. Some factors in a business situation change over a period of time.
2. A number of aspects of the organization that once fit the situation and worked well no longer are appropriate.
3. Organizational problems begin to surface.
4. Managers become aware of the problems and attempt to take some corrective actions.
5. The management initiative runs into resistance.
6. The managers eventually overcome the resistance, but at a large cost to the organization (and often to themselves).

Though managers may encounter many potential problems while initiating an organizational change, the one that seems to emerge most often is related to human resistance.[1] To understand how managers can successfully manage organizational change, we must begin by examining this central problem area.

---

[1] See Jay Lorsch, "Managing Change," in *Organizational Behavior and Administration*, ed. Paul Lawrence, Louis B. Barnes, and Jay Lorsch (Homewood, Ill.: Richard D. Irwin, 1976), pp. 669–72.

Human Resistance to Change

Human resistance to change takes many forms, from open rebellion to very subtle, passive resistance. And it emerges for many reasons—some of which are rational and some of which are not. Some reasons are primarily self-centered; others are relatively selfless.

Politics and Power Struggles

One major reason that people resist organizational change is that they see they are going to lose something of personal value as a result of the change. Resistance in these cases is often called "politics" or "political behavior," because people are focusing on their own best interests and not that of the total organization.[2]

After a number of years of rapid growth, for example, the president of one organization decided that its size demanded the creation of a new staff function—new-product planning and development—to be headed by a vice president. Operationally, this change eliminated most of the decision-making power that the vice presidents of marketing, engineering, and production had over new products. Inasmuch as new products were very important in this organization, the change also reduced the status of the marketing, engineering, and production VPs. Yet status was important to those three vice presidents. During the two months after the president announced his idea for a new-product vice president, the existing vice presidents each came up with six or seven reasons why the new arrangement might not work. Their objections grew louder and louder until the president shelved the new job idea.

In another example, a manufacturing company had traditionally employed a large group of personnel people as counselors, "father confessors," and friends to its production employees. This group of counselors exhibited high morale because of the professional satisfaction they received from the "helping" relationships they had with employees. When a new performance appraisal system was installed, the personnel people were required to provide each employee's supervisor with a written evaluation of the employee's emotional maturity, promotion potential, etc., every six months. As some of the personnel people immediately recognized, the change would alter their relationship with most employees—from a peer/friend/helper to more of a boss/evaluator. Predictably, they resisted the new system. While publicly arguing that the new system was not as good for the company as the old one, they privately put as

[2] For a discussion of power and politics in corporations, see Abraham Zaleznik and Manfred F. R. Kets De Vries, *Power and the Corporate Mind* (Boston: Houghton Mifflin, 1975), chap. 6; and Robert H. Miles, *Macro Organizational Behavior* (Santa Monica, Calif.: Goodyear Publishing, 1978), chap 4.

much pressure as possible on the personnel vice president until he significantly altered the new system.

Political behavior emerges in organizations because what is in the best interests of one individual or group is sometimes not in the best interests of the total organization or of other individuals and groups. The consequences of organizational change efforts often are good for some people and bad for others. As a result, politics and power struggles often emerge throughout these change efforts.

While this political behavior sometimes takes the form of two or more armed camps publicly fighting it out, it usually is much more subtle. In many cases, it occurs completely under the surface of public dialogue. In a similar way, although power struggles are sometimes initiated by scheming and ruthless individuals, they more often are fostered by those who view their potential loss as an unfair violation of their implicit, or psychological, contract with the organization.[3]

Misunderstanding and a Lack of Trust

People also resist change when they incorrectly perceive that it might cost them considerably more than they will gain. Such situations often occur when people are unable to understand the full implications of a change or when trust is lacking in the change initiator–employee relationship.[4]

For example, when the president of a small midwestern company announced to his managers that the company would implement a flexible working schedule for all employees, it had never occurred to him that he might run into resistance. He had been introduced to the concept at a management seminar and decided to use it to make working conditions at his company more attractive, particularly to clerical and plant personnel. Shortly after the announcement to his managers, numerous rumors began to circulate among plant employees—none of whom really knew what flexible working hours meant and many of whom were distrustful of the manufacturing vice president. One rumor suggested that flexible hours meant that most people would have to work whenever their supervisors asked them to—including weekends and evenings. The employee association, a local union, held a quick meeting and then presented the management with a nonnegotiable demand that the flexible hours concept be dropped. The president, caught completely by surprise, decided to drop the issue.

Few organizations can be characterized as having a high level of

---

[3] Edgar Schein, *Organizational Psychology,* (Englewood Cliffs, N.J.: Prentice-Hall, 1965), p. 44.

[4] See Chris Argyris, *Intervention Theory and Method,* (Reading, Mass.: Addison-Wesley Publishing, 1970), p. 70.

trust between employees and managers; consequently, it is easy for misunderstandings to develop when change is introduced. Unless misunderstandings are surfaced and clarified quickly, they can lead to resistance.

Different Assessments of the Situation

Another common reason people resist organizational change is that their own analysis of the situation differs from that of those initiating the change. In such cases, their analysis typically sees more costs than benefits resulting from the change, not only for themselves but for their company as well.

For example, the president of one moderate-sized bank was shocked by his staff's analysis of their real estate investment trust (REIT) loans. Their complex analysis suggested that the bank could easily lose up to $10 million and that possible losses were increasing each month by 20 percent. Within a week, the president drew up a plan to reorganize that part of the bank that managed REITs. However, because of his concern for the bank's stock price, he chose not to release the staff report to anyone except the new REIT section manager. The reorganization immediately ran into massive resistance from the people involved. The group sentiment, as articulated by one person, was "Has he gone mad? Why in God's name is he tearing apart this section of the bank? His actions have already cost us three very good people [who quit] and have crippled a new program we were implementing [which the president was unaware of] to reduce our loan losses."

Those who initiate change sometime incorrectly assume that they have all the relevant information required to conduct an adequate organizational analysis. Further, they often assume that those who will be affected by the change have the same basic facts, when they do not. In either case, the difference in information that groups work with often leads to differences in analysis, which in turn can lead to resistance. Moreover, insofar as the resistance is based on a more accurate analysis of the situation than that held by those initiating the change, that resistance is obviously good for the organization, a fact which is not obvious to some managers who assume that resistance is always bad.[5]

Fear

People sometimes resist change because they know or fear they will not be able to develop the new skills and behaviors required of them. All human beings are limited in their ability to change their behavior,

---

[5] See Paul R. Lawrence, "How to Deal with Resistance to Change," *Harvard Business Review,* May–June 1954.

with some people much more limited in this respect than others.[6] Organizational change can inadvertently require people to change too much, too quickly. When such a situation occurs, people typically resist the change—sometimes consciously but often unconsciously.

Peter Drucker has argued that the major obstacle to organization growth is managers' inability to change their attitudes and their behaviors.[7] In many cases, he points out, corporations grow to a certain point and then slow down or stop growing because key managers are unable to change as rapidly as their organizations. Even if they intellectually understand the need for changes in the way they operate, they sometimes are unable to make the transition.

In a sense, all people who are affected by change experience some emotional turmoil, because change involves loss and uncertainty—even changes which appear to be positive, or "rational."[8] For example, a person who receives a significantly more important job as a result of an organizational change will probably be very happy. But it is possible that such a person feels uneasy. A new and very different job will require new and different behavior, new and different relationships, as well as the loss of some current activities and relationships that provide satisfaction. It is common under such circumstances for a person to emotionally resist giving up certain aspects of the current situation.

Still Other Reasons

People also sometimes resist organizational change to save face; to go along with the change would be, they think, an admission that some of their previous decisions or beliefs were wrong. They may resist because of peer group pressure or because of a supervisor's resistant attitude. Indeed, there are many reasons why people resist change.[9]

Because of all the possible reasons for resistance to organizational change, it is hardly surprising that organizations do not automatically and easily adapt to environmental or technological or strategic changes. Indeed, organizations usually adapt only because managers successfully employ strategies and tactics for dealing with potential resistance.

---

[6] For a discussion of resistance that is personality based, see Goodwin Watson, "Resistance to Change," in *The Planning of Change,* ed. Warren Bennis, Kenneth Benne, and Robert Chin (New York: Holt, Rinehart & Winston, 1969), pp. 489–93.

[7] *The Practice of Management* (New York: Harper & Row, 1954).

[8] See Robert Luke, "A Structural Approach to Organizational Change," *Journal of Applied Behavioral Science,* 1973.

[9] For a general discussion of resistance and reasons for it, see Gerald Zaltman and Robert Duncan, *Strategies for Planned Change* (New York: John Wiley & Sons, 1977), chap. 3.

Tactics for Dealing with Resistance

Managers may use a number of tactics to deal with resistance to change. These include education/communication, participation, facilitation and support, negotiation, co-optation, coercion, and manipulation.[10]

Education/Communication

One of the most commonly used ways of dealing with resistance to change is education and communication. This tactic is aimed at helping people see the need for the logic of a change. It can involve one-on-one discussions, presentations to groups, or memos and reports. For example, as a part of an effort to make changes in a division's structure, measurement system, and reward system, the division manager put together a one-hour audiovisual presentation that explained the changes and the reasons for the changes. Over a four-month period, he made this presentation no less than a dozen times to groups of 20 or 30 corporate and divisional managers.

Education/communication can be ideal when resistance is based on inadequate or inaccurate information and analysis, especially if the initiators need the resister's help in implementing the change. But this tactic requires at least a minimally good relationship between the initiators and the others, or the resisters may not believe what they hear. It also requires time and effort, particularly if a lot of people are involved.

Participation

Participation as a change tactic implies that the initiators involve the resisters or potential resisters in some aspect of the design and implementation of the change. For example, the head of a small financial services company once created a task force to help design and implement changes in the company's reward system. The task force was composed of eight second- and third-level managers from different parts of the company. The president's specific request to them was that they recommend changes in the company's benefits package. They were given six months and were asked to file a brief progress report with the president once a month. After making their recommendations, which the president largely accepted, they were asked to help the firm's personnel director implement them.

Participation is a rational choice of tactics when change initiators believe they do not have all the information they need to design and

---

[10] Conceptually, there are a number of ways that one can label change tactics. This list of seven tactics is one useful approach. Other writers on this subject have used different variations on that list.

implement a change or when they need the wholehearted commitment of others in implementing a change. Considerable research has demonstrated that participation generally leads to commitment, not just compliance.[11] But participation does have its drawbacks. Not only can it lead to a poor solution if the process is not carefully managed, but it also can be enormously time consuming.

Facilitation and Support

Another way in which managers can deal with potential resistance to change is through facilitation and support. As a tactic, it might include providing training in new skills, giving employees time off after a demanding period, or simply listening and providing emotional support.

For example, one rapidly growing electronics company did the following to help people adjust to frequent organizational changes. First, it staffed its human resource department with four counselors, who spent most of their time talking to people who were feeling "burned out" or who were having difficulty adjusting to new jobs. Second, on a selective basis, it offered people "minisabbaticals," which were four weeks in duration and which involved some reflective or educational activity away from work. And finally, it spent a great deal of money on education and training programs conducted in-house.

Facilitation and support are best suited for resistance due to adjustment problems. The basic drawback of this approach is that it can be time consuming and expensive, and still fail.[12]

Negotiation

Negotiation as a change tactic essentially involves buying out active or potential resisters. This could mean, for example, giving a union a higher wage rate in return for a work rule change, or it could involve increasing an individual's pension benefits in return for an early retirement.

Effective use of negotiation as a change tactic can be seen in the activities of a division manager in a large manufacturing company. The divisions in this company were very interdependent. One division manager wanted to make some major changes in the division's organization. Yet, because of interdependencies, she recognized that she would be forcing some inconvenience and change on other divisions. To prevent top managers in other divisions from undermining her efforts, she negotiated

---

[11] See, for example, Alfred Marrow, David Bowers, and Stanley Seashore, *Management by Participation* (New York: Harper & Row, 1967).

[12] Zaltman and Duncan, *Strategies for Planned Change,* chap. 4.

with each division a written agreement that promised certain positive outcomes (for them) within certain time periods as a result of her changes and, in return, specified certain types of cooperation expected from the divisions during the change process. Later, whenever other divisions began to complain about the changes or the change process itself, she pulled out the negotiated agreements.

Negotiation is particularly appropriate when it is clear that someone is going to lose out as a result of a change and yet has significant power to resist. As a result, it can be a relatively easy way to avoid major resistance in some instances. Like the other tactics, negotiation may become expensive—and a manager who once makes it clear that he or she will negotiate to avoid resistance opens up the possibility of being blackmailed by others.[13]

Co-optation

A fifth tactic managers use to deal with potential or actual resistance to change is co-optation. Co-opting an individual usually involves giving him or her a desirable role in the design or implementation of the change. Co-opting a group involves giving one of its leaders, or someone it respects, a key role in the design or implementation of a change. A change initiator could, for example, try to co-opt the sales force by allowing the sales manager to be privy to the design of the changes and by seeing that the most popular salesperson gets a raise as part of the change.

To reduce the possibility of corporate resistance to an organizational change, one division manager in a large multibusiness corporation successfully used co-optation in the following way. He invited the corporate human relations vice president, a close friend of the president's, to help him and his key staff analyze some problems the division was having. Because of his busy schedule, the corporate VP was not able to do much of the actual information gathering or analysis himself, thus limiting his own influence on the diagnoses. But his presence at key meetings helped commit him to the diagnosis and the solution the group designed. The commitment was subsequently very important because the president, at least initially, did not like some of the proposed changes. Nevertheless, after discussion with his human resource VP, he did not try to block them.

Co-optation can, under certain circumstances, be a relatively inexpensive and easy way to gain an individual's or a group's support (less expensive, for example, than negotiation and quicker than participation). Nevertheless, it has its drawbacks. If people feel they are being tricked into not resisting, they obviously may respond negatively. And if they use

---

[13] For an excellent discussion of negotiation, see Gerald Nierenberg, *The Art of Negotiating* (New York: Cornerstone, 1974).

their ability to influence the design and implementation of changes in ways that are not in the best interests of the organization, they can obviously create serious problems.

Manipulation

Manipulation, in this context, refers to covert influence attempts. In a sense, therefore, co-optation is a form of manipulation. Other forms do not have specific names but involve, for instance, the selective use of information and the conscious structuring of events so as to have some desired (but covert) impact on the participants.

Manipulation suffers from the same drawbacks as co-optation, but to an even greater degree. When people feel they are not being treated openly or that they are being lied to, they often react negatively. Nevertheless, manipulation can be used successfully—particularly when all other tactics are not feasible or have failed.[14] With one's back to the wall, with inadequate time to use education, participation, or facilitation, and without the power or other resources to use negotiation, coercion, or co-optation, a manager might resort to manipulating information channels to scare people into thinking there is a crisis coming which they can avoid only by change.

Coercion

The seventh tactic managers use to deal with resistance is coercion. Here they essentially force people to accept a change, explicitly or implicitly threatening them with the loss of jobs or promotion possibilities or raises or whatever else they control. Like manipulation, coercion is a risky tactic because people strongly resent forced change. Yet coercion has the advantage of overcoming resistance very quickly. And in situations where speed is essential, this tactic may be one's only alternative.

For example, when assigned to "turn around" a failing division in a large conglomerate, the chosen manager relied mostly on coercion to achieve the organizational changes she desired. She did so because she felt, "I did not have enough time to use other methods, and I needed to make changes that were pretty unpopular among many of the people."

Using Change Tactics

Effective organizational change efforts are almost always characterized by the skillful use of a number of these change tactics. Conversely, less

---

[14] See John P. Kotter, "Power, Dependence, and Effective Management," *Harvard Business Review*, July–August 1977, pp. 133–35.

effective change efforts usually involve the misuse of one or more of these tactics.

Managers sometimes misuse change tactics simply because they are unaware of the strengths and limitations of each tactic (see Figure 7–1). Sometimes they run into difficulties because they rely only on the same limited number of tactics regardless of the situation (e.g., they always use participation and persuasion, or coercion and manipulation).[15] Sometimes they misuse the tactics simply because they are not chosen and implemented as a part of a clearly considered change strategy.

Change Strategies

In approaching an organizational change situation, managers explicitly or implicitly make strategic choices regarding the speed of the effort, the amount of preplanning, the involvement of others, and the relative emphasis of different change tactics. Successful change efforts seem to be those in which these choices both are internally consistent and fit some key situation variables.

The strategic options available to managers can be usefully thought of as existing on a continuum (see Figure 7–2).[16] At one end of the continuum, the strategy calls for a very rapid implementation of changes, with a clear plan of action and little involvement of others. This type of strategy mows over any resistance and, at the extreme, would involve a fait accompli. At the other end of the continuum, the strategy would call for a much slower change process that is less clearly planned from the start and that involves many people in addition to the change initiators. This type of strategy is designed to reduce resistance to a minimum.[17]

With respect to tactics, the farther to the left one operates on the continuum in Figure 7–2, the more one tends to use coercion and the less one tends to use the other tactics—especially participation. The opposite is true the more one operates to the right on the continuum—the less coercion tends to be used and the more the other tactics tend to be used.

---

[15] Ibid., pp. 135–36.

[16] See Larry E. Greiner, "Patterns of Organizational Change," *Harvard Business Review*, May–June 1967; and Larry E. Greiner and Louis B. Barnes, "Organization Change and Development," in *Organization Change and Development*, ed. Gene Dalton and Paul Lawrence (Homewood, Ill.: Richard D. Irwin, 1970), pp. 3–5.

[17] For a good discussion of an approach that attempts to minimize resistance, see Renato Tagiuri, "Notes on the Management of Change," Working Paper, Harvard Business School.

Figure 7–1
Tactics for Dealing with Resistance to Change

Tactic	Best for:	Advantages	Drawbacks
Education/ communication	Resistance based on lack of information or inaccurate information and analysis.	Once persuaded, people will often help with the implementation of the change.	Can be very time consuming if large numbers of people are involved.
Participation	Situations in which initiators do not have all the information needed to design the change and where others have considerable power to resist.	People who participate will be committed to implementing change. And any relevant information they have will be integrated into the change plan.	Can be very time consuming. Participators could design an inappropriate change
Facilitation and support	Dealing with people who are resisting because of adjustment problems.	No other tactic works as well with adjustment problems.	Can be time consuming, expensive, and still fail.
Negotiation	Situations where someone or some group will clearly lose out in a change and where they have considerable power to resist.	Sometimes is a relatively easy way to avoid major resistance.	Can be too expensive in many cases. Can alert others to negotiate for compliance.
Co-optation	Very specific situations where the other tactics are too expensive or are infeasible.	Can help generate support for implementing a change (but less than participation).	Can create problems if people recognize the co-optation.
Manipulation	Situations where other tactics will not work or are too expensive.	Can be a relatively quick and inexpensive solution to resistance problems.	Costs initiators some of their credibility. Can lead to future problems.
Coercion	When speed is essential and the change initiators possess considerable power.	Speed. Can overcome any kind of resistance.	Risky. Can leave people angry with the initiators.

Figure 7–2
Strategic Options for the Management of Change

←	→
Rapid changes Clearly planned Little involvement of others Attempt to overcome any resistance	Slow changes Not clearly planned initially Lots of involvement of others Attempt to minimize any resistance

Key Situational Variables
- The amount and type of resistance that is anticipated.
- The position of the initiators vis-à-vis the resisters (in terms of power, trust, etc.).
- The locus of relevant data for designing the change and of needed energy for implementing it.
- The stakes involved (e.g., the presence or absence of a crisis, the consequences of resistance and lack of change).

Exactly where a change effort should be strategically positioned on the continuum in Figure 7–2 seems to be a function of four key variables:

1. *The amount and type of resistance that is anticipated.* The greater the anticipated resistance, other factors being equal, the more appropriate it is to move toward the right on the continuum.[18] The greater the anticipated resistance, the more difficult it is to simply overwhelm it and the more one needs to find ways to reduce some of it.

2. *The position of the initiator vis-à-vis the resisters, especially with regard to power.* The greater the initiator's power, the better the initiator's relationships with the others; and the more the others expect that the initiator might move unilaterally, the more one can move to the left on the continuum.[19] On the other hand, the weaker the initiator's position, the more he or she is forced to operate to the right.

3. *The locus of relevant data for designing the change and of needed energy for implementing it.* The more the initiators anticipate they will need information from others to help design the change and commitment from them to help implement it, the more they must move to the right.[20] Gaining useful information and commitment requires time and the involvement of others.

---

[18] Jay Lorsch, "Managing Change," pp. 676–78.

[19] Ibid.

[20] Ibid.

4. *The stakes involved.* The greater the short-run potential for risks to organizational performance and survival, the more one must move to the left.

Organizational change efforts that are based on an inconsistent strategy, or ones that do not fit the situation, tend to run into predictable problems. For example, an effort that is not clearly planned but is quickly implemented will almost always run into unanticipated problems. Efforts that attempt to involve large numbers of people and at the same time try to move quickly will virtually always end up sacrificing either speed or involvement. Efforts in which the change initiators do not have all the information they need to correctly design a change but which nevertheless move quickly and involve few others sometimes encounter enormous problems.

Implications for Managing Organizational Change

Organizational change efforts can be greatly aided by an analysis and planning process composed of the following three phases:

1. Conducting a thorough organizational analysis—one which identifies the current situation, any problems, and the forces which are possible causes of those problems. The analysis must clearly specify:
   a. The actual significance of the problems.
   b. The speed with which the problems must be addressed if additional problems are to be avoided.
   c. The types of changes that are generally needed.
2. Conducting a thorough analysis of factors relevant to implementing the necessary changes. This analysis focuses on questions of:
   a. Who might resist the changes, why, and to what extent.
   b. Who has information that is needed to design the change and whose cooperation is essential in implementing it.
   c. The position of the change initiator vis-à-vis other relevant parties in terms of power, trust, normal modes of interaction, etc.
3. Selecting a change strategy based on the analysis in Phases 1 and 2, and a set of change tactics, and then designing an action plan that specifies:
   a. What must be done.
   b. By whom.
   c. In what sequence.
   d. And within what time frame.

When initiating and managing an organizational change, it is conceivable that some or all of these steps will need to be repeated if unforeseen events occur or if new and relevant information surfaces. At the extreme, in a highly participative change, the process might be repeated a dozen times over a period of months or years. The key to successful organizational change is not whether these steps are repeated once or many times but whether they are done competently and thoroughly.

Case 7–1

First National City Bank Operating Group (A)

John A. Seeger, Jay W. Lorsch, Cyrus F. Gibson

John Reed paced along the vast glass walls of his midtown Manhattan office, hardly noticing the panorama of rooftops spread out below him. One of 41 senior vice presidents of the First National City Bank, Reed, at 31, was the youngest man in the bank's history to reach this management level. He headed the bank's Operating Group (OPG)—the back office, which performed the physical work of processing Citibank's business transactions and designing its computer systems, as well as managing the bank's real estate and internal building services. Today, musing about the forthcoming 1971 operating year and his plans for the next five years, John Reed was both concerned and angry.

He was concerned that his recent reorganization of the Operating Group, though widely recognized as a success, was not sufficient. His area still followed the traditional working procedures of the banking business, and OPG was still seen by the rest of the bank as a necessary evil which, tolerated by its more intelligent brethren, should muddle along as it always had. After a year with OPG and five months as its head, he still had few concrete measures of its performance. But most of all, John Reed was concerned that his initial concept of what OPG needed—massive new computerized systems for coping with a growing mountain of paper-based transactions—might be both impractical and

Harvard Business School case 474–165.

irrelevant. Reed's new staff assistant, Bob White, had been pushing hard for a change in management approach, to emphasize budgets, costs, and production efficiency instead of system development.

And, uncharacteristically, John Reed was angry. He looked again at the management report he had received the day before. Only now, in September, had he learned that his manpower had grown by 400 people in July and August. Maybe Bob White really had something in his stress on control and management.

First National City Bank

The Operating Group was one of the six major divisions established in a reorganization of Citibank at the end of 1968. The five market-oriented divisions, shown in the organization chart in Exhibit 1, generated varying demands for OPG services; all of them were looking forward to continued

Exhibit 1
Institutional Organization, 1970

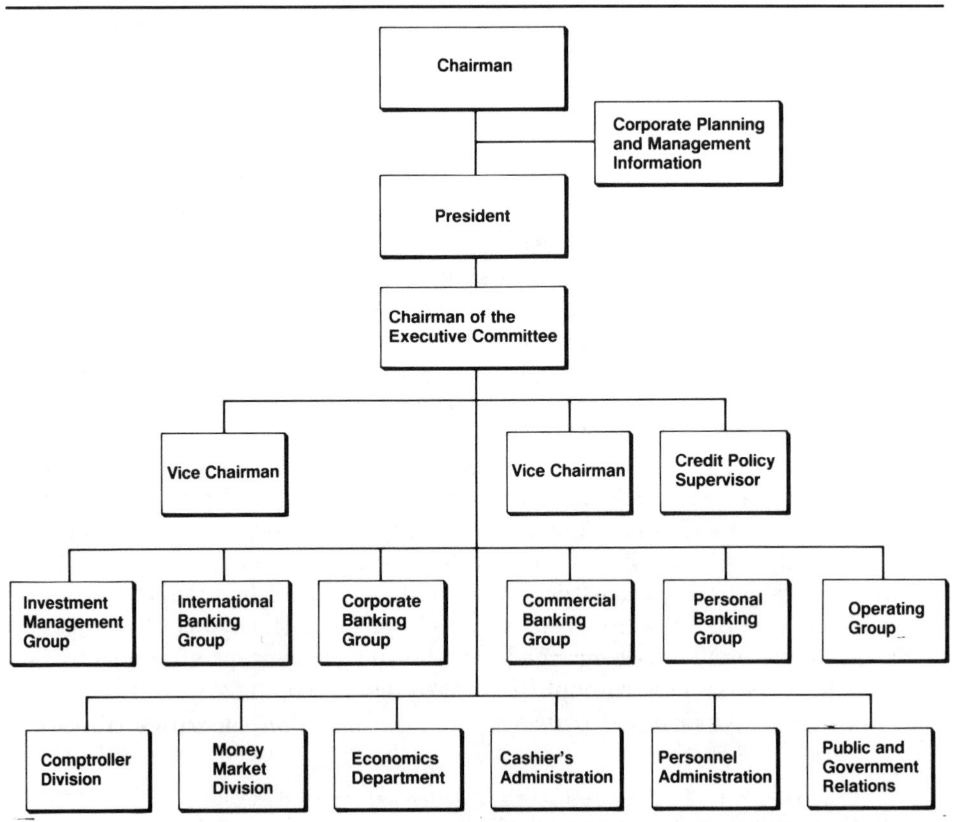

growth in 1971, and all were pressing for improved performance by the Operating Group.

Citibank's Personal Banking Group (PBG), with 181 branches and 6,000 employees, provided a full range of services to consumers and small businesses in the metropolitan New York area. As the area's leading retail bank, PBG projected a 3 percent annual growth in checking account balances and a 2 percent annual growth in savings accounts over the next several years; in addition to an increase in number of accounts, PBG anticipated continuation of the recent trend toward more activity per account.

The Investment Management Group, with 1,700 employees, managed assets for personal and institutional investors, and provided full banking services to wealthy individuals. In the latter category, the group currently carried some 7,000 accounts, and it hoped to increase this figure by 25 percent in the next four years.

The Corporate Banking Group (CBG), itself subdivided into six industry specialist divisions, served big business (generally, companies with more than $20 million in annual sales), financial institutions, and government accounts within the United States. CBG aimed at an annual growth rate over 5 percent, but qualified its ambitions: In order to gain market share in the increasingly competitive world of the major corporations, the bank would have to improve both its pricing structures and the quality of its services. Operating Group errors, CBG said, had irritated many major accounts, and OPG's reputation for slow, inaccurate service made expansion of market share very difficult.

The Commercial Banking Group operated 16 regional centers in the New York area to serve medium-sized companies, most of which did not employ their own professional finance executives and thus relied upon the bank for money advice as well as banking services. The fastest-growing group of the bank, Commercial Banking projected an annual growth rate of about 10 percent.

The International Banking Group (IBG) operated some 300 overseas branches, in addition to managing several First National City Corporation subsidiary units concerned with foreign investments, services, and leasing. Although IBG conducted its own transaction processing at its overseas centers, still its rapid growth would nevertheless present new demands on the Operating Group in Manhattan. All business originating in New York was handled by Reed's people, and the IBG complement of 160 New York-based staff officers was expected to double in five years.

Worldwide, First National City Corporation had shown assets of $23 billion in its financial statement of December 31, 1969. Earnings had been $131 million after taxes (but before losses on securities traded). The corporation employed 34,000 people, having doubled its staff in the previous 10 years, while tripling its assets. Citibank's published goals for financial performance presented another source of pressure for improvement in OPG: Board Chairman Walter B. Wriston had recently committed the bank to an annual growth rate of 15 percent in earnings per share of common stock. President William Spencer had made it clear to Reed that OPG was expected to contribute to this gain in earnings.

The Operating Group's Functions

As the bank had grown, so had its back office. Increases in services offered, in customers, in volume per customer, and in staff all meant added transactions to be processed by OPG. As the volume of paper flowing through the bank increased, so did the staff and budget of the back office. In 1970, John Reed had some 8,000 people on his group payroll, and he would spend $105 million on the direct production of the bank's paperwork. For several years, transaction volume had increased at an annual rate of 5 percent; OPG's total expenditures had grown faster, however, at an average of 17.9 percent per year since 1962.

OPG headquarters was a 25-story building at 111 Wall Street, several miles south of the bank's head offices at 399 Park Avenue. The volume and variety of work flowing through this building were impressive; in a typical day, OPG would:

- Transfer $5 billion between domestic and foreign customers and banks.
- Process $2 billion worth of checks—between 1.5 million and 2 million individual items.
- Start and complete 900 jobs in the data processing center, printing 5 million lines of statements, checks, and other reports.
- Process $100 million worth of bill and tax payments for major corporations and government agencies. (During the 16 weeks between February 1 and May 30, the group also processed 50,000 income tax returns per day for the City of New York.)
- Handle 102,000 incoming and outgoing telephone calls and 7,000 telegrams and cables.
- Mail out 30,000 checking account statements and 25,000 other items, requiring postage expenditures of $10,000 a day.

Operating Group Organization

In 1969, John Reed transferred into OPG from the International Banking Group to become a vice president of the bank and to set up a task force pointed toward reorganization of the group. He had assembled a team of young, technically oriented managers (most of them relatively new to OPG) to analyze and rearrange the basic functions of the group. Systematically, this task force had examined the structure and function of each OPG subdepartment, working with the line managers to question where the subgroups fit in the organization; to whom their managers reported and why; what processes and technologies they shared with other groups; and how the physical output of each group affected the operation of the next sequential processing step. The result of this study was a complete realignment of reporting responsibilities, pulling together all those groups doing similar work, and placing them under unified management.

A leading member of OPG's systems management team during this reorganization effort was Larry Small, who had followed Reed from the planning staff at the IBG in 1969. Small, a 1964 graduate of Brown University (with a degree in Spanish literature), set the keynote for the task force approach with his concept of basic management principles:

> *Managing simply means understanding, in detail—in* meticulous *detail—where you are now, where you have to go, and how you will get there. To know where they are now, managers must measure the important features of their systems. To know where they are going, managers must agree on their objectives, and on the specific desired values of all those measured factors. And to know how to get there, managers must understand the processes which produce their results. Significant change demands the participation of the people involved, in order to gain the widespread understanding required for success. Management is essentially binary; all change efforts will be seen as either successes or failures. Success follows from understanding.*

Few major changes in equipment or physical space were required by the new organization, and the approach characterized by Small's statement made the transition an easy one. By late 1969, OPG was running smoothly under a four-area structure as shown in Exhibit 2.

Area I was the operating part of the Operating Group; it included the people who processed the transactions that constituted the bank's business. Area I operated the computer systems, processed checks for collection from other banks, posted the accounts for Citibank's customers, transferred funds from one customer to another, and prepared customers' bank statements.

Area II encompassed system design and software for computer operations; it was the intellectual side of OPG, developing new computer systems for the use of Area I. The subgroups in charge of operations analysis, management information systems, and data control also belonged to Area II, as did the programming group in charge of ALTAPS, a new automated loan and time payment processing system.

Area III, quite removed from OPG's paper-oriented processing groups, was a freestanding organization in charge of Citibank's real estate, physical facilities, and building services. (When he was not concerned about processing transactions in the back office, Reed could worry about the quality of cafeteria food and the cleanliness of the bathrooms.)

Area IV was composed of the relatively low-volume, high-value trans-

Exhibit 2
Basic Organization: Operating Group

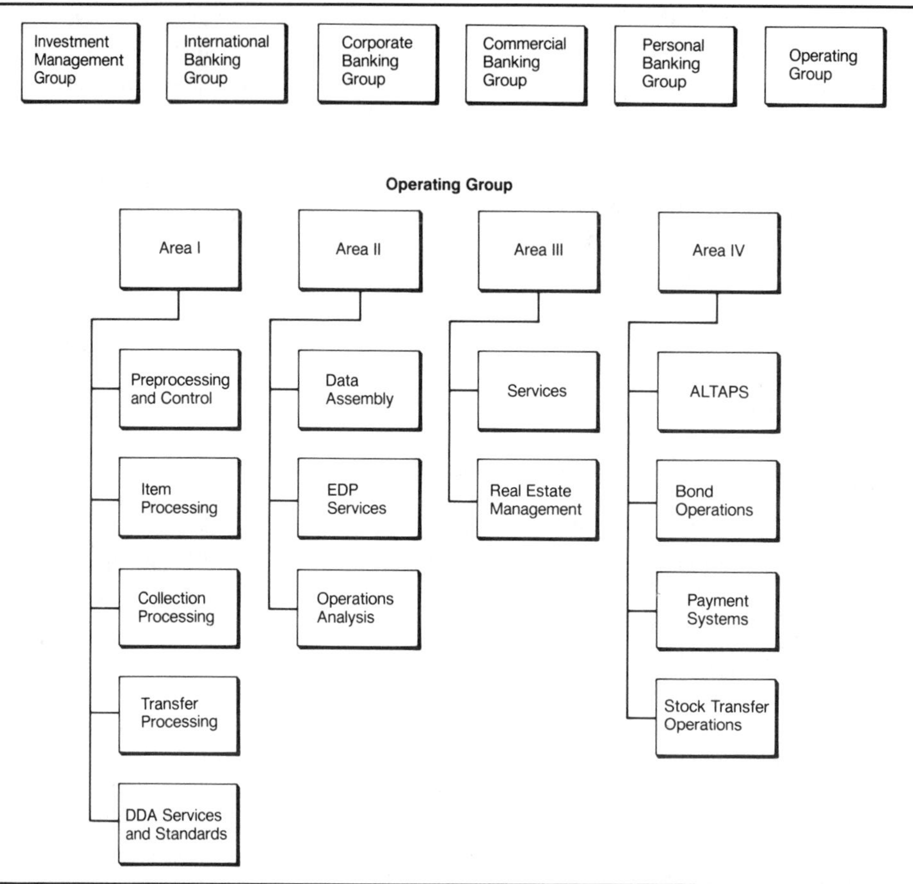

action-processing departments—stock transfer, corporate bonds, corporate cash management, mutual funds, and government services.

In addition to the routine of day-to-day operations, Reed was responsible for the long-range development of both hardware and software systems. For several years, a subsidiary of the bank—with operations in Cambridge, Massachusetts, and California—had been working on the kind of on-line systems and terminals that would be required to support the checkless society which the financial community expected would some day replace paper-based record processing. Reed had decided to maintain the separation of this advanced research and development activity from OPG. "Let's face it," he said, "the computer systems we have now will never evolve into the systems needed for point-of-sale transaction processing. When those new systems come, they'll come as a revolution—a total replacement of existing technology. We should develop the new systems, sure. But we shouldn't let them screw up the systems we need today and tomorrow in the meantime."

In September 1970, John Reed, feeling comfortable with the overall structure of OPG but impatient with its lack of measured progress, had assigned Small to head Area IV. Small's demonstrated skills in management of change held out the promise that this highly sensitive area, where any errors could cause major problems for the bank's most important customers, would soon be under more effective control. Now Reed was considering the future course of Area I, where even more people and dollars were involved.

Area I: The Demand Deposit Account System

The largest single job performed by OPG was demand deposit accounting (DDA), the complex process of handling the physical flow of paper and communications, posting transactions, distributing processed items, and producing the bank's daily statement of operating condition. Some 2,000 employees in Area I performed this work. The process was composed of three parts: the "front end," which received, encoded, and read transactions onto magnetic computer tapes; the data center, which sorted the data and printed statements; and the "back end," which microfilmed and filed the checks of Citibank's own customers, prepared and mailed their statements, and handled accounting exceptions.

Around the clock, mail sacks containing checks, deposit slips, travelers' checks, transfer vouchers, credit memos, and other paper transaction records arrived in the eighth-floor receiving room at 111 Wall Street to enter the front end of the demand deposit accounting system. The first step of that process was to weigh the bags, gauging the volume of work coming in: one pound of mail equaled about 300 items to be processed.

Each incoming mailbag contained a control sheet, listing the various bundles of checks and the aggregate total of the bundles. Contents were checked against control sheets to ensure that all bundles listed were actually received. From this point onward in the DDA system, each batch of material was signed for whenever it moved from one area of responsibility to another. The records of these transfers, together with any changes in batch totals as discrepancies were discovered or generated, were accumulated by a proof clerk on each operating shift. The following morning, these proof worksheets were consolidated into the bank's daily report of its operating condition, as required by the Federal Reserve System.

Materials arriving from other banks and check clearinghouses were already partly processed, but items from domestic Citibank branches, the head office, mail deposits, and lockboxes had to be encoded with machine-readable information. These papers were distributed to one of the 150 magnetic-ink encoding machines, where operators would key the dollar amounts into a keyboard. The machines would print these amounts on the checks, accumulating batch totals for each 300 checks processed. Some machines had several pockets, and sorted the work into different pockets for different kinds of media, adding up separate control totals for each pocket. As the pockets filled up, the paper was unloaded into conveyor trays, to be transported to the next operation, where the checks were read by machines and sorted by their destination, while the information from the checks was recorded on computer tape.

Encoder operators were generally women, who worked on an incentive pay arrangement and processed 800 to 1,100 items per hour. No direct record of keypunching accuracy was kept, and operators were not penalized for errors. About 600,000 checks each day entered the back end of Citibank's process, where they were microfilmed, screened for exceptions, and filed by customer for rendition and mailing of statements.

At the read/sort machines, on the floor above, the paper media were sorted into two major classifications. "On us" checks—those written against the accounts of Citibank's own customers—were directed to the back end of the DDA system; "transit" checks, written on other banks, were directed to the various check clearinghouses and exchanges. Firm deadlines held for these exchanges. For example, the major Manhattan banks met at 10 A.M. each morning to trade checks with each other, and to settle the differences between the checks paid and collected for other banks. This meeting had been a New York tradition for well over a hundred years; banks were not late for the exchange.

Overdrafts, stop payment orders, and "no-post" items were listed by the computer and referred to exception clerks, who searched through the incoming paper for the offending items, in order to route them to the proper offices for special handling. No-posts were especially troublesome; about 1,300 items per day, with an average value of $1,000 each, would flow into the back end, destined for accounts that had been closed, or were burdened by attachments, or had invalid numbers, or belonged to recently deceased owners, or were suspected of fraudulent activity. On a typical day, the exception clerks would fail to find between 50 and 100 of these checks, and the cases would be referred to the investigations unit.

In the filing and and signature-checking section, women worked at 158 large filing machines, where each operator was responsible for 5,000 to 7,000 accounts. In addition to simply filing the day's flow of checks, each operator handled telephoned check-cashing authorizations; reconciled "full sheets" (the first pages of multipage monthly statements); compiled the daily activity of medium-volume accounts (between 25 and

125 items per day) into so-called SMUT listings;[1] and ruled off the accounts scheduled for next-day statement rendition.

Nine clerks in the breakdown section received the checks for the next day's statements from the filing clerks, collated them with the statements arriving from the computer printer, and prepared the work for the rendition group for the following day. The 60 women in rendition confirmed the count of checks to go with each statement, observed special mailing instructions, and sorted the outgoing mail into heavy, medium, and light weight classifications.

Throughout the DDA process, errors could be generated in a variety of ways. If out of adjustment, any of the machines could eat a check. Multipocket encoders could add a check into the total for one pocket, but sort the paper into a different pocket, creating a shortage in one batch of material and a corresponding overage in another. Conveyor trays could be spilled, and loose paper could be stored in desk drawers, or shoved under furniture, or swept out in the trash. The bank's proofing system recorded variances in all the processing steps, and accumulated the errors in the "difference and fine" account—commonly called the D&F.[2]

The Operating Group Staff

By tradition, OPG was a service function to the customer-contact divisions of the bank. Citibank's top management attention was directed outward—toward the market. OPG was expected to respond to change as generated and interpreted by the customer-contact offices. As a consequence, tradition held that the career path to the top in banking led through line assignments in the market-oriented divisions. "The phrase 'back office' is commonly assumed to mean 'backwater,' " said Reed. "Operations is a secure haven for the people who have grown up in it; it's a place of exile for people in the other divisions."

In 1970, most of OPG's management was made up of career employees who had spent 15 to 25 years with the group, often beginning their service with several years of clerical-level work before advancing to supervisory jobs. Through years of contact with "their" outside divisions of the bank, managers had built up rich personal acquaintance with the people they served. Frequent telephone contacts reinforced these rela-

---

[1] The Citibank executives interviewed for this background material were generally young men who had served with OPG for only two or three years. They did not know the antecedents of the acronym SMUT.

[2] The source of the name "D&F" for the variance account was obscure—one manager thought that a monetary fine once may have been levied against the bank that failed to balance its accounts perfectly.

tionships. Dick Freund, OPG's vice president for administration and a veteran of 42 years' service with the group, commented on the close interaction between OPG people and the customer-contact offices:

Problem solving here is typically done on a person-to-person basis. For example, an account officer in International Banking, faced with tracing some amendment to a letter of credit, would know that Jerry Cole, an assistant vice president on the 22nd floor, could find the answer. He'd call Jerry, and yes, Jerry would get him an answer. Whatever else Jerry was doing in the Letter of Credit Departments could wait; when a customer needs an answer, our men jump. They're proud of the service they can give.

Recruits for the managerial ranks of the bank typically came directly from the college campus. Freund described the process:

We hire people straight out of college—most of them without business experience—and shuttle them around in a series of low-level jobs while they learn the bank. The Yale and Princeton and Harvard types eventually settle in the customer-contact offices; the Fordham and St. John's and NYU types come to Operating Group. We don't have the glamorous jobs that IBG and Corporate can offer, but even so there's a lot of prestige to working for First National City, and the security we offer means a lot to some of these people. I know one officer who bases his whole employment interview on security. "You come to work for us," he says, "and put in a good day's work, and you'll never have to worry about your job. Never."

Management Succession and the Changing Role of the Operating Group

Freund traced the recent succession of top managers at OPG:

From 1964 to 1968, when he retired, we had a top man who convinced the Policy Committee that our operating capabilities were becoming more and more important—that we simply couldn't afford to take them for granted. There was a tidal wave of paperwork coming—the same wave that swamped so many brokerage houses in 1968—and we had to pay attention. Until 1968, nobody cared much.

The first clear signals that management attitudes towards the Operating Group were changing came in 1968, when Bill Spencer was appointed executive vice president in charge of Operations. Mr. Spencer was generally regarded as a prime candidate for the bank's presidency. It was plain that his appointment wasn't some form of punishment. He had to be here for a reason, and the reason had to be that Operations was, after all, an important part of the corporation.

It was Spencer who recruited John Reed to move from the International Banking Group to Operations, and who promoted Reed to senior vice president, in 1969. "And that was another sign that things were changing," Reed said. "For one thing, nobody my age had ever made SVP before. But more important, I wasn't a 'banker' in the traditional sense. Most of Operations' management had been in the group for 15 to 30 years; I'd only been with Citibank for 5, and none of that was with OPG."

Reed's undergraduate training had been in American literature and physical metallurgy. After a brief job with Goodyear Tire and Rubber and a tour in the army, he had taken a master's degree in management at Massachusetts Institute of Technology, and then joined the IBG planning staff, where he applied systems concepts to the international banking field with impressive results. His rise in the organization was not at all the usual pattern of career development, as the experience of other bank officers suggests. For example, a gray-haired senior vice president from the Corporate Banking Group reported: "I've spent all my life in the bank. I was trained by assignment to different departments every two years; then, when I went into a line position, I had enough experience to correct something by doing it myself. At the very worst, I always knew people in the other departments who could straighten out any problem."

A PBG vice president said: "I started with Citibank as a night clerk in Personal Banking. It was 10 years before I reached supervisory ranks, and by then I'd had a lot of experience in Credit and in Operations as well."

A newly appointed assistant vice president in the Operating Group added: "I joined the bank as a naive liberal arts graduate, and spent three years in clerical work before making first-line supervision. After eight years as a supervisor, you get a pretty good feeling for what's happening around you."

In May 1970, to the surprise of no one, William Spencer was named president of First National City Corporation. Reed—youth, nonbanking background, and all—was selected to head the Operating Group.

Operating Group Costs

By tradition, the method of meeting increased workloads in banking was to increase staff. If an operation could be done at the rate of 800 transactions per day, and the load increased by 800 pieces per day, then the manager in charge of that operation would hire another person; it was taken for granted. Financial reports would follow, showing in the next month-end statement that expenses had risen, and explaining the rise through the increased volume of work processed.

But in the late 1960s, the workload began to rise faster than the hiring rate could keep up; moreover, operator productivity decreased. Backlogs of work to be done would pile up in one OPG department or another, and they could not be cleared away without overtime. Even with extensive reassignment of people and with major overtime efforts, some departments would periodically fall behind by two or even three weeks, generating substantial numbers of complaints from customers.

Three or four times a year, special task forces would be recruited from other branches of the bank to break the bottlenecks of these problem departments. Trainees, secretaries, junior officers, and clerks would be drafted for evening and weekend work, at overtime pay rates. "The task force approach is inefficient, annoying, and expensive, but it gets us out of the hole," said Freund. "A lot of these people don't *want* to work these hours, but it has to be done." In 1970, OPG spent $1,983,000 on overtime pay.

There were other sources of expense in the Operating Group that did not show up on financial reports. Reed described a major area of hidden costs:

If we have cashed a $1,000 check drawn on the Bank of America in California, we are going to be out $1,000 until we send them the check. If we miss sending the check out today, it will wait until tomorrow's dispatches to the West Coast, and we'll wait a day longer for that $1,000. There are rigid deadlines for each of the clearinghouses; even a relatively small number of checks missing these deadlines can cost us a great deal of money. If each day only 3 percent of the $2 billion we handle is held over, then we will lose the interest on $60 million for one day. That turns out to be something like $3 million a year in lost earnings. We call it "lost availability."

That's a big number. Yet, until a few months ago we were making no effort to reduce it, or even to measure it. No one had thought of it as a cost. Check processing has always been treated as a straight-line operation, with bags of checks going through the line as they were received. Whatever wasn't processed at the end of the day was held over, and cleaned up the following day. It was just another clerical operation.

In 1970, lost availability amounted not to 3 percent of the value of checks processed, but to 4 percent.

Operating Group Quality

"Quality is something we really can't measure," said Freund. "But we can get perceptions that the level of service we're providing isn't acceptable. For all our outlay of expenses, it seems we are not improving, or even maintaining, our performance."

Indications of poor service came to OPG in the form of customer complaints, usually voiced through account officers from the market-contact divisions of the bank. Failures could take many forms, including loss of checks after they had been posted, late mailing of statements, miscoding of checks, payment of checks over stop orders, misposting of transfers, and, on occasion, loss of whole statements. Since any kind of error could cause inconvenience to the customer, the people in direct touch with the market were highly sensitive to quality. These account officers frequently assumed the role of problem solvers on the customer's behalf, traveling to the Wall Street office to work directly with OPG staff to remedy specific errors affecting their accounts. A separate section had been set up to analyze and correct errors in customer accounts; its backlog of unsolved inquiries was a major indicator to management of OPG's quality level. In the fall of 1970, this investigations department faced a backlog of 36,000 unsolved cases.

The importance of error-free operation to the customer-contact officers was pointed out by several officers from outside of OPG. A vice president from Corporate Banking Group said:

Sure, I know the volume of paper has gone up. I know we have 750,000 accounts, and most of them are handled for years without a mistake. But Operations has to perform at 100 percent, not at 99 percent. Errors can be terribly embarrassing to the customer; repeated errors can lose customers for us. I have 600 checks missing from last month's statement for a major government account . . . and there were 400 missing from the previous month's statement. Now how can I sell additional services to that account, when we can't even produce a correct monthly statement for him?

An assistant vice president from Personal Banking added:

We tell the customer that his canceled check is his legal receipt, and then we lose the check. What am I supposed to tell the man then? I can get him a microfilmed copy of the check, but that's not very useful as a legal document, is it?

An account officer in the International Banking Group said:

Just getting a simple transfer through the books can generate a whole family of problems. Here's a typical case. A translator at 111 Wall Street miscodes the original transaction (it was written in Portuguese), and the transfer goes to the wrong account. When that customer inquires, we trace the error and reverse it. But before the correction goes through, a follow-up request comes in from Brazil; it's a duplicate of the first request, and our people don't catch the fact it's a follow-up, so they put through another transfer. Now the same item has gone through twice. Where does it all end? My customer is tired of writing letters about it.

And a CBG vice president sighed: "If our operations were perfect, we'd have a tremendous tool to go out and sell against the competition."

The Technological Fix

An important issue for OPG was the extent to which its problems could be remedied through technology. Reed explained:

The customer-contact side of the bank, and to some extent the top management group, shows a natural tendency to press in the direction of great, massive, new, total computer systems—bringing the ultimate promise of technology into instant availability. It has been natural for all of us to blame mistakes and daily operating problems on inadequate systems; after all, if the systems were perfect, those mis-

takes would be impossible. But maybe we've all been brainwashed. Maybe we expect too much.

Fifteen years before, Citibank had acquired its first computer—a desk-sized Burroughs machine used to calculate interest on installment loans. Over the next four years, OPG had cooperated in an extensive research program on automated check processing, based on equipment developed by ITT to encode and sort mail in European post offices. This experimental system had progressed to the point of pilot use on the accounts of First National City's own employees when, in 1959, the American Banking Association adopted magnetic ink character recognition (MICR) as an industrywide standard approach to check processing. Citibank immediately dropped the ITT system and installed MICR equipment.

Although the computer facilities had grown immensely in the ensuing decade, the basic process performed by OPC remained the same. "For example," said Reed, "people used to verify names and addresses against account numbers by looking them up in paper records. Now they sit at cathode-ray tubes instead, but they're still doing the same operation."

Reed's computer people had reported to him that Citibank's use of machines was already highly efficient. The Operating Group was—and had been for several years—at the state-of-the-art level of computer use. A new survey by the American Bankers Association seemed to verify this conclusion: whereas the average large bank spent over 30 percent of its back-office budget on machine capacity, OPG spent less then 20 percent.

Reed paused beside his corner window and said:

Think about this for a minute. We've been running this operation as if it were a computer center. We've been hoping for some Great Mother of a software system to come along and pull the family together. Well, she's slow. None of us children has heard one word from her. Maybe she's not coming. What if it's not *a computer center we have here? What other point of view could we take that would result in running the Operating Group differently? Better? What if it's a* factory *we've got here?*

The Factory Concept

Through much of August 1970, Reed had worked with Small and White to develop the implications of viewing OPG as a high-speed, continuous-process production operation. White, working without an official title, had just joined Reed's staff after six years with Ford Motor Co., most recently as manager of engineering financial analysis for Ford's product development group. At the age of 35, with an Ohio State bachelor of science degree and an M.B.A. from the University of Florida behind him, White brought a firm conviction to OPG that the McNamara philosophy of budgets, measurements, and controls was the only way to run a production operation.

Now, in early September, Reed was trying some of these ideas on Freund to get a sense of their impact on the traditional banker. Freund, with more than four decades in the organization, was serving as a sounding board; Reed had almost decided to carry a new program to the Policy Committee of the bank, and he wanted to anticipate their reactions:

We know where we want the Operating Group to be in five years' time. For 1971 and 1972 we want to hold expenses flat; in spite of the rising transaction volumes, we'll keep the same $150 million expense level as this year, and after that we'll let costs rise by no more than 6 percent a year. By 1975, that will mean a $70 million annual saving compared to uncontrolled growth at 15 percent. At the same time, we want to improve service, and eliminate our bottlenecks and backlogs like the jam-up in investigations.

To accomplish those goals, though, we will have to put over a fundamental change in outlook. We must recognize the Operating Group for what it is—a factory—and we must continually apply the principles of production management to make that factory operate more efficiently.

It is not important for the people in the factory to understand banking. We'll take the institutional objectives and restate them in terms of management plans and tasks that are quite independent of banking. The plain fact is that the language and values we need for success are not derived from banking, and we couldn't achieve what we want in terms of systems development and operations if they were.

To control costs, we must think in terms of costs. That means bringing in management people trained in production management—tough-minded, experienced people who know what it is to manage by the numbers and to measure performance against a meaningful budget. We have to infuse our management with a new kind of production-oriented philosophy, and the process has to start with new, outside points of view. Good production people in here can provide a seed crystal, and the present management staff can grow around the seed. Some of them will make it; others won't. Our headhunters can find the top factory management people to start the reaction. From there on, it's up to us.

Out costs are out of control because we don't know what they are, let alone what they should be. Our quality is criticized when we don't have any idea what quality really is, or how to measure what we're already doing. Our processes run out of control and build up backlogs because our efforts are aimed at coping with transactions instead of understanding what made them pile up in the first place.

I'm not talking about turning the Operating Group into *a factory. I'm talking about recognizing that it is a factory, and always has been. The function isn't going to change, but the way we look at it and manage it must.*

Reed turned to Freund, who had been listening intently, and said: "What will they say to that, Dick?"

Freund smiled and his eyes sparkled:

They'll go for the stable budget idea, and in spite of skepticism they will hope you can do it. They'll love the idea of improved service, but they'll know you can't pull that one off if you're holding costs down. And the factory management idea?

There's one other bit of history you should know, John. The first engineer we ever hired came to work here in 1957, the year after we bought our first little computer. He was an eager guy, really impressed by the challenge of managing back-office operations. He poked around for a few days and then came back to the head office to declare that this wasn't a bank at all. It was a factory, he said. Nothing but a goddamn paperwork factory. That was after just two weeks on the job. It was his last day on the job, too.

Reed grinned broadly and turned to face White. "Are you ready to move out of the office, Bob? This concept is going to fly, and we're going to need someone down at Wall Street who can make it happen. Why don't you get yourself ready to take over Area I?"

Case 7–2

First National City Bank Operating Group (B)

John A. Seeger, Jay W. Lorsch,
Cyrus F. Gibson

Picture a high-pressure pipeline, five feet in diameter, carrying money to dozens of different distribution pipelines. Your job is to make a lot of plumbing changes in the pipes, but you can't shut off the flow of money while you work. If anything goes wrong and the pipe breaks, all those dollars are going to spill out on the floor. In a week's time, you'll be wading around in $10 billion. You'll be up to your eyebrows in money. Other people's money.

John Reed, one of six executive vice presidents of Citibank and the officer in charge of the bank's Operating Group (OPG), was reflecting on the process of change in a continuous-process, high-volume production operation. It was January 1973, and Reed was reviewing the accomplishments of the past two and a half years. On the surface, it was easy to document progress; OPG had numbers to show for its efforts. But Reed was anticipating criticism, too, as he prepared for the policy committee meeting at the end of the month. After all, the group's performance hadn't been perfect; the money pipeline had broken down for the second time only four months ago. Several customer-contact divisions still complained that service and quality levels in OPG were going downhill, in spite of numeric measurements that showed substantial improvement. And Reed's fellow EVPs and division heads on the policy committee had tenacious memories.

Harvard Business School case 474–166.

Added to his other concerns was a new situation, highly visible to the bank as a whole. Organizers for the Office and Professional Workers Union (OPWU) were handing out thousands of leaflets to workers at 111 Wall Street, OPG's office building. Citibank's pay scales were competitive with other Manhattan employers' rates, but there were some indications of dissatisfaction in the work force. The previous year, for example, 125 women had walked off the job with a list of grievances; bringing the situation back to normal had required four months' full-time effort by one of OPG's most experienced assistant vice presidents. There was little feeling among top management that unionization was an immediate threat, but still the OPWU leaflets could not be ignored.

How, Reed wondered, could changes in the bank's back office be evaluated in terms of their impact on the rest of the institution? How could the new nonbanking approach of the Operating Group be made meaningful to the traditional bankers from the market-oriented divisions? For that matter, how could Reed himself picture the full impact of his changes on OPG and on the bank?

He stood at the window of his Manhattan office, high above the early morning traffic on Park Avenue. Behind him on his huge desk lay the two documents he had studied the night before. One was a draft of a speech that Robert White, senior vice president in charge of the production areas of OPG, would soon deliver to the American Bankers Association (ABA). The speech outlined the management approaches Citibank had applied to its back-office operations over the previous two years. Citibank's success in gaining control of its paperwork had attracted industrywide attention; in 1971 and 1972, OPG had handled substantial increases in volume of work, while reducing its expenditures below the 1970 level. The chairman of the First National City Corporation had been widely quoted as crediting the Operating Group for a major share of the bank's increased earnings. Judging by the numbers, John Reed had few reasons for concern.

The second document on his desk, however, seemed to tell a different story. It was a consultant's report, which Reed had commissioned in order to hear an outside viewpoint on the effects of the changes he and his colleagues had engineered in the past two years. The report was based largely on interviews the consultants had conducted with some 70 officers of the bank, both inside OPG and in the market-contact divisions; it focused sharply on some undesirable side effects of OPG's changes. The imposition of tight control policies, the report suggested, could lead to anxiety and insecurity in middle management. These fears could lead, in turn, to the establishment of unrealistic goals (as an effort to please the new bosses), and to increased resistance to change (as middle management's effort to protect itself). The consequence of these two factors could be poor performance, seen as missed deadlines and crises, and as a sensed need by top management for still tighter controls. It was a classic vicious circle.

Placed side by side, the two documents made interesting reading. Reed wondered how OPG could learn from the comparison—how it could avoid unanticipated consequences of change in the future.

Change in the Operating Group, 1970–1972

Soon after his promotion to head OPG in May 1970, Reed had faced the question of defining just what OPG was. Was it, as banking tradition dictated, simply a mechanical support group for the customer-contact offices of the bank? Or could it be seen as an independent, high-volume production operation—a factory—which designed and controlled its own processes and products in the style of a manufacturing organization?

Reed decided that OPG was a factory. As such, it badly needed managers who knew how to run factories—people skilled in planning and controlling mass-production processes. Dick Freund, OPG's vice president for administration and a veteran of 45 years' service with the bank, described the group's first effort to recruit professional production management:

> *What industries do you think of when you want examples of outstanding factory management? Well, automotives have to be close to the top of the heap. And what companies do you think of? The winners: General Motors and Ford. The first headhunter Reed turned loose on the job happened to have his foot in the door at Ford. You should have seen the first man who came to interview; we really went all the way to impress him. Reed had the fellow out to his home to talk, and so did Spencer (the bank's president). The guy was obviously impressed, and went back to Detroit to think it over. Then he told us "no." His family was well established in their present home, and he didn't want to bring them to New York. His kids had put on a very convincing flip-chart presentation, he told us. Can you imagine it? Reed and Spencer were just incredulous—couldn't believe it. Here's a really top guy, and he lets his kids decide what he's going to do! We were flabbergasted.*

Succeeding efforts at recruiting production-oriented executives were more fruitful, and OPG began to fill its management ranks with young, aggressive talent. One of the early arrivals was Bob White, who left Ford Motor Co. to work as John Reed's assistant. For several months, the two men worked intensively to build a specific action framework around the 1971 goals of OPG. Then White, supported by other newly recruited executives—three of them from Ford—moved into the line organization to take charge of the transaction-processing responsibilities of OPG's Area I. (See Case 7–1.)

Top-Down Management

The draft of Bob White's speech for the ABA explained how the change process began with a fundamental look at the group's whole philosophy of management:

In general terms, we can say that "administering" connotes a passive mode, while "managing" bespeaks an active mode. An administrator is, in a sense, a bystander, keeping watch on a process, explaining it if it goes awry. But managing means understanding your present world, deciding what you would like it to be, and making your desired results happen. A manager is an agent of the future, of change.

The fact is that, traditionally, banking operations are not really managed at all. In a sense, the people in charge are running alongside the processing line, instead of being on top of it pressing the process levers. All you can do in such a situation is react. At Citicorp, we decided that this was unacceptable. We wanted to manage our back office, not administer it.

There are two critical prerequisites for this: conviction and orientation toward results. Each manager must be absolutely convinced that he can control all factors relevant to his operation. That conviction must begin at the top, and must carry with it a willingness to spend for results. I am talking about spending in terms of change to the organization, its structure, its fabric—about the amount of top management time and energy expended, and about the type of people you are willing to accept in your culture.

To ensure an environment that will foster the kind of dedication and commitment we need, we use a pass/fail system as a management incentive. A manager passes or fails in terms of result objectives he himself has set within the top-down framework. He is rewarded or not rewarded accordingly. No excuses or rationalization of events "beyond one's control" are accepted.

I've been treated better in the past three years than in all of the previous nine years.[1]

Reed has been very fair with everybody who has produced, in a salary sense.

The feeling was we should do things, especially make or beat budget, and that if we didn't we should expect to be out.

The ABA speech continued:

The style of management we sought was top-down management. Each manager sets his own objectives for his own level in translating objectives set from above. Although people felt initially constrained by a top-down approach, I am fully convinced that it is the *only* approach. Each manager is not only free to exercise his vision—he is expected to do so. He is unfettered by what is traditional, by what is the norm. Nothing is sacred. The real problem is that the top-down system *strains* people, but it does not *constrain* them. Good people thrive in such an environment.

This job is exciting, like working for a glamour company, almost like having your own company. I really like being a "maverick."

---

[1] Italicized quotations used throughout this case are representative comments of other managers who were involved in or affected by the OPG reorganization, as reported to the consultants whom Reed had hired. These quotations, of course, did not appear in the ABA speech.

I like the opportunity to work for change, and to have responsibility for it. What I don't like is the incompetence of those who resist.

I work 10 to 12 hours a day. I guess Reed works 24 hours.

OPG has lived in crisis for the past six years, but it's worse now, especially the hours and pressure that everyone is under. I spent the whole summer working six days a week and never saw the kids. Finally got up the courage to tell my wife I was working Labor Day week-end. She put it to me; well, I called and said I wasn't coming in. The guys I used to work with say to me now, "Congratulations," even though my new job isn't a promotion. They see me as being better off, just to be out of that place.

White's speech continued:

> If you start your management process with the first-line supervisors and accumulate upward, you are assuming that the smartest people and the strategic direction for the business come from the bottom of the management pyramid. If this is true, we need to reverse the present salary structure so that the first-line people are paid the most money. It is not a question of brightness or ability, it is rather that top management has a better view of the overall organization, its direction, goals, strengths, weaknesses, and so forth.

The speech went on to outline the basic management theories that OPG had formalized and applied to its functions in the past three years. "Management 101," it was called, and it was simply stated as "knowing *where we are, where we want to be, and how we plan to get there.*" Responsible managers were expected to know, in formal terms, the current state of their world and all the processes that were producing their current results; the *desired* state of their area and the processes that would produce *those* results; and finally the changes they would make in today's processes to turn them into tomorrow's processes. "It is not results we are managing, but processes that achieve the results." After defining the 1970 situation of the Operating Group and its three goals for 1971 (flat costs, improved service, and elimination of the investigations backlog), the speech proceeded:

> What was left was to design the action plan—the processes that would get us to the results we wanted. [See Figure A, which reproduces a slide shown to the audience at this point in the speech.]
>
> We planned to build a strong management team, to hire managers who had the conviction and motivation to control their own operations with management skills as opposed to administrative skills.
>
> We planned in 1971 to cut out all the fat accumulated during the prior 10 years of 18 percent annual cost rises—at that rate we knew there was some fat.
>
> We planned to develop and install a financial control system, emphasizing simplicity and the major cost elements: (1) people, (2) overtime, (3) process float, or lost availability, and (4) equipment and computers.

Figure A
Phase I Action Plan, November 1970–June 1971

- Hire the right "top management" people to build up a new style of management team
- Squeeze out the "Fat"
- Implement major new computer systems
- Develop a-Financial Control System that **forecasts**
  - —People and annual salary rates
  - —Overtime
  - —Lost availability
  - —Inventory
- Define the "rock" cleanup process
  - —Separate backlog from current work
  - —Do today's work today

We planned to define a process for cleaning up "rocks," such as the 36,000 backlogged investigations, so that we could come out from under the crisis environment and get control of our processing. This meant designing the techniques to separate rocks out from current work so that we could both dissolve the rock and do today's work today so that the rock would not grow.

In fact, the real significance of the Phase I action plan was that it enabled us to get a handle on the operating environment. With this program, we started to get on top of the back office so as to control and manage it.

The whole management team was brought in cold, predominantly from Ford. So you had this whole new team applying industrial concepts to paper flow. It has worked. But people took affront that these bright young stars were coming along and changing the whole new world.

The number of people actually severed from the bank was actually very small for the organization—only 179—but the image is very negative.

The fear of a cut—a layoff—wasn't a very realistic one. In fact, there have been very few—but the perception of it was the important thing.

The key issue in the bank today is job security.

There was a language problem. The buzz words used by the new guys differed from the language the old managers used and understood.

Lots of people close to retirement retired early. People at the AVP level are running scared.

The bank no longer offers security to old-timers. My chance to become a VP is almost nil, regardless of performance; I just don't have the right background.

People have really put out in this place, some of them have really worked. But when some old-timers were pushed out, it hurt a lot of us. We said, "Is that what's in store for us if we keep going here?" Also, when the old-timers who knew other parts of the bank left, we lost a way to get a lot of contacts with the other groups.

> To gain control of costs, it was necessary to forecast what our expenditures would be *before* we were committed. We developed a one-page expense summary report based on forecast, rather than on history. [See Exhibit 1.] The manager is in control of all his variables. We do not recognize any type of expense as uncontrollable or institutional. Forecasts are updated monthly and are met.

We have a tendency now to try to meet due dates at all costs.

Due dates for changes are, in most cases, absurd. Time commitments are ridiculous, and the consequences of not meeting due dates aren't made known beforehand.

People try to be optimistic to please the boss. When they miss the milestones, they get screwed.

> But when we set about implementing new computer-based systems, we learned a very important lesson: We hadn't gone back to basics enough. We found we did not really understand the present processes completely.
>
> And so a second action plan, Phase II, was devised in June of 1971. We called it the performance criteria system, PCS. What we were aiming at was breaking up the operations into manageable, controllable, understandable pieces. These were the key approaches to defining the back-office dynamics.
>
> 1. Define the products/services as recognized by the customer.
> 2. Develop a customer-to-customer flowchart and procedures for processing each product/service.
> 3. Develop the organization to match and support the product definition and process flow on a customer-to-customer basis.
> 4. Develop our physical layout into a closed-room, one-floor layout that matched the flows, procedures, and organization so as to enhance control and minimize movement.
> 5. Decentralize all peripheral equipment.
> 6. Incorporate support functions into the responsible line organization.
>
> Our processing had always been conceived of in functions, rather than in system processes. All the work flowed into one pipeline of processing functions; for example: preprocessing, encoding, read-to-tape, sorting, reconcilement, repair, and dispatch. You can visualize the functions along a vertical axis, and the people and time frame along a horizontal axis [see Exhibit 2], giving us a very wide pipe carrying 2–3 million transactions per day. If the one pipe breaks, all the work in the pipe before the break stops or spills out. That shouldn't happen often; but when it does, the whole operation stops.
>
> We aimed to break down that pipeline into several smaller lines, each carrying a different product and each supervised by a single manager who

Exhibit 1 1973 Expense Forecast ($000s)

AREA: AREA I	DIVISION: DDA RECAP	DATE	EXHIBIT

	Month of January				Month of February			March–December			Full Year 1973			
	Actual	Actual (O)/U Budget	Actual (O)/U Forecast	Actual (O)/U 1972 Actual	Forecast	Forecast (O)/U Budget	Forecast (O)/U 1972 Actual	Forecast	Forecast (O)/U Budget	Forecast (O)/U 1972 Actual	Forecast	Forecast (O)/U Budget	Forecast (O)/U Prior Forecast	Forecast (O)/U 1972 Actual
Salaries														
Official and nonofficial														
Part time														
Fringe benefits														
Overtime														
Temporaries														
Severance														
Subtotal salaries														
Other operating (including 799s)														
Education and training														
Computer time—outside vendors														
Consultants														
Computers														
Furniture and equipment														
Insurance and legal														
Postage														
Stationery and Supplies														
Telephone, telegrams, and cables														
Travel, memberships, and subscriptions														
Business, promotions and entertainment														
Food														
Operating losses and losses not insured														
Difference and fine														
Lost availability														
Rent														
Rental income														
OPC occupancy expense														
Real estate taxes														
Building depreciation														
Utilities														
Freight and cartage														
Other														
1972 related expense														
Provisions														
Subtotal other operating														
Total Expense														

Exhibit 2
Functional Organization Pipelines

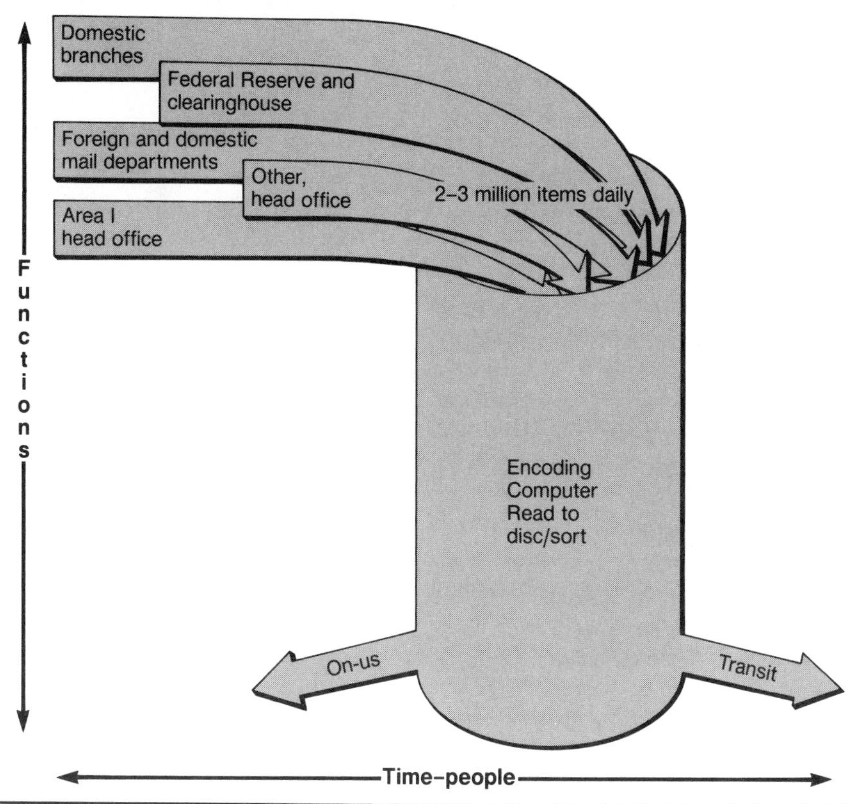

controlled every aspect of his process, from the time a customer originates a transaction all the way through a straight line until we dispatch the results back to the customer. [For an example of this straight-line flow, see Exhibit 3.]

We began by breaking the operations out on the basis of six separate input streams: two flows from our domestic branches, separate domestic and international mail deposit flows, one flow from our head office department, and one from incoming exchanges. Each of these became a separate processing line [see Exhibit 4]. These flows are not mere theory; they exist in documented fact.

In came flowcharting and the product-line concept. We had a flowchart that stretched across the room and back. White had an incredible ability to understand the whole thing—to point to something and just ask the critical question about how something worked, or why it was part of our activity and not somewhere else. The result was a definition of 11 different products, and a full reorganization in one month. It's the only way to run a bank.

Exhibit 3
Straight-Line Organization

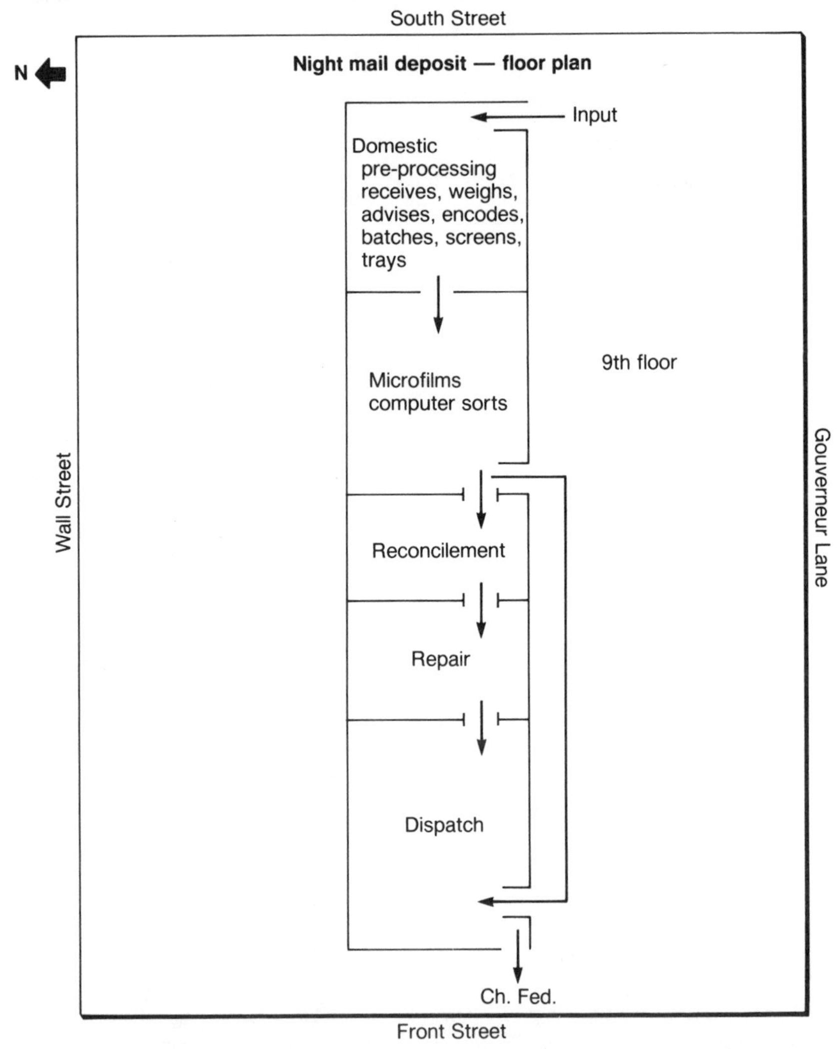

Changes were viewed differently by different people. People started flowcharting everything, and Bob White was going over everything, step by step. But lots of people got the feeling that they didn't know what to do. They didn't fit in this new environment.

The Blowup: September 1971

In August of 1971, White decided it was time to act on the new organization of Area I. "We had been talking a lot about reorganizing the flows,"

Exhibit 4
Product/Process Organization Pipelines

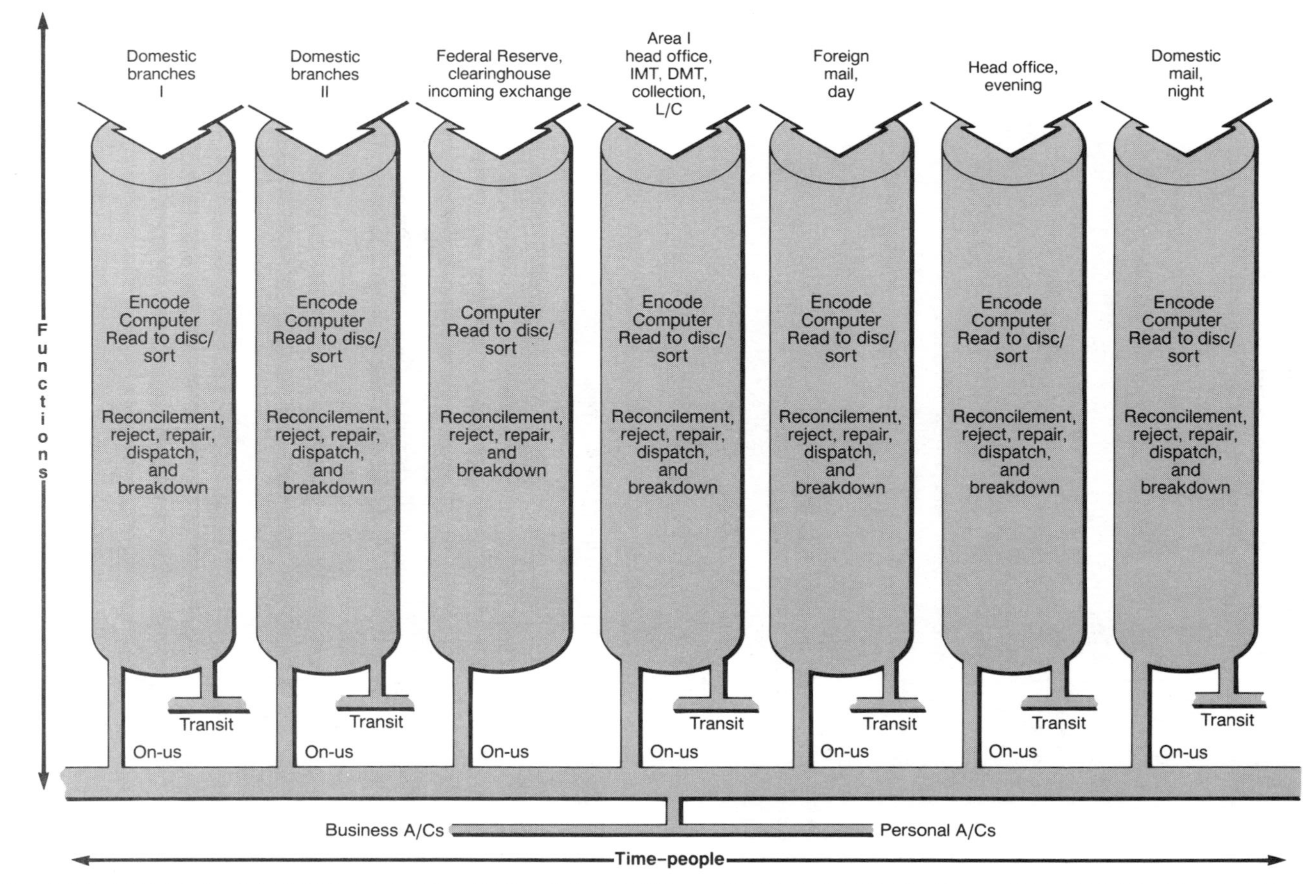

he said, "but nothing was actually happening. We had spent months with people, talking about implementation, and we thought they understood. It was time to move."

On a hot September Friday evening, when the regular work shift went home, equipment crews began the job of rearranging the facilities at 111 Wall Street. By Monday morning the physical layout was set up for six separate lines, each with its own full complement of peripheral equipment, ready to begin work. And soon after the work force reported on Monday, it became clear that the demand deposit accounting (DDA) system had problems. Equipment had been moved and connected, but technicians had not had time to check operations before it went back into service; some of the machines refused to operate at all. Machine operators, informed on Friday that they would still have their same machines but in different locations on Monday, arrived at work with questions, and there were not enough supervisors to answer them. Leftover work from Friday's processing, tucked away in accustomed corners by machine operators, was nowhere to be found; the customary corners were gone.

The money pipeline creaked and groaned under the strain.

As the week wore on, new problems came to light. The three proofing clerks, who had handled three shifts of consolidated front-end operations, could not keep up with the load generated by decentralized work streams. With new people in charge of new areas, proof clerks did not know whom to call to resolve apparent discrepancies; the "Difference & Fine" (D&F) account of accumulated variances began to grow alarmingly. By the end of the week, it was apparent that Citibank's problems were greater than just debugging a new system. OPG's managers were inventing new systems on the spot, attempting to recover. By the second weekend of September, the disturbance had grown to tidal wave proportions. The D&F account hit $1.5 billion on each side of the ledger before heroic weekend work by the group's middle managers brought it back down to $130 million. First National City Bank failed to meet the other New York bankers at the 10 A.M. exchange, and it failed to file its Federal Reserve reports.

The money pipeline had burst.

Geoffrey MacAdams, the grey-haired head of the proofing operation, walked into the computer room, waving his hands in the air. "Stop the machines," he said haltingly to the computer operations head. "Stop the machines. It's out of control."

"I remember walking through the area and finding a pile of work, out on a desk top, with a note on the top saying, 'This is out by a million, and I'm just too sleepy to find it,' " said one manager. "There was maybe $20 million or $30 million in the stack. At least the girl was good enough to put a note on it. We were learning, the hard way, not to put papers like that into desk drawers."

Larry Stoiber, operations head for four of the six processing lines, looked up slowly one morning when White greeted him, and he delayed several seconds before showing signs of recognition. Stoiber had been at work for 55 hours without a break. White sent him home in a Citibank car, with instructions not to let him back into the bank until he was coherent.

In two weeks' time the new production processes began to work. Within a month of the change, routine operations once more ran routinely (note the difference between White's memo of August 30 and the status report of October 8 on lost availability, included as Exhibits 5 and 6). But it was five months before the backlog of work and problems generated by the DDA blowup were resolved.

In early October, as the DDA system began to return to normal, and its managers turned their attention to the problems of cleaning up the side effects of the blowup, Reed visited the Wall Street building to talk to Small and White. "I wanted to be the first to tell you this news," he said. "The promotions committee met this morning. You have

Exhibit 5
White's Memorandum of August 30, 1971

MEMORANDUM TO: J. Cavaiuolo, operations head
L. Stoiber, operations head
F. Whelan, operations head

Effective Tuesday, August 31, I would like a report (attached) from each of you showing lost availablity and deferred debits and credits for each of your operations:

— Branch—Whelan.
— Domestic mail—Stoiber.
— Foreign mail—Stoiber.
— Head office—Stoiber.
— Lockbox—Stoiber.
— Exchanges—Cavaiuolo.

The first lost-availability report should cover the period from the first city-country deadline on Monday to the New York–New Jersey deadline on Tuesday. The deferred debits and credits report should be based on one DDA update to the next.

The report should be completed and on my desk by 1:45 P.M. daily. Initially the report will be in addition to the regular lost-availability daily report—I assume you will ensure the report will tie. You are now each *personally* responsible for ensuring that all lost availability is measured. I would rather not *ever* find any more "undiscovered" lost availability.

If you have any questions or any problems in meeting this deadline, see me today. If not, I will expect the first report at 1:45 P.M. on Tuesday.

Robert B. White
Vice President
August 30, 1971

Exhibit 6
Excerpt from October 8, 1971, Internal Report on the Status of "Rocks" in the Demand Deposit Accounting System

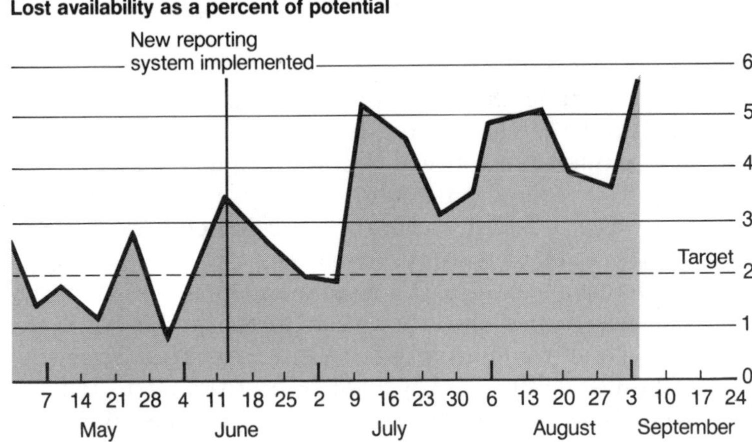

Float

Float statistics for the month of September were not available due to incomplete data as a result of procedural changes caused by the recent reorganization. A data-capturing network has now been developed and implemented; and reliable and complete data were reported on October 1 and thereafter, indicating an average 3.2 percent lost availability for the three-day period October 1–5.

both been named senior vice presidents of the bank." He smiled broadly. "Congratulations."

The design for change from the top just cannot anticipate all the problems that are going to arise at the first-line supervisor level; those people have to know more than just the before-and-after job description.

I'll tell you why people didn't protest the change, or question their instructions. We were scared—afraid of losing our jobs if we didn't seem to understand automatically.

The changes were accompanied by a great fear that people would get fired. Most lower managers and clerical workers felt management—that's AVP level and above—was highly insensitive to people.

Reed and White and the new guys know what they're doing; they're good at setting up cost and quality measures and conceptualizing the system. But at the practical level, things haven't worked. In the past, new instructions would be questioned and worked through until they were either understood or the designer was convinced there was a problem. For example, if I go out there and tell Mary to start writing upside down and backwards on what she is doing, she'll look at me and say "Why?" because she knows me and to her it doesn't make sense. If one of the new guys tells her to write upside down and backwards, she'll do it and not say a word. If anything a little unusual starts to happen, she won't know why it's important, and she won't say a word about it. When the "Ford kids" say do it, people do it. But they're scared.

It hurt us, credibilitywise, with the rest of the bank. The sharks smelled blood in the water and came at us from all directions. But things are better now—an order of magnitude better.

Just a year later, in September 1972, the demand deposit accounting system blew up again, this time centered in the back end of the process, where the filing and telephone authorization process was being changed to anticipate the installation of computer voice answer-back equipment. The changes altered the way accounts were ruled off in preparation for statement rendition, making it impossible for the file clerks to select the proper checks to match with the computer-printed last pages of customers' statements. Unlike the 1971 crisis, this blowup affected customers directly and immediately. "The problem looked critical to the branch people, who had customers standing in line at the tellers' windows waiting for answers that never came. And it seemed critical to account officers in corporate banking, who couldn't get statements for their customers. But it was actually much less serious than the 1971 episode, because it didn't involve the proofing system," said White. "We were able to react much more quickly, and we were pretty much recovered from it within a month and a half."

Achievements in the Operating Group

The draft speech for the American Bankers Association summarized the results of Operating Group's improvement efforts in two charts reproduced as full-color slides (see Exhibits 7 and 8). By the end of 1973, according to the forecast, personnel in the group would be reduced by 30 percent from 1970 levels; overtime would be down by 71 percent; lost availability would be down by 75 percent; and the backlog of investigations would be shrunk from 36,000 to 500 cases—one day's load. The speech elaborated:

> The real achievement here, though, is that we forecasted what we would achieve and then made it happen. Moreover, we *did* put together the kind of management team we wanted, and we *did* get hold of the processes within our shop. At the same time, we developed a control system to measure the two facets of service to our customers: quality and timeliness. Quality measures error rate; it is the number of errors as a percentage of the total work processed on a daily basis.
>
> We currently measure 69 different quality indicators, and we are meeting the standards 87 percent of the time. When a given indicator is met or

Exhibit 7
Expense Forecast Summary

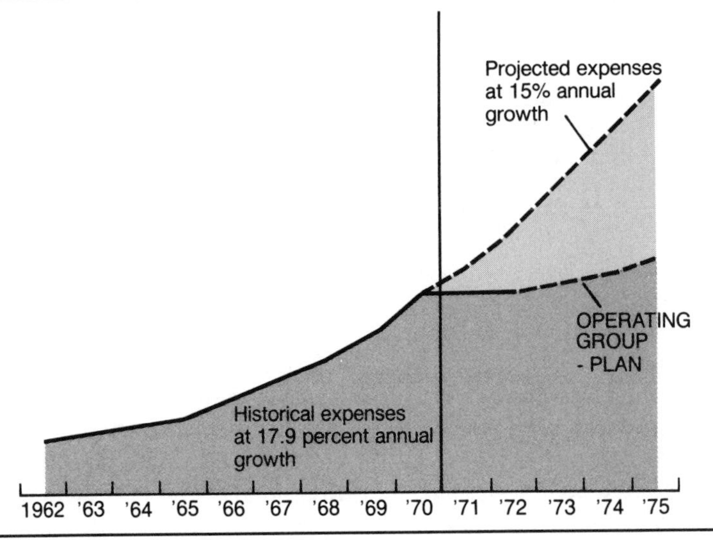

Source: Slide taken from ABA speech.

beaten consistently, we tighten the standard; we expect to continue this process indefinitely.

Timeliness is the percentage of work processed in a given time period—generally a 24-hour time period. At the moment, we have defined 129 different standards for timeliness, and we expect that number to continue to grow. Today, we are meeting 85 percent of these standards. Moreover, we also

Exhibit 8
Results: 1970–1973

	Headcount		Overtime		Lost availability	
Year	Number of Employees	Cumulative percent decrease from 1970	$ (000)	Cumulative percent decrease from 1970	$ (MMs)	Percent of potential
1970	7,975	—	1,983	—	56.4	4.0%
1971	6,610	17%	1,272	35%	32.8	2.0%
1972	5,870	26%	845	57%	26.5	1.8%
1973	5,528	30%	564	71%	14.2	0.5%

Source: Slide taken from ABA speech.

> continually tighten these standards as soon as we prove they can be consistently met. I think it is fair to say that our service performance has improved greatly since we began to hold costs flat—if for no other reason than that we now *really* know what we are doing.

In order to make progress, we had to be firm with the other divisions of the bank. We used to interrupt anything in order to handle a special request. No more. We're consciously shutting them out, so we could work on the basic processes here. Now we have no people wandering in here to distract our clerks.

Changes were also evident from outside of OPG. Three officers from the customer-contact divisions commented as follows:

My frustration is I wish there were more old-time bankers in there and fewer systems and organization types. There is a huge loss of old guys I can turn to for help in getting things done, people who know banking. Maybe they should keep just a few. Some. A few cents a share might well be worth it.

People over here say that if those guys are so good, why do they keep screwing up? You'd think they'd learn something in two years.

In the old days, when the old guys were running things, you knew who to go to. Now we don't know. Even if we find somebody, he's faced with a process where he couldn't give special service even if he wanted to.

White's speech concluded:

> These, then, were the achievements of two years of fundamental change. They are, I think, substantial, and they provide us with the solid base we need to focus in on the future.

One of John Reed's magazine articles that came around said something about people being replaceable, like machines. That hurt. You lose solidarity.

Somebody asked me once if I liked it that we were working in what Reed called a factory. That really struck home. So, maybe it is like a factory. Why do they have to say it?

Case 7–3

Corning Glass Works (A): The Electronic Products Division

Michael Beer

In July 1968, Don Rogers, vice president and general manager of the Electronics Products Division (EPD) of Corning Glass Works, requested a meeting with Corning's director of organization development. He began the discussion by reflecting on the state of his organization.

I asked you to get together with me so that I could discuss a serious problem. We have had some difficult times in my division over the past two years. [See Exhibit 1 for EPD's operating data.] *Sales have been down due to the general economy and its effects on the electronic industry. But our problems are greater than that. Our business is becoming fiercely competitive. To deal with the downturn in business we have reduced the number of people and expenses sharply. This has been painful, but I think these actions have stemmed the tide. We are in control again. But the business continues to be very competitive, morale is low, there is a lot of conflict between groups that we can't seem to resolve. There is a lack of mutual confidence and trust. The organization is just not pulling together, and the lack of coordination is affecting our ablity to develop new products. Most of my key people believe that we are having conflicts because business is bad. They say that if business would only get better we will stop crabbing at each other. Frankly, I am not sure if they are right. The conflicts might be due to the pressures we are under but more likely they indicate a more fundamental problem. Can you and your group determine if the conflict between groups is serious and if so, what I might do about it?*

Harvard Business School case 477–024.

Exhibit 1
EDP Sales and Operating Margin, 1961–1968 ($000)

	1961	1962	1963	1964	1965	1966	1967	1968
Sales	$12,723	$21,745	$22,836	$20,036	$25,320	$26,553	$23,852	$24,034
Operating margin*	3,011	5,449	5,826	2,998	5,075	4,170	1,559	1,574

* Operating margin equals sales less manufacturing, administrative, and sales expenses.
Source: Company records.

The Larger Corporation

Corning's Business

The Electronic Products Division was one of eight line divisions in Corning Glass Works (CGW), a leading manufacturer of specialty glass. (See Exhibit 2.) Corning's growth and reputation were based on a strong technological capability in the invention and manufacture of glass products. This technological capability was supported by a Technical Staffs Division (R&D) which conducted basic research and product and process research in glass and related technologies. The company had been the first to establish an industrial laboratory in the early 1900s, and by 1968 its investment in R&D as a percent of sales was quite significant in comparison with that of other companies in the industry. Corning's growth, which had been running at an average of 10 percent a year over the previous 10 years, was based on its capacity to invent new glass products which were competitively unique in technology or capability. Many of these products were invented in response to requests from original-equipment manufacturers (OEMs) who wanted Corning to apply its research and development strength to meet their needs. Strength in manufacturing also contributed to Corning's technological edge. Thus the company was in the enviable position of growing profitably without substantial competitive pressures. Patents, technological know-how in manufacturing, and the requirement of substantial capital investment prevented others from offering serious threats.

Exhibit 2
Corning Organization Chart

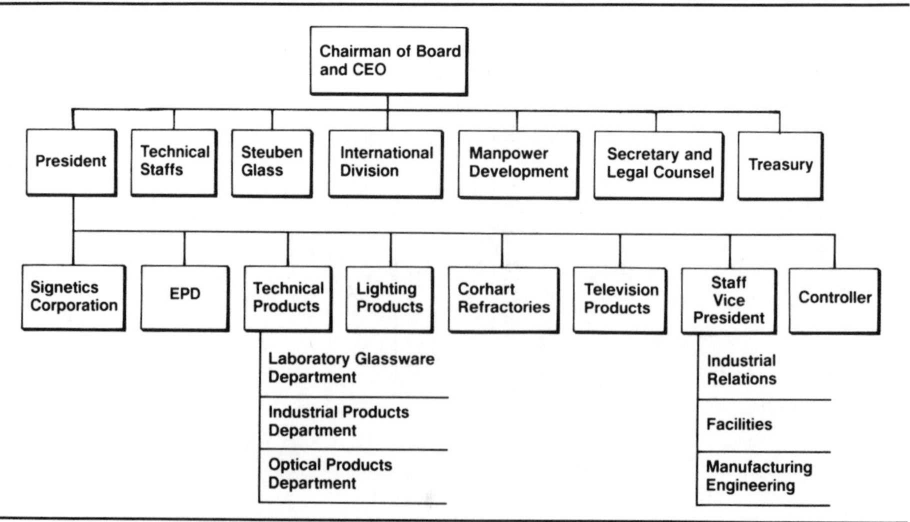

Source: Company records.

Corning's R&D capability led to major businesses in the manufacture of glass envelopes (bulbs) for incandescent lamps and television tubes. Other businesses included glass lenses for optical and ophthalmic use, laboratory glassware, refractories for glass and steel furnaces, and many other specialty glass items sold to a wide variety of industries in a wide variety of markets. Although much of Corning's business was with OEMs, it also had a significant position in the manufacture and sale of consumer products for use in the kitchen. Pyrex® pie plates were an early entry into this business, followed in the 1950s by the development of Corning Ware® (heat-resistant, cook-and-serve ovenware) and Centura® (break-resistant tableware).

Corning's unique technological strengths resulted in very profitable growth for the firm in the 20 years preceding 1968, though this growth had been uneven because of it dependence on invention in the laboratory. In 1968, Corning was in a strong financial and profit position. (See Exhibit 3 for financial history.)

How the Corporation Operated

The organization of the corporation reflected the close link between Corning's growth and its technology. The Technical Staffs Division (R&D) was regarded as very important by top management. Its vice president reported directly to the chairman of the board. Next to R&D, Corning's strongest functional area was manufacturing. Many of the company's top executives had been promoted from the ranks of manufacturing, which was widely regarded as the function through which one could advance to the top. To complement a strong manufacturing orientation, the company had developed a control system in which plants were viewed as profit centers. Thus bottom-line results were measured at the plant level by gross margin (plant sales less cost of manufacture) and at the divisional level by operating margin (total gross margin for the division less selling and administrative expenses). Financial results were reported every 28 days and were reviewed 13 times a year. These period reviews were conducted at all levels of the corporation.

Because of the nature of Corning's business, most divisions maintained relatively small sales departments, with a few salespeople servicing the small number of important accounts. These salespeople maintained close relations with their customers and could supply virtually all the information needed by a division about its markets. Thus many of the divisions had limited marketing efforts. Major sales transactions between Corning and its customers were conducted at high levels of the corporation since major Corning investments were often involved. Similarly, decisions about new products were also made at a high level in the division or the corporation.

Corning Glass Works was established in Corning, New York, in the

Exhibit 3

CORNING GLASS WORKS
Consolidated Income Statement
1959–1968
(in thousands)

	1968	1967	1966	1965	1964	1963	1962	1961	1960	1959
Net sales	$479,089	$455,220	$444,139	$340,471	$327,612	$289,217	$262,200	$229,569	$214,871	$201,370
Dividends, interest, and other income	17,733	15,639	15,404	12,489	10,093	10,554	9,593	8,835	10,160	8,071
	496,822	470,859	459,543	352,960	337,705	299,771	271,793	238,404	225,031	209,441
Costs and expenses:										
Cost of sales	335,957	310,798	291,669	237,048	229,432	199,211	184,100	160,773	158,293	138,128
Selling, general, and administrative expenses	67,251	63,253	61,172	45,612	44,525	40,012	35,088	28,972	25,538	25,380
Interest and state taxes on income	8,961	9,210	6,333	2,622	1,505	1,708	1,408	1,243	1,119	1,297
U. S. and foreign taxes on income	37,886	37,779	47,195	28,989	27,221	27,264	23,100	21,490	18,026	20,300
	450,055	421,040	405,369	314,271	302,683	268,195	243,696	212,478	202,976	185,105
Net income	$ 46,767	$ 49,819	$ 54,174	$ 38,689*	$ 35,022	$ 31,576	$ 28,097	$ 25,926	$ 22,055†	$ 24,336

* Exclusive of nonrecurring net gain of $1,279,499 on contribution of investments in associated companies.
† Exclusive of nonrecurring net loss of $2,334,024 on sales of investments in associated companies.

mid-1800s. For many years all of its operations were based in Corning, but as the company grew, plants and sales offices were established throughout the country. In 1968 most of its 40 plants were located east of the Mississsippi River. Headquarters for all but two of its divisions were in Corning, New York. Thus, for most of the divisions, business problems could be discussed on a face-to-face basis. People from the several divisions saw each other frequently on Corning's premises, on the streets of the town, and on social occasions. In a sense, the corporation operated like a relatively close-knit family. People at all levels and from diverse parts of the corporation interacted informally. Even top officers were addressed on a first-name basis. It would not be uncommon for top-level corporate officers to meet divisional personnel in the main office building and to engage them in informal discussions about the state of their business—asking about orders, shipments, sales, and profits for the period.

History of EPD

The Business

The Electronic Products Division manufactured passive components[1] for several markets. More than half of EPD's sales in 1968 were to OEMs who bought resistors and capacitors in large volume for use in a variety of their products. The remainder of the division's sales were to distributors who resold the components in smaller quantities.

Much like other Corning businesses, the components business had grown on the basis of Corning's unique capabilities in glass, which when used as a substrate[2] gave the components desirable electrical qualities. In the late 1950s and early 1960s, the growth of the space program and the increasing reliance on missiles for defense created demand for highly reliable components, since failure threatened the integrity of very sophisticated and expensive systems. The government was willing to pay premium prices for components that met its very strict specifications, and Corning's knowledge base enabled it to serve this market well. In response to market demand, EPD expanded its plant operations in Bradford, Pennsylvania, and in the early 1960s built a new plant in Raleigh, North Carolina. Bradford manufactured resistors, and Raleigh produced capacitors.

In the early 1960s the nature of EPD's business began to shift. As the military market leveled off, EPD concentrated more of its efforts

---

[1] A passive component is a device used in electrical circuitry, that does not perform an electrical function by itself but acts upon or modifies an external electrical signal.

[2] A substrate is the material (e.g., carbon or glass) on which various coatings are deposited to make a resistor or capacitor of given electrical quality.

in new commercial markets. For example, color television was emerging as a significant market, and color sets required more components, with more stringent specifications, than were needed for black and white. The growth of the data-processing industry also provided a new market for EPD components. Using its unique technological capabilities in product development and manufacturing, EPD was able to enter these new markets and quickly establish a major position in them. In 1965, EPD built a plant in Wilmington, North Carolina, to supply high-volume demands in the consumer electronics and data-processing markets. By 1968, 60 percent of EPD's sales were to the data-processing, consumer electronics (primarily TV), and telecommunication (telephones) markets.

Between 1966 and 1968 commercial customers' need for low-cost components prompted increased and often fierce competition among a number of firms. As companies competed for large-volume contracts from major OEMs, prices fell sharply, putting pressure on costs. To managers in EPD it appeared as if EPD was in a commodity business.

In addition, there was continual pressure on component manufacturers to extend existing product lines as OEMs developed new end-use products for their growing markets. Thus, added to the price competition for large contracts was a need to respond to customers with new-product extensions that met their unique specifications. A component manufacturer could not bid on a contract until its product had passed tests conducted in its own and the customer's laboratories. Often it was also necessary to meet military specifications, since commercial customers sometimes ordered against these specifications.

Responding to customer needs with new-product extensions was a competitive necessity because new products commanded higher prices in their early stages of development and thereby offered an opportunity for growth. As the technology of integrated circuits was introduced in the early 1960s, top management in EPD feared that the total volume of components sold would decline, making an increase in market share mandatory for survival. EPD's poor performance in 1967 and 1968 was a reflection of a major shakeout in the electronic components industry compounded by a weakening of demand. A large number of component manufacturers were competing for what they perceived to be a declining total market in the future. Competition hinged primarily on price, but quality and service were also important. Customers were giving special consideration to manufacturers that could assure short delivery lead times (usually no more than four weeks) while efficiency in manufacturing operations demanded longer lead times. Stricter quality standards were also being demanded because poor quality often could shut down an OEM production operation.

The new Wilmington plant had opened just at the outset of this era of intense competitive pressures within a declining economy. The future looked bleak indeed. Some managers in EPD wondered whether the division could meet Corning's high expectations for profitability and growth, or even survive.

Management History

Until 1966, EPD was headed by Joe Bennett, who had been in charge of the division in its infancy and nurtured it into a significant business for Corning. He was an entrepreneur who was always seeking to get EPD into new businesses. Recognizing the importance of the new integrated circuit technology in the early 1960s and its threat to the passive components business, Bennett prevailed on Corning to purchase Signetics Corporation, a small company which was then on the forefront of the new integrated circuits technology. Similarly, EPD had started a major effort to develop a new product and market using microcircuit technology—a technology that bridged both passive components and integrated circuits, and offered opportunities for further growth.

Scott Allen, the division's controller until 1966, felt Bennett exemplified the division's strengths:

> *We always try new things. We always experiment. We set a fast pace. There is a feeling of urgency and commitment and dissatisfaction with the status quo. As an example, we are 14 steps ahead in computer applications. This stems from Bennett and the dynamic industry we are in.*

The entrepreneurial spirit, the desire to grow, and the spirit of experimentation fostered by Bennett created an air of excitement and anticipation about the future. People talked about growth and opportunity being "around the corner." These expectations were not always met. After its acquisition, Signetics was operated as a separate organizational entity, so that its acquisition resulted in relatively few promotional opportunities for EPD personnel. The microcircuit project proved an even greater disappointment, and was dropped as a failure after large sums of money had been spent in development.

Joe Bennett

Joe Bennett was 48 years old in 1966. A big man with a quick and creative mind, he ran the division almost single-handedly. Many of the key decisions were made by him, and none were made without his knowledge and approval. People respected and also feared him.

Tom Reed, product development manager for capacitors and the new microcircuit project, described Bennett and his style:

> *Joe is very authoritarian with me and others. As a result, those working for Bennett who are most successful are political and manipulative.*
>
> *People around here do not extend themselves very much to disagree with Bennett. The way to disagree with him is in a manipulative way. If he wants*

something done, tell him you'll do it and carry it out immediately. Then after a period of time go back to him and tell him that following through on his suggestion is going to cost us X number of dollars and we could make more the other way; but if he still wants to do it his way, it will be done.

Bennett has a significant impact on our organization, with all of us reflecting him in our managerial styles. We are all more authoritarian than before. I am less willing to let my people make mistakes, even though I think it is important that people learn from their mistakes. The pressure and unrealistic standards are transmitted down to people throughout the organization. This results in our commitments often being unrealistic.

There is little group activity and decision making by the top team except where there is a specific problem. It is not a natural group. We are never together. I don't think we have been together, except at formal managers' meetings, once in the last three months or so. There is no cohesiveness in the group reporting to Bennett.

Joe Bennett was a man of paradoxes. Although most people felt he was extremely directive in his management style, he had an intense interest in the behavioral sciences and their applications to management. Mark Bell, Corning's industrial psychologist, claimed that Bennett was better read in the field than he was. Bennett had also attended several sensitivity training sessions, in which participants spent a week in an unstructured group learning about themselves through the eyes of others.

Participation in the Managerial Grid Program

Bennett's interest in the subject stimulated a number of attempts to apply behavioral sciences to management within the division. In 1965, EPD undertook a divisionwide management and organization development program called the Managerial Grid.[3] The program was to include an examination of individual management styles, group effectiveness, intergroup relations, and organizationwide problems. In all phases, action plans for improvement were to be developed.

Originally intended to span a three-year period, the Grid program was discontinued after Joe Bennett's untimely death from cancer. Dr. Don Rogers, a director in Corning's Technical Staffs Division, took over as vice president and division manager. He requested a report on the current state of the Managerial Grid in EPD, and was told that Grid had had a positive impact on the division but that the uncompleted Phase III, dealing with the improvement of intergroup relations, was particularly needed.

In light of business difficulties and his relative newness to the division, Rogers decided to discontinue the program.

---

[3] For more information on the Managerial Grid, see R. R. Blake and J. S. Mouton, *The Managerial Grid* (Houston: Gulf Publishing, 1964), and *Corporate Excellence through Grid Organization Development* (Houston: Gulf Publishing, 1968).

EPD in 1968

The Division Manager

Don Rogers' promotion to vice president was considerd unusual because he lacked line experience, but his knowledge and background were relevant to EPD's business and he had a number of qualities that indicated his potential for a top management position.

As director of physical research, Rogers had responsibility for all research and development work going on in Technical Staffs in support of EPD's business. He was therefore knowledgeable about EPD's technology. He often sat in on EPD's meetings and had a general knowledge of the electronics business. He had even served as a member of the board of Signetics.

Don Rogers also had considerable personal assets. He was tall and had a commanding presence. He was very bright, quick thinking, and could express himself extremely well in both small and large groups. EPD managers were impressed by his capacity to grasp a wide variety of complex problems ranging from technical to managerial. He was always very pleasant and friendly and could get people to be open with him, since he was also ready to share information and his own thoughts. In fact, people were often surprised by the things he was willing to reveal and discuss. He also involved people in problems and consulted them on decisions.

Despite these very positive attributes and managers' genuine liking and respect for Rogers, some aspects of his management style attracted criticism. His personality and his superior intellectual capabilities almost always assured that he was a dominant force in meetings. Some also had questions about how much confronting he did, how much he tolerated, and how much leadership he took in difficult situations. Some managers made the following comments:

He does not listen too well. His interruptions of others prevent him from hearing others' opinions and make it seem as if he really does not want criticism. What's more, he has been too soft on me. He should be holding me to my goals. I have not met some of these goals, and he should be climbing all over me.

He is not involved enough in the problems that arise from differences in the goals of functional departments. This may be because he spends too much time away at Ion Physics and Signetics. But it doesn't change the fact that he is not involved enough.

You get the same record back from him regardless of what you say. It is safe to be open with him and tell him what's on your mind, but he does not listen.

Rogers is too gentlemanly, is not tough enough, has not demonstrated risk taking, and is encumbered by Corning Glass Works' philosophy and standards. I am not sure how well he fences with others in the company.

Wave makers are not wanted in the division and are being pushed out. People at the top do not create and confront conflict.

EPD's Organization

In June 1968, EPD employed 1,200 people, 250 of whom were salaried managerial and professional employees. It had three plants and four sales districts and, with the exception of some R&D support from Corning's Technical Staffs Division, was a self-contained, multifunctional organization. Reporting to Don Rogers was a controller, a manufacturing manager, a marketing manager, a sales manager, and a product development manager. (Exhibit 4 shows an organization chart for EPD.)

EPD's organization resembled that of most divisions, with two exceptions. First, the marketing and sales functions were separated by Rogers shortly after he became division manager. As he said later:

It seemed to me that marketing and sales had sufficiently different responsibilities to justify their separation. Sales, I felt, should be concerned with knocking on doors and getting the order while marketing should be concerned with strategies for pricing, new products, and identification of new opportunities for the future. Marketing is a strategic function, as opposed to a day-to-day function.

Exhibit 4
Electronic Products Division: Organization Chart

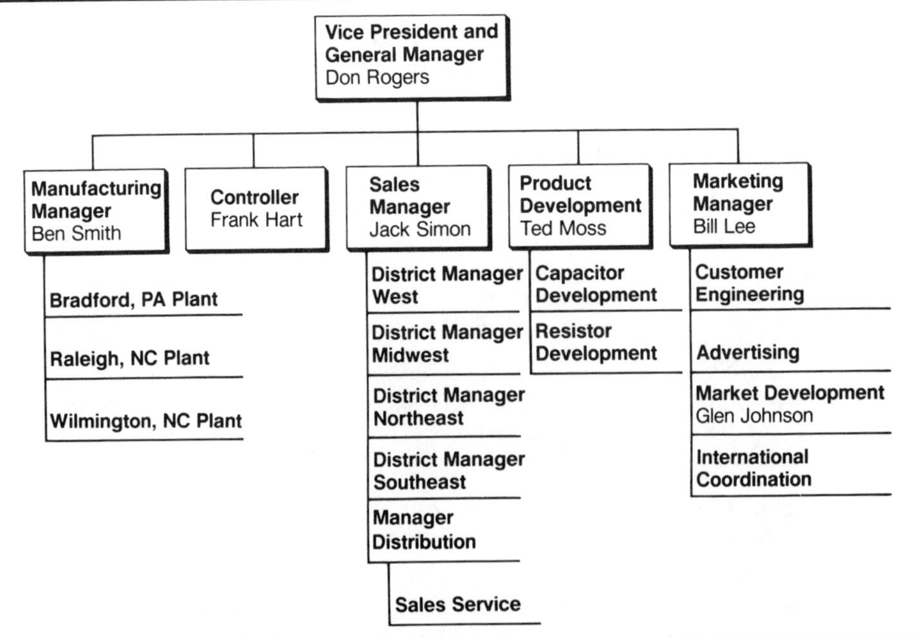

Source: Company records.

A second difference was the existence of a product development group. Most other divisions relied totally on the Technical Staffs Division for technical product development support and only had engineering groups for manufacturing staff support. EPD's Product Development Department was responsible for developing new products, although they also relied on Technical Staffs for research and development support. The Product Development Department often became involved in manufacturing-process development as well.

Don Rogers made a number of additional organizational changes shortly after his takeover.

1. EPD had been one of the two Corning divisions with headquarters outside Corning, New York—a source of some pride to Joe Bennett. At the urging of top management, and believing that EPD had to learn to relate more closely to the corporation, Don Rogers moved the headquarters from Raleigh to Corning.

2. Before 1966, the division had been geographically decentralized. The Raleigh plant, which manufactured capacitors, also housed a market development group and a product development group for capacitors. Similarly, the Bradford plant had an onsite market development group and a product development group for resistors. The product development managers had reported to Bennett, the market development managers to the general sales and marketing manager. In 1968 product development was consolidated under Ted Moss, who was located in Corning, New York, though the groups themselves remained at the plants. The market development groups were brought back to Corning, New York.

3. Rogers also replaced all of his key managers with the exception of Ted Moss, the product development manager. Ben Smith, the new manufacturing manager, had held a similar job in Corning's Laboratory products Department. Bill Lee, the new marketing manager, had held positions in manufacturing in Corning's other divisions and had recently been in charge of corporate market planning. Frank Hart, the new controller, had worked in plants in Corning's Lighting Products Division. Of the new division staff only Jack Simon, the new sales manager, came from within EPD. He had been a district sales manager. (See Exhibit 5 for a listing of key managers and their backgrounds.)

4. Before 1966, a market planning function had reported to Joe Bennett. As part of the cost-cutting efforts in 1967 and 1968, this function had been eliminated and its responsibilities given to the new marketing function.

5. One of EPD's major problems in 1966 and 1967 had been poor service to customers. The number of missed commitments was very high; EPD's reputation for delivery and service was slipping. Under Rogers's

Exhibit 5
Background of EPD Executives

Don Rogers—vice president and general manager, Electronic Products Division, 40 years old. He received a Ph.D. in chemistry from the University of Cincinnati, a master's in chemistry from St. Johns University, and a B.S. from Queens College in New York City. He joined Corning in 1957 as a chemist in its Technical Staffs Division (R&D). In 1961 he became manager of electronic research and in 1964 director of physical research in the same division. He was appointed EPD's division manager in June 1966.

Bill Lee—marketing manager, 39 years old. He received a B.S. in chemical engineering from Rutgers. He joined Corning Glass Works in 1950 as a staff engineer, and subsequently held several engineering and supervisory positions in glass plants. Following an assignment in corporate market planning, he became manager of marketing in EPD in 1967.

Ben Smith—manufacturing manager, 43 years old. He received an engineering degree from Clarkson College. He became EPD's manufacturing manager in 1967 following numerous manufacturing positions in Corning's Lighting Products and Technical Products Divisions. He had started as a plant engineer, department foreman, production superintendent, and plant manager in several glass plants in these divisions. Just before moving to EPD he had been manufacturing manager in the Laboratory Glassware Department.

Ted Moss—product development manager, 45 years old. After receiving a degree in mechanical engineering from City College in New York City, he joined Corning Glass Works as a staff engineer. After five years in other divisions he joined EPD in its early infancy. He served as a project engineer first and then held several managerial positions in product and process development. He became manager of product development for EPD in 1968.

Frank Hart—division controller, 31 years old. He joined Corning Glass Works in 1962 after completing a B.S. in industrial administration at Yale, serving in the U. S. Army, and completing an M.B.A. at the Harvard Business School. Before joining EPD as its division controller in 1967, he served in a variety of plant accounting positions in Corning's Lighting Products and Television Divisions.

Jack Simon—sales manager, 34 years old. He went to St. Bonaventure University where he received a degree in sociology. He joined Corning Glass Works in 1960 as salesman in the Electronic Products Division. All of his experience with Corning was with EPD, where he became a district sales manager before taking over as sales manager in 1967.

direction, EPD improved its service. The manufacturing manager held plant managers responsible for meeting specific goals for delivery commitments and shortening delivery lead times. In addition, an information system was developed by the sales service function in an effort to improve service.

EPD and the Corporation

Don Rogers reported to the president of Corning (see Exhibit 2). He was responsible for managing all aspects of the division's operations, and for achieving profitability and growth goals. These goals were established at the end of each year (September–October) for the following year through a process of negotiation. The division would generate its sales budget through a bottom-up process in the Sales Department, using price guidelines from Marketing. The plants would then generate their gross margin budget based on their estimate of plant sales and costs. These would be consolidated at the top of the division and submitted to corporate staff. After forecasting corporate sales and profits, the corporate staff would invariably ask the division to modify its sales and profit plans. If corporate sales were forecast to be lower than desired, the division might be asked to increase its sales goals. The same procedure was followed for profits. This process often caused great consternation at the division level as budget proposals, which took a lot of time and energy to generate, had to be modified to meet corporate needs.

EPD, along with the other divisions, was expected to grow at an average rate of 10 percent a year, the corporation's historical average growth rate. Profits were expected to approach the levels the corporation had come to expect of its more traditional OEM businesses. These typically were higher than the prevailing profitability levels among electronic component manufacturers. The ability of EPD to attain these objectives was a subject of much discussion and controversy in the division. A number of key people wondered whether both growth and profit objectives could be met. Volume could always be increased by taking low-price business, but this reduced profitability. Most people within EPD looked to new products as a major source of both new volume and profits.

The Functional Departments in 1968

Manufacturing

Resistors and capacitors were manufactured in high volume at three plants—located in Wilmington, North Carolina (resistors), Bradford, Pennsylvania (resistors), and Raleigh, North Carolina (capacitors). Each of these plants had a plant manager and a full complement of line and staff functions including production, engineering, quality control, purchasing, accounting and control, and personnel. Because all line production operations were under him, the production superintendent had greater power than other members of the plant manager's staff. The head of engineering was second in line of influence. These plants (like other plants in Corning) were held responsible for gross margin and thus were profit centers.

The plant managers, with one exception, had grown up in EPD. Their performance was evaluated on the basis of gross margins and assorted other manufacturing variances, including delivery lead times and missed commitments to customers.

The plant managers felt that their reputations and therefore their promotability were dependent on plant growth and good gross margin performance. All saw their future advancement within the manufacturing hierarchy of the company leading to the possibility of promotion to general manager of a division. Since manufacturing was the dominant function, such an expectation was not unrealistic.

Because plants were profit centers, their performance was well known around the corporation. There were many opportunities for exchanges at plant managers' meetings, and the corporation had established an informal system for comparing plant performance. All of this heightened the individual plant manager's concerns about plant gross margin and growth.

EPD's plant managers were extremely upset by the lack of growth in the division's business. In the last two years, their volume had shrunk and, because of price cuts, their dollar volume had dropped substantially. Managers were thus under enormous pressure to reduce costs in order to maintain their gross margins. While they were able to reduce some costs, gross margins still declined. With some exceptions, EPD's plants had the lowest gross margins in the company. Plant managers expressed the following statements:

> *We're experiencing price erosion in our product lines, and I don't see a large number of new products. We need something new and unique. I don't see growth potential in our existing products.*
>
> *We need direction on resistors. We cannot afford two plants. We need a process to allow us to make low-cost resistors.*
>
> *There are no operational objectives. I get the feeling that everyone is concerned, but* no *objectives are set.*

The frustration experienced by the manufacturing people was expressed most in their attitudes toward the marketing and sales functions. They felt Sales focused exclusively on volume with no concern for gross margin. They blamed Sales for getting low gross margin business and not fighting hard enough to get better prices. Sales, in other words, was giving the store away at the plant's expense, and Sales wasn't penalized for it.

A production superintendent said, "There is a breakdown in common agreement when it comes to pricing. Sales will sell for anything, and the plant won't buy it unless 40 percent margin is involved."

The manufacturing manager, Ben Smith, commented, "There is a feeling of mutual distrust between Sales and Manufacturing because Manufacturing believes Sales is not putting enough of a price on the products. This is a typical problem that results when two groups have different goals."

Manufacturing was still more critical of the marketing function. They felt that Marketing had failed in its responsibility to provide direction to the division for profitable growth. They particularly blamed Bill Lee, the marketing manager, for lack of "strong leadership." They were upset by what they called the "disappearing-carrot syndrome." As Manufacturing saw it, Marketing would come to the plant and project a market of several million dollars for a new resistor or capacitor (the carrot). On the basis of this projection, Manufacturing would run samples and make other investments in preparation for the new product only to find out six months or a year later that Marketing was now projecting much smaller sales and profits. Manufacturing concluded that marketing lacked the ability to forecast marketing trends accurately and was generally incompetent. They saw a need to replace the marketing manager and many others in Marketing.

A production superintendent explained, "What is slowing down EPD is weak marketing, lack of marketing direction, and a very narrow product base. You can't sell what you do not have, and if you do not have it and you do not know where you are going to be in two years, you probably will not sell what you have."

Another production superintendent commented, "The last five years have left people quite cold as far as strategies are concerned. For example, Marketing does not have the same strategy as we do, and they give us no direction."

Ben Smith, the manufacturing manager, said, "No one has confidence in Marketing people. Plant managers don't believe them now since they have been wrong so many times."

Manufacturing was also unhappy with Product Development, which they felt had not always given them products that would run well on their production lines. They looked to Product Development to develop low-cost components and saw nothing coming. When Product Development requested special runs on their manufacturing lines to develop new products, Manufacturing wondered what benefits would compensate for this sacrifice in their efficiency.

Marketing

Marketing comprised several activities, including customer engineering and advertising. Its most important function was market development.

Under Glen Johnson, Market Development was responsible for developing sales projections for the next year, market plans for the next three years, analyses of market share, and plans for improving market position. One of the primary means for increasing market share was the development of new types of resistors and capacitors (product extensions). It was Market Development's responsibility to identify these new opportunities and to assure the development of new products in coordination with other functions. Marketing specialists reporting to Johnson had responsibility for scanning and analyzing different market segments and for developing new products in them. They used measures of profitability and growth by market segment to assess their progress. Because the identification of new market opportunities was primarily their responsibility (with help from Sales), as was the development of the new product plan, Marketing felt the pressure for new-product development fell on them.

The marketing function had many new people, since it had been established as a separate function just a year earlier. Most of the people had transferred from the Sales Department, where they had been salesmen or in sales service. Johnson, for example, had been a district sales manager. The marketing specialists were generally recent technical or business graduates with one or two years of sales experience.

Overwhelmed by the tough job of forecasting, planning, and formulating strategy in a very turbulent marketplace, the marketing people felt that no one appreciated their difficulties. The marketing manager, Bill Lee, complained, "We have not defined the resistor business. When the government business dropped, we did not face up to a need to produce at lower cost."

A marketing specialist remarked, "You can't be stodgy in this business. You must be fast moving and quick acting. You must be decisive, adaptable, a long-range thinker, and deal with a very ambiguous situation."

Some felt that Corning had such high standards for profitability on new products that it was impossible to meet them in the components business. The market development manager, Glen Johnson, said:

> *While corporate financial people will admit that we need a different set of criteria, they informally convey to us that we are doing a lousy job, and it makes us run conservatively. The corporate environment is not a risk-taking one. We tend to want to bring a proprietary advantage to our business which we cannot do. This is slowing us down.*
>
> *Glass K* [a new product] *took seven years in product development. Technological development of unique characteristics is not an effective strategy in a dynamic environment. There were some original conceptions, but these quickly passed by the boards, as the development process took seven years instead of the original three years projected for it.*

Marketing people were also critical of Product Development and its responsiveness to divisions' needs. As marketing people saw it, Product

Development's priorities were wrong and their projects were always late. According to the market development manager, Glen Johnson, "Moss bootlegs projects. There are no ways to establish priorities in development; no criteria have even been set up. Seventy percent of his time is in process development."

Marketing felt most resentful about the lack of cooperation and the continual sniping from Manufacturing. They saw the plants as conservative and unwilling to take risks. This was particularly aggravating because many marketing people felt they were distracted from their primary responsibility by having to spend inordinate amounts of time dealing with the plants. Glen Johnson indicated that he would not have taken the marketing job had he known that it would involve the many frustrations of getting Manufacturing and others to do things.

Sales

EPD products were sold through a direct selling force of approximately 25 salesmen, organized into four sales districts. Each district was managed by a district sales manager who reported to the national sales manager. The direct sales force visited manufacturers whose products incorporated passive components, with the objective of learning about the customer's needs by talking to purchasing agents and design engineers, and then obtaining contracts for resistors or capacitors.

In addition to direct sales, products were sold in small lots through distributors. Distributor strategy and relations were the responsibility of the distributor sales manager, who also reported to Jack Simon. It was the distributor sales manager's job to coordinate the efforts of field salesmen in support of his objectives.

A sales service manager reported to the distribution manager. The sales service group was divided geographically, with a sales service group located in each plant. They worked with the plant to expedite order processing and keep the plant informed about customer needs for delivery and service.

The sales force consisted of college graduates interested in sales or marketing careers, and older and experienced salesmen who had worked in this industry for a long time. Salesmen identified strongly with their industry. Jack Simon, the national sales manager, had come up through Sales, as had all of the district sales managers.

In comparison with other Corning divisions that sold to OEM customers, EPD served a much larger set of customers in several markets. The EPD sales force had to develop many relationships with purchasing agents and engineers, and relied on good relationships to obtain market intelligence and an opportunity to bid on contracts. But salesmen also had to negotiate with these same people to obtain the best possible price. Since their performance was evaluated on the basis of sales volume, they worked hard to beat their budgeted sales targets. Despite some discussion and discontent, the sales force was not paid on a commission basis.

Jack Simon reported mistrust, gamesmanship, maneuvering, and politicking between Sales and Marketing. "Most people [in Marketing] do not believe that Sales' competence is high," he said. "On the other hand, we in Sales do not believe that the information Marketing gives us is the best."

Major conflict arose in budget-setting sessions, partly because Sales based its forecasts on customer canvassing while Marketing used analytical tools to develop its projection. Simon said, "Conflicts are not resolved based on facts. Instead there are accusations. I don't trust them [Marketing] and I don't trust that they have the capability to do their jobs."

His view of Manufacturing was somewhat more positive:

Relations with Manufacturing are personally good, but I have a number of concerns. I do not know and no one knows about actual cost reductions in the plant. I don't think Manufacturing gets hit as hard for lack of cost reduction as Sales takes it on the chin for price reductions. Another problem is Bradford's service. Its putrid! There is constant gamesmanship in the Bradford plant.

At lower levels of the organization, relationships between Sales and Manufacturing seemed even worse. There were shouting matches over the telephone between the Midwest district sales manager and the Wilmington plant manager. In one instance Sales had requested quick delivery to meet a major customer's needs, feeling that a slow response would damage EPD's position with the customer. The plant said it could not provide delivery on such short notice without upsetting plant operations. The sales service manager commented, "The relationship with the Bradford plant is bad. Measurement for plant managers has to change. They are not really measured on service. Things have improved somewhat, however, and they are a bit more concerned about service."

Product Development

Product Development was responsible for extensions of the current product line. Usually, between 10 and 12 new-product development projects were under way, often requiring significant technological development. The development group was divided into two parts: one for resistors, located in the Bradford plant, and one for capacitors, located in Raleigh. The manager of product development was based in Corning, New York, along with the rest of the divisional staff.

The product development group was composed of technical people who had spent their careers in research and development work. While some of these people had come from the corporate R&D group, many had worked in the division for most of their careers or had held technical positions in other companies in the electronic industry.

Ted Moss, manager of product development, described his relationship with other groups:

In general, my department's relations with the plants are pretty good, although some problems existed at Bradford. My biggest concern is with Marketing. I do not feel that Marketing provides detailed product specification for new products. In addition, marketing people do not understand what is involved in specification changes. I think that writing specifications jointly with Marketing would help this problem. Another problem is that marketing people have to look ahead more and predict the future better. They always need it yesterday. We need time!

Moss was also critical of Corning's Technical Staffs Division, which also did some product development work for EPD.

It is difficult to get a time schedule from them. Their direction is independent of ours since they report elsewhere. They will not wring their hands if they are behind schedule. They will more quickly try to relax requirements for the development if it is behind schedule. I need more influence on specifications when it comes to things they are working on. I often have to go upstairs to solve the problems that occur with this group.

Moss also cited problems with the sales group.

We need comments from the sales group on our new products. I wanted to get the call reports they write and asked Simon for copies. His argument for not giving them to me is that the Marketing Department has the responsibility for interpretation. I finally had to go to Rogers to resolve the problem.

The Controller

It was the division controller's responsibility to maintain all accounting records for the division, provide a financial summary every 28 days, and report on performance to the division staff and the corporate controller. Frank Hart, the controller, also developed quarterly forecasts of business performance. He commented, "In most cases three-period forecasts are extremely inaccurate. It is very difficult to forecast the business this way. Our forecasts are always off. Yet it is a corporate requirement." EPD had difficulty not only in forecasting its business but in explaining the reasons for upturns and downturns.

The New-Product Development Process

Most new-product development effort concentrated on extensions of the current product line—that is, resistors and capacitors with special technical characteristics that were intended to meet new market needs.

The course of EPD product development was far from smooth. A new product for the television market, for example, had been killed and resurrected four times with different parts of the organization having differing knowledge of its status at given points in time. Marketing clearly saw this new product, the focus divider, as an opportunity, and Product Development thought it was technically feasible. But Sales questioned EPD's ability to compete in the marketplace, in view of Manufacturing's cost quotes. As discussions progressed on needed product modifications to reduce costs, Marketing's estimate of the potential market changed, as did Product Development's assessment of technical feasibility. Because each function's management independently judged the viability of the product, the status of the project was never clear-cut. At one time, salesmen were obtaining orders for samples of the focus divider while Manufacturing and Marketing had decided that the product was not feasible and had killed the idea. Similar problems occurred on other projects, since Product Development sometimes made samples of products for Sales people that did not have the commitment of Manufacturing or even Marketing.

In another case, severe conflict between marketing and plant personnel erupted over a new coating for resistors. Marketing had determined that a new, uniform coating was needed for competitive and efficiency reasons. They presented their views to the division's management and received what they thought was a commitment to change resistor coatings. But the plants were reluctant to convert their operations. They questioned whether Product Development had proved that the new coating would work and could be manufactured to meet product specifications at no additional cost. Moreover, the plants completely distrusted Marketing's judgment of the need for this change. In 1968, after two years of foot dragging, the conversion was nowhere near completion. The Marketing specialist in charge of the project would return from plant meetings angry and completely discouraged about his ability to influence plant people to advance the project.

Two daylong meetings were held in Corning, New York, once each accounting period (28 days) to discuss, coordinate, and make decisions about new products. Separate meetings were held for capacitors and resistors. In all, approximately 20 people attended each meeting, including the division manager, his immediate staff, plant managers, and a few other key people in the other functions.

The meetings were chaired by Glen Johnson, the market development manager, who typically sat at the head of the table. At the other end of the table sat Don Rogers. Johnson would publish an agenda ahead of time and would direct the discussion as it moved from one project to another. For each project, progress was checked against goals agreed to by each function at the previous review. Each function would describe in some detail what had been done in its area to support the project (for example, what equipment changes had been made in a plant). If a function had not met its goals, as was often the case, new deadlines would be set. While problems encountered were always described, the issue of slippage in goals and the underlying reasons for it were rarely discussed. Differences in opinion usually proved very hard to resolve. People would end them by agreeing to disagree and moving on to the next item on the agenda. While tempers flared occasionally, open hostility or aggression was rarely expressed in the meetings. Afterward, however, people often met in pairs or small groups in the hallways, over coffee, or in other offices to continue the debate.

A continual stream of people flowed in and out of these meetings to obtain information from subordinates in their functional area. It was not uncommon for a plant manager to leave the meeting to call an engineer in his plant for details about a project's status. At one meeting Ted Young, a marketing specialist, was repeatedly cited as the person who knew the most about the project under discussion, yet he was not present. On other occasions, marketing specialists (who were located in Corning, New York) were called in to share their information about a project. If necessary, plant people and product development people were also sometimes brought to Corning for the meeting.

In the past, the division manager had not attended product development meetings. In 1968, Marketing asked Don Rogers to attend these meetings to help in moving decisions along. Rogers took a very active part in the meetings. He often became involved in the discussion of a new product, particularly its technical aspects. Frequently he explained technical points to others who did not understand them. His viewpoints were clearly heard and felt by others, and people thought that meetings had improved since he decided to sit in. Nevertheless, Glen Johnson still dreaded the product development meetings.

> *I never sleep well on the night before the meetings. I start thinking about the various projects and the problems I have in getting everyone to agree and be committed to a direction. We spend long hours in these meetings, but people just don't seem to stick to their commitments to accomplish their objectives by a given date. Projects are slipping badly, and we just can't seem to get them moving. In my opinion, we also have some projects that should be killed, but we can't seem to be able to do that, either. Frankly, if I had it to do over again, I would not take this job. After all, how much marketing am I really doing? I seem to spend most of my time in meetings getting others to do things.*

The Outlook for 1969

As 1968 drew to a close, Don Rogers and the top management group were preparing for their second GLF (Great Leap Forward) meeting. This meeting had been instituted the year before as a forum for discussing major problem areas and developing commitment to division objectives for the coming year. Now it was time to look ahead to 1969.

In a memo to the key managers, Rogers summarized the problems that needed to be addressed in the coming year:

> *It is obvious that division growth is our major problem and that we need to develop new products to get growth. Achievement of budgeted operating margin*

is a close second. Morale has become a more acute problem, and the need for communication, coordination, and the proper balance of long- and short-range efforts continues to require our attention.

As the top managers in EPD prepared for the two-day meeting in Ithaca, New York, it was clear that they had survived the shakeout in the industry. But they also knew that many major problems remained. They all wanted growth and saw it as their major problem, but they were not developing new products fast enough to meet this objective, nor did they agree about strategies, priorities, or criteria for profitability.

To complicate matters, morale was low, risk taking was down, and significant problems in communication and coordination existed. In the external environment, price/cost squeezes continued, and competition was as fierce as ever.

As key managers prepared for their GLF meetings, the Corning organization development staff was preparing to present the findings of their study of EPD to Don Rogers.

Case 7–4

*Corning Glass Works (B): The Electronic Products Division**

Michael Beer

In January 1969, Tom Noles, director of organization development for Corning Glass Works, met with Don Rogers, vice president of Corning's Electronics Products Division (EPD) to present his diagnosis of the problems facing EPD. In July 1968, Rogers had asked Noles to study his division to ascertain the root causes of various problems Rogers perceived and to recommend solutions. The division's sales and profits had declined drastically in 1967 and 1968 from previous levels (see Exhibit 1). Although severe cost savings measures had been taken, Rogers remained concerned about the fierce competition in the components market, low morale in the division, and the lack of mutual confidence and trust between groups, which often led to conflicts that were difficult to resolve. He was particularly concerned about the impact of poor relations between functional groups on business decisions, product development, and divisional performance as a whole.[1]

Noles and two members of his department had agreed to undertake a three-month study of the division and to report their findings and recommendations. The study included several phases. Initially Noles and his associates became acquainted with EPD's business and the key members of the organization by sitting in on a variety of meetings held at

* All names have been disguised.

Harvard Business School case 477–073.

[1] See Corning Glass Works (A), HBS Case Services No. 477–024, for a description of the situation in the Electronic Products Division in late 1968.

Exhibit 1
EPD Sales and Operating Margin, 1961–1968 ($000)

	1961	1962	1963	1964	1965	1966	1967	1968
Sales	$12,723	$21,745	$22,836	$20,036	$25,320	$26,553	$23,852	$24,034
Operating margin*	3,011	5,449	5,826	2,998	5,075	4,170	1,559	1,574

* Operating margin equals sales less manufacturing, administrative, and sales expenses.
Source: Company records.

the divisional and plant levels. This included a two-day product development meeting held each month.[2] The consultants also conducted many informal conversations with individuals. In the second phase some 40 in-depth interviews were conducted with individuals at the top three levels of the organization in all functional areas and plants. The final phase involved the administration of a questionnaire aimed at measuring more precisely certain salient findings that were emerging from the interviews.

The process had taken longer than anticipated but now Corning's Organizational Development (OD) Department was ready with its diagnosis and recommendations. Flip charts were prepared, and Noles was about to begin the presentation to Rogers. Bits and pieces of the internal consultants' observations had been discussed throughout the four and one half months of the study, but Rogers now waited in anticipation for a comprehensive report.

The Diagnostic Findings

The presentation was long and reviewed the findings in detail. A comparison with companies in other industries suggested EPD had serious problems in cross-functional conflict and coordination. As shown in Exhibit 2, EPD managers rated coordination between functions in EPD lower than did managers from poorly performing companies in plastics, foods, and containers. These poor relations hurt the division's performance through their effects on new product development, service, morale, and decision making. Some on Rogers' staff had held that the conflict in the division was due to declining market conditions and poor divisional performance. They felt that if business got better they would stop crabbing at each other. The OD staff felt otherwise. They saw the poor relations between functional groups as a symptom of some fundamental organizational problems that had been building in the division for a long time and were associated with changes in the division's markets and recent changes in management. The OD group presented 11 major conclusions about the causes of intergroup problems:

1. EPD markets have been shifting as a result of a decline in space and military spending by the federal government and the growth course charted by the division. The result has been increasing sales in the data-processing, telecommunications, and consumer electronics markets, which required the rapid development of product extensions at competitive prices and good service–not unique technological advantage in product, which had been the initial basis of entry into the components busi-

---

[2] Ibid.

Exhibit 2
Integration: Electronic Products Division Comparison with Other High and Low Performers in Three Industries, 1968

Industry	Organization	Average Integration*
Plastics	High performer	5.6
	Low performer	5.1
Foods	High performer	5.3
	Low performer	5.0
Container	High performer	5.7
	Low performer	4.8
Electronic	Electronic Products Division	4.3

* All ratings were on an eight-point scale with high score indicating high integration.

Source: Company records. Comparison scores from three industries obtained from P. R. Lawrence and J. W. Lorsch, *Organization and Environment: Managing Differentiation and Integration* (Boston, Mass.: Harvard University, Graduate School of Business Administration, Division of Research, 1967).

ness. EPD's environment was now more uncertain than in the past, and management rated its predictability as very low [see Exhibit 3]. Other indicators of uncertainty were the inability to forecast and the inability of Marketing to develop accurate estimates of the market size for new products.

2. EPD operates in an uncertain environment. Yet in terms of management and organization, it is very similar to Corning divisions that participate in much more certain and stable original equipment manufacture businesses where Corning has a technological advantage and where capital requirements have prevented serious competition. This is not surprising, since all but one of EPD's key managers have spent most of their careers in other divisions.

[The research of Lawrence and Lorsch[3] was presented as a conceptual framework for understanding EPD's problems and led to the following interpretations of the root causes of the problem.]

3. The division has larger differences [differentiation] between functions than most other Corning Glass Works divisions–differences in structure, goals, time horizons, and personal orientations of people. Rogers' decision to split marketing and sales reflects an intuitive understanding that these differences are necessary to cope with the business. The needs for a product development group and corporate R&D support are other

[3] P. R. Lawrence and J. W. Lorsch, *Organization and Environment: Managing Differentiation and Integration* (Cambridge, Mass.: Harvard University, Graduate School of Business Administration, Division of Research, 1967).

Exhibit 3
Ratings of EPD's Environment by People in Division, 1968

High						Low
Stability Predictability Certainty						Stability Predictability Certainty
1	2	3	4	5	X 6	7
					Mean = 5.7	

Source: Company records.

examples. Yet in some places there is not yet enough differentiation. Market planning as a function has been eliminated as a cost-saving step, and Product Development in the division is working on projects similar to those of corporate R&D.

4. High levels of differentiation have brought a greater need for coordination [integration] in the division. Yet there are no mechanisms for integration other than the organization's hierarchy and Rogers' own involvement in many decisions. Most integration and decision making is handled at the top as in the monthly product development meetings. But this mechanism is being frustrated by the relatively large number of new-product projects and the diversity of information required to make decisions. This information simply does not exist at the top.

5. Poor integration is exacerbated by the demise of mechanisms that existed in the past. Marketing groups previously located at the plants have been moved to Corning, New York, reducing opportunities for communication. Bennett, Rogers's predecessor, achieved some coordination through his single-handed management of the division. Now this is no longer appropriate, nor is Rogers inclined to manage that way.

6. The natural differences between groups, the absence of mechanisms for bringing them together, and the historical competitive atmosphere of the division has led to some very poor relationships between groups.

[The consultants presented questionnaire data showing that the poorest relationships were between groups that people perceived as requiring particularly high levels of coordination—for example, Manufacturing and Marketing (see Exhibit 4).]

Marketing is already attempting to coordinate [integrator role] the work of other functions in developing product extensions and other profit-

Exhibit 4
Required and Actual Integration as Seen by People in EPD, 1968

	Required Integration			Actual Integration		
	Rank	Mean	Standard Deviation	Rank	Mean	Standard Deviation
Sales and Marketing	1	6.6	.60	16	4.4	1.10
Marketing and Product Development (resistors)	2	6.4	.79	18	4.3	1.37
Marketing and Product Development (capacitors)	3	6.3	.78	7	4.7	1.00
Manufacturing and Product Development (resistors)	4	5.8	.97	20	4.1	.99
Manufacturing and Sales	5	5.6	1.09	19	4.1	.91
Product Development (capacitors) and Manufacturing	6	5.5	1.01	17	4.3	.75
Manufacturing and Marketing	7	5.5	1.24	21	3.8	1.02
Product Development (resistors) and Technical Staffs (R&D)	8	5.3	1.10	9	4.6	.98
Manufacturing and Controller	9	5.3	1.28	1	5.3	.84
Product Development (capacitors) and Technical Staffs (R&D)	10	5.2	1.05	6	4.7	.91
Technical Staffs (R&D) and Marketing	11	5.0	1.16	15	4.4	.90
Marketing and Fluidics*	12	5.0	1.71	14	4.5	.96
Technical Staffs (R&D) and Fluidics	13	4.6	1.14	13	4.5	.83
Product Development (resistors) and Sales	14	4.6	1.36	11	4.5	.68
Sales and Product Development (capacitors)	15	4.6	1.60	5	4.7	.79
Controller and Sales	16	4.5	1.15	3	5.0	.84
Marketing and Controller	17	4.4	1.14	10	4.6	1.00
Fluidics and Controller	18	4.2	1.03	2	5.0	.74
Product Development (resistors) and Controller	19	4.0	1.12	8	4.6	.73
Product Development (capacitors) and Controller	20	3.8	1.00	4	4.9	.87
Technical Staffs (R&D) and Manufacturing	21	3.1	1.25	12	4.5	.83

Note: All ratings were on a seven-point scale with high scores indicating high required or actual integration.

* The Fluidics Department was a small, $2 million business which reported to Rogers but was not part of the components business and operated independently of it.

Source: Company records.

oriented projects. [Marketing chairs the product development meetings.] But Marketing is staffed by young and inexperienced people who are seen as sales oriented and incompetent; they are *not* formally acknowledged as having the responsibility for integrating. This makes it difficult for Marketing to get other functions to do things in support of product development. There is considerable resentment of Marketing because they are thought to have great influence on what happens in the division, despite their perceived incompetence [see Exhibit 5]. Resentment is particularly strong in Manufacturing, the function that historically has been

Exhibit 5
Influence of Functional Groups in EPD and Corporate R&D as Seen by People in Division, 1968

Function	Influence Score
Marketing	4.1
Sales	3.9
Production	3.8
Controller	3.1
Product Development	2.9
Technical Staffs (Corporate R&D)	2.0

Note: Ratings were on a five-point scale with high score indicating high influence.
Source: Company records.

most important and most powerful in the division and in Corning Glass Works.

7. Product Development and R&D have relatively low influence in the division. Yet EPD needs to develop products to meet its growth and profit objectives.

8. The fact that marketing personnel are not evaluated in terms of profits reduces their sensitivity to cost/price trade-offs in managing new-product introductions and reinforces their tendency to be sales oriented. On the other hand, Manufacturing's responsibility for gross margin gives them a final club in any conflict with Marketing, thus worsening the relationship between the two and reducing chances for cooperative problem solving.

9. The culture of EPD, shaped by Bennett's single-handed management style, is one in which differences are ignored [smoothing] or resolved by pressuring one party to the other's will [forcing]. Relatively little use is made of the open dialogue and problem solving [confrontation] that have been noted in other successful companies in uncertain environments. The questionnaire data [Exhibit 6], observations, and interviews confirmed this conclusion.

10. People do not have a common understanding of division objectives, strategies, and business philosophy—even at the top. They differ about what the primary markets are and about realistic profit and growth expectations. This disagreement contributes to poor integration.

11. The differences between EPD's business and Corning's traditional glass business create some problems. The division needs distinctive goals, strategies, and managerial approaches in certain areas, yet the close physical proximity and control by Corning's management and staff groups leads to some difficulties.

Exhibit 6
Modes of Conflict Resolution in EPD as Seen by People in Division, 1968

Mode of Conflict Resolution	Amount*
Forcing	3.1
Smoothing	3.0
Confrontation	2.9

Note: All scores are on a five-point scale.
* In organizations studied by Lawrence and Lorsch, confrontation was almost always rated significantly higher than forcing or smoothing—even when the company operated in a certain environment.
Source: Company records.

As Noles finished presenting the findings, he knew that he had captured his audience's attention and interest. Rogers had asked many incisive questions, reflecting his intelligence and grasp of complex issues, and was now sitting forward in anticipation of the OD group's recommendations. Both short- and long-range recommendations were to be made, urging major changes in the division's structure and management process.

As Noles proceeded, he wondered how the recommendations would be received. He had been convinced that it was best to be direct and make specific recommendations, although his staff was concerned that by forging their own recommendations the consultants were precluding participation by Rogers's staff, thereby triggering resistance among those most affected by the findings and recommendations. Their view had been that recommendations should be jointly forged with EPD's management after a presentation of the findings.

OD Department Recommendations

A project team organization was recommended for EPD, especially for new-product development tasks.[4] It was suggested that members of these project teams be selected differently, depending on the function represented. For example, functions such as research and/or development would be represented by bench scientists or development engineers, while manufacturing would be represented by individuals at higher levels in the organization, such as the production superintendent or the manufacturing engineer.[5] Sales should also be represented, but it was less clear

---

[4] Parts of the next three sections are based on Gerald R. Pieters, "Changing Organizational Structures, Roles and Processes to Enhance Integration: The Implementation of a Change Program," a paper presented to the Division of Industrial and Organization Psychology of the American Psychological Association, September 3, 1971, in Washington, D.C.

[5] These positions were generally regarded as the two most important jobs in the plant, in the order listed.

by whom. Unlike Manufacturing and Product Development, Sales was organized geographically rather than by product (see Exhibit 7). Moreover, it was not obvious whether salespeople or district managers should represent Sales on the team. The controller function was to be represented by the controller of the plant associated with the given product.

Marketing, it was recommended, should be the integrating function. Earlier in the presentation, the consultants had noted that people in the division, particularly Manufacturing, had great concerns about the competence of Marketing's personnel, their inexperience, and their sales orientation. Nevertheless, they now urged that the marketing specialists in the Market Development Department under Glen Johnson (see Exhibit 7) should serve as project team integrators. Project team integrators were to be trained in their roles through seminars and group discussions. Additionally, OD specialists would sit in on the early project team meetings as process consultants,[6] observing the functioning of the team, feeding back their observations, raising issues, and facilitating the confrontation of conflict. They were also to provide feedback to the integrators on their effectiveness and help train them.

It was further recommended that Rogers and his staff modify their roles by withdrawing from the detail of product development projects, delegating project planning and action responsibility to the teams, and reserving for themselves the review of projects and resource allocation. They were to be referred to as the Resource Allocation Team, or RAT. A director from the corporate R&D laboratory who was responsible for electronic research was to be asked to join Rogers's staff for these reviews.

Each project team was to develop its own objectives for the project, plan the project (it was recommended that PERT[7] be used as a program management tool), and report to the top team on a quarterly basis through the integrator. At these quarterly meetings, which would replace the monthly product development sessions, the progress of the projects would be reviewed along with money and manpower resource requirements.

It was recommended that the top group spend some time (several days away from the office) developing itself into an effective management team that would be able to provide unified direction to the division. First, they were to reexamine the present strategies and direction of the division and develop a set of commonly agreed-to goals, strategies, and a business philosophy to be communicated to the division's membership. Later, they were to observe how they functioned as a group, the quality of their meetings, how the behavior of individuals (including Rogers) influenced group effectiveness, and what and who had to change.

---

[6] See E. H. Schein, *Process Consultation: Its Role in Organization Development* (Reading, Mass.: Addison Wesley Publishing, 1969).

[7] PERT is a program management technique invented and used by the U.S. Navy during the development of the Polaris submarine.

Exhibit 7
Electronic Products Division: Organization Chart

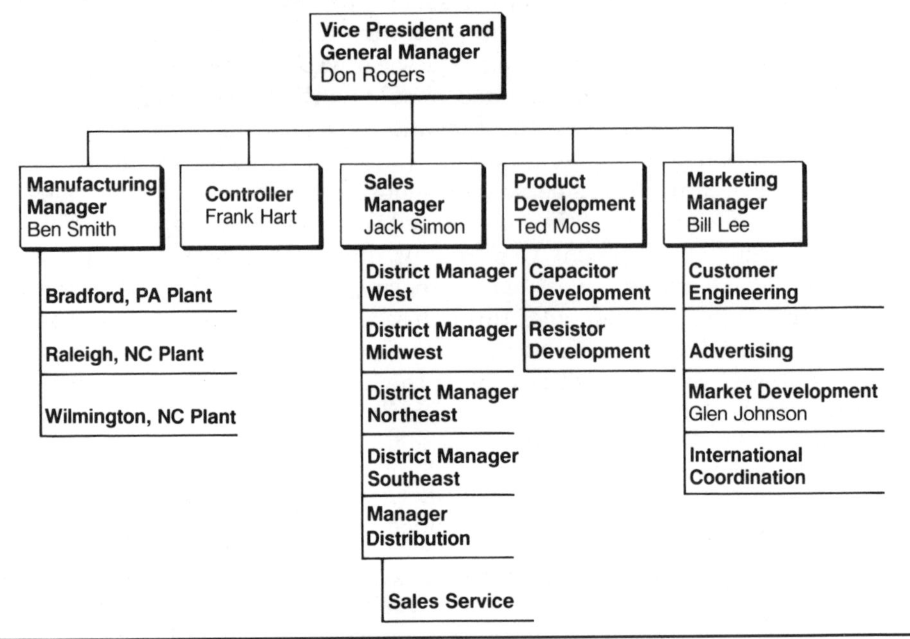

Source: Company records.

These meetings were to be attended by Noles as a facilitator and were referred to as team development meetings.

The consultants recommended to Rogers that he adopt a stronger management style. They felt that the motivation of EPD staff would be improved if he budgeted more time for direct contact with his subordinates and other key people, molded a cohesive staff by clarifying his expectations, set a tone and direction as well as settled conflicts, and inspired enthusiasm for projects and the direction of the division by "talking them up." At the same time, he was asked to do more listening and be more receptive to conflict. The consultants offered Rogers help on this personal agenda through further feedback as the program of change developed.

To deal directly with the intergroup relations problems, it was recommended that "intergroup laboratory meetings"[8] be held for the groups that had the worst relations. In these meetings (typically two days) pairs

[8] See R. R. Blake, H. A. Shepart, and J. S. Mouton, *Managing Intergroup Conflict in Industry* (Houston: Gulf Publishing, 1964); and R. Beckhard, *Organization Development: Strategies and Models* (Reading, Mass.: Addison Wesley Publishing, 1969).

of groups were to come together to exchange perceptions of each other, obtain clarification of these perceptions, and develop an action plan for improving relationships. The intent of the meetings would be to develop better mutual understanding and trust between groups and improve integration.

Several longer-range recommendations were also made:

- A program should be developed for identifying potential integrators and consciously developing them through cross-functional work experiences and various types of training. Laboratory training, Kepner-Trego rational problem-solving training, and technical marketing seminars were recommended.
- For the long-range development of greater interpersonal competence and collaboration, many of the EPD salaried personnel assigned to project teams should receive laboratory training (sensitivity training or a more structured program called the Managerial Grid).[9]
- The division should consider hiring a full-time organization development professional to carry on these activities and help the division make the changes recommended.

In addition to their formal recommendations, the OD consultants also suggested a future change in the accounting and control system, which placed gross margin responsibility (sales less cost of manufacture) at the plant. They felt that Marketing should be the profit center and the plants should be cost centers. The consultants discussed these views with Rogers, but did not press their ideas, nor did Rogers encourage them. Both parties recognized the corporation's commitment was to the plant profit center concept and the near impossibility of obtaining an exception for EPD.

Implementation

By the time the presentation of the recommendations had been completed, it was clear that Rogers was not only receptive but enthusiastic. His frequent questions and comments throughout the presentation had shown an understanding of the analysis, its conceptual foundations, and the rationale for the actions recommended. He was less enthusiastic about the consultants' analysis of the relationship between the division and the corporation and the implication that the corporation was somehow responsible for part of EPD's problems. Rogers also disagreed with the implication that the division should maintain some differences (e.g.,

---

[9] For information on these and other techniques referred to, see M. Beer, "The Technology of Organization Development," in *Handbook of Industrial and Organizational Psychology,* ed. M. P. Dunette (New York: Rand McNally, 1976).

in profit objectives, types of people, control system) between itself and the corporation. He felt that such a policy could undermine corporate support for EPD, without which the division could not survive. Rogers supported the bulk of the recommendations, however, and suggested that they be presented to his staff. When Noles asked if this presentation should include the findings about Marketing and his (Rogers's) own style, he quickly said yes.

The OD group made its presentation to Rogers's staff in February; the meeting went smoothly. Many questions were asked about the findings, particularly those relating to perceptions of Marketing. Throughout the discussion, the marketing manager asked questions and did not behave defensively, while the manufacturing manager remained fairly quiet. On occasion someone would come to Marketing's defense, but no one used the negative data about them to attack them further. There was relatively little discussion of Rogers's style of management. When the meeting ended, Rogers's enthusiasm seemed to have carried the day, and the staff committed itself to getting to work immediately on the development of a strategy and implementation of the project organization. The other recommendations also appeared to be accepted, although no specific implementation steps had been planned.

In March the top management group met offsite for two days to examine and reestablish the goals, strategies, and direction of the division. At this meeting it became clear that they all had slightly different views of what the division direction should be. With the very strong guidance of Rogers, the meeting ended by setting priorities for markets (e.g., data-processing, military) based on their growth and potential profitability, and drawing up a list of projects that reflected these priorities. In yet another meeting, the management group considered which of these projects should be handled by a project team, and selected nine projects to begin with. They chose members for each team, including the integrators from Market Development and, where appropriate, a representative from corporate R&D. In addition, several "evaluation and recommendation" projects were identified that required study and analysis by a cross-functional team. These teams would report to the RAT with their analysis and recommendations on whether the division should launch a full-fledged project.

During April and May the decisions reached by Rogers and his staff were communicated widely. Rogers personally briefed Corning's president about what he was intending to do in EPD. All of the salaried, exempt employees of the division in all plant locations, sales districts, and in Corning, New York, as well as members of related staff groups (e.g., corporate R&D, Controller's Division, Manpower Development Division) were asked to attend a three-part presentation lasting up to four hours. Most of Rogers's staff were present for each of these presentations, which covered:

- The division's redefined objectives and strategies, presented by Rogers.
- The diagnostic findings and recommendations of the OD Department, including the perceptions of Marketing and Rogers, presented by Noles. This part included the conceptual framework of Lawrence and Lorsch, which had guided the diagnosis and recommendations.
- Bill Lee, the marketing manager, described the nine high-priority projects and named the project team members. He emphasized the marketing specialists' role as integrators and what that meant. He also explained how Rogers and his staff would move away from a direct, detailed involvement in development projects to assume a review and resource allocation role, with specific project responsibility delegated to project teams.

Following the presentation, extended informal meetings were held for discussion and clarification of the actions being initiated. These were often followed by drinks and dinner with at least the key people at each location. The formal and informal give-and-take sessions elicited a variety of reactions to the proposed changes.

- In the formal meetings at the plants, many sharp questions were asked about the choice of Marketing to integrate project teams and about the advisability of the project team concept. The questions and comments reflected a deep distrust of Marketing and concern about loss of influence by Manufacturing:

  Will anyone in Manufacturing have a chance to head up project teams? Why should it be just Marketing?

  What does this integrator concept in Marketing mean for the role and importance of Manufacturing?

  What is in it for a plant person to be on a project team? Why should I go to meetings and put in a lot of time? As far as I can see, I still get evaluated on the same thing I have always been evaluated on within the plant.

  It looks to me as if the members of the project team are going to be dependent on the marketing integrator's ability to sell the project to the resource allocation team. If he can't sell it effectively, the project fails, and we all fail with it.

  How do we get projects started now? In the past, if we saw an opportunity to consolidate products or make some changes in order to reduce costs, we would get our Manufacturing Engineering Department to start work on the project. Now it looks like we have to go through Marketing to get a project started. They can screen out a lot of projects that we think are important to increasing our gross margin.

- In several of the meetings with sales personnel, district sales managers indicated considerable concern about the impact of the organization change on the sales group. One district manager said:

  Why can't salesmen be integrators on the project teams? They have as much contact with the customer as marketing people, and we have some pretty good people who can do the job. If salesmen are not made integrators, they will feel that the sales function has been downgraded. Anyway, I don't feel that the market development people have done that good a job. Why should they be given this assignment?

- Over drinks and dinner in Wilmington, North Carolina, after one of the presentations, several plant people indicated that they felt the marketing group was weak and lacked the ability to take on the responsibility for integrating. Rogers and his staff responded that the people in Market Development were going to be given the chance to do this job and that many of them could handle it. Those that couldn't would not stay. Rogers said, "We have to start someplace, and Marketing appears to be the logical group to pull things together because of their role and position in the organization."
- The presentation in Corning, New York, which included the Market Development Department, revealed considerable concern on the part of the market specialists who were to be the integrators. One of them commented:

  I am very anxious about the changes you are talking about. Frankly, I don't know if I can do the job, if I have the capability. This job is going to put me in the spotlight. What happens if I don't succeed? We have several strikes against us already, judging by what people have said about us. Also, how are we going to get the plants to do what has to be done? Those idiot manufacturing people can't get the costs down.

  A corporate staff manager who had recently been a production superintendent in EPD said in an informal discussion after the presentation, "The whole thing might fail if you don't get heavyweights into the integrator jobs."

The series of communication meetings required two months. Rogers and his staff made 14 different presentations and traveled to eight different locations from Wilmington, North Carolina, to Los Angeles, California. Everywhere, the same presentation was given and reactions were obtained. Rogers took charge in these presentations and in the meetings that followed, answering questions as candidly as he could. The management of EPD and the OD specialists came away from the presentations chastened. At the conceptual stage, the ideas had seemed right and sensible. But the reactions to the communication meetings indicated that a lot of people would have to change to make it happen. The magnitude of the change for EPD became apparent. Now it was time to see if it would all work.

The First Year of Change

By June 1969 the project organization was in place. Project teams were beginning to meet, and the first reviews with the resource allocation team were being scheduled. People were beginning to understand how the new organization was to function and were changing their approach to running EPD's business. Rogers himself was strongly supportive of the changes and was seen as providing the impetus for the program. Despite this progress, there were problems.

In the early stages of implementation, the OD specialists held several meetings with the project integrators to explore and discuss the implications of the role of integrator. At these meetings the marketing specialists showed their anxieties about their new assignment, which they saw as an additional load on top of their existing marketing job. They were also uncomfortable with the title of "integrator." Although they recognized that successful performance of the role, with its additional visibility, promised added growth potential, they were equally aware of their handicaps, e.g., youth, inexperience in the division, currently negative perceptions of the marketing function, and concerns, particularly on the part of Manufacturing, that Marketing was too sales oriented, ignoring costs and profits. In addition, the task of managing a cross-functional project team without formal authority seemed overwhelming. They had a hard time understanding how to develop other sources of influence and how to handle nonresponsiveness by other functions.

Some frustrations developed in many of the project team members. In their first meetings, project teams often became entangled in long discussions about the background of the projects in the functional groups represented. They had trouble getting to the stage where they could set goals and outline the task. Some people began to wonder if project team management meant long, unproductive meetings that accomplished nothing.

Several of the people on Rogers's staff became uncomfortable about not having frequent, detailed feedback on project status. The manufacturing manager, Ben Smith, requested copies of all the memos that were generated by teams. In another instance, Rogers and his staff received some rather sketchy information that seemed to suggest a catastrophic problem. They quickly scheduled a meeting to "resolve the problem." The integrator of the team voiced his concern that such a meeting would undermine the activities of the team and not give the team concept a chance to work. Rogers and his staff held the meeting, and the integrator was asked to describe the situation. He related what was going on and what the team was doing about it. Management seemed to go away from the meeting satisfied that something was being done.

Over time, it became apparent that not all of the people who had been assigned to teams were going to have or make the necessary time. For example, production superintendents and manufacturing engineers soon delegated their roles on the team to lower-level people in the plants. District sales managers delegated their responsibility to salespeople (generally senior salespeople). Sometimes the senior and junior people from a function would both come to a meeting, and the group would become large and unwieldy.

In the past, plant managers had been involved personally in planning and decision making for all projects in their plants. Soon after the change to a project organization, they began complaining that they were left uninformed and "out of the loop." Project teams were planning and making decisions affecting the plant with the understanding and consent of the plant representative, but often the plant managers and others in the plant learned about these decisions only after the fact. This increased the plant managers' concern about the organizational change, and their complaints about Marketing continued; if anything, discontent seemed to increase because it was voiced more openly. Complaints were often carried to Ben Smith, the manufacturing manager, who would raise these concerns with Rogers and his staff.

For some time after the implementation of the new organization, it seemed as if every situation requiring coordination between two or more departments was perceived as requiring a formal project team. As the distribution manager in Sales said, "It seems as if we form a team every time we go to the men's room." He and others began to complain that people weren't taking responsibility for making hard decisions. It also seemed to take a long time to reach decisions. As one person said, "Previously I could make a decision and run with the ball; now I have to sit in a meeting for a day and get six other guys to agree that I ought to do it before I can go ahead. This slows things down."

As the year of change progressed, several problems became apparent in the relationship between EPD and the corporation. Because the addition of the integrator role had expanded the scope and responsibility of the job of marketing specialist, the people in Marketing felt that its wage and salary level should be raised. They felt higher salaries were needed, both to ensure equitable compensation and to attract into the job the kinds of experienced people everyone agreed were required in the long run. Marketing's management ran into problems, however, as they tried to explain their reasoning to the Wage and Salary Department in Corning's personnel function. This department had not encountered the integrator role before. They had heard the presentation by Rogers and staff but did not fully understand it, and were not convinced that the market specialist's job in EPD should be rated higher than similar jobs in other divisions.

There were other problems, too. As Rogers and his staff began to delegate more and more responsibility to lower levels, two aspects of their relation to the corporation began to emerge as somewhat troublesome. Several people saw a conflict between their efforts to delegate within the division and corporate management's formal and informal requests for information about what was going on in EPD. As the marketing manager, Bill Lee, said:

I run into top corporate people in the lobby, in the cafeteria, or on airplanes, and they ask me questions about projects, customers, shipments, and orders that require more details than I feel I should have, given our new approach to management. They are important people and expect me to know these things, and so I will continue to try to have the information at my fingertips, but it runs counter to what we on staff are trying to do when we say we want to be more strategically oriented.

Feeling caught in the middle, Rogers's staff often vented their frustrations on the OD consultants, who continued to emphasize the importance of delegation.

In the area of budgeting, Jack Simon, the sales manager, saw a similar conflict. He complained that yearly sales budgets, which were increasingly developed through a bottom-up process within Sales, were being changed at the corporate level on the basis of corporate estimates and needs. He wrote a long memo to Rogers on this issue, expressing his concern about asking salespeople and district managers to come up with budgets only to change them later arbitrarily. Though this concern was not new, its intensity seemed to increase.

But project team meetings continued throughout 1969. Rogers and his staff set aside two or three days each quarter for reviews of the project team activity. Project team integrators, though initially poorly prepared for these reviews, began to improve their presentations. They liked the exposure that their new role gave them to top management. They felt the project team concept gained visibility for their problems and made it easier to secure top management support for the directions they were proposing.

The project team organization also gave lower levels more exposure to what was going on at the top as they interacted with Rogers and his staff during the reviews. People sometimes came away from these meetings feeling that the RAT did not solve problems openly. They did not always confront conflicts, and were not operating as a team as much as they should be. Moreover, the top group was criticized for a lack of direction. It was felt that they were not fulfilling their resource allocation responsibility. Project integrators still had problems getting people they needed to work on their projects because of the competition of other activities. One person complained, "They are not setting priorities and communicating these." Another said, "I don't know what they do in RAT meetings."

Throughout 1969, the OD consultants sat in on project team and RAT meetings, counseled with integrators and individual managers, and kept Rogers and his staff informed on the progress of the whole change effort. But this too was behind schedule. Rogers and his staff had not had a second meeting to deal with how they worked as a group (team development). The demands of working with project teams and the RAT were so great that there had not been time to hold the intergroup meetings for pairs of groups that were having difficulty. Similarly, no change in the control or evaluation system had been made. The plant was the profit center, and there was no way to account for profit by products. Individuals on teams were evaluated by their functional bosses. No laboratory training for people on teams had taken place, and no plans for upgrading the people in the integrator role had been developed.

By December 1969 when Rogers and his staff met for their annual GLF (great leap forward) meeting, EPD was operating as a project organization. Project teams and the RAT were meeting as scheduled. Marketing people were enthusiastic about the impact of the reorganization on their role and influence in the company, but complaints about Marketing were still being heard, particularly from Manufacturing. Bill Lee, the marketing manager, was sometimes attacked for providing no direction and for weaknesses in the marketing function. Throughout, Rogers held firm to the concept of the project organization and supported Bill Lee and the marketing function in their efforts to adopt the integrator role and exert more influence in the management of the division.

Case 7–5

CORNING GLASS WORKS (C): The Electronic Products Division*

Michael Beer

By the end of 1970, the change process moving EPD to a project/matrix organization had been under way for 18 months. The organizational changes introduced in 1968 were still in place. The division had a banner year in 1969. Sales were the highest in the division's history, and profits had improved significantly (see Exhibit 1). In 1970, sales had dropped slightly, but profits continued to be much better than the pre-1968 levels.

The management of the division was becoming very committed to changes in organization and management that they had introduced in 1969. At the request of the president of Corning Glass Works, Rogers made a presentation to all officers and key executives of the company about what had been done in EPD and how, in his (Rogers') view, it had contributed significantly to improvements in the division's performance. Rogers' staff was equally enthusiastic about the changes, although there were differences between individuals in degree of enthusiasm. Despite their enthusiasm, the top group wanted an objective reading on the impact the new organization was having on EPD. They commissioned a rediagnosis of the division by the Organization Development Department. A number of significant improvements in EPD's management process and performance were found.

The target of the change program had been to improve integration in the division, with a clear expectation that such improvements would

---

* All names have been disguised.

Harvard Business School case 477–074.

Exhibit 1
EPD Sales and Operating Margin, 1961–1970 ($000)

	1961	1962	1963	1964	1965	1966	1967	1968	1969	1970
Sales	$12,723	$21,745	$22,836	$20,036	$25,320	$26,553	$23,852	$24,034	$31,100	$26,900
Operating margin* . . .	3,011	5,449	5,826	2,998	5,075	4,170	1,559	1,574	6,400	3,400

* Operating margin equals sales less manufacturing, administrative, and sales expenses.

effect better product development performance. Prior to 1968 the division had developed five new products. This was considered inadequate if the division was to maintain or improve its position in the marketplace. In 1970, nine new products were introduced, more than in the previous five years (see Exhibit 2).

Questionnaire data and interviews showed an increase in overall integration between functional groups. People all over the division felt that teams had greatly facilitated coordination and that intergroup relations were improved. As one person, representative of many others, said: "Problems are shared and understood. If things don't happen, I don't start placing blame. I have a better understanding of why it didn't happen. Now I ask how I can help to make it happen. It is important to have empathy for the other guy, but not sympathy." Despite these overwhelmingly positive reports of change, the relationship between Manufacturing and Marketing had not improved significantly.

People reported that higher-quality decisions were being made because "the team supports openness, and all relevant information is being pooled for decision making." The locus of decision making shifted dramatically after the introduction of project teams. Responsibility (as it related to product development and other cross-functional profit improvement programs) was being delegated from upper management to project teams who had the information and data necessary to solve the problems and make decisions. People thought that teams facilitated the development of a more objective approach to problems. More commitment to decisions was also reported.

An unexpected but positive outcome of the change was that people on project teams felt that the experience had been the best and the most management development they had received since being with Corning. Many felt that they understood for the first time how different functions operated and the complexity of business problems and decision making.

Exhibit 2
Electronics Products Division:
Introduction of New Products*

Year	Resistors	Capacitors
1966	1	0
1967	0	0
1968	4	0
1969	0	0
1970	6	3

* New products are defined as those which meet the following three requirements:

1. Produced within the last five years.
2. Have major significance to customer.
3. Not an obvious one-for-one replacement.

The handling of conflict in the division changed dramatically. Confrontation problem solving increased and in 1970 was the primary mode of resolving differences. Forcing dropped to second in frequency of use, and smoothing dropped significantly and was third in the frequency with which it was used (see Exhibit 3). The following anecdote illustrates the type of changes that took place.

In June 1971, one of the OD consultants received a telephone call from Joe Black, a marketing specialist and integrator of a major product team working on the development of a new product. The team had been in operation for less than a year and had both technical and organizational problems. The following is the gist of his remarks:

> *Sam, our team has been having some problems, and I have decided it is time to get to the causes. We are just not working together effectively, and we all see a need for improvement. For example, I find myself "going around the system" to get things accomplished. Instead of going to a team member to get something done, I am going over his head.* [Other symptoms of an unhealthy situation were given.] *I think we should all get together and put the technical tasks aside and take a closer look at our "process"* [his word].

If Joe Black were in the same situation in 1968, he would most likely have continued to go to his boss to get pressure exerted on people in other functions.

Another area where noticeable change had occurred was in the recognition of Marketing as the integrating function. Marketing was now more involved in the communication network related to product development and introduction and played a more central role in business decisions. The young integrators were seen as having matured over the 18-month period, and their legitimacy and acceptance by others had increased. Those who could not handle the increased responsibility were moved out of Marketing. However, some people in the division still had concerns over the competence of the integrators and Marketing in general. Manufacturing in particular was still critical of Marketing and the lack of direction they gave. They still viewed the integrators as too young and too inexperienced, and indeed they still were. Bill Lee, the marketing manager, increasingly came under attack for his lack of leadership in moving the division into profitable product lines. Other influ-

Exhibit 3
Conflict Resolution Styles in EPD before and after Changes

	Amount	
Mode of Resolution	**1968**	**1970**
Confrontation	2.9	3.5
Forcing	3.0	2.8
Smoothing	3.0	2.5

ence patterns did not change. Product Development continued to be low in influence and Manufacturing and Sales high. Of all the functions, Manufacturing was still the most powerful and dominant function.

The improvements in integration extended beyond EPD to the corporate R&D group. This came about through participation on project teams by R&D people. One comment heard over and over again was that "scientists are now out of their labs and know how their work fits into the overall project." As one scientist said, "My blinders have been taken off."

Coordination at the top was seen as improved. Integrators felt that they were getting most of the resources they needed and liked being exposed to the top group. However, some concerns about the top group continued. People wondered what they did at RAT meetings, since there were often no visible products or communication to the division. Some felt the top group was not together, confronting conflict, or operating as a team.

On the whole, however, there had been many positive changes in the division, and these outweighed continuing and new problems: increased numbers of new products introduced; improved integration and intergroup relations; high degree of commitment to decisions made; improved morale; improved problem solving; increased use of confronting as a means of resolving conflict; Marketing in a stronger position to integrate and seen by some at least as doing a better job; and a better interface with corporate R&D.

In 1970, Rogers was promoted to be a group vice president of Corning's Technical Products Division—a much larger and more important division. A new vice president who had no familiarity with the division and was known to be hard nosed and tough was taking over. Many in the division were quite concerned about the impact this would have on the changes in management which had taken place in EPD.

Reading 7–1

Organizational Change Techniques: Their Present, Their Future*

Stephen R. Michael

The French say that the more things change, the more they remain the same. George Odiorne's law says that things that do not change remain the same. These two views suggest that, change or no, life will go on. I would like to suggest another possibility: Things that do not change may not remain at all. Translated into a management context, lack of change may endanger the survival of organizational life itself.

It seems reasonably clear, for example, that the change from a Democratic to a Republican administration at the federal level is bringing about some drastic alterations in the political environment of business. Changes in government regulation, subsidies for business, and assistance to state governments are just a few changes that are occurring. The implications of these changes for business may be obvious because they are so well publicized. Ignorance as such may not impede organizational adaptation.

But other changes that occur in the environment are not so obvious, such as gradual shifts in population, in social and business conventions, and in attitudes. The implications of these changes are not only not obvious; they may be difficult to forecast even after serious study. Adaptation, therefore, may be difficult.

---

* Reprinted, by permission of the publisher, from *Organizational Dynamics,* Summer 1982 © 1982 AMACOM, a division of American Management Associations, New York. All rights reserved. The data reported in this study were obtained during a research project funded by the Graduate School of the University of Massachusetts/Amherst.

The Manager's Two-Front Job

This continuum of change in the environment—from the obvious to the unpredictable—is merely one way of emphasizing the developing responsibilities of managers. While the manager has historically had what can be referred to as an "inside job"—keeping operations going—that role is changing. Management is now a two-front job. There is an outside as well as an inside responsibility. The first front is the traditional one—guiding the organization to achievement of its goals by getting on with its tasks. The second front is a newer responsibility—maintaining a watch on the external environment for problems that will afflict and opportunities that can be exploited for the organization. These two responsibilities can be seen to merge in the new role of managers as change agents. Drastic changes in technology, the proliferation of new products and the obsolescence of old, tough international competition, as well as inflation and energy problems: All of these events, trends, and changes in the environment will require managers in the 1980s to spend more time than they did in the 1970s acting as agents of organizational change.

As they do, they will find that they have a variety of organizational change techniques from which to choose in carrying out their tasks. It will not be necessary—indeed it may be inadvisable—to proceed in a haphazard, trial-and-error approach to implementing change.

In what follows, the nature of organizational change will be discussed; the available organizational change techniques will be reviewed, compared, and contrasted; and data showing the relative use of the various techniques by a sample of *Fortune* 500 companies will be presented.

Organization-Environment Fit

Organizational change is the process of adjusting the organization to changes in the environment. It is carried out when there is reason to believe that there is a poor fit between the organization and the environment. The result, if done properly, should be a better organization-environment fit. Exhibit 1 illustrates the major factors and actions involved. In summary, the environment gives rise to problems that the organization has to face and opportunities that it can exploit. The organization's potential responses are a function of its strengths and weaknesses. Analysis of the organization's strengths and weaknesses in the light of environmental problems and opportunities suggests the nature of the organization-environment fit. A poor fit should give rise to a problem definition. The definition, in turn, should point the way toward developing alternative strategic solutions. The choice of a strategic solution is a function of the relative payoffs—money, morale, goodwill, time, productivity, and so forth—that the alternatives offer. Implementation of the chosen solution should bring about a better organization-environment fit.

Exhibit 1
Model of Organizational Change: Adjusting the Organization to Its Environment

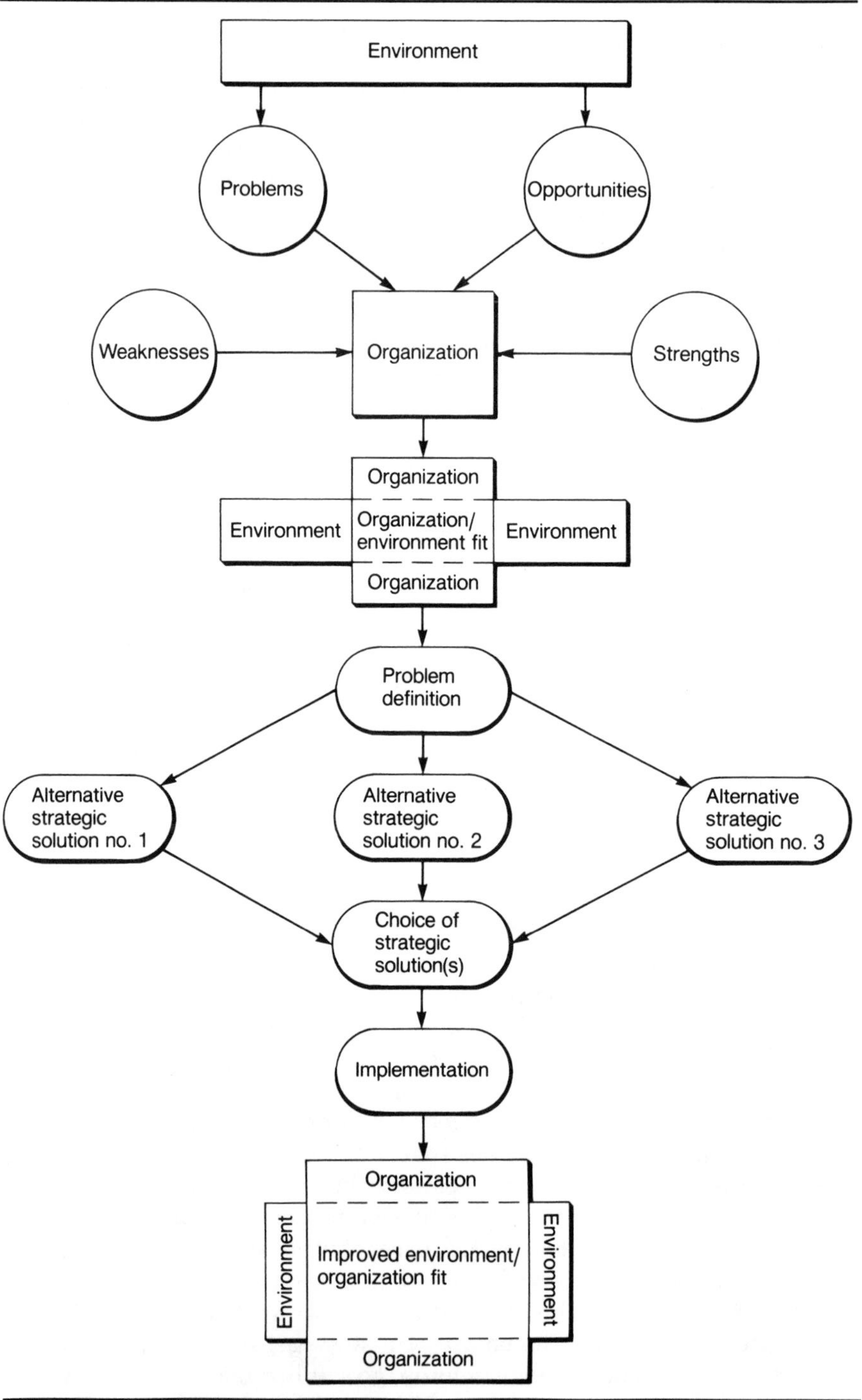

Source: Stephen R. Michael, et al., *Techniques of Organizational Change* (McGraw-Hill Book Co., © 1981). Reproduced by special permission.

When making organizational change, bear these problem areas in mind:

1. Even under the best of circumstances, organizational change isn't easy.
2. Because of the intricate web of organizational interrelationships and dependencies and the large-scale financial and human investments in the existing order, organizational change cannot be implemented on a catch-as-catch-can basis; it must be highly systematized.

The difficulty in bringing about organizational change is well documented in management literature and will be remembered by managers who have had to introduce changes in technology, launch a new product, or drastically change the division of labor under their jurisdictions—just to cite a few examples. What is involved here is the age-old conflict between bureaucratization and innovation.

Bureaucratization is the formalization of the organizational structure in terms of routine, standardized work. Its most obvious manifestations are a finer and more rigid division of labor and the proliferation of policies and procedures. These outcomes represent the learning derived from experience. The consequences should include lower costs. But the lessons learned become work habits and expectations, and therefore they become very resistant to change.

Innovation involves the substitution of a new idea for an old idea. New ideas require new work habits and different expectations. Hence the conflict between bureaucratization and innovation.

It is easier initially, of course, to take an unplanned, uncoordinated approach to organizational change. Like other people, managers are reluctant to spend time thinking and proceeding in a formal, orderly fashion so long as it appears unnecessary to do so. The consequence is a tendency to tinker. A slight change here, a slight change there; such small steps seem easy and safe. Small steps are also reversible. But the danger here is the inevitable losing sight of the forest because of the trees.

The solution is not to take one big step instead of several little ones. Rather, it is the taking of necessary steps in an orderly format of change. Such structured formats are provided by the organizational change techniques to be discussed below. They provide programmed approaches that enable managers to control the changes they wish to bring about. Not only do the techniques provide coordination; the procedures involved in the techniques make it possible to get meaningful participation from personnel who will be affected by changes. Such participation is likely to reduce the resistance to change and to facilitate successful implementation.

Techniques of Organizational Change

Exhibit 2 describes and compares the six commonly used techniques of organizational change: organizational behavior modification, management by objectives, management development, organization development, management auditing, and the control cycle of planning, implementing, and evaluating operations. Some of these are more familiar than others because managers react to fads and fashions just as other people react to new hemlines and hairdos. The current popularity of a particular technique may derive from publicity rather than its appropriateness for the tasks at hand. Their simultaneous presentation here is in accord with the contingency theory of management: The proper solution to a management problem depends on the situation. As we shall see, the techniques are not interchangeable, though they are complementary.

These techniques have not always been viewed as change processes, although they help bring change about. For example, management by objectives (MBO) is often viewed as a technique for improving communications between superiors and subordinates and for providing a basis for performance appraisals. But MBO is also a vehicle for change. The way in which each technique helps bring about change will be described. Then the techniques will be compared and contrasted.

Organizational Behavior Modification

Organizational behavior modification (OBMod) is based on B. F. Skinner's theory of learning. In brief, this theory holds that people as well as laboratory animals learn to change behavior through the feedback they get from the environment in response to overt behaviors. OBMod, therefore, is concerned with identifying desirable or undesirable behaviors and maintaining or changing such behavior by manipulating the environment and/or providing positive reinforcement.

This technique is implemented in a series of five steps. The first involves the identification of critical behaviors—those that have a significant impact on organizational performance and results. Only such overt, observable behaviors as absenteeism and tardiness in turning in reports are important here. Attitudes, motivations, and other inner states of individuals are not considered. To quote Fred Luthans, "(1) Can it be seen? and (2) Can it be measured?"

The latter question leads to the second step, measurement of the critical behaviors. The frequencies of specific behaviors will indicate whether there is a problem.

If the frequencies show a problem, the third step is to make a functional analysis of the behavior. This step is to determine the antecedent events and the consequences of the behavior. For example, the arrival of a mail clerk in an office (antecedent) could serve as a stimulant for the office employees to stop working and begin to socialize. The consequence would be a pleasant but unscheduled work break.

Once the analysis is completed, the fourth step requires an intervention in the situation. Basically, the intervention should involve positive reinforcement. For example, the supervisor could enter the work area at the same time as the mail clerk and make complimentary remarks to any personnel who do not interrupt their work. The others will get the message.

Step five, the last step, consists of evaluating the results of this process. Four factors are evaluated: the reaction to the use of OBMod, the extent to which supervisors have learned to use the techniques, the degree to which behaviors have changed, and the improvement in performance.

Management by Objectives

MBO achieves change by using superior-subordinate discussions to plan a subordinate's work. During such discussions, objectives, plans, and programs are established for changes in routine work, the resolution of problems, and the introduction of innovation.

The rationale behind MBO stems from observations that supervisors and subordinates usually fail to agree on the subordinate's expected level of output, on the subordinate's major problems, and on the ways in which the subordinate's job can be improved. Note that each of these areas of disagreement may involve change unless the superior agrees to the status quo—which is not likely.

Consequently, superior and subordinate look at the subordinate's tasks from the standpoints of routine work, unresolved problems, and opportunities for innovation. Task objectives and performance standards are set on the basis of mutual agreement in these three areas. Strategies and budgets, among other managerial considerations, are usually on the collaborative agenda.

The subordinate manager, therefore, has information about his or her job that permits and encourages self-control. This reduces the superior's control tasks. Nevertheless, superior and subordinates do meet periodically to review interim results. At the end of the MBO period, they also meet to look at final results to appraise subordinate performance, as a preliminary to the next cycle.

To underscore what may be an obvious point, management by objectives is a technique used primarily with managerial, professional, and technical personnel. The more routine the work, the lower the probability that MBO can help produce benefits that exceed its costs.

Management Development

Training and development lead to organizational change by altering the capabilities of managerial personnel. Such a process may be implemented

Exhibit 2
Comparison of Organizational Change Techniques

	Types of Techniques					
Characteristic	**Organizational Behavior Modification**	**Management by Objectives**	**Management Development**	**Organization Development**	**Management Auditing**	**Control Cycle**
Focal point	Individuals.	Individuals.	Individuals.	Entire organization or part.	Entire organization or part.	Entire organization or part.
Symptoms of problems requiring attention	Undesirable behaviors of workers resulting in substandard performance.	Different expectations and interpretations by superiors and subordinates of subordinates' performance.	Deficiencies in performance of tasks requiring mental or social skills to do present job and/or lack of skills to do future job.	Destructive conflict and lack of cooperation among individuals and groups.	Existing or anticipated problems or opportunities in product demand and supply, structure, functions, and processes.	Inability to adapt organization to changing environment using feedback control on product demand and supply, structure, functions, and processes.
Kinds of changes sought or achieved	Improved fit between individual and job, primarily at nonmanagerial levels.	Improved fit between individual and job at managerial and professional levels.	Improvement in mental and social skills at managerial and professional levels.	Improved interpersonal and intergroup behavior.	Improvements in product demand and supply, structure, functions, and processes.	Improvements in product demand and supply, structure, functions, and processes.
Theoretical bases	Behavioral theory.	Behavioral and management theories.	Behavioral theory.	Behavioral theory.	Management theory.	Management theory.

Type of control	Feedback to resolve problems.	Feedforward/ feedback to forestall problems or exploit opportunities.	Feedforward/ feedback to forestall problems or exploit opportunities, or feedback to resolve problems.	Feedback to resolve problems.	Feedforward/ feedback to forestall problems or exploit opportunities, or feedback to resolve problems.	Feedforward/ feedback to forestall problems and exploit opportunities.
Continuity	Intermittent.	Continuous.	Intermittent or continuous.	Intermittent.	Intermittent.	Continuous.
Change agent	Superiors and/or inside and outside consultants.	Superiors; inside and outside consultants can assist.	Superiors, with personnel or training department to coordinate.	Outside and/or inside consultants with backing of higher management.	Outside and/or inside consultants with backing of higher management.	All managers, with assistance of staff group and/ or outside consultants.

Source: Stephen R. Michael, et al., *Techniques of Organizational Change* (McGraw-Hill Book Company, © 1981). Reproduced by special permission.

to bring managers up to some set standard of performance or to prepare them for higher-level duty. Development of new or more highly developed skills provides the foundation for altered behavior.

The felt need for management development may arise from any aspect of managerial behaviors. A major source, however, is likely to be performance appraisals and other, less formal appraisals of management performance and potential. Any change in technology and tasks, as well as policies and strategies, could also trigger the need for management development.

Some firms routinely put all those who are hired for entry-level managerial jobs through a company training and development program. In such cases, the intent is to acculturate new employees to the organization's unique mode of operations—in effect, to domesticate them.

If a person survives that initial training program, other needs or opportunities for training will usually arise. Essentially, there will be a need for training to bring about a better fit between the individual and the current or future job. The former situation arises when the individual doesn't measure up to an existing job or when the job is enlarged or changed in some other way. On the other hand, the individual may be groomed to take on a higher-level job as vacancies occur. Management development does not merely fit a person to an existing role, however. More likely than not, the trained manager will find ways to change the job and the associated tasks. The usual sequence of change in the manager is the acquisition of new knowledge, the translation of the knowledge into new skills, and the transformation of new skills into new behaviors.

Training and development range from the casual to the formal; they range from on-the-job training to coaching and counseling by a superior, to special but short programs and seminars, and finally, to extended periods of residence at a business school or institute.

Organization Development

Collective behaviors of all or of some subset of organizational members are changed through the use of organization development (OD). The results are accomplished by improving interpersonal skills, the mutual resolution of common problems, and team building—among other methods.

As implied above, organization development relies upon knowledge of the behavioral science field. The intent is to improve organizational effectiveness by applying this knowledge to organizational members' behavior. This treatment includes six major stages.

- OD begins with the *entry* stage in which a particular organization suffers the symptoms of poor interpersonal relationships among organizational members. An outside consultant or internal OD expert is then called in.

- The second stage involves some form of *contract* between the organization and the OD expert. The commercial form of contract is ideally supplemented by informal agreements that emphasize open communications and the exploration and classification of mutual expectations.
- At this point *data collection and diagnosis* signal the beginning of the actual study. Data are collected through observation, from documents and questionnaires, and from interviews. The data are collected, analyzed, and evaluated.
- *Feedback* to organizational members follows. The information is summarized according to the pattern of collection, then it is categorized conceptually, and finally, the OD consultant synthesizes the observations, impressions, and emotional reactions that characterize the data gathering.
- The change process itself is termed *intervention.* Typical interventions include structural change, team building, intergroup conflict resolution, role analysis, training, and the like.
- Finally, there is an *evaluation* stage to assess the results of organization development. The evaluation should be both quantitative and qualitative. The former would include such things as turnover, grievances, and productivity. The latter would be subjective reactions of organizational members, especially top management.

Management Auditing

Management auditing is a survey technique that is used to anticipate or solve organizational problems having to do with product demand and supply, structure, functions, and processes. The audit results in recommendations for changes that are implemented at the appropriate management level.

The management audit resembles the financial audit; only the focal issues are different. The financial audit is concerned with organizational operations exclusively from the financial perspective. The management audit is concerned with questions of management efficiency and effectiveness. Of course, one may lead to the other. Financial audits sometimes point up the need to conduct a management audit. Some public accounting firms recommend management audits when the financial audit suggests difficulties that have financial consequences, but whose origins actually lie outside the financial realm.

Management audits may also be compared with a physical checkup. Indeed, management auditors typically conduct their investigations armed with a checklist of factors to be reviewed and evaluated. These usually include an array of specific topics to be checked in terms of general management and functional areas. In organizations with product divisions and subsidiaries, the checklist would be applied to each organizational unit as well as the total corporate entity. Included in the checklist are such factors as products, prices, production control, capital requirements, and a host of others.

The auditors must be well versed in management knowledge and practices. Eventually they prepare a report recommending ways in which the organization's operations can be improved. If it approves, top management may implement the recommendation itself or retain the auditors to help carry out the changes.

The Control Cycle

Finally, the control cycle provides for the planning, implementation, and evaluation of changes in operations and organizational arrangements to bring about or maintain an appropriate fit between the organization and its environment.

Overall, the control cycle is used to monitor on a continuous basis and to change the organization, focusing primarily on demand for the organization's products, programs, and services. Change is then brought about in the organization's supply capabilities to maximize efficiency and effectiveness. To achieve a new equilibrium between supply and demand may require adjusting output, adding to or deleting from the product line, changing organizational structure, making personnel changes, increasing long-term debt, opening new facilities or closing old plants, and so forth.

Although the technique of the control cycle includes planning, implementing plans, and evaluating results, most oral and written commentary emphasizes planning. Thus, for example, there is short-range (or tactical) planning that usually covers the next year, and long-range (or strategic) planning that generally covers five years, but possibly more or less. The short range tends to emphasize the consequences of the current organizational state while the long range emphasizes strategic or discretionary choices about the organization's future course.

Differences and Similarities in Techniques

These six techniques are used to achieve a better organization-environment fit in different ways. Organizational behavior modification focuses on individual behaviors. If successful, the result should be greater productivity at the work level by the individuals affected. Management by objectives focuses on managerial, professional, and technical personnel and is intended to achieve greater effectiveness (thus making a better organization-environment fit) by assuring that superiors and subordinates are in harmony about the subordinate's task objectives and performance standards. Such agreements should result in maximum goal-seeking behavior by both superior and subordinate. Management development makes a somewhat more indirect contribution to organization-environment fit. It does this by first changing the manager; then the manager is expected to change the organization as the need arises.

Like management by objectives, organization development focuses on increasing harmony among organizational members; but the focus is on larger numbers than MBO's two-by-two in the chain of command. Improved cooperation should result in increased ability to deal with the environment. Management auditing is a problem-solving, opportunity-exploiting technique that, as problems are solved and opportunities exploited, helps bring about a better organization-environment fit whenever it is used. Finally, the control cycle constitutes a constant watch on the environment to maintain a dynamic equilibrium between it and the organization.

As this review of organizational change techniques shows, there are considerable differences among them. There are more differences than mentioned thus far; there are also some similarities.

For example, some techniques focus on personnel as individuals. That is, the individual is the unit of change. Organizational behavior modification, management by objectives, and management development are in this category. The other techniques—organization development, management auditing, and the control cycle—focus on the whole organization or some major part.

In terms of timing of organizational change, the techniques also differ among themselves. Organizational behavior modification and organization development utilize feedback control and are typically used to correct or resolve organizational problems that already exist. The other techniques rely upon both feedback and feedforward control. Feedback control is remedial in nature, while feedforward is anticipatory; feedback is used to correct an existing problem, while feedforward is used to prevent or mitigate a potential problem. While feedback control can be used alone, feedforward cannot. This is because the feedforward actions taken to forestall a problem cannot fully anticipate all details; unanticipated details are left to be corrected through the use of feedback control.

As a common example of the above differences in control, consider the use of the control cycle of planning, implementing, and evaluating organizational change that utilizes both feedforward and feedback control. The control cycle is used for a variety of purposes, including the anticipation of changes in product demand and the concomitant need to change supply capabilities. In the course of planning next year's operation, demand is expected to increase by 10 percent. Therefore, the organization makes plans to increase operational levels to produce the additional goods. This is the feedforward aspect of control. The forecast of increased demand, however, is obviously only an estimate. Therefore, to more closely tailor supply to actual demand, feedback on product flow must be provided periodically, and further changes made in supply capabilities if actual demand is significantly different from the forecast. The typical result is that the difference between demand and supply is less when feedforward and feedback control are combined than when only feedback control is used.

The differences in the controls used in various techniques also have an impact upon continuity of use. The techniques that depend primarily on feedback control—organizational behavior modification, organization development, and management auditing—are used intermittently, as required when feedback shows a problem exists. The other techniques can, or of necessity must, be used continuously for maximum effectiveness. For example, management by objectives and the control cycle typically are incorporated into the organization's routine processes.

There are also differences and similarities in the identity of the change agents. Organization development and management auditing require, for example, the services of either internal or external experts and the active backing of higher management. Some other techniques must be applied by the manager whose operations are affected by the technique—for example, MBO, management development, and the control cycle; in organizational behavior modification, however, managers and/or consultants implement the process. These points are summarized in Exhibit 1.

The variations in the techniques reinforce a point made earlier in connection with the contingency approach to management; each is most appropriate for specific situations. They are also complementary; management by objectives and the control cycle, for example, are mutually supportive in anticipating and dealing with related aspects of organizational change.

Fortune 500 Use of Techniques

A survey conducted among *Fortune* 500 companies indicates that all of these organizational change techniques are currently used in the business world. The survey, sent to a randomly selected sample of 50 percent of this group, elicited a response rate of 28 percent (71 respondents). The organizations surveyed were asked the question that is spelled out in Exhibit 3.

Exhibit 4 summarizes the incidence of usage of these techniques among the responding companies. To state a summary fact, more than 10 times as many companies were currently using one or more of the techniques as had tried and given up on any one of them. Among the companies that had stopped using the techniques, the average usage was four companies per technique. Among the firms that are currently

Exhibit 3
Question on Organizational Change Techniques Posed to *Fortune* 500 Companies

Have you in the past five years used, or are you now using, any of the following organizational change techniques? (Check all applicable.)

Techniques	Used in Past Five Years, but Not Using Now	Using Now
Organizational behavior modification	( )	( )
Management by objectives	( )	( )
Management development	( )	( )
Organization development	( )	( )
Management auditing	( )	( )
Control cycle (planning, directing, and evaluating results)	( )	( )

using one or more of the techniques, the average usage was 41 companies per technique. The greatest disillusionment was with management by objectives, tried and given up by eight companies. Users seemed least disillusioned with organization development and the control cycle. One company tried and gave up the former; none of the companies had given up the latter—and all of them are currently using this technique.

We do not have background facts to explain why various techniques were dropped after being tried. In some, perhaps most, instances, it may be that the particular problem or problems dealt with were resolved satisfactorily, and there was no further need for the technique. On the other hand, it is possible that the choice of a technique may have been dictated by selective exposure rather than a thorough evaluation of the situation—an evaluation that might have suggested the use of a different technique.

In terms of current usage, some interesting facts emerge. Organizational behavior modification is the least used technique and organization

Exhibit 4
Use of Organizational Change Techniques by *Fortune* 500 Companies*

	Used in Past Five Years, Not Using Now		Using Now	
Technique	**Number**	**Percent**	**Number**	**Percent**
Organizational behavior modification	5	7	8	11
Management by objectives	8	11	53	75
Management development	2	3	54	76
Organization development	1	1	33	46
Management auditing	4	6	38	53
Control cycle	0	0	71	100

* Number of responses—71; response rate—28 percent.

development the second least used. The fact that the incidence of being tried and dropped is higher for organizational behavior modification than for organization development may be because the former is newer than the latter, with less experience to guide its use. But both may be used less than the other techniques because they are the newest of the six. We can also speculate that the practically equal usage of management by objectives and management development is more than a coincidence. MBO may very likely be the technique that reveals the need for management development. Eighty-five percent of the companies using MBO also use management development. Finally, the sample's 100 percent use of the control cycle of planning, directing implementation, and evaluating results indicates that it is the organizational change technique of choice. The other, less popular techniques may very well be used to deal with problems and opportunities uncovered through the control cycle.

The success of the *Fortune* 500 companies is undoubtedly based on a great variety of factors: capable management, up-to-date technology, large domestic markets, a highly educated work force, and the like. But it is quite reasonable to assume that the resort to organizational change techniques—rather than uncoordinated trial-and-error approaches—may very well have contributed substantially to their success.

The simultaneous use of various techniques also attests to a level of sophistication in these firms that warrants comment. Management literature tends to reflect the fads and fashions of academic research, and management practice follows as well as leads these movements. Currently, organizational behavior modification and organization development are in the limelight more than the other techniques, if only because they are newer. They therefore may appear more seductive to managers seeking an approach to organizational change. The results of this survey suggest that the best criterion for choosing a technique is its suitability for dealing with a specific problem or situation, rather than its current popularity in the literature and at management seminars.

Summary and Conclusions

Previous comments have suggested that our ideas about organizational change are continually changing. In addition, our identification and understanding of what constitutes an organizational change technique also change.

Are the above-mentioned techniques here to stay? One tentative conclusion we can draw from the usage data is that there is an apparent inverse correlation between the "age" of a technique and its use by the *Fortune* 500 companies. The control cycle is the oldest and most widely used; organizational behavior modification is the newest and least used.

Because the companies constitute a select sample of large, well-managed firms, it is also reasonable to assume that the data show a higher incidence of usage than would be the case for a purely random sample of companies, which would include smaller firms and a larger array of industries. From the foregoing (keeping in mind the expected increase of turbulence in the environment), we can sensibly predict that the use of the organizational change techniques will increase.

That does not mean that such techniques will not change in form and content, however. For example, one such change may occur in management by objectives. Some critics point out that MBO is a one-sided arrangement. It commits the subordinate to do certain things but does not call for a concomitant commitment by the superior to provide adequate resources and other forms of support. A possible change might be the transformation of MBO into management by contract to overcome this deficiency.

Furthermore, there may be more productive, incipient techniques lurking on the management horizon. As a matter of fact, over 20 years ago, Jay W. Forrester began to write about what he called "industrial dynamics." This is a mathematical and computer-based approach to simulating the firm, with the focus on informational and operational delays that result from business fluctuations. While industrial dynamics can be thought of as a particular form of planning and control covered in the control cycle, these two techniques differ from each other at least as much as organizational behavior modification and organization development.

Despite the fact that it has been around for some time, industrial dynamics does not appear to be particularly popular. But then, neither is organizational behavior modification, at least as compared with the other techniques. There may be a common reason for the slow adoption of each.

Management is a set of skills that are learned on the job, from management literature, and from training. The willingness and ability to learn the art of management depend in part on previous learning in the basic disciplines from which management derives its content. A manager deficient in knowledge about the social sciences is probably not likely to be attracted to organizational behavior modification and organization development. Similarly, a manager repelled by mathematics and the computer is unlikely to delve into industrial dynamics.

Ultimately, these more recently developed organizational change techniques may become more popular as a newer breed of lower-level managers works their way up the hierarchy in their organizations. This newer breed will be better versed in the social sciences, mathematics, and the computer. Therefore they will probably expand the use of existing techniques and perhaps even help spawn new ones.

Selected Bibliography

Organizational change has always been a concern for organizational managers. It predates the days when Moses gave up trying to adjudicate all disputes among his Hebrew followers and delegated authority to do so to levels of lesser officials. But organizational change increasingly became a concern and, for some, an obsession after World War II. The bulk of the literature, however, consists of articles and reports, and these have not been systematically compiled in book form. One such book, however, is Newton Margulies and John Wallace's *Organizational Change* (Scott, Foresman, 1973).

The organizational change techniques, on the other hand, have been much publicized, both in articles and books—but always one technique at a time. A discussion of all the techniques has finally been brought together by Stephen R. Michael, Fred Luthans, George S. Odiorne, W. Warner Burke, and Spencer Hayden in *Techniques of Organizational Change* (McGraw-Hill Book Company, 1981). This book includes comprehensive bibliographies for each technique. Many writings on Jay W. Forrester's industrial dynamics have been brought together in Edward B. Roberts's (ed.) *Managerial Applications of System Dynamics* (MIT Press, 1978).

These techniques are options, and their effective use is governed by the contingency approach to management, a rather simple idea with enormous ramifications. An early collection of writings illustrating contingency is contained in Fremont D. Kast and James E. Rosenzweig's *Contingency Views of Organization and Management* (Science Research Associates, 1973). A brief introduction to the subject is given in Stephen R. Michael's "The Contingency Manager: Doing What Comes Naturally" (*Management Review,* November 1976).

Part Five

Part Five expands our scope from relatively short time periods (a few months to a few years), to much longer time periods. Like Part Four, it addresses change in any kind of organizational unit, but focuses on change that is directed at developing an organization which is capable of being effective in the long run.

Managing the development of organizations usually involves—as the text, cases, and readings illustrate—attempts to increase adaptability so that the organizations can cope with future growth and/or environmental changes. The text in this part identifies the characteristics of highly adaptive and flexible organizations, as well as the tools and strategies available to managers for developing these characteristics. The cases describe managers whose primary interest is in ensuring long-term positive outcomes as an outgrowth of necessary immediate organizational decisions. The readings provide an overview of organization development—a long-term managerial and organizational effectiveness strategy—as well as frameworks for conceptualizing and managing the growth of organizations over the long run.

Chapter 8

Developing an Organization that Contributes to Long-Run Effectiveness

Effective management is more than the production of immediate results. For companies that want to continue operating in the future, effective management includes creating the potential for achieving good results over the long run. The manager who as president of a company produces spectacular results for a 3- to 10-year period can hardly be considered effective if, at the same time, he or she allows plant and equipment to deteriorate, creates an alienated and militant work force, gives the company a bad name in the marketplace, and ignores new-product development.

Our focus up to this point—dealing with current problems or potential problems of the immediate future—reflects a key reality of managerial behavior in almost all modern organizations. That is, coping with the complexities associated with today and the immediate future absorbs the vast majority of time and energy for most managers.[1] In this chapter, however, we shift our concern to a longer-run time frame: How do managers develop their human organizations to assure that they have the potential for facilitating organizational effectiveness in the long run?

The Long Run

Most managers will readily admit that their ability to predict their company's future is very limited. Indeed, with the possible exception of death and taxes, the only thing that seems entirely predictable is that things

[1] See Henry Mintzberg, *The Nature of Managerial Work* (New York: Harper & Row, 1973), chap. 3.

will change. Even for the most bureaucratic company in the most mature and stable environment, change is inevitable.[2]

Over a period of 20 years, it is possible for a company, even one that is not growing, to experience numerous changes in its business, its product markets, its competition, government regulations, available technologies, its labor markets, and its own business strategy. These changes are the inevitable product of its interaction with a world that is not static.

Growing organizations tend to experience even more business-related changes over a long period of time. Studies have shown that they not only increase the volume of the products or services they provide but also tend to increase the complexity of their products or services, their forward or backward integration, their rate of product innovation, the geographic scope of their operations, the number and character of their distribution channels, and the number and diversity of their customer groups. And while all of this growth-driven change occurs, competitive and other external pressures also increase.[3] Companies that grow rapidly experience even more and faster changes.[4]

From a manager's point of view, these types of business changes are important because they generally require organizational adjustments. For example, a company's labor markets might change over time, subsequently requiring it to alter its selection criteria and make other adjustments to fit the new type of employee. New competitors might emerge with new products, thus requiring renewed new-product development efforts and a new organizational design to support that effort. In a growing company, business changes tend to require major shifts periodically in all aspects of its organization (see Figure 8–1 and 8–2).

The inability of an organization to anticipate the need for change and to adjust effectively to changes in its business or in its organization causes problems, as we have seen in the previous examples in this book. Sometimes these problems take the form of poor collaboration and coordination. Sometimes they involve high turnover or low morale. Always, however, they affect the organization's performance, in that goals are not achieved and/or resources are wasted.

Because change is inevitable and because it can so easily produce problems for companies, the key characteristic of an effective organization from a long-run point of view is that it is able to anticipate needed organizational changes and to adapt as business conditions change. Anticipatory skills can help prevent the resource drain caused by organiza-

---

[2] Warren Bennis, *Changing Organizations* (New York: McGraw-Hill, 1966), chap. 1.

[3] Donald K. Clifford, Jr., "Growth Pains of the Threshold Company," *Harvard Business Review,* September–October 1973, p. 146.

[4] George Strauss, "Adolescence in Organizational Growth: Problems, Pains, and Possibilities," *Organizational Dynamics,* Spring 1974.

Figure 8–1
Greiner's Summary of Required Changes in Organization Practices during Evolution in the Five Phases of Growth

Category	Phase 1	Phase 2	Phase 3	Phase 4	Phase 5
Management focus	Make and sell	Efficiency of operations	Expansion of market	Consolidation of organization	Problem solving and innovation
Organization structure	Informal	Centralized and functional	Decentralized and geographical	Line-staff and product groups	Matrix of teams
Top management style	Individualistic and entrepreneurial	Directive	Delegative	Watchdog	Participative
Control system	Market results	Standards and cost centers	Reports and profit centers	Plans and investment centers	Mutual goal setting
Management reward emphasis	Ownership	Salary and merit increases	Individual bonus	Profit sharing and stock options	Team bonus

Source: Larry E. Greiner, "Evoluation and Revolution as Organizations Grow," *Harvard Business Review*, July–August 1972, p. 45.

Figure 8–2
Summary of Changes during Three Stages of Organizational Development

Company Characteristics	Stage I	Stage II	Stage III
The business:			
1. Product	Single product or single line.	Single product line.	Multiple product lines.
2. Distribution	One channel or set of channels.	One set of channels.	Multiple channels.
3. R&D	Not institutionalized—oriented by owner-manager.	Increasingly institutionalized search for product or process improvements.	Institutionalized search for *new* products as well as for improvements.
4. Strategic choices	Needs of owner versus needs of firm.	Degree of integration. Market share objective. Breadth of product line.	Entry and exit from industries. Allocation of resources by industry. Rate of growth.
The organization:			
1. Organization structure	Little or nor formal structure—"one-man show."	Specialization based on function.	Specialization based on product/market relationship.
2. Product/service transactions	Not available	Integrated pattern of transactions. □→□→□↓ Market	Not integrated. A B C ↓ ↓ ↓ Markets
3. Performance measurement	By personal contact and subjective criteria.	Increasingly impersonal, using technical and/or cost criteria.	Increasingly impersonal, using *market* criteria (return on investment and market share).
4. Rewards	Unsystematic and often paternalistic.	Increasingly systematic with emphasis on stability and service.	Increasingly systematic, with variability related to performance.
5. Control system	Personal control of both strategic and operating decisions.	Personal control of strategic decisions, with increasing delegation of operating decisions based on control by policies.	Delegation of product/market decisions within existing businesses, with indirect control based on analysis of "results."

Source: Adapted from Bruce Scott, "Stages of Corporate Development" (Boston: Intercollegiate Case Clearing House, 1971).

tional problems, while adaptability helps an organization avoid the problems that change can produce. Over long periods of time, this ability to avoid an important and recurring resource drain can mark the difference between success and failure for an organization.

A Case of Organizational Decline

To fully appreciate the importance of anticipatory skills and adaptability in the long run, consider this somewhat extreme case. The company involved was founded in the late 1920s, primarily through acquisitions. It was created as the response of an entrepreneur to a variety of changing market conditions. Over a 5- to 10-year period, he established an enormously successful venture; in its market it became the largest and most profitable organization of its kind.

It is difficult to tell from historical records how much, if anything, the entrepreneur did to develop the company's long-run organizational adaptability. Two facts, however, are known. The ongoing operations were so profitable that he submitted to the demands of the national union just to avoid a disruption of operations. This resulted in the establishment of innumerable "work rules" and the entry of first-line supervisors into the union. Second, he did almost nothing to bring in or develop middle- and top-level managers. As an extremely talented person, capable of making a large number of effective business decisions himself, he saw no need for assistance from others.

In the mid-1940s the entrepreneur died. His brother took over as president and tried to maintain the company's existing policies and profitability. For the first few years of his tenure, everything seemed to work well.

Nevertheless, the company's industry, like many others, began to undergo significant changes after World War II. These changes occurred gradually but continuously over at least a 10-year period. During this time the company made very few organizational adjustments to adapt to these changes, for what appear to be a number of reasons. First, the few people who had any real decision-making authority in the company did not seem to see any need for many changes. They simply did not have the information that would have showed them what was happening in their industry and in their market area. Second, when they did have information on the changes that were occurring, they often had difficulty deciding how to adjust to them. They were, for example, completely unaware of the typical developmental sequences shown in Figures 8–1 and 8–2. The intuitively brilliant leadership once supplied by the original entrepreneur was gone, and nothing had taken its place. Finally, when they did identify a change and saw what response was needed, the managers were generally unable to implement it. For one thing, union rules prohibited a great deal of change; for another, there was no middle management to help them implement it. The firm was not at all flexible.

Some of the company's competitors were successful in identifying and reacting to the industry and market changes. As a result, the rate of increase of this company's sales and profits began to decrease. At the same time, problems with employees and the union began to surface.

The company's president initially focused his efforts on trying to stop the profit decline. In this endeavor, he was somewhat successful, yet in slowing the profit decline, he was forced to hold salaries and maintenance budgets down, thereby adding to the problems with his employees and the union. A climate of antagonism and distrust developed.

Between 1956 and 1965 the company's real (noninflated) annual growth in sales declined from 5 percent to 0 percent. Its profits leveled out and then fell to a net loss in 1965. By that time, the company's stock price was so low that a larger corporation successfully acquired a controlling interest. This corporation brought in its own top management group (which included a number of extremely successful managers) and predicted a quick turnaround.

The company resumed profitable operations in 1969 and, with the exception of 1973, has remained profitable to this time. Nevertheless, its profitability levels remain below the industry average, and its 1975 sales were, in real dollars, about the same as in 1965. It has gone through two more presidents since 1965, and the current one has been quoted in the business press as saying that the job of organizational "renewal" that is ahead of them is still very large.

Characteristics of an Effective Organization—From a Long-Range Point of View

It is possible to infer the characteristics that contribute to long-run effectiveness by looking for what was missing in the previous example. If we consider our discussion of the difficulty of organizational change in the Citibank cases, we can deduce other characteristics. The picture that emerges is one of an organization where changes in its business are anticipated or quickly identified, where appropriate responses are quickly designed, and where the responses are implemented at a minimum cost.[5] This behavior would be possible because the company is staffed with talented managers who are skilled at organizational analysis, as well as with relatively adaptable employees. Informal relations among these people would be characterized by trust, open communications, and re-

[5] The many social scientists who have approached the topic of organizational adaptability from different perspectives all tend to agree, in general terms, with this conclusion. See, for example, Edgar Schein, *Organizational Psychology* (Englewood Cliffs, N.J.: Prentice-Hall, 1965), p. 99.

Figure 8–3
Characteristics of a Highly Effective Organization: A Long-Run Point of View

Employees:
1. The company is staffed with more than enough managerial talent.
2. Managers are skilled at organizational analysis and understand typical stages of organizational development.
3. A large number of employees are relatively adaptive and have skills beyond a narrow specialty.
4. Employees have realistic expectations about what they will get from, and have to give to, the company in the foreseeable future.

Informal relations:
1. There is a high level of trust between employees and management.
2. Information flows freely, with a minimum of distortion within and across groups.
3. People in all positions of responsibility are willing to listen to, and be influenced by, others who might have relevant information.

Formal design:
1. The organizational structure includes more than enough effective integrating mechanisms for the current situation and relies minimally on rules and procedures.
2. Measurement systems thoroughly collect and distribute all relevant data on the organization's environment, its actions, its performance, and changes in any of these factors.
3. Reward systems encourage people to identify needed changes and help implement them.
4. Selection and development systems are designed to create highly skilled managerial and employee groups and to encourage the kinds of informal relations described above.

spect for others' opinions. The formal design would include effective integrating devices, sensitive and well-designed measurement systems, reward systems that encourage adaptability, and selection and development systems that help support all the other characteristics (see Figure 8–3).

Unlike the declining company described earlier, an organization with the characteristics listed in Figure 8–3, as well as other characteristics that specifically fit its current business, could successfully respond to growth, industry changes, top management turnover, and virtually anything else that came its way. Its adaptability would allow it to continue changing its organization to fit its changing business, and it would both survive and prosper over long periods of time.

Bureaucratic Dry Rot

Very few companies or nonprofit businesses have organizations with characteristics even close to those described in Figure 8–3. This fact has been emphasized by a number of social scientists who, in the past decade, have expressed serious concern over what they call "bureaucratic dry rot."[6] We all pay a heavy price, they note, for the large, bureaucratic,

[6] See Warren Bennis, *Beyond Bureaucracy* (New York: McGraw-Hill, 1966), chap. 1.

upadaptive organizations that are insensitive to employees' needs, ignore consumers' desires, and refuse to accept their social responsibilities.

Existing evidence suggests that although most contemporary organizations cannot be described as very adaptive, many managers nevertheless appreciate the benefits of adaptability. When polled, managers often respond that "ideally" they would like to have the kind of organization suggested by Figure 8–3, but they also admit that their current organization does not have some or all of these characteristics.[7]

There are at least five reasons for the inflexibility and shortsightedness of most contemporary organizations. The first and most significant is related to resources. Creating a highly adaptive organization requires time, energy, and money. For example, in the case of the company that went into decline, creating an adaptive organization early in its history might have required:

- Hiring, assimilating, and training a management team, both at the top and in middle-level ranks.
- Careful selection and training of all other personnel.
- Concentrated effort from the managers to develop integrative devices, measurement systems, and the like.
- Steady effort from the managers to develop and maintain good, informal relationships among themselves and their employees.

Possibly the organization did not have the resources to invest in these systems. Had it tried, it might have been necessary to divert resources from some of its current operations; and if its competitors did not choose to follow its lead but continued to invest as heavily as possible in current operations, perhaps the company would have lost market share and income and even gone out of business long before it could enjoy the benefits of its long-term investment in adaptability.[8]

A second reason for the unadaptive and bureaucratic behavior of modern organizations is that their managers are not very skilled at producing the characteristics of an effective organization in the long run. Because organizations generally invest resources in current operations and not in producing adaptive human systems, the on-the-job education of managers is usually focused on current operations, not on producing adaptability. Generating the characteristics shown in Figure 8–3 requires skills that have to be developed and nurtured.[9]

---

[7] Rensis Likert's "System 4" organization is very similar to what we have called a highly adaptive organization. He asked many managers, via a questionnaire, what type of organization they would like to have, and they usually answered "System 4." See Likert's *The Human Organization: Its Management and Value* (New York: McGraw-Hill, 1967), p. 28.

[8] See John P. Kotter, *Organizational Dynamics* (Reading, Mass.: Addison-Wesley Publishing, 1978).

[9] Chris Argyris, *Increasing Leadership Effectiveness,* (New York: John Wiley & Sons, 1976).

Still a third reason for the inflexibility of many contemporary organizations is that some people clearly benefit from a static situation. The entrepreneur who established the unadaptive organization described earlier, thoroughly enjoyed the way he ran the company. It is doubtful that he would have invested resources in developing a management team, or developed one even if it cost him nothing. Furthermore, financial backers approved of how he ran the business, which included passing on a large share of the firm's earnings in dividends. Had he tried to cut the dividends to invest more in something as nontangible as adaptability, they undoubtedly would have protested.

A fourth reason for unadaptive behavior can also be seen from the case of decline. Once an organization reaches a certain size, if it has not developed a certain minimally adaptive human organization, it becomes very difficult to turn things around without a gigantic infusion of resources. Considerable effort is required simply to overcome the "organizational entropy"[10] that makes the organization even more unadaptive and rigid.

A fifth reason why more companies do not have organizational characteristics like those in Figure 8–3 is that their management has decided they are unnecessary. Based on their projection of what the future has in store for their company, they estimate how much adaptability they will need and then invest resources that produce only that level of adaptability. If they are growing very quickly or if they are in a very volatile market, and if they expect that rapid changes will continue in their business, they invest considerable resources in creating an adaptive human organization. If they are not growing, if they are in a stable market, and if they feel the future will not demand many changes from them, they invest relatively few resources.

In short, the forces that prevent organizations from developing a high level of adaptability are strong. The forces that can push successful organizations into decline are numerous as well. As a result, one of the most difficult of all management tasks involves developing an organization that has *enough* adaptability to promote effectiveness in the long run.

Organizing for the Future

Developing an organization that is adaptive enough to ensure a company's continued success requires, most of all, a dedicated and skilled top manager or top management group—one both willing and able to make decisions that will balance the needs of the present and the needs of the future. Deciding whether to use an available resource to solve a current problem or to develop flexibility for the future is generally very

---

[10] Chris Argyris, *Intervention Theory and Method,* (Reading, Mass.: Addison-Wesley Publishing, 1970), chap. 3.

difficult.[11] Without serious dedication to success in the long run, short-run pressures often take precedence.

Deciding exactly how to develop future adaptability best, but at minimum cost, can also be difficult. Obviously the words and deeds of the people on top are important. If they stress learning, planning, adaptability, open communications, and the like, that behavior will clearly help set norms for others. Training and development activities are also undoubtedly important. So are periodic reviews of the state of the human organization, which identify more and less adaptive components. In each of these cases, however, managers have many options regarding exactly how to stress learning or to design training or to review the organization.

Organizational Development (OD)

A new management specialty called organization development (OD) has emerged in the past 15 years. OD specialists focus mostly on methods for increasing the adaptability of human organizations.[12] Although the total number is still relatively small, more and more businesses have established OD functions, usually within the personnel or human resources department.[13] People who work in these functions utilize a variety of techniques to help managers develop human organizations with the characteristics shown in Figure 8–3. The most commonly used techniques include:

1. Kepner-Trego clinics,[14] Phase One Managerial Grid sessions,[15] T-groups,[16] and other training seminars designed to improve a manager's ability to work with others, solve problems, and lead.
2. Methods of resolving conflict and improving relationships in organizations, such as team building,[17] intergroup labs,[18] confrontation meetings,[19] and third-party consultations.[20]

---

[11] See Peter Drucker, *Management* (New York: Harper & Row, 1976), pp. 43–44.

[12] People who call themselves OD specialists sometimes also help solve short-run organizational problems and involve themselves in other activities as well.

[13] Fred Luthans, "Merging Personnel and OD," *Personnel,* May 1977.

[14] Kepner-Trego Inc., Princeton, NJ. Problem-solving–decision-making classes.

[15] R. R. Blake and J. S. Mouton, *Building a Dynamic Corporation through Grid Organization Development* (Reading, Mass.: Addison-Wesley Publishing, 1969).

[16] Chris Argyris, "T-Groups for Organizational Effectiveness," *Harvard Business Review,* March–April 1964, pp. 84–97.

[17] Shel Davis, "Building More Effective Teams," *Innovation* 15 (1970), pp. 32–41.

[18] R. R. Blake, H. A. Shepard, and J. S. Mouton, *Managing Intergroup Conflict in Industry* (Houston: Gulf Publishing, 1964).

[19] Richard Beckhard, "The Confrontation Meeting," *Harvard Business Review,* March–April 1967, p. 45.

[20] Richard Walton, *Interpersonal Peacemaking: Confrontations and Third-Party Consultations* (Reading, Mass.: Addison-Wesley Publishing, 1969).

3. Methods for designing formal organizational structure,[21] spatial arrangements,[22] pay systems,[23] jobs,[24] and performance appraisal systems.[25]
4. Methods for measuring the current state of employee attitudes,[26] small-group functioning,[27] organizational climate,[28] and organizational processes.[29]
5. Broad approaches to the whole development process, such as process consultation[30] and survey feedback.[31]

Applied appropriately, all of these techniques can help develop more adaptive human organizations, although they are not a panacea for long-run effectiveness and can be misused like any other managerial tool.[32] Organizations that have been most successful in using these techniques have usually had a competent OD staff or set of OD consultants, as well as a talented top management group that generally guided their efforts.

OD Change Efforts

Efforts to change an organization for developmental purposes, using any of the techniques previously listed, tend to be different in two important

---

[21] Paul R. Lawrence and Jay W. Lorsch, *Developing Organizations* (Reading, Mass.: Addison-Wesley Publishing, 1969).

[22] Fritz I. Steele, *Physical Settings and Organizational Development* (Reading, Mass.: Addison-Wesley Publishing, 1973).

[23] F. G. Lesieur, ed., *The Scanlon Plan: A Frontier in Labor-Management Cooperation* (MIT Industrial Relations Section, 1958).

[24] W. J. Paul, K. B. Robertson, and F. L. Hertzberg, "Job Enrichment Pays Off," *Harvard Business Review,* March–April 1969, pp. 61–78.

[25] H. H. Mayer, E. Kay, and J. R. P. French, "Split Roles in Performance Appraisal," *Harvard Business Review,* January–February 1965, pp. 123–29.

[26] M. E. Shaw and J. M. Wright, *Scales for the Measurement of Attitudes* (New York: McGraw-Hill, 1967).

[27] J. K. Hemphill, *Group Dimensions: A Manual for Their Measurement* (Columbus: Ohio State University, Bureau of Business Research Monograph 87, 1956).

[28] G. H. Litwin and R. A. Stringer, *Motivation and Organizational Climate* (Boston: Harvard Business School, Division of Research, 1968).

[29] Likert, *The Human Organization.*

[30] Edgar H. Schein, *Process Consultation: Its Role in Organization Development* (Reading, Mass.: Addison-Wesley Publishing, 1967).

[31] P. Chase, "A Survey Feedback Approach to Organization Development," *Proceedings of the Executive Study Conference* (Princeton: Educational Testing Service, November 1968).

[32] For a good general discussion of OD, see Raymond E. Miles, "Organization Development" in *Organizational Behavior: Research and Issues,* ed. George Strauss et al. (Industrial Relations Research Association, 1974).

ways from organizational change efforts aimed at solving a current problem.

First, developmental change efforts are of a more ongoing nature. Unlike problem-solving organizational change, they tend not to begin and end in a period of months.

Second, developmental change efforts generally use coercive tactics to a lesser degree than other change efforts. For a variety of fairly obvious reasons, coercion simply cannot be used constantly over long periods of time to create an effective organization.

Summary

Developing a human organization that contributes to long-run effectiveness means developing enough flexibility and anticipatory ability so that the organization can adapt to inevitable changes in its environment. Creating and maintaining such an organization requires that managers be willing to invest resources in its human organization beyond what is needed merely for current operations. It also requires skill in making decisions that affect the human organization's adaptability.

A process that can help managers make effective developmental decisions requires periodic consideration of the following questions:

1. How much change is our organization likely to experience in the next 5, 10, 20 years? In what directions will these changes probably take us? How certain are we of our estimates of change? How much flexibility is needed to respond to these estimated changes?
2. How flexible is our human organization currently? That is, what is its current state on the dimensions shown in Figure 8–3? Is this adequate to cope with the change estimates?
3. If more flexibility is needed, how much is needed and how quickly? Where is additional flexibility needed: everywhere, in top management, or in just the formal systems?

With perceptive answers to those questions, managers can develop and implement over time a set of interventions that keeps a company's organization adaptive enough to cope with its probable future.

Case 8–1

Webster Industries (A)*

R. Roosevelt Thomas, Jr.

On Friday, October 17, 1975, Bob Carter, a 32-year-old graduate of the Amos Tuck School, was observing his first anniversary as manufacturing manager in the Fabrics Division of Webster Industries. Except for 2 years spent earning his M.B.A., he had been with the company for 10 years, and he was very satisfied with his Webster experiences. Before being selected for his current position, he had spent two years as a plant production superintendent, three years as a plant manager, and two years as assistant to the president, Abe Webster. On a day that should have been one of celebration, Carter sat at home in a very somber mood and started on his third martini of the afternoon.

Earlier in the day, Ike Davis, head of the Fabrics Division, had told Carter that Fabrics would have to reduce its personnel by 20 percent and that the manufacturing department, in particular, would have to make a cut of 15 percent at the managerial level. This meant that Carter would have to trim his 289 managers by 43 individuals. Davis's request stemmed from reduction plans presented to him by Abe Webster. Because Abe had set the following Friday as the deadline for the submission of termination lists, Davis wanted his top divisional managers to begin a review as a group on the preceding Wednesday of all proposed Fabrics separations. Davis concluded his conversation with Carter by listing the five guidelines that Abe Webster had provided:

1. No one with over 20 years of Webster service and 50 years of age should be terminated without a review by the president.

* All names and places have been disguised.

Harvard Business School case 476–110.

2. Since the last reduction (approximately one year before) had affected primarily hourly and weekly workers, this go-around was to focus on managerial levels.
3. Seniority was not to be a major determining factor as to who would be separated.
4. Early retirement should not be relied on as a mechanism for meeting reduction targets.
5. Blacks, women, and other minorities were not to be terminated more aggressively than other employees.

After speaking with Davis, Carter went home to ponder the situation.

Carter spent the afternoon in his den thinking about the task before him. He remembered the first time he had terminated an employee. Early in his career he had fired a secretary—it had taken him a week to muster enough courage to do it and a week to recover. Since that experience, however, he had found each successive termination increasingly easy. But never before had he been involved in releasing so many individuals at once, especially so many people with whom he had worked and developed social relations. Though he had been in his present position for only a year and had no previous experience in the Fabrics Division, Carter knew most of his managers by name and considered several to be friends. Furthermore, he and his family dealt with many of these individuals and their families in various community and civic activities. In addition to the likelihood of having to recommend the termination of personal and family friends, Carter worried about the possibility of having to release employees with significant lengths of service. He knew that any person with over 10 years of Webster employment would be very surprised by termination. While pondering the possible consequences of the reductions, Carter became more and more anxious as he realized that he had few firm ideas on how the cuts should be made. The only certainty was that he must conform to Abe's guidelines.

General Information on Webster Industries

Location

Located on 17 acres of rolling red Georgia hills on the northern outskirts of Clearwater, Georgia, Webster's headquarters resembled a college campus with plantationlike buildings. Top management was housed in the refurbished "Big House" of the old Webster Plantation, while middle-level corporate managers were situated in a modern three-story office building that was known as the "Box." Built a thousand yards from the Big House, the modern structure appeared out of place in the plantation setting. The Big House and the Box were the heart of one of America's most successful textile companies.

Clearwater was unabashedly a company town. Of its population of about 35,000, one half of the employed residents worked for Webster, one third engaged in serious farming, and the remainder labored in several small factories around the town. Not only was Webster the dominant employer, Websterites held all important community positions. The company stressed community involvement and encouraged its people to accept civic responsibilities.

Because Webster attracted highly educated employees from a variety of places, Clearwater differed from the typical small, rural Georgia town. For example, Georgia educators ranked its school system ahead of Atlanta's. The town had experienced much success in attracting quality teachers by offering generous salary schedules and excellent facilities. Another unique feature of the town was a thriving set of cultural and entertainment events, from regular appearances by the Atlanta Symphony and various theater groups to exhibition games featuring the Atlanta professional athletic teams. As one Clearwaterite put it, "Clearwater is not your run-of-the-mill mill town."

Company History

Colonel Jeremiah Webster, an officer in the Confederate army, founded the company after the Civil War. When the colonel retired from the operations, his youngest son assumed the leadership. He in turn was followed by his oldest male offspring, Mark Webster, who presided over the company from 1941 to 1960. Under Mark's tenure, Webster grew and branched into other fabric markets. By 1960 the company produced fibers for carpeting and for home and industrial furnishings. Sales rose from $150 million in 1941 to approximately $900 million in 1960. During this period Webster opened its first plants outside of Clearwater. Growth and geographical dispersion of operations greatly strained the company's management.

In the 1950s Mark Webster recognized his company's need for skilled management. Convinced of management's importance for the future of Webster, he set out to attract M.B.A.s to his organization in 1955. Though trained as a lawyer, he had considerable respect for professional business education. This respect had been fostered by consulting relationships with professors from some of the leading national and regional business schools. Mark also encouraged his son, Abe, to attend the Wharton School.

After earning his M.B.A. at Wharton, Abe served five experience years before assuming the presidency. Until that time, Webster's president had also served as chairman of the board of directors. After Abe's five years of experience, however, Mark decided to split the jobs. Abe became president, and Mark concentrated on the chairmanship. Mark still kept regular hours, but emphasized that Abe was running the business. Under Abe the company continued to grow, primarily through di-

Exhibit 1
Webster Industries: Partial Corporate Organization Chart

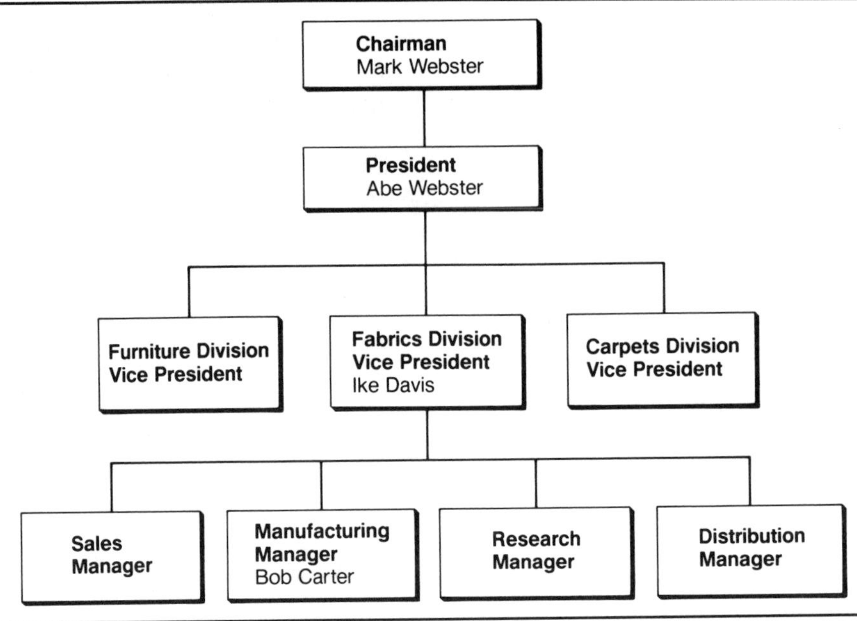

versification by acquisition of several small furniture and carpet manufacturers. Following these acquisitions, Webster's management adopted a divisional structure (see Exhibit 1). Despite its diversification, Webster was very much a textile company. Of its 1974 sales of approximately $1.7 billion, 70 percent came from the Fabrics Division. The carpet and furniture lines each accounted for 15 percent.

The Fabrics Division's products were categorized as fibers for apparel, home furnishings, carpeting, and industrial furnishings. Organizationally, Fabrics had a functional structure of Sales, Manufacturing, Distribution, and Research. Within Sales, the organization was by markets; the sales force was organized around the different fiber classifications. Comparable to Sales, the manufacturing plants were grouped by markets with three in apparel and two in each of the other areas. Each group reported to a production manager, who in turn reported to the assistant production superintendent, Cecil Stevens (see Exhibit 2).

Organizational Climate

Websterites described the company as a first-class place to work. Employees took great pride in the company's nationally known products and

Exhibit 2
Fabrics Division: Organization Chart

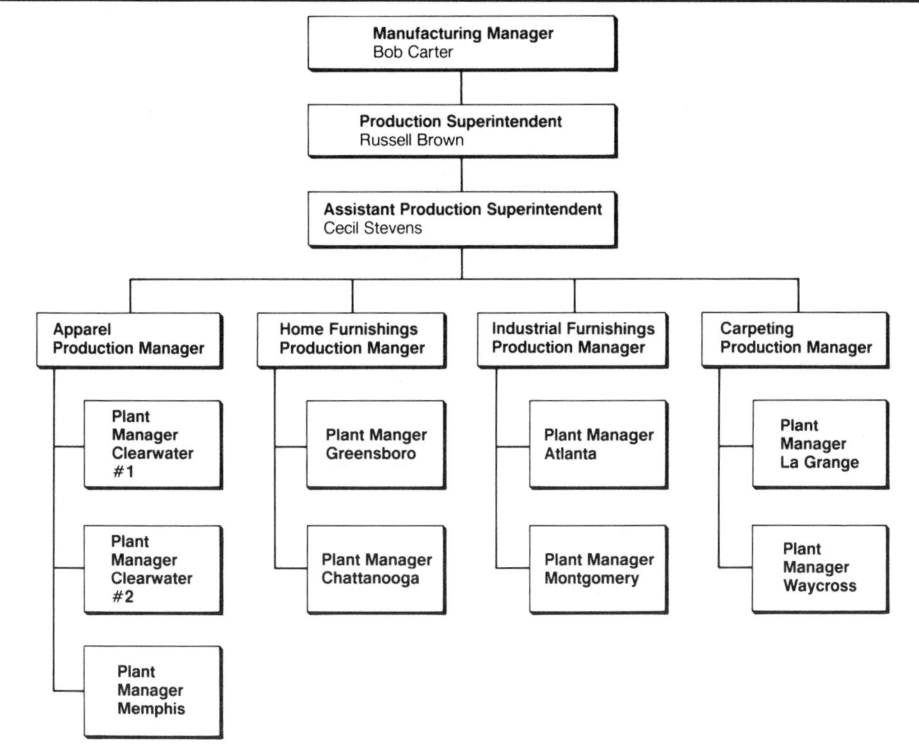

frequently remarked, "You can tell Webster fabrics from a mile away!" The organization consistently won industry awards for superior products, which were displayed in the Big House lobby. Webster also maintained excellent relations with its employees.

Management spared little in its efforts to make work at Webster rewarding *and* productive. The organization's facilities and working conditions excelled those of its competitors. Webster's pay and fringe benefits systems offered attractive financial packages and served as models for several firms located throughout the country. Further, because of its rapid growth, Webster had been able to provide its people with challenging work and opportunities for advancement. The company pioneered in establishing a Human Resources Division which performed the regular personnel functions along with a number of activities intended to facilitate the employees' growth and development. As part of its development projects, the Human Resources Division designed both a performance appraisal system (PAS) and an information system capable of tracking each employee's career and development. Top management gave the division much credit for the fact that no Webster plant was unionized.

Company officials also pointed to the firm's paternalistic culture as another factor contributing to good employee relations. They used the term *constructive paternalism* when describing the organization's attitudes and activities. For example, there were the annual company picnics, luncheons, dinners, and parties centered around special occasions. The employees' belief structure also reflected paternalism. Typically, the Webster employee believed, "If you make it through the 10th year, you can be reasonably assured that Webster always will have a place for you." Many employees expected this reciprocal agreement to hold even for individuals who had developed drinking and/or emotional problems. In more than one instance, Webster had kept an employee long after alcoholism had impaired his or her effectiveness, primarily because of top management's feeling that the person had no other place to go. Similarly, the company had paid the psychiatric bills of several employees rather than dismiss them as ineffective performers. Some viewed the open-door policies of the chairman and the president as another illustration of paternalism. All decisions could be appealed to the highest levels. A few managers expressed concern that employees with the appropriate connections had tended to use the open-door policies to secure undeserved promotions. Finally, the company on several occasions had financed the education of local youths—obviously with hopes that they would return to Clearwater and Webster, but with no strings attached. Two benefactors of this practice were the present Montgomery plant manager (Harvard B.A. and M.B.A.) and the chief corporate counsel (Yale B.A. and J.D.). Neither had ever worked for any other organization than Webster.

Clearwaterites openly spoke of the firm's paternalism, as shown here in the words of one plant controller:

There is a sense of family here. An expectation that if you are loyal to the company, it will be loyal to you. An expectation that if you have a problem, you can take it to Papa Webster [the company] and it will be at least seriously considered. Twelve years ago, a tornado came through and fiercely hit Clearwater. Those new houses you see along Webster Drive are a result of the company's generous response.

I could go on and on. Fringe benefits also reflect how the company takes care of its people. The whole fringe benefits package is oriented toward taking care of the employee's family. We were the first to ensure the education of a worker's children should he or she die. We continually upgrade retirement benefits to offset inflation. The company's hiring and promotion practices are also paternalistic. The offspring of employees always have first shot—if they are qualified—at openings. Webster—along these same lines—promotes from within. Rare is the case of someone being hired from the outside for a top position. What more is there to say? Webster is a darn good company.

Webster's Employees

Webster's managerial employees came from several areas of the United States. Typically, they had received degrees from schools on the East Coast. The M.B.A.s were from the top national and regional schools. Managers without M.B.A.s had sophisticated technical training. The backgrounds of Webster's managers differed significantly from those of its typical plant laborers, who tended to come from the area around the plant and to have at least a high school diploma or at most an associate degree from a community college. Despite these differences, Webster had experienced little class conflict. Most attributed this harmony to the Human Resources Division, the many opportunities for advancement, and Webster's practice of having M.B.A.s (especially those in manufacturing) spend some time in low-level plant positions.

Manufacturing in the Fabrics Division had 1,787 people located at headquarters and in nine plants. Of these, 289 served as managers. Managers worked either at corporate headquarters on the manufacturing manager's staff, or functioned in a managerial, supervisory, or staff capacity at one of the plants. The background of manufacturing managers was similar to that described above for Webster managers in general. Of the 289 managers, 160 lived in and around Clearwater.

Webster's Troubles

The symptoms that set off the alarm at Webster were second-quarter earnings of less than 50 percent of 1974 earnings and a threatened cash position. The economy and Webster's sloppy growth habits contributed to each of these difficulties.

The economy, especially the slowdown in the construction industry, hit Webster's furniture and carpeting businesses hard. The softening of the demand for furniture and carpeting caused Webster's sales to decline from a 1973 peak of $2.1 billion. Simultaneously, inflation exerted upward pressure on costs. The dips in sales and earnings reduced Webster's cash flow considerably, so much so that money became extremely tight for the first time in 35 years. Though Mark and Abe Webster had expected the current earnings and cash troubles, they were unnerved by the extent of the problems. In addition to the troubled economy, the firm's phenomenal growth had complicated matters further.

The production manager in the largest Clearwater plant offered the following observations:

> *We grew too fast. We wanted diversification but were not ready to handle it. With the acquisitions of the 1960s we became a different company almost overnight. Truthfully, we definitely were not prepared to break the billion-dollar level in sales. We grew too fast to consolidate. Only now are we learning the*

basics of managing a multibusiness enterprise. Controls were poor, especially in some of the plants we acquired. Staffing was done sloppily, so we ended up with a lot of fat. Plus we were—in my opinion—lax in our evaluation of performance.

The economy and the problems of diversification combined to slow Webster's growth and to threaten its financial integrity.

Bob Carter's Evening

By 6 P.M. Carter began to overcome his initial shock and to realize that, while painful, the reduction was probably needed and probably best for the company. He had known for some time that his department had fat at the managerial levels. Just six months earlier he had sought to demote three individuals—including his second in command. In denying his recommendation, Ike Davis had told Carter, "These men have too much service to be treated as you have proposed." So Carter was stuck with them; at least that had been the case until then. Carter reasoned that one benefit of the reduction in force would be an opportunity to make some long-needed changes. He saw his task as that of making the best reductions possible in the least painful manner.

After dinner Carter returned to his den to address the issue of how to cut 43 individuals from his managerial payroll. Because of his relatively brief tenure, he wanted to consult at least one other individual. The logical choices were the number two and three persons in his hierarchy; however, Carter wanted to demote the production superintendent, Russell Brown, and to promote the assistant production superintendent, Cecil Stevens. He had been impressed with Stevens and had decided some time back that he should have Brown's job. The reduction presented an opportunity to make the change.

Carter concluded that Stevens should be involved initially and perhaps others later on some basis. At 8:30 P.M. he called Stevens, who lived four miles away, and asked him to come over to discuss the critical situation. Cecil arrived an hour later. Carter informed him of the reduction plans and of his intention to recommend him for promotion to production superintendent. Stevens was both delighted by his promotion and shocked by the magnitude of the proposed separations. After relating details of his session with Davis, Carter asked Stevens to aid him in developing a strategy for determining the individuals to be released. Specifically, he requested that Stevens be prepared by Monday morning to identify and discuss issues that should be considered in formulating a reduction plan.

Carter and Stevens spent another 45 minutes discussing their perceptions of the company's situation and the need for the reduction. They also raised some questions about Webster's PAS. Stevens wondered how much weight should be given to performance ratings. Carter admitted that he had not gotten around to using PAS on a regular basis, but indicated that he would be interested in hearing Stevens's views of the system and its usage in the department. Stevens asked if they should consider inviting others to the session on Monday morning. After some discussion, they agreed to invite the production managers with the exception of the home furnishings manager, who was a likely candidate for demotion or termination. Carter and Stevens ended their meeting by agreeing on a timetable: Monday, 8 A.M.—develop strategy; Monday, 1 P.M.—begin to implement strategy; and Wednesday, 2 P.M.—present list to divisional managers.

The Monday Morning Meeting

On Monday morning, Carter, Stevens, and three of the four production managers met as planned. Stevens began the meeting by presenting his thoughts on possible criteria for developing a termination list:

The following represents my thinking on possible options open to use. I see five.

The first is seniority. *Though guidelines prohibit much use of this criterion, there are a few individuals who might be receptive to offers of early retirement.*

The second is fairness. *Should this be a criterion? Operationally, I do not know what it means except that we would not do anything that would be perceived as grossly unfair. I do know, however, that our people will expect fairness.*

The third is fat. *The list would be determined by the elimination of "fat" or excess positions. This approach has legitimacy. The difficulty, however, is that some good people are in "fat" positions. The use of this criterion alone could result in a net quality-downgrading of manufacturing personnel.*

The fourth is performance. *The basic question here is, "How do we measure performance?" How much weight do we give to PAS data? Some individuals feel that the PAS data are hopelessly biased, because of the managers' tendency to give everyone good ratings. How much weight do we give to the personnel audit data?*[1] *If we were to give significant weight to the audit data, would we be compromising the future effectiveness of the auditor? When making field visits, the auditor not only gathers data on performance from managers but also talks to individuals about their careers and problems. Many employees have been very frank with the auditors. If we use audit data as input in making termination decisions, the employee may feel betrayed and become reluctant to trust the auditors in the future. This would be especially likely if managers tried to make the auditors scapegoats. I can hear a manager telling a terminated employee, "I wanted to keep you, but our auditor Jack had too strong a case against you."*

Additionally, to what extent are we constrained by past practices? In the past, few managers have been diligent and responsible in talking with their people

[1] Personnel auditors from the Human Resources Division visited each manager at least once a year to discuss his or her employees' performances. During these discussions they obtained a performance rating for each employee. This process was separate from Webster's performance appraisal system (PAS).

about performance; as a consequence, many employees are not aware of their relative standing with respect to performance. If these individuals are terminated, they will likely be shocked and feel that they have been treated unfairly. Can we fairly terminate on the basis of performance?

The fifth is potential. *Again, the basic questions are around measurement and the weights to be given to PAS and audit data. How do we measure potential? How much weight do we give to PAS data? Audit data? Should we terminate an individual with little potential but capable of doing his or her present job fully satisfactorily? I am thinking about one plant controller in particular. He is an excellent assistant plant controller, but he does not have the potential to advance further. Would he be a candidate?*

I consider this large reduction to be a one-shot deal. As such, the reduction represents a beautiful crisis opportunity to make moves that would be difficult under normal circumstances. We can seize the opportunity not only to meet our termination target but also to upgrade our department. Other divisions are releasing competent people. Some will be better than those that we will propose to keep. This means that we could upgrade by reducing a larger number than our target, and then hiring replacements from our sister divisions' terminations. For example, our target is 43. If after meeting this target we identified 5 available individuals who were better than persons we were planning to keep, we could terminate 48 and hire the 5 former employees of the other divisions. However, if we are to seize this opportunity, we will have to develop sound ways of evaluating performance and potential.

A lively discussion of PAS and the personnel audit followed Stevens's remarks. During these deliberations the group relied heavily on Stevens's memorandum on performance appraisal at Webster (see the appendix).

Appendix: Memorandum on Performance Appraisal

Memorandum

TO: Bob Carter

FROM: Cecil Stevens

RE: Performance Appraisal at Webster

DATE: October 20, 1975

Since leaving your home on Friday evening, I have had an opportunity to talk with a number of individuals. Specifically, I saw Ed Johnson, the designer of our PAS system, at the club and had a good conversation; talked with Jack Bryant, our personnel auditor, about his work with the division; and spent two hours after church discussing the reduction with the manufacturing managers of the other divisions. Immediately below are my impressions of PAS and also the personnel audit function of the Human Resources Division.

Performance Appraisal System (PAS)

Bob, PAS was designed three years ago and has been used primarily on a voluntary basis. My discussion of the system is based primarily on conversations with its designer, Ed Johnson.

Purpose

The system is intended to help the manager act as a:

- Manager responsible for attaining organizational goals.
- Judge responsible for evaluating individual performance and making decisions about salary and promotability.
- Helper responsible for developing subordinates.

One problem in the past has been failure to recognize the three roles cited above, or a tendency to emphasize one over the others. PAS is based on the assumption that each role is equally important and is intended to help the manager do justice to each.

Components

PAS components are three in number: management by objectives (MBO), a developmental review, and an evaluation and salary review.

MBO. This component focuses on results and is intended to help the manager realize organizational goals. Though each manager is expected to adapt MBO to his or her situation, there are typically six steps:

1. *Identification of objectives.* Here, objectives are identified and prioritized. Also, review periods are set.
2. *Establishment of measurement criteria.* The basic question here is, "What monetary measures, percentages, and/or other numbers will be used to measure the achievement of objectives?" For example, if we in manufacturing were to establish "greater production effectiveness" as one of our objectives, we would have to decide how to measure the extent of achievement. Total unit costs? Total direct labor costs? Total production?
3. *Planning.* Plans are made for achieving the identified objectives. What is to be done? Who is to do it? When is it to be done? How is it to be done?
4. *Execution.* Plans are implemented.
5. *Measure.* Secure actual monetary figures, percentages, and/or other numbers so that results may be reviewed.
6. *Review results.* Compare actual measurements to plan. The frequency of measurement and review will depend on the number of review points within a year. Typically, the entire MBO cycle is repeated once a year, with intermittent reviews in between.

MBO is essentially a system for identifying what is to be done and ensuring that it is done. As such, MBO has a major weakness in terms of the managerial role: It does not aid the manager in observing, evaluating, or improving the behavior of subordinates. If the manager is to help his employees improve their behavior, he will need a behavior-oriented tool. The developmental review was designed to meet this need.

The Developmental Review. As indicated above, the review is intended to help the manager observe, analyze, and improve subordinate behavior. There are three subcomponents: the performance description questionnaire, the performance profile, and the developmental interview.

1. Performance Description Questionnaire. The questionnaire contains 70 behavioral statements, each describing a behavior determined through research to be indicative of effectiveness. Supervisors are asked to rate the extent to which the subordinate exhibits the behavior described. The 70 behavioral statements are grouped into a smaller number of dimensions such as openness to influence, priority setting, formal communications, organizational perspective, decisiveness, delegation/participation, support for company, unit productivity, and conflict resolution. The manager is asked to complete a questionnarie for each subordinate. He or she is asked to indicate on a six-point rating scale how descriptive the statement is of the employee's actual behavior. Also, under each statement is space for the recording of any critical incidents supporting the manager's judgment. (See Attachment 1.) The performance profile is produced by computer from the questionnaire data.

Attachment 1

Sample Items from Performance Description Questionnaire

1. Involves subordinates in decision-making process. ______
2. Makes a special effort to explain Webster policies to subordinates. ______
3. Molds a cohesive work group. ______
4. Fails to follow up on work assignments given to others. ______
5. Works closely with subordinates who lack motivation. ______
6. Selects and places qualified personnel. ______
7. Subordinates accomplish a large amount of work. ______
8. Objects to ideas before explained. ______
9. Is accurate in work. ______
10. Gives poor presentations. ______

Ratings

Number	*Definition*
1	Strongly agree
2	Agree
3	Somewhat agree
4	Somewhat disagree
5	Disagree
6	Strongly disagree

2. Performance Profile. The profile is intended to serve as a tool to help managers discriminate among a subordinate's performances on a number of performance dimensions. An individual's profile shows net strengths or weakness for each dimension in terms of the person's own average. The profile line represents the average of the employee's ratings on all performance dimensions. The number and location of X's show the extent to which the employee's score for a particular dimension is below or above his or her average for all dimensions. Dimensions with X's to the left of the profile line are those where the individual is relatively weak (compared to his or her average). Dimensions with X's to the right are those where the subordinate is relatively strong. The number of X's indicates the extent of the weakness or strength. (See Attachment 2.) The tool is designed to facilitate analysis of a subordinate's performance and is not valid theoretically for comparison of individuals.

3. Developmental Interview. The purposes of the developmental interview are to provide the subordinate with a performance analysis based on the performance questionnaire and profile, to identify areas of weaknesses, and to translate these weaknesses into an appropriate developmental program. Tools are available to help the manager and subordinate in designing developmental plans.

The reasoning behind the design of the developmental review was a hope that the performance description questionnaire and profile would

Attachment 2

Sample Profile Interpretations

Dimension	*A*		*B*		*C*	
1. Openness to influence	XX		XXXXX			XX
2. Priority setting		XX		XXX		XXXXXX
3. Formal communications		XX		XXX	XXXXXX	
4. Organizational perspective	XX		XXXXXXXXXX		XX	
5. Decisiveness		XX		XX		XX
6. Delegation/participation	XX			XX	XXXXXX	
7. Support for company		XX	XX			XXXXXX
8. Unit productivity	XX			XXX	XX	
9. Conflict resolution		XX	XX		XX	
10. Team building	XX			XXX	XX	
11. Control		XX		XX		XXX

A. Implication is that manager is well balanced *dimensionally.*

B. Implication is that this manager has one *very* significantly weak *dimension,* another relatively weak *dimension,* contrasted to the remaining favorably balanced *dimensions.*

C. Implication is that this manager has two relatively weak dimensions, two relatively strong *dimensions,* with remaining *dimensions* relatively balanced.

CAUTION: Remember that you are only comparing the individual to himself and *not* with other people. IF an individual is "well balanced dimensionally," it means there is not much difference between what he does best and what he does the poorest; it does *not* necessarily mean he is a "well-balanced manager."

help the manager and his subordinates distinguish development from MBO and evaluation, and thereby reduce subordinate defensiveness that typically characterizes feedback sessions where developmental and evaluative issues are handled simultaneously.

Evaluation and Salary Review. This review is separate from the MBO and developmental reviews. Its basis is a form which asks the manager to rate the employee's overall performance and his or her potential. (See Attachment 3.) The overall rating should reflect the MBO sessions and the development review data and interview. In short, the two other components of PAS provide important inputs for the evaluation review. Possible overall ratings are unsatisfactory, fair, full satisfactory, excellent, and outstanding.

Once the overall rating has been given, the salary matrix may be used as a *guide* in determining recommendations for salary adjustments. The matrix approach is straightforward and used by several organizations. Under this method, salary adjustments are a function of the subordinate's rating and the relative standing of the employee's salary within his or her pay range. (See Attachment 4.)

Usage of PAS

Bob, as I indicated earlier, the system has been used on a voluntary basis so far. In the corporation as a whole, the usage rate is 29 percent; in manufacturing it is 40 percent. The only group using it 100 percent is Fabrics' sales force.

The Personnel Audit

In addition to PAS the Human Resources Division is also responsible for conducting the personnel audit. The purposes of the audit are to secure performance data that will facilitate corporate manpower planning, to encourage and improve communications between superiors and subordinates, and to provide career development counseling. There is a potential conflict among the purposes in that the auditor is required to perform both evaluative and counseling roles. Some individuals who "pour out their souls" to the auditors are unaware of their evaluative function.

Our auditor, as you know, is Jack Bryant. At least once a year Jack visits each manager and talks about their subordinates. He also talks with subordinates about their development and their perceptions of where they stand. Where there are discrepancies between a subordinate's perception and what his or her manager has said, Jack works with the

Attachment 3

Detach and sent to: **Private**

POSITION PREFERENCE

Employee name ______ Date ______

Division ______ Employee number ______

Position ______ Location ______

Supervisor ______

Supervisor and subordinate develop *together*. Indicate below subsequent positions for your subordinate *that you both can agree* are realistic, appropriate, and interesting. Specify both functional area (e.g., Sales, Personnel, etc.) and, whenever possible, type of job.

ORDER OF PREFERENCE FOR NEXT JOBS:

Short Term
First Choice:
Second choice:

Long term (within next 5 years)
First choice:
Second choice:

SUPERVISOR'S SUMMARY:

Supervisor fills in by himself *after* the developmental interview. The subordinate should be shown these ratings after the supervisor has coordinated the rating with the *second*-level supervisor.

A. CHANGE OF STATUS: Indicate by your choice of the statements below (check one) the change of status you recommend for this person during the next 12 months.

______ Should be separated as soon as possible. (SEP)

______ Should be reassigned to position with a decreased responsibility. (DEM)

______ Should be reassigned to a position with a similar level of responsibility. (LAT)

______ Need more experience before reassignment can be considered. (EXP)

B. CAREER POTENTIAL: Based on current knowledge, indicate in the spaces below (check one) the level this person has the greatest probability of achieving. Note: Potential ratings do *NOT* imply a person's readiness for promotion now.

______ Potential division manager or equivalent. [must be Group 50 or above.] (BLUE)

______ Potential to higher supervisory/managerial level. (GREEN)

______ Potential is best utilized within a specialty or as an individual performer. (BROWN)

______ Good performer; no indication to date of potential for a higher level. (YELLOW)

Attachment 3 (*concluded*)

________ Should be reassigned to a position with more responsibility. (RDY)

________ Should remain in present position. (STA)

________ Questionable performance. (RED)

C. OVERALL JOB PERFORMANCE during the past 6–12 months may be characterized as: (check scale)

Unsatisfactory	Fair	Satisfactory	Excellent	Outstanding

D. COMMENTS:

....

ENDORSEMENT OF SECOND LEVEL SUPERVISOR

________ I agree with all of the above recommendations.

________ I disagree with some (or all) of the above recommendations and would make the following recommendations:

____

Signature

Attachment 4

Salary Matrix

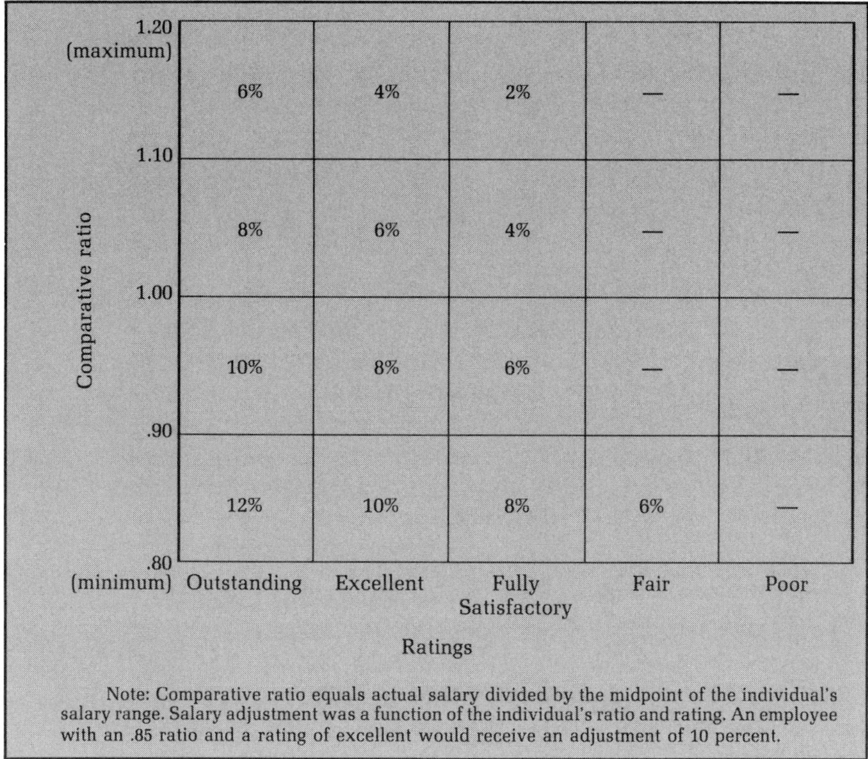

Comparative ratio	Outstanding	Excellent	Fully Satisfactory	Fair	Poor
1.10–1.20 (maximum)	6%	4%	2%	—	—
1.00–1.10	8%	6%	4%	—	—
.90–1.00	10%	8%	6%	—	—
.80 (minimum)–.90	12%	10%	8%	6%	—

Ratings

Note: Comparative ratio equals actual salary divided by the midpoint of the individual's salary range. Salary adjustment was a function of the individual's ratio and rating. An employee with an .85 ratio and a rating of excellent would receive an adjustment of 10 percent.

manager in developing a plan for correcting the employee's misperceptions. Jack, however, has no enforcement power; consequently, some managers fail to give accurate—if any—feedback to their employees. The audit has been very successful in securing information for the central corporate data bank, but has had somewhat less success in getting managers to be honest with subordinates. Though individual employees may see their central file, few avail themselves of the opportunity; consequently, many subordinates remain in the dark as to how they are actually perceived by their bosses. I, however, understand that a computer-based system capable of providing each employee with performance data has been designed and implemented below managerial levels. Reportedly, the system annually provides each employee with a printout showing—among other things—performance ratings and career history. April 1, 1976, is the target date for full implementation in the managerial ranks.

Currently, the form used by the auditors asks for a rating of the individual's performance and potential. There also are sections dealing

Attachment 5

Employee Name ____________ Supervisor ____________ Date ____________

PERFORMANCE
1 2 3 4 5 NR (circle one)

POTENTIAL
(Circle one) 1 2 3 4 5 NR

COMMENTS: (Supervisor should define significant strengths and weaknesses [development needs] and accomplishments.)

CHANGE OF STATUS—for the next 12 months (check one):

1. ________ Should be separated as soon as possible (termination).
2. ________ Should be reassigned to a position of decreased responsibility (demotion). Which function(s) (comment)? ____________
3. ________ Should be reassigned to a position with a similar level of responsibility (lateral move). Which function(s) (comment)? ____________
4. ________ Needs more experience before reassignment can be considered (not ready). Which function(s) (comment)? ____________
5. ________ Should be reassigned to a position of more responsibility (promotion). Which function(s) (comment)? ____________
6. ________ Will probably remain in present position indefinitely (leveled).

Performance

Number	*Definition*
5	Outstanding
4	Excellent
3	Fully satisfactory
2	Fair
1	Unsatisfactory

Potential

Color	*Number*	*Definition*
Blue	5	Potential division manager or equivalent (for individuals currently at the "A" payroll level).
Green	4	Potential to higher supervisory position.
Brown	3	Potential is best utilized within a specialty or as an individual performer.
Yellow	2	Good performer; no indication to data of potential for a higher level.
Red	1	Questionable performer.

with the employee's strengths and weaknesses and the manager's recommendations for future reassignments. (See Attachment 5.)

I have checked with Jack, and he has assured me that there are audit ratings on file for at least 97 percent of our personnel.

Bob, hopefully these remarks on PAS and the personnel audit will stimulate discussion leading to an appropriate reduction plan.

Case 8–2

Worldwide Typewriter Company*

Donald J. Gogel, Leonard A. Schlesinger

Starting with a prototype electric typewriter developed by its founder in a basement laboratory in 1957, Worldwide Typewriter Company developed increasing technological sophistication and market presence in its first decade of corporate existence. Based in a suburb of Chicago, Illinois, the company expanded its product line into electronic word processing, established a direct sales force, and gained a reputation for product quality and customer service.

During the 1970s, the company continued its rapid growth. Its European operations became increasingly important. Its direct sales force grew to become one of the largest in the United States. And, on the strength of its 1972 acquisition of the Minicomp Corporation of San Raphael, California, it established a beachhead in the minicomputer and "office of the future" industry (Exhibits 1 and 2).

Kendrick R. Smith, president and chief executive officer, had joined the company in 1965 as vice president, marketing. He left a similar position with a competing typewriter manufacturer, frustrated that the manufacturer's top management lacked the vision and the will to adapt to the new electronic technologies. Smith performed well and moved to Brussels to manage Worldwide's European headquarters in 1972, where he remained as managing director until 1976. In late 1976, Smith returned to the United States with a new title of executive vice president and chief operating officer of the Minicomp Corporation subsidiary.

* All data, names, and organizational relationships have been disguised.

Harvard Business School case 483–076.

Exhibit 1
Worldwide Typewriter Company Sales ($ millions)

	1972	1973	1974	1975	1976	1977	1978	1979	1980	1981
United States	$628	$739	$ 869	$1,023	$1,203	$1,420	$1,720	$1,960	$2,312	$2,566
Europe	170	198	250	310	388	485	570	672	840	1,050
Latin America	20	40	70	86	105	120	140	167	195	230
Asia	8	15	20	27	32	37	40	44	49	55
Total	$826	$992	$1,209	$1,446	$1,728	$2,062	$2,470	$2,843	$3,396	$3,901

Exhibit 2
Worldwide Typewriter Company: Sales by Product Category ($ millions)

	1972	1973	1974	1975	1976	1977	1978	1979	1980	1981
Typewriters	$614	$740	$ 882	$1,041	$1,201	$1,410	$1,662	$1,833	$2,134	$2,322
Minicomputers	212	252	327	425	527	652	808	1,010	1,262	1,578
Total	$826	$992	$1,209	$1,466	$1,728	$2,062	$2,470	$2,843	$3,396	$3,900

When Smith stepped up to Worldwide's chief executive officer job in 1980, he inherited a basically strong company. Yet, as he knew, the company was beginning to show the strains of increasing conflict between the Typewriter and Minicomputer Divisions, particularly between their independent sales forces. And, as he had anticipated during his years in Brussels, the whole concept of a European headquarters was open to question.

In his Executive Committee meeting to kick off 1982, Smith raised these two concerns explicitly to his top management team.

Gentlemen, he began, *look at this organization chart* [Exhibit 3]. *Does the management approach implicit in this organization structure do justice to our strategic view of the future? Does it still make sense to maintain two independent sales forces, one for minicomputers and one for typewriters, when we are committed to being the premier company offering a fully integrated office products line? And should we continue to manage both our typewriter and minicomputer businesses through a European headquarters when we are committed to maintaining close ties between our field organizations and our product development units?*

The Twin Sales Force Dilemma

Worldwide Typewriter had developed one of the best direct sales forces in the United States. Fifteen hundred strong, the sales force had 40 branches in major markets around the country. A 1,000-person technical service organization, based in the same branches, provided aftersales service.

Worldwide had followed a policy of recruiting college graduates right off the campus to seed its sales force. Based on its reputation as a pro-

Exhibit 3
Worldwide Typewriter Company: Organization Chart

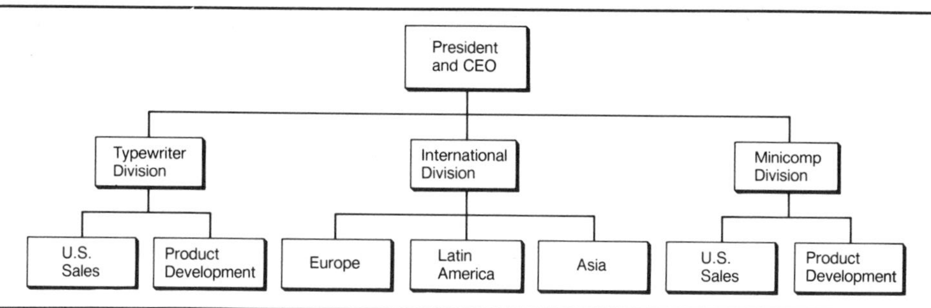

gressive employer in an opportunity-rich industry, the company had been able to attract honors graduates from some of the best state university systems in the country. Promotion was almost entirely from within the ranks of the existing sales organization, and able salespeople were able to move rapidly up the sales management hierarchy. Formal performance appraisals of all sales reps were used to determine individual development needs and identify candidates for promotion. While sales volume performance was weighted heavily, skills such as interpersonal relations and problem solving were also carefully assessed.

Worldwide had always maintained a highly leveraged compensation plan, with salespeople earning approximately 40 percent of their compensation as salary, with 60 percent derived from sales commissions. At least through 1980, Worldwide's high-performance salespeople earned as much as any of their counterparts in the office equipment industry.

At Worldwide, sales management had always been centralized and disciplined. Headquarters staffs did the first drafts of annual plans and budgets, setting targets for units sold, establishing national pricing programs, determining sales force call and coverage ratios (e.g., one sales rep should make 2.2 calls a day and be responsible for a sales territory of 50 accounts or potential accounts). As a result, branch managers operated within very tightly defined boundaries; they managed against line item budgets and product-by-product quotas. "How many boxes this month?" was sales management's favorite question.

Minicomp Corporation, on the other hand, followed a dramatically different approach to sales force management. These differences appeared in terms of recruitment, promotion, training, compensation, branch structure, as well as in ties of the sales force to product development organization.

The Minicomp sales force has been wholly separate from the Typewriter sales force, with virtually no cross-divisional mobility. Minicomp liked to hire from the outside, seeking people with four to seven years of intensive selling experience in a computer environment. Although a policy of promotion from within was a long-term objective, the rapid growth of Minicomp as well as the need to bring in experienced salespeople, has led to multiple external hires at high levels in the sales organization.

The desire for experienced-person recruiting rather than campus-based hiring in part reflected the enormous training costs required to provide an inexperienced college graduate with a basic education in computer technology. Minicomp had found that a 10-month intensive training course, designed specifically for college graduates, was required to bring recruits up to speed as a sales rep. The training needs were so high not only because of the difficulty in mastering computer technology but because Minicomp salespeople were meant to be problem solvers first and salespeople second. Specifically, tailoring a Minicomp solution to customer needs was an "application" sell as much as a "hardware" sell. Minicomp's top personnel manager also believed hiring experienced people was more efficient because turnover would be higher among campus recruits than among experienced reps. Such turnover would be expensive in view of the large investment in training.

Compensation plans in Minicomp were much less leveraged than in the Typewriter Division. Salespeople typically received 80 percent of their compensation as salary, with the remainder as commission. Compensation levels for sales reps in Minicomp had been kept in line with the Typewriter Division by the corporate staff until 1978, when Minicomp management insisted that this policy was beginning to prevent them from attracting and retaining people with computer experience. By 1982, Minicomp sales reps' pay levels averaged 25 percent above Typewriter reps'.

Given the nature of their sales, Minicomp sales reps were organized into selling "teams" of four to six people. Although a formal branch structure existed for Minicomp in about 20 major markets, the effective unit for budgeting, planning, and account control was the selling team. (Each branch had about five teams.) These teams, consisting of an account executive, a systems representative, and two or more systems analysts, had much greater latitude in choosing how to serve customers. Operating within a "sales-expense-to-revenue ratio," team leaders had considerable power to configure and price installations within the guidelines defined by the corporate marketing department.

In the first few years, after the acquisition, the differences in sales approaches between Typewriter and Minicomp appeared to be minor philosophical quibblings over how to manage a sales force effectively. Increasingly, however, these differences reflected fundamentally incompatible approaches to the business. Nowhere were these differences more evident than in comparing the "box" versus "system" selling skills or in contrasting the Typewriter versus the Minicomp relationships to national accounts.

1. "Box" versus "System" Selling Skills. The difference between selling stand-alone hardware (the typewriter "boxes") and software-based systems (the minicomputer networks) has had significant impact on the way the respective products are sold. (Exhibit 4 illustrates some of these differences in product delivery; Exhibit 5 summarizes some of their impact on different elements of selling.)

Increasingly over the past five years, electronic typewriters have been sold as word processors and as part of larger office automation systems—e.g., they have been sold as local secretarial stations linked to a centralized, high-speed printer in a company's centralized reproduction center.

Smith was becoming concerned about these trends because they threatened to make obsolete the skill base of the Typewriter sales force. As soon as his boxes were linked into larger systems, Typewriter sales force management would break down—the company would have the wrong people, with the wrong education and training levels, recruited

Exhibit 4
Differences in "Box" and "System" Product Delivery

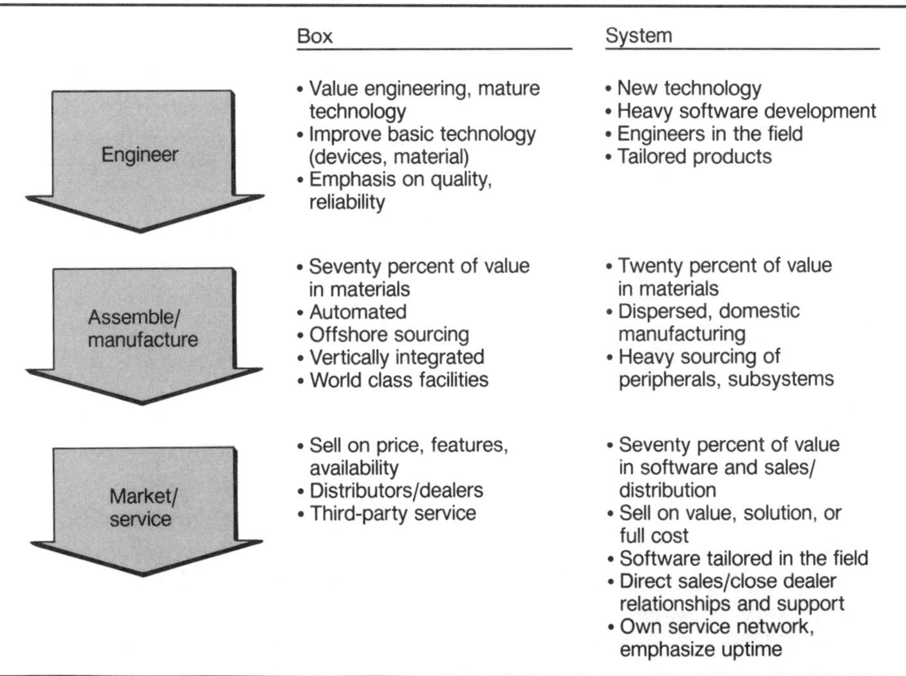

Exhibit 5
Comparison of "Box" and "System" Selling Requirements

Legend: High / Moderate / Low

Element of selling	Requirements: Box	Requirements: System
Information processing knowledge of salesperson	Low	High
Specialized training	Moderate	High
Specialized systems applications knowledge	Low	High
Understanding of customer's business	Low	High
Need for contact with senior executive decision maker	Low	High
Need to commit customer to major investment	Low	High
Time required to complete selling cycle	Low	High

from the wrong sources, compensated on the wrong basis, and motivated toward wrong objectives.

Moreover, as the systems world was emerging ever more clearly, the typewriter sales force was beginning to lose more and more of its top performers to competitors who were offering entry on the ground floor.

2. National Accounts Relationships. Both Typewriter and Minicomputer sales were heavily concentrated in larger accounts, but typewriters are sold to many more accounts than minicomputers (Exhibit 6). Each, however, followed independent paths. Each planned, priced, covered, sold, serviced, billed, and contracted according to its own desires. As a result, there was no coordination or consistency in terms and conditions (e.g., cancellation penalties, credit and return policies, pricing plans) among Typewriter and Minicomp sales forces. Customers dealt with the sales forces as though they represented wholly unrelated companies.

In accounts where Typewriter and Minicomp sold to different buyers, there usually were few, if any, direct conflicts. Thus, to a customer where typewriters were sold to the vice president, general services, and minicomputers sold to the vice president, data services, the dual sales approach raised no issues.

By and large, Typewriter buying decisions were made locally by a

Exhibit 6
Concentration of Sales

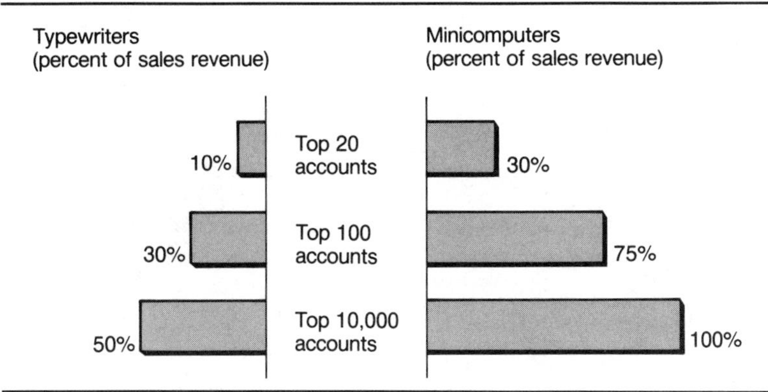

relatively low-level manager. Minicomp decisions, however, were more frequently made on a centralized basis.

However, as customers began to take an integrated look at all their office automation needs, they were increasing the degree of their centralized buying. Whether through approved vendor lists or more formal office automation committees that negotiate directly with suppliers, the trend was toward seeking an integrated product offering/solution from a supplier that could fulfill virtually all office automation needs.

To date, the direction of this trend was clear, but not the pace of change. A recent survey commissioned by Typewriter to determine customer buying processes found no single pattern emerging (Exhibit 7). However, as the trend toward centralized buying continued, Smith saw the challenge as one of moving customers toward higher degrees of integration (Exhibit 8).

Given all these facts, Smith knew he had to be moving toward integrating the Typewriter and Minicomp sales forces. But he certainly was not sure how to get there.

The European Dilemma

In 1962, Worldwide opened a small sales office in Brussels. Hoping to capitalize on its low-cost position and high-quality technology compared to European manufacturers of electric/electronic typewriters, the sales office opened its doors with eight salesmen (two Belgians, two Englishmen, a Frenchman, a Dutchman, and two Americans) and an American director.

Over the course of the next decade, the small sales office grew into the regional headquarters for over a dozen direct sales organizations,

Exhibit 7
Customer Survey Results

Question	Summary Evidence	Comment
1. How centralized is your buying process:	Nineteen different patterns of centralized/decentralized decision making identified. Increasing use of office automation committees.	No common approach. Tendency toward greater central control.
2. How integrated/compatible are your products?	Issue of little interest to top executives. Data processing groups usually evaluate separately from office administrators. Most vendor guidelines do not specify compatibility.	Integration/compatibility of products an increasing but still limited concern.
3. What is the technical sophistication level of your decision maker?	Some customers pushing state of the art. Most customers willing to let supplier provide technical solution/expertise.	Wide variety of customer skill levels.
4. Who makes the decision?	Typewriter decisions mostly remain at office manager level. Minicomputer decisions often require data processing executive <u>and</u> CEQ support.	Relative differences in size of purchase seem to control level of decision maker.
5. How would you describe your company's commitment to office automation?	Tremendous variations between customers. Highly committed companies tend to be: —In technology-based businesses. —Internal sponsor/champion. —In healthy industrial sectors.	Market needs still largely latent.

Exhibit 8
Moving Customers to Higher Degrees of Freedom

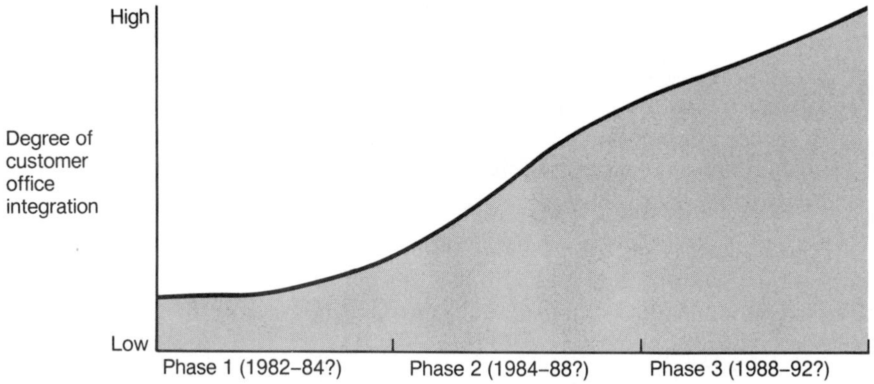

High

Degree of customer office integration

Low

	Phase 1 (1982–84?)	Phase 2 (1984–88?)	Phase 3 (1988–92?)
Challenge to Worldwide	Identify stage of maturity/sophistication of company buying process Develop marketing approach to suit customer needs	Monitor evolution of buying processes within each grouping Use leading-edge companies to learn successful approaches Utilize vertical marketing to focus resources	Satisfy needs of totally integrated purchasing process in most organizations

each established as a corporation in its own country. The European headquarters was itself a duly incorporated entity.

At first, the country sales organizations were no more than branches reporting to Brussels headquarters. Virtually all decisions—from hiring and firing to pricing plans and advertising campaigns—were made in Brussels. Even after the country sales organizations began to grow and develop into full-fledged operating companies, run by local nationals, the legacy of centralized control from Brussels remained.

The Brussels staff performed multiple functions.

1. *Control.* There was a large central finance and control staff.
2. *Administration.* Since the Brussels headquarters was in fact a wholly owned subsidiary corporation of Worldwide Typewriter, it maintained a large central administrative staff in such areas as personnel, legal, and corporate affairs.
3. *Planning.* The European organization was viewed by Worldwide Typewriters as a single profit center. Although each country was allocated a portion of the headquarters profit target, profit tradeoffs among countries were made in Brussels—e.g., headquarters decided whether to invest in Italy in this year or to derive as much profit as possible.

4. *Functional services.* Headquarters personnel provided basic staff functions to the operating companies for planning, pricing, marketing, training, and personnel.
5. *Logistics.* Headquarters managed its own procurement, warehouse, materials, and supply functions.
6. *Data systems.* To provide the necessary information flows from country operations to Brussels and from Brussels to Chicago, headquarters invested heavily in computer-based management information administrative systems.

The structure of these headquarters staffs changed continuously. But the organization chart in Exhibit 9 describes the staff structure well; Exhibit 10 contains a measure of the head count and direct personnel costs of Brussels headquarters.

In 1972, when the Minicomp Corporation was acquired, Worldwide management decided to place Minicomp's European sales force under the control of Brussels headquarters. Since the Minicomp European sales force was very small compared to the Typewriter sales force, the decision represented more of an administrative convenience than a strategic initiative. (Exhibit 11.)

However, by 1982, there were significant strains in the reporting relationship. The Minicomp sales force had always felt the stigma of second-class citizenship in the Brussels headquarters. They believed, with some justification, that the headquarters staff was dominated by people brought up in the typewriter business—people with little appreciation for the unique characteristics and problems of the small-computer business. Moreover, they were openly resentful of the way that the Brussels management squeezed the minicomputer business to generate additional profits needed to earn their bonuses when typewriter sales fell below target.

During the last year, the Minicomp sales organizations in the major European countries have become increasingly outspoken about their dissatisfaction with their relationships with Brussels. On a number of occasions they have argued that they should be allowed to report directly to the Minicomp Division in San Raphael. A letter from the French Minicomp sales manager presents the case for this move in some detail (Exhibit 12).

Smith believes the French sales manager makes a number of valid points. But he is unwilling to concede the issue for three primary reasons.

1. *Span of control.* Smith is concerned that the Minicomp Division in San Raphael will have too many direct reports if all the major European sales organizations report directly. The normal considerations about span of control are compounded by the large physical distances and time zones between Europe and California.

Exhibit 9
European Headquarters: Organization Structure

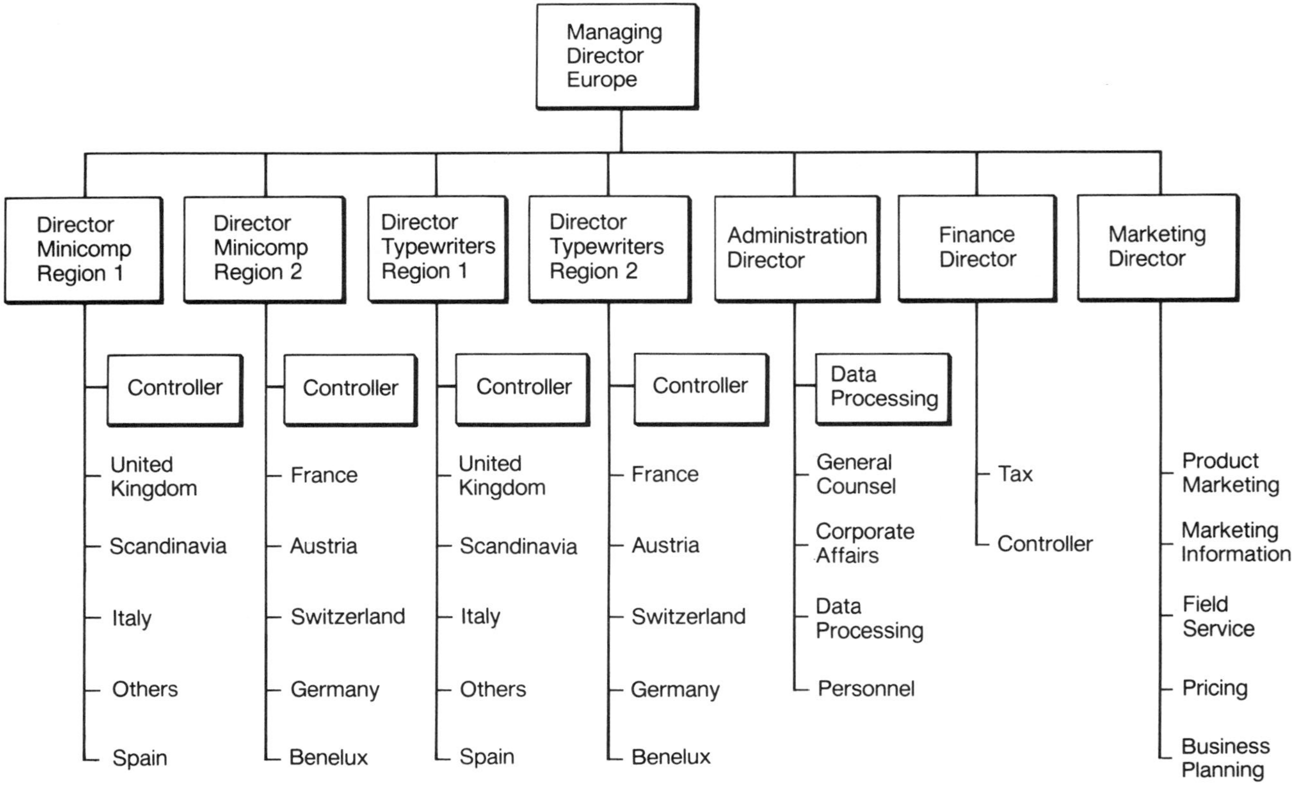

Exhibit 10
European Headquarters: Head Count and Direct Cost by Staff Role, 1981

Roles	Head Count (number of people)	Cost ($000)
1. Control	75	$ 3,185
2. Administration	25	1,250
3. Planning	60	2,600
4. Functional services	115	4,825
5. Logistics	90	4,008
6. Data systems	65	2,175
Total	430	$18,043

2. *Potential financial and political costs of redundancies.* Moving Minicomp out of headquarters would lead to a reduction in the size of the Brussels staff. This could be costly in both financial and political terms. Under the relevant Belgian laws, for example, a senior planning analyst earning $30,000 per year would be entitled to almost $18,000 in lump-sum severance pay. Perhaps more damaging, an American company laying off several hundred white-collar workers in the city that houses the commission of the European Economic Community would find itself in a very bad political light.

3. *Apparent inconsistency with the movement toward integrating the U. S. sales forces.* Moving the reporting of Minicomp European sales organizations back to the U. S.-based division goes against the direction of sales force integration in the United States. After all, in some ways, Europe already has a form of sales force integration.

As of late 1982, no action had been taken to change the reporting relationship of the Minicomp European sales organizations.

Exhibit 11
European Sales Forces: Head Count

	Typewriters	Minicomp	Total
United Kingdom	140	45	185
Scandinavia	31	12	43
Italy	50	19	69
Spain	41	14	55
France	95	34	129
Austria	22	10	32
Switzerland	23	8	31
Germany	115	49	164
Benelux	42	15	57
Other	36	6	42
Total	595	212	807

Exhibit 12
Reporting of Minicomp European Sales Force

November 11, 1982

TO: Kendrick T. Smith
FROM: Jean Pierre Rampal

Ken, as you know, I have been lobbying for some time to have the Minicomp sales organizations in our major European companies report directly to the Minicomp Division in California. My primary motivation for recommending this change arises from my conviction that our minicomputer sales forces require closer ties to and support from the product units in San Raphael than can be achieved under today's arrangements.

As I see it, such a change would help us in a number of ways.

1. *Provide more direct communication* between our product designers and planners and the salespeople closest to customer needs.
2. *Enhance the technical support, training, and documentation* available to our salespeople by having a direct pipeline to California.
3. *Speed decision making.* We cannot wait in France for questions to be routed through Brussels to California and back to us via Brussels. We need the authority to act more on our own after conferring directly with the division.
4. *Build local capabilities.* With a big headquarters staff in Brussels, our sales operations have never developed the capabilities they need to run their country businesses. To get a strong cadre of managers in the operating companies, we must be able to offer them real responsibility, without the constraint of close supervision and support from Brussels.
5. *Offer more attractive career paths.* Our salespeople feel stunted here. With a headquarters that is hostile or indifferent to the minicomputer sales force, our best people have no sense that they can move up within the corporation. If we reported to San Raphael, at least individuals could see a visible track up through the division.
6. *Develop more responsive systems.* I know this is a sore point in the company, but I am still not a believer in the $70 million investment in Brussels centralized systems. Pricing, billing, inventory management, and other systems need to be responsive to minicomputer purchaser needs that are not the same as typewriter purchaser needs. The centralized economies of scale we are chasing just are not worth it.
7. *Reduce costs substantially.* It goes without saying that there are substantial savings if we can reduce our headquarters operations as a result of this change.

I know that your positive experience in managing the Brussels headquarters years ago has led you to keep the status quo. But the environment has changed, and we should change in response.

I hope to raise the question with you directly when I meet with you in Chicago in early December.

Case 8–3

Litton Microwave Cooking Products (C)*

Vijay Sathe

In October 1976, Bill George, president of Litton Microwave Cooking Products, one of 112 divisions of Litton Industries, Inc., was concerned about several issues related to the company's middle and lower management levels. The division had grown from $19 million in sales in 1971 to $186 million in the fiscal year just ended. This tremendous sustained growth, averaging 60 percent compounded annually, had created stresses and strains for people, particularly those in lower and middle management levels. In many cases, their jobs were growing faster than they could handle them, leading to frustration and anxiety for the individual managers, with serious implications too for the company's future well-being. If extremely rapid growth years continued, as projected, into the late 1970s, the company would soon approach the $.5 billion sales mark. It was clear to George that as the division grew to this size and beyond, the nature of the business would require considerable delegation of authority to middle and lower management levels. Would these managers be ready to handle the new responsibilities?

Nature of the Business

Litton Microwave Cooking Products was the world's largest producer of microwave ovens, commanding 30 percent of the 1976 consumer market and 70 percent of the commercial market in the United States. Micro-

* Some of the information has been disguised for reasons of confidentiality.

Harvard Business School case 477–085.

wave penetration in the U. S. consumer oven market was estimated to be a mere 6 percent, and sales were expected to surpass those of conventional ovens by 1978, continuing strong through the late 1970s (Exhibit 1A). The performance of the microwave oven was particularly impressive against the backdrop of the lackluster major appliance industry and had attracted the attention of several domestic and foreign manufacturers. Amana, Tappan, General Electric, Panasonic, and Sharp were already strong competitors, and others could conceivably decide to enter the market. Although competition was expected to intensify in the years ahead, market saturation and an industry shakeout were not expected until the mid-1980s.

The spectacular success of the microwave oven business was due largely to three factors. First, the initial concerns about the safety of microwave ovens had been largely laid to rest. In 1973, Consumer's Union had raised the possibility of radiation leakage but the Food and Drug Administration's Bureau of Radiological Health (BRH) had not supported the charge. The BRH had set tough standards on allowable leakage in 1971 and had followed up with strict enforcement. Manufacturers' facilities were inspected every six months, and all new designs had to be reviewed by the BRH. Second, rising energy costs had made the microwave oven more economical. With its low power consumption and cool operation, the microwave oven used about 50–75 percent less energy than a conventional oven for the average family of four. Finally, new features had greatly increased the microwave oven's versatility. Variable power settings, special browning devices, and temperature controls permitted the microwave oven to cook almost as broad an array of foods as conventional devices; it could now be positioned in the market as a *complete* cooking device.

Litton's leadership in this market was attributed to its aggressive marketing and distribution programs backed up by innovative product design and competitive prices. About 90 percent of the company's business was in consumer ovens (70 percent in countertop models and 20 percent in ranges); the remaining 10 percent of the business was in commercial ovens. The countertop business included some private-label sales, mainly under the Sears label. (Pictures of a representative sample of the company's products are shown in Exhibit 2.)

Litton was a recognized leader in the technology of microwave cooking. Patent protection was of limited value since the technology was changing rapidly and success hinged on the ability to be first on the market with new-product innovations. An important determinant of Litton's technological leadership was its engineering design department, believed to be the world's largest microwave engineering group. The company's task team organization, comprising members drawn from various functional areas, had been credited with offering the flexibility needed to achieve a rapid response to the demands of the marketplace. In con-

Exhibit 1
Industry Sales of Consumer Ovens

A. Microwave Ovens' Growing Share of Major Cooking Appliance Market

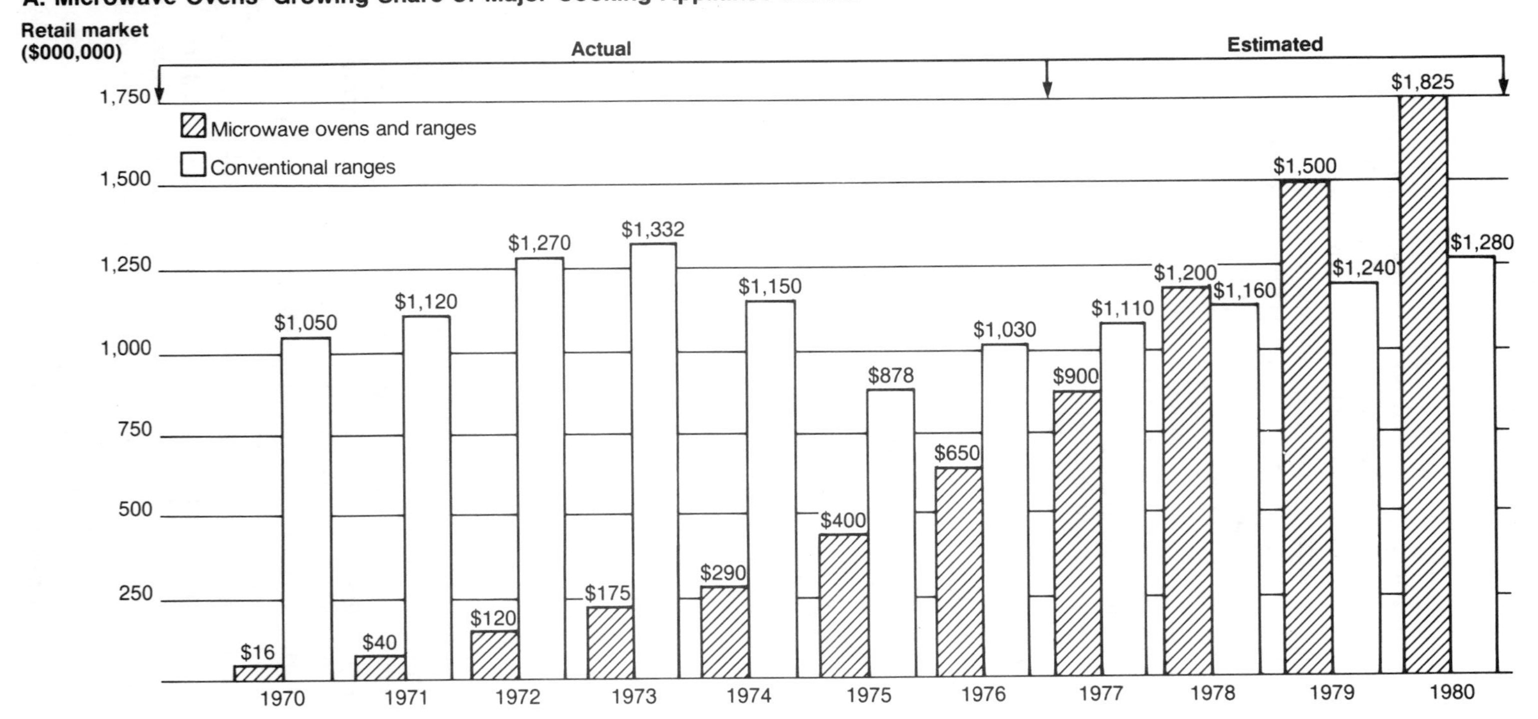

Exhibit 1 ***(concluded)***

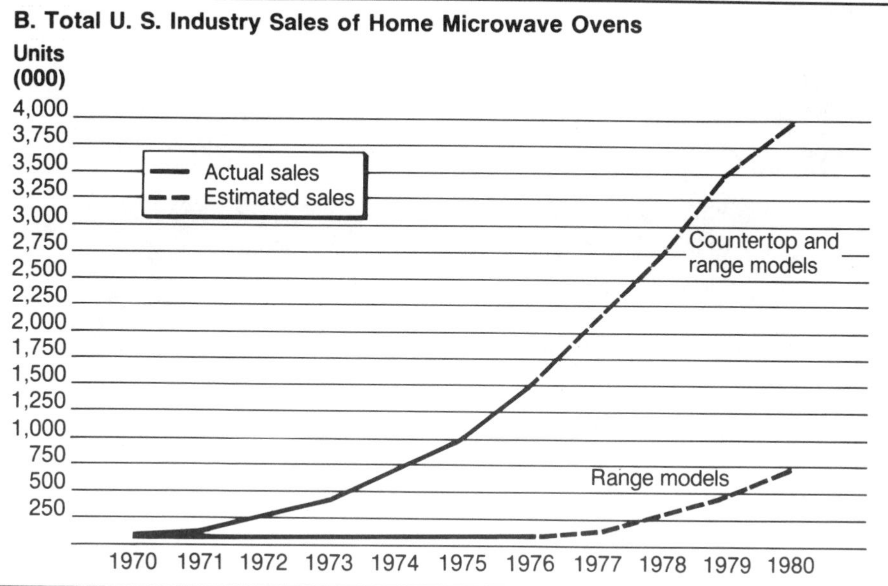

Source: Litton Microwave Cooking Products.

trast, major competitors were characterized as being in the appliance industry tradition—conservative, and slow to respond to market changes. For example, Litton Microwave executives described GE's appliance division as an organization where things tended to get bogged down.

Production of ovens involved the subassembly and assembly of parts purchased to design specifications. About 80 percent of the cost of the manufactured product was in the purchase price of parts. The direct labor component, involving relatively unskilled labor, was small. Thus, manufacturing cost depended largely on design specifications and the ability to obtain low prices from suppliers, and only secondarily on production efficiencies.

Dedicated to microwave ovens, the Litton division had achieved greater production experience than any of its competitors, which were generally more diversified. Litton took considerable pride in having manufactured more microwave ovens than anyone else.

History

The consumer market for microwave ovens was relatively undeveloped through 1965. In 1966, sales reached 12,000 units. In 1967, Amana, a newly acquired subsidiary of Raytheon, introduced the first 115-volt coun-

Exhibit 2
Pictures of Products

Litton 419 Minutemaster® microwave oven

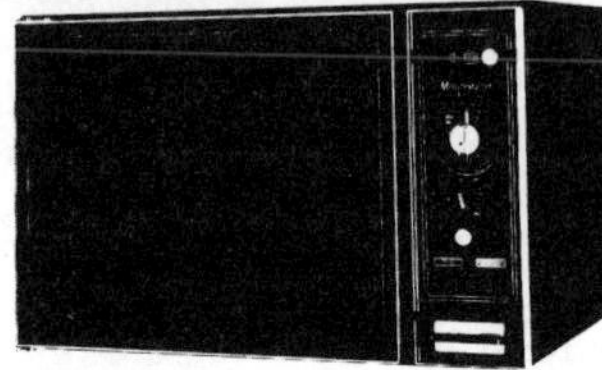

Special Features
- Solid state Vari-Cook oven control for slow-cooked goodness at microwave speeds
- Vari-Temp automatic food temperature control
- 99-minute Micro-Timer digital timer
- Bright, easy-clean acrylic interior
- Sealed-in ceramic shelf
- See-through oven door
- Modern, attractive styling
- Extra-large 1.2 cubic foot usable oven interior

Litton 460 Memorymatic™ microwave oven

Special Features
- 99-minute electronic timer
- Solid state Vari-Cook oven control
- Vari-Temp control
- Memorymatic oven control with an additional 99 min. of memory time
- Solid state touch control
- Lighted digital display
- Minute Timer
- Automatic on/off control
- Extra-large 1.2 cubic foot usable oven interior
- Easy-clean acrylic interior and sealed in ceramic shelf
- Separate Time and Temp, Memory, and Vari-Cook touch controls
- Free Vari-Cook Microwave Cookbook

Automatic Conventional oven timer
Push to turn infinite heat controls
Automatic Defroster
Microwave Step Saver Timer™
Time of day clock Minute Minder
8" quick heat element
Black glass door
Mini-Food shelf
Closed-door smokeless broil
Self-cleaning oven

Litton Combination 650 microwave range

("Single Oven Cavity" Range)

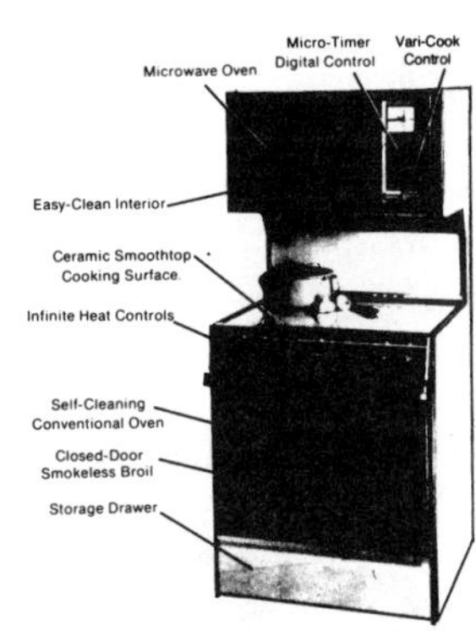

Litton Micromatic 989 microwave range

("Double Oven Cavity" Range)

Source: Litton Microwave Cooking Products.

tertop microwave oven, and by 1969, demand had grown to 45,000 consumer units per year. The subsequent growth of the consumer oven business had been spectacular, and rapid growth was expected to continue through 1980 (Exhibit 1B).

In late 1969, Litton Microwave Cooking Products began the first phase of its long-range plan for entering the consumer microwave oven business. Countertop units were produced for sale under private label for Admiral, Tappan, and Montgomery Ward. In 1970, public concern over possible microwave radiation leakage and the economic recession put a damper on industry sales. As a result, Litton's sales under the private-label program fell short of the company's projections in its first year in the consumer oven market.

In August 1971, 28-year-old Bill George was appointed executive vice president of the Litton division with responsibility for all internal activities, including profitability. (Bob Bruder was president and had overall charge of the division.) After completing a bachelor's degree in industrial engineering from Georgia Institute of Technology, and an M.B.A. from Harvard Business School, Bill George worked as a civilian in the Department of Defense, first as an assistant to the assistant secretary of defense (comptroller) and then as a special assistant to the secretary of the navy. During the transition between administrations in 1969, Bruder asked George to join Litton as director of long-range planning for the company's food services group. His first assignment was to study whether Litton should enter the consumer microwave oven business. Shortly after its entry into the private-label end of the consumer business, Litton had encountered start-up problems, and George was asked to move to the microwave division as vice president in early 1970. In this position he had responsibilities for each major area of the business. Excerpts from magazine articles on his career are included in Exhibit 3.

Exhibit 3
Excerpts from Magazine Articles on Bill George

YOUNG TOP MANAGEMENT: The New Goals, Rewards, Lifestyles

How dedicated under-40 executives are making it big—and richly—running some of the country's major corporations

The new organizations built by these young executives are often more participative than traditional businesses. "I don't want to be controlled by an organization, and I don't want my organization to control other people," says 32-year-old William W. George, president for two years of Litton Industries, Inc.'s Microwave Cooking Products Division. "We get together as peers. It doesn't matter whether you're president or an engineer. Authority goes to competence." George holds what he calls "sensing sessions" at least monthly with the company's 600 hourly employees. "I don't believe in waiting for contract time. I want to avoid a we-they attitude."

***

Change is bound to come in the flexible new organizations. As a rule, major appliance makers take 24 to 40 months to introduce a new product. "That's just the way it is in the industry, and nobody changed the rules," says George. "I insisted we make product introductions in 9 to 18 months. I can afford to take the risk and break the rules. I'm at an age where if I make a major mistake, I have time to go out and redeem myself."

***

Acceptance of a youthful executive outside the company is sometimes more difficult still. "My age is no problem within the company," says Litton's George. "But on the outside, people often have trouble accepting me. They ask pointed questions like: 'Who was your father?' " George has found being a president at 32 so cumbersome that on social occasions he evades the issue. "When someone asks, I just say I'm in general management."

Exhibit 3 *(concluded)*

***

Litton's George practices transcendental meditation 20 minutes every morning and afternoon to unwind.

***

Many young executives make special efforts to allocate more time for their families, which often has the side effect of providing some needed rest and recreation. Some, like Litton's George, have even found time to help with the chores. Since his wife puts in a 55-hour week as an educational psychology teacher at the University of Minnesota, he cooks 40 percent of the family's meals and makes about one third of the trips to the baby-sitters and day-care centers where the Georges leave their two-year-old son.

***

Litton's George, who makes more than $75,000 a year, takes a different approach. "No matter what our income, I should be able to live on $20,000 a year," says George, who lives in a 40-year-old house valued at about $50,000. "I don't want to be locked into a high income. Someday I may want to go into teaching or government service and live on that kind of income."

BUSINESSMEN IN THE NEWS

The major appliance industry is pretty slow these days, but microwave ovens are burning up the business. An insignificant seller five years ago, they fetched about $300 million at retail last year.

In this youthful business a young man is king. William George, 32, heads the Microwave Cooking Products division of Litton Industries, which ranks number one in sales of home and commercial units. Litton's microwave sales are expected to reach $85 million in 1975, and George says his group has been a "very strong profit contributor." Litton, which lost $40 million as a whole last year, can use the money.

An engineer and Harvard Business School graduate, George worked at the Defense Department for three years before joining Litton. "Every business today is affected by the government," he says. "I wanted to understand governmental processes from the inside."

As it happened, the night he was packing to join the division in Minneapolis in 1970, he heard a government warning on the radio that microwave ovens might be hazardous. For the next six months at Litton, George worked with HEW to establish acceptable safety standards. These days the government reviews all new designs and inspects Litton's factories twice a year.

One of the most significant steps taken under the leadership of Bob Bruder and Bill George was the decision to market a consumer microwave oven under the Litton brand name despite the disappointing results in the private-label market in 1970. This move represented Litton Industries' first entry in the consumer products field. The division had a strong position in commercial microwave ovens, but the consumer market represented an entirely different type of sale, to different people, and for different reasons. A key concern was the division's ability to compete successfully with a powerful force like GE.

In January 1971, Bill George selected Dan Cavalier to spearhead the company's entry into the consumer field. Cavalier's long track record included extensive experience in consumer marketing with companies such as RCA, Philco, Caloric, and GE. Within three weeks of joining

Litton, Cavalier hired his former associate, Si Ware, who had been with Westinghouse for 20 years, to assist him as national sales manager of consumer products.

By the end of 1971 the division had established a 20 percent share of the consumer market through sales of its own brand and private label sales. Although some competitors, notably Amana, had an advantage in consumer brand awareness, Litton was able to penetrate the market by emphasizing salesperson training, retail demonstrations, special cookbooks, and the introduction of new convenience features. The company then employed about 400 people, half of them hourly workers. Total revenue was $19 million, and the division made a profit contribution to Litton Industries.

In 1972, 300,000 consumer microwave ovens were sold in the United States, and Litton maintained its 20 percent share of the market. The division had established an impressive national distribution network for its consumer products via 50 distributors and about 2,000 dealers. In the fiscal year ended July 31, 1973, revenues almost doubled over the previous year, and the division held its share of the market. Total employment increased 37 percent during the year. In August 1973, Bill George was promoted to president, and Bob Bruder was made a group vice president of the Litton Industries Medical Products Group.

Both revenues and total employment doubled between July 1973 and July 1975. Revenues totaled $99 million for the fiscal year ended July 31, 1975, and the division made a strong profit contribution to Litton Industries, which was recovering from a $40 million net loss the previous year. Revenues and total employment almost doubled again between July 1975 and July 1976, and the microwave operation remained a leader among Litton divisions. The trends in revenue, production capacity, and employment over the years are shown in Exhibit 4. In August 1976, Bill George was elected a corporate vice president of Litton Industries and continued as president of Litton Microwave Cooking Products.

The division expected its recent success to continue into fiscal 1977. Forecast sales were about 450,000 countertop units (30 percent of the projected market) and about 55,000 range units (55 percent) for an overall 32 percent share of the domestic consumer market for microwave ovens. In addition, Litton expected to hold its commanding 70 percent share of the $30 million commercial microwave oven market. If these projections were accurate, total revenue would reach $260–290 million in fiscal 1977.

Corporate-Divisional Relations

The fundamental building blocks of Litton Industries were its decentralized divisions, which were treated as individual profit centers. The division manager played a key role in the Litton system and enjoyed a great deal of autonomy. With the exception of capital expenditure decisions

Exhibit 4
Trends in Revenue, Unit Production, and Employment: 1971–1976

	Fiscal Year					
	1971	1972	1973	1974	1975	1976
Revenue ($ millions)	19	32	53	72	99	186
Increase over previous year (%)		68	66	36	38	88
Production capacity (thousands of units)	43	79	202	288	432	936
Increase over previous year (%)		84	56	43	50	116
Employment at end of fiscal year						
Indirect workers (managerial, professional, secretarial, and support)	200	389	495	567	812	1,167
Increase over previous year (%)		95	27	15	43	44
Direct workers (hourly, unionized)	213	290	434	482	957	1,994
Increase over previous year (%)		36	50	11	99	108
Total employment	413	679	929	1,049	1,769	3,161
Increase over previous year (%)		64	37	13	69	79

above $35,000 and executive salary decisions above $45,000, decisions made at the divisional level did not require specific corporate approval. Nor was the division manager required to buy from other Litton divisions. The only mandatory interaction in the Litton organization was vertical; horizontal interaction developed on the basis of the mutual self-interest of divisions. Thus, the corporate level made no attempt to interfere with the divisions to achieve centralized planning efficiencies. It was felt that divisional autonomy offered advantages in increased motivation that outweighed any benefits that could be gained by imposing "slide rule" efficiencies from the corporate office.

There was no human resources function at corporate headquarters. The industrial relations department was staffed with lawyers concerned mainly with labor negotiations and employment contracts.

Planning at Litton was considered a line rather than a staff activity. Most of Litton's plans were generated at the division level. Once a year, the division manager was required to submit to his or her corporate group vice president a business plan describing proposed activities during the coming 12-month period. It included projected revenue, profit, and capital requirements. The plan was discussed, evaluated, and modified at the group level before being submitted for corporate approval. Once the plan was approved, the division drew up a set of detailed, interlocking financial plans to execute the business plan. These plans contained profit and loss statements, balance sheets, and supporting data for the coming 12-month period on a month-by-month basis. Financial data were also included for a 24-month period on a quarterly basis and for a 36-month period on a yearly basis. After being checked for accuracy by corporate headquarters, these plans became the charter for the division's operations and were updated quarterly.

In addition to the business and financial plans, the division submitted a monthly report to corporate headquarters showing actual performance against the financial plan. Corporate expected each division to meet the monthly targets. Four performance indicators received special attention: profits, cash generated or used, return on gross assets (including capitalized leases), and return on capital utilized (net assets minus current liabilities). If performance was out of line, the division was expected to notify corporate management immediately rather than waiting to submit the monthly report. In addition, corporate executives visited each division periodically to keep in touch with divisional activities. Telephone meetings were frequently arranged to discuss problems and exchange information.

The division retained its autonomy only as long as it met its performance targets. If it missed its monthly targets, the division would receive increasing corporate attention, including more than the usual number of corporate visitors. Continued inability to meet targets would result in replacement of the division's general manager, unfavorable corporate resource allocation, and possibly even divestiture of the division.

The Litton Microwave division was a consistent high performer and had met its monthly targets for profit, cash generation, and return on investment during each of the past 24 months.

Organization at Litton Microwave

Between August 1971, when Bill George joined the division as executive vice president, and August 1976, revenue and total employment at Litton Microwave increased 10-fold and profits increased 17-fold. The company's organization played an important role in ensuring this dramatic success. Although the division was formally organized into the traditional functional departments under the president (see Exhibit 5 for a list of these departments, and for background information on the department heads), most of its activities were managed by informal task teams that did not appear on the formal organization chart but operated within the functional structure. Bill George explained:

Back in 1971 our long-range plan called for building our sales volume to $100 million in five to seven years, representing a compound growth rate of 40 percent per year. I was convinced that the only limitation on our revenue and profit growth was our organization's ability to grow as rapidly as the market opportunities. The organizational challenge was to create a structure and climate which would facilitate such growth. In evaluating whether our functional organization could meet these needs, I became concerned about the ability of this structure to respond to changes in a volatile market and to encourage and stimulate creativ-

Exhibit 5
Backgrounds of Functional Heads

Doug Baker—vice president of human resources, 42 years old. Bachelor of business administration (Texas), M.B.A. (Stanford). Joined Litton Microwave in present position in July 1973. Responsible for all activities involving employee planning, development, and organizational structure. Prior experience included positions as senior associate with Willson Associates, vice president of Jones and Byrd, manager of training for Pillsbury Company, and assistant to the president at the Kitchell Corporation.

Jack Blake—vice president of engineering, 48 years old. Bachelor of science in business and engineering (Minnesota), M.B.A. (Minnesota). Joined the division in 1970, promoted to current position in July 1972. Responsible for engineering research, new-product development, product engineering, and all technical support of the division's operations. Previous experience included position as director of manufacturing at Litton's applied science division and key engineering-management positions with General Mills and General Motors.

Dan Cavalier—president of marketing and sales division, 58 years old. Undergraduate education at the University of Maryland and the University of Georgia. Joined the division in 1971, promoted to present position in July 1975. Responsible for marketing, sales, and sales-related activities for the company's consumer, commercial, and private-label activities. Past experience included positions as vice president and general manager at Salespower, manager of market development at GE, vice president of marketing for Caloric, and merchandising manager for consumer products at Philco Ford.

Don Colt—vice president of international division, 40 years old. A.B. (Stanford), M.B.A. (Harvard). Joined Litton Microwave in current position in October 1975. Responsible for all of the division's international activities. Prior experience included marketing and general management positions with the international group of Lawry's Foods for 14 years.

Richard Jones—senior vice president of finance and administration, 34 years old. Bachelor of science in engineering (Michigan), M.B.A. (Michigan). Joined the division as assistant controller in 1969, promoted to current position in April 1973. Responsible for all financial activities within the division, including financial control, data processing, financial planning, and international finance. Prior experience included position of financial analyst with Litton's corporate staff in Beverly Hills from 1967 to 1969.

Paul Westgard—vice president of operations, 40 years old. Bachelor of science in industrial administration (Minnesota). Joined the division in April 1974, promoted to current position in December 1974. Responsible for the division's manufacturing operations, materials, and facilities expansion. Previously he was director of operations for Josten's, Inc.

ity. Functions tended to take a narrow view of their respective roles rather than to see the overall needs of the business. On the other hand, the functional organization was simple and efficient. It provided specialists a point of focus and a feeling of security. As such, we developed the concept of using task teams composed of people from the various functional areas to carry out the bulk of the work.[1]

Task teams were formed to address such issues as new-product development, manufacturing of products, new marketing programs, cost reduction activities, facility planning, private-brand sales, and new business ventures. Each team had a designated leader, generally a member of middle management, and representatives from several functional areas; members of top management participated as required. Bill George spent a great deal of time attending task team meetings.

Although task teams cut across the various functional areas, they tended to become associated with one functional area more than with others. For example, most members of the new-product development teams were usually engineers, and these teams were under the general supervision of the engineering vice president. Similarly, manufacturing teams were under the vice president of operations, and new marketing programs teams were under the marketing head. The activities of several of these teams are discussed below in the context of the appropriate functional departments.

Engineering

The 90-person engineering department was composed of 14 task teams working on approximately 40 new-product development projects in four areas: advanced engineering, design engineering, product engineering, and commercial engineering. Each area was headed by a department manager. The design engineering area was the largest of the four and included managers for the range line, the Litton countertop line, and the private-label countertop line.

Advanced engineering represented the company's research activity. This area originated a few projects that eventually proceeded to the appropriate product engineering group, i.e., commercial, range, countertop, or private-label. The majority of the design activity originated in these respective areas and represented refinement, modification, and development of the existing product lines.

The progress of a typical product development project is charted in Exhibit 6. A team usually began with an engineer and two technicians. A designer, a stylist, a buyer, a home economist, draftspeople, and quality control and manufacturing personnel were added as the project developed. The transition from preproduction to production following the final

[1] This passage and several others were taken from an article by Bill George, "Task Teams for Rapid Growth," *Harvard Business Review*, March–April 1977.

Exhibit 6
Product Development System

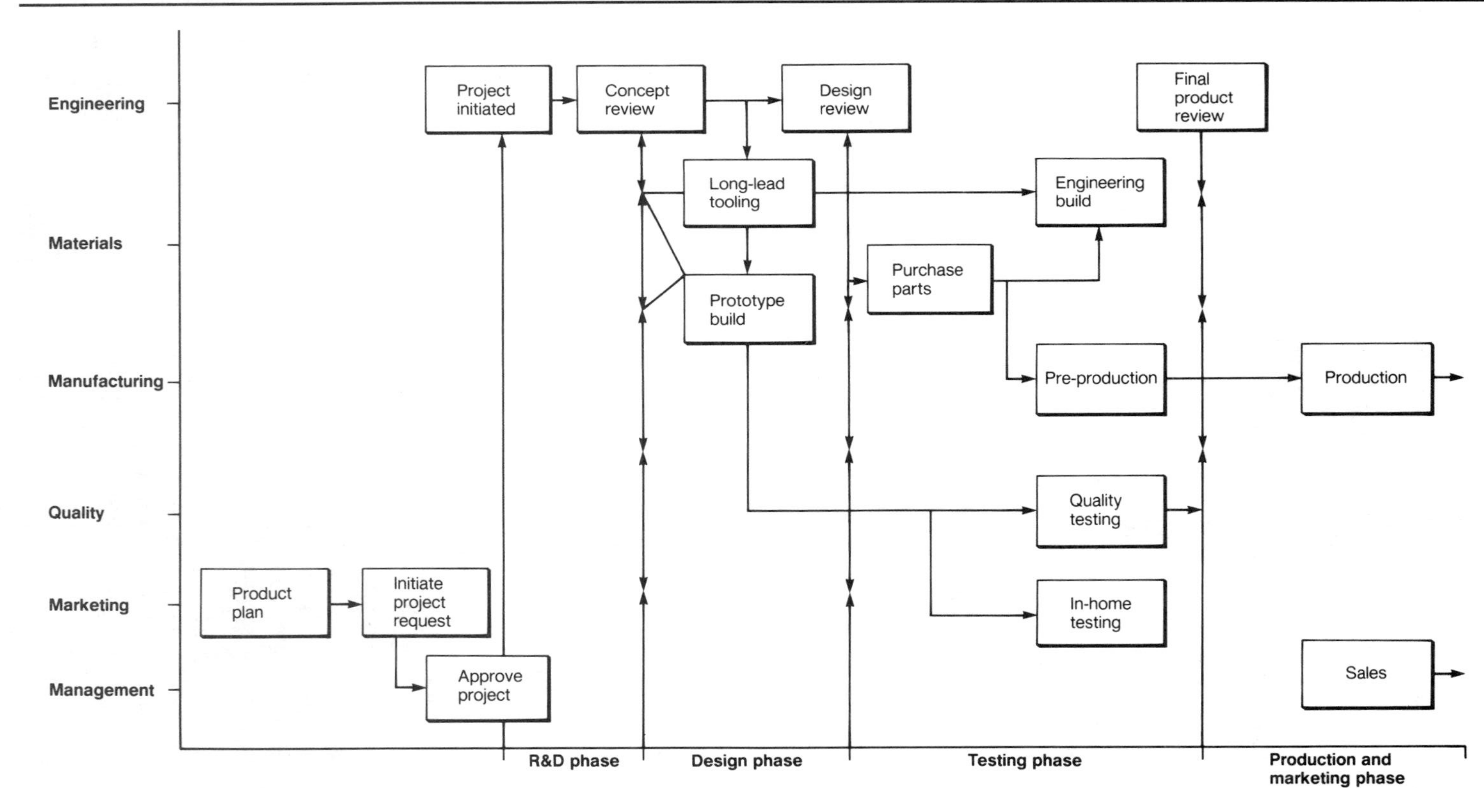

Source: Bill George, "Task Teams for Rapid Growth," *Harvard Business Review,* March–April 1977.

product review was typically handled by personnel in the product engineering area, but engineers on the original design team would stay on board as needed. The product engineering group was also involved in firefighting projects when engineering design or redesign was needed on an emergency basis to overcome problems in an existing product. In addition, members of the product engineering group participated in cost reduction and product improvement projects. Thus most of the day-to-day interaction between engineering and operations was handled by this group. The relationship was described as being "as good as can be expected between engineering and operations." The majority of the problems arose in products in the range line, which was being continually developed.

In engineering, the major organizational concern was whether the group could expand rapidly enough to keep up with the new-product development requirements generated by marketing. On the average, it took six months to fill authorized openings because of the tight hiring market for engineers. In the words of one engineering executive:

> *Individuals will give you 12 hours a day for only so long. Then batteries begin to discharge. If they are not recharged, a lot of them will leave. It is the inflow of new people that keeps this place charged with energy.*

An engineering manager who had been at Litton Microwave for many years had this reaction, however:

> *I work more hours than perhaps anyone else in engineering. I wouldn't want it any other way! The average engineer is putting in about 50 hours per week. There is some complaining, but not a great deal. This is an exciting place to work because we are at the forefront of microwave engineering technology.*

Jack Blake, vice president of engineering, attempted to put the problem in perspective:

> *We have not been able to staff up to the authorized level because the hiring market for engineers is extremely tight and we are very demanding in selecting the people we want. Typically, about 10 candidates are interviewed in Minneapolis for every 1 that we hire. Only two engineers have left in the last three years. About a year ago a competitor hired one of our best engineers away by offering him a $10,000 salary increase. Two months ago this person called me and asked if he could return to work with us at his old salary. He said he missed the professional excitement of being at the forefront technologically. I was glad to have him back.*

The Engineering Department generally recruited persons with prior work experience. For project manager positions, it sought M.B.A.s with engineering backgrounds and 7 to 15 years' work experience. Others hired typically had 3 to 5 years of experience. Fewer than 5 percent were fresh engineering graduates. Talent was located through newspaper advertisements and the services of headhunters, rather than campus visits. A human resources manager assigned to engineering assisted in the recruitment process.

Bill George's Involvement in Task Team Meetings. Bill George took part in several engineering task team meetings. Some felt his participation furthered the development of middle managers because he would ask probing questions and demand thorough analysis and well-thought-out recommendations. Others, however, felt George was stifling middle management development and undermining the team leader's authority by his awesome presence in these meetings.

The casewriter sat in on a few task team meetings to observe Bill George's involvement. Subsequent conversations with various participants indicated that the observed meetings were fairly typical. The team leader sat at the head of the table and led the meeting. Bill George sat in one corner and listened more than he talked. But whenever the task team was reaching a consensus or the team leader a decision that George disagreed with, he would jump in with a volley of penetrating questions: What about the ____ problem? How are we going to cope with ____? Have you thought about the consequences of ____? If the questioning revealed problems that had not been anticipated or well thought through, he would suggest that additional work be done before any decisions were made. Occasionally when deliberation reached an impasse, Bill George would take a position: "I think we ought to ____."

Some felt that this kind of behavior was the best form of management development. As one of them stated:

> *Bill George is not saying, "Do this because I am the president." He doesn't have the "correct solution" figured out in advance, nor does he play the "I've got the answer, you guess it" game that some managers like to play. He is saying, "I think your analysis is faulty, and this is why. Show me that I am wrong or do something about it." If this is not the best form of coaching and development, I don't know what is. And I don't think this hurts the team leader either. The good team leader will ask: "Why didn't* I *think of asking those questions?" Everyone should be better prepared the next time.*

Others, however, wondered whether Bill George's presence in the meetings might not impede the development of the very managers he hoped to assist. Given his formal power within the organization and the fact that he was right 90 percent of the time, it was very difficult for middle management to challenge his analysis. In effect, they felt they had little opportunity to translate their own thinking into actions and learn from the consequences of those actions. George's critics conceded that errors would definitely impose certain costs in the short run if these managers were allowed to make more decisions, but believed that the development of middle management would be enhanced in the long run. This would become a crucial factor when the company passed

$500 million in sales, as was expected to happen within the next few years. Because of the sheer size and technological complexity of the business, any one person, no matter how bright and energetic, would then be unable to oversee all the important business decisions. One manager remarked:

> *An informal organization with one man in firm control can work under the $50 million sales level. The transition from $50 to $100 million is gear wrenching. The organization becomes formalized. Beyond $500 million the organization becomes totally structured. Bill George is a "hands-on" manager and has done an exceptional job so far with his attention to detail. He must now learn to adopt a different style. It calls for sitting in the office and managing people via budgets and numbers rather than by direct involvement in operating decisions.*

Operations

Production workers were paid on an hourly basis, with no incentive compensation. For most the job was a relatively low-skill assembly operation, and wage rates ranged between $4 and $5.50 an hour. The 1,400 members of the hourly labor force at Litton Microwave were represented by the United Electrical and Machine Workers Union, which had successfully negotiated a new 41-month contract with the company effective May 10, 1976. Union and management had always had a good working relationship.

Turnover among the hourly workers had always been rather high, averaging 25 percent per year. It was not difficult to find the needed replacements locally, and it did not take long to get new workers up to speed since relatively little skill was needed for the light assembly work to be done. Capable first-line supervisors, however, were extremely hard to recruit. Because of the task and the composition of the hourly work force, good supervisory interpersonal skills were needed in addition to technical skills. One unit manager commented:

> *Most jobs are growing faster than we can define or staff them. What is unique to growth is that experience is measured in months rather than in years. Because of the tight market for good first-line supervisors, many of those we recruit are not only new to Litton but new to the trade and new to the job as well.*

New supervisors were sent to short outside training programs, covering both technical subjects and topics such as leadership training. The prevailing view among managers, including Bill George, was that more needed to be done to strengthen the first level of management.

Each of the product lines (range, commercial, and countertop), was headed by a plant manager who reported to the vice president of operations. Reporting to the plant manager were one or more unit managers responsible for all aspects of manufacturing one or more of the company's product lines. Each unit manager was in charge of a self-contained task team, which typically comprised two to four first-line supervisors, a product engineer, production engineers, quality inspectors, material handlers, schedulers, and 75–200 production workers. It was the task team under the unit manager that made the day-to-day decisions involved in the manufacturing process. They were responsible for product quality, direct and indirect costs, product schedules, scrap, etc., and were assisted on an as-required basis by specialists in design and product engineering (under the vice president of engineering), cost accounting (under the vice president of finance), and human resources.

Some managers within the operations area were also concerned about top management involvement in task team meetings. One of them observed, "I have the responsibility but not the authority to make decisions. We go through a lot of turmoil because the president and the vice presidents have failed to delegate authority." Another pointed to a related concern:

> *Growth offers the unwritten promise of advancement opportunities, but the promotion we anticipate may never come. There is no time to train us, and untested people are being brought in from outside. That's frustrating. If this keeps up, there may be a mass exodus of middle management.*

Within operations, there was no consensus on the adequacy of staffing authorizations. One manager dwelled on the virtues of running lean: "You need tight budgets. I feel secure running lean. I feel good running lean." Another remarked, "Obtaining staffing authorization is no problem if I can justify my needs. The difficulty is in finding the right people soon enough after I get staffing approval. *That* has been a problem." One senior manager with a broad overview of the operations area held a somewhat contrary view:

> *Our plans are more aggressive than the resources that are available. Marketing and finance have been staffed in such a way that their organizations are now in place. One of the last areas to go that way is operations.*

Marketing and Sales

Reporting to the president of the marketing and sales division, Dan Cavalier, were directors of market planning, marketing communication, and marketing services (including consumer affairs, sales administration and transportation, and service and parts warranty), and vice presidents responsible for commercial, private-brand, and consumer sales.

As vice president of consumer sales, Si Ware headed the biggest group within marketing and sales. Consumer sales, including both countertops and ranges, were handled by 52 independent distributors as well as by appliance dealers in 12 major metropolitan areas. The consumer sales force was organized into four regions (west, central, east, and south), each headed by a regional manager (in Los Angeles, Chicago, New York, and Dallas). Each region had four to seven district managers, one or two distributor sales managers, and a home economist who handled product demonstrations.

The district managers, who were the field salespersons, were responsible for direct market sales in the major metropolitan areas, which represented 40 percent of Litton's consumer sales. Each district manager handled 30 to 40 accounts. They had to spend time with the dealer demonstrating microwave ovens, helping to plan the merchandising of the products, and training retail salespeople. Scheduling calls on accounts was entirely up to each district manager but the company insisted that all calls be preplanned. A monthly call report plan had to be sent in advance to the regional manager, and daily call report sheets were submitted at the end of each week.

Independent distributors in other markets represented 60 percent of Litton consumer sales. Distributor sales managers called on these accounts once a month, encouraging them to purchase in accordance with a quarterly sales plan.

Finance

The senior vice president of finance and administration reported directly to Bill George and also had a dotted-line relationship with Litton's corporate vice president for finance. Reporting to Litton Microwave's senior vice president of finance were a director of business planning, an operations controller, a general controller, and a director of management information systems.

The director of business planning was responsible for developing the details of the division's annual business plan. A distinction was made between the Sales Plan, which represented the volume level that could be realized with aggressive marketing, and Plan I, a more conservative estimate for which corporate approval was sought.[2] Except for the engineering and sales departments, staffing authorization levels were based on the sales level of Plan I rather than the Sales Plan. Bill George explained the rationale for adopting this procedure:

> *We are staffing based on a conservative level of sales because if we staffed at the Sales Plan level and the projected increases of 60–70 percent were not realized, we would have to lay people off. I believe management has a strong obligation not to lay people off. That is one of the reasons I admire the management at IBM—they haven't had a layoff in 37 years.*

In January 1976, a new manpower planning and flexible budgeting procedure was introduced. Essentially, function heads were asked to esti-

---

[2] In fiscal 1976, for example, the Sales Plan level was $176 million and Plan I was $125 million. Actual sales in fiscal 1976 were $186 million.

mate their staffing requirements for several revenue levels, e.g., $250, $350, and $500 million, rather than at Plan I levels only. It was hoped that this procedure would make it easier and quicker to obtain additional staffing authorization as the business grew. In the past, function heads had been reluctant to seek budget exceptions. When they did, it usually took some time to justify the need for additional personnel and obtain approval. The flexible budgeting procedure did not constitute a staffing approval but was designed to expedite such approval by forcing function heads to look ahead and anticipate their staffing needs at various volume levels. Except in engineering and sales, staffing authorization at the beginning of the fiscal year continued at the Plan I level.

International

Exports of consumer countertop ovens and commercial units to Canada and several industrialized nations in Europe accounted for approximately 10 percent of the company's total revenue. There were no assembly operations outside the United States.

Human Resources

The presence of a human resources department at the same organizational level as operations, finance, engineering, and marketing gave formal recognition to Bill George's conviction that human resources were every bit as important as physical, fiscal, technological, and market resources. Human resource managers were assigned to work with each of the functions, with responsibility for all the people issues in that function. Each function was responsible for hiring, performance review, compensation, promotion, and termination decisions in its own area. The human resources manager assigned to that function provided staff assistance. In addition, the department of human resources handled team-building sessions, training, and career development.

Team Building. The task team concept used at Litton Microwave had its beginning in the team-building program that Bill George initiated soon after becoming executive vice president of the division in August 1971. The program began with a series of offsite seminars with the top management group conducted by Doug Baker, a local consultant. The purpose of the program was to develop the general management skills of top managers and facilitate communication between the various functions. A variety of learning devices was used, including an exercise written especially for the company, general management case studies, and a questionnaire on organization issues. Reflecting on these sessions, Bill George observed:

Particular attention was directed to my management style and to my willingness or unwillingness to delegate greater decision-making authority. The inputs from these sessions helped me adapt my style to the needs of the emerging organization.

The initial program was so successful that it was extended to all managers within the company and expanded to include a broad range of organizational development activities. Soon after Bill George was promoted to president of the division in August 1973, he convinced Doug Baker, the outside consultant, to join the company on a full-time basis to set up the human resources function and to extend the team-building program throughout the division (Exhibit 7).

As of October 1976, all five function heads and several managers reporting to these heads had held team-building sessions for their own groups. The top four levels of management had met several times for group team-building sessions. In addition, the team concept had been spread to other levels of the organization through a series of meetings involving all employees—crew meetings held by unit managers, dialogue sessions between the president and 12–15 employees at various organizational levels, quarterly business reviews for production and office workers, etc. Recently the human resources department had introduced interaction sessions between two functions. Five to 10 key managers from each function got together for a day to identify and work on overcoming barriers between them. The top management group continued offsite team-building sessions about twice a year.

The meetings at the various organizational levels amounted to a considerable investment of time not only for Bill George (who spent more than 75 percent of his working time in meetings) but for other managers as well. Many people, including all of top management, believed that this investment of time had helped foster a feeling of openness and "oneness" within the company and had played a crucial role in the company's dramatic success. One person remarked, "Jealousy is almost nonexistent in this company. Individuals feel free to share their problems and frustrations with others." Another said, "There is very little 'politics.' People are open and direct rather than scheming and spiteful." These views were widely shared.

Although most credited the team-building sessions with developing the feeling of openness, there were some skeptics. One engineering manager commented:

Jobs are growing faster than people. How do you handle those without the needed horsepower as the job grows? Training programs can *help, but human resources needs to first get their own show together and then begin to do more follow-up with other functions. Last month, for example, we had a three-day meeting of all eight engineering department heads. The human resources manager was invited to come along, but it was a meeting arranged at* our *initiative and* by us. *It went very well.*

Exhibit 7
Organizational Development Activities at Litton Microwave*

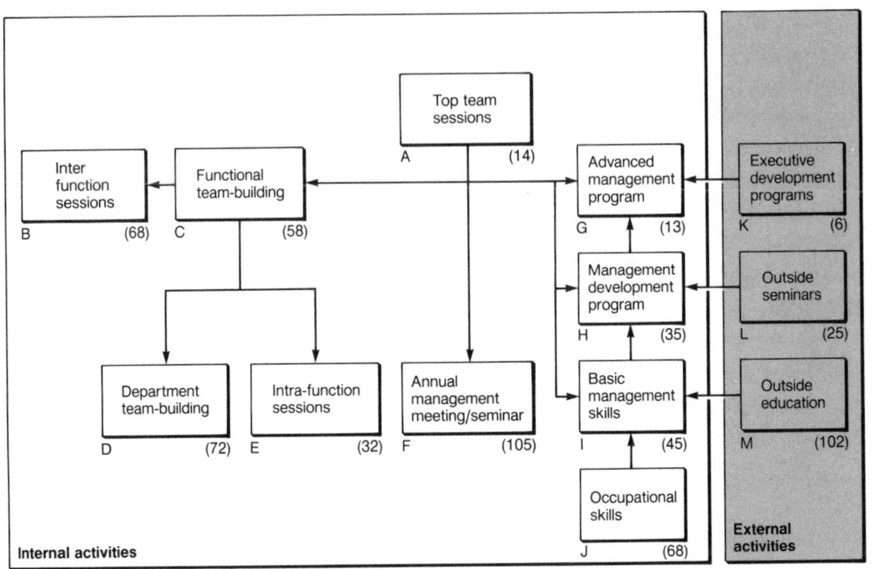

Note: Numbers in parentheses indicate the number of people that participated in each of the activities during fiscal 1976.

* Explanatory notes keyed to alphabetical designations:

A. Team-building sessions for president and functional heads.
B. Team-building sessions involving managers from two different functions. One day or less in duration.
C. Functional head and the department managers reporting to the functional head. One day or less in duration.
D. Department head and key managers reporting to the department head. One day or less in duration.
E. Team-building sessions involving a functional head, department managers, and other managers in the functional area. One day or less in duration.
F. President, functional heads, department managers, and lower-level managers. One day in duration. Dealing with issues of organization, use of time, etc. Frequently involved an outside consultant.
G. Functional heads and key managers. Six days spread over several weeks, using a couple of outside consultants. Dealt with high-level managerial skills.
H. Orientation program for new managers. Three and a half days in duration.
I. First-line supervisors. Four and a half days in duration. Interpersonal skills and leadership training.
J. Secretarial and factory personnel (e.g., forklift truck operators). One to three days in duration.
K. Such as Harvard's two-week summer programs. Management of organizational effectiveness, production management, etc.
L. Such as American Management Association's one- or two-day programs for management development.
M. Tuition reimbursement for evening courses.

Source: Litton Microwave Cooking Products.

Recruitment, Selection, and Training. Human resources had to spend a great deal of time in staffing the ever-increasing number of positions to be filled. The hiring market for experienced engineers and first-line supervisors was extremely tight, and these positions were hard to fill. Most of the recruiting was done in the Midwest. The division's location in Minneapolis–St. Paul proved to be a selling point in recruiting. Several individuals who had been recently hired commented on how pleased they were with their new community. A typical comment was, "It is a great place to raise a family. We have good schools, clean air, low crime, and plenty of activities outdoors. The Twin Cities' metropolitan area also provides excellent cultural events." Many people who had initial reservations liked the Minneapolis–St. Paul area once they settled in. Several of those recently hired were either from the area originally or had lived there before and had chosen to return.

The selection process was generally perceived as effective. Even those who were sorry to see top jobs going to outsiders agreed that those hired were capable and productive. A recently hired unit manager observed:

> *The selection process is as thorough as I have seen it anywhere. I was interviewed on four different occasions, including sessions with Doug Baker (vice president of human resources), Ron March (manager of human resources—operations area), Steve Dill (the recruiter), and Paul Westgard (vice president of operations).*

Several managers, especially in operations and engineering, complained bitterly about the length of time it took to fill key positions. An operations manager remarked, "It has sometimes taken six months to fill supervisory and managerial positions under me, and I have had to raise holy hell with human resources." A manager in engineering echoed the same theme: "The average time taken to fill authorized staff openings in engineering is six months. It should take no longer than three months in spite of the relatively tight job market in engineering."

The lag in hiring in fiscal 1976 was generally attributed to the fact that the human resources department itself was short on staff. In July 1976, Bill George authorized a major expansion of the employment department within the human resources function.

An important staffing issue was the recruitment of outsiders to fill high positions. During the past three years, 43 percent of all managerial openings had been filled by hiring from the outside. The remaining positions were filled by promotions from within the division. Managers who were passed over in filling new openings felt doubly frustrated: they were not being promoted, and at the same time they had to run lean. Bill George was well aware of this predicament:

> *Above-average performers have problems when we bring people in from the outside to fill positions that they aspire to. We like to promote from within whenever possible, but I do not believe in putting people in positions for which they are not qualified. With our rapid growth we have to be sure the individual can handle the position in two or three years when it will likely double in size and complexity.*
>
> *We should do more to help our people develop. For example, by providing lateral moves when promotion is not possible. But the rapid growth we are experiencing prevents us from promoting as much as we would like to from within.*

Hard data on the average tenure of nonhourly employees at Litton Microwave were not available, but estimates varied between 12 and 18 months for the nonmanagerial staff, and between 18 and 24 months for the 180 managerial employees. Turnover had not been high; rather, the short average tenure reflected the large number of new hires needed to sustain the division's rapid growth.

The large influx of people from the outside presented the division with the problem of socializing the newcomers and bringing them up to speed rapidly. New hires were given a one- to three-day general orientation by human resources (the longer sessions were for those at higher levels in the organization). Most new recruits found these sessions very useful. One recently hired manager commented:

The company is extremely open to the newcomer, and that helps speed up the socialization process. But we need a more formalized training program for our new hires. At present, the company uses on-the-job training only. Some form of job-rotation training would help.

Doug Baker, vice president of human resources, responded as follows:

Every new managerial employee participates in a three and one half day, offsite team-building seminar no later than six months after joining us. The seminar has a very strong orientation flavor and involves about 18–25 persons who are new to their jobs, to Litton Microwave, or both. It would be nice to have a formalized training program that goes beyond this, but we cannot afford that luxury. We run a tight ship and a fast pace around here and on-the-job training provides the most efficient means of getting a new employee up to speed.

Career Development. In early 1976, a comprehensive career development program was introduced along with the manpower planning and flexible budgeting procedure. The program was aimed at developing the management, professional, and staff capabilities required to support the growing needs of the company, meshing the career desires and interests of the individual with the job requirements identified in the annual manpower planning process. At the heart of the program was a job-posting system to enable the individual to participate actively in his or her own career planning. Although the career development program was generally well received, both employees and management had some concerns. Employees felt they did not always get a good explanation of why they were not selected for a given position they had sought. Some top managers, including Bill George, were worried that employees and young managers might develop unrealistic expectations about just how much a growth company could offer in terms of career opportunities. For this reason, one department head chose not to discuss with his subordinates the potential career paths and openings he had in mind for them before they were actually appointed to these positions.

Performance Evaluation. The evaluation program was used both as a communication and counseling tool in performance planning and as a basis for performance evaluation. Its specific objectives were to achieve an understanding with the employee as to what was expected, how expectations were being met, and ways to improve performance; to establish a written record of employee accomplishments, future job expectations, training and development needs, and career goals; and to provide the manager a means of rating the employee's overall performance as a primary consideration for salary purposes. There was a general sense of satisfaction with the performance evaluation program.

Rewards. Employees generally described the pay scales as "competitive, but not great." Several people reported a sense of intrinsic satisfaction in working at Litton Microwave, and hoped that the company's growth in the future might offer them a considerable payoff in the form of greater responsibility and career advancement opportunities.

Most professional and managerial personnel were paid a straight salary. Only a few key employees were selected for participation in an incentive compensation program tied to individual contribution and company profitability. Selection criteria included: scope of managerial responsibility (generally department heads and above qualified); relative level of earnings; and the individual's potential contribution to division profits.

At the beginning of the fiscal year, those selected for the incentive compensation program were informed of their "base award percentage," i.e., the proportion of the individual's annual base salary that would be paid as incentive compensation. The actual base award percentage used in computing incentives was dependent on the level of actual pretax profit achieved (no awards were made if profits fell below 85 percent of the Plan I target) and was tied explicitly to the individual's performance rating. The marketing area offered a similar program, in which the base award percentage was influenced equally by performance against profit and sales targets.

The Situation in October 1976

A University of Minnesota research team had conducted an employee attitude survey of all nonunion employees at Litton Microwave in May 1976. Several feedback sessions were conducted during August and September 1976 to report survey results to the employees and ask them to define specific problems and solutions.

The substantive issues raised by most groups during these feedback sessions revolved around questions of delegation, staffing, and compensation. There was a general employee perception that not enough decision-making authority was delegated downward to allow middle managers the latitude necessary for solving the problems of a rapidly growing organization. The problem of inadequate staffing was generally attributed to budgeting based on too conservative a level of sales. Compensation was an issue because of unmet employee expectations and a feeling that individual contributions to divisional success were not properly recognized. These findings were presented to Bill George and the various function heads by the research team on October 4, 1976.

In a memo to all function heads dated October 22, 1976, Bill George described in detail the areas requiring review and approval by various executives (Exhibit 8), concluding as follows:

> *Comments we receive from middle management indicate to me that this delegation system (and its intentions) is not well understood by them. I hope you will take advantage of this opportunity to review the delegation* within *your function, develop the delegation of authority* and *responsibility to get the job done, yet retain control for yourself of the most crucial areas.*

The University of Minnesota survey had indicated that some employees attributed the delegation problem to the management level immediately above them. Others, however, pointed higher. George responded:

> *We are delegating not out of necessity as growth occurs but as management talent develops and broadens its outlook.*
>
> *When I took over this division back in 1971, my first order of priority was to build a strong top management team. We did that by 1973. Since then we have been concentrating on the middle management level. With the actions to date, this area is now okay in my view. Our need today is for building a strong first-line supervisory level.*
>
> *Overall, the key issue is managing growth under control. Our growth has not only been high over a long period of time, it is in a technologically complex business. Rapid growth in a simple business like the manufacture of metal chairs is one thing. Continuing rapid growth in a business requiring constant innovation is a different game altogether. About 90 percent of our products are new every year!*

Looking to the future in October 1976, Bill George was wondering whether a change to a product-line organization would help alleviate some of the division's difficulties. Under this arrangement, each major product line (range, commercial, and countertop), would be headed by a "mini general manager" with the appropriate engineering, marketing, operations, and human resources personnel reporting directly to him or her. Such a change would represent a major reorganization.

George had seriously considered this alternative earlier but had decided against it, feeling that the division was not large enough to make a product-line organization economically viable. Moreover, he had felt that the needed management talent was not available. Now that the company was much larger and top management had been built up, Bill George was once again contemplating the question of moving to a product-line organization:

> *In this business, the key organization question is how one achieves integration between the functions. Delegating authority* within *a given function is relatively*

Exhibit 8
Areas Requiring Review (R) and Approval (A) by Various Executives, Fiscal Year 1977

	President	President Marketing/ Sales Division	Vice President and General Manager International*	Function Head	Senior Vice President Finance and Adminis- tration	Vice President Human Resources
A. Hiring						
1. Requisitions						
In Plan I, approved Sales Plan or flexible budget				A		R
Head count or budget exceptions	A			A		A
2. Salary offers						
$24,000 base salary and up	A			A		A
$15,000–$24,000				A		A
3. Interviews						
Managers on incentive compensation or marketing commission	A			A		A
B. Salary/compensation						
1. Salary increases						
$24,000 and up	A			A		A
$15,000–$24,000				A		A
2. Incentive compensation or marketing commission						
Eligibility	A	A	A	A		R
Payout	A	A	A	A		R
3. Sales commissions						
Plan		A	A		A	A
Payout						

Exhibit 8 *(continued)*

	President	President Marketing/ Sales Division	Vice President and General Manager International*	Function Head	Senior Vice President Finance and Adminis- tration	Vice President Human Resources
C. Job classifications						
1. New positions and changes in existing positions						
Grade 60 and above	A			A		A
Grade 59 and below				A		A
D. Budgets						
1. Plan I	A			A	A	
2. Budget exceptions						
Advertising						
In Sales Plan		A			R	
Above Sales Plan	A	A			A	
Department						
In approved Sales Plan or flexible budget				A	R	
Exempt managers	A			A	R	
Other than exempt managers					A	R
Not in approved Sales Plan or flexible budget	A				A	
3. Budget transfers (other than advertising)						
Over $25,000	A			A	A	
Under $25,000				A	A	
4. Advertising budget transfers						
Over $100,000	A	A			A	

Under $100,000		A			A
E. Capital and tooling expenditures 1. Within department Plan I budget $25,000 and up	A			A	A
$10,000–$25,000				A	A
2. Above department Plan I budget Above $10,000	A			A	A
Under $10,000				A	A
F. Engineering projects 1. In Plan I $15,000 and up	A			A	
Under $15,000				A	
2. Not in Plan I Over $5,000	A			A	
Under $5,000				A	
G. Marketing programs 1. Marketing plans (annual)	A	A	A		R
2. National advertising Creative concept	A	A			
Budget Media schedules		A			
Creative implementation		A			
3. Sales promotions In Plan I/Sales Plan budget $300,000 and up	A	A	A		R

Exhibit 8 ***(concluded)***

	President	President Marketing/ Sales Division	Vice President and General Manager International*	Function Head	Senior Vice President Finance and Adminis-tration	Vice President Human Resources
Under $300,000		A	A		R	
Not in Plan I/Sales Plan budget $30,000 and up	A	A	A		A	
Under $30,000		A	A		A	
H. Pricing 1. Suggested list prices	A	A	A		A	
2. New discount schedules	A	A	A		A	
3. Price exceptions		A	A			
4. Customer classifications		A	A			
I. Warranties 1. Revisions to terms	A	A	A		A	
J. Terms of sales		A	A		A	
K. Computer projects (major) 1. In Plan I					A	
2. Not in Plan I	A				A	
L. 12-month production plan	R			A (VP Ops)	R	
M. Purchase orders 1. Over $500,000				A (VP Ops)		

N. Press releases				
1. National	A	A	A	
2. Local Trade		A	A	
O. Product planning and development				
1. Product plans	A	A	A	R (VP Engr)
2. Feature decisions	A	A	A	A (VP Engr)
3. Styling	R	A	A	R (VP Engr)
4. Major technical decision	R			A (VP Engr)
5. Schedules	A	R	R	{A (VP Engr) R (VP Ops)}
6. Costs	R	R	R	{A (VP Engr) R (VP Ops)}

* Outside the United States.
Source: Litton Microwave Cooking Products.

easy to do. Achieving the necessary coordination across *the various functions is much more difficult. So far, I have played that key role, with much of the integration at lower levels being carried out by task team leaders. We are now reaching the point at which we may need four or five top-level integrators like myself. I am wondering whether a move to a product-line organization will help achieve the necessary cross-functional coordination in the most efficient manner.*

Reading 8–1

Evolution and Revolution as Organizations Grow*

Larry E. Greiner

A small research company chooses too complicated and formalized an organization structure for its young age and limited size. It flounders in rigidity and bureaucracy for several years and is finally acquired by a larger company.

Key executives of a retail store chain hold on to an organization structure long after it has served its purpose, because their power is derived from this structure. The company eventually goes into bankruptcy.

A large bank disciplines a "rebellious" manager who is blamed for current control problems, when the underlying cause is centralized procedures that are holding back expansion into new markets. Many younger managers subsequently leave the bank, competition moves in, and profits are still declining.

The problems of these companies, like those of many others, are rooted more in past decisions than in present events or outside market dynamics. Historical forces do indeed shape the future growth of organizations. Yet management, in its haste to grow, often overlooks such critical developmental questions as: Where has our organization been? Where is it now? And what do the answers to these questions mean for where we are going? Instead, its gaze is fixed outward toward the environment and the future—as if more precise market projections will provide a new organizational identity.

---

* Reprinted by permission of the *Harvard Business Review.* "Evolution and Revolution as Organizations Grow" by Larry E. Greiner (July/August 1972). This article is part of a continuing project on organization development with the author's colleague, Professor Louis B. Barnes, and sponsored by the Division of Research, Harvard Business School.

Companies fail to see that many clues to their future success lie within their own organizations and their evolving states of development. Moreover, the inability of management to understand its organization development problems can result in a company becoming "frozen" in its present stage of evolution or, ultimately, in failure, regardless of market opportunities.

My position in this article is that the future of an organization may be less determined by outside forces than it is by the organization's history. In stressing the force of history on an organization, I have drawn from the legacies of European psychologists (their thesis being that individual behavior is determined primarily by previous events and experiences, not by what lies ahead). Extending this analogy of individual development to the problems of organization development, I shall discuss a series of developmental phases through which growing companies tend to pass. But, first, let me provide two definitions:

1. The term *evolution* is used to describe prolonged periods of growth where no major upheaval occurs in organization practices.
2. The term *revolution* is used to describe those periods of substantial turmoil in organization life.

As a company progresses through developmental phases, each evolutionary period creates its own revolution. For instance, centralized practices eventually lead to demands for decentralization. Moreover, the nature of management's solution to each revolutionary period determines whether a company will move forward into its next stage of evolutionary growth. As I shall show later, there are at least five phases of organization development, each characterized by both an evolution and a revolution.

Key Forces in Development

During the past few years a small amount of research knowledge about the phases of organization development has been building. Some of this research is very quantitative, such as time series analyses that reveal patterns of economic performance over time.[1] The majority of studies, however, are case oriented and use company records and interviews to reconstruct a rich picture of corporate development.[2] Yet both types of research tend to be heavily empirical without attempting more generalized statements about the overall process of development.

---

[1] See, for example, William H. Starbuck, "Organizational Metamorphosis," in *Promising Research Directions,* ed. R. W. Millman and M. P. Hottenstein (Tempe, Ariz.: Academy of Management, 1968), p. 113.

[2] See, for example, the *Grangesberg* case series, prepared by C. Roland Christensen and Bruce R. Scott (Boston: Intercollegiate Case Clearing House, Harvard Business School).

A notable exception is the historical work of Alfred D. Chandler, Jr., in his book *Strategy and Structure.*[3] This study depicts four very broad and general phases in the lives of four large U.S. companies. It proposes that outside market opportunities determine a company's strategy, which in turn determines the company's organization structure. This thesis has a valid ring for the four companies examined by Chandler, largely because they developed in a time of explosive markets and technological advances. But more recent evidence suggests that organization structure may be less malleable than Chandler assumed; in fact, structure can play a critical role in influencing corporate strategy. It is this reverse emphasis on how organization structure affects future growth which is highlighted in the model presented in this article.

From an analysis of recent studies,[4] five key dimensions emerge as essential for building a model of organization development:

1. Age of the organization.
2. Size of the organization.
3. Stages of evolution.
4. Stages of revolution.
5. Growth rate of the industry.

I shall describe each of these elements separately, but first note their combined effect as illustrated in Exhibit 1. Note especially how each dimension influences the other over time; when all five elements begin to interact, a more complete and dynamic picture of organizational growth emerges.

After describing these dimensions and their interconnections. I shall discuss each evolutionary/revolutionary phase of development and show *(a)* how each stage of evolution breeds its own revolution, and *(b)* how management solutions to each revolution determine the next stage of evolution.

Age of the Organization

The most obvious and essential dimension for any model of development is the life span of an organization (represented as the horizontal axis

---

[3] *Strategy and Structure: Chapters in the History of the American Industrial Enterprise* (Cambridge, Mass.: MIT Press, 1962).

[4] I have drawn on many sources for evidence: *(a)* numerous cases collected at the Harvard Business School; *(b) Organization Growth and Development,* ed. William H. Starbuck (Middlesex, England: Penguin Books, 1971), where several studies are cited; and *(c)* articles published in journals, such as Lawrence E. Fouraker and John M. Stopford, "Organization Structure and the Multinational Strategy," *Administrative Science Quarterly* 13, no. 1 (1968), p. 47; and Malcolm S. Salter, "Management Appraisal and Reward Systems," *Journal of Business Policy* 1, no. 4 (1971).

Exhibit 1
Model of Organization Development

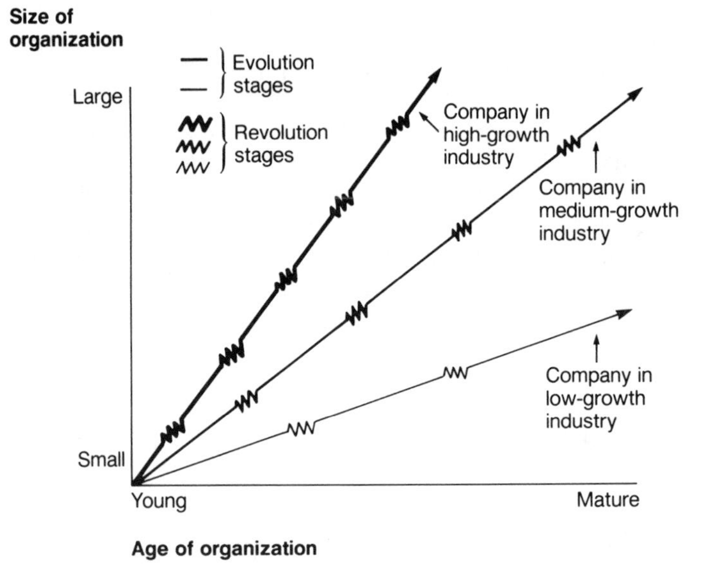

in Exhibit 1). All historical studies gather data from various points in time and then make comparisons. From these observations, it is evident that the same organization practices are not maintained throughout a long time span. This makes a most basic point: management problems and principles are rooted in time. The concept of decentralization, for example, can have meaning for describing corporate practices at one time period but loses its descriptive power at another.

The passage of time also contributes to the institutionalization of managerial attitudes. As a result, employee behavior becomes not only more predictable but also more difficult to change when attitudes are outdated.

Size of the Organization

This dimension is depicted as the vertical axis in Exhibit 1. A company's problems and solutions tend to change markedly as the number of employees and sales volume increase. Thus, time is not the only determinant of structure; in fact, organizations that do not grow in size can retain many of the same management issues and practices over lengthy periods. In addition to increased size, however, problems of coordination and communication magnify, new functions emerge, levels in the management hierarchy multiply, and jobs become more interrelated.

Stages of Evolution

As both age and size increase, another phenomenon becomes evident: the prolonged growth that I have termed the evolutionary period. Most growing organizations do not expand for two years and then retreat for one year; rather, those that survive a crisis usually enjoy four to eight years of continuous growth without a major economic setback or severe internal disruption. The term *evolution* seems appropriate for describing these quieter periods because only modest adjustments appear necessary for maintaining growth under the same overall pattern of management.

Stages of Revolution

Smooth evolution is not inevitable; it cannot be assumed that organization growth is linear. *Fortune*'s "500" list, for example, has had significant turnover during the last 50 years. Thus we find evidence from numerous case histories which reveals periods of substantial turbulence spaced between smoother periods of evolution.

I have termed these turbulent times the periods of revolution because they typically exhibit a serious upheaval of management practices. Traditional management practices, which were appropriate for a smaller size and earlier time, are brought under scrutiny by frustrated top managers and disillusioned lower-level managers. During such periods of crisis, a number of companies fail—those unable to abandon past practices and effect major organization changes are likely either to fold or to level off in their growth rates.

The critical task for management in each revolutionary period is to find a new set of organization practices that will become the basis for managing the next period of evolutionary growth. Interestingly enough, these new practices eventually sow their own seeds of decay and lead to another period of revolution. Companies therefore experience the irony of seeing a major solution in one time period become a major problem at a later date.

Growth Rate of the Industry

The speed at which an organization experiences phases of evolution and revolution is closely related to the market environment of its industry. For example, a company in a rapidly expanding market will have to add employees rapidly; hence, the need for new organization structures to accommodate large staff increases is accelerated. While evolutionary periods tend to be relatively short in fast-growing industries, much longer evolutionary periods occur in mature or slowly growing industries.

Evolution can also be prolonged, and revolutions delayed, when profits come easily. For instance, companies that make grievous errors in a rewarding industry can still look good on their profit and loss statements; thus they can avoid a change in management practices for a longer period. The aerospace industry in its infancy is an example. Yet revolutionary periods still occur, as one did in aerospace when profit opportunities began to dry up. Revolutions seem to be much more severe and difficult to resolve when the market environment is poor.

Phases of Growth

With the foregoing framework in mind, let us now examine in depth the five specific phases of evolution and revolution. As shown in Exhibit 2, each evolutionary period is characterized by the dominant *management style* used to achieve growth, while each revolutionary period is characterized by the dominant *management problem* that must be solved before growth can continue. The patterns presented in Exhibit 2 seem to be typical for companies in industries with moderate growth over a long time period; companies in faster-growing industries tend to experience all five phases more rapidly, while those in slower-growing industries encounter only two or three phases over many years.

It is important to note that *each phase is both an effect of the previous phase and a cause for the next phase.* For example, the evolutionary management style in Phase 3 of the exhibit is "delegation," which grows out of, and becomes the solution to, demands for greater "autonomy" in the preceding Phase 2 revolution. The style of delegation used in Phase 3, however, eventually provokes a major revolutionary crisis that is characterized by attempts to regain control over the diversity created through increased delegation.

The principal implication of each phase is that management actions are narrowly prescribed if growth is to occur. For example, a company experiencing an autonomy crisis in Phase 2 cannot return to directive management for a solution—it must adopt a new style of delegation in order to move ahead.

Phase 1: Creativity

In the birth stage of an organization, the emphasis is on creating both a product and a market. Here are the characteristics of the period of creative evolution:

- The company's founders are usually technically or entrepreneurially oriented, and they disdain management activities; their physical and mental energies are absorbed entirely in making and selling a new product.
- Communication among employees is frequent and informal.

Exhibit 2
The Five Phases of Growth

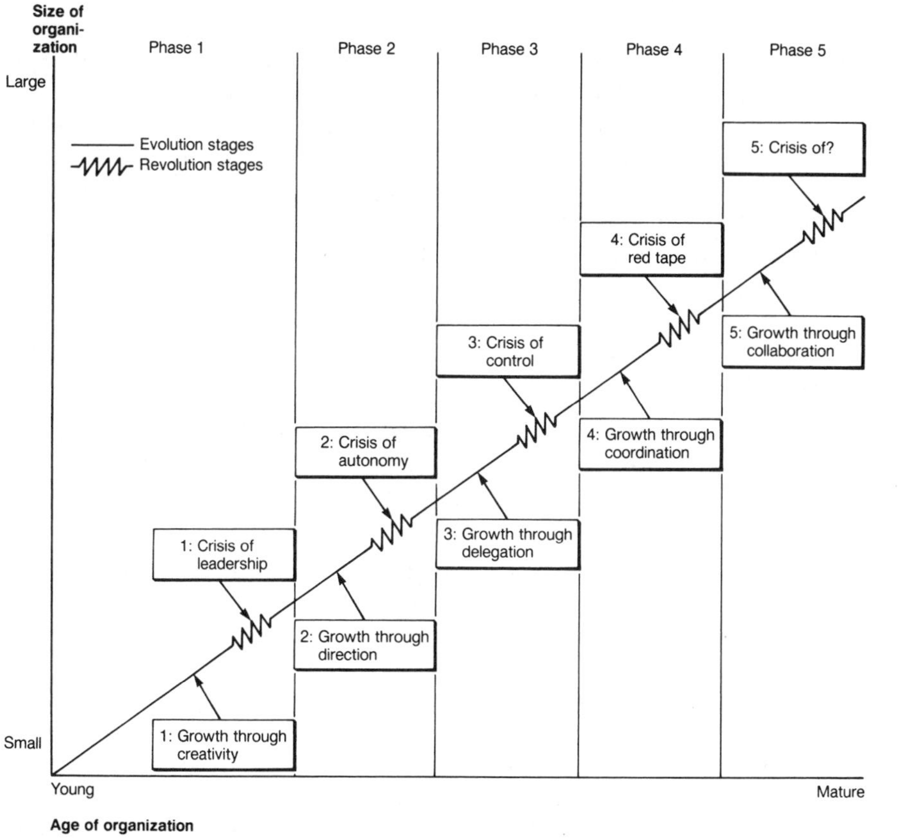

— Long hours of work are rewarded by modest salaries and the promise of ownership benefits.
— Control of activities comes from immediate marketplace feedback; the management acts as the customers react.

The Leadership Crisis. All of the foregoing individualistic and creative activities are essential for the company to get off the ground. But therein lies the problem. As the company grows, larger production runs require knowledge about the efficiencies of manufacturing. Increased numbers of employees cannot be managed exclusively through informal communication; new employees are not motivated by an intense dedication to the product or organization. Additional capital must be secured, and new accounting procedures are needed for financial control.

Thus the founders find themselves burdened with unwanted management responsibilities. So they long for the "good old days," still trying to act as they did in the past. And conflicts between the harried leaders grow more intense.

At this point a crisis of leadership occurs, which is the onset of the first revolution. Who is to lead the company out of confusion and solve the managerial problems confronting it? Quite obviously, a strong manager is needed who has the necessary knowledge and skill to introduce new business techniques. But this is easier said than done. The founders often hate to step aside even though they are probably temperamentally unsuited to be managers. So here is the first critical developmental choice—to locate and install a strong business manager who is acceptable to the founders and who can pull the organization together.

Phase 2: Direction

Those companies that survive the first phase by installing a capable business manager usually embark on a period of sustained growth under able and directive leadership. Here are the characteristics of this evolutionary period:

- — A functional organization structure is introduced to separate manufacturing from marketing activities, and job assignments become more specialized.
- — Accounting systems for inventory and purchasing are introduced.
- — Incentives, budgets, and work standards are adopted.
- — Communication becomes more formal and impersonal as a hierarchy of titles and positions builds.
- — The new manager and his key supervisors take most of the responsibility for instituting direction, while lower-level supervisors are treated more as functional specialists than as autonomous, decision-making managers.

The Autonomy Crisis. Although the new directive techniques channel employee energy more efficiently into growth, they eventually become inappropriate for controlling a larger, more diverse and complex organization. Lower-level employees find themselves restricted by a cumbersome and centralized hierarchy. They have come to possess more direct knowledge about markets and machinery than do the leaders at the top; consequently, they feel torn between following procedures and taking initiative on their own.

Thus the second revolution is imminent as a crisis develops from demands for greater autonomy on the part of lower-level managers. The solution adopted by most companies is to move toward greater delegation. Yet it is difficult for top managers who were previously successful at being directive to give up responsibility. Moreover, lower-level managers are not accustomed to making decisions for themselves. As a result, numerous companies flounder during this revolutionary period, adhering to centralized methods while lower-level employees grow more disenchanted and leave the organization.

Phase 3: Delegation

The next era of growth evolves from the successful application of a decentralized organization structure. It exhibits these characteristics:

- — Much greater responsibility is given to the managers of plants and market territories.
- — Profit centers and bonuses are used to stimulate motivation.
- — The top executives at headquarters restrain themselves to managing by exception, based on periodic reports from the field.
- — Management often concentrates on making new acquisitions which can be lined up beside other decentralized units.
- — Communication from the top is infrequent, usually by correspondence, telephone, or brief visits to field locations.

The delegation stage proves useful for gaining expansion through heightened motivation at lower levels. Decentralized managers with greater authority and incentive are able to penetrate larger markets, respond faster to customers, and develop new products.

The Control Crisis. A serious problem eventually evolves, however, as top executives sense that they are losing control over a highly diversified field operation. Autonomous field managers prefer to run their own shows without coordinating plans, money, technology, and manpower with the rest of the organization. Freedom breeds a parochial attitude.

Hence, the Phase 3 revolution is under way when top management seeks to regain control over the total company. Some top managements attempt a return to centralized management, which usually fails because of the vast scope of operations. Those companies that move ahead find a new solution in the use of special coordination techniques.

Phase 4: Coordination

During this phase, the evolutionary period is characterized by the use of formal systems for achieving greater coordination and by top executives taking responsibility for the initiation and administration of these new systems. For example:

- — Decentralized units are merged into product groups.
- — Formal planning procedures are established and intensively reviewed.

- Numerous staff personnel are hired and located at headquarters to initiate companywide programs of control and review for line managers.
- Capital expenditures are carefully weighed and parceled out across the organization.
- Each product group is treated as an investment center where return on invested capital is an important criterion used in allocating funds.
- Certain technical functions, such as data processing, are centralized at headquarters, while daily operating decisions remain decentralized.
- Stock options and companywide profit sharing are used to encourage identity with the firm as a whole.

All of these new coordination systems prove useful for achieving growth through more efficient allocation of a company's limited resources. They prompt field managers to look beyond the needs of their local units. While these managers still have much decision-making responsibility, they learn to justify their actions more carefully to a "watchdog" audience at headquarters.

The Red-Tape Crisis. But a lack of confidence gradually builds between line and staff, and between headquarters and the field. The proliferation of systems and programs begins to exceed its utility; a red-tape crisis is created. Line managers, for example, increasingly resent heavy staff direction from those who are not familiar with local conditions. Staff people, on the other hand, complain about uncooperative and uninformed line managers. Together, both groups criticize the bureaucratic paper system that has evolved. Procedures take precedence over problem solving, and innovation is dampened. In short, the organization has become too large and complex to be managed through formal programs and rigid systems. The Phase 4 revolution is under way.

Phase 5: Collaboration

The last observable phase in previous studies emphasizes strong interpersonal collaboration in an attempt to overcome the red-tape crisis. Where Phase 4 was managed more through formal systems and procedures, Phase 5 emphasizes greater spontaneity in management action through teams and the skillful confrontation of interpersonal differences. Social control and self-discipline take over from formal control. This transition is especially difficult for those experts who created the old systems as well as for those line managers who relied on formal methods for answers.

The Phase 5 evolution, then, builds around a more flexible and behavioral approach to management. Here are its characteristics:

— The focus is on solving problems quickly through team action.
— Teams are combined across functions for task group activity.
— Headquarters staff experts are reduced in number, reassigned, and combined in interdisciplinary teams to consult with, not to direct, field units.
— A matrix-type structure is frequently used to assemble the right teams for the appropriate problems.
— Previous formal systems are simplified and combined into single multipurpose systems.
— Conferences of key managers are held frequently to focus on major problem issues.
— Educational programs are utilized to train managers in behavioral skills for achieving better teamwork and conflict resolution.
— Real-time information systems are integrated into daily decision making.
— Economic rewards are geared more to team performance than to individual achievement.
— Experiments in new practices are encouraged throughout the organization.

The ? Crisis. What will be the revolution in response to this stage of evolution? Many large U. S. companies are now in the Phase 5 evolutionary stage, so the answers are critical. While there is little clear evidence, I imagine the revolution will center around the "psychological saturation" of employees who grow emotionally and physically exhausted by the intensity of teamwork and the heavy pressure for innovative situations.

My hunch is that the Phase 5 revolution will be solved through new structures and programs that allow employees to periodically rest, reflect, and revitalize themselves. We may even see companies with dual organization structures: a "habit" structure for getting the daily work done, and a "reflective" structure for stimulating perspective and personal enrichment. Employees could then move back and forth between the two structures as their energies are dissipated and refueled.

One European organization has implemented just such a structure. Five reflective groups have been established outside the regular structure for the purpose of continuously evaluating five task activities basic to the organization. They report directly to the managing director, although their reports are made public throughout the organization. Membership in each group includes all levels and functions, and employees are rotated through these groups on a six-month basis.

Other concrete examples now in practice include providing sabbaticals for employees, moving managers in and out of "hot spot" jobs, establishing a four-day workweek, assuring job security, building physical facilities for relaxation *during* the working day, making jobs more interchangeable, creating an extra team on the assembly line so that one team is always off for reeducation, and switching to longer vacations and more flexible working hours.

The Chinese practice of requiring executives to spend time periodically on lower-level jobs may also be worth a nonideological evaluation. For too long, U. S. management has assumed that career progress should be equated with an upward path toward title, salary, and power. Could it be that some vice presidents of marketing might just long for, and even benefit from, temporary duty in the field sales organization?

Implications of History

Let me now summarize some important implications for practicing managers. First, the main features of this discussion are depicted in Exhibit 3, which shows the specific management actions that characterize each growth phase. These actions are also the solutions which ended each preceding revolutionary period.

In one sense, I hope that many readers will react to my model by calling it obvious and natural for depicting the growth of an organization. To me this type of reaction is a useful test of the model's validity.

But at a more reflective level I imagine some of these reactions are more hindsight than foresight. Those experienced managers who have been through a developmental sequence can empathize with it now, but how did they react when in the middle of a stage of evolution or revolution? They can probably recall the limits of their own developmental understanding at that time. Perhaps they resisted desirable changes or were even swept emotionally into a revolution without being able to propose constructive solutions. So let me offer some explicit guidelines for managers of growing organizations to keep in mind.

1. *Know where you are in the developmental sequence.*

Every organization and its component parts are at different stages of development. The task of top management is to be aware of these stages; otherwise, it may not recognize when the time for change has come, or it may act to impose the wrong solution.

Top leaders should be ready to work with the flow of the tide rather than against it; yet they should be cautious, since it is tempting to skip phases out of impatience. Each phase results in certain strengths and learning experiences in the organization that will be essential for success in subsequent phases. A child prodigy, for example, may be able to read like a teenager, but he cannot behave like one until he ages through a sequence of experiences.

I also doubt that managers can or should act to avoid revolutions. Rather, these periods of tension provide the pressure, ideas, and aware-

Exhibit 3
Organization Practices during Evolution in the Five Phases of Growth

Category	Phase 1	Phase 2	Phase 3	Phase 4	Phase 5
Management focus	Make and sell	Efficiency of operations	Expansion of market	Consolidation of organization	Problem solving and innovation
Organization structure	Informal	Centralized and functional	Decentralized and geographical	Line-staff and product groups	Matrix of teams
Top management style	Individualistic and entrepreneurial	Directive	Delegative	Watchdog	Participative
Control system	Market results	Standards and cost centers	Reports and profit centers	Plans and investment centers	Mutual goal setting
Management reward emphasis	Ownership	Salary and merit increases	Individual bonus	Profit sharing and stock options	Team bonus

ness that afford a platform for change and the introduction of new practices.

2. *Recognize the limited range of solutions.*

In each revolutionary stage it becomes evident that this stage can be ended only by certain specific solutions; moreover, these solutions are different from those which were applied to the problems of the preceding revolution. Too often it is tempting to choose solutions that were tried before, which makes it impossible for a new phase of growth to evolve.

Management must be prepared to dismantle current structures before the revolutionary stage becomes too turbulent. Top managers, realizing that their own managerial styles are no longer appropriate, may even have to take themselves out of leadership positions. A good Phase 2 manager facing Phase 3 might be wise to find another Phase 2 organization that better fits his talents, either outside the company or with one of its newer subsidiaries.

Finally, evolution is not an automatic affair; it is a contest for survival. To move ahead, companies must consciously introduce planned structures that not only are solutions to a current crisis but also are fitted to the *next* phase of growth. This requires considerable self-awareness on the part of top management, as well as great interpersonal skill in persuading other managers that change is needed.

3. *Realize that solutions breed new problems.*

Managers often fail to realize that organizational solutions create problems for the future (i.e., a decision to delegate eventually causes a problem of control). Historical actions are very much determinants of what happens to the company at a much later date.

An awareness of this effect should help managers to evaluate company problems with greater historical understanding instead of "pinning the blame" on a current development. Better yet, managers should be in a position to *predict* future problems, and thereby to prepare solutions and coping strategies before a revolution gets out of hand.

A management that is aware of the problems ahead could well decide *not* to grow. Top managers may, for instance, prefer to retain the informal practices of a small company, knowing that this way of life is inherent in the organization's limited size, not in their congenial personalities. If they choose to grow, they may do themselves out of a job and way of life they enjoy.

And what about the managements of very large organizations? Can they find new solutions for continued phases of evolution? Or are they reaching a stage where the government will act to break them up because they are too large?

Concluding Note

Clearly, there is still much to learn about processes of development in organizations. The phases outlined here are only five in number and are still only approximations. Researchers are just beginning to study the specific developmental problems of structure, control, rewards, and management style in different industries and in a variety of cultures.

One should not, however, wait for conclusive evidence before educating managers to think and act from a developmental perspective. The critical dimension of time has been missing for too long from our management theories and practices. The intriguing paradox is that by learning more about history we may do a better job in the future.

Reading 8–2

*How to Decipher and Change Organizational Culture**

Vijay Sathe

Two basic arguments are presented here. First, behavior change does not necessarily produce culture change. Second, managers can benefit by taking this into account when conceiving and implementing organizational change.

The following topics will be covered in this discussion:

1. Definition of culture.
2. How to decipher culture.
3. How to assess the resistance to culture change.
4. How to influence culture change.
5. How to know if the attempted culture change is occurring.
6. The alternatives to major culture change.

Accounts from the experiences of several companies and managers who have succeeded or failed in creating culture change will be presented for purposes of illustration. In addition, the case of Cummins Engine Company and its operating head, Jim Henderson, will be used to provide one in-depth illustration of successful culture change.[1] It describes how Jim Henderson, chief operating officer of Cummins Engine Company, managed a difficult inventory situation in the mid-1970s, and succeeded eventually in modifying the company's management culture.

---

* In R. H. Kilman and Associates, *Managing Corporate Cultures* (San Francisco: Jossey-Bass, 1985). Reprinted by permission.

[1] A detailed written account of this case, along with two companion video tapes, has been published elsewhere (Browne, Vancil, and Sathe, 1982). Only the essential story line is reported here.

Cummins Engine Company and Jim Henderson

Background

Incorporated in 1919, Cummins had its headquarters in Columbus, Indiana. From modest beginnings as a machining shop, the company had become a major industrial firm by the mid-70s, with some 20,000 employees worldwide, net sales of $800 million, and after-tax profit of $25 million.

The company was founded by Clessie Cummins, but it was Irwin Miller, chief executive officer, and Don Tull, chief operating officer, who had the most profound influence on the Cummins organization during a period spanning 30 years, from the mid-30s to the mid-60s. During this time the company was closely directed from the top. Tull was constantly present on the plant floor, checking the work flow, quality control, employee morale, inventory levels, and shipment schedules. Because the company was largely under one roof during these years, costly and cumbersome management systems were not required.

In the mid-60s, as the company grew and the facilities expanded, Miller realized the need to build a management team. He began to turn top management responsibilities over to younger, more professionally trained managers. When Tull stepped up as chairman of the Executive Committee in 1969, Jim Henderson became executive vice president for operations. Henderson, one of a number of young managers whom Miller attracted into the company in the 60s, continued this hiring policy; but the bulk of the senior operating management and staff positions were still filled by older managers with proven track records.

As the 70s rolled along, plant capacity in Columbus was woefully inadequate to meet the rising demands of the engine business. Facilities expansion was first undertaken on a crash basis in Columbus in 1970, but the rationalization and development of formal management and control systems to support a multiplant operating mode had to wait until later. For example, inventory control for all three plants in Columbus continued to be carried out at the main engine plant.

In spite of its dramatic growth, in many ways Cummins Engine Company still remained a small-town company in the mid-70s. It was the largest employer in Columbus, and its history of close relations with an independent local union fostered a sense of special concern for local issues.

Perhaps the most salient management process in the mid-70s was still the traditional exercise of the art of expediting. The company emphasized extraordinary service to its customers, which was an important competitive edge over other suppliers, and a good manager in top management's eyes was one who could always find a way to expedite a special customer request.

Since the mid-60s, top management had been pushing to professionalize management and build a more rational and systematic set of organizational systems. The reality, however, was that demand was growing so fast that only the expert old hands who knew how to coax the last ounce of productivity out of the operating system could keep the production schedule from slipping.

The Inventory Crisis

Anticipating a sharp downturn, top management viewed the company's rising inventory levels, approaching 80 days' supply, with growing concern in late 1974. In addition, there was a major discrepancy between the materials management records and the financial accounting records on inventory levels.

Miller and Tull urged Henderson to take the old, hard-line approach to controlling inventories: During the periodic business cycle downturns which hit the truck manufacturing industry and its component suppliers especially hard, Tull had not hesitated to batten down the hatches. He would let part of the work force go, cut off all capital spending, and cancel orders to suppliers. Tull and the controller could be found on such occasions out on the receiving dock, turning away deliveries.

Henderson asked for an opportunity to solve the problem in his own way, however. The practice of managing each downturn in the economy with a top-down, "firefighting" approach made it difficult to get managers to take more personal initiative for solving such problems; they had learned to wait for the guy at the top to tell them what to do. This Band-Aid approach also delayed the installation of formal systems, such as materials requisition planning, that the company needed in order to prevent the periodic recurrence of this problem. Henderson had concluded that the old way of operating which had worked in a single-plant environment would not work in the existing multiplant environment. He wanted to solve the inventory problem in such a way that it also yielded the desired outcomes in the longer term (his managers taking more personal responsibility for solving such problems, and becoming committed to installing and using appropriate information and control systems.)

Henderson's Actions. Henderson began to meet weekly with his group heads, their plant managers, and the controller to monitor the inventory situation. Henderson also made some unannounced plant visits to draw attention to the inventory problem and to signal to his managers that he was not going to do it for them. These actions helped the company's managers to cope in a manner that went somewhat against the grain of their culture. Over the next several years, two shared assumptions were changed. First, the assumption that "top management will tell us what to do when there is a problem" was replaced by the assumption that "all managers should take personal responsibility for solving problems." Second, the important shared assumption, "operate informally without systems," was modified to "use systems to do the routine work, operate informally to expedite."

In this case, behavioral changes led to cultural changes. Why this occurred here, but may *not* always occur, will be explained. First, we need to better understand culture and how it can be deciphered.

Definition of Culture

There are many definitions of culture (Kroeber and Kluckhohn, 1952). Early authors (e.g., Taylor, 1871) defined culture rather broadly to include knowledge, belief, art, law, morals, and customs. Two major schools in cultural anthropology have influenced later work. The view of culture favored by the "adaptationists" is based on what is directly observable about the members of a community—that is, their patterns of behavior, speech, and use of material objects. The "ideational school" prefers, in defining culture, to look at what is shared in the community members' *minds*—that is, the belief, values, and other ideas people share in common (Keesing, 1974; Swartz and Jordan, 1980).

This is one reason the subject is confusing: Different people think of different slices of reality when they talk about culture. To integrate various views of culture, Edgar Schein (1983) has proposed a three-level model that we will adapt for use here.[2]

The first level of culture is composed of technology, art, audible and visible behavior patterns, and other aspects of culture that are easy to see but hard to interpret without an understanding of the other levels. This is the slice of cultural reality that the adaptationists have been most interested in. We will denote this level by the term *organizational behavior patterns,* or *behavior.*

The second level of culture reveals how people explain, rationalize, and justify what they say and do as a community, how they "make sense" of the first level of culture. We will denote this level with the term *justifications of behavior.*

---

[2] This conceptualization is based on the model proposed by Schein (1983), but two points should be noted. First, Schein uses the term *values* to denote espoused values, whereas the terms *beliefs* and *values* are used here to denote those assumptions that people actually hold, that is, the ones they have internalized (Bem, 1970; Rokeach, 1968). Second, Schein focuses on preconscious and unconscious assumptions because these are powerful and people may not even become aware of them until they are violated or challenged. Such assumptions are hard to discover and debate because they are taken for granted. Conscious assumptions have also been included in the definition of culture used here because although these are easier to detect and debate, they too have a strong influence on behavior and are hard to change. People do not easily give up internalized beliefs and values, whether consciously or unconsciously held (Bem, 1970; Rokeach, 1968), as opposed to beliefs and values that they merely espouse or comply with (Kelman, 1958).

The third level of culture goes deeper still and is the level that the ideational school has been most interested in. It consists of people's ideas and assumptions that govern their justifications and behavior. We will denote this level by the term *culture,* which we will define specifically as *the set of important assumptions (often unstated) that members of a community share in common.* Two basic types of assumptions are people's beliefs and values—not what they *say* their beliefs and values are or those they will comply with because of the demands of others, but those beliefs and values they consider to be their own, that is, those they have *internalized.* People may not become conscious of these held true beliefs and values until they are violated or challenged and even then will resist changing them (Bem, 1970; Kelman, 1958; Rokeach, 1968). Thus, the effects of culture defined in this way are not only subtle and powerful but persistent as well.

This definition does not imply that the other two levels of culture are unimportant. Rather, the levels are interrelated but sufficiently distinct so that combining them is not analytically advantageous (Geertz, 1973). Managers are interested in how people behave as well as in what they believe, but we know a lot more about how to create behavior change (Beer, 1980; Schein, 1980) than we do about how to create belief change. We will see that behavior change does not necessarily produce belief change, in part because of the intervening level of justification of behavior. These processes cannot be understood and managed if all three levels are included under the culture label. Organizational insight and analytical power are to be gained by using different terms for each level and examining all three levels. Let us now take a closer look at this definition of culture by examining two of its major elements—content and strength.

The content of a culture influences the *direction* of behavior. Content is determined not by an aggregate of assumptions but by how the important ones interrelate and form particular patterns. From the variety of beliefs and values that the people in a community may hold, the important assumptions are those that are widely enough shared and highly enough placed relative to other assumptions in the community so as to be of major significance to the life of the community. A key feature of the pattern of a culture is the *ordering* of its cultural assumptions, which indicates their relative importance.

As Schein (1983) has explained, the content of a culture ultimately derives from two principal sources: (1) the pattern of assumptions that founders, leaders, and organizational employees bring with them when they join the organization (which in turn depends on their own experience in the culture of the regional, national, ethnic, occupational, or professional community from which these people come) and (2) the actual experience that people in the organization have had in working out solutions for coping with the basic problems of adaptation to the external environment and internal integration. In short, the content of culture derives from a combination of prior assumptions and new learning experiences.

The strength of a culture influences the *intensity* of behavior. Three specific features of culture determine its strength: *thickness* (how many important assumptions there are), *extent of sharing* (how widely they are shared in the organization), and *clarity of ordering* (how clearly some are more important than others). The stronger cultures are thicker, more widely shared, and more clearly ordered and consequently have a more profound influence on organizational behavior. Such cultures are also more highly resistant to change.

What makes some cultures stronger than others? Two important factors are the number of employees in the organization and their geographical dispersion. A smaller work force and more localized operations facilitate the growth of a stronger culture because it is easier for beliefs and values to develop and become widely shared. But larger organizations with worldwide operations, such as IBM, can also have strong cultures that derive from a continuity of strong leadership which has consistently emphasized the same beliefs and values, as well as a relatively stable and longer-tenured work force. Under these conditions, a consistent set of enduring beliefs and values can take hold over time and become widely shared and clearly ordered.

Deciphering a Culture

The internalized beliefs and values that members of a community share in common cannot be measured easily or observed directly. Neither can one simply rely on what people say about it in order to decipher a culture. Other evidence, *both historical and current,* must be taken into account to infer what the culture is.

The managers at Cummins seemed to share five important assumptions, ordered as follows:

1. Provide highly responsive, quality customer service.
2. Get things done well and quickly ("expediting").
3. Operate informally without systems.
4. Top management will tell us what to do if there is a problem.
5. The company is part of the family.

The procedure used to decipher this culture is now presented.

Inferring the Content of Culture

Each important shared assumption may be inferred from one or more manifestations of culture, that is, the shared things, shared sayings, shared doings, and shared feelings one experiences in the organization. The aim is to discover a pattern of important assumptions that help "make sense" of the cultural manifestations. The challenge is to ensure that the "making sense" is from the point of view of the "natives," that is, those whose culture is being deciphered (Swartz and Jordan, 1980). With this in mind, three basic questions may be explored to infer the content of culture from its manifestations:

1. What is the background of the founders and others who followed them? An understanding of the background and personality of the founders and others who helped mold the culture offers important clues about the content of culture. For example, Irwin Miller at Cummins strongly believed in community service and in "rooting out bureaucratic behavior," which led to two important cultural assumptions (the company is part of the family, and operate informally without systems). Also, most of the Cummins employees came from the local community, and many were from families whose members had previously or currently worked at the company, further reinforcing the cultural belief that the company was part of the family.

2. How did the organization respond to crises or other critical events? What was the learning from these experiences? Since culture evolves and is learned, focusing on stressful periods of an organization's history can provide two types of important clues to help decipher culture. First, this may reveal how particular assumptions came to be formed. For example, the inventory crisis at Cummins ultimately caused the belief in operating informally without systems to get transformed into a new belief in using systems to do the routine work and relying on informal operation to expedite. Second, by focusing on such periods in history, particularly those that were traumatic for the organization, one also has the opportunity to discover the *ordering* of the cultural assumptions, which is hard to decipher because such assumptions may not ordinarily conflict with each other. The organization may be forced to choose between two important assumptions during a stressful period.

For example, although Cummins did not like to lay people off, it did so during periodic downturns. This suggests that the first four cultural assumptions, which were not affected by these traumatic events, were more important than an assumption which was violated to some extent—Assumption 5 (the company is part of the family). Similarly, the 1974 inventory crisis brought Assumptions 3 and 4 into conflict with Assumptions 1 and 2. Since the former were questioned and were eventually modified but the latter were not, Assumptions 1 and 2 must be considered more central than Assumptions 3 and 4.

The people at Cummins had so thoroughly bought into the values of (1) highly responsive, quality customer service and (2) expediting behavior, that these ideals had become more than strategic objectives and operational directives. They had become taken-for-granted, shared assumptions that were a central part of the Cummins management culture. These assumptions were never questioned by the managers at Cummins, even during times of stress such as the economic downturn and the inventory crisis. Indeed, the purchasing managers went so far as to *ignore* higher management directives and ordered extra parts because they believed customer service would otherwise be adversely affected.

3. Who are considered deviant in the culture? How does the organization respond to them? In a sense, deviants represent and define a culture's boundaries. An understanding of who and what is considered deviant in a culture helps in deciphering it. For instance, Cummins hired lots of M.B.A.s from among the brightest and the best in the early 1960s, many of whom didn't make it in the company. Those that survived were culturally compatible. Many of those who disappeared were deviants—people who believed in systems and procedures, and those who believed their talent and professional education gave them special status in the company ("I am a hot-shot M.B.A.; I'll teach these guys how to do it right"). These people violated important cultural assumptions (expedite, operate informally without systems, the company is part of the family) which are revealed by trying to understand why these people were rejected by the culture.

A cultural assumption may be so consistently adhered to and taken for granted that almost no one ever violates it. Such an assumption may be particularly hard to discover. Its centrality and power may only be revealed on those rare occasions when someone knowingly or inadvertently violates it, incurring the wrath and fury of the entire community. An example of such an assumption in academia is intellectual integrity. A recent case in point is the disbelief and heated controversy surrounding the chairman of medicine of a prestigious school, who has been accused of plagiarism ("Stanford," 1984). Much can be learned about a culture by looking for such infrequent but critical incidents that deeply offend the people in the community. There is no indication of such a critical incident at Cummins.

Investigator's Skill and Status

It is also important to consider who is doing the investigation, because this also determines what is revealed. Some people are more skilled at reading culture than are others. Skill comes with practice; those who have been exposed to different cultures will have had greater opportunity to develop these skills, because culture is more readily deciphered *in contrast* to other cultures one has experienced (Louis, 1980).

The investigator's status relative to those whose culture is being read also affects what is revealed. Consider three important cases: established member, newcomer, and outsider. The established member has the benefit of experience in the culture and the native's point of view. The irony is that this great asset is also a liability in that some of the cultural assumptions may be so taken for granted by the established member that he or she may find it difficult to surface them. Both newcomers and outsiders can help in such identification.

Since newcomers are not deeply immersed in the culture and have the benefit of contrast from comparing it with the culture of the organization they are coming from, they are more likely to notice the cultural manifestations, and *perhaps* the underlying assumptions, than the established members who take them for granted. The qualifier is important because the newcomer may not as yet have access to all the information (especially that which is considered sensitive and embarrassing by the established members), and the newcomer may also misinterpret the culture's content if he or she has not yet understood the native point of view. On the other hand, if the newcomer can team up with one or more established members (and conversely if an established member can rely on one or more newcomers) to *jointly* explore the culture, the advantages that each party brings could considerably strengthen the process of discovery (Schein, 1983).

Outsiders are likely to be at an even greater disadvantage than the newcomer in terms of access to sensitive information and in understanding the native point of view, but they have the benefits of greater objectivity and contrast. Accordingly, outsiders may find it difficult to decipher the cultural content from its surface manifestations, which they can readily notice, unless they can enlist the help of those who are inside the culture. Conversely, established members of a culture can ask for help from outsiders and assist them in deciphering their culture.

The author is very familiar with the Cummins situation, but is an outsider. The culture has been deciphered from information provided by company insiders, including Jim Henderson, the president of Cummins. However, since I did not jointly explore the Cummins culture with these people, the description given may be deficient and might have been improved had such a process been undertaken at the time of the case.

Estimating the Strength of Culture

In inferring the content of culture, it already has been determined how many important shared assumptions the company's culture has and how clearly they appear to be ordered. The *extent of sharing,* the third property that affects the strength of culture, remains to be assessed.

One clue is how extensive the cultural manifestations are from which the inferences are made—the *proportion* of people in the organization who demonstrate that they share the same physical attributes, slogans, practices, and feelings. In general, a higher proportion indicates that the beliefs and values are more widely shared. Other clues may be obtained by examining the factors mentioned earlier that influence the strength of culture.

The Cummins culture was relatively strong because there were several important assumptions that appeared to be widely shared and clearly ordered. History, leadership, organizational size, geographical dispersion, and the stability of the work force all had an impact. In its 60-year history, Cummins had only two generations of top management, and the first, highly influential generation (Irwin Miller and Don Tull) were still serving as chairman of the board and chairman of the executive committee, respectively, at the time of the case. Cummins was medium sized; most of its operations were close together; and employee and management turnover was relatively low.

How to Assess the Resistance to Culture Change

Culture change may involve a change in (1) the content and/or (2) the strength of the existing organizational culture. Let us examine each separately before considering their joint effect.

Incremental versus Radical Change in Culture's Content. A greater change in culture's content is involved to the extent that:

1. The change involves a *greater number* of important shared assumptions.
2. The change involves *more central* (highly ordered) shared assumptions.
3. The change involves a movement *toward more "alien"* (less intrinsically appealing) shared assumptions.

"Alien" versus Intrinsically Appealing Beliefs and Values. Three interrelated considerations help determine the intrinsic appeal of the beliefs and values in question. First, beliefs and values that are shared at some level by members of an organization are more intrinsically appealing than those that are not. At Cummins, the value of a close working relationship with the union was not shared widely enough nor was it placed high enough in the company's ordering of beliefs and values to be considered a cultural value. However, this value was more intrinsically appealing for Cummins managers than an "antiunion" value because many of them valued the role of the union and desired close relationships with it.

Second, beliefs and values that were once part of the organization's culture but have since atrophied and are no longer important shared assumptions are more intrinsically appealing than beliefs and values that were never part of the organization's culture. At Cummins, the assumption that "small is beautiful" was part of the company's heritage, but this value had atrophied after the expansion of the war years and was not part of the company's culture by the mid-70s. This "dormant" value could have been more easily adopted by the people at Cummins than the value "bigger is better," for instance, which was never part of the company's culture.

Third, beliefs and values that are supported by the cultures of the regional, national, ethnic, occupational, and professional communities to which the people in the organization belong are more intrinsically appealing than beliefs and values that do not find such support in the cultures of the relevant wider communities. For example, "service to the community" was an important value in the local community from which many of those at Cummins came. Accordingly, beliefs and values consistent with the notion of community service were more intrinsically appealing to the Cummins managers than beliefs and values that ran counter to this notion.

Resistance to Culture Change. A radical change in culture's content is more difficult to accomplish than is an incremental change. Further, for a given degree of change in culture's content, cultural resistance will be greater in strong culture than in a weak culture because the former involves change for a larger number of organizational members than does the latter. Thus, the degree of cultural resistance may be economically represented as follows:

Resistance to culture change	=	Magnitude of the change in the content of the culture—radical versus incremental change in culture's content	×	Strength of the prevailing culture—strong versus weak culture

The culture change at Cummins involved two of the five important shared assumptions. Assumption 3 (operate informally without systems) underwent a moderate change to "use systems to do routine work, operate informally to expedite." Assumption 4 (top management will tell us what to do if there is a problem) was substantially altered to "all managers should take personal responsibility for problem solving." Overall, the magnitude of the change in the content of the culture is more than incremental but less than radical. However, because Cummins had a relatively strong culture, the overall resistance was considerable, and these cultural changes took four to five years to accomplish. In general, the greater the cultural resistance, the more difficult and time consuming the culture change will be.

How to Influence Culture Change

Managers interested in producing culture change must understand and intervene in each of the basic processes that cause culture to perpetuate itself (Exhibit 1). There are two basic approaches for effecting a desired culture change: *(a)* getting people in the organization to buy into a new pattern of beliefs and values, (Processes 1, 2, and 3) and *(b)* adding and socializing people into the organization and removing people from the organization as appropriate (Processes 4 and 5). Let us consider each of these processes in turn.

Behavior

The process by which culture influences behavior is consistent with the conventional wisdom—that is, that beliefs and values influence behavior (Process 1, Exhibit 1). However, the opposite is also true. A considerable body of social science literature indicates that *under certain conditions* (to be discussed shortly), one of the most effective ways of changing people's beliefs and values is to first change their corresponding behavior. The general techniques for creating behavior change are well covered in the existing management literature (Beer, 1980; Schein, 1980), but these methods must be used more restrictively if culture change is to be produced. As elaborated below, the motivation to change behavior must be based on intrinsic motivators rather than relying exclusively, or even excessively, on extrinsic forms. For example, consider the experience of one company and its chief executive officer Matt Holt:

Exhibit 1
How Culture Perpetuates Itself

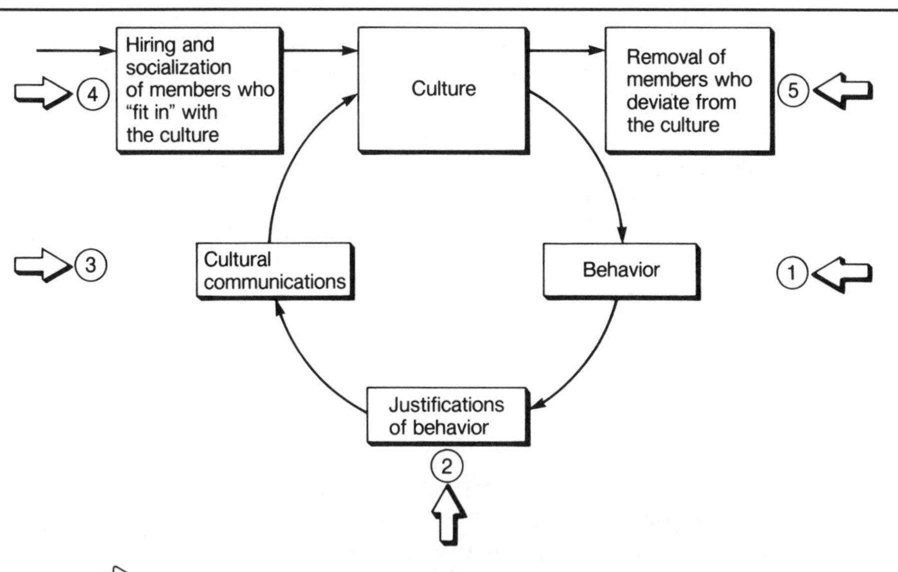

> Buffeted by shifting market forces and management turnover, the corporate business strategy had lacked coherent direction. Matt Holt's mandate was to take a longer-term view of the business and to create a technology-driven organization. Analysis conducted with the help of outside consultants indicated that a "cultural metamorphosis" was needed to accomplish this. A reorganization followed, including changes in the measurement and reward system to "encourage the required behavior."
>
> Matt realized there would be a "wait and see" period while people tried to figure out "whether they really mean it." He knew that his "true intentions" would be judged on the basis of what he did, not just what he said. Accordingly, he tried to ensure that the management systems inspected and rewarded the required behavior, and he conducted his own affairs (that is, use of his time, visits, "pats on the back") to reinforce and support what the new formal systems were signaling. Two years later, there had been some improvements. People appeared to be "doing the right things," allocating their time and resources as prescribed by the new systems. Missing, however, was the missionary zeal, the sense of commitment and excitement that Matt had hoped to inject into the life of the company as people came to identify with and share his vision of the mission.

Some behavior change had occurred here, but no culture change. The problem was the heavy reliance on extrinsic motivation, as explained below.

Justifications of Behavior

Behavior change does not *necessarily* produce culture change, because of the intervening process of justification of behavior (Process 2, Exhibit 1). This is what happened in the case of Matt Holt. People were behaving as called for by the new formal systems, but they continued to share the old beliefs and values in common and "explained" their new behavior to themselves by noting the external justifications for it (Aronson, 1976; Bem, 1970)—for example, "We are doing it because it is required of us," and "We are doing it because of the incentives." There was behavior compliance, not culture commitment. In a very real sense, people in this case were behaving the way they were because they felt they had no choice, not because they fundamentally believed in it or valued it.

Thus, one reason culture perpetuates itself is that even if behavior is changed (Process 1, Exhibit 1), people tend to rationalize it in terms of external justifications (Process 2) and continue to adhere to the prevailing pattern of beliefs and values. Managers attempting to create culture change must remain alert to this danger and try to counteract it by using each of the following three approaches.

The first recommendation, which may appear counterintuitive, is to minimize the opportunity for external justification by inducing the appropriate behavior change with a *minimal* use of rewards, punishments, and other *extrinsic* forms of motivation (Aronson, 1976, pp. 109–

17). This doesn't "feel right" at first for many of us who have become used to offering incentives to get what we want. However, others are likely to be going along just for the incentives rather than because they fundamentally believe in what we are asking them to do. This is exactly what happened in the case of Matt Holt. In contrast, Jim Henderson at Cummins offered no financial incentives and relied minimally on other extrinsic motivators (principally some unannounced plant visits to draw attention to the inventory problem in order to produce the desired behavior). This approach took time and exposed him to personal risk and criticism from his superiors, Irwin Miller and Don Tull, for not acting more forcefully to solve the growing inventory crisis. Henderson understood that the recommended "strong measures" would indeed solve the short-term inventory problem but would not help bring about the new culture he was seeking to create in which his managers would take more personal responsibility for the problem (rather than waiting for directives from the top) and introduce and use the systems required to prevent its periodic recurrence.

The second recommendation follows from the first: To the extent possible, the necessary behavior change should be induced by using *intrinsic* forms of motivation. Essentially, this means that one must get people to see the inherent worth of what it is they are being asked to do. As Schein (1973) has explained, one way to do this is to persuade people to unlearn or question their current pattern of beliefs and values by helping them to see that their assumptions either are not confirmed by reality testing or are actually disconfirmed. This lack of confirmation, or disconfirmation, which is typically accompanied by pain, guilt, anxiety, and lack of self-confidence, provides the necessary intrinsic motivation to learn the new behavior. Matt Holt, for instance, did very little in this area. In contrast, the weekly inventory meetings that Henderson instituted at Cummins provided a forum for joint exploration that led people to see the value of the new approach he was advocating.

Some use of extrinsic motivators may be unavoidable. A third approach, then, that managers interested in producing culture change must use is to *nullify inappropriate rationalizations* of the new behavior. A somewhat drastic technique for doing this is to give people an "out"—those who do not "buy into" the new pattern of beliefs and values may be given the option to leave or transfer to a different organization. If it is perceived as a feasible and a real option, giving people the opportunity to leave can be a powerful tool in producing culture change, not only because it weeds out those who are unlikely to buy into the new pattern of beliefs and values (Process 5, Exhibit 1) but also because those left behind will find it more difficult to come up with inappropriate rationalizations—the perception of choice helps build commitment (Salancik, 1977). This technique is somewhat risky in that some valued people may choose to leave before one has had a chance to convert them. However, such people tend to be marketable and may leave anyway if they feel coerced.

Another technique is to attempt to directly nullify inappropriate rationalizations. Matt Holt made no attempt to do so. In contrast, Jim Henderson helped remove the inappropriate rationalizations used by his subordinates at Cummins ("Why change? Those above will tell us what to do," and "The guy at the top will act sooner or later to get us out of this crisis.") He did so by demonstrating that he was going to operate differently from the way Don Tull had managed the Cummins operations over the past 30 years. Henderson was not going to issue orders in the old way to quickly fix the problem, even if this meant that the inventory problem would worsen and thereby expose him to personal risk and criticism from above for not acting decisively according to the proven methodology.

Managers engaged in culture change must also communicate the new pattern of beliefs and values and get people to adopt them. Let us now turn to this process.

Cultural Communications

Culture is communicated via both implicit and explicit forms (Process 3, Exhibit 1). The former include rituals, customs, ceremonies, stories, metaphors, special language, folklore, heroes, logos, decor, dress, and other symbolic forms of expression and communication (Pondy, Frost, Morgan, and Dandridge, 1983). Examples of the latter are announcements, pronouncements, memos, and other explicit forms of expression and communication. Both forms must be relied on to persuade people to adopt the new cultural beliefs and values.

If the new pattern of beliefs and values in question is more intrinsically appealing to the people in the organization than is the prevailing pattern, the main problem in getting their adoption is the credibility of the communication, as in much political campaign rhetoric ("I like what I am hearing, but is this what the communicator really believes?"). However, if the new pattern of beliefs and values being communicated is *less* intrinsically appealing to the audience than is the prevailing pattern, as it was in the cases of both Matt Holt and Jim Henderson, credible communications about the new pattern of beliefs and values result in their being believed to be true intentions rather than mere corporate propaganda (for example, "I think management is really serious about this"). But this doesn't mean the new pattern will be adopted. The audience may remain aware of the new beliefs and values, and even comply with them, without internalizing them. Let us consider each of these processes in turn.

Credible Communication of New Beliefs and Values. This is a difficult task; explicit communications by managers of the new beliefs and values that they hope the people in their organization will buy into, such as "We believe people are our most important asset," may fall on deaf ears or be seen as mere corporate propaganda. How can communications be made more credible?

First, backing up words with deeds gains credibility, especially for individuals who in the past have consistently lived by what they said. A leader who has lost his or her reputation for credibility cannot reestablish it immediately. A considerable period of demonstrated consistency between the communicator's espoused beliefs and actual behavior must elapse before explicit communications are accepted as true intentions rather than mere fluff.

Second, communications tend to be accepted with less skepticism when they are not apparently espousing something that is in the communicator's self-interest. Explicit communications about new beliefs and values are more credible if their advocates apparently stand to lose in some meaningful way if the organization adopts these beliefs and values, or when they entail significant personal sacrifice for the proponents.

Given these difficulties and limitations of explicit communication, two indirect means exist to get across a new pattern of beliefs and values so that they seem credible. One is to spread the word by more informal means of communication, including reliance on neutral intermediaries (especially those who formerly had been cynical). This is because people receive communications less skeptically when they don't feel that the communicators are *trying* to persuade them (Aronson, 1976). Second, research shows that communications are not only more memorable but also more believable when implicit forms, such as telling stories and anecdotes from company history or individual experience, are used to communicate intended beliefs and values (Martin, 1982).

Why are stories more credible? Essentially, it is their concreteness, as well as the fact that the moral of the story is not explicitly stated. The listener draws his or her own conclusions, and is more likely to believe them. The problem with such communications is that a different moral may be inferred than the one intended. One way to guard against this danger is to pick stories which minimize the potential for misinterpretation. Ultimately, however, the way to increase the credibility of communications is to ensure that they are backed by consistent action that is in keeping with the intended beliefs and values. Both Matt Holt and Jim Henderson did a good job in this area.

Internalization of New Beliefs and Values. If they are credibly communicated, a new pattern of beliefs and values that is more intrinsically appealing than the present pattern will be accepted and eventually internalized. However, to the extent that the new pattern of beliefs and values is *less* intrinsically appealing—that is, perceived as "alien" by the people in question—communications about them must be not only emphatic and credible but persuasive as well. Such "culture persuasion" cannot rely on statistics and other facts alone, for alien beliefs and values are not necessarily accepted and internalized on the basis of hard evidence. (McMurry, 1963, p. 139; Pfeffer, 1981, p. 325). This was the challenge that both Matt Holt and Jim Henderson faced.

There are two basic approaches for getting people to accept and eventually internalize new beliefs and values, especially alien ones: identification and "Try it, you'll like it."

The first approach relies on the audience's identification with one or more persons who credibly communicate their attachment or conversion to the pattern of beliefs and values in question. Such a person could be the manager directing the culture change, or it could be anyone else whom the audience not only believes but *identifies with.* Here is one example:

> In a company with a long tradition of authoritarian management, a new CEO with a strong belief in participative management was having a great deal of difficulty getting managers to do more than go through the motions. One of the senior executives from the "old school," who was widely respected and admired as a company folk hero who would never say or do anything he didn't really believe in, then began to come around. As word of his conversion spread informally, others began to change their beliefs. It got to the point that this "idol's" department became a model of the intended culture. The belief in participative management began to seep to the rest of the company and gradually became more widely shared.

There was no indication that this mechanism was at work in the case of either Matt Holt or Jim Henderson. The following account of how the "folk hero" just mentioned came to change his belief in participatory management in the first place indicates the second approach (try it you'll like it) to getting the acceptance and eventual internalization of new beliefs and values, especially alien ones:

> He began to try the approach being advocated because he was a company loyalist who had an even stronger value: "I owe the new boss a fair shake." He was skeptical at first, but then came a few fairly dramatic changes having to do with the improved morale of certain valued but difficult employees, changes that he attributed to the new philosophy. Gradually, he changed his mind about participative management. Advocacy followed, and eventually he became a "culture champion."

If people can be persuaded to give it a fair chance and they like the experience that they attribute to it, they may buy into the new beliefs and values being advocated. This is the approach that Jim Henderson used successfully at Cummins. As mentioned previously and as illustrated by contrasting the cases of Matt Holt and Jim Henderson, such persuasion to try the new behavior must not rely too heavily on financial and other extrinsic forms of motivation; otherwise the incentives may serve as external justification for the new behavior and may produce no changes in the prevailing beliefs and values. This is especially important when the beliefs and values in question are alien. Where the intrinsic appeal of the beliefs and values in question is greater, one can rely more on extrinsic motivators to induce the new behavior without increasing the risk of inappropriate rationalizations. Further, both appeals and challenges can be effective tools in getting people to "give it a try" without heavy reliance on extrinsic motivators and their attendant risk of external justification.

In the case just cited, the value of participative management was not intrinsically appealing to the folk hero, but he decided to give it a try because the appeal was to his higher value (I owe the new boss a fair shake). A more general form of this appeal is to ask people to "give it a try" in more tentative, exploratory, and relatively nonthreatening ways, like "Let us try it as an experiment" or "Let us try it; we can always go back if it doesn't work." Another general form of appeal is to show people that the proposed changes are really nothing new ("We have done it before, it is part of our heritage"). One may also be able to get people to try the new behavior without heavy reliance on incentives by challenging them to do so.

Hiring and Socializing Newcomers and Removing Deviants

A final set of processes that are important to consider if culture change is being attempted is (1) the hiring and socialization of newcomers to fit into the intended culture and (2) the weeding out and removal of existing members who do not (Processes 4 and 5, Exhibit 1). Neither of these processes was relied on to any great extent in the cases of Matt Holt and Jim Henderson.

Changes in the *content* of culture (in the number of important shared beliefs and values and the way they are ordered) require appropriate changes in administrative philosophy—changes in human resource management policies and practices that alter the "breed" of people hired and socialized into the company as well as those who are removed.

Strength of culture is increased by adhering to a consistent philosophy to guide human resource management policies and practices over time. Keeping down the rate at which people are brought in and turned over also strengthens the culture. With a more stable work force, there is greater opportunity for the beliefs and values to become more clearly ordered and widely shared.

There is a limit to how rapidly culture can be changed by adding, socializing, and removing people from the organization. It is difficult to effectively assimilate a large member of new people in a short period of time. A large influx of people can also lead to political infighting, ploys, and counterploys in the organization as people jockey for position, especially where large numbers of new people are brought in at higher levels.

How to Know if Culture Change Is Occurring?

If the prevailing culture is fairly open, as it was in the cases of both Matt Holt and Jim Henderson, it will be easier to see whether people are buying into the new beliefs and values. Where the culture is not so open, people may "put on the airs" that they feel they must, making the detection of culture change tricky. Consider the following situation:

> Over a period of three years, Winn Hughes, an innovative division general manager responsible for 2000 people and $200 million in annual revenues, attempted to create an "entrepreneurial division culture." Several new ventures were launched by the division during this period, and one was highly successful. When Winn was promoted to a different part of the company, he felt he had left behind several promising ventures in the pipeline and, more important he felt, many "product champions." Within one year of his departure, however, he learned that all these ventures had "died in the tracks" or had been killed.
>
> It *wasn't* the case that Winn's replacement had ordered these actions, nor even that his successor was antientrepreneurial. Instead, the new head, who called himself a "balanced asset and growth" manager, said he would fund deserving projects and starve others—it was up to the people who believed in their projects to stick their necks out for them. No one had come forward.
>
> "Where are my product champions?" Winn asked himself with great disappointment when he heard about this. "They have disappeared into the woodwork!" he thought.

The real answer was that there never were any product champions in that division, which had witnessed three general managers in five years. Under Winn's predecessor, a cost-cutting "hatchet man," these managers played the cost and efficiency game. During Winn's tenure, they played the entrepreneurial game. And under Winn's successor, the "balanced" DGM who they perceived was an asset manager deep down, they played the "this year's return on investment" game. In short, these managers believed in playing the game that happened to be in town. That was their principal shared value, along with security consciousness and risk aversion—these were the underlying constants that explained these people's actions under three different general managers over a period of five years. Winn had been fooled because he mistook compliance for commitment.

Behavior change does not necessarily indicate a corresponding culture change, because the organization's leadership and systems (structures, measurements, controls, incentives, etc.) can effect behavior change without any culture change, as they did in the case of Matt Holt. It is also what happended in this case. Culture change can be positively inferred only if the new behavior can be attributed neither to the organization's leadership nor to its systems. A good test of culture change is whether the new behavior persists after the leadership that helped create the culture change leaves or after the systems used to create the culture change are further altered.

Although this is a good test of culture change, it is of little use to current leadership that wants to know if the culture change they are attempting to create is in fact taking hold. That is what Winn Hughes should have asked himself and, in retrospect, says he would have liked to have known. They are not foolproof, but three types of tests may be used to make some reasoned judgments about whether culture change is occurring:

1. Is There Evidence of Intrinsically Motivated Behavior? Would the new behavior persist if extrinsic motivators (administered by the organization's leadership and systems) were somewhat diminished? Winn could have eased off a bit on the bonuses and the public recognition he was giving product championing, to see how many were really committed to the concept. If this is deemed too risky a test (Let's not mess with what is working well"), one can look for opportunities that impose greater demands on the organization to see if the people respond appropriately *without* a corresponding increase in the extrinsic motivators. In the case cited, the deadlines on two key projects had to be advanced a bit for competitive reasons. The managers involved argued that the new deadlines could not be met without additional resources, resources that were not forthcoming because of a budget crunch. They said they would do their best, but there were no indications that they were stretching themselves to try. No one was putting in longer hours, for example. Both the projects failed to meet the slightly advanced deadlines.

2. Is There Evidence of "Automatic Pilot" Behavior? If a crisis or a novel situation is encountered, do the people involved "automatically" do what seems to be appropriate in light of the desired culture without waiting for directions from the organization's leadership or prodding from the organization's systems? In Winn's case, one of the new ventures was an outdoor product that encountered unexpected breakage on the customers' equipment on one particularly cold winter night during its first year on the market. Rather than acting immediately and offering free replacements, the managers involved took 48 hours to "investigate the problem" and reached a decision only after consulting with Winn (who was on an overseas field trip and was difficult to reach), while irate customers waited. Winn was upset that they had waited to consult with him on this relatively straightforward issue but didn't probe further for the significance of this critical incident. Had they been product champions, these managers would have taken the modest personal risk of acting without the boss's input to do what had to be done.

3. Is There Evidence of "Countermandated" Behavior? Do people behave in ways that run counter to established cultural values and/or organizational directives but that make sense in light of the desired culture? There was no evidence of such behavior in Winn's division. For example, the managers involved might have bootlegged resources from other parts of the company (which would have been counter to the company culture) or ignored certain policy directives (for example, 20 percent of engineering time had to be devoted to research projects rather than development projects) in an attempt to meet the advanced project deadlines.

While it may be infeasible or inadvisable to conduct these tests as planned experiments to determine if culture change is in fact occurring, one can look for occasions and situations that offer the opportunity to learn from such "natural experiments" that provide tell-tale signs of culture change, or of lack thereof. Thus, with detective work and opportunistic testing, a manager can make reasoned judgments about whether culture change is occurring.

The Alternatives to Major Culture Change

Since major culture change is difficult to effect and generally takes a relatively long time to accomplish, why bother to create such change? Why not rely on the organization's leadership and systems instead to create the necessary changes in organizational behavior patterns?

The answer is that, under certain conditions, creating behavior change without culture change may not work at all or may work but at very high costs to the organization. The reason for this is that creating culture change in the organization is analogous to gaining the commitment of the individual. Just as it is possible to secure an individual's compliance without gaining his or her commitment, so also it is possible to secure behavior change without culture change and with essentially the same kinds of costs and risks, of which there are basically three types:

1. *Inefficiency:* The costs of monitoring behavior to secure compliance and the costs of rewards and punishments (administered via the organization's leadership and systems) required to sustain it. These costs rise sharply as the organization gets larger and geographically more dispersed, because monitoring and rewarding/punishing appropriate behavior becomes increasingly difficult. In contrast, these costs are much smaller when behavior change is accompanied by appropriate culture

change, because the behavior is self-monitored and the rewards and punishments driving the behavior are at least partly self-administered.

2. *Insufficiency:* Compliance is often characterized by the "just enough" syndrome—people will do just enough to get by. Committed people, on the other hand, will put in the energy, time, and effort to do what needs to be done, not just what they are minimally required to do. Compliance can be a problem also, because the organization's leadership and systems can never fully anticipate every contingency that can arise. When something novel or unforeseen happens, the organization is at the mercy of the individual to do what is appropriate, which may be different from or even contrary to the specified behavior. Thus, where energy and commitment are critical and where novel or unplanned responses are frequently called for, behavior change without a corresponding culture change may be inadequate.

3. *Irrelevancy:* Finally, there are considerations which are simply not addressed by behavior change alone. These relate to mental processes, such as perception and thinking, which are only affected by culture change, not by behavior change. Where changes in such mental processes are an important aspect of the organizational changes being sought, behavior change by itself is not a viable option.

Unless the considerations mentioned above make it essential, a major culture change may not be worth the time, costs, and risks associated with it. Whenever possible, it makes sense to ask whether the desired results can be achieved without a major onslaught on the prevailing culture, especially a strong one. Indeed, this is one of the creative aspects of management. It is recommended that the following questions be seriously considered before embarking to radically transform a strong culture.

1. Can the Desired Results Be Obtained by Behavior Change without Culture Change? This is a particularly attractive option where only temporary changes in behavior are required to deal with a transient situation. It may also be a better alternative where the culture is weak, but appropriately so, because the business environment is unstable and requires abrupt changes in the organization's behavior patterns.

There are also times when the necessary behavior changes must be effected quickly and culture change is less critical. At Citibank in the early 70s, for instance, John Reed converted the operating group from a service-oriented "back office" to a "factory" in order to cope with the rising tide of paper (see cases 7–1 and 7–2). Reed had little time to spare and relied on a core group of managers with expertise in production management (many of them recruited from Ford Motor Co.), heavy use of extrinsic motivators (threats and punishments), as well as the removal of several middle managers to effect the required behavioral changes. Culture change did not follow, but this was not essential in this case, as evident from applying the three critical tests just mentioned. Inefficiency was not great, because all the people were located on two floors in one building and behavior compliance could be relatively easily monitored. Insufficiency was not a big problem, because the changes were toward a predictable, routine technology with little room for novelty or possibility of having to deal with the unexpected once the operations were debugged and running. Finally, irrelevancy was not a major consideration, because the important changes involved skills and behavior rather than perceptions and other mental processes.

2. Can the Desired Results Be Obtained by Creatively Utilizing the Existing Potential of the Prevailing Culture? Rather than viewing culture as something to be changed, one can look upon it with the frame of mind that says: "Culture is my friend. How can I rely on it to accomplish the desired ends?" For example, in a professional consulting group with a "Lone Ranger" culture (each on his or her own), several attempts to transform the group's culture into a more collaborative one failed. Finally, the business strategy and organization were reconceptualized as several "independent entrepreneurs," each with his or her own "fiefdom," in lieu of the failed attempts to get them to collaborate and dominate a preferred market segment. Results improved dramatically and were sustained for a longer period of time than ever before.

3. Can the Desired Results be Obtained by Utilizing the Latent Potential of the Prevailing Culture? Rather than look upon culture as something to be changed, one can ask: "What hidden part of this culture can I awaken to achieve the intended results?" If appropriate dormant values can be detected and activated (constituting an incremental rather than a radical change in culture's content, as explained earlier), the desired results may be more easily achieved. For example, the newly appointed head of a demoralized unit ("We are not as good as the competition") decided to challenge the group on what he correctly perceived to be their two hidden "hot buttons": values of self-confidence and pride in the group. The group responded tentatively at first, but these values were strengthened and reinstilled in the group as the new leader repeatedly showed the group how performance improved when these dormant values were adhered to.

4. Can the Desired Results Be Achieved via a Culture Change toward More Intrinsically Appealing Beliefs and Values Rather Than toward More Alien Ones? This also constitutes a less radical change in culture's content. For example, a highly successful U. S. family business that had built a strong corporate culture around the central value of family spirit ("This company is a family") had considerable difficulty getting new offices in southeast Asia to buy into this value. When the head of international operations, a son of the founder, took it upon himself to build a stronger "international culture" by preaching this value in his visits to the new offices, he met with reactions ranging from apathy to hostility. He learned that most of his host country employees viewed the term *family* as an almost sacred symbol of kinship ties and resented its use in the context of their employment with a foreign company. There was greater receptivity to the notion that the employees were "invited guests" of the U. S. company, and eventually these people bought into the values of concern and caring for the U. S. "host," which helped to generate the spirit the company was seeking.

In sum, an understanding of these approaches and methods can help managers decide how best to utilize the prevailing culture to the extent possible and how to transform it to the extent necessary to most effectively achieve the desired results.

References

Aronson, Elliot. *The Social Animal.* 2d ed. San Francisco: W. H. Freeman, 1976.

Beer, Michael. *Organization Change and Development.* Santa Monica, Calif.: Goodyear Publishing, 1980.

Bem, Daryl J. *Beliefs, Attitudes, and Human Affairs.* Monterey, Calif.: Brooks/Cole Publishing, 1970.

Browne, Paul C., Richard F. Vancil, and Vijay Sathe. *Cummins Engine Company: Jim Henderson and the Phantom Plant.* Harvard Business School case 9–182–264, 1982. There are two videotapes accompanying the case: *(a)* "Managerial Philosophy, Personal Style, and Corporate Culture" (Videotape 9–880–001, 28 minutes) and *(b)* "The Phantom Plant" (Videotape 9–880–002, 14 minutes). Both videotapes and the case are available from Case Services, Harvard Business School, Boston, MA 02163.

Geertz, Clifford. *The Interpretation of Cultures.* New York: Basic Books, 1973.

Keesing, Roger M. "Theories of Culture." *Annual Review of Anthropology* 3 (1974), pp. 73–79.

Kelman, H. C. "Compliance, Identification, and Internalization: Three Processes of Attitude Change." *Conflict Resolution* 2 (1958), pp. 51–60.

Kroeber, A. K., and Clyde Kluckhohn. *Culture: A Critical Review of Concepts and Definitions.* New York: Vintage Books, 1952.

Louis, Meryl. "Surprise and Sense Making: What Newcomers Experience in Entering Unfamiliar Organizational Settings." *Administrative Science Quarterly,* June 1980, pp. 226–51.

Martin, Joanne. "Stories and Scripts in Organizational Settings. In *Cognitive Social Psychology,* eds. A. Hastorf and A. Isen, 1982.

McMurray, Robert N. "Conflicts in Human Values." *Harvard Business Review,* May–June 1963, pp. 131–32.

Pfeffer, Jeffrey. *Power in Organizations.* Marshfield, Mass.: Pitman, 1981.

Pondy, Louis R., Peter J. Frost, Gareth Morgan, and Thomas C. Dandridge, eds. *Organizational Symbolism.* Greenwich, Conn.: JAI Press, 1983.

Rokeach, Milton. *Beliefs, Attitudes, and Values.* San Francisco: Jossey-Bass, 1968.

Salancik, Gerald R. "Commitment Is Too Easy." *Organizational Dynamics,* Summer 1977, pp. 62–80.

Schein, Edgar H. *Organizational Psychology.* 3d ed. Englewood Cliffs, N.J.: Prentice-Hall, 1980.

Schein, Edgar H. "Personal Change through Interpersonal Relationships." In *Interpersonal Dynamics,* eds. W. G. Bennis, D. E. Berlew, E. H. Schein, and F. L. Steele. Homewood, Ill.: Dorsey Press, 1973.

Schein, Edgar H. "Organizational Culture: A Dynamic Model." Working Paper No. 1412–83, Massachusetts Institute of Technology, February 1983.

Seeger, John A., Jay W. Lorsch, and Cyrus F. Gibson. *First National City Bank Operating Group (A) and (B).* Cases 9–474–165 and 9–474–166, 1975, Case Services, Harvard Business School, Boston, Mass. 02163

"Stanford Investigates Plagiarism Charges." *Science,* April 6, 1984, p. 35.

Swartz, Marc, and David Jordan. *Culture: An Anthropological Perspective.* New York: John Wiley & Sons, 1980.

Taylor, E. B. *Primitive Culture.* London: J. Murray, 1871.

Reading 8–3

Problems of Human Resource Management in Rapidly Growing Companies*

John P. Kotter, Vijay Sathe

Rapid growth companies—that is, companies that grow at an average rate greater than 20 percent per year (in number of employees) for at least four or five years in a row—are of considerable importance to managers, investors, and the public at large. They offer managers an exciting place to work and significant career advancement opportunities. It is not uncommon to find young managers in top spots in these companies. They offer the investor the chance for a much greater than average financial return. It boggles the mind to think how much money was made by those who bought large blocks of IBM, Polaroid, or Xerox stock around 1950. And rapid growth companies offer the public at large a significant source of expanding employment. Just a few rapidly growing companies in the same geographic region can sometimes make the difference between a stagnant economy with high unemployment and a robust economy with low unemployment.

Those interested in rapid-growth companies would agree that most of them share a common key to their success—their high rate of growth is sustained by virtue of their position of leadership in a rapidly expanding product/market area. This leadership position is typically achieved and maintained via the aggressive marketing of new and technically sophisticated goods or services. Through good fortune or shrewd calculation, these companies tend to be at the right place, at the right time, with the right set of capabilities.

People interested in rapid-growth companies seem to be much less aware of the fact that most of these firms share at least one other important pattern in common. These companies tend to experience similar human resource problems.[1] These problems are important because the way in which managers deal with them typically determines whether or not the company will be able to sustain its rapid growth over time.

In this article we will first identify the common problems that seem to plague rapid-growth companies, and then discuss solutions that some of the more successful ones have used to deal with them. This article is based on our experiences with 12 companies that have grown on the average at 40 percent per year for five or more years.

Problems Caused by the Need for Rapid Decisions

The president of one rapidly growing firm told us the following story, which highlights one of the problems created by rapid growth:

I was having lunch with an acquaintance of mine who is the president of a company that is about twice our current size. His firm has been growing at between 5 and 7 percent per year for the last 10 years. I was telling him about some of the decisions I had made during the previous two weeks and some of the decisions I had to make in the upcoming week. At one point he stopped me and said something like—"You know, you make as many important business decisions in a month as I do in a year." And while he may be exaggerating a bit, I think he's basically right. Since we grow at about 5 percent per month, I end up making decisions in a month that he gets nearly a year to make.

The speed with which decisions must be made in rapid-growth companies puts a strain on managers that many people simply cannot cope with. Many of us intellectually and emotionally need more time to make decisions than is available in such situations. We need time to get relevant information, to analyze that information, to identify alternative decisions, and to select a decision. Especially when the decision stakes are high, many people need time to emotionally come to grips with their intellectual choice. For some managers, this needed time runs into months or even years.

The required decision-making speed in rapid-growth companies also places the organizational structure under stress. The need for quick new-product design, development, manufacturing, and marketing decisions, which is characteristic of these companies, requires a rapid flow of information across departmental lines and close cross-functional coordination. The traditional functional structure is not designed to cope with these

---

[1] Two recent articles deal with some of this subject. One is based on a study of five small (100–200 employees) but rapidly growing firms: George Strauss, "Adolescence in Organizational Growth," *Organizational Dynamics* (Spring 1974). The other is based on the experience of one rapidly growing firm: William George, "Task Teams for Rapid Growth," *Harvard Business Review* March–April 1977).

requirements. It is best equipped to handle a more stable set of tasks. When it is small, a rapidly growing company can achieve the necessary cross-functional coordination because of the flexibility afforded by its small size. As it grows, however, the traditional functional structure will start to cause problems for a rapid-growth company. Decisions will begin to "fall between the cracks." Decisions will not be made. And certain activities will get "bogged down" because the structure cannot cope with the rapidly changing environment.

The need for rapid decisions has a similar impact on informal structure and culture. The informal relationships among individuals and groups in organizations almost always include some distrust, suspicion, bad feelings, and misunderstandings. All of these factors impede smooth information flow, effective collaboration, and rapid decision making. When a company is small, these relationships can be managed so as not to undermine effective decision making. But growth makes such management more difficult because the number of relationships to be managed increases more rapidly than the number of employees.

Problems Caused by Rapidly Expanding Job Demands

Similar organization positions in companies of very different size obviously place quite different demands on the incumbents. The job of the chief financial officer in a $10 million company, for example, is significantly different from that of the person holding the same position in a $150 million company. Internal reporting and control, data processing, financial planning, annual budgeting, and internal auditing all would probably be a significant part of the responsibilities of the chief financial officer of the larger company. Most, if not all, of these functions would probably be absent in the smaller company. Since a rapid-growth company's annual sales could grow from $10 million to $150 million in just a few years, the chief financial officer's job in such a company could change dramatically in a relatively short time period. Some people can adjust to such a change. Many cannot.

Peter Drucker has said that one of the biggest impediments to successful growth is the inability of key managers to change their attitudes and behavior to fit the changing needs of the organization.[2] And while Drucker is talking about all growth situations, we believe this is especially true in high-growth situations.

The problem of people not being able to change as rapidly as their jobs typically creates two more problems. First, it often leads to a shouting match between various levels of management regarding questions of delegation and development. For example:

---

[2] Peter Drucker, *The Practice of Management* (New York: Harper & Row, 1954), pp. 246–252.

A middle-level manager: *The biggest problem we have in this company is top management's unwillingness to delegate more. My boss is still making the same kinds of decisions in the same ways he did five years ago. But the company today is three times as large as it was then. He should be doing other things today and delegating many of those decisions to me.*

A top manager: *Our biggest problem today is somehow getting middle management to the point where they can handle their ever-increasing responsibilities. I'm still making some decisions that I should not be making. But I have no qualified person beneath me to whom I can delegate those decisions.*

A middle-level manager: *Top management says that we are not ready to handle more delegation. But how are we ever going to get ready if they don't allow us to make some of those decisions. Sure we would probably make a few errors, but we would learn a lot in the process.*

A top manager: *We can't afford mistakes around here. We cannot take chances with the record of success we have had here.*

People's inability to grow and change as quickly as their jobs creates a second problem related to unmet career expectations. Managers often join rapid-growth companies for the advancement opportunities. But many of these companies find it necessary to fill between 10 and 50 percent of their nonentry-level openings from the outside because people with the necessary experience are not being developed as rapidly as needed within the company. When an ambitious person sees numerous higher-level jobs filled from the outside, he or she often becomes frustrated.

Finally, people's inability to grow with job demands can place key managers in difficult, guilt-eliciting positions. The following story has been repeated to us in varying forms literally dozens of times:

Jerry was my fourth employee. I hired him in 1966 to be my first full-time salesman. He worked long hours for us and got two key contracts that saved the company in 1967.

When we hired our seventh salesman, I made Jerry sales manager. And in 1971, I made him vice president for sales. Today, in 1977, we have revenues of 25 million on a yearly basis, the marketing department has nearly 100 employees, and Jerry is way over his head.

In retrospect, I should never have made him vice president of sales in 1971. But he expected the title change since I had just made my engineering manager the vice president of engineering. And I didn't want to hurt his feelings or make him think I didn't fully appreciate the loyalty and long hours he had given the company.

Today his inability to manage his department is hurting us severely, but I have delayed moving him for months. I know I have to act soon. But god, it's hard. I really think that as much as I love my wife, throwing her out of the house would not be as emotionally demanding.

Problems Caused by Large Recruiting and Training Demands

Perhaps the most obvious problems faced by fast-growing companies are recruiting and training. Fast growth requires the recruitment, selection, and assimilation of large numbers of people. And for most rapidly growing companies, satisfying this need at an affordable cost is difficult.

The slow-growing company in a mature industry can often satisfy its hiring needs by waiting for the right people to walk in the door. It can satisfy its assimilation needs by osmosis; the relatively few new people learn the ropes from those they interact with.

Rapidly growing companies, however, cannot rely on such a passive stance. Such firms often have to hire 5 to 10 times as many people each year as do slow-growing companies of equal size. They are forced to aggressively seek out possible employees. Because they are often in new industries or have new products or services, they may need somewhat atypical combinations of talents, which makes recruiting even more difficult. As a result, the typical high-growth company spends considerable time and energy in recruitment and selection of new employees, but is still unable to hire people as quickly as required. A personnel officer in one such company told us:

I go through a hundred resumes a day. So do other people here, including some line managers. Our whole department is constantly involved in recruiting and hiring. And that's not necessarily good, because we neglect other duties like training and organizational development activities. But even though we are so focused on just recruiting, we still do not bring people in as quickly as many of our line managers want. To get the kind of engineers we need, for example, it usually takes us six months. In the company I worked for 10 years ago, which wasn't growing very fast at all, six months for hiring was fine. Here it's not. Our engineering vice president says the strain we put on his department by hiring so slowly is enormous.

Assimilating and training new employees is equally difficult in rapid-growth firms. Unlike the situation is a slow-growth company, the new employees are seldom put in a group where they are surrounded by "old-timers" who can informally teach them the job, the company's goals and values, and the structure and procedures. It is quite possible that the average seniority of the people they interact with is a year or less. This situation can cause a number of problems, such as those described by one company president:

Our new recruits out of college can sometimes get lost in here. We had one last year that nearly cost us a $100,000 order because he was not trained or being supervised closely.

The people we hire with 10 to 20 years of prior experience can cause another type of problem. They bring with them a whole set of ideas about corporate goals, personnel philosophy, how to do things, and the like, which sometimes are quite different from our own. In their cases, we not only have to teach them our ways, we have to get them to unlearn what we consider "bad habits."

The difficulty of achieving quick assimilation is particularly important because of its crucial role in rapidly growing companies. When only 2 or 3 percent of the employees are relatively new, it really doesn't matter much if they are not fully on board for six months to a year. However, when 20 to 50 percent of the employees are relatively new, how quickly they get on board matters a great deal.

Problems Caused by Constant Change

"Change is inevitable in a situation like ours," one president of a rapidly growing company told us, "and it's a fact of life we just have to learn to accept and live with. But that's easier said than done."

Rapid-growth situations tend to be full of uncertainty and ambiguity caused by constantly changing employees, job demands, structures, systems, products, and markets. And uncertainty can create problems. It is not possible, for example, to do career planning, as in a more stable and certain environment. It is very difficult to devise clear rules and procedures to help guide people's actions. Some individuals like this type of an environment, but many do not. If there are too many employees of the latter type in a high-growth situation, the strain they feel will affect organizational performance.

Constant change also means perpetual loss of the familiar, including aspects of it that were valued, and the constant need for readjustment. Psychological research shows that loss and readjustment cause stress, even on people who like change because of the challenge or the material rewards associated with it. And stress, beyond a point, creates its own problems. As one executive in a rapid growth firm told us: "Lots of people around here are on edge. The stress sometimes shows in their work, and in their marriages. The divorce rate in our management group is considerably above the national average."

Finally, change usually creates the need for even more change to keep the organization in balance. Increased revenues require more employees, which requires more recruiting and training. Increased size eventually requires new systems to be developed, which often requires more specialists to be hired and trained. And all of these activities consume resources, which tend to be scarce in high-growth situations.

Problems Caused by a Constant Strain on Resources

Rarely are high-growth companies such a "sure bet" in the long run that investors are willing to run up operating losses in the short run. As such, the stockholders or the corporate management of these companes typically expect them to turn in at least a modest profit every year. But profit generation can be incredibly difficult, for two major reasons. First, because of constant change, these companies cannot realize the efficiencies that are possible in more stable situations. Second, rapid-growth firms typically have to plan for and operate in business environments that are always larger than their current financial resources. As the controller of one company so aptly put it:

We are currently doing planning and development as if we were a $100 million-a-year company, which we will be in two years. In terms of sales orders and manufacturing capacity, we are operating like a $50 million-a-year company. But the money we are putting in the bank as a result of deliveries is equivalent to yearly sales of about $35 million.

Financial analysts are familiar with this paradox—companies experiencing a substantial revenue growth are frequently cash starved. What is often overlooked, however, is that the simultaneous strain on the company's human resources is often equally or more severe.

It is not uncommon for managers and professionals in high-growth companies to complain of being "burned out," and of being unfairly compensated relative to their contributions:

We never have enough people. Everybody works 60 to 80 hours a week. After a while it really gets to you, especially since the pay isn't that great.

I joined the company in 1973, which means I've been here for 10 years! [From an interview in 1977.]

My wife keeps asking me why I haven't gotten much larger bonuses. Given my contribution to the company and its success, she has a good point.

The relentless resource strain also means that people do not have the time to do anything but what is required immediately. Important activities that are not cloaked in urgency tend to fall by the wayside. Thus, the tasks of assimilation, training, and development of the ever-growing numbers of employees typically receive the short shrift from line managers who are constantly preoccupied with more pressing matters. These tasks also are often ignored by personnel people who are fully occupied with the more urgent demands of recruitment and hiring, and with routine but necessary functions such as employee benefits and payroll. Tasks associated with the design and implementation of new information, control, and operating systems are also easily ignored. And planning of all types gets neglected.

Interaction Effects

The problems already described are difficult in themselves. If unattended, however, these problems can interact to produce a vicious circle in which

Exhibit 1
The Consequences of Unattended Human Resource Problems in Rapid-Growth Companies

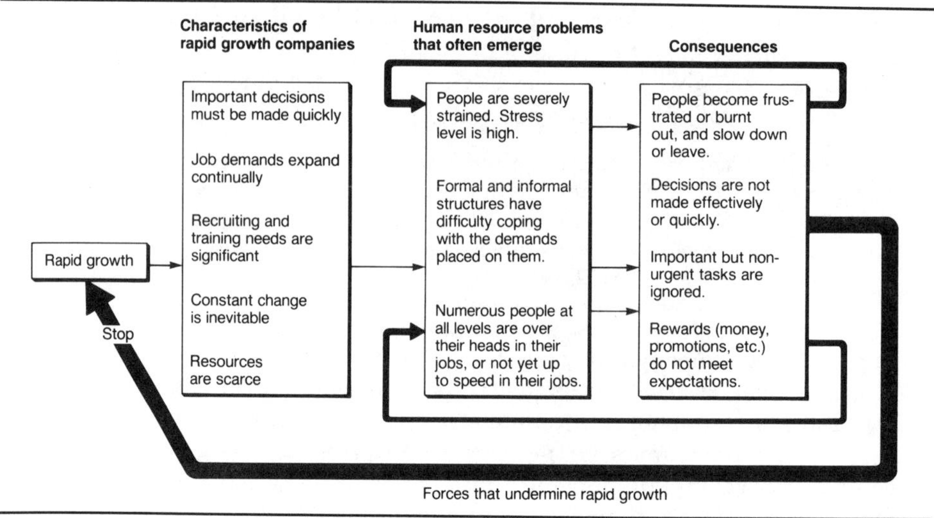

the situation can get completely out of hand (see Exhibit 1). The following detailed case history illustrates what can happen:

> Three years ago a company we are familiar with was highly effective and growing rapidly. The ability of the professional and managerial employees and the flexibility possible because of its small size enabled the firm to develop and market new products rapidly. As the company grew, so did the job demands. Some people grew with their jobs, but others began to strain under the ever-growing number of responsibilities. Most, however, were satisfied and highly motivated because the company was achieving its objectives in ways that could clearly be related to their own efforts. There was a personnel manager but no formal human resource function. However, human resource problems were generally handled effectively on a personal basis by top management.
>
> As the company's growth continued, a point was reached at which there was a clear need for considerable human resource development activity. Although many persons were being promoted, an equally large number were being brought in from the outside to fill high-level openings. Those not promoted were skeptical when told they were passed over because they lacked the necessary experience. They felt they deserved a chance and could learn quickly if given the opportunity. Top managers, however, were unwilling to take chances with those who, in their opinion, were not yet ready for promotion. At one point consideration was given to establishing a human resource function to aid in the assimilation of the ever-growing number of newcomers and to help in the training and career development of all employ-

ees, particularly those not promoted. Given the demands on the company's resources that this entailed, however, the plan was "temporarily" shelved.

The situation remained as described for about one year. Those affected waited to see what action management would take. When it appeared that there would be no major change in the handling of these problems, some employees that management considered to be valuable but unpromotable began to leave. Others wondered why they were putting in such long hours without any promotion. They began to cut back their contribution to a level they perceived as equitable with the recognition and rewards received.

The turnover and diminution of effort predictably hurt the company's performance and resulted in a greater strain on its financial and human resources. The high turnover meant that even more people had to be hired from the outside. This, in turn, led to further problems of assimilation, on the one hand, and more frustration for those not receiving promotion, on the other. Turnover continued to increase, and performance fell dramatically. The company was trapped in a vicious circle.

Today this firm's rate of growth has dropped to 12 percent per year. Profitability remains poor. Morale is low. Competition has moved in, and the initial momentum has been lost. A new president has taken over recently and is in the process of deciding how best to get the company fired up again.

Solutions

Successful rapid-growth companies we know rely on some or all of the following solutions to cope with the problems we have described.

Recruiting, Selection, and Training. Despite the short-run problems created, the more successful rapid-growth companies tend to be very selective in their hiring. They screen large numbers of people, sometimes hundreds for each opening, in order to hire a large percentage of people who *(a)* can perform the job without a great deal of training—as a result, they do not hire large numbers of people right out of college; *(b)* have obvious potential for growth; *(c)* like volatile environments; *(d)* are willing to work long hours; *(e)* are flexible; *(f)* have philosophies and personalities consistent with the company "culture."

To keep the cost of finding these types of people within bounds, a number of firms actively encourage their employees to do informal recruiting and screening whenever they can. As one human resource person told us: "You can always spot our people at cocktail parties. They will have some guy pinned in the corner while they get information about him or while they try to sell him on the company."

To help get these new people assimilated, the more successful rapid-growth firms often hold one- to three-day orientation sessions. These sessions are typically run by line executives—not staff personnel people—who outline the company's history, philosophy, strategy, structure, and compensation system. In one firm, the chief executive officer plays a central role in these sessions.[3]

Team or Matrix Structures, and Team Building. After they have reached a certain size, most successful rapid-growth companies adopt an organizational structure that relies heavily on teams or a matrix.[4] Unlike most traditional structures, these types of organizational arrangements are capable of successfully handling a volatile, rapid decision-making environment.

Team and matrix structures can be difficult to implement, however. They completely undermine the "authority must equal responsibility" dictum that most managers follow. The resulting ambiguity can be frustrating and difficult to live with. This is probably why some rapid-growth companies try to do without these structures despite the fact that they are needed.

To help make their team or matrix structure work, successful rapid-growth companies usually rely on team-building activities.[5] With the aid of outside consultants or experts within their human resource department, they periodically have managers in natural work teams (which might involve people within or across departments) go away from the firm for a few days to clear up any problems that are hampering the group's effectiveness. Team-building activities help members maintain good working relationships despite the ambiguity inherent in the organizational structure and assist in increasing a work team's ability to make effective decisions quickly.

Managing the Culture. All of the more successful rapid-growth companies we have encountered emphasize the importance of creating and maintaining a certain type of informal company culture. The characteristics of this culture include a shared belief in openness, a shared sense of what the company is and where it is going, a clearly perceived commitment to employee welfare, and norms supporting flexibility and change.

To help keep information flowing efficiently and accurately, an atmosphere of open doors, unlocked desks, and approachability is usually encouraged. "We want no secrets around here," one person told us, "and we work hard to convince people that we mean it."

People we have talked to sometimes refer to their company's "philoso-

---

[3] For a more detailed description of this type of orientation session, see John P. Kotter, "The Psychological Contract: Managing the Joining Up Process," *California Management Review* (Spring 1973), pp. 91–99.

[4] See George, "Adolescence"; and William Goggin, "How the Multidimensional Structure Works at Dow Corning," *Harvard Business Review* (January–February 1974).

[5] For a further description of team building, see Shel Davis, "Building More Effective Teams," *Innovations* (1970), pp. 32–41.

phy" or their company's "religion." To create this shared sense of goals and values, one firm spent considerable time and energy communicating a new corporate strategy to virtually all employees. The president of another firm had actually written a paper, which was widely circulated in the firm, on the company's philosophy. Such a shared vision, he believes, helps bind people together and helps coordinate their actions without the need for more formal rules, procedures, and structures.

The employees in the successful rapid-growth companies we know of generally believed that the company really cared about its people. As one person put it: "One of the reasons I've worked as hard as I have and feel as strongly as I do about the company is because I know it really cares about me and others." This belief is created through many different kinds of actions. In two of these firms, job openings are always posted, and insiders are always considered before hiring someone from the outside. In another company, people are given time off whenever the long hours seem to be affecting them physically.

Finally, the culture in these companies tends to be supportive of flexibility and change. This is fostered by the words and deeds of top people. One CEO, for example, has told groups of employees on numerous occasions that he is not sure he will be the right person for the CEO job in four to five years: "If I'm not, so be it. I'll find a more appropriate replacement for myself and try to contribute here in some other way."

Planning. Successful rapid-growth companies manage to find the time to do organizational and human resource planning. Being aware of the potential problems described in this article, their leaders periodically look into the future and modify current decisions if they see important problems developing. They recognize that change is inevitable and try to plan for it. They work to project human resource needs so as to keep staffing demands consistent with available resources.

This type of planning activity does not have to be time consuming. The key to its success is largely attitudinal; that is, if managers understand the problems of rapid growth and anticipate their potential negative impact, they can devise various means of overcoming them.

Organizing and Staffing the "Personnel" Function. Because of the potential severity of human resource problems in rapid-growth firms, the more successful companies generally have a full-time, formally designated human resource function. The less successful ones seem to resist this. Instead, they cling to the more traditional role of the personnel function—recruitment, hiring, fringe benefits, and so forth.

Even when quite small ($30 million per year in revenues for manufacturing firms), successful rapid-growth companies typically have a head of human resources who is unusually talented and well paid in light of the company's size. This person generally reports directly to the president and often has a very close informal relationship with the president. Because of this relationship and the person's own competence, the human resource function is perceived as powerful and important in these companies.

In many of the more successful firms, the human resource function is also staffed below the director with a very capable group of people. Organizationally, these people are often deployed such that each of the other departments in the company has one or more human resource personnel assigned to it. Each of these staff people then works closely with the assigned department to recruit and train people, to run team-building sessions, to help manage the culture, to plan, and to help people both understand and adjust to the inevitable stresses and strains.

Being Sensitive and Tough at the Top. The top managers of successful rapid-growth companies tend to be unusually sensitive to human resource problems and are willing to deal with them with toughness if necessary.

Without a high level of sensitivity to potential organizational and human resource problems, top management will tend either to ignore them or to relegate them to a low order of priority. And toughness is needed to deal with tasks that can be unusually unpleasant. An example is the frequent need to replace or reassign individuals (including those at the very highest levels) whose jobs have outgrown them. Another example is the willingness to do battle with a corporate management group that may be unfamiliar with, and hence insensitive to, the special challenges and needs of human resource management in a rapidly growing company.

One of the more impressive examples of sensitivity and toughness we have seen was when a CEO replaced himself, long before retirement, with an outsider. He sensed that he was no longer appropriate for the job and that no one who reported to him could handle it then or in the foreseeable future. So he hired an outsider and explained his actions at length to a number of disappointed insiders.

There is no question that it takes a very capable group of people, and one that can absorb a lot of physical and emotional strain, to manage a high-growth company successfully. To maintain its record of success, the management of such a company needs to understand, anticipate, and overcome the problems described in this article. An awareness of the solutions used by companies that have successfully sustained high growth over long periods of time should help in devising remedies that best fit a particular situation.